THE STAMP ATLAS

To the memory of
Stuart Rossiter (1927-1982)
Without whose inspiration
and initial work
this atlas might never
have appeared.

THE STAMP ATLAS

W. RAIFE WELLSTED & STUART ROSSITER

CARTOGRAPHY BY

JOHN FLOWER

Facts On File Publications

New York, New York • Oxford, England

This edition published in America by Facts on File Publications, 460 Park Avenue South, New York, N.Y. 10016

First published in Great Britain in 1986
by Macdonald & Co (Publishers) Ltd
London & Sydney

A member of BPCC plc

Reprinted 1987

Library of Congress Cataloguing-in-Publication Data

Wellsted, Raife
The stamp atlas.
Includes Index.
1. Postage-stamps
2. Postage-stamps — collectors and collecting.
I. Flower, John, *1929-*
II. Title
HE6182.W4 1986 769.56 86-8843

ISBN 0-8160-3146-2

Filmset by Flairplan Photo-typesetting Ltd

Printed and bound in Great Britain by
Purnell Book Production Ltd, Paulton, Bristol
A member of BPCC plc

Edited for the publishers by Lund Humphries
Designer: Colin Lewis
Photographer: John Heseltine
Indexer: H.K. Bell

CONTENTS

Cartographer's Acknowledgements

I am indebted to John Taylor of Lund Humphries for his encouragement and wise counsel over the long years that this project has been maturing;

To his assistant Eveline van Rooy whose conscientiousness and perseverance has overcome the unenviable task of checking and re-checking the maps and tackling the task of the indigenous names;

To Jack and Mick at DEP Ltd., Tadworth, Surrey;

To Chris and Pete at Corydon Press, Southwater, Sussex, who put up with my sometimes unreasonable demands for instant photographic processing; and lastly

To some of my former peers, without whom I could not have coped with this task. Some are listed below.

Major Reference works consulted

Atlas of African History, Edward Arnold 1978

Cambridge Modern History Atlas, C.U.P. 1970

Cassell's Atlas, 1909, 1928.

Citizen's Atlas, J. Bartholomew 1935, 1943.

Hammond's Historical Atlas of the USA, 1968.

Muir's Historical Atlas, George Philip 1963.

Penguin Atlas of World History, 1974.

Reader's Digest Wide World Atlas, Rand McNally 1982.

Recent History Atlas, Gilbert & Flower, Weidenfeld 1967.

Shepherd's Historical Atlas, George Philip 1965.

Times Atlas of the World, 1895, 1923, 1967, 1972.

Illustration Acknowledgements

Stamps and overprints are reproduced by kind permission of the National Postal Museum, London.

For permission to reproduce other illustrations appearing on the pages listed the Publishers are indebted to:

Ace Photoagency *31* (photo: Howard Phillips), *39* (photo: Jim Kinnear), *51* (photo: Brian Nash), *54* (photo: B. Beattie), *57* (photo: John Panton), *61* (photo: A. Dobravska), *73* (photo: John Panton), *79* (photo: Carlo Chinca), *93* (photo: A. Dobravska), *136* (photo: Neville Melmore), *187* (photo: R. Walker),

Alitalia *93* (Susan Chislett, Publicity)

Anne Conway, Photographer *46, 46, 241, 249, 249, 260*

Aspect Picture Library *202* (photo: Tom Nebbie), *202* (photo: Vince Streano).

Bryan and Cherry Alexander Photography *205, 205 208*

Bundespostmuseum Frankfurt am Main *73* (photo: DBP Frölich Frankfurt

Camerapix Hutchison Library *196, 288*

Commonwealth Secretariat *191, 195*

Compix (Commonwealth Institute) *149, 149, 149, 180, 180, 191, 237, 241, 297*

DAS Photo (photos: David Simson) *51, 59, 59, 61, 103, 104, 104, 104, 168*

Hellenic Post (Aspioti-Elka) *125* (photo: N. Mavrogenis and N. Kontos)

The Illustrated London News Picture Library *84, 208, 237, 277, 279*

Mary Evans Picture Library *15, 19, 19, 21, 21, 23, 23, 27, 27, 27, 31, 31, 31, 45, 45, 46, 63, 98, 103, 106, 135, 146, 168, 185, 231, 297*

Mepha (Middle East Photographic Archive) *219* (photo: M. Sparrow), *219* (photo: J. Brown), *219* (photo: Malcolm Hoare), *231* (photo: A. Ramsey), *277* (photo: T. Hariwell), *277* (photo: C. Osborne)

Museo Postal Argentino *173*

National Portrait Gallery, London *196* (painting by J. Webber)

National Postal Museum, London *57*

P & O Group Library *95, 237* (painting by R. H. Neville Cumming), *260*

Postal & Telecom Museum, Portugal 53 (watercolour by Luis Jardin Portela 1962), *53* (watercolour by Luis Jardin Portela 1962)

Poztmuseum, Stockholm *98* (photo: Portens Thrycker)

PTT Museum, Bern *80* (photo: Saurer), *80* (poster by Emile Cardinaux)

Robert Harding Picture Library *288* (photo: Sassoon)

The Ryohei Ishikawa Collection (published by Sotheby Parke Bernet 1980) *210* (collection by Major A. E. Hopkins)

Swiss National Tourist Office *78* (photo: Schwab)

Sylvia Pitcher Photography *136*

Thill A. Bruxelles Edit. *59*

Tim Graham Picture Library *95* (photo: Tim Graham)

Victoria & Albert Museum, London *88* (pastel by James Huntley)

W. Raife Wellsted *84, 173, 316*

Yugoslav National Tourist Office, London *119*

INTRODUCTION

It is almost impossible to assemble a collection of stamps without some knowledge of or interest in the political history of the country or countries by which the stamps were issued. Moreover, the introduction of an increasing number of commemorative and other special issues will lead the student and general collector alike to an interest not only in the stamps but in the postal and social history of the territory or area concerned.

For the postal historian, a knowledge of geographical changes and history is an essential part of his study, and this calls for an understanding of the political changes and military intervention which have led to changes in boundaries and allegiances. It was this problem of locating the relevant information which led the late Stuart Rossiter and John Flower who had collaborated on the famous Blue Guides to propose a Stamp Atlas. In particular, Stuart, who was a student of the postal history of East Africa, recognized the difficulties which face many collectors because of the frequent and apparently unconnected changes which took place in the stamp-issuing territories of the African continent. As a result he developed his ideas and began to prepare a manuscript on a country by country basis detailing the boundary changes and the political pressures which gave rise to them. These first thoughts were committed to paper and it was intended that they should be supported by maps prepared by John Flower and stamps or covers from Stuart's collection.

Sadly, in 1982, Stuart died and for two years the project lay fallow with only three of the five continents completed. In 1984 the work began again when the outstanding sections were completed and the others were brought up to date. Thus the project which began as an idea in 1978 has at last been completed; it is hoped that the volume which has resulted will be a valuable addition to the general research library of many collectors.

Apart from Europe, the treatment of the continents follows a similar pattern and deals with each country in turn. The sequence within each continent varies as appropriate. The American continent, including the Caribbean islands, is dealt with from north to south. Australia and New Zealand are followed by the Pacific Islands. Asia is covered from the Middle East eastwards to Japan. Africa is treated in a clockwise direction, commencing with North Africa. Finally, the territories in the South Atlantic, Indian Ocean and Antarctica round off the Atlas.

Europe, which opens the Atlas, is more complex. The wars of the 17th and succeeding centuries have given rise to massive and complicated boundary changes. The text for European countries, therefore, has been broken down into a series of ten time bands. These bands have been selected so that the main changes in the principal countries can if necessary be considered together. The bands used are up to 1660, 1660-1793, 1793-1815, 1815-50, 1850-71, 1871-1914, 1914-18, 1918-39, 1939-45 and since 1945. The story of each territory is narrated chronologically, but it can be cross-referenced to any other country by using similar time bands in other territories. At the beginning of the European section, there are 10 time band maps which graphically illustrate the changes which have occurred to that continent and reference to these from the text is desirable.

Throughout, political changes are illustrated by the use of stamps issued by the various territories, and other illustrations have been selected principally for their postal or philatelic significance.

A book of this size and scope cannot hope to answer each and every question. It is intended as a work of general reference and one which will lead to a greater understanding of the boundary changes, stamp issues, and policies which have taken place. However, it is also hoped that it will motivate collectors to look behind the simple facts of stamps issues and to think in more detail about the background history of the countries whose stamps they have chosen to collect.

For those sections which Stuart Rossiter wrote, he would obviously wish to acknowledge the assistance he received from his many friends, but, unfortunately, no record remains of his literary references. For the balance, no single work of reference was used, but the compilation would not have been possible without reference to the following books: *The Encyclopaedia of British Empire Postage Stamps*, Volumes I to V by Robson Lowe; *The International Encyclopaedia of Stamps*, edited by James Mackay; *The Times Atlas of World History; The History of the British Army Postal Service*, Volumes I to III, published by Edward Proud; *Haydn's Dictionary of Dates*, 1903; *Stanley Gibbons Catalogues*, both Simplified and Specialized and the *Encyclopaedia of Military History* by Dupuy and Dupuy. The remainder of the core of knowledge used in this work has been gleaned from many different and, in some cases, unremembered sources.

Stamp collecting in all its facets is probably the most popular indoor hobby that exists. If this book adds in any way to the reservoir of general knowledge about stamps and history, it will have matched up to the original intent of both Stuart Rossiter and John Flower. It will have served its purpose.

W Raife Wellsted

The American Philatelic Society

Beginning a Second Century of Service

The American Philatelic Society, founded in 1886 as the United States' first national philatelic organization, today is the largest such group in the nation. The APS has more than 50,000 members in the United States and 100 other countries.

The Society publishes a 100-page monthly journal, *The American Philatelist,* that is the oldest continuously published philatelic magazine in the world. The APS also publishes books on varied aspects of philately. *The Stamp Atlas* is only the second book offered by another publisher to be endorsed by the American Philatelic Society.

The APS offers its members seminars and correspondence courses in philately, the opportunity to buy and sell stamps through a Sales Division, translation services, and, for members living in North America, moderately priced insurance for stamp collections. The American Philatelic Expertizing Service provides expert opinions on the genuiness of philatelic material for a small fee.

The services of the American Philatelic Research Library are available to members, who may visit the library or borrow materials by mail. The library publishes a quarterly journal, *The Philatelic Literature Review.*

Information about membership in the American Philatelic Society and the American Philatelic Research Library, or about any of their services, may be obtained by writing to:

The American Philatelic Society, P.O. Box 8000, State College, Pennsylvania 16803

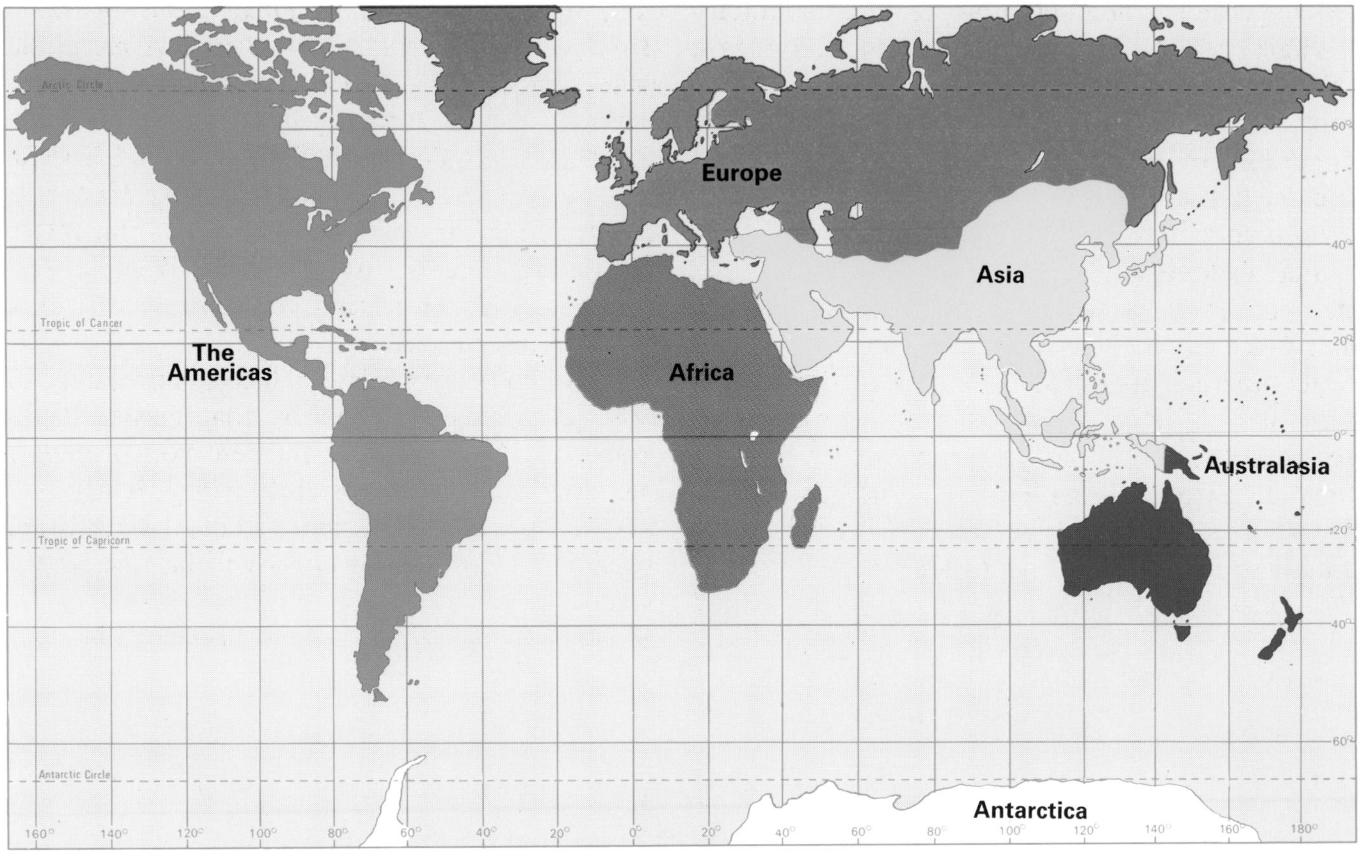
Arctic Circle
Europe
Asia
Tropic of Cancer
The Americas
Africa
Australasia
Tropic of Capricorn
Antarctic Circle
Antarctica
160° 140° 120° 100° 80° 60° 40° 20° 0° 20° 40° 60° 80° 100° 120° 140° 160° 180°
60° 40° 20° 0° 20° 40° 60°

HOW TO USE THE MAPS

The maps in this Atlas have been designed to illustrate and augment the text. In the main, they are based on political developments particularly with regard to changes in frontiers stemming from imperialism and conquest on the one hand, and independence movements on the other. Facts drawn from postal history are superimposed on this policital background.

Where dates and comments have been used for general historical purposes, they are set within parentheses. Postal history information – as distinct from philatelic information – generally appears without parentheses.

Stamp (philatelic) information is symnbolized thus:

1890 shows dates when stamps on the maps were **FIRST USED** i.e. when a province or state began using stamps issued by another territory, usually an imperial or occupying power.

1894 shows dates when stamps were **FIRST ISSUED** specifically for a province or state and, in some cases, towns.

1903 shows dates when stamps were **SUBSEQUENTLY ISSUED** or re-issued for a particular territory, after a 'natural break' (for example, after a *coup d'état*). These dates tend to reflect particularly important events in the history of the country concerned.

1888 shows when a Post Office or Postal Agency opened.

Other pertinent information is given in keys for each map.

HOW TO USE THIS BOOK

All stamp information which appears on the maps is duplicated in the text for ease of reference.

The maps have been designed to demonstrate clearly the geographical and historical aspects of each region, with a main map in colour providing an overall outline at the opening of each continental section. Maps for individual countries or areas follow, and these incorporate the chronology of stamp issues.

The European section differs slightly in style in that it incorporates a set of ten 'time-band' maps specially designed to show the ebb and flow of Empires and occupying powers from 1650 onwards as well as, after 1840, information on stamp issues. These are divided at major moments in history though there are, naturally, substantial compromises within the broader time spans.

Where possible place names using the Latin alphabet are given their indigenous form – e.g. København (indigenous) rather than Copenhagen (in English) – to emphasize the transitory nature of governments and occupying powers during the century and a half throughout which stamps have been issued, and during which the inscriptions appearing on stamps have reflected political changes. This formidable task was tackled with some apprehension and much hard work. We hope that we have, for the most part, been reasonably successful.

All sea and other water names are shown in light italic type. Maps are orientated throughout with North to the top. The exceptions to this rule bear a North point.

Notes on the text and stamp illustrations

Headings

The system of headings for political entities is as follows:

Large bold type – territories which are currently issuing stamps (in 1986).

Small bold type – sub-divisions of these territories.

Small bold type preceded by a roundel – territories that once issued stamps but do so no longer.

Currency

For nearly all territories currency tables are included in the text which show the primary denomination and currency changes since stamps were first issued there. Such denominations often appear on the stamps themselves, hence their inclusion here.

Stamp Illustrations

All stamps are reproduced same size except where otherwise indicated.

Map Abbreviations

Austr.	Australia
Auton.	Autonomous
Belg.	Belgium
Br. or Brit.	British
BSA	British South Africa
Bulg.	Bulgaria
Cap.	Capitol
Cr.	Crown
Col.	Colony
CPR	Canadian Pacific Railway
Czech.	Czechoslovakia
Comms.	Communists
Dem. Rep.	Democratic Republic
Den.	Denmark
Domin.	Dominion
Equat.	Equatorial
Fr.	French
GB	Great Britain
Grk.	Greek
Ger.	Germany
Hung.	Hungary
Ind.	Independent
Ital.	Italy
Jap.	Japanese
King.	Kingdom
Lith.	Lithuania
Lux.	Luxembourg
Mand.	Mandate
Milit.	Military
Nats.	Nationalists
NSW	New South Wales
NW	North West
NZ	New Zealand
Occ.	Occupied
OFS	Orange Free State
Ott. Emp.	Ottoman Empire
Pen. Col.	Penal Colony
Pol.	Poland
Port.	Portugal
PO	Post Office
Prot.	Protectorate
Rly.	Railway
Rep.	Republic
Sep. Col.	Separate Colony
Sard.	Sardinia
Self. Govt.	Self Government
SA	South Africa
Terr.	Territory
TPO	Travelling Post Office
Unit. Neth.	United Netherland
UK	United Kingdom
UN	United Nations
US	United States

EUROPE

THE ROYAL POSTS

The need for rulers to maintain control over and contact with every corner of their dominions led to the creation of the Royal Posts.

Before 1660, European posts for use by the public were virtually non-existent and correspondence between countries depended on the need either for the Royal courts or the rulers to transmit messages or for the maintenance of commercial information between merchants. At that time, many of the countries which we recognize today did not exist at all or existed in a different form. Certainly many of the boundaries were ill-defined and subject to change. Provinces, and indeed even countries, could transfer their loyalty by the marriage of a prince or princess to another royal family, and conquest commonly led to changes of allegiance.

The system of Royal messengers sprang from this need to oversee newly acquired territory or to maintain contact with armies in the field. The messengers were horsed and required to travel at considerable speed, which reduced the number of items which could be carried. Horses had to be changed at regular intervals and staging posts were provided on the main routes to minimize the delay. However, the use of these messengers was limited solely to the King and his court; outside that privileged few the regularity of any means of communication depended on the commercial development of the nation.

Merchants had had to develop their own postal network in parallel. They had no access to the Royal Posts and, commencing in Italy, the Merchants' Posts had spread throughout Europe by the end of the 15th or early 16th centuries. Initially developed by the Venetians to the Levant, Italian trading links were established further and further north and reached England early in the 16th century. By the end of the 16th century, regular services were operated by the Merchants both nationally and internationally. The cost of the letters was paid by the recipient and was usually charged in Italian currency regardless of the country of origin or delivery.

For the general public, neither of these two services was available. The one was forbidden and the other was too expensive. Literacy was at a low level and depended on clerks at court or in great households or on monastic influence. The transmission of letters, which were usually written from dictation, was by private servant or public carrier. Formal transmission of letters from the general public hardly existed.

However, the demand for such a service was growing and as the boundaries of the nations became more settled, the need to develop contact on a social plane as well as for reasons of state or mercantile purposes led to the opening of the Royal Posts to the public. By 1660, both the French and the British services had been made available, and in the latter case was a monopoly to prevent the operation of a mail service other than through the Royal Mail.

The sections for the nations which developed into the major powers of the 18th and 19th centuries examine the state of their postal development up to 1660. Details of the opening of the posts are also included where they are known to exist, but the exact structure of the formal services is not always clear. The map of Europe up to 1660 shows the state of affairs at a moment when, postally, the new nations were needing to develop their links for alliance and trade, and the first postal conventions were being created.

Pre 1650

Boundary of the Holy Roman Empire
Spanish
Swedish (Habsburg)
Austrian (Habsburg)
Venetian
Ottoman Empire
Ottoman influence
0 kilometres 400
0 miles 200
ISLAND (Den.)
FAROE ISLANDS (Den.)
SHETLANDS
ORKNEYS
Atlantic Ocean
DANMARK & NORGE
SVERIGE
SUOMI
Carelia
Gulf of Bothnia
Lake Ladoga
Helsingfors
St Petersburg
Christiana
ALAND IS
Stockholm
Estonia
RUSSIAN EMPIRE
Livonia
GOTLAND
OLAND
Skagerrak
Kattegat
North Sea
Scotland
GREAT BRITAIN (1603)
IRELAND
Ulster
Connaught
Leinster
Munster
Drogheda
Dublin
Holyhead
Chester
Wales
England
Bristol
London
Baltic Sea
Lithuania
København
PREUSSEN
Sweden (1648)
Danzig
Sweden (1648)
Elbe
Brandenburg
Berlin
Vistula
POLSKA
Warszawa
Kiev
Dneiper
VEREENIGDE PROVINCIEN (1648)
English Channel
Bruxelles
NEDERLAND
CHANNEL IS (Brit.)
Rhine
Sachsen
Schlesien
Böhmen
Prag
Gleschien
Dneister
Bessarabia
Moldavia
Pruth
Odessa
Paris
Danube
Mähren
Wien
HUNGARISCHE KÖNIGREICH
München
FRANCE
Dijon
Mâcon
ÖSTERREICH
Buda
Pest
Transilvania
Bay of Biscay
HELVETISCHE REP. (1648)
Tirol
Lake Balaton
Drava
Danube
Wallachia
Lyon
Bordeaux
Rhone
Savoie
Po
STATI ITALIANI
Venezia
Sava
Belgrad
Black Sea
Danube
Toulouse
Navarre
MONACO
Genoa
Stati Papali
ANDORRA
MONTENEGRO
PORTUGAL (1640)
ESPAÑA
Madrid
Aranjuez
Aragon
LA CORSE (Genoa)
Adriatic Sea
Costantinopoli
OTTOMAN EMPIRE
Lisboa
Roma
Salonika
Napoli
NAPOLI
MALLORCA
MENORCA
Tyrrhenian Sea
SARDEGNA
Castilla
ISLAS BALEARES (Sp.)
Aegean Sea
Smyrna
IONIAN IS (Venice)
Ionian Sea
Granada
Athinai
Morea
Mediterranean Sea
Gibraltar
Tanger (Port.)
Cueta (Sp.)
Sicilia
RHOD
Oran (Sp.)
Mellila (Sp.)
MALTA (Knights of St John)
KRITI (Venice)

1650-1793

Boundary of the Holy Roman Empire
Spanish (Bourbon 1714)
Austria-Hungary 1793
Prussia 1793
Russia 1793
Venetian
Ottoman Empire
Ottoman influence
0 kilometres 400
0 miles 200
ISLAND (Den.)
Reykjavik
FAROE ISLANDS (Den.)
SHETLANDS
ORKNEYS
Atlantic Ocean
North Sea
Scotland
GREAT BRITAIN & IRELAND (1707)
Carrickfergus
Drogheda
Dublin
Limerick
I. OF MAN
Wales
England
Bristol
Exeter
London
English Channel
CHANNEL IS
DANMARK & NORGE
Christiana
SVERIGE
SUOMI
Carelia (1721)
Viborg
Gulf of Bothnia
Helsingfors
St Petersburg
Ingria
ALAND IS
Stockholm
Estonia (1721)
GOTLAND
RUSSIAN EMPIRE
Moskva
Livonia
Riga
OLAND
Baltic Sea
København
SCHLESWIG
HELGOLAND (Den.)
HOLSTEIN
Elbe
Lithuania
(to Russ. 1795)
(1772)
(1667)
Danzig
PREUSSEN
(1772)
(to Prussia 1795)
(1793)
PREUSSEN
Berlin
POLSKA
Warszawa
(1795)
(to Austria 1795)
(1667)
Dneiper
VEREENIGD NEDERLAND
Rhine
Sachsen
Schlesien (1742)
Vistula
Gleschien (1772)
(1762)
ÖSTERREICHISCHE NEDERLAND
Paris
Böhmen
Praha
Mähren
Dniester
Pruth
(1791)
Danube
Wien
Bukovina (1775)
Bessarabia
Moldavia
(1783)
REPUBLIQUE FRANCAISE (1793)
ÖSTERREICH
Buda
Pest
Danube
Transilvania
Bay of Biscay
HELVETISCHE REP.
Tirol
Drava
Lyon
Bordeaux
Rhone
VENETIA
Sava
SLAVONIA
Wallachia
La Coruña
Po
Venezia
Beograd
Danube
Black Sea
Bilbao
San Sebastián
SARDEGNA
STATI ITALIANI
Genoa
MONACO
Bosnia
Servia
ANDORRA
Stati Papali
BULGARIA
LA CORSE (Fr.)
MONTENEGRO
Costantinopoli
PORTUGAL
Madrid
Barcelona
Tarragona
Adriatic Sea
Roma
Albania
OTTOMAN EMPIRE
ESPAÑA
Lisboa
Tyrrhenian Sea
Napoli
Salonika
MENORCA (Brit. 1713)
SARDEGNA
Aegean Sea
REGNO DELLE DUE SICILIE
Smyrna
IONIAN ISLANDS
Jerez
ISLAS BALEARES (Sp.)
Ionian Sea
Athínai
Cadiz
Gibraltar (Brit. 1713)
Morea
Mediterranean Sea
Tangier
Cueta (Sp.)
Sicilia
RHODOS
Mellila (Sp.)
MALTA
KRITI (Turk. 1669)

Britain

CURRENCY

sterling to 1971
1971 decimal currency

Up to 1660

Following the conquests of Edward I in the 13th century, Wales had become a principality of England, but in spite of constant wars unification with Scotland had to wait until the death of Queen Elizabeth I in 1603. The Wars of the Roses, a civil war between the Houses of York and Lancaster, prevented any real stability until after 1487, when the Tudor dynasty began. Under Henry VIII (1509-47) the first Master of the Posts, Sir Brian Tuke, was appointed in 1516. It was his responsibility to ensure that the King's messages were speedily and efficiently handled and that horses were provided at the staging posts. This was a responsibility for the Royal Post and no public mail, except from courtiers, and then only by special favour, was carried. Because of this, the merchants, particularly those with overseas connections, had to establish their own service, and before the end of the 16th century both the Merchant Stranger and the Merchant Venturers Post were operating in London.

When Elizabeth died in 1603, she was succeeded by James VI of Scotland who became James I of England, and a union of the two countries was effected. This was followed by a period of growing unrest as greater control of the government was sought by the people. By restricting the King's ability to raise taxes, Parliament, when it sat, was able to exercise some control over the King. To counteract this, Charles I tried to create monopolies which would pay him for the right to produce and merchandise a particular product.

In 1635, partly to extend this source of tax, partly to defray the costs of the Royal Courier service and partly to establish an intelligence system, Charles, by proclamation, opened the Royal Post to the public. A fixed range of charges based on the distance carried was established and, in 1637, a second proclamation excluded the carriers from any monopoly. Thus for a time two quite separate postal systems operated in the country, and although the King's post went three times each week to Edinburgh, there was enough mail being carried outside the Royal Mail to warrant the publication in 1637 of a *Carriers Cosmographie*. This shows clearly the number of regular routes used by those who were outside the King's Post.

However, the first public post, 'To Foreign Parts', had been opened even before 1635, in 1632. At that time, by decree, Thomas Witherings was appointed as the Postmaster to Foreign Parts and the first letters carried by the British Post Office with charge marks appeared. The rate from Calais was 4*d*.

Within seven years of the opening of the post to the public, the Civil War broke out and continued until the King himself was executed in 1649. During this period, the posts were severely curtailed, if they ran at all, and the carriage of letters by carriers was often disrupted by seizure by opposing forces. However, normal social and business correspondence had to continue and a number of small local posts grew up. It is believed that in certain areas, notably East Anglia, the service was more or less normal during these years, but the state of affairs in the Midlands and in the other principal areas of fighting would have been very difficult.

By 1647 the situation within the country had returned more or less to normal and the posts were re-established. However, with the King defeated, the control of the mail was changed. For the first time, the post was 'farmed', that is to say it was auctioned to the highest bidder, and, after payment of a sum to the government, the successful applicant was allowed to take his profit from the postal service. That this was a lucrative source of income can be gathered from the example of the first holder of the office, John Manley, who in 1653 bid £10,000 per annum for this right. At his request the smaller posts which had sprung up had to be suppressed, and in the following year Oliver Cromwell, by then Lord Protector, passed an order in council which made it an offence for anyone else to charge for carrying letters. Although it had always been the King's original intent that the post should be a monopoly, it was thus in fact under the Commonwealth that there was the start of the monopoly system which still holds good to this day.

1660-1793

Under the Commonwealth, an Act for the Post Office was passed in 1657. This set up the monopoly of the post in more general form and also established the rights of those who operated the post. For the first time the position of Postmaster-General was created and the first incumbent was John Thurloe. In 1660 Charles II was restored to the throne and a further Post Office Act largely confirmed the Act of 1657, which had been declared illegal. The new Postmaster-General was Henry Bishop, and he was responsible for setting up the General Letter Office near the present site of the Mansion House and also for the introduction of postal markings on letters. He stated that 'A stamp is to be put on every letter', the purpose of which was that any delay in the handling of the mail would clearly be seen. This first marking, a simple circle with the date in the upper half and the month in the lower, was used for many years.

With the growth in commerce following the Restoration, the size of the Post Office increased as did the amount paid for 'farming' the post. In 1680 a local post was established in London by William Dockwra; this was speedily suppressed, though his service was used as the basis of the London post until the middle of the 19th century.

By early in the 18th century, markings for provincial towns began to appear and these clearly show the extent of commerce, and the main centres of industry as they were at that time. Special marks similar to the London Bishop Mark were used in Bristol

Royal Mail coach, 1830s

and Exeter and straightline names without date were widely used.

Acts affecting the rates of postage were passed in 1660 and 1765, but these were all based on letters coming into London and out again. While this might have been advisable for security purposes in the 17th century, as the country became more settled it was obvious that a more equitable system would have to be devised. Ralph Allen of Bath is attributed with the bulk of the work in the establishment of the Cross Posts; although postal markings continued to carry the mileage from London as part of their general format, the speeding of the service achieved by his reforms was substantial.

The carriage of mail between post towns was a haphazard affair in the 18th century. The work was mainly carried out by postboys who rode from town to town delivering and collecting letters on their way. They were notoriously slow, drunken and insecure. The Post Office advised anyone who wished to send valuables through the post that they should cut bills or money drafts in half and hold the second half until they knew that the first had arrived.

By the 1780s with the dawn of the Industrial Revolution the need for a quicker and more secure mail service was apparent. The man who eventually provided the spark which created the new system was another West Country man, John Palmer. He was the manager of the Theatre Royal in Bath, and Bristol was also within his responsibility. With his need to move troupes of actors to and from each place and London some better means of transport had to be devised. Against resistance from the Post Office, he managed to persuade William Pitt that the Post Office should operate a series of mail-coaches which would travel quickly and directly between centres and, as the mail guard would be armed, with security. The first trial was carried out between Bristol and London on 2 August 1784 and was followed by the development of a complete service throughout the country by 1790.

Although John Palmer was responsible for this leap forward in speed and security of the mail, his idea would not have been possible without the provision of better roads as a result of the introduction of turnpikes. So in 133 years the Post Office in Britain had moved from its beginnings to a structure which survived as a basis for its remarkable development throughout the 19th century.

Abroad, the changes had been less startling. The development of the colonial empire in the 17th and 18th centuries had meant that the giant trading concerns such as the East India Company had had to maintain continuous contact with their agents abroad. Major colonial and European wars had seen many British troops in service both at home and overseas and their needs for communication had also had to be provided for. This growth had led to the Ship Letter system and the Post Office packets, which are dealt with elsewhere.

During the War of the Austrian Succession (1739-45), British forces fighting with their German allies (the King of England had also been the Elector of Hanover since 1714) had received the first overseas postal marking on their mail. The letters AB [Armée Britannique] had been applied to their letters in 1743-4.

The loss of the American colonies following their Revolution and the American War of Independence (1776-83) had been a blow not only to Britain's worldwide prestige but also to the expansion of the colonial empire. This growth had been severely affected, although both India and Canada had been largely established as British spheres of influence by the middle of the 18th century. However, the map of Europe was about to change. The French Revolution of 1789 and the effect on Europe of the overthrow of royal power led on to the wars of Napoleon.

1793-1815

The French Revolutionary and Napoleonic wars of this period had little direct effect on the British postal service at home. The mail-coach service which had been inaugurated in

1793-1815
Austro-Hungarian Empire
Prussia
Russia
Ottoman Empire
German Confederation 1815
0 kilometres 400
0 miles 200
ISLAND
(Den.)
FAROE ISLANDS
(Den.)
SHETLANDS
ORKNEYS
Atlantic Ocean
North Sea
NORGE & SVERIGE
(From 1814)
DANMARK & NORGE
(Separated 1814)
Christiana
Gulf of Bothnia
SUOMI
(Russ. 1809)
Vyborg
Helsingfors
St Petersburg
ALAND IS
Stockholm
GOTLAND
OLAND
Baltic Sea
Moskva
RUSSIAN EMPIRE
GREAT BRITAIN
& IRELAND
DANMARK
(From 1814)
København
Dublin
Kingstown
(Dun Laoghaire)
Holyhead
HELGOLAND
(Brit. 1814)
RÜGEN
Danzig
Lübeck
Hamburg
Elbe
Vistula
Hannover
Hannover
Berlin
Warszawa
POLSKA
Kiev
Dneiper
PREUSSEN
Amsterdam
VEREENIGDE
NEDERLAND
London
Falmouth
English Channel
Rhine
Sachsen
CHANNEL IS
(Brit.)
Lux.
Prag
Lemberg
REP. KRAKÓW
ÖSTERREICHISCHE KAISERLICHE
KONIGREICH
Dneister
Pruth
Bessarabia
Moldavia
Odessa
Paris
Bay of Biscay
FRANCE
Danube
Bayern
München
Wien
ÖSTERREICH
Buda
Pest
Transilvania
MAGYARORSZAG
SCHWEIZ
Lyon
Bordeaux
Rhone
Savoie
Piemonte
SARDEGNA
Lombardia - Venetia
Po
Venezia
Drava
Sava
Wallachia
Bucuresti
Black Sea
Beograd
Bosnia
Servia
Dalmatia
STATI ITALIANI
Stati
Papali
Nice
MONACO
(Sard.)
ANDORRA
Sofia
MONTENEGRO
Costantinopoli
OTTOMAN EMPIRE
LA CORSE
(Fr.)
Roma
Adriatic Sea
PORTUGAL
Madrid
ESPAÑA
Lisboa
Albania
Salonika
Tyrrhenian Sea
Napoli
SARDEGNA
Aegean Sea
CORFU
IONIAN
ISLANDS
(Fr. 1807;
Brit. 1815)
Ionian
Sea
REGNO DELLE DUE SICILIE
ISLAS BALEARES
(Sp.)
Morea
Athínai
Gibraltar
(Brit.)
Tanger
Cueta
(Sp.)
Mediterranean Sea
Sicilia
RHODES
Mellila
(Sp.)
MALTA
(Fr. 1788; Brit. 1800)
KRITI

1815-1850

Austro-Hungarian Empire
Prussia
Russia
Ottoman Empire
German Confederation 1839
0 kilometres 400
0 miles 200
ISLAND
(Den.)
FAROE ISLANDS
(Den.)
SHETLANDS
ORKNEYS
Atlantic Ocean
UNITED KINGDOM
OF GT BRITAIN
& IRELAND
1840
Dublin
London
Falmouth
North Sea
NORGE
&
SVERIGE
Christiana
Gulf of Bothnia
SUOMI
Helsingfors
St Petersburg
ALAND IS
Stockholm
GOTLAND
OLAND
Moskva
DANMARK
København
Baltic Sea
Memel
Schleswig
Holstein
Cuxhaven
Lubeck
Hamburg
Elbe
RUSSIAN EMPIRE
P R E U S S E N
1850
Berlin
Vistula
Warszawa
POLSKA
(Russ. Prov. 1849)
Lublin
Kiev
Dneiper
Amsterdam
NEDERLAND
Bruxelles
BELGIE
1849
English Channel
CHANNEL IS
1840
LUX.
(to Belg. 1839)
Rhine
Sachsen
Dresden
Kraków
Lemberg
Prag
Paris
ÖSTERREICHISCHE KAISERLICHE
KONIGREICH
Bayern
1849
Danube
Wien
Munchen
ÖSTERREICH
1850
Buda
Pest
Dneister
Pruth
Bessarabia
Moldavia
Odessa
Bay of Biscay
FRANCE
1849
SCHWEIZ
1843
Tirol
Transilvania
MAGYARORSZAG
1850
(to Russ. 1829)
Drava
Bordeaux
Lyon
Savoie
Lombardia -Venetia
Po
Venice
Sava
Wallachia
Rhone
SARDEGNA
STATI ITALIANI
Beograd
Servia
(Ind. 1829)
Black Sea
Vigo
Nice
MONACO
Stati
Papali
Oporto
ANDORRA
LA CORSE
(Fr.)
Adriatic Sea
MONTENEGRO
Costantinopoli
PORTUGAL
Madrid
Albania
OTTOMAN EMPIRE
ESPAÑA
Roma
isboa
Tyrrhenian Sea
Napoli
Salonika
SARDEGNA
REGNO DELLE DUE SICILIE
Aegean Sea
Sevilla
ISLAS BALEARES
(Sp.)
IONIAN
ISLANDS
(Brit.)
Athinai
Cadiz
Málaga
Gibraltar
(Brit.)
Peninsular Line
Mediterranean Sea
Ionian Sea
HELLAS
Tanger
Cueta
(Sp.)
Sicilia
Navarino
(1827)
RHODOS
Mellila
(Sp.)
MALTA
(Brit.)
KRITI
(Egypt 1824-40)

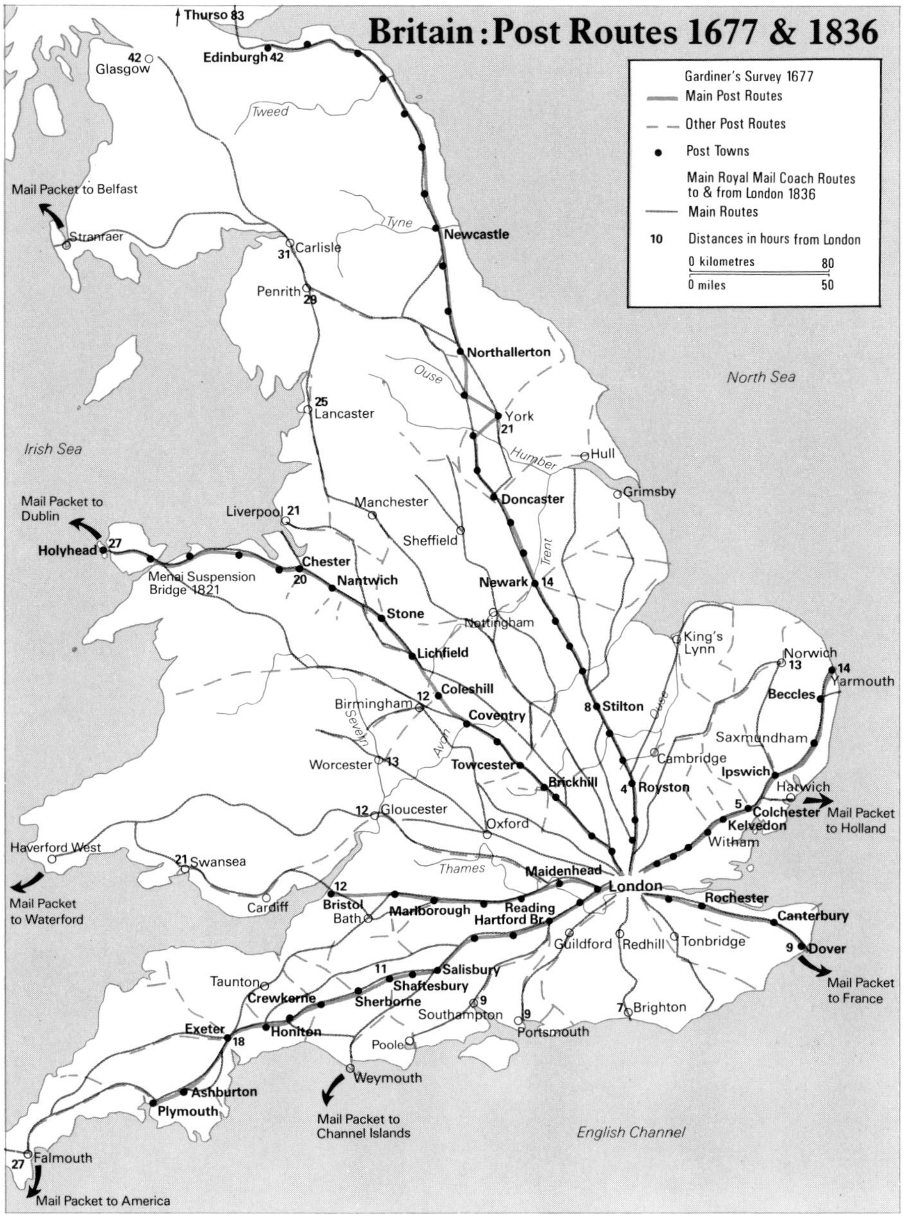
Britain: Post Routes 1677 & 1836
Gardiner's Survey 1677
Main Post Routes
Other Post Routes
Post Towns
Main Royal Mail Coach Routes to & from London 1836
Main Routes
10 Distances in hours from London
0 kilometres 80
0 miles 50
Thurso 83
Glasgow 42
Edinburgh 42
Tweed
Mail Packet to Belfast
Stranraer
Tyne
Newcastle
31 Carlisle
Penrith 29
Northallerton
Ouse
North Sea
25 Lancaster
York 21
Irish Sea
Humber
Hull
Grimsby
Mail Packet to Dublin
Liverpool 21
Manchester
Doncaster
Sheffield
Holyhead 27
Chester 20
Menai Suspension Bridge 1821
Nantwich
Trent
Newark 14
Stone
Nottingham
Lichfield
King's Lynn
Norwich 13
14 Yarmouth
Coleshill
Birmingham 12
Severn
Coventry
8 Stilton
Beccles
Saxmundham
Worcester 13
Avon
Towcester
Cambridge
Ipswich
Brickhill
4 Royston
Harwich
Mail Packet to Holland
12 Gloucester
5 Colchester
Kelvedon
Witham
Oxford
Haverford West
21 Swansea
Thames
Maidenhead
London
Mail Packet to Waterford
Cardiff
12 Bristol
Bath
Marlborough
Reading
Hartford Br.
Rochester
Canterbury
Guildford
Redhill
Tonbridge
9 Dover
Mail Packet to France
11 Salisbury
Shaftesbury
Taunton
Crewkerne
Sherborne
9 Southampton
9 Portsmouth
7 Brighton
Exeter 18
Honiton
Poole
Weymouth
Ashburton
Plymouth
Mail Packet to Channel Islands
English Channel
27 Falmouth
Mail Packet to America

1784 continued to grow and by the end of this period was in its heyday. It had proved itself to be speedy and reliable as well as secure and the robbery of the postboys, which had been a major problem before its introduction, was not repeated with the mail-coaches. Acts of Parliament led to increases in letter charges again in 1796, 1801 and 1812, partly to increase the revenue and provide funds for the continuance of the war, and partly to meet the increase in the cost of living.

The most significant introduction during this period was the local Penny Post service, which enabled mail in a small area to be collected together and passed on to the main mail routes. It was this network of receiving houses that led to the wide range of sub-post offices, which have been a feature of the British Post Office ever since.

The type of postal markings became more formalized at this time and general standard types can be found and identified. In the 1790s almost all markings included the date, and, for the first time, the year was also included as a general rule.

As Britain was not invaded, there was no disruption of the internal mails, but it was a different matter overseas. The Post Office packet service and many of the smaller, lightly armed vessels were prey to the attacks of French and Spanish privateers. Many of the smaller colonies were occupied by enemy forces. At the same time, especially in the West Indies, British forces took control of many of the French islands. Because of distance, and the length of time for intelligence to reach Britain, the public were in difficulty in knowing how best to route their letters. At the same time Britain had large forces abroad and supply lines were subject to frequent attack. Nevertheless, the service was maintained, especially to Lisbon as the base of the Peninsular Army, and mail was carried in both directions.

Early in this period the British Army invaded the Low Countries and was accompanied by Henry Darlot, the first Postmaster-General to the Forces. He set up a service with a special postmark 'Army Bag' and this was used on mail in 1799. However, the bulk of the mail from officers and other ranks in other campaigns was carried without special markings, and was placed in the Ship Letter arrival system.

The first decade of the 19th century saw the growth of what was to become one of the major abuses of the postal system — the right of free mail. This system had been established for government departments and for members of both Houses of Parliament in the 17th century, but, although the number and weight of letters were restricted, it still gave a privilege to many people who were only too glad to take advantage of it. To prevent some of the abuse, the sender was required to sign the outside of the cover, but in 1784 this was changed so that the place

Above
Mail coaches outside the GPO, London, c.1830

Right
The Post Office, London, 1809

of posting and the date had also to be in the superscription of the address. It is fortunate that many of these 'fronts' have survived, preserved by the autograph collectors of the last century, but the volume of this free mail was a burden under which the Post Office had to struggle for many years.

1815-50

FIRST STAMPS ISSUED 6 May 1840

Although there were many troubles in Europe during this period, Britain entered into a period of relative stability. Apart from the Crimean War and many colonial wars, it was not until 1914 that it was again required to take part in a European war.

However, during these 35 years two of the most significant changes in the postal service occurred. First was the demise of the mail-coach service. This mainstay of the transmission of letters within the kingdom had been based on the turnpike roads and the provision of a fast and reliable service. However, though the coaches had been built to a Post Office specification they had been owned by the contractors who operated the service. Therefore, when railways came on the scene, there was no capital investment involved on the part of the Post Office and no vested interest in retaining the coaches. By the late 1820s coaches were at their peak and over 40 mail-coaches were leaving Post Office headquarters each night. By 1846 no mail coaches were entering London and by 1855 there were no coaches at all.

The first train ran on the Stockton-Darlington railway in 1825; in 1830 the Liverpool and Manchester Railway was opened and in November that year it began to carry mail. The Post Office had to face a number of serious problems. There was the question of security and safety, problems over moving mail from stations to POs in the towns, and the cost of carriage itself. But all of these could be solved and the overriding advantages of quick and direct service meant that deliveries could be speeded up dramatically.

Linked with the advance in the means of transport was the advantage of being able to pre-sort mail while in transit. As early as 1826 Rowland Hill, whom we shall discuss later in this section, had proposed that letters could be sorted on mail-coaches to save time and improve the service. This proposal was not followed through because coaches could not provide the space which would be required, and, more important, any loss of passenger accommodation would adversely affect the contractors. However, the same constraint did not apply to the railways. By 1838 a trial was run on the Grand Junction Railway between Birmingham and Warrington using a modified cattle truck. It was an immediate success and it was claimed 'that it enabled the travelling and sorting to be done at the same time'. Immediately, the Post Office ordered four special carriages to be run from Euston. In the early stages these ran to Bletchley and mail went on by coach to Birmingham, but by 1842 the service was through direct

A
POSTAGE
ONE PENNY
B
C
HALF PENNY
FIVE PENCE
75P
D
TEN PENCE
E

A Britain:King George V 1913; **B** Britain:Queen Victoria 1840; **C** Britain:King Edward VII 1901; **D** Britain:Queen Elizabeth 1980; **E** Britain:King George VI 1938.

from London to Preston. The days of the Travelling Post Offices (TPOs) had arrived.

The second change was much more far reaching, with implications not only in Britain but throughout the world. This was Rowland Hill's reform, which was introduced in 1839-40. Before we look at the far-sighted changes he proposed, it is as well to be clear on the system as it stood in Britain in the mid-1830s. The Act by which the Post Office had been founded and on the basis of which it had developed over 200 years since Charles I's proclamation had calculated all charges for carriage on the distance carried and the number of sheets of paper used. As an envelope counted as another sheet of paper, this system had delayed the introduction of commercial envelope manufacture for over 50 years. A further problem was that it was difficult for the sender to assess the distance that the letter had to be carried and, unless he wished to visit the nearest post town, it was usual for the recipient to pay for the letter on arrival.

Rowland Hill, a schoolmaster in North London, proposed a series of changes to this procedure: free franking should be abolished, a uniform postage rate should apply to all parts of the kingdom, the sole increment should be dependent on the weight of the item and payment should be made by the sender. It was part of his plan that *all* letters would have to be prepaid — but this was not accepted. In none of his early papers was the question of adhesive stamps mentioned, but this appeared later and led to the introduction of the first postage stamp, the Penny Black, on 6 May 1840.

The reforms proposed by Rowland Hill were debated throughout the land. The growth in the volume of mail, which had reached 50 million items in 1838, was a result of the need for commercial contact during the Industrial Revolution and the growth of literacy in the population. It was now a period of social as well as commercial correspondence and cost was an important factor.

As a trial, the 4*d* Uniform Post was introduced on 5 December 1839, but as it was public knowledge that the cost was soon to be reduced to 1*d*, pressure led to the introduction of 1*d* postage on 10 January 1840, four months before the stamps were ready. During the interim period between January and May many handstamps were introduced to indicate the prepayment of postage until these were replaced in May by the new stamps.

In April 1840 it was discovered that the red cancelling ink provided for marking the stamps to prevent re-use could be removed too easily. As a result the recipe was modified and a Post Office notice issued on 28 April 1840 gave details of the way in which the ink was to be mixed. The cancellation to be used and issued to each of the post towns was a so-called 'Maltese Cross', though this had rounded corners and is not strictly as described. This cancellation was first struck in red on the black stamp, but in early 1841 this was replaced by a black ink which was more difficult to remove. The colour of the stamp was changed to red. All the early stamps were printed by Perkins Bacon, who held the contract for all values up to and including 2*d* until 1880. The Maltese Cross continued as the cancellation until 1842. Many of these crosses, which appear to have been made locally, are distinguishable from each other and can also be found struck in a variety of colours, though red and black were the only ones officially approved.

In 1842 a series of numbers was issued on an alphabetical basis to the post towns in England and Wales with a further series for Scotland. These styles of markings and numbers were used until the end of the century.

By 1846 a demand for higher value stamps had been created, although few other countries had so far issued stamps. The Post Office, as previously, was worried about the re-use of stamps and, as a result, selected the embossing process for the 1*s* value (1847) and 10*d* value (1848). In the recommendation it was stated that 'the Queen's head being free from ink, and thus unvarnished, readily imbibes the cancelling ink'.

As part of Rowland Hill's original scheme the public was to be able to purchase envelopes and letter sheets with the postage prepaid. These were

Post being delivered in the Scottish Highlands, 1848

Left
London Postman, 1819

British Numeral Postmarks used abroad

During the period up to 1892, lists of numerals issued to British POs show many examples issued to overseas locations. Many of these never used British stamps and, although in the British series, they were essentially the colonial issue. Some of these numbers were also issued in the United Kingdom so care must be taken to ensure that these stamps are truly 'used abroad'. Below are listed those numbers and locations where British stamps are known to have been used.

247 –	Fernando Po
582 –	Naguabo – Port Rico
942 –	Larnaca
969 –	Nicosia
974 –	Papho
975 –	Famagusta
981 –	Limassol
982 –	Kyrenia
098 –	Platres
A01 –	Kingston – Jamaica
A02 –	Antigua
A03 –	Demerara – British Guiana
A04 –	Berbice – British Guiana
A05 –	Bahamas
A06 –	Belize – British Honduras
A07 –	Dominica
A08 –	Montserrat
A09 –	Nevis
A10 –	St Vincent
A11 –	St Lucia
A12 –	St Kitts
A13 –	Tortola – Virgin Islands
A14 –	Tobago
A15 –	Grenada
A18 –	English Harbour – Antigua
A25 –	Malta
A26 –	Gibraltar
A27 – A79 –	Jamaica
B01 –	Alexandria – Egypt
B02 –	Suez – Egypt
B32 –	Buenos Aires
C28 –	Montevideo – Uruguay
C30 –	Valparaiso – Chile
C35 –	Panama
C36 –	Arica – Peru
C37 –	Caldera – Chile
C38 –	Callao – Peru
C39 –	Cobijo – Bolivia (now in Peru)
C40 –	Coquimbo – Chile
C41 –	Guayaquil – Ecuador
C42 –	Islay – Peru
C43 –	Payta – Peru
C51 –	St Thomas – Danish W.I.
C56 –	Carthagena – Colombia
C57 –	Greytown – Nicaragua
C58 –	Havana – Cuba
C59 –	Jacmel – Haiti
C60 –	La Guaira – Venezuela
C61 –	Puerto Rico
C62 –	Santa Martha – Colombia
C63 –	Tampico – Mexico
C81 –	Bahia – Brazil
C82 –	Pernambuco – Brazil
C83 –	Rio de Janeiro – Brazil
C86 –	Porto Plata – Dominican Rep.
C87 –	St Domingo – Dominican Rep.
C88 –	St Jago de Cuba – Cuba
D22 –	Ciudad Bolivar – Venezuela
D26 –	St Thomas – DWI Mail packet
D47 –	Polymedia, Cyprus
D48 –	Headquarters Camp
D65 –	Pisagua – Peru
D74 –	Pisco & Chiuca Islands – Peru
D87 –	Iquique – Peru
E18 –	Colon – Colombia
F69 –	Savanilla – Colombia
F83 –	Arroyo – Porto Rico
F84 –	Aguadilla – Porto Rico
F85 –	Mayaguez – Puerto Rico
F87 –	Smyrna – Turkey
F88 –	Ponce – Puerto Rico
G06 –	Beirut – British Levant

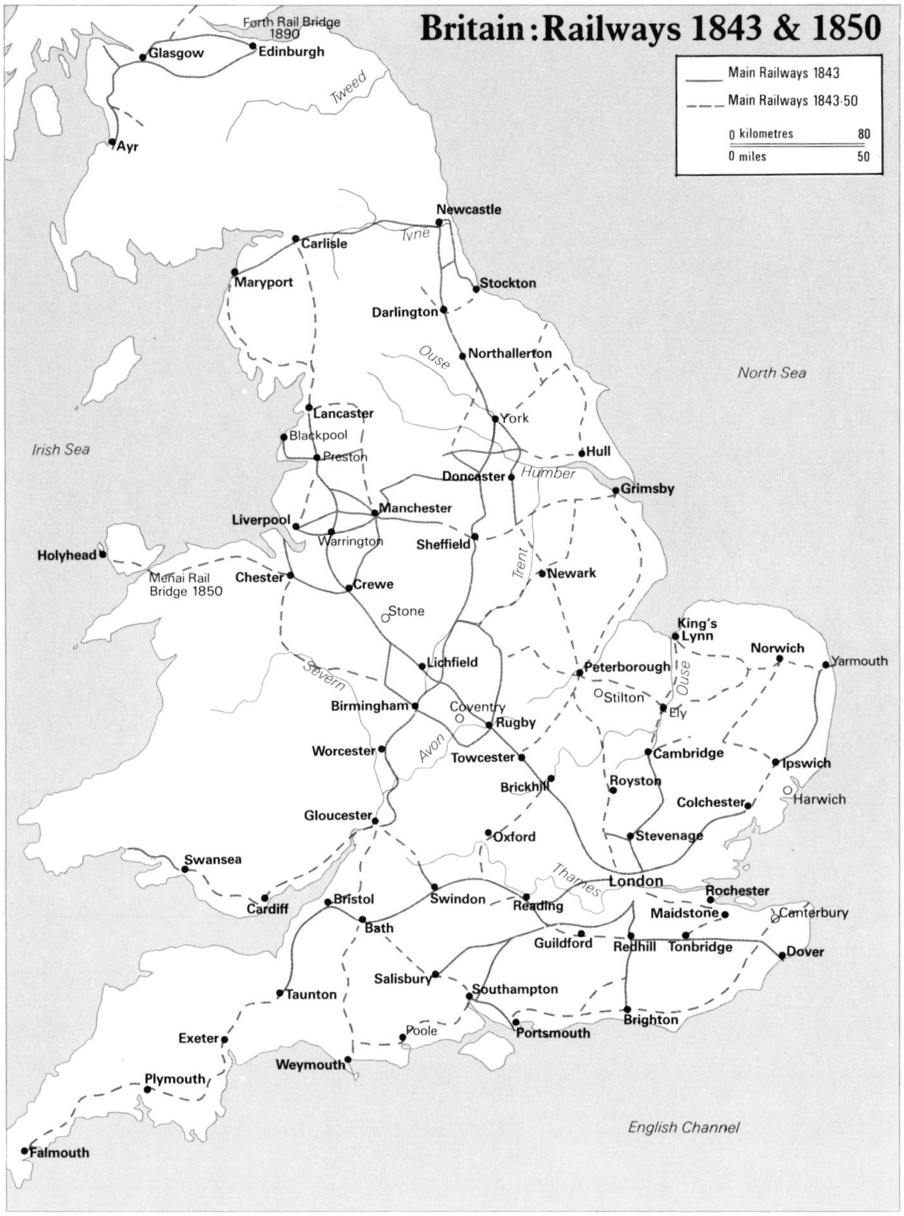
Britain: Railways 1843 & 1850
Main Railways 1843
Main Railways 1843-50
0 kilometres 80
0 miles 50
Forth Rail Bridge 1890
Glasgow
Edinburgh
Tweed
Ayr
Newcastle
Tyne
Carlisle
Maryport
Stockton
Darlington
Ouse
Northallerton
North Sea
York
Lancaster
Blackpool
Preston
Irish Sea
Hull
Doncaster
Humber
Grimsby
Manchester
Liverpool
Warrington
Sheffield
Holyhead
Menai Rail Bridge 1850
Chester
Crewe
Trent
Newark
Stone
King's Lynn
Norwich
Yarmouth
Lichfield
Severn
Peterborough
Stilton
Ely
Birmingham
Coventry
Rugby
Worcester
Avon
Towcester
Cambridge
Ipswich
Brickhill
Royston
Harwich
Colchester
Gloucester
Oxford
Stevenage
Swansea
Thames
London
Rochester
Cardiff
Bristol
Swindon
Reading
Maidstone
Canterbury
Bath
Guildford
Redhill
Tonbridge
Dover
Salisbury
Southampton
Taunton
Brighton
Poole
Portsmouth
Exeter
Weymouth
Plymouth
English Channel
Falmouth

produced in 1840 as the Mulready envelopes. They met with universal criticism and as a result were quickly withdrawn and replaced by envelopes with a 1*d* or 2*d* stamp embossed. The former remained in use until the turn of the century.

Although the changes and reforms had major and far-reaching effects on the internal post, the impact on overseas post, which was affected as much by industrial and technical development as it was by new postal systems, was less dramatic. The interchange of mail for foreign destinations was still regulated by individual treaties and the methods of accounting were both complex and costly. But the development of steam for ships meant that more regular and reliable services could be devised. Linked with this was the growing need for Britain to be able to communicate quickly and reliably with the colonies which were beginning to provide the raw materials on which the new affluence was to be based.

Under Rowland Hill's postal reforms, the Ship Letter Office was closed, but during this period the Post Office packets had disappeared and been replaced by contract shipping lines, which undertook to make regular trips to specified destinations. The most important of these were Cunard on the Transatlantic service, and Peninsular and Orient to the Mediterranean and beyond Egypt to India, Australia and the Far East.

1850-71

During these years, only overseas wars impinged on the boundaries of Empire. Europe was going through a period of nationalistic change, but Britain remained aloof and avoided any of the European wars. The stability which was gained enabled Britain to develop its resources and the growth of commerce led to massive increases in the volume of post carried. This was compounded by the growth of literacy and the fact that cheap postage had made the post available to all but the poorest.

The first stamps had appeared in 1840, with higher values being issued before the end of the decade. The convenience which the use of adhesives and the prepayment of postage had brought led to new values being required as time progressed. Many of these were issued to meet specific overseas requirements, as with the 4*d* stamp of 1854, which was designed to pay the new reduced rate for France. At the same time, the method of production of stamps had to be reconsidered. The system used in the 1840s, line engraving for values up to 2*d* and embossing for the higher values, was expensive and, in the latter case, slow. When the new Act controlling the use of fiscal stamps was introduced in 1853, De La Rue — a firm of playing-card manufacturers — obtained the contract for surface-printing the new issue, largely owing to the friendship between Ormonde Hill and Thomas De La Rue. Their production was so quick, efficient and low-priced that

POST OFFICE
LETTER BOX
Nº I
MILES FURLONGS YARDS
3 215
FROM THE GENERAL POST OFFICE

Above
First letter-box, sited at the corner of Fleet Street and Farringdon Street, London, 1855

GENERAL POST OFFICE

Right
London postmen overburdened on St Valentine's Day, 1866

they were also given the opportunity to provide the values above 2*d*. Therefore until 1880 when De La Rue began to print all British stamps, they printed all values above 2*d*, and during this period a wide range of colours and values were used.

Major problems during this period for the internal mail service were, first, the establishment of a means of mechanically separating stamps and, second, securing a better and quicker means of cancelling the ever-growing volume of letters and, by the end of 1871, postcards.

Early stamps were not perforated. They were cut from sheets by the clerks, usually in horizontal strips (vertical strips are much scarcer) and sold singly or as required by the customer. It is known that a machine for the separation of a single stamp from a strip of 20 or more by use of a small guillotine was displayed at the Great Exhibition in 1851 but no such machine has survived.

In 1848, Henry Archer had patented a machine for perforating sheets on a flatbed system and trials led to the introduction of perforated stamps in 1850, though early roulettes had been tried in 1848. This was followed in 1854 by a modified design by W. Bemrose and Son, who invented a rotary perforating machine. In the interim other trials had been carried out with a roulette machine of the Treasury, which produced a distinctive serpentine edge to the stamps.

When postage stamps were first introduced, the handling of letters continued on much the same basis. The initial volume increases were coped with and hand-cancelling of the stamps continued as the only means of preventing the re-use of stamps. However, the continuing increase in the number of letters posted led to the need for some quicker means of cancellation. The first machine trials were held in London in 1857 on a machine designed by Pearson Hill, the son of Rowland Hill. This type was not fully successful, but a revised design using the 'parallel motion' system was successful and was brought into use in a number of POs in the 1860s. Other designs and types of hand-operated machines were introduced after trials but the Pearson Hill machine remained the first choice with British and colonial administrations until the introduction of electrical or power-driven machines later in the century. Most of these were developed in Scandinavia or the USA and were imported or made under licence in Britain.

In October 1869 the Austrian PO introduced postcards, a pre-printed card with an impressed stamp which passed through the post at a reduced rate. The demand for the issue of similar items in Britain was instantaneous and the new cards were introduced on 1 October 1870, the same day as the new printed paper rate. This service was an immediate success and 70 million of the new cards were

1850-1871

Kingdom of Italy 1870
Germany 1871
0 kilometres 400
0 miles 200
ISLAND (Den.) 1870
FAROE IS (Den.) 1870
SHETLANDS
ORKNEYS
Atlantic Ocean
UNITED KINGDOM
Scotland
North Sea
IRELAND
Dublin
Wales
England
London
English Channel
CHANNEL IS
NORGE & SVERIGE 1855
Christiana
Stockholm
GOTLAND
OLAND
Gulf of Bothnia
ALAND IS
Helsingfors
St Petersburg
SUOMI 1856
Riga
Baltic Sea
Memel
-1867
1868 -71
DANMARK 1851
København
HELGOLAND 1859 1867
Lübeck
Hamburg
Danzig
Ost Preussen
RUSSIAN EMPIRE 1858
NEDERLAND
Amsterdam
1852
Elbe
Berlin
Poznań
Vistula
Warszawa
POLSKA 1860
Dneiper
DEUTSCHLAND
Bruxelles
BELGIË
Rhine
LUXEMBURG 1852
Paris
Alsace-Lorraine (to Ger.1871) 1870
Tours
FRANCE
Bay of Biscay
Bordeaux
Prag
Kraków
Lemberg
Dneister
ÖSTERREICHISCHE KAISERLICHE KONIGREICH 1867
Danube
München
Wien
ÖSTERREICH 1850
Buda
Pest
MAGYARORSZAG 1850 1868
Moldavia (1859)
Pruth
Odes
(to Moldavia 185
HELVETIA 1850
LIECHTENSTEIN 1850 -1912
Lyon
Rhone
Lombardia-Venetia 1850
Po
Trieste
Venezia
Drava
Sava
Beograd
ROMANIA 1862 1862
Wallachia (1859)
Bucuresti
(to Ott. Emp 1856)
Black Se
(to France 1860)
SARDEGNA
STATI ITALIANI
SERVIA 1866
BULGARIA
ACORES 1868
MADEIRA 1868
Nice
MONACO 1851-60 1860-85
Stati Papali
MONT
LA CORSE (Fr.)
Adriatic Sea
Costantinopoli
PORTUGAL 1853
Lisboa
Madrid
ESPAÑA 1850
Il Patrimonio
Roma (Cap. 1870)
Albania 1870
OTTOMAN EMPIRE 1863
ITALIA 1862
Napoli
SARDEGNA
Tyrrhenian Sea
Aegean Sea
ISLAS BALEARES (Sp.)
REGNO DELLE DUE SICILIE
IONIAN ISLANDS 1859 (to Greece 1863)
Athinai
HELLAS 1861
Gibraltar (Brit)
Tanger Brit.1857
Cueta (Sp.)
1857
Mediterranean Sea
Ionian Sea
Sicilia
Mellila (Sp.)
MALTA 1854 1860
KRITI (Egypt 1824-40)
RHC
Mos

1871-1914

ISLAND
(Den.)
1873
Seydisfiordur
Reykjavik
FAROE IS
(Den.)
SHETLANDS
ORKNEYS
Atlantic Ocean
UNITED KINGDOM
Scotland
IRELAND
Dublin
Wales
England
London
North Sea
NORGE
(1905)
Christiana
SVERIGE
(1905)
Stockholm
Gulf of Bothnia
ALAND IS
Helsingfors
St Petersburg
SUOMI
GOTLAND
OLAND
Riga
Moskva
Baltic Sea
1871-1919
Memel
DANMARK
København
HELGOLAND
Danzig
Ost Preussen
RUSSIAN EMPIRE
Hamburg
Elbe
NEDERLAND
Amsterdam
Berlin
Poznań
Vistula
Warszawa
POLSKA
Dneiper
DEUTSCHLAND
1872
English Channel
Bruxelles
BELGIË
LUX.
Rhine
CHANNEL IS.
Prag
Bohemia
Kraków
Galicia
Lemberg
Dneister
Pruth
ÖSTERREICHISCHE KAISERLICHE
KONIGREICH
Wien
Budapest
Danube
Paris
München
FRANCE
Odessa
(to Russ 1878)
Bay of Biscay
SCHWEIZ
LIECHTENSTEIN
1912
Tirol
Carinthia
Drava
Lyon
Rhone
Bordeaux
Po
Venezia
Trieste
Croatia-Slavonia
Sava
Beograd
ROMANIA
(1878)
Bucuresti
(to Rom. 1878)
Black Sea
(to Rom. 1913)
Dalmatia
Bosnien
1879
Sarajevo
Hercegovina
(1878)
(1878)
BULGARIA
(Ind. King. 1908)
1879
1850-70
1870-7
SAN MARINO
1877
1902
SERVIA
Sofia
E. Rumelia
(1878)
(1913)
MONACO
1885
ITALIA
Adriatic Sea
(1913)
Adrianople
Costantinopoli
Thrace
(1913)
LA CORSE
(Fr.)
Roma
MONT
1874
TURKISH EMPIRE
PORTUGAL
Madrid
ESPAÑA
Lisboa
Napoli
ALBANIA
1913
Epirus
Macedonia (1913)
(1881)
Thessaly
Aegean Sea
Tyrrhenian Sea
SARDEGNA
(Ital.)
CORFU
HELLAS
Smirna
ISLAS BALEARES
(Sp.)
Ionian Sea
Athinai
Gibraltar (Brit.)
1886
Mediterranean Sea
Palermo
Sicilia
DHODHEKANISOS
(to Italy 1912)
Tanger
Cueta
(Sp.)
(Sp. Prot. 1912)
Mellila
(Sp.)
ALGERIA
(Fr. Prot.)
MALTA
TUNIS
MOROCCO
KRITI
(Auton. 189g)
(to Greece 1913)
1899
1899
1900

sent in the first 15 months. It should be emphasized that there was nothing new in being able to send cards through the post. It had been quite usual for many years. The innovation was the reduced rate and it was this service which was to revolutionize the writing and collecting habits of the nation in the first decade of the 20th century.

During this whole period the growth in the number of letters continued to give problems to the Post Office. In 1840-1, the first full year after the introduction of 1*d* postage, the number was 169 million. By 1871 this figure had risen to 917 million. At this time, the number of letters delivered to individual houses was probably less than 50 per cent but the percentage was growing rapidly, and was up to 97 per cent by the end of the century.

Abroad, the complications of new countries issuing stamps, together with the growth of international trade, made the archaic system of individual treaties and conventions almost impossible to administer. In 1863 a postal congress was held in Paris to attempt to rationalize the situation. Although this congress provided few concrete results, the personal contacts which were made led to a substantial easing in the regulations and highlighted the need for a permanent body. Work to this end carried on during this period and a date was set in 1870. However, the Franco-Prussian war prevented the meeting from taking place and it was not until 1874 that the General Postal Union met for the first time.

In 1854 the Crimean War broke out, initially between Russia and Turkey. France and Britain came to the aid of Turkey and an expeditionary force was sent to the Dardenelles, ostensibly to drive the Russians out of Silistria. The Russians retreated, but it was decided to destroy Sebastopol on the Crimean peninsula and the war dragged on for a further 18 months. On the postal side, a Post Office official was sent out as postmaster-general to the forces and, again, a special cancellation was used to cancel the forces mail. At the same time a number of supporting Army POs were established, including one in Constantinople; this was subsequently the basis for the British POs in the Turkish Empire (q.v), which were in operation until World War I and even later in the case of Constantinople.

1871-1914

This was a period of stability for Europe and for Britain. At the start, having been free from major wars for 65 years, Britain had benefited from the constant growth in national and international trade, the reduction in the power of France, and the development of the British Empire. The volume of mail through the Post Office in the Jubilee year of 1890 was 2000 million items, approximately 50 per person per year or one letter each week for every person in the country; this was 40 times more than in 1838. The increase in volume had led to the need for new techniques for cancelling the mail and, following the trials of the period up to 1870, these were taken, in the years up to World War I, to their completion, with the installation of high-speed machines in all major POs.

Although the telephone had by now been invented, it was not until the period between the world wars that it made any significant impact on the passing of personal messages. However, with the increasing sophistication of the population and the growth of commerce there was a need to develop faster communications. Individual telegraph and cable companies had been established in the 1850s and the Post Office quickly found that they were beginning to win a lucrative portion of the mail market. In 1870 the Post Office took over the existing telegraph companies by Act of Parliament and incorporated them into their service (there they remained until the split between the Post Office and British Telecom in the 1970s). This went some way towards responding to the public's need, but with a minimum cost of 1*s*, an even cheaper means which could carry a longer message was required. The answer was the introduction of the Express Service in 1891. By this means, letters could be carried specially to an address at a cost of 3*d* per mile; largely used by commercial interests, it provided a means of transmission which though it has been varied in many ways, still exists today.

These two services — telegraph and express post — helped the public to communicate more quickly, but the most significant increase in volume was in postcards. When these were introduced in 1870 only pre-printed cards were accepted and this led to constant friction with the stationers who wanted to introduce their own cards. It was forbidden to stick stamps on cards so manufacture was effectively vested in the Post Office. Following pressure from Parliament and public alike, the Post Office modified the rules in 1894 and the picture postcard was introduced. The effect was instantaneous. In the next 15 years it seemed that everyone collected cards. By 1913 almost 1000 million postcards passed through the post, though this was probably less than half the actual number of cards sold because of the number which people would buy to place, unused, in their collection.

A number of significant changes occurred in stamp production. In 1880 De La Rue attained a monopoly of supply to the British Post Office and they maintained this position until 1910. At the end of that year, part of the contract passed to Harrison & Sons (½*d*, 1*d*, 2½*d*, 3*d*, and 4*d*), and the rest was produced by Somerset House, the headquarters of the Board of Inland Revenue.

Colours of stamps were also varied during this period for a number of reasons. The General Postal Union, which met for the first time in 1874, became the Universal Postal Union in 1878, and at its first Congress in Paris suggested to members that certain stamps — in Britain's case, ½*d*, 1*d* and 2½*d* — should be green, red and blue respectively. The Post Office tried to comply and by 1880, with the first De La Rue printing of the two lower values, this was achieved. However, the Treasury had made other changes which meant that the situation could not last.

Above
Country postman, 1860s

Left
Postman 1867 — an illustration from a child's gift book

Right
Letter-carrier, mail-guard and driver in GPO uniforms, 1860

The first involved telegraph stamps. When the Post Office telegraph service had started in 1870, special stamps had been issued for pre-payment of the charges. In 1881 the Treasury decided that these stamps were no longer necessary and that postage stamps could also serve for the payment of telegraph charges. This increased the need for higher value stamps though most of these were used telegraphically.

The second and more far-reaching change was to make postal stamps also available for fiscal or revenue purposes. From 1881 most British stamps were inscribed 'Postage and Revenue'. This simple change in principle meant that the Post Office could no longer control the ink used to cancel stamps. When cancellation had been done by postal officials there had been little difficulty, but once this cancellation could be applied by anyone, often with simple writing ink, the stamps could become prone to cleaning and re-use. To avoid this the Post Office had to resort to special inks, known as 'doubly fugitive', which were more susceptible to cleaning agents. In 1881 there were only two such inks, lilac and green. It became impossible to remain with the UPU-recommended colours and by 1884 all values were changed to one or other of these colours. This was the situation until 1902, when the stamps of King Edward VII were issued: as by then ink technology had improved to the stage where less fugitive inks could be used, these were amended to green, red and blue. These changes in colour and design produced a series of interesting issues and paved the way for new colours and standards with the first stamps of King George V's reign in 1911.

In 1883 the Post Office parcel post service had been introduced. From the inception of the postal service in the 17th century, carriers had been allowed to continue the carriage and delivery of parcels and by the middle of the 19th century a number of special parcel companies had been introduced. Some of their business had been taken by the Post Office book post, which was introduced in 1847. This service was both quicker and cheaper than the carriers, but it was limited by weight. Inevitably, the system was subject to abuse and on 1 August 1883 the Post Office parcel service began. Although there was no monopoly, packages were prepaid with stamps on special forms and many of these rates had to be prepaid with a single adhesive. This led to new values being issued — the 10*d* in 1890, 4½*d* in 1892, 7*d* in 1907, 8*d* in 1913.

Overprinted stamps for Government departments had begun in 1883 to meet the requirements of the Inland Revenue. Similar overprints were also used for Government parcels. As time went on, other departments were included: Office of Works, Army, Admiralty and Board of Education. In these series exists the rarest of all British stamps, the 6*d* IR Official of 1904. The overprints were discontinued in 1904, but they had started a pattern which was also implemented for use in overseas territories. The reasons for these issues will be discussed under each country, but during this period overprinted stamps were released in British Levant (1885), British Bechuanaland (1887), Bechuanaland Protectorate (1888), Oil River Colonies (1892), East Africa (1890), Morocco Agencies (1907) and Zululand (1888).

The overseas post of this period was overshadowed by the early work of the

1914-1919
German-Russian Boundary 1914
Germany 1914
Austro-Hungarian Empire 1914
Poland 1921
0 kilometres 400
0 miles 200
ISLAND
(Den.)
FAROE ISLANDS
(Den.)
SHETLANDS
ORKNEYS
Atlantic Ocean
UNITED KINGDOM
Scotland
IRELAND
Dublin
Wales
England
London
Folkestone
North Sea
NORGE
Christiana
SVERIGE
Stockholm
SUOMI
Gulf of Bothnia
Helsingfors
ALAND IS
Leningrad
ESTONIA
1916-8
1918
GOTLAND
Riga
LATVIA
1916
1916-8
1918
OLAND
Baltic Sea
LITHUANIA
1916-8
1918
Memel
(1921)
Vilna
USSR
White Russia
Mosk
DANMARK
København
HELGOLAND
Danzig
Ost Preussen
Tannenburg
Hamburg
Elbe
NEDERLAND
Amsterdam
Berlin
(1919)
Poznań
Vistula
POLSKA
(Rep. 1918)
Warszawa
1918
Kiev
Dneiper
Ukraine
DEUTSCHLAND
Koln
Boulogne
Bruxelles
BELGIË
CHANNEL IS
Eupen
Malmedy
LUX.
Coblenz
Mainz
Saar
Schlesien
Kraków
Gleschien
Dneister
Praha
Le Havre
Paris
Rhine
Alsace-Lorraine
CESKOSLOVENSKO
1919
1919
Danube
Bukovina
Bessarabia
Jassy
Moldavia
Odes
München
Wien
Budapest
Pruth
FRANCE
1918
1919
ÖSTERREICH
MAGYARORSZAG
Transilvania
ROMANIA
Bay of Biscay
SCHWEIZ
Danube
Drava
1919
Caporeto
Bosnia
Wallachia
Dobruja
Lyon
Bordeaux
Rhone
Veneto
Vittoria
Trieste
Venezia
Venetia Giulia
Po
Sava
Beograd
Bucuresti
Danube
Black Sea
Sarajevo
Herzegovina
Nice
MONACO
SERVIA
MONT.
BULGARIA
Sofia
ANDORRA
ITALIA
Costantinopoli
Thrace
Adriatic Sea
TÜRKIY
PORTUGAL
Madrid
LA CORSE
(Fr.)
Roma
ALBANIA
Salonicco
Lisboa
ESPAÑA
Macedonia
Napoli
Tyrrhenian Sea
SARDEGNA
HELLAS
Aegean Sea
ISLAS BALEARES
(Sp.)
IONIAN IS
Ionian Sea
Athinai
Mediterranean Sea
Gibraltar(Brit.)
Tanger
Cueta
(Sp.)
Sicilia
DHODHEKANISOS
(Ital.)
(Sp.)
Mellila
(Sp.)
MALTA
Algerie
(Fr.)
Tunis
(Fr.)
KRITI
Maroc
(Fr.)

1919-1939

German acquisitions 1938-39
Russian-German Boundary Sept 1939
0 kilometres 500
0 miles 300
ISLAND
(Den.)
FAROE ISLANDS
(Den.)
SHETLANDS
ORKNEYS
Atlantic Ocean
NORGE
Oslo
SVERIGE
Stockholm
SUOMI
(1920)
Olonetz
Gulf of Bothnia
Helsinki
ALAND IS
Leningrad
N. Ingermanland
ESTONIA
GOTLAND
Riga
LATVIA
Moskva
Scotland
GREAT
BRITAIN
Ulster
(1925)
IRISH FREE
STATE
1922
Dublin
North Sea
DANMARK
København
OLAND
Baltic Sea
Memel
1920
LITHUANIA
USSR
1923
White Russia SSR
(1922)
Vilna
Schleswig
1920
HELGOLAND
Danzig
1920
Ost
Preussen
Marienwerder
Grodno
West
Preussen
1920
Allenstein
1920
Wales
England
Hamburg
Elbe
Berlin
Vistula
Poznań
Warszawa
Kiev
Dneiper
London
NEDERLAND
Amsterdam
DEUTSCHLAND
(WEIMAR REP)
1919
Schlesien
1920
POLSKA
Bruxelles
BELGIË
English Channel
CHANNEL IS
Rhine
Rhineland
Praha
Bohemia-Moravia
Kraków
Terschen
Ukraine SSR
(1922)
Dneister
LUX
Paris
Saar
1920
Alsace-
Lorraine
SLOVENSKO
Ruthenia
Danube
München
Komarno
Debrecen
Wien
Budapest
1919
Odessa
Bessarabia
Moldavia
Bay of Biscay
FRANCE
ÖSTERREICH
MAGYARORSZAG
Transilvania
ROMANIA
SCHWEIZ
Szeged
Danube
1919
Banat
Bacska
Wallachia
Temesvar
1919
Lyon
Bordeaux
Rhone
Drava
Trieste
Fiume
Venezia
Po
Sava
Beograd
Bucuresti
Danube
Black Sea
CORES
1929
ADEIRA
1929
MONACO
JUGOSLAVIJA
1921
Zara
(Ital. 1920)
E.Thrace
(Gk. Mand. 1920)
(returned to Turk.
1922)
BULGARIA
Sofia
ANDORRA
1928
ITALY
Adriatic Sea
Montenegro
(to Yugo. 1922)
Adrianople
Istanbul
(Costantinopoli)
PORTUGAL
Madrid
ESPAÑA
LA CORSE
(Fr.)
LAGOSTA
(Ital. 1920)
1939
Tiranë (Cap. 1920)
Dedeagach
TÜRKIYE
Roma
CITTA DEL
VATICANO
1929
ALBANIA
(King. 1928)
(Ital. 1939)
Salonicco
Gallipoli
Durazzo
Napoli
Tyrrhenian Sea
SASENO
1923
SARDEGNA
HELLAS
Smyrna
Aegean Sea
ISLAS BALEARES
(Sp.)
IONIAN IS
Ionian Sea
Athínai
(to Gr. 1920-2)
Mediterranean Sea
Gibraltar (Brit.)
Tanger
Cueta
(Sp.)
Sicilia
DHODHEKANISOS
(Ital.)
Sp. Maroc
Mellila
(Sp.)
MALTA
(Self-govt. 1922)
KRITI
Casablanca

Universal Postal Union. Although delayed by the Franco-Prussian War, the UPU was eventually established in 1874. Its first decision was to regularize the postage rates between the 22 founder members, which were set at 25 gold *centimes* (or 2½*d* in Britain), with postcards at half that rate. This agreement was effective from 1 July 1875, which was the first time that a postcard rate had been introduced for cards going abroad.

Apart from easing the accounting and all other aspects of the transfer of international mail between member countries, a number of new international services and consolidation of postal rates took place under the auspices of the UPU. International Express mail was introduced in 1885, though the British Post Office did not follow suit until 1892; insured mail followed in 1899, and the introduction of International Reply Paid Coupons in 1907-8.

During this period the British Army was involved in several campaigns abroad, and in 1882 the Army Postal Service was established. This was based on the 24th Middlesex Rifle Volunteers (the Post Office Rifles). The unit was raised originally in 1868 as part of the Volunteer force and comprised employees of the Post Office. On the suggestion of its commanding officer, they were to be made available to the War Office for deployment with the army when expeditions were sent abroad. The first of these was to Egypt in 1882, followed by the Sudan in 1884, where they were also joined by a telegraph company. The Army Postal Corps were also heavily involved in the Boer War of 1899-1902 and the many army manoeuvres in the first decade of the 20th century. In 1908, the Territorial Army was created, and at that time the Army Postal Corps became part of the Royal Engineers, (as the Army Postal Service), and the Post Office Rifles became an infantry unit, the 8th Bn, the London Regiment.

1914-19

The war had little effect on the internal mail service. Although there were some early German attempts to shell towns on the East Coast and some raids by zeppelins, the strength of the Royal Navy and the ineffectiveness of aerial assault prevented any prolonged attacks. The main effect on internal services was a dramatic reduction in the number of postcards in the mails. From 1000 million in 1913 the figure had fallen to less than half when the next return was published in the mid-1920s. The volume of mail had increased but the 'craze' for postcards had gone, never to return to the same extent.

The use of high-speed cancellation machines, which was well established by the outbreak of war, continued and in 1917 for the first time a slogan advertising BUY WAR BONDS NOW was included in the cancelling die. Three different designs were used in the last year of the war but these were then withdrawn and no new designs used until 1922.

The work of the UPU had been largely suspended by the war, but many countries continued to implement the agreements reached at the Rome Congress of 1906, the last one to have been held. When the British Post Office increased the rates for internal postage in 1917, the overseas rates were retained until the next Congress of 1920.

The war created major disruption in the overseas mail service. The introduction of censorship on a wide scale for the first time led to many major delays as did the submarine campaigns and the sinking of many ships. The problems of censorship led to the introduction of a unique service in 1915 which enabled the public to have letters accelerated through the censor by pre-payment of a fee of 2*s* 6*d*. This applied particularly to mail for the Americas and neutral Europe.

The Army Postal Service was involved in all the many campaigns fought during the war. Numbered Field PO handstamps were issued down to brigade level, and in general terms, the original number issued was the number of the brigade itself. Detailed summaries of the allocation of numerals have been published.

In 1915 Army Intelligence discovered that, from a similar system used by the Germans, they were able to establish the order of battle. As a result, on the Western Front the numbers were interchanged as a security measure. Such systems did not apply in other theatres of war. British troops served in Italy, Greece, Egypt and Palestine as well as France. In 1919 an expeditionary force was sent to Russia to assist against the Bolsheviks. All of these had Field POs allocated. In addition the Army operated a number of TPOs in areas where transport by road had became too difficult or dangerous.

During unrest in Egypt in 1919 an aerial service was established to fly mail within Egypt and from Palestine to Cairo, the beginning of a new service which led to the establishment of the service in Germany after the war had ended. The improvement in the reliability of aircraft during the war was quickly noted by forward-thinking members of the Government and the Post Office. Although the Air Ministry refused all proposals on the grounds that aircraft were required for war purposes, the demand for an air service across the Channel was established and would operate once the war was over.

1919-39

Improvements in technology occasioned by the war led to improvements in the handling of mail. As we have seen, it had never been the policy of the Post Office to own its vehicles. Whether the carriage of mail was based on mail-coaches, railways, or motor vehicles, the use of contractors had avoided a massive investment in machinery and people. However, attitudes were changing, and from the 1920s onwards the Post Office began to purchase its own vehicles and the black-bonnetted red vans became a feature of the roads of the country.

The volume of mail continued to grow but the complementary increase in the number of telephones owned by the public began to reduce the interchange of short personal messages on paper.

Within the United Kingdom a num-

Above
Yorkshire postman, 1908

Above right
Two automatic stamp-machines (1907) which supplied penny stamps and packets of postcards

Below right
Post-box in Cornwall

Left
Postwoman during World War I

ber of changes occurred during this period. Ireland, which had been part of Great Britain and Ireland since the Act of Union in 1707, became independent as the Irish Free State in 1922. The organization of the Irish post was no longer under control from Britain, but initially the stamps of Britain were used overprinted.

Although three postal slogans had been used in the war, no further examples were introduced until 1922. The first commemorative stamps were issued in Britain in 1924 for the British Empire Exhibition at Wembley. These were repeated in 1925 when the Exhibition was continued for a further year owing to bad weather and resulting low attendances in the opening year. Further sets of stamps were issued in 1929 for the UPU Congress, in 1935 for the Silver Jubilee of King George V and in 1937 for the Coronation of King George VI.

Although many European countries suffered from serious inflation in the inter-war years, Britain was affected to a much lesser extent. However, many changes of postal rate occurred during the first few years after the war; it was not until 1923 that stable charges were re-established and these remained in force until 1940.

In 1928 a special airmail conference of the UPU was held in Holland. During the conference a delegation paid a visit to a firm which was manufacturing a machine for automatic sorting of letters. As a result, one of these machines, a Transorma, was installed in Brighton in 1935, the start of automatic sorting in Britain.

Towards the end of World War I, demand had arisen for the use of aircraft to carry mail. After the collapse of the German Army in 1918, the British army of occupation in the Rhineland found it difficult to get the mail to and from Germany because of the damage to roads and railways. As a result, an airmail service was established; initially from Marquise near Boulogne to Cologne with a number of stops, it was eventually opened direct from Hawkinge near Folkestone to Cologne.

Although this service ended after some eight months because the roads and railways had been improved and the size of the occupation force had been reduced, its success in its later stages inspired confidence to start the first direct service from London to Paris in November 1919. Throughout the early stages of the growth of the airmail service up to 1930 the mail was always charged an additional fee for carriage. This varied from country to country and ranged from an initial rate of 2*s* 6*d* to Paris in 1919 (reduced to 2*d* in 1920) to 8*d* to Russia. Similar charges to other continents were introduced as links were established to Africa and through Asia to Australia.

In the mid-1930s a proposal was

1939-1945
Axis Powers Sept 1939
Territory occupied by Axis 1940-42
0 kilometres 400
0 miles 200
ISLAND
(Dem. Rep. 1944)
FAROE ISLANDS
SHETLANDS
ORKNEYS
Atlantic Ocean
North Sea
NORGE
Oslo
SVERIGE
Stockholm
SUOMI
Helsinki
(1940)
(Russ. 1940)
(regained by Finland 1941-4
Russian 1945)
Gulf of Bothnia
ALAND IS
GOTLAND
OLAND
Baltic Sea
Leningrad
Novgorod
Moskv
Estonia SSR
(1940)
Riga
Latvian SSR
(1940)
Memel
Lithuanian SSR
(1940)
Vilna
White Russia SSR
USSR
Scotland
GREAT BRITAIN
Ulster
EIRE
Dublin
England
Wales
London
DANMARK
København
HELGOLAND
Danzig
Ost Preussen
Grodno
(1939)
NEDERLAND
Amsterdam
Hamburg
Elbe
Berlin
Poznan
Poznań
Vistula
Warszawa
POLSKA
Gen. Govt. of Poland
1939
Kiev
Dnieper
Ukraine SSR
English Channel
CHANNEL IS
1941
(Ger. Occ.)
Bruxelles
BELGIË
Aachen
Rhine
Rheinland
LUX.
Saar
DEUTSCHLAND
Dresden
Sachsen
Schlesien
Praha
Bohemia-Moravia
Kraków
Terschen
Slovensko
Ruthenia
Moldavia SSR
Dniester
Prut
Bessarabia
Odess
Paris
Tours
FRANCE
Alsace & Lorraine
1940
Bayern
Danube
München
1945
ÖSTERREICH
Wien
Komarno
Debrecen
Budapest
(1941)
MAGYARORSZAG
Szeged
Danube
ROMANIA
Cri
(Russ. 1940)
Bay of Biscay
Vichy
Lyon
Bordeaux
Vichy France
1940
Rhone
SCHWEIZ
Campione
1944
Po
1945
Trieste
Lubliana Slovenia
1941
Drava
Hrvatska Croatia
1941
Sava
Fiume & Kupa
1941
Venezia
Istria
1945
Banat Bacska
Bucuresti
(Bulg. 1940)
Black Sea
Beograd
Danube
Dalmatia
1943
JUGOSLAVIJA
Servia
1941
SAN MARINO
MONACO
ITALIA
Brac
1944
Montenegro
1941
BULGARIA
Sofia
Adrianople
Istanbu
ANDORRA
PORTUGAL
Madrid
Lisboa
ESPAÑA
LA CORSE
(Fr.)
Roma
Adriatic Sea
Gulf of Kotor
1944
Tirane
ALBANIA
(Ital. Occ. 1939)
Macedonia
1944
E. Thrace
Dedeagach
TÜRKIY
Gallipoli
Napoli
Tyrrhenian Sea
SARDEGNA
HELLAS
Aegean Sea
Smyrna
ISLAS BALEARES
(Sp.)
IONIAN IS
Ionian Sea
Athinai
Gibraltar (Brit)
Tanger
Cueta
Mediterranean Sea
Sicilia
Sp. Morocco
Mellila
MALTA
KRITI
DHODHEKANISO

After 1945

ISLAND
FAROE ISLANDS
1975
SHETLANDS
ORKNEYS
Atlantic Ocean
Scotland
1958
North Sea
GREAT BRITAIN
Ulster
1958
EIRE
Dublin
I. OF MAN
1958
England
Wales
1958
London
HELGOLAND
NORGE
Oslo
SVERIGE
Stockholm
SUOMI
Gulf of Bothnia
Helsinki
ALAND IS
Leningrad
GOTLAND
Riga
Moskva
OLAND
USSR
DANMARK
København
Baltic Sea
Memel
Vilna
Gdansk
Grodno
NEDERLAND
Amsterdam
Hamburg
Elbe
Berlin
POLSKA
Poznań
Warszawa
Vistula
Kiev
Dneiper
Rhine
DEUTSCHE DEMOCRATISCHE REPUBLIK
1949
English Channel
Bruxelles
BELGIË
BUNDESREPUBLIK DEUTSCHLAND
Bonn
1949
Krakow
CHANNEL IS
1958
ALDERNEY
1983
Praha
CESKOSLOVENSKO
Dneister
Paris
UNITED NATIONS (SWITZERLAND)
1950-69
1969
UNITED NATIONS (AUSTRIA)
1979
Danube
München
Wien
Pruth
FRANCE
OSTERREICH
Budapest
Odessa
MAGYARORSZAG
Bay of Biscay
Berne
SCHWEIZ
ROMANIA
Danube
Drava
Lyon
Rhone
Bordeaux
Trieste
Po
Venezia
Sava
Beograd
Bucuresti
Black Sea
Danube
JUGOSLAVIJA
ACORES
1980
MADEIRA
1980
MONACO
SAN MARINO
BULGARIA
ANDORRA
ITALIA
Sofia
Adriatic Sea
Istanbul
LA CORSE
(Fr.)
PORTUGAL
Madrid
ESPAÑA
Roma
Tirane
TÜRKIYE
ALBANIA
Lisboa
Tyrrhenian Sea
Napoli
SARDEGNA
HELLAS
Aegean Sea
CORFU
ISLAS BALEARES
(Sp.)
IONIAN IS
Athinai
Ionian Sea
ZANTE
Mediterranean Sea
Sicilia
Gibraltar (Brit.)
Tanger
Cueta
(Sp.)
RHODOS
Mellila
(Sp.)
MALTA
1964
KRITI

made for an 'all-up' mail service to the Empire which was designed to bring airmail charges within the reach of everyone. As early as July 1930 a consolidated rate for mail to Europe (4*d*) had been introduced and this was followed by the 'all-up' rate of 1½*d*, which gradually spread across the air links of the Empire. It reached India in February 1938 and Hong Kong later the same year. The 'all-up' service was discontinued on the outbreak of war.

No direct air service existed to the USA until 1939. Attempts to fly the Atlantic from Newfoundland after 1920 had varying success, but the services in the reverse direction were not possible until flying boats were introduced from the west coast of Ireland. The service was barely started before it was closed by World War II.

The UPU had not met since 1906 when it assembled for the first time after the war at Madrid in 1920. The main outcome was the increase in the freedom to amend overseas rates. This enabled a number of anomalies to be removed and the subsequent Congresses at Stockholm (1926), London (1929) and Cairo (1935) all continued the work of the Union. In addition, a number of meetings were introduced on the international transfer of airmail, a growing problem.

1939-45

War was declared in September 1939 (the dates differed throughout the Commonwealth but in Britain the date was 3 September). It was the first total war to be fought in Europe, except for the Spanish Civil War of 1936-8, and brought the danger of death through bombing to every corner of the nation. For the first time for centuries there was a real danger of invasion and the whole country was affected by the blitz.

The Post Office had to face up to massive disruption within the country. In past wars the post at home had been almost unaffected, but this time the damage to transport systems, destruction of POs and the deployment of national assets to the general good all led to major changes in the usual patterns. Additionally, large numbers of the staff enlisted or were called up and new staff had to be recruited and trained.

The comparative calm of the first nine months of the war gave the necessary breathing space to enable the planning to commence, but when the bombing of London started in earnest in the autumn of 1940, delays were inevitable. In December 1942 the PO at Moorgate in the City was destroyed in a night raid; by mid-January a temporary PO had been set up in an open space in Eldon Street and the service was back. This means of showing the nation that, despite all, there was a superficial normality did much to maintain the morale which was one of the highlights of this period of the war.

Before the war, steps were in hand for the celebration of the centenary of the first postage stamp in May 1940. The intrusion of the war prevented any major exhibition, but a special set of stamps was issued. At much the same time the rates were increased for the first time since 1921. Before this there had been some discussion on the possibility of a special surcharge on internal postage rates to help pay for the war effort, but with the increase this plan was dropped.

Restriction on the supplies of raw materials led to changes in the inks used for printing stamps. The deep colours used for the common values were reduced in content, and lighter versions were issued in 1942. At the same time essays were produced for smaller stamps, though these were never issued.

The TPOs were discontinued but mail continued to be carried and delivered despite all the damage; constant reviews of the ways in which the mail routes could be shortened or improved continued throughout the war.

The foreign and colonial mail were greatly affected. In the early days of the war the only major changes were the increase in rates (the all-up service was discontinued in September 1939) and the re-introduction of censorship; however, this did not last long. With the fall of France in June 1940 the main routes to Africa, the Far East and Australia were closed, as was the service to South America, which had been flown via France. Mail was then flown to the USA and thence via Clipper across the Pacific. This route, though expensive, was even used for mail to Cyprus and Palestine — almost circumnavigating the globe.

When Japan entered the war at the end of 1941 many services were interrupted or ceased altogether. Several alternatives were tried as the improvement in the range and reliability of aircraft enabled new routes to be considered. Through all these problems, which affected both sides in the war, the UPU based in Berne remained neutral and continued to provide help to both sides on the most suitable routes which were available.

The Forces Postal Service operated throughout and had Field POs in all theatres of war. Although some concessions in postal rates continued, the airmail services were charged. Later in the war the Airgram service was introduced, which enabled messages to be microfilmed, carried to the UK, enlarged and delivered. This enabled vast numbers of servicemen to maintain contact with home, a vital element for their morale.

1946 to date

When World War II ended, Britain was faced with an enormous task of reconstruction. This was accompanied by a period of austerity which, in terms of rationing, was more severe than during the war. The return to some degree of normality allowed the Post Office to introduce its own plans for expansion and development.

To the public the most obvious changes were in the telecommunications field. The development of the telephone service had by now begun to erode the use of postcards and short letters. The boom in industry balanced this loss, but over the next 25 years the continued improvement in verbal communications eventually led to the end of the internal telegraph service in 1982.

The shadow of inflation began to appear in the 1960s but it was not until the 1970s that the increase in the postal charges began to be seriously affected. The main letter rate had remained at 2½*d* from 1940 until 1958 and was still only 4*d* in 1968, when two-tier postage was introduced. This new system of first- and second-class services, which were initially introduced at 5*d* and 4*d*, most seriously affected the postcard service. There was no longer a special reduced rate and the volume slumped to less than 80 million cards in the early 1980s.

In 1971 the currency was decimalized: 100 new pence to £1. The rate at the time of the introduction was 3p and 2½p (7.2*d* and 6*d*), but the pressure of inflation caused all costs to increase rapidly. The rates were increased regularly on an annual basis until some degree of stability was achieved in 1982-3, when the first-class rate was raised to 16p. From 1984 onwards the ½p coin was demonetized and increments of increase had to be in units of 1p.

The public face of the Post Office had changed in many other ways. The number of collections and deliveries had been reduced. Partly this was due to union pressure and partly because the channels of communication had changed. The telephone was increasingly used for contact and the letter service suffered accordingly. The increasing costs of labour also had implications for the Post Office, which had always been a labour-intensive industry. The introduction of postcodes as an aid to automatic sorting was a feature of the 1960s, and by 1978 the use of phosphor dots on covers and phosphorized paper on stamps led to an increased ability to sort letters electronically.

However, the pressures on the Post Office following its final separation from telecommunications in 1981 led to a modification in the Post Office monopoly. For the first time deliveries of Christmas cards could be organized on a local basis and Express Delivery services were also opened to competition. Nevertheless, the strength of the Post Office was not seriously affected and it still remains as an important social force in the nation.

Britain: MLOs 1985
Postal Districts
Mechanised Letter Offices (MLOs)
0 kilometres 80
0 miles 50
Aberdeen
Perth
Glasgow
Edinburgh
Tweed
Tyne
Newcastle
Carlisle
Belfast
Cleveland
Darlington
North Sea
Ouse
York
Bradford
Leeds
Humber
Hull
Preston
Huddersfield
Irish Sea
Bolton
Oldham
Doncaster
Liverpool
Manchester
Sheffield
Chester
Crewe
Trent
Stoke
Derby
Nottingham
Shrewsbury
Leicester
Peterborough
Norwich
Wolverhampton
Birmingham
Coventry
Ouse
Severn
Northampton
Cambridge
Worcester
Avon
Ipswich
Milton Keynes
Stevenage
Gloucester
Oxford
Hemel Hempstead
Chelmsford
Swansea
Newport
Swindon
LONDON
Southend
Cardiff
Bristol
Thames
Reading
Bath
Guildford
Maidstone
Canterbury
Redhill
Tonbridge
Southampton
Portsmouth
Brighton
Exeter
Bournemouth
Plymouth
English Channel
London
1. Watford
2. Harrow
3. Twickenham
4. Kingston-on-Thames
5. Croydon
6. Dartford
7. Romford

Overseas the main changes were in the continued transfer of mail from ships to aircraft. This had been foreshadowed by improvements in the performance of long-distance flying during the war. By 1951 the mail to Europe was all carried by aircraft and no supplement was paid; the Atlantic service was no longer a problem and the whole world was criss-crossed by airmail-carrying services. The time taken for mail by ships became increasingly unacceptable.

The UPU continued to meet regularly every five years but, although its importance for the standardization of international rates continued, its effect on new services began to decline. Its most important contribution continued to be the regularization of international accounting systems and simplification of the transfer of mail between countries.

Militarily, the post-war period witnessed many minor campaigns in which British troops and the Forces

POSTAGE
REVENUE
4d
A
8P
P
POSTAGE
REVENUE
4D
C
8½P
D
E
10½P
F
ER
POSTAGE REVENUE
4D

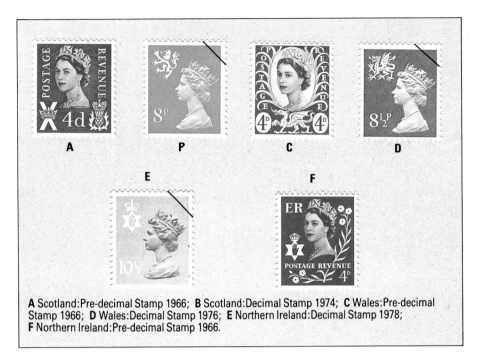

A Scotland:Pre-decimal Stamp 1966; **B** Scotland:Decimal Stamp 1974; **C** Wales:Pre-decimal Stamp 1966; **D** Wales:Decimal Stamp 1976; **E** Northern Ireland:Decimal Stamp 1978; **F** Northern Ireland:Pre-decimal Stamp 1966.

Postal Service were involved. Field POs were operating throughout the world, and most notably in Hong Kong, Korea, Kenya, Aden, Cyprus, with British Forces in Germany, and, more recently, in Ascension Island and the Falkland Islands.

In 1985 the Post Office celebrated the 350th anniversary of the opening of the inland Post Office to the public. Over three and a half centuries it has changed from a largely social and political intelligence network to a major force in the transmission of commercial information. It has been the spearhead of many technical innovations and, despite the many changes in the size and format of the service, has faced up to the needs of the public in peace and war alike.

Scotland

FIRST STAMPS British Stamps from 1840
FIRST REGIONAL STAMPS ISSUED 18 August 1958

Independent kingdom in the north of Britain which became unified with England and Wales when James VI of Scotland became James I of England on the death of Queen Elizabeth in 1603. Although the culture of the country has remained separate, government operations have been integrated, and apart from the Jacobite revolts of 1715 and 1745 control has been vested in London. Attempts to establish a separate devolved government in the 1970s failed on a referendum. Scotland has a Postal Board, which is responsible for the postal service.

Early posts in Scotland followed much the same pattern as their English counterparts and, although different styles of postmark were used, the method of operation between the two countries remained the same. One slightly different feature in the pre-1840 rates was the additional ½*d* tax, which was applied to all vehicles with more than two wheels that crossed the border. This tax was instituted to help pay for the maintenance of roads.

Agitation for different stamp designs for the region started in the 1940s and received support from the Post Office. However, these did not appear until the general issue of regional stamps in 1958. They now take the form of the standard 'Machin Head' design with the inclusion of the 'Lion of Scotland'.

Wales

FIRST STAMPS British Stamps from 1840
FIRST REGIONAL STAMPS ISSUED 18 August 1958

Principality in the west of Britain which was subdued by Edward I in 1283-4. His son, subsequently Edward II, was the first Prince of Wales. Despite subsequent revolts, the Welsh have remained part of Britain ever since.

Wales has remained part of the British Post Office since its inception. It has generally used British types of marking and has been particularly important as the base for Irish mail. The first regional issues for Wales and Monmouthshire were introduced in 1958 and now show the 'Machin Head' incorporating the 'Dragon of Wales'.

Northern Ireland

FIRST STAMPS British Stamps from 1840
FIRST REGIONAL STAMPS ISSUED 18 August 1958

Separated from the rest of Ireland (q.v.) in 1922 when the Irish Free State was formed. Has remained an integral part of the United Kingdom and is one of the Regions of the British Post Office.

Integrated with Ireland before 1922, Northern Ireland, or Ulster, has been part of the British Post Office for more than 200 years. Complete sets of special stamps have not been issued but a selection of the most popular values have been released with the insignia of the 'Hand of Ulster'.

Since 1970 British Forces POs have operated to provide the service for the garrison which has been stationed there.

Ireland

Before 1650

CURRENCY	
1922	sterling
1971	decimal currency
Later currency devalued against sterling	

Ireland, unlike the rest of the British Isles, was not conquered by the Romans. However, there was a well-established tribal system there in pre-Christian times. The four provinces of Leinster, Munster, Connaught and Ulster date from that period. During the 6th and 7th centuries, Irish tribes settled in the eastern part of Scotland.

The Norman conquest of Ireland began in 1169, and by 1172 the Irish chiefs were forced to accept the control of Henry II. The efforts of Henry VIII to impose the Reformation of the Church on Ireland began a period of brutal repression which led to several uprisings against the British Crown. Elizabeth and, later, Cromwell put down minor rebellions, but the wars of the 1630s and early 1640s set the pattern of religious intolerance which has persisted to the present day.

Communications with Ireland prior to 1598 were irregular and depended on occasional vessels or the official ships which maintained contact between the King and Governor of Ireland. In that year a regular post was fixed via Holyhead or Bristol. Roads through Wales proved difficult and the route was changed to Chester and the River Dee by 1640.

During the English Civil War Charles I tried to move his Irish army to Britain to fight on his side, but for some time such moves were frustrated by Parliamentary control of the northern ports. By the time that the troops were transferred, the Parliamentary army had become too strong and severe defeats were inflicted. In 1649 Cromwell and Ireton invaded Ireland, massacred the garrison at Drogheda, and reduced the whole island. By then the separation of Catholics in the southern part of the island and Protestants in Ulster had already begun.

1650-1793

During this period, Ireland remained part of the British Crown, but was garrisoned by British troops. Following his abdication by flight on 11 December 1688, James II landed in Ireland on 12 March 1689. He was pursued by William of Orange, who landed at Carrickfergus on 14 June 1690. They met at the Battle of the Boyne on 1 July 1690 and James was completely defeated. The war was finally ended after the surrender of Limerick in October 1691. A period of peace followed, broken in 1760 during the Seven Years' War when a French commodore called O'Farrell or Thurst (his mother's name) invaded Carrickfergus and plundered the town. He was trapped by a British squadron and defeated on 28 February 1760.

The first post in Ireland was established at Dublin in the last quarter of the 17th century. It is generally agreed that the Dublin dated mark, similar to the London mark, was introduced about 1670. Later types of mark throughout Ireland followed the general pattern of British provincial types until 1840. Mileage marks were calculated from Dublin instead of London. The Dublin Penny Post was organized in 1773-4 and was extended to the outskirts of the city within a four-mile radius as a Twopenny Post.

In 1784, following an Act of Parliament, the Irish Post Office was separated from the British Post Office and remained a separate entity until 1831 despite the Act of Union in 1800.

1793-1815

During the Napoleonic Wars, there was one serious attempt to raise Ireland against the British with the support of the French navy and some French troops. The Irish leader, Wolfe Tone, landed in May 1798 and this led to a rebellion against British control. The rising was gradually suppressed during 1799 but not before large numbers on both sides had been killed.

By 1798 considerable improvement in communications with Britain had been achieved and the regular packet from Holyhead to Kingstown was sailing five times per week. The mail packets were very punctual and were vital to the government for the maintenance of contact with the local administration.

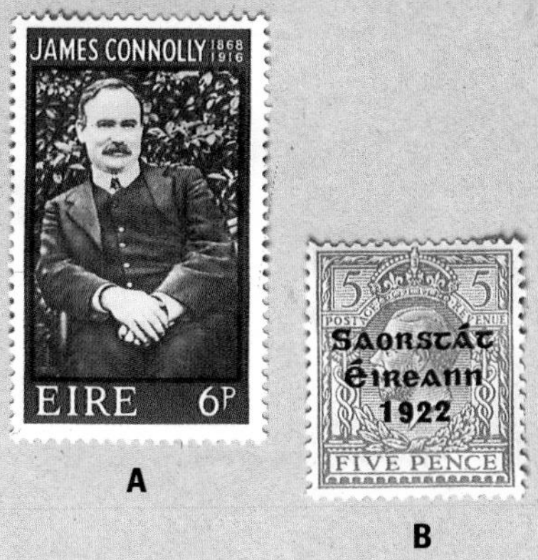
JAMES CONNOLLY 1868 1916
EIRE 6P
A
SAORSTÁT ÉIREANN 1922
FIVE PENCE
B

A Eire:Republic 1968;
B Eire:Irish Free State 1922.

1815–50

FIRST STAMPS British Stamps from 6 May 1840

In the period of peace after the war Britain did not forget the rising by the Irish and their garrisons were regularly maintained. However, the great Anglo-Irish families who tended to be absentee landlords did little to endear themselves to the Irish people. In 1846 the failure of the potato crop led to the great famine which resulted in hundreds of thousands of deaths and the beginning of the mass immigration of Irish families to the colonies and America.

None of this was reflected in the postal history of the period. Ireland continued to operate as a separate unit until 1831, when it was combined again with the British Post Office.

Numerical cancellations of a design specific to Ireland were introduced in 1844, but otherwise the postal markings followed the normal pattern of a British provincial PO.

1850-71
During these years the question of Home Rule for Ireland dominated British politics, as it did for many years to come. There was constant unrest, and riots and murders took place as well as political assassination.

The Post Office, operated from London, remained aloof from these troubles and maintained an adequate service. This was supported by improvements in the standard of vessels used for the carriage of mail across the Irish Sea.

1871-1914
The difficulty of controlling Ireland continued unabated during the Victorian and Edwardian eras. The demand for Home Rule increased during this period and led to open revolution in 1916. Nevertheless, the postal service was maintained and British stamps continued to be used. The normal British postmark types were used and British pillar boxes were erected in Irish towns.

1914-18
Ireland, as part of Great Britain, was involved in World War I from 4 August 1914. British stamps continued to be used and normal services continued. However, on Easter Monday 1916 the Irish Republicans seized the Post Office and the rebellion broke out in earnest. Although this first rebellion was put down by British troops and the leaders were executed, the demand on resources for the maintenance of the war on the Western Front meant that Irish garrisons had to be reduced and it became possible for more trouble to be fermented.

A national parliament was established at the end of 1918 and it affirmed the independent status of Ireland in January 1919.

No adhesives were issued at this period, though some propaganda labels were produced.

1919-39

FIRST STAMPS ISSUED FOR FREE STATE (EIRE) 17 February 1922

The Irish Free State was formed following elections in 1921. In 1925 the boundary between Ireland and Ulster (Northern Ireland) was settled. After that date the ties both constitutional and political were gradually relaxed. In 1937 a new constitution was confirmed giving the Free State the status of a republic within the Commonwealth. This was terminated in 1949 when the country became the Republic of Ireland.

A supply of British stamps printed by Harrisons (low values) or Bradbury Wilkinson (*2s 6d*, *10s*) were overprinted in Ireland by Dollard Limited or Alex Thom & Co. A small number were also overprinted in England by Harrisons, but this was mainly on coils.

The definitive issue of Ireland began to appear in December 1922, but some British unoverprinted items, notably postal stationery and registered envelopes, continued to be used unoverprinted until they were superseded in 1924.

The first airmail connection with Britain began experimentally in May 1924, but all other mail was routed via London until 1939 when the regular Pan American Service from Foynes (near Shannon) to New York was introduced on 30 June. Imperial Airways followed on 5 August 1939 but the service terminated at the outbreak of war.

1939-45
Ireland remained neutral during World War II and the internal postal service operated normally. The names of most towns had by now been changed to their Gaelic equivalents and most of the handstamps too were changed during this period. The links by air for mail to the rest of the world were controlled by Britain, but Irish mail was accepted after censorship.

1946 to date
Although stamps have been inscribed EIRE since 1922, the official name of the territory did not take this form until the Republic of Ireland was formally established in November 1949. Since that date, Ireland has continued to issue stamps in the normal way.

Isle of Man

Before 1850

FIRST STAMPS British Stamps from 6 May 1840

CURRENCY

sterling to 1971
1971 decimal currency

Island in the Irish Sea about 60 miles from Liverpool; changed hands on several occasions up to 1610, when it was granted to the Earl of Derby. Through inheritance passed to the Duke of Athol in 1735, who received £70,000 for all his rights in 1765. The parliament of the island, the Tynwald, is an independent legislative body, probably the oldest continuous parliament in the world.

There is little knowledge of the postal arrangements while the island was in the hands of the Earl of Derby. In 1765 the Act of Revestment which returned the island to the British Crown led to an official packet service from Whitehaven to Douglas. Until 1822 Douglas was a sub-office of Whitehaven, but in that year the packet service was moved to Liverpool and Douglas became a post town.

The first handstamp is known to have been issued before 1767 and markings continued in the normal British provincial style, though worded 'Isle of Man'. Between 1832 and 1840 there was a Penny Post in operation in the Isle of Man with receiving offices at Castletown, Peel and Ramsey, as well as Douglas itself.

Issued with a Maltese Cross postmark to begin with, the numeral 407 was used in Douglas from 1844 and later (1851) 036 and 037 were allocated to Ramsey and Castletown.

1914-18
During World War I a number of prisoner-of-war camps were estab-

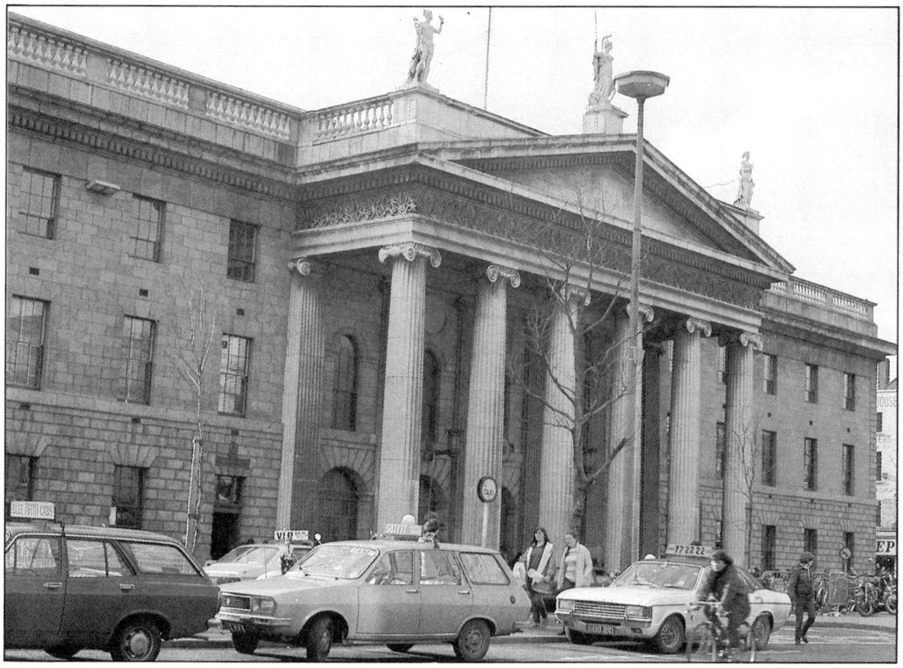

General Post Office, Dublin : headquarters of the Easter Rising in 1916

lished on the island. The only one which had its own PO was Knockaloe, though others had their own cachets. Douglas Holiday Camp was also used as an aliens' detention camp.

1939-45
Island served a similar purpose in World War II when camps at Knockaloe and Douglas Holiday Camp were re-opened. Because of the influx of internees, the number of camps and cachets were increased in this period.

1945 to date

FIRST REGIONAL STAMPS ISSUED 18 August 1958

Continued to use British and regional stamps under control of the North West Postal Region until postal independence was achieved on 5 July 1973. A new special issue of stamps was released on that day.

Channel Islands

CURRENCY

sterling to 1971
1971 decimal currency

Group of islands in the English Channel close to the Cotentin Peninsula. Came to the British Crown in 1066 with the Norman invasion. Main islands are Jersey, Guernsey, Alderney and Sark. Although they are within the British Isles, each island retains its own local administration and collects its own taxes. There were no official postal services until late in the 18th century. All mail was carried on a casual basis by the trading vessels which plied from Weymouth or St Malo in France.

1793-1815
Because of their proximity to the French coast, the garrison was increased during the Napoleonic Wars. The led to the opening of POs on Jersey and Guernsey on 15 February and 22 March 1794 respectively. Cancellations similar to those on the mainland were introduced and continued to be used in succeeding years. Ship letter markings were introduced in the early 1800s.

1815-50

FIRST STAMPS ISSUED 6 May 1840

When stamps were issued, they were brought into use immediately in the Channel Islands. Maltese Cross cancellations were issued and a distinctive cross, probably made locally, was used in Alderney, which had opened a PO in 1843. Subsequently cancellations followed the trend of the British provincial offices. The numerals issued in 1844 were 324 for Guernsey, 409 for Jersey and (in 1848) 965 for Alderney.

Handstamps in France were also used at this period to cancel stamps which were carried direct to France or were cancelled on board ship.

1850-71
One of the provisions of the Anglo-

A
B
C
JERSEY £2
VISIT OF H.M. THE QUEEN AND H.R.H. THE DUKE OF EDINBURGH JUNE 28-29 1978
7p
TO THE BAILIWICK OF
GUERNSEY
MANX CAT
10
ISLE OF MAN
POSTAGE 5P
Postage 4D
POSTAGE 4D
D
E
F

A Jersey 1969.
B Guernsey 1969.
C Isle of Man 1973.
D Guernsey 1968.
E Jersey 1968.
F Isle of Man 1969.

French Postal Convention of 1856 allowed for the transport of letters between British and French ports by private ships. The captains of such ships were to be paid 1*d* per letter. As a result, movable boxes were provided either at the quayside or on vessels and their contents would receive a special cancellation on arrival at the port. This provision particularly applied to mail passing between the Channel Isles and France.

In France these letters were often cancelled with a lozenge of dots and a numeral – the number relating to the port of arrival: Granville was 1441, St Malo 3176 and Le Havre was 1496. Letters in the reverse direction were cancelled with a British-style postmark inscribed: 'Jersey/France/MB'. This type was used from 1858 until World War II.

1871-1914

Continued to use British adhesives throughout the period with standard British postmarks. During this period and during World War I many high values can be found cancelled with the postmarks of the two main POs. These relate to the payment of tobacco tax on the island and are not, strictly, postal usage.

1919-39

Between the wars the Channel Islands continued to use British stamps, and these can be distinguished by their postmarks. POs had been established on Sark and in 1925 a PO was opened on Herm Island. These were both sub-offices of Guernsey. The Herm office was closed in 1938.

Between the wars, attempts were made to establish regular air services to the islands and these were finally inaugurated to Jersey in 1937 and to Guernsey in 1939. They operated from Southampton and carried a GPO contract until the outbreak of war.

1939-45

FIRST LOCAL ISSUE Jersey 1 April 1941
FIRST LOCAL ISSUE Guernsey 7 April 1941

After the fall of France, the invasion of the islands by the Germans could not long be delayed and the unopposed occupation took place on 30 June 1940. British stamps continued to be used, but stock quickly ran out and had to be replaced with local issues. The shortage of penny stamps on Guernsey led to the provision of bisects of the 2*d* stamp. These were officially allowed between 27 December 1940 and 22 February 1941. The 1940 Centenary issue is most often seen but the other 2*d* values of King George V and George VI were also used.

When the islands were liberated on 10 May 1945, the British Post Office allowed full validity to the local issues for one year. Previously these had only been valid for local and inter-island postage.

1945 to date

FIRST REGIONAL STAMPS ISSUED
18 August 1958

By 1947 there was some pressure to have special stamps for the islands, and, although no postage stamps were produced, fiscal stamps were issued. In 1948 a special issue was made to commemorate the third anniversary of the liberation of the Islands. These two values were available in the Channel Islands, and also at certain selected offices on the mainland. They were valid for postage throughout Britain.

Administered by the South West Region of the Post Office until 1969, on 1 October that year, Jersey and Guernsey (which incorporated Alderney, Sark and Herm) issued their own stamps as an independent PAdmin.

• Herm Island

Herm Island PO was closed as Guernsey sub-office in 1938. After the war, the owner of the island issued a series of carriage labels for payment for letters carried from the island to Guernsey. These were suppressed when Guernsey became postally independent in 1969. A sub-office was re-opened at that time.

Alderney

FIRST STAMPS ISSUED 14 June 1983

Used the stamps of Guernsey after regional issues were released in August 1958. It became a sub-office of Guernsey when it became postally independent, and released its own stamps for the first time in 1983.

Stamps of Alderney can be used throughout the Bailiwick.

France

CURRENCY	
	100 centimes = 1 franc
1960	100 (old) francs = 1 new franc

Before 1660

During the 14th and 15th centuries France was dominated by the English, who, through marriage and conquest, had gained control over large areas of what is modern France. Following the battle of Agincourt in 1415, Henry V of England married the daughter of the French king and briefly became king of France and England. On his death in 1422 the regency set up for his infant son was not strong enough to combat the growing sense of unity in France. In the later part of the 15th century the Wars of the Roses began in England and this diversion helped Louis XI of France to bring under his control many of the provinces, dukedoms and baronies which, through ever-changing allegiances, had prevented the formation of a unified nation.

The nucleus formed at that time grew in strength and national identity until Henry of Navarre welded the country into a single unit in 1589. After this period Cardinals Richelieu and Mazarin converted France into the most powerful nation in Europe, though religious difference led to civil wars which tended to split the country when it was not fighting a common enemy.

The first mail service was set up on 19 June 1464 by decree of Louis XI but it only operated for the king and the royal court. The first international couriers were established by the Count of Thurn and Taxis in 1490. Over the years the mail service developed, and in 1576 a tax was established for sending letter under the control of the French government, the first such charge for a post which was not directly for the court. At the direction of Fouquet de Varennes the organization became more precise and was made available to the public in 1603. However, it was a regulation of Pierre d'Almeras, General of Posts, on 16 October 1627, approved by letters patent of the king on 12 May 1628, which established the first postal tariff for the public. The first service was from Paris to Dijon or Macon (2 *sous*), Lyons, Bordeaux or Toulouse (3 *sous*). These tariffs were changed in April 1644 and by then the services had extended very considerably. The 2-*sou* rate disappeared, but 41 places were listed with rates between 3 and 5 *sous*. In May 1644 the rates for letters to overseas destinations were approved. The rate to England was 10 *sous* and to other adjacent territories from 9 to 16 *sous*. Letters were marked in manuscript.

Further development of the service began in 1630 under the Marquis de Louvois, who was Superintendent of Posts until 1668.

1660-1793

Under Louis XIV, the 'Sun' king (1643-1715), the internal disputes were largely suppressed and the boundaries with Italy and Spain confirmed. The wars of the later 17th and early 18th centuries were designed to extend the French eastern frontier to the Rhine. The region between Switzerland and the North Sea continued to be a battlefield until World War II, with only short periods of peace.

The reforms of Louvois continued in the early part of this period. In 1673 the tariffs were altered so that they were in direct relation to the distance carried. There were four zones: up to 25 leagues, 25-60 leagues, 60-80, and over 80 leagues. The rates for a letter ranged from 2 to 5 *sous*.

In 1676 the rate was again revised but on this occasion to allow for the use of an envelope. In England the policy was that a letter should be a folded sheet and an envelope was considered to be a second sheet and the charge was doubled. However, in France the charge for an envelope was set at only 1 *sou* and this allowed the manufacture of envelopes to develop while in England no such industry existed until the 1820s.

Letters were endorsed in manuscript until the start of the 18th century, when the larger offices adopted straight-line marks. The markings of the French postal service can be classified in three different types: those using the word 'De', which were the *cachets de départ*; 'Port Paye' which were the prepaid markings; and 'Deb', which were arrival marks (*Debourse*). These words appear beside the name of the town.

By 1789 a complete network of postal services had been extended to cover the whole country. Established relationships with neighbouring countries were continued and access was given to the entry of French mail into the imperial service operated by the Counts of Thurn and Taxis.

In 1789 the nation rose against the feudal abuses in France and the royal government was overthrown. After four years of terror, including the execution of the king and queen in 1793, the French revolutionary wars began. However, before this, there had been disruption of the postal service, partly by execution of the senior officials and partly because of uncertainty of control in some districts.

Tariff alterations had been made for internal letters in 1704, when the distances carried were increased to 150 leagues; in 1759, when the rates were raised to 4-14 *sous*; and in 1792, when a major change was made. By this legislation, payment by distance remained (5-15 *sous*) but mail in the same *département* was carried at a fixed rate of 4 *sous*. In 1759 a special 'poste' was opened in Paris.

1793-1815

The execution of the king and the

Napoleon's Conquests to 1814

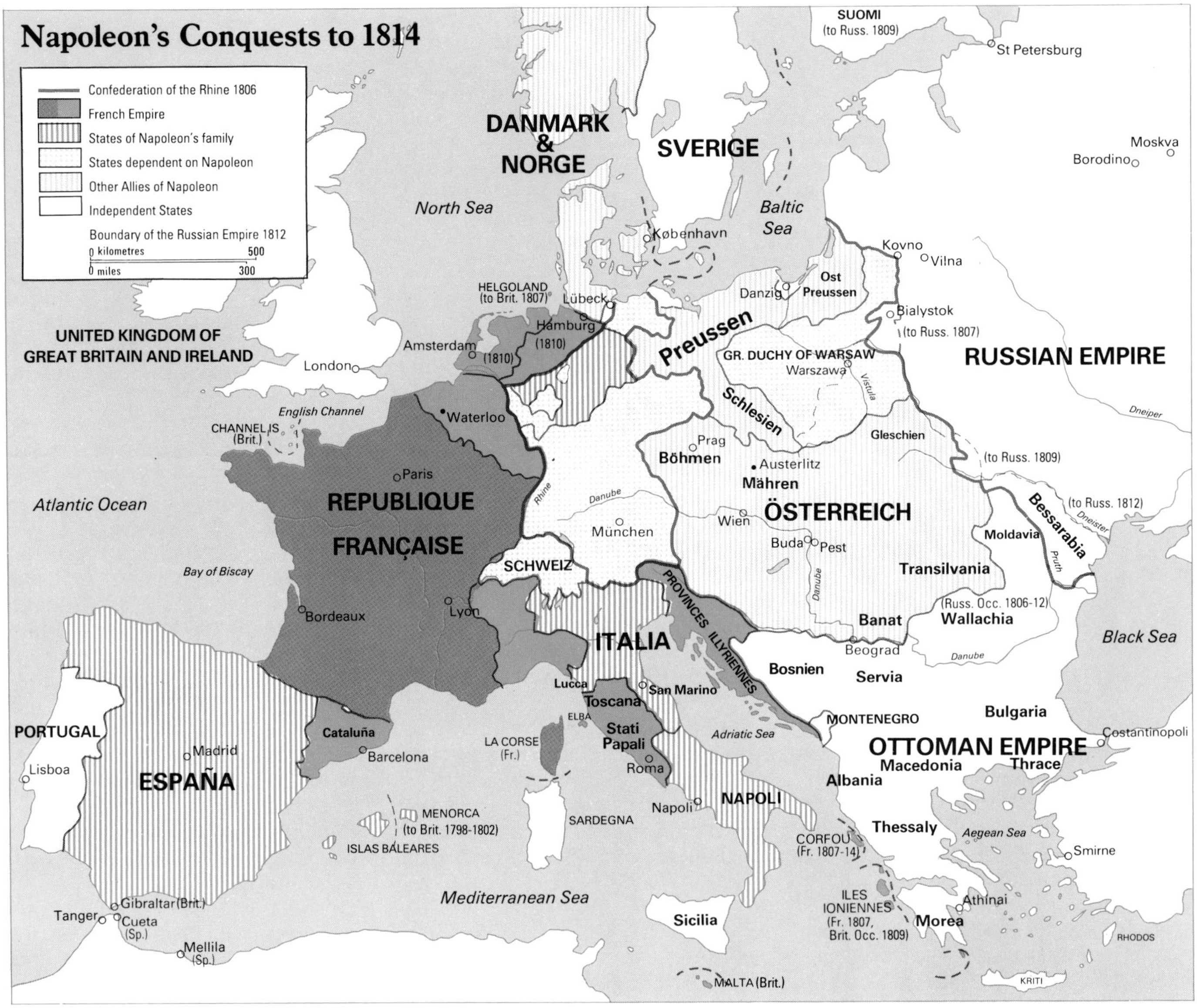
Confederation of the Rhine 1806
French Empire
States of Napoleon's family
States dependent on Napoleon
Other Allies of Napoleon
Independent States
Boundary of the Russian Empire 1812
0 kilometres 500
0 miles 300
SUOMI
(to Russ. 1809)
St Petersburg
Moskva
Borodino
DANMARK & NORGE
SVERIGE
North Sea
Baltic Sea
København
Kovno
Vilna
HELGOLAND (to Brit. 1807)
Lübeck
Danzig
Ost Preussen
Bialystok
(to Russ. 1807)
UNITED KINGDOM OF GREAT BRITAIN AND IRELAND
London
Amsterdam
Hamburg (1810)
(1810)
Preussen
GR. DUCHY OF WARSAW
Warszawa
Vistula
RUSSIAN EMPIRE
Dneiper
English Channel
CHANNEL IS. (Brit.)
Waterloo
Schlesien
Prag
Böhmen
Gleschien
(to Russ. 1809)
Austerlitz
Mähren
Paris
Atlantic Ocean
REPUBLIQUE FRANÇAISE
Rhine
Danube
München
Wien
ÖSTERREICH
Bessarabia
(to Russ. 1812)
Dneister
Moldavia
Pruth
Buda
Pest
Bay of Biscay
SCHWEIZ
Transilvania
Bordeaux
Lyon
PROVINCES ILLYRIENNES
(Russ. Occ. 1806-12)
Wallachia
Banat
ITALIA
Black Sea
Beograd
Danube
Bosnien
Servia
Lucca
San Marino
Toscana
ELBA
Stati Papali
MONTENEGRO
Bulgaria
PORTUGAL
Cataluña
LA CORSE (Fr.)
Adriatic Sea
Costantinopoli
Madrid
Barcelona
Roma
OTTOMAN EMPIRE
Macedonia
Thrace
Lisboa
ESPAÑA
Albania
NAPOLI
Napoli
MENORCA (to Brit. 1798-1802)
SARDEGNA
Thessaly
CORFOU (Fr. 1807-14)
Aegean Sea
Smirne
ISLAS BALEARES
ILES IONIENNES (Fr. 1807, Brit. Occ. 1809)
Athinai
Morea
Mediterranean Sea
Gibraltar (Brit.)
Tanger
Cueta (Sp.)
Sicilia
RHODOS
Mellila (Sp.)
MALTA (Brit.)
KRITI

formation of the Directory after the country had been declared a republic led to pressure from the major powers in Europe, which advanced to attack France. In 1793 wars began, and lasted almost without interruption for the next 22 years. Initially the loss of many officers traditionally drawn from the aristocracy weakened the leadership of the army, but the spirit of the troops led to many early successes and the frontiers were not only preserved but extended into Belgium and towards the Rhine.

Following the successes of the Italian campaigns in 1796-7, Bonaparte's climb to the emperorship of France began. After the expedition to Syria and Egypt, Bonaparte returned to France and overthrew the council of 500, which had replaced the Directory, and on 10 November 1799 Napoleon Bonaparte was declared first consul. In 1802 he became consul for life and on 18 May 1804 he was proclaimed emperor. The seeming relentless advance of the French armies continued until 1812, at which time the armies were stretched from Portugal to Moscow but the growing strength of the Allies led to defeat of the French in a series of campaigns in 1813. By early 1814 France had been driven back to its original frontiers and Paris was entered by the Allies on 31 March 1814. Napoleon abdicated and was exiled to Elba. The Bourbons were restored.

On 1 March 1815 Napoleon left Elba and returned to France. He arrived at Fontainebleau on 20 March — the start of the '100 Days'. He was defeated at Waterloo on 18 June 1815 and returned to Paris, where he was forced to abdicate. The Bourbons were again restored and Napoleon was exiled to St Helena.

The reorganization of France under the Code Napoleon led to many changes in the postal services. Changes in the method of payment had begun under the Directory and in 1795, after many alterations in the system of weights and distances, a new series of rates was issued. These increased all stages by 1 *sou*, so that the rates for distance ranged from 6 to 18 *sous* and the rate for the same *département* became 5 *sous*. In December the same year changes were again made. The costs were greatly increased and the number of stages for distance was reduced. The minimum cost was now 50 *sous*, but this was reduced to 6 *sous* in July 1796.

Obviously these fluctuations could not be allowed to continue, and in 1800 a revised series of charges was introduced, which with minor changes remained in force until 1815. Initially a letter up to 7 grammes (¼ oz) was 2 *decimes* for 100 kilometres. This related to a previous rate of about 4 *sous* for 20 leagues. An interesting factor is that the maximum distance was increased from 180 leagues 850 kms (530 miles) to 1000 kms (620 miles) — a measure of the advances which the French had already made.

During the wars France occupied and absorbed into French territory Belgium and Holland, Germany to the Rhine, Savoy, Piedmont and Tuscany. Satellite regimes were established with the Helvetic Confederation (1803), the Kingdom of Italy and the Kingdom of Naples (1805), the Confederation of the Rhine (1806), the Grand Duchy of Warsaw (1807) and Spain (1808). Under the Napoleonic reorganization all the *départements* were given numbers which were included in the postmarks. Numbers were also given to the occupied territories (some of these are listed under individual territories) which took the numbers of *départements* from 84 to 129.

Dated postmarks were introduced in France from the early years of the century and there were many marks issued to the Grande Armée for use by the French armies in the field. Marks of entry into France and the route by which they had arrived were also indicated on the postmarks at this time.

1815-50

FIRST STAMPS ISSUED 1 January 1849

The Congress of Vienna reduced France to its original boundaries and, in particular, ensured that the eastern frontier was moved back from the Rhine. The Bourbons continued to exercise control of the country until 1830, when, following a revolt, Charles X was deposed in favour of Louis Philippe, Duke of Orleans. He reigned until 1848, when another rising deposed him and the Second Republic was declared.

The postal service was consolidated into the new reduced area. Rates were reset in 1828, when the distance was reduced from 1000 km (620 miles) to 900 km (560 miles), and this remained essentially the rate until stamps were issued in 1849. The currency was also reformed and the present format of 100 *centimes* to 1 *franc* was introduced.

Postal markings continued to show the different types of markings for arrival and despatch and the military service continued to develop — mainly in connection with France's colonial expansion.

First stamps were printed in values of 20 *centimes* and 1 *franc*, the rate for letters having been set at 20 *centimes* for 7½ grammes (¼ oz). The stamps were inscribed REPUB. FRANC.

1850-71

With the introduction of adhesive stamps, a series of new marks was introduced to obliterate the new labels. Initially these were in various forms of diamonds or circles with parallel lines or bars. Between 1853 and 1876 a series of new cancellations, consisting of a diamond of dots containing a number, was used by French POs. Two series were produced with small and large numerals — each one indicating the offices of despatch. These cancellations were also used in POs abroad.

Further stamps were added to the range between 1850 and 1852. Initial tariffs introduced at the time stamps were issued were quickly changed and the internal rate became 25 *centimes* in 1850, though this reverted to 20 *centimes* in 1854. This tariff remained the basis until 1871.

Meanwhile major political changes were occurring. At the beginning of December 1851, Prince Louis–Napoleon Bonaparte, President of the Republic, organized a military coup which led to the dissolution of the National Assembly. Election of the president for ten years was proposed. In October 1852 the Senate was called to decide on the future of the constitution. The restoration of the empire was proposed and agreed subject to a vote by the people. The vote was held on 21 November 1852 and was carried by 7¾ million votes to ¼ million against. Napoleon III was declared emperor on 2 December. Initially stamps appeared with Napoleon's head replacing 'Ceres' but with the inscription remaining as REPUB. FRANC. However new stamps appeared in August 1853 inscribed EMPIRE. FRANC.

In 1854 France joined England in the war against Russia fought in the Crimea. In the later stages they were supported by the Sardinians. The French army was particularly successful in the assault on Sebastopol. Because of the shortage of British ships, much of the early mail from British forces was carried by French vessels. Mail from this campaign was marked 'Armée d'Orient'.

In 1859 France, allied with Sardinia, fought the Austrians for control of northern Italy. In return for their support, France gained Savoy and the Alpes Maritimes.

In 1870 Napoleon led his country into a disastrous war with Prussia. He was unaware of Bismarck's plan to form a buffer on the west bank of the Rhine. The trigger which started the war was the agreement that a Prussian prince should become king of Spain. This was unacceptable to Napoleon and war began on 28 July 1870. The

B
EMPIRE FRANC
25 C POSTES 25 C
DES SOCIETES PHILATELIQUES
0,50
C
REPUBLIQUE FRANÇAISE
REPUB FRANC
20 C POSTES 20 C
D
EMPIRE FRANCAIS
80 C POSTES 80 C
A
REPUBLIQUE FRANÇAISE
15c
POSTES
E
4F50
F

A France:French Empire 1863; B France: French Empire 1852; C France:French Republic, New Currency 1974; D France: French Republic 1849; E France:French Republic 1903; F France:Vichy France 1941.

French were defeated, the emperor was captured at Sedan on 2 September, and the empire was dissolved. The Third Republic was declared immediately and a provisional government established at Bordeaux.

Stamps supplied to the provincial POs quickly ran out and new printing was made at Bordeaux mint. The 'Ceres' design of the Second Republic was re-introduced and the inscription REPUB. FRANC.

The Prussians advanced into France, Paris was invested by 19 September, and capitulated on 28 January 1871. During the siege, several attempts were made to get mail in and out of the city. Letters were sent out in manned balloons (*balons montés*) and attempts were made to send letters by floating metal canisters down the Seine (*boule de moulin*). However, the most successful system for incoming letters made use of pigeons from Tours. Messages reduced in size were read by projecting the paper onto a screen (this service was also available from Britain).

Under the terms of the peace agreement, France lost Alsace-Lorraine (q.v.) to Prussia and subsequently to the German empire. Bismarck had gained his foothold on the west bank of the Rhine.

1871-1914

After the disaster of the Franco-Prussian War, it took time for France to recover and to regain its place as a major power in European politics. The various alliances of this period enabled France to rely on its new allies for common defence while it gradually rebuilt its own strength. It was a time when the French gradually expanded their empire in Africa and began to develop a colonial policy throughout the world.

At home the postal organization remained much as before, but new tariffs were introduced in September 1871, partly as a result of the war, and the basic internal rate returned to 25 *centimes*. It remained at this level until after World War I.

Postcards were introduced with a rate of 15 *centimes* in January 1873 and an express service was started in March 1892 at a cost of 50 *centimes*. Registration had been suspended during the Prussian occupation and this was re-established in February 1873.

France was one of the original signatories of the UPU in 1874. The first meeting had been planned in Switzerland in 1870 but was delayed because of the Franco-Prussian War. Even when it was eventually held, the French delegation was late and many of the decisions were approved in its absence. Rates for the UPU countries were introduced in October 1875 at a rate of 30 *centimes*, but this was reduced to 25 *centimes* in May 1878 after the first congress of the UPU, which was held in Paris.

The extension of the French colonies led to rapid development of the French mailboat service during this period. The division of Africa between the main European powers was completed by 1900, through France was still in conflict in North and West Africa.

The Entente Cordiale with Britain was declared in 1907 and a Franco-British exhibition was held at White City, London in 1908. The alliance of the two powers in combination with Russia seemed to provide a balance of power, to offset the strength of the Central Powers, but this was not to be. In 1914 the assassination of the Austrian Archduke led to the outbreak of World War I.

1914-18

France entered the war with Germany after the invasion of Belgium, and immediately moved into Germany in the area of Alsace. However, the strength of the German drive through Belgium broke the French northern armies, and the army in Alsace withdrew. After the battle of the Marne, the Germans were driven back and the war settled down to a stalemate of trench warfare for the next three years. Apart from Germany and Russia, the French forces suffered the greatest losses and part of northern France was occupied by the Germans for most of the war. In 1916 German stamps overprinted for the Western Military Command were used in these occupied areas, and it was not until 1918 that all these areas were regained by France.

French forces also fought in Italy

POSTES

Far left
Aged French post-box

Left
Post-box beside a church, Yonne, Burgundy

and in the Salonica campaign. Forces postmarks were used from these areas. The French commander at Salonica distinguished himself in 1918 by making the longest and quickest advance of World War I. With the British holding his flank against attack from the Turks, the French advanced through the Balkans and up to the line of the Danube. This led to French forces markings being used throughout this area and, later, overprinted stamps were introduced for civilians in these areas. At the end of the war, France regained Alsace-Lorraine (q.v.) from Germany and, apart from re-occupation in World War II, they have remained French ever since.

1918-39

The peace conferences of World War I were held in Versailles and at St Germain en Laye. Special postmarks were used on the mail from the delegates. The many changes in the boundaries in Europe are detailed under each country; French forces were employed in peace-keeping in areas of unrest and Field PO marks were used by the French army. Overprinted French stamps were used in Memel (q.v.) until the French were forced to withdraw in 1923.

At home France was not so seriously affected by the inflation in Germany as some other countries, but the decline in the value of the *franc* led to several increases in postal rates in the 1920s.

The rate for internal postage had been reduced to 15 *centimes* in 1917 but returned to 25 *centimes* in April 1920, 30*c* in July 1925, 40*c* in May 1926 and 50*c* in August 1926, where it remained until 1937. It moved to 65*c* in July 1937, to 90*c* in November 1938 and to 1 *fr* in December 1939.

In November 1919, after successful trials during the peace conference, the first airmail service was introduced between London and Paris. The rate for this service was initially 3 *fr* in addition to the normal postage. The French, like the British, needed to develop quicker mail services to the colonies abroad. In particular, France pioneered the flights to West Africa — initially from Toulouse to Casablanca and then to South America. The British Post Office used the Air France service until it was suspended in 1940.

The service to the Far East was more difficult to sustain because so many countries had to be overflown on the route. The need to complete a service to Indo-China was the main objective for the French, and this line was completed in 1934.

The building of the Maginot Line in the late 1920s gave France a feeling of security against any growth of power in Germany. With the resurgence of the German army after 1933 when Hitler became chancellor, it was obvious that the French army and the Western Allies needed time to rebuild their forces, particularly their air strength. The Munich Agreement of 1938 gave both countries a breathing space of one year but, despite this, war was declared in September 1939 after the German invasion of Poland.

1939-45

France entered the war on 3 September with Britain and immediately prepared for assault from Germany. Because of the strength of the Maginot Line, Germany did not attack immediately. In April 1940 Denmark and Norway were invaded and a French force formed part of the Allied

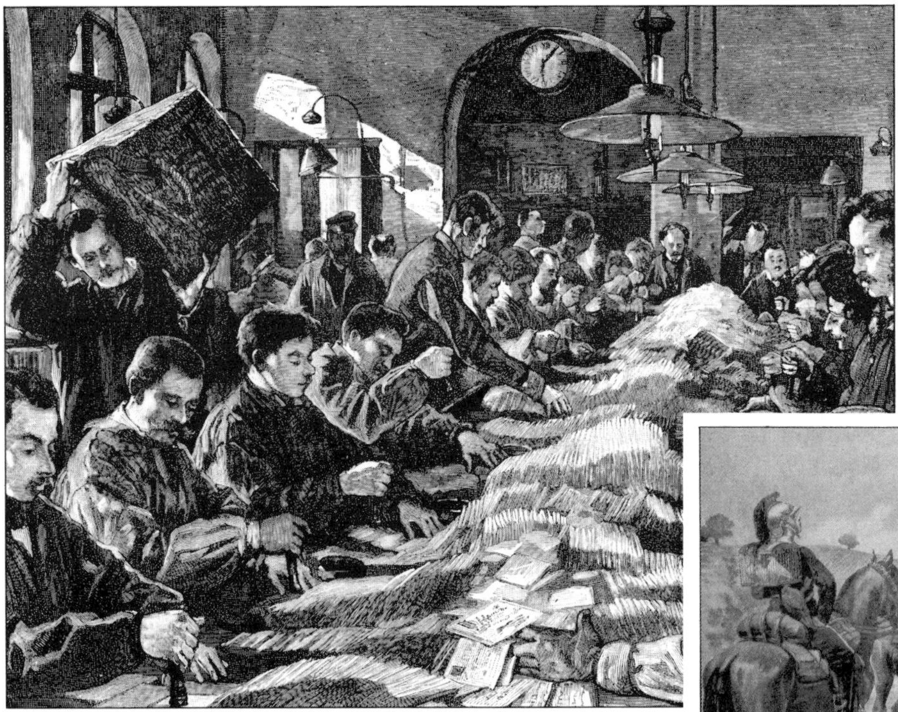

Stamping in Hôtel des Postes, Paris, 1880

Above
Parisian post-box, c.1818

Left
Messenger pigeons used by French Army, 1897

Expeditionary Force to north Norway.

In May the Germans invaded Holland and Belgium and quickly passed through to enter France from the north-east and directly south of Luxembourg, which by-passed the Maginot Line. The French army fell back and its British allies, pinned to the Channel coast, were forced to withdraw from Dunkirk.

On 10 June Italy declared war and moved into the undefended region of southern France. On 12 June Paris was declared an 'open city', and the government was moved first to Tours and then to Bordeaux. On 17 June Marshal Pétain asked the Germans for an armistice and on 22 June France was forced to accept the harsh terms imposed by Hitler.

France was divided into occupied and unoccupied areas. The latter was roughly south of the Loire but included no part of the Atlantic coast. Vichy was the new seat of government.

The war seriously disrupted the mail service, and although the basic structure remained it was now separated by the new boundary. Alsace and Lorraine (q.v.) were returned to German direct control. French stamps which had been issued by the Third Republic remained in use throughout France, and the first issue of the new French state appeared on 12 November 1940.

The rates of postage were increased from 1 *franc* to 1*f*50*c* in January 1942. Overseas contact with the French colonies was particularly difficult because of the action of the Allies and many places declared for Free France under General de Gaulle. A mail service continued with Britain from unoccupied France, which was nominally neutral. An air service via Lisbon and Madrid operated during 1941 and 1942, but when Britain and America invaded North Africa in November 1942, the Germans occupied the whole of France and this external link was discontinued.

On 6 June 1944 the Allies invaded Normandy and in August, southern France. By the end of 1944 virtually all of France had been liberated and Paris became the capital again in August. Stamps of a new design were printed in Washington and brought to France by the Allies in June. These were used in liberated areas as the forces advanced. They were placed on sale in Paris in October 1944. A further series, which had been printed in Algiers, was first placed on sale in Corsica in 1943, and was also released in Paris in November 1944.

A provisional government had been formed on 25 August 1944 and in September some of the pre-war designs of 'Iris' were released in new colours and, in the same month, a new

'Marianne' design, which had been printed in London, was also released. This issue was used until late in 1945. The complication of these four different issues all being used at the same time was compounded by the overprinting of many French stamps captured by the advancing Allies with the letter RF. The postage rates were again increased on 1 March 1945 and the basic rate was increased to 2 *fr*.

1945 to date

As a result of the war, France regained all the territory which had been lost in 1940 and also some small area on the frontier with Italy north of Menton. The provisional government of August 1944 was replaced in October 1946 by the Fourth Republic.

Normal postal links, both internal and external, had been quickly reformed and by September 1944 overseas mail was being delivered in southern France. However, France now began to suffer from inflation and the postal rates rapidly increased. From 2 *francs* in 1945, the rate reached 20 *francs* in 1957.

Because of the failure of French military policies in both Indo-China and Algiers, coupled with changes in government of the Fourth Republic, General de Gaulle was again asked to take control and the new constitution came into effect with the Fifth Republic on 4 October 1958. The rate of postage continued to climb; in 1959 it was 25*fr* and when the new currency was introduced in January 1960, this rate was confirmed. As elsewhere in Europe, this rate has continued to escalate since that date.

France has been a member of the EEC since its formation and, though a member of NATO when it was formed, withdrew in the 1960s.

• Alsace-Lorraine

CURRENCY

Stamps as France
German occupation of Alsace-Lorraine
1940 As Germany

FIRST STAMPS ISSUED 1870

During the Franco-Prussian War, some areas of France were occupied by the Prussian Army and a provisional issue was released on 10 September 1870. This was also used in Alsace-Lorraine after it was ceded to Prussia. By the convention of 14 February 1871, the rate from Alsace-Lorraine to France was set at 40 *centimes* – 20 *centimes* local stamps and 20 *centimes* French. On 31 August the rate was increased to 45 *centimes* with 25 *centimes* in French adhesives required. On 1 January 1872 the rate was re-established at 45 *centimes* but the German portion of 20 *centimes* could also be paid with 2 silver *groschen*. On 5 May the need for double franking ceased. From then until 1918 stamps of the Empire were used throughout both provinces.

1918-1939

After World War I the two provinces were returned to France and French stamps were reissued and used from 1919 onwards.

1939-45

Provinces of France reconquered by Germany in May 1940. On 29 July 1940 the french *départements* of Haut Rhin and Bas Rhin in Alsace were combined with Baden to form the new province of Elsass-Baden. Similarly, part of Lorraine was combined with Saarpfalz to form Westland.

Overprinted stamps for Elsass (Alsace) were issued on 15 August 1940 and Lothringen (Lorraine) on 21 August. Both issues were used until 31 December 1941, when they were fully integrated into Germany, and German stamps were used until reconquest by Allied forces late in 1944. Stamps of France have been used in these areas ever since.

Monaco

FIRST STAMPS Sardinia 1851-60
France 1860-85
FIRST STAMPS ISSUED 1 July 1885

CURRENCY

1885 As France

Independent principality on the south coast of France which has been ruled by the Grimaldi family since the 10th century. It was recognized by France in the 16th century and in 1793, during the French revolutionary wars, it was annexed by France. It was then co-ordinated into the French postal service and given a departmental number.

In 1815, after the Congress of Vienna, it was placed under the protection of Sardinia, but it became completely independent on 2 February 1861. When France gained Savoy and the Alpes Maritimes in 1858, Monaco became an enclave in French territory.

A Sardininan-style postmark was allocated to Monaco and was used on French stamps when they were first introduced. French postmarks including numeral 4222 in a lozenge of dots were introduced in September 1860. Monaco has continued to issue its own stamps since 1885 though French stamps remained valid in Monaco until 31 March 1886.

Andorra

FIRST STAMPS Spain or France to 1928
FIRST STAMPS ISSUED Spanish overprinted — March 1928

CURRENCY

1928 French PO As France
1928 Spanish PO As Spain

Province in the Pyrenees which in 1278 was placed under the joint protection of the Spanish Bishop of Urgel and the French Count of Foix. As a result, Andorra had two overlords and today still plays a nominal tribute to the Bishop and to the French President. Andorra has remained aloof from all the troubles of the succeeding centuries.

A
B
POSTES
2
CENTIMES
C
D
:-: CORREOS :-:
ANDORRA
ANDORRE
POSTES

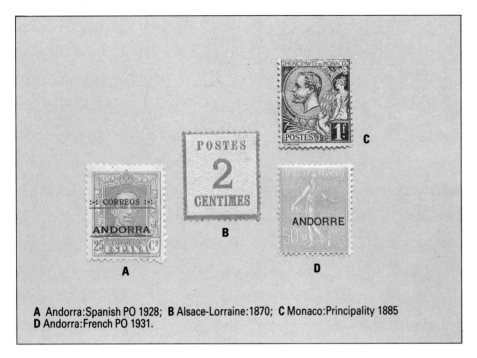

A Andorra:Spanish PO 1928; **B** Alsace-Lorraine:1870; **C** Monaco:Principality 1885
D Andorra:French PO 1931.

Spanish stamps overprinted and special issues in Spanish currency were used until June 1931 when France, having obtained approval from the UPU Congress in London in 1929, established its own postal administration and issued overprinted stamps. Since that date issues of both Spanish and French currencies have been in use for external mail, but uniquely there is no charge for internal mail in the province.

Spain (España)

CURRENCY

1850	8½ (later 8) cuartos = 1 real
1866	80 cuartos = 100 centimes de escudo = 1 escudo
1867	1000 milesimas = 100 centimos de escudo = 80 cuartos = 1 escudo
1872	100 centimos = 1 peseta

Before 1650

Country which at various times has occupied most or all of the Iberian Peninsula. Originally a loose alliance of kings and dukes which fell prey to the Muslim invasion in the 8th century following an invitation to the Moors to assist in a civil war in Spain. Southern Spain was held by the Moors until they were driven out in the 15th century. In 1469 Ferdinand of Aragon married Isabella of Castille and nearly all the Christian dominions in Spain were united under their control by 1479.

In 1492 Columbus was sent from Spain on his voyage of discovery which led to the establishment of the Spanish empire in the Americas in the 16th century. In 1516 the Habsburgs of Austria became kings of Spain, and in 1519 Charles I of Spain also became Holy Roman Emperor. Although this direct connection was short-lived, it led to Spain's involvement in European power politics. Philip of Spain married Mary of England in 1554, but he returned to Spain when she died in 1558. Portugal was united with Spain in 1580, and from this base Philip launched the armada against England.

The Moors were banned from Spain at the start of the 17th century and over 900,000 were forced to leave for North Africa. Portugal was lost in 1640 and never regained.

During this period the postal service was a royal courier service only. The main cities of the country were linked by this service, which reported to the capital, Madrid, or further south to the royal palace of Aranjuez. The Moors to the south had their own links with Africa but no regular service. However, connections with the Holy Roman Empire led to a ship-borne link being created in the Mediterranean, as relations with France generally made it impossible for couriers to cross the mainland. This in turn led to Spanish influence in Italy.

1650-1753

Spain was constantly involved in European and foreign wars during this period, and although its maximum power had passed in the 16th century, it still played a leading part in power politics. In 1700 the Habsburg line died out and a Bourbon was nominated as king. The link between the Spanish and French royal houses was unacceptable and the War of the Spanish Succession was fought from 1700 to 1713.

By this time a public postal service had been introduced and the earliest postal markings appeared: Barcelona and Tarragona in 1717, Jerez in 1718, Cadiz and San Sebastian in 1721, Bilbao in 1722; and by 1732 twelve different towns are recorded. Surprisingly, Madrid did not issue handstamps until 1763, but thereafter many different types were used.

Contact was maintained with the overseas empire by the galleons which sailed on an annual basis from Spain or South America. The link with the Far East colony of the Philippines was maintained by a route through Mexico from Corunna to Vera Cruz, overland to Acapulco and then by galleon to Manila. Incoming letters were marked FILIPINAS on arrival in Spain.

In 1759 the King of the Two Sicilies became King of Spain, which reinforced the link with Italy.

By 1793 the Spanish postal service was fully developed and all the main cities were linked on a regular basis.

85
PTA
ESPAÑA
CORREOS
A
ESPAÑA
CORREOS
B
6
PTAS
ESPAÑA
CORREOS
C
ESPAÑA
CORREOS
15
CENTIMOS
D
6 CUARTOS
CORREOS
1850
E

A Spain:King Juan Carlos 1981; **B** Spain:Civil War 1938; **C** Spain:Franco 1955; **D** Spain:King Alfonso XIII 1930; **E** Spain:First Issue 1850.

1793-1815

Spain did not support the revolutionary forces of France, but war with Britain broke out again in 1796. In 1805 the Spanish and French fleets were destroyed at Trafalgar. In 1807 the French entered Spain and a Spanish army was sent to the Baltic to support the French forces there. The French took Madrid in March 1808. The king abdicated in favour of Napoleon in May, and Napoleon's brother Joseph became king in July.

The Spanish people never accepted French control and a guerilla war broke out, supported by British forces landed in Portugal (q.v.) in 1808. A British presence remained until 1813 when the last French forces were driven from Spain.

French forces used the postal markings of the Grande Armée, but the British army relied on the packet service from Falmouth to Lisbon. the Spanish internal service was completely disrupted throughout the period of the Peninsular War but was quickly re-established in the areas which were liberated by allied forces. More straight-line postmarks were introduced during this period and by the full restoration in 1814 the service was in a stronger position than before. Even small villages were now linked to the main service.

Although the king was restored in May 1814, the American empire had begun to break up by 1810, with a revolt in Mexico. Although this was suppressed, the state in Mexico prevented the use of the route to the Philippines after that date.

1815-50

Following the defeat of France and the restoration of King Ferdinand, the constitution was set aside and the king ruled autocratically for several years. In 1820 a new constitution was placed before the Cortes. The king was forced to retire to Seville and later in 1823 to Cadiz. As a result, the French entered Spain, and in June invested Cadiz. The French remained in Cadiz until 1828 and military marks were used by the French garrison.

In 1833 Ferdinand died and was succeeded by his infant daughter, but Don Carlos, the King's brother declared himself to be the legal successor to the throne and the First Carlist War began. It lasted until 1840, and the young queen's party was supported by a British legion which fought in northwest Spain. Letters from this force bore no special markings but can be recognized by arrival marks in England.

In the early 1840s a complete new series of standard postal markings was introduced. These were large double circles with the name of the office at the top, the district in the lower part and a number on each side. These numbers represented the province in which the town was situated and ranged from 1 (New Castille — the area about Madrid) to 26 (Cadiz). Other numbers were used for colonies and dependencies abroad including 27 (Africa), 28 (Balearic Islands), 29 (Canary Islands), 30 (Cuba and Puerto Rico) and 31 (Philippine Islands).

In the period from 1832 to 1853 there was a British Consulate Office in Cadiz which was responsible for the transmission of mail for Britain. It had two different cancellations inscribed 'B.C./Cadiz'.

1850-71

FIRST STAMPS ISSUED 1 January 1850

The first series, showing the head of Queen Isabella, consisted of five values based on the currency of 8 *cuartos* = 1 *real*. Some contained the inscription 'Certificado' because they were intended for registered mail. Initially the series of dated handstamps introduced in the 1840s was used on stamped letters, but generally was not used to obliterate the stamps — these were cancelled with a lozenge-shaped network of lines. Additionally, other types of cancellation were used, including laurel wreaths, numerals and straight-line markings.

A further issue in the same currency was issued in 1856, but in 1866 the currency was changed to 1000 *milesimas* = 100 *centimos* = 1 *escudo*. This led to some unusual inscriptions on the succeeding stamp issues.

In 1868 Isabella was deposed by the Cortes and fled to France. She was obliged to abdicate in favour of her son Alfonso in 1870, but he was not accepted by the Spanish parliament, who offered the crown to Amadeo, the

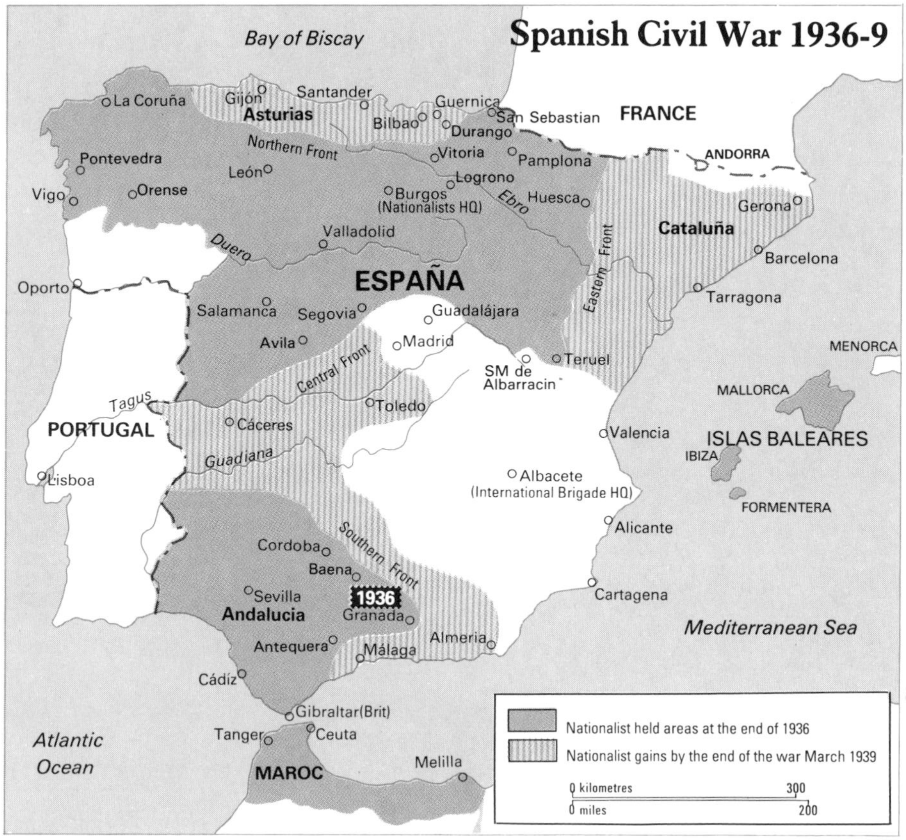
Spanish Civil War 1936-9
Bay of Biscay
La Coruña
Gijón
Santander
Asturias
Guernica
Bilbao
Durango
San Sebastian
FRANCE
Northern Front
Vitoria
Pamplona
ANDORRA
Pontevedra
León
Logrono
Vigo
Orense
Burgos
(Nationalists HQ)
Ebro
Huesca
Gerona
Cataluña
Valladolid
Duero
Eastern Front
Barcelona
Oporto
ESPAÑA
Tarragona
Salamanca
Segovia
Guadalájara
Avila
Madrid
MENORCA
Central Front
SM de Albarracin
Teruel
MALLORCA
Tagus
Toledo
PORTUGAL
Cáceres
Valencia
ISLAS BALEARES
IBIZA
Guadiana
Lisboa
Albacete
(International Brigade HQ)
FORMENTERA
Alicante
Southern Front
Cordoba
Baena
Sevilla
1936
Granada
Cartagena
Andalucia
Mediterranean Sea
Almeria
Antequera
Málaga
Cádiz
Gibraltar(Brit)
Atlantic Ocean
Tanger
Ceuta
Melilla
MAROC
Nationalist held areas at the end of 1936
Nationalist gains by the end of the war March 1939
0 kilometres 300
0 miles 200

son of the King of Italy. He accepted the crown on 4 December 1870, and the scene was set for the Second Carlist War.

1871-1919

The Carlist War continued until 1875, and this was the start of a period of political instability from which Spain suffered for the following 70 years. King Amadeo abdicated in 1873. A republic was proclaimed on 11 February 1873 and fighting continued between government forces and the Carlists who supported the grandson of Don Carlos for the throne.

Disruption of the postal service was inevitable and many different stamp issues appeared during this period. In 1872 the currency was again changed to 100 *centimos* = 1 *peseta* and after Amadeo abdicated stamps were issued by the republic and by the Carlists.

In 1874 Alfonso was proclaimed king but he died in November 1885 and was succeeded initially by his daughter, Mercedes, but later by his posthumous son, Alfonso XIII, when he was born on 17 May 1886 . In 1898 the Spanish-American War broke out and was conducted mainly in the Philippines and Cuba. As a result, Spain lost its remaining major colonies. Spain was a signatory of the UPU at its first meeting, the colonies in 1877. Spain remained neutral throughout World War I.

1919-39

Madrid was the site of the VIIth Congress of the UPU in 1920, the first Congress since 1906.

The reign of King Alfonso XIII ended with the collapse of the monarchy in 1931 and a republic was proclaimed. Political parties ranging from royalists to anarchists were unable to agree on any policy and for five years there was no real direction to the country.

At that time, there was a military uprising in the North African garrison town of Melilla and this was associated with a general rebellion by the army. The rebels, or Nationalists, quickly captured most of Andalusia, but were not supported in the north or near Madrid. In 1937 Asturias in the north of Spain fell to the Nationalists and after fierce fighting the following year, the army broke through to the sea. Barcelona fell in January 1939. The country was re-united under Franco in March of that year when the government surrendered.

During the war many issues of a provisional nature were prepared by both sides. As the nationalists advanced, they were faced with demands for postage stamps and republican stamps were overprinted with patriotic slogans both with and without official permission. The postal service was totally disrupted and stamps of both types were used concurrently.

The use of Republican stamps in the Nationalist areas was forbidden after 1 August 1937, but they continued to be overprinted when captured. The first stamps produced by the Nationalists appeared in Granada in August 1936 within a month of the outbreak of hostilities.

The Republicans were running short of foreign currency in 1938 and a philatelic bureau was established in Barcelona. Both parties experienced shortages of stamps during the war; the Nationalists because they had limited facilities for printing, and the Republicans because they were unable to supply the towns still nominally under their control. Fiscal stamps were used when possible in some of the towns which had been cut off by the Nationalists.

Local war tax stamps were issued by the Nationalists and these, though intended to be used in addition to normal postage stamps, were often used on their own.

Military marks on mail are numerous and indicate the battalion of each regiment. The Nationalists were supported by the Italians and Germans

MADRID-CAPITAL
PROVINCIAS Y EXTRANJERO

Above
Spanish post-box

Left
Road from Madrid to Portugal which would have been used by postal authority

while the Republicans were supported by the Russians and the International Brigade, which comprised nationals from many countries including Britain. First stamps portraying General Franco appeared in 1939, at the end of the civil war.

1939-45
Spain remained neutral during World War II. It was necessary to rebuild the economy which had been so severely affected by the civil war.

1945 to date
Spain continued its recovery throughout the early years after the war. It became a major tourist area in the 1960s and when Franco died in 1975, the royal family was re-instated, King Juan Carlos being crowned in the same year.

Dispute with Britain led to the closing of the boundary with Gibraltar in 1969, and it was not re-opened until February 1985.

• Canary Islands

FIRST STAMPS Spain from 1854
FIRST STAMPS ISSUED 1936

Island group off the north-west coast of Africa. A Spanish province since 1483. Used stamps of Spain from 1854 except in 1936-38 when overprinted airmail stamps were issued for the Lufthansa transatlantic service to Brazil. This service was curtailed before the end of the Civil War in 1939.

Portugal

CURRENCY

1853	1000 reis = 1 milreis
1912	100 centavos = 1 escudo

Before 1815
Maritime nation on the west coast of the Iberian Peninsula which was responsible for much of the exploration of the world in the 15th and 16th centuries.

Territory was cleared of the Moors in 1145 and was then co-ordinated under its first king. Prince Henry the Navigator established a school of navigation at Sagres in the Algarve and the first gradual but planned exploration of the coast of Africa was started. Madeira was colonized in 1420, the

Azores in 1437, and the Cape Verde Islands in 1456. Bartholomeu Dias rounded the Cape of Good Hope in 1487.

Vasco da Gama reached the west coast of India in 1498, and in 1500 Cabral reached the coast of Brazil. Colonization spread down the coast of Africa, to India and in 1512 to Malacca. However, growth of the colonial empire was halted in 1580 when Spain invaded Portugal, and it became a vassal state until 1640. In 1668 the Spaniards tried to regain Portugal but were defeated at Vila Vicosa near the frontier. During the period under Spanish domination some of the overseas colonies were either lost or reduced in size and importance.

During the next 125 years Portugal remained independent but its influence continued to wane. Problems of succession to the throne were overcome by close intermarriage of the royal family. The Spanish and French invaded the country in 1762 but with the assistance of the British they were forced to withdraw.

Portugal was able to remain aloof from the early stages of the Napoleonic wars except for a brief clash with Spain from March to June in 1801. However, in 1807 Spain and France signed a treaty for the division of Portugal following the entry of a French army into Spain. Portugal was invaded and Lisbon was taken on 27 November 1807. The court and royal family fled to Brazil.

In June and July 1808 the Portuguese rose against the French forces and in July a British Expeditionary Force arrived off the mouth of the Mondego River, and defeated the French at Vimiero on 21 August. Under the Convention of Cintra, the French army was allowed to return to France. The Peninsular War under Arthur Wellesley (later Duke of Wellington) had begun.

Portugal operated a royal post from early times and during the Spanish occupation of 1580-1640 this was incorporated into the Spanish service. After Portuguese independence was re-established the internal service was re-organized on national lines, but was operated until 1787/8 by a private family. In 1787 the overseas postal service was taken over by the government and this was followed by the internal service on 1 January 1788. Handstamps for the major towns followed.

The king left for Brazil in November 1807 and from then until 1813 Portugal was the base of the British army and a battlefield for the French and the Allies. Periodically the British would advance into Spain but each winter would withdraw to Portugal. A packet service was organized by the British Post Office and mail was carried from Falmouth to Lisbon during this period.

1815-50

After the Congress of Vienna the boundaries of Portugal were confirmed and independence from Spain was agreed. The postal service was re-established, in part assisted by British advisors. However, the royal succession was in some doubt and the court did not return from Brazil until 1821. King John VI, who had been regent since 1791, died in 1826 and was succeeded by his son. In 1828 the king became ruler of Brazil — on election — and abdicated in favour of his daughter, who was only seven years of age.

A civil war ensued until 1834 and was supported by a British brigade that fought for the young Queen against her uncle, who had usurped the throne. Although the Queen re-established control, unrest continued and periodic revolutions which disrupted the postal service occurred until her death in 1853.

1850-71

FIRST STAMPS ISSUED July 1853

First issue showed the head of Queen Maria and was printed in the Mint at Lisbon. When the Queen died later in the year, the stamps were replaced by a new issue with the head of the new king, Pedro V. The postal service had been closely allied to the British service since the Napoleonic wars and many innovations which were introduced in Britain are reflected in similar changes in Portugal. Perhaps the most obvious of these are the pillar boxes on street corners, which are not only of a similar design but orginally were made in British foundries.

1871-1914

Stamps were issued for each of the reigns which followed. King Carlos was assassinated in 1908 and was succeeded by King Manoel. Two and a half years later he was deposed, and a republic was established in October 1910. The stamps of the royal period were overprinted REPUBLICA between 1911 and 1912. The currency was changed from *reis* to *centavos* and *escudos* in 1912.

1914 to date

Portugal entered World War I on the side of the Allies on 9 March 1916 and sent a force to France which had its own FPO. It has remained an independent republic ever since. After a period of dictatorship in the 1950s and 1960s a revolution followed in 1974 and a socialist government has ruled since then.

Madeira

FIRST STAMPS ISSUED 1868

Island of the north-west coast of Africa, administered as part of Portugal. Originally settled in 1421. Issued standard Portuguese colonial overprints and designs from 1868 to 1929; since then has used stamps of Portugal. In 1980, new stamps for Madeira were introduced and are used concurrently with issues of Portugal.

Azores (Acores)

FIRST STAMPS ISSUED 1868

Group of islands in the Central Atlantic which have been a Portuguese colony since 1457, though they were subject to Spain from 1580 to 1640. Issued standard Portuguese colonial overprints and designs from 1868 to 1929; since then has used stamps of Portugal. In 1980, new stamps for the Azores were introduced and are used concurrently with issues of Portugal.

Gibraltar

CURRENCY	
1886	sterling
1971	decimal currency

Before 1650
The Rock of Gibraltar together with the heights near Ceuta in Morocco form the Pillars of Hercules. Captured and fortified by the Moors under Tarig in 711, this fortress, known as Gebel Tarig, has given the colony its present name. Retaken by Spain in 1309 but subsequently held by many local dignatories. Generally believed to be impregnable to assault. No mail of this period has survived, nor was there sufficient trading to have established a service.

1650-1793
During the War of the Spanish Succession a British fleet under Sir George Rooke attacked Gibraltar on 21 July 1704 and the fortress fell on 24 July. It was besieged almost immediately by Spanish and French forces, who were unsuccessful, losing some 10,000 men compared to 400 British. Ceded to Britain in 1713 under the Treaty of Utrecht. The Spaniards were not happy with this result and made assaults in 1720 and 1727. Neither were successful.

In 1779 Spaniards and French began a further assault and this developed into one of the most famous sieges in history. Starting on 16 July 1779, it lasted until 5 February 1783. Throughout, British forces held firm and finally the blockade was withdrawn. Although letters from the gar-

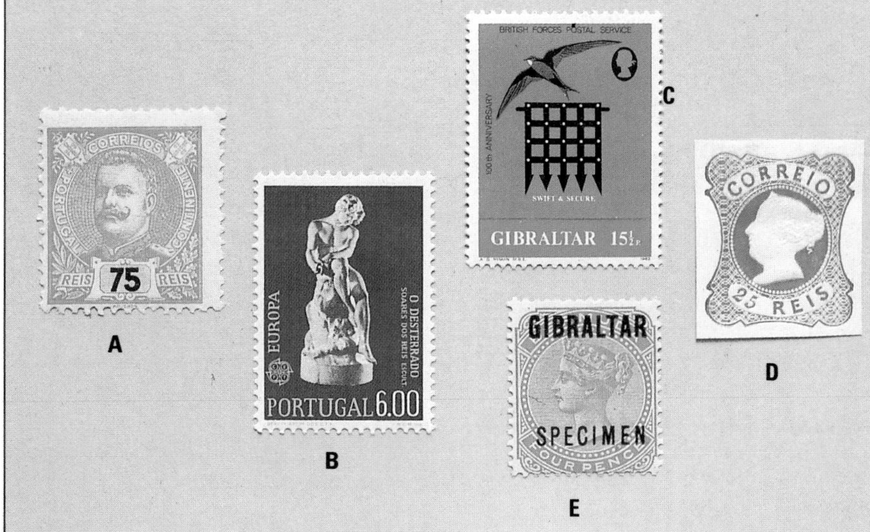
CORREIOS
REIS
75
REIS
A
EUROPA
O DESTERRADO
PORTUGAL 6.00
B
GIBRALTAR 15½p
C
CORREIO
25 REIS
D
GIBRALTAR
SPECIMEN
E

A Portugal:King Carlos 1895; **B** Portugal:Republic 1974; **C** Gibraltar:Colony 1982; **D** Portugal: Queen Maria 1851; **E** Gibraltar:Colony 1886.

Far right
Portuguese mail-wagon chief, 1893

Right
Portuguese mail distributor, 1893

The Rock of Gibraltar

rison exist, no official postal service was introduced until the early part of the 19th century.

1793-1815

For the first time in many wars to come, Gibraltar was an important naval base for Britain. Used by the Royal Navy to maintain their southern blockade of France and their command of the Mediterranean after the Battle of the Nile in 1798.

In the early years of the century the PO established in Gibraltar was a branch of the GPO in London. By Act of Parliament of 2 December 1806 the Postmaster-General was authorized to operate a packet to Gibraltar and Malta from Falmouth. Handstruck markings were introduced at this time and are known from 1809.

1815-50

Gibraltar continued to use handstruck markings even after stamps were issued in Britain. In August 1835 the GPO packet was withdrawn and replaced by a contract service operated by the Peninsula line. This operated from Falmouth until 1862. Stops were also made at Vigo, Malaga and Cadiz as well as Lisbon and Oporto. In February 1843 the *Great Liverpool* left Southampton with the first passengers for the Far East. This service became monthly and later, in 1853, twice monthly.

1850-71

FIRST STAMPS British 1857

In 1857 British stamps were placed on sale in Gibraltar and numeral 'A26' was allocated for the cancellation of adhesives as well as the letter 'G' in an oval of bars. Use of British adhesives continued until the PO was handed over to the colonial administration in 1886.

P & O shipping line continued to use Gibraltar as a port of call for transfer of mail and it was also used for Spanish mail which was transferred to the Spanish PO at San Roque.

By convention with Spain it was agreed that mail between Spain and Gibraltar should be regarded as local post. As a result the British internal *½d* postcard was placed on sale and can be found used to Spain.

1871-1914

FIRST STAMPS ISSUED Bermuda overprinted 1 January 1886

In 1885 approval was given to hand over control to the colonial authorities and the British GPO ceased to exercise any authority. The effective date was 1 January 1886 and, as there was insufficient time to introduce a new issue before that date, stamps of Bermuda were overprinted for Gibraltar.

Overprinted stamps were in new colours and were replaced by Gibraltar's own adhesives in December 1886.

In 1857 the first British PO in Morocco had been opened in Tangier. No stamps were provided but mail was passed to Gibraltar and cancelled. On the transfer of the Gibraltar PO from London to the Colonial Office in 1886 control of the Tangier PO was also transferred and Gibraltar stamps were placed on sale there and in other ports where consular offices continued to act as PAs. Stamps of Gibraltar continued to be used in Morocco until 1898, when stamps overprinted 'Morocco Agencies' were placed on sale. These in turn were replaced in 1907, when the British GPO resumed control of the PAs in Morocco.

Gibraltar joined the UPU in 1876.

1914-18

During World War I Gibraltar acted as a naval base for the Allied Mediterranean fleets. The garrison was enlarged and the volume of mail from the forces increased.

1939-45

Major naval supply base throughout World War II and particularly during the siege of Malta. Field POs operated within the colony and were used to cancel Gibraltar stamps. Owing to problems of perforating supplies of stamps when the printers were damaged by bombs in 1941-2, a number of unusual compound perforations appear on Gibraltar stamps. Some of these are rare.

1945 to date

A new constitution was granted in 1950 and revisions occurred in 1964 and 1969. However, Gibraltar remained a British possession and a referendum in 1969 showed that Gibraltarians were almost 100 per cent against any link with Spain. In 1969 Spain closed the frontier which was not re-opened until February 1985.

Netherlands

CURRENCY

1852 100 cents = 1 gulden (florin)

Before 1650

Country bordering the North Sea in north-west Europe. It was a pattern of duchies and earldoms in the Middle Ages but gradually became consolidated under the Counts of Holland and in 1416 gained the region of Brabant along the border with what is now Belgium. The territory was annexed by Burgundy in 1436 and control passed to Austria by marriage in 1477. This passing to the Hapsburg family led to its control by Spain in the 16th century.

The misrule of the Spanish Habsburgs, coupled with the religious persecution of the Reformed Dutch Church by the Inquisition, led to the revolt under William the Silent, Prince of Orange, in 1572. Although William was the lieutenant of the Spanish king for the Low Countries, he supported the Dutch Lutherans and fought with them against the Spanish. The crown was offered to Queen Elizabeth of England in 1575, but was declined, though with promises of support.

In 1576, at the Pacification of Ghent, the northern and southern provinces created a union. In 1579 the seven northern provinces joined together in the League of Utrecht and declared their independence three years later. In 1584 William was assassinated by an agent of the Spanish king but the war was continued by his sons. The struggle was supported by England until 1648, when the Republic of the United Provinces was recognized by the Peace of Westphalia at the end of the Thirty Years War.

During this period no formal mail service existed but complex courier routes were established for the passage of reports and instructions. There is evidence that the service to Belgium organized by the Counts of Thurn and Taxis was also used to provide communications for the public in the more northern region.

1650-1793

Following the Peace of Westphalia, Holland entered into a period of maritime and trading supremacy. Wars with England developed from the clash of commercial interests between these two maritime powers but after war with France in 1670, William of Orange married Princess Mary of England in 1677 to cement an alliance of the two countries with Sweden. In 1688 James II of England was forced to abdicate because of his Catholic religion when William landed in Torbay. William and Mary were proclaimed king and queen of both kingdoms in February 1689.

Wars with France continued and after William's death in 1702 the alliance led to the suport of Holland in the War of the Spanish Succession (1702-15). Dutch power began to decline at this time, civil war was always possible between the religious factions, and after a disastrous war with England in 1781-3 there was a major religious civil war in 1787.

The postal service was still not formalized within the nation at this time and although postal communication was possible for the public, this was either carried by favour or by the Thurn and Taxis post into central Europe.

1793-1815

In 1793 French revolutionary forces marched into Belgium and Holland. The Dutch declared in their favour, and a British force was landed to try to expel the French.

In 1795 the Batavian Republic was formed in alliance with France and the Dutch fleet was used against the British navy. However, with defeat for the Dutch at the Battle of Camperdown in 1797, the British established naval supremacy and the remainder of the Dutch fleet surrendered.

In 1806 Louis Bonaparte, brother of Napoleon I and father of Napoleon III, was declared king. He abdicated on 1 July 1810 and immediately the region was incorporated into France. In 1813 after the defeat of the French

A
B
C
D
E
F
20 CENT
DIX CENTS
50 C
NEDERLAND

A Netherlands:King William III 1852; **B** Belgium:First Issue 1849; **C** Netherlands:Queen Wilhelmina 1924; **D** Belgium:King Baudouin 1973; **E** Belgium:King Leopold 1931; **F** Netherlands:Queen Juliana 1949.

the House of Orange was restored, and in 1815 Belgium and Luxembourg were added to the dominions of the King of the Netherlands.

A national postal service was created in the country in 1803 and a system of mounted postillions was used to collect and deliver the mail. Handstruck markings were introduced for all the large cities. When the country was incorporated into France, a French system of postal organization was introduced and this continued until the defeat of Napoleon in 1813-14.

1815-50

The Kingdom of the Netherlands, which was granted to the House of Orange after the Congress of Vienna, controlled both Belgium and Luxembourg until 1830. At that time the Belgians rose against the rule of William Frederick following several years of religious discord. Belgium separated from the Netherlands in July 1831 and a war began. In 1839 the Treaty of London guaranteed the neutrality of Belgium, but the Netherlands still retained titular control of Luxembourg.

The use of handstamps was extended to the smaller villages. The railway service was used to speed the mail and the Hook of Holland was used as a transit port for mail to and from Britain.

1850-71

FIRST STAMPS ISSUED 1 January 1852

First stamps were printed in the Mint at Utrecht and did not show the name of the territory. It was not until 1867 that stamps appeared which included the name NEDERLAND.

Belgian independence made Dutch control of Luxembourg difficult, particularly as Luxembourg joined the German Confederation in 1830. The King of the Netherlands received an offer from France to buy the duchy in 1867 but this was prevented by the Prussians.

1871-1918

During this period of alliances among the great European powers, the Netherlands declared their neutrality and supported neither the entente between England and France nor the Central Powers.

The Netherlands was one of the original signatories of the UPU in 1874.

The Netherlands remained neutral throughout World War I and, although there was substantial disruption of the overseas mails, the internal services were maintained. Allied and German troops that entered Holland during the war were interned.

1918-39

Between the two wars the Netherlands was one of the pioneers of mechanized letter-sorting and the Transorma machine installed at Brighton in 1936 — the first British sorting machine — was developed in Rotterdam.

As a nation with a worldwide empire, especially in the East Indies, the use of air traffic to maintain commercial communication was important. The Royal Dutch Airline (KLM) was formed in 1919 and had expanded the direct link to Batavia before any other airline managed a regular service of this length. Special stamps for this route were issued in 1933.

In 1934 stamps overprinted for use in the International Court of Justice at the Hague were released but were withdrawn during World War II.

1939-45

Again declared neutrality at the outbreak of World War II, but in May 1940 the country was invaded by the Germans and was quickly overrun. Holland was occupied until the early part of 1945, though the southern provinces were liberated in the summer and autumn of 1944.

Stamps inscribed 'Nederland' continued to be issued by the occupying powers, but without the Queen's head. A government-in-exile was established in London and stamps were issued on 15 June 1944. These were intended for use on Netherlands warships serving with the Allied fleet. However, following the restoration of independence in May 1945 the same stamps were released in Holland, though they were not valid for postage until 1 April 1946.

POSTERIJEN

Above
Post-box, Amsterdam

Left
British packet-boat from Harwich arriving at Helvetsluys, Netherlands, 1794

1945 to date
Since World War II the Netherlands has not tried to maintain its stance of neutrality and has been an active member of NATO and the Western Alliance. It was an original signatory of the Treaty of Rome which created the EEC.

In 1947 stamps for the International Court of Justice were re-introduced and continued to be used during succeeding years.

Belgium

CURRENCY

1849 100 centimes = 1 franc
German occupation of Belgium
1914 As Belgium

Before 1650
Belgium as it is known today is a comparatively young country, having gained its independence from Holland in 1830, but its history as part of the Low Countries and earlier as part of the Spanish Netherlands has made it an important factor in the European power struggle.

When Belgium was a province of Austria a postal service was established to link Brussels to the parent state as early as 1 March 1500. This was operated by the Count of Thurn and Taxis (Tour et Tassis) and, later in the century, an internal service linking Malines, Ghent and Bruges was added to the Brussels link. In 1543 a second service was established from Liège through the Tyrol to Italy. These services had originally been intended for official mail but prepaid private mail was also allowed. All postal markings were handwritten on the reverse of the letters.

After the death of Charles V in 1558, a Protestant uprising disrupted the postal system and this continued on and off for many years.

1650-1793
During the War of the Spanish Succession in the early part of the 18th century, British troops as well as Austrian fought with the French for control of the country. The French invaded Belgium in 1701 and a new service to replace the Austrian-dominated Thurn and Taxis service was introduced. This operated on French lines. However, in 1714 Belgium, except for the principality of Liège reverted to Austria.

At this time there were 104 receiving offices open to the public, some of which used handstamps as well as manuscript markings.

In 1725 the postal monopoly was returned to the Counts of Thurn and Taxis and Prince Anselme François de

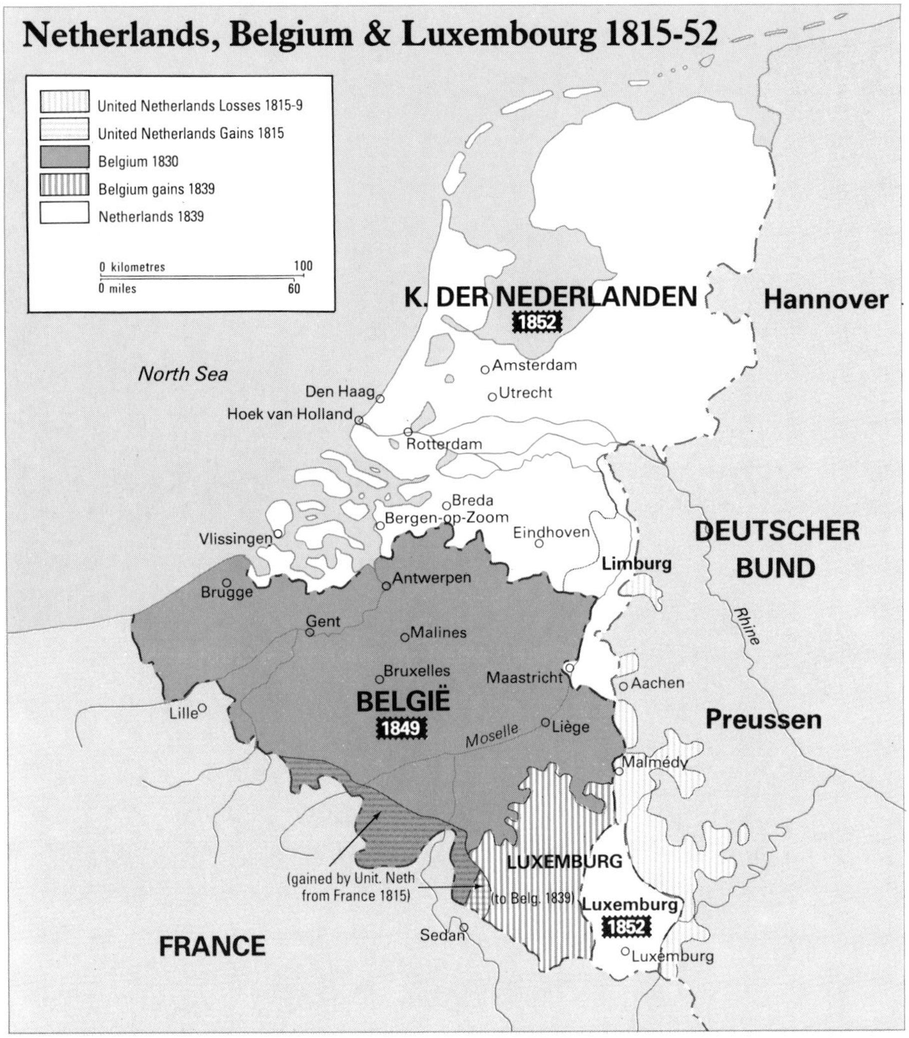
Netherlands, Belgium & Luxembourg 1815-52
United Netherlands Losses 1815-9
United Netherlands Gains 1815
Belgium 1830
Belgium gains 1839
Netherlands 1839
0 kilometres 100
0 miles 60
K. DER NEDERLANDEN
1852
Hannover
North Sea
Amsterdam
Utrecht
Den Haag
Hoek van Holland
Rotterdam
Breda
Bergen-op-Zoom
Eindhoven
Vlissingen
DEUTSCHER
BUND
Limburg
Brugge
Antwerpen
Gent
Malines
Rhine
Bruxelles
Maastricht
Aachen
Lille
BELGIË
1849
Moselle
Liège
Preussen
Malmédy
LUXEMBURG
(gained by Unit. Neth from France 1815)
(to Belg. 1839)
Luxemburg
1852
Sedan
Luxemburg
FRANCE

Taxis was made 'General des Postes'.

In June 1744 the French again invaded Belgium during the War of the Austrian Succession. The Belgian postal system was placed under the French service and all funds were passed to the French Treasury.

By the Treaty of Aix-La-Chapelle in 1748 Austria regained control of Belgium and Prince Anselme replaced the French postal agents with officers of his own. During this war the first military markings appeared on British mail with the introduction of a number of handstruck marks reading AB [Armée Britannique], AA [Armée Autrichienne] and AHO [Armée Hollondaise]. Although usually struck in Germany, examples are also known on letters from Belgium. The Belgian postal service appears to have escaped serious disruption during the Seven Years War (1756-63).

1793-1815

At the outbreak of the French revolutionary war in 1793, Belgium was invaded and became a French province until 1814. It was divided into 9 *départements*, which used the number 86 and 91-98. These numbers were included in the handstamps, and the Belgian postal service operated as part of the French postal administration. Town handstamps similar to those in use in France were introduced.

After Napoleon abdicated in 1814 the postal service was administered from Prussia, but in June 1815, Napoleon, who had landed in southern France, crossed the frontier into Belgium and was finally defeated at Waterloo.

1815-50

FIRST STAMPS ISSUED 1 July 1849

By the Congress of Vienna, Holland and Belgium with Luxembourg were united under the King of the Netherlands. The King proclaimed that all territories under his government belonged to the kingdom of the Netherlands. Postal services were amalgamated under the Dutch Director-General and in the following 15 years most handstruck markings were translated from French into Dutch or Flemish. These straight-line markings were in turn replaced at the main POs by circular marks which included the dates.

This rapid change from French influence was greatly resented by the Belgians, especially in the southern provinces, and led to a rising against the Dutch in September 1830. On 18 November 1830 a national council proclaimed the country's independence and in the following year Prince Leopold of Saxe-Coburg-Gotha became King of Belgium.

Postal services were reorganized: the 9 provinces were grouped into 2 regions and many places reverted to their French names. As there was a Prussian garrison in Luxembourg, the Belgians were alarmed that the Dutch might use their territory to attack. A Belgian force was maintained to cover this possibility and, by 1837, the first Belgian military marking had appeared.

At the same time, the first mail was being carried on the Belgian railroad system. In 1841 the 'Service des Postes sur le Chemin de Fer' was inaugurated and subsequently many train marks began to appear.

Leopold was interested in all modern reforms and in 1849 he decided that Belgium should use postage stamps. This followed his close study of the reforms of Rowland Hill.

1850-71
Belgian stamps followed the British tradition and did not have the name of the country included in the design until after Leopold died in 1865. He was succeeded by Leopold II, and from 1869 the designs included the word 'Belgique'. First stamps were printed in sheets of 200, but these were increased to 300 stamps per sheet from 1863.

Handstamps issued to offices after stamps had been released are interesting. Initially they were circular with the number allocated to the office in a rectangle surrounded by parallel lines. The offices (1-208) and TPOs had horizontal bars and the distributions (1-145) had vertical ones. Marks without number, using horizontal bars, were issued to postmen to cancel letters handed to them for delivery on the same route. These circular obliterators were replaced in April 1864 by a lozenge of dots similar to French types.

1871-1914
Belgium was one of the first signatories of the GPU in 1874, which became the UPU in 1878.

The Flemings complained that the French name for Belgium — 'Belgique' — was the only name on the stamps, and from 1893 'Belgie' was added. The name has appeared in both languages ever since.

Between 1893 and 1914 an innovation was tried. All stamps were produced with a detachable label inscribed 'Do not deliver on a Sunday' in both French and Flemish. All stamps were printed with these detachable *bandalettes*, which enabled the sender to indicate whether delivery was to be made on a Sunday.

Belgium's neutrality was guaranteed by the Treaty of London (1839). It was a breach of this treaty which led to the entry of Britain into World War I.

1914-18
Belgium was invaded by the Germans

TAXIPOST

Above
Sign on side of Belgian postal van

Left
Belgian post-box

Below
Post office, Brussels

on 1 August 1914 and quickly occupied except for a small area, the Ypres salient, which remained in Allied hands throughout most of the war, and the enclave of Baarle Hertog surrounded by Holland which remained in Belgian hands throughout the war. Britain entered the war on 4 August.

The government moved to Le Havre in France on 13 October 1914 and continued to print stamps for use in that locality and in unoccupied Belgium. The Germans issued stamps for use in occupied Belgium on 1 October 1914. These continued in use throughout the war and were used concurrently with the stamps of German Western Military Command from 1916. The latter were also used in the occupied area of northern France.

British Field POs were used in Belgium and, in particular, when a force was sent to Antwerp in October 1914.

Following the collapse of the German army, King Albert re-entered Brussels on 22 November 1918.

1919-39

Belgian troops occupied part of the Rhineland until 1930 and overprinted stamps were issued for this area (*see* Germany 1919-39). The troops themselves had free postage so no stamps were used. Having withdrawn from occupation, Belgium hoped that neutrality would be maintained, especially with the building of the Maginot and Siegfried Lines further south.

1939 to date

Invaded by Germany on 10 May 1940 and quickly overrun. Some British units were moved up from France but once the king surrendered the Belgian army, withdrawal to Dunkirk was necessary. Several British Field POs were either captured or had their handstamps destroyed by staff.

No overprints were issued: King Leopold remained in Belgium at the start of the German occupation though eventually imprisoned in Germany. The liberation began in August 1944, and in September the king submitted to a regency under his brother Charles. When Leopold was released, the Belgian parliament would not accept him and the regency continued until July 1950, when Leopold again tried to return to Belgium. This caused widespread rioting and the king abdicated in favour of his son — Baudouin.

Belgium is a member of NATO and a founder member of the EEC.

Luxembourg

CURRENCY

1852	124 centimes = 1 silver groschen
	100 centimes = 1 franc
1940	100 pfennig = 1 reichesmark
1944	100 centimes = 1 franc (Belgian)

Before 1815

Strategically-sited territory bordered by Belgium, France and West Germany. At various times it has been controlled by Germany, France, Austria, Spain and Holland. In the Middle Ages the Counts of Luxembourg were elected rulers of many European states, including Germany, Poland, Bohemia and Hungary.

In 1795 Luxembourg was occupied by French forces and became an occupied *département* until 1815. It was integrated into the French postal service, having earlier been served by the Counts of Thurn and Taxis, as Luxembourg was on the route down the Moselle into France.

1815-50

After 1815 Luxembourg, by then a grand duchy, was awarded to the King of Holland along with Belgium. Dutch types of postal markings were allocated during this period.

In 1830, following the revolt of the Belgians against Dutch control, Luxembourg joined the German Confederation and was garrisoned by Prussian troops, who brought their own 'Feldpost' with them. Pre-adhesive markings distinctive to Luxembourg were used until stamps were issued in 1852. The King of the Netherlands remained the titular head until 1890.

1850-71

FIRST STAMPS ISSUED 15 September 1852

First two stamps issued were in different currencies: 10 *centimes* in Belgian currency and 1 silver *groschen* in Prussian currency. However, Prussian influence waned and later issues were only in Belgian currency. In 1867, by the Treaty of London following the war between Prussia and Austria, Luxembourg became an independent grand duchy. Luxembourg remained neutral during the Franco-Prussian War, though much of the fighting took place close to its southern border.

1871-1914

Last links with Holland were severed on 23 November 1890 when William III, King of the Netherlands and Grand Duke of Luxembourg, died. The duchy passed to the Dukes of Nassau and has been ruled by them ever since.

1914-18

Luxembourg was overrun by the Germans and occupied throughout World War I. Grand Duchess Marie Adelaide remained in the duchy throughout the war.

Stamps of Luxembourg unoverprinted were used throughout this period, though German troops garrisoned there used their own Field POs.

1919-39

When World War I ended in November 1918 Luxembourg was freed and again became an independent grand duchy. In 1922 Luxembourg formed an economic union with Belgium and the currencies have been held at par except during World War II.

Luxembourg was the site of the eleventh Congress of the Federation International de Philatelie (FIP) in 1936 and issued a set of stamps for the occasion. This was the first such set issued for the body which has subsequently become the controlling authority for international philately.

1939-45

Remained neutral until invaded by

Germany in May 1940. German stamps were issued, overprinted for use in Luxembourg, on 1 October 1940 and stamps of Luxembourg were overprinted in German currency in December 1940. Luxembourg was incorported into the German province of Moselleland in May 1941 and used German stamps from January 1942 until liberation in 1944. Stamps of Luxembourg were re-issued in Belgian currency on 6 November 1944. At the same time a customs union of Belgium, Netherlands and Luxembourg (Benelux) was created.

1945 to date

Regained full independence after World War II but once Allied forces were withdrawn declared its neutrality and did not join the NATO. However, this decision was revoked in the 1960s and Luxembourg has been a member ever since. It joined the EEC when it was formed in 1958.

A
10 Pf
BAYERN
B
BAYERN
EIN
KREUZER
FRANCO
C
1F
LUXEMBOURG
D
20 centimes 20
E

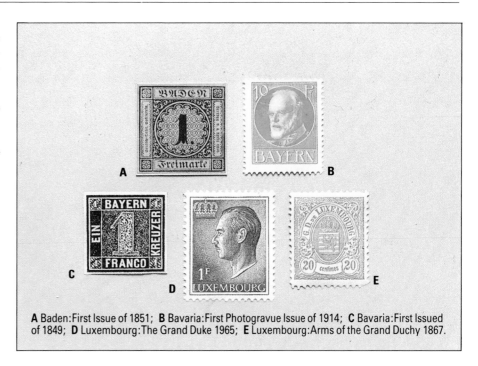

A Baden: First Issue of 1851; **B** Bavaria: First Photogravue Issue of 1914; **C** Bavaria: First Issued of 1849; **D** Luxembourg: The Grand Duke 1965; **E** Luxembourg: Arms of the Grand Duchy 1867.

Right
Belgian postman at Dinant-sur-Meuse

Below
EEC building and viaduct, Luxembourg

Germany before and after unification

A region of northern central Europe which has been one of the battlefields of Europe. The German tribes resisted the attempts of Rome to subdue the area and although some parts were administered, the Romans were expelled in the third century. Charlemagne subdued the Saxons and other tribes, and was crowned emperor at Rome in 800. After the collapse of his dynasty control was vested in successive elected rulers until it became hereditary again under the Habsburgs from 1437 to 1804.

By the 18th century, there were hundreds of petty German states paying nominal allegiance to the Holy Roman Empire, but still trying to retain a measure of independence. The Thirty Years War (1618-1648), which was one of the great religious conflicts between protestants and catholics, led to some depopulation of the area and laid waste enormous territory. This in turn severely affected the development of the social structure of the region.

Although some postal services had been established by the Italian merchants and the Counts of Thurn and Taxis in the 16th century, these were massively disrupted by the successive wars of the following centuries and remained essentially transit posts without handstamps until late in the 18th century.

In the early part of the French Revolutionary Wars, the Emperor quickly lost the Netherlands and all his territories west of the Rhine. In 1806, after having created the Kingdoms of Bavaria, Wurttemberg and Westphalia, (1807), Napoleon dissolved the German Empire and formed the Confederation of the Rhine on 12 July. Northern Germany fell in 1810-11 and was incorporated into the French postal service using many handstamps which included departmental numbers.

The ports on the North coast including Bremen, Hamburg and Lûbeck had formed a League in the 12th century and became the Hanseatic League in 1241. These were essentially trading ports and were also centres of mail transmission in receipt from Scandinavia and Britain. The League lost much of its importance in the 17th and 18th century, but Hamburg remained a free port until 1888.

The Prussian influence to unite Germany into a single empire began in the 18th century under the leadership of Frederick the Great (1749-1786). In 1818, Prussia was the originator of the *Zollverein* or Customs Union which, by 1844, included all of northern Germany. This led initially to the ease of transfer of goods but inevitably towards postal union which was finally agreed with Austria and most German states in 1850.

• Allenstein

FIRST STAMPS ISSUED Overprinted Germany 3 April 1920

CURRENCY

As Germany

Area of East Prussia which used Prussian, North German Confederation and German stamps to the end of World War I. There followed a dispute over the administration of the land and, under the Treaty of Versailles, a plebiscite was held on 11 July 1920. In the plebiscite, 98 per cent of the votes were in favour of remaining part of Germany. International use of the overprinted stamps ceased from 20 August 1920 and German stamps were used thereafter.

The district was occupied by Soviet troops in 1945 and was then transferred to Poland, which has administered the area ever since under the name of Olsztyn.

• Baden

FIRST STAMPS ISSUED 1 May 1851

CURRENCY

1851 60 kreuzer = 1 gulden

Grand duchy in south-west Germany created by Napoleon in 1806. Survived the Napoleonic wars and became part of the German Empire, by treaty in 1870.

Earliest postal markings appeared during the Confederation of the Rhine in 1806. After Napoleon's defeat in Russia, Baden joined the allies against France and hence was not reduced in size at the Congress of Vienna.

In May 1848 there was a major uprising against the Grand Duke and he was forced to flee the country. He was restored by Prussian intervention in August 1849. In April 1850 a postal union was formed between Prussia and Austria in which Baden was included. Separate issues for Baden ceased in 1871 when the Baden postal administration was incorporated into the German Empire and new stamps were issued in January 1872. (For issues during the French occupation after World War II see Germany 1945 to date.)

• Bavaria (Bayern) Before 1850

FIRST STAMPS ISSUED 1 November 1849

CURRENCY

1849 60 kreuzer = 1 gulden
1874 100 pfennig = 1 mark

Kingdom in southern Germany established in 1804. Became part of Confederation of the Rhine in support of Napoleon to avoid continuous attacks by Austria and France while it tried to remain neutral. In 1813, after the French retreat from Russia, Bavaria changed sides and, like Baden, emerged from the Napoleonic wars in a comparatively strong position. New constitution was granted in 1818 by forward-thinking Maximilian I, which reconciled monarchic authority with demands for reform.

Earliest postal markings were name-stamps of towns to indicate the route or town from which the letters had come, either in French or German:

thus 'de Munique' indicated that the letters had come from Munich.

During the French occupation the *département* number was included in the postal marking. Most places used the number 100 but Landau was placed in *département* 67. After 1815 other pre-adhesive markings were used for each town until adhesives were issued. Bavaria issued stamps before either Prussia or Austria.

1850-71
First adhesives were usually cancelled with identifying numerals and these were allocated to individual towns. In June 1866 Bavaria, like Hanover, sided with Austria against Prussia, but made peace on 22 August 1866. The country was forced to pay a large indemnity and changed allegiance. Sided with Prussia against France in 1870. In December 1871 King of Bavaria proposed that King of Prussia should become Emperor of Germany. The kingdom became part of the German Empire but continued to issue its own stamps.

1871-1914
Kingdom continued within the German Empire throughout this period, but with its own stamps. A new issue was released in March 1914 and these were the first stamps in the world to be printed by the photogravure process.

1914-18
Bavaria entered the war in August 1914. However, during the strains of the later war years the monarchy collapsed. Revolution broke out on 7 November 1918 and a republic was proclaimed the following day.

1918-39
Stamps of Bavaria overprinted 'Volksstaat' were issued in 1919 but the leader of the new government, Kurt Eisener, was assassinated on 1 February 1919. There followed a Communist uprising and this was only quelled after fierce fighting. On 5 May 1919 Bavaria became a 'Freistaat' and new

Letters from the Front, Franco-Prussian War, 1870

overprinted stamps appeared on 17 May. A new, unoverprinted issue appeared on 14 February 1920 and the PO was incorporated into that of the Weimar Republic on 29 April 1920.

Bavarian stamps ceased to be valid on 30 June 1920. However, official stamps for Bavaria had been issued on 1 April by overprinting Bavarian officials 'Deutsches Reich' and a similar overprint for use in the whole of Germany was applied to remaining stocks of Bavarian stamps on 6 April 1920.

• Bergedorf

FIRST STAMPS ISSUED 1 November 1861

CURRENCY

1861 16 schilling = 1 Hamburg mark

Small town south-east of Hamburg which was jointly owned by the Free Cities of Hamburg and Lübeck from 1420. It followed the rise and fall of the power of the Hanseatic League and was part of one of the occupied *départements* of France during the Napoleonic wars.

Stamps were issued while Bergedorf was still under the joint control of Hamburg and Lübeck. The design showed the arms of the two cities. On 8 August 1867 Hamburg bought Bergedorf outright from Lübeck and from that date stamps of Hamburg were used.

• Bremen

FIRST STAMPS ISSUED 10 April 1855

CURRENCY

1855 22 grote = 10 silbergroschen
72 grote = 1 thaler

City and port in Germany which from the 13th century gained increasing importance. Joined the Hanseatic League in 1276 and became a Free City of the Holy Roman Empire in 1646.

Post operated by the Counts of Thurn and Taxis had an office in Bremen from 1784. In 1802 the postal convention with the French government allowed the Thurn and Taxis service to continue. Bremen was annexed to the French Empire in 1810, but it became a Free City again in 1813. By 1814 Bremen was operating a service to North America.

There were several POs in operation in Bremen in the 19th century and these included the Duchy of Berg, Hanover and Prussia. These offices used their own postmarks and were responsible for handling the foreign mail of the relevant territories.

Bremen joined the North German Confederation (q.v.) on 31 December 1867 following the Austro-Prussian war of 1866, and used the Confederation's stamps until incorporated into the German Empire in 1871; German stamps were issued in January 1872.

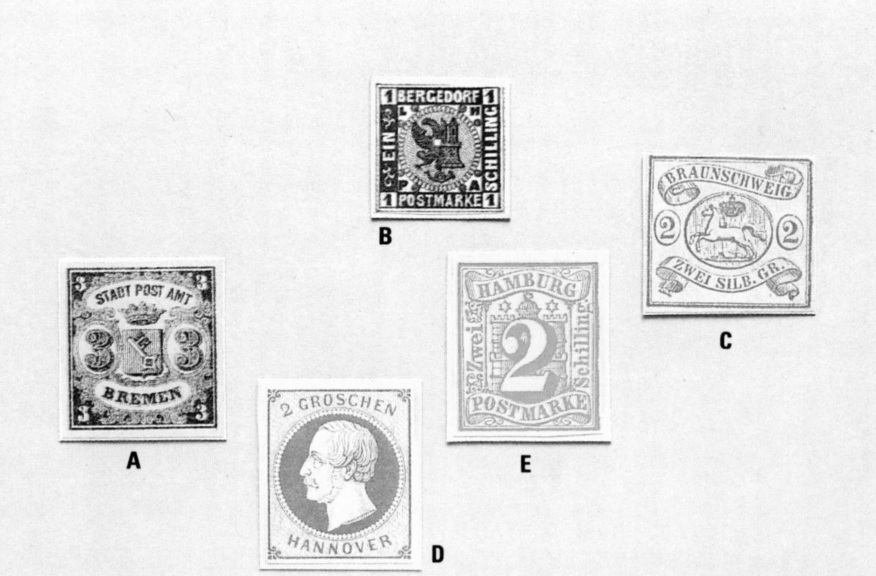
BERGEDORF
POSTMARKE
B
BRAUNSCHWEIG
ZWEI SILB. GR.
C
STADT POST AMT
BREMEN
A
2 GROSCHEN
HANNOVER
D
HAMBURG
POSTMARKE
E

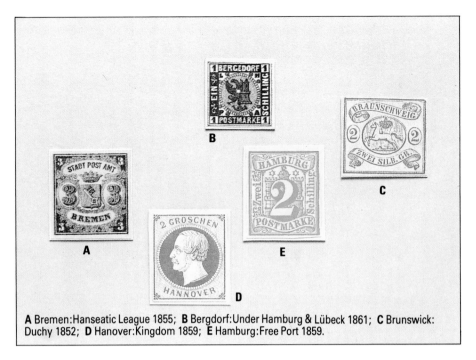

A Bremen:Hanseatic League 1855; **B** Bergdorf:Under Hamburg & Lübeck 1861; **C** Brunswick: Duchy 1852; **D** Hanover:Kingdom 1859; **E** Hamburg:Free Port 1859.

• Brunswick (Braunschweig)

FIRST STAMPS ISSUED 1 January 1852

CURRENCY

30 silbergroschen = 1 thaler

Duchy in Lower Saxony which was included in the kingdom of Westphalia by Napoleon in 1806. The then Duke of Brunswick had been mortally wounded at the battle of Auerstadt in October 1806. He was succeeded by his fourth son (the older sons being blind), who assumed the dukedom after the defeat of Napoleon at the Battle of Leipzig in 1813. He, in turn, was killed during the Waterloo campaign in 1815.

Brunswick joined the North German Confederation and used stamps of the Confederation after 31 December 1867 until incorporated in the German Empire in 1871; German stamps were issued in January 1872.

• Hamburg

CURRENCY

1859 16 schilling = 1 mark

Before 1850

Important city and port on the River Elbe which, with Lübeck, formed the nucleus of the Hanseatic League in 1241. It became a Free City in 1510 and was a flourishing commercial city. With Bremen, it was the centre of trade for Scandinavia and America. It was occupied by the French in 1806 following the defeat of Prussia at the Battle of Jena, and was incorporated into France in 1810. After the Congress of Vienna in 1815, its freedom was confirmed, though the French had ceased to control the city from 1813.

The city was incorporated into the postal system run by the Counts of Thurn and Taxis in 1615, but, later, Hamburg allowed the following states to open POs:

Denmark in 1651 (including Sweden)
Brandenberg in 1654 (later became the Prussian office)
Mecklenberg-Schwerin in 1674
Hanover in 1684 (also used as the link with Britain until 1798)
Sweden in its own right in 1685
Schleswig-Holstein in 1695
Brunswick in1706
Britain from 1798 to 1806

All the foreign POs were closed during the French occupation in 1806. Postal affairs were transferred to the Duchy of Berg, which was under Joachim Murat who became King of Naples in 1808. France annexed Hamburg in 1810 and gave it a *département* number (128), which was incorporated into the postmark.

1850-71

FIRST STAMPS ISSUED 1 January 1859

As a free city, Hamburg did not join the Prussian-Austrian Postal Union in 1850 and continued to allow the foreign offices to handle mail which was funnelled through the city to and from Scandinavia.

Stamps of the city were used until Hamburg joined the North German Confederation in 1867 and were withdrawn and replaced by those of the Confederation in 1868. Stamps of Hamburg were also used in Bergedorf (q.v.) from 8 August 1867.

Stamps of the Confederation were withdrawn in 1871 when the Confederation joined the German Empire, and German issues were used thereafter. However, Hamburg remained a Free City until 1888, the last of the German Free Cities to be incorporated fully into the German Customs Union (Zollverein).

Before Hamburg issued its own stamps in 1859, six territories used their own stamps in Hamburg which can be recognized by datestamps or numeral obliterators. These were: Schleswig-Holstein, Hanover, Prussia, Denmark, Mecklenburg and Thurn and Taxis.

• Hanover

CURRENCY	
1850	12 pfennig = gutengroschen
	20 gutengroschen = 1 thaler
1858	10 (new) pfennig = 1 (new) groschen
	30 (new) groschen = 1 thaler

1815-1850

After the problems of the Napoleonic wars, Hanover became a kingdom in 1814, the King of England being also King of Hanover. During the regency of the Prince of Wales in England (1810-20), the Duke of Cambridge was appointed regent for Hanover. The Royal Great Britain Hanoverian Post Office was independent of any British involvement. The servants of the PO in Hanover wore distinctive red uniforms and the design of handstamps was of a British rather than Germany type. Hanover had a PO in Hamburg, and the British Army had a pension office in Hanover for payment to the survivors of the King's German Legion. This remained open until 1862.

In 1837 Queen Victoria was unable to accept the Hanoverian Crown because there was no descent through the female line. Ernest, Duke of Cumberland became King of Hanover on 20 June 1837.

1850-71

FIRST STAMPS ISSUED 1 December 1850

In 1866 Hanover took the side of the Austrians in the war against Prussia. Prussian troops entered Hanover on 13 June, but the Hanoverian army defeated a Prussian force on 27 June. Defeat of the Austrians at Königgratz (Sadowa) on 3 July caused the alliance to collapse, and the Hanoverians were forced to surrender. Hanover was annexed by Prussian law on 20 September 1866. Prussian stamps were placed on sale on 1 October 1866; Hanoverian stamps remained valid until the end of that month. Covers with mixed franking of Prussian and Hanoverian stamps can be found. Hanover has remained part of Germany ever since.

A Oldenburg: Embossed Issue of 1862; **B** Marienwerder:International Commission 1920; **C** Mecklenburg-Strelitz:Embossed Issue of 1864; **D** Lübeck:Arms of the City 1859; **E** Mecklenburg-Schwerin:Only Sold in Blocks of Four 1856.

A
B
C
D
E

• Heligoland (Helgoland)

CURRENCY	
1867	16 schilling = 1 mark
1875	100 pfennig = 1 mark

1793-1815

Island in the North Sea near the mouth of the River Elbe. Danish until 1807 as part of the Duchy of Holstein, but was then captured by the British and retained by them after the Napoleonic Wars. Their annexation was confirmed by the Treaty of Kiel (14 January 1814). Population was largely German-speaking and from 1796 the postal service had been operated by the administration of the Free City of Hamburg.

1815-50

By 1826 the island had become a fashionable bathing resort, and regular steamers made the run from Hamburg to the island. Up to 1830 mails were carried weekly to and from Cuxhaven for transmission to Hamburg or the island. After that date more numerous sailings were made by steam vessels.

1851-90

FIRST STAMPS Hamburg 1859
FIRST STAMPS ISSUED 15 April 1867

When the Hanseatic cities joined the North German Confederation on 1 January 1868, the Hamburg-Heligoland conventions were transferred to them, as they were to the German Empire in 1871.

The currency was changed from Hamburg to German currency on 1 January 1876 and Heligoland became a member of the UPU in 1879. It was ceded to Germany on 18 June 1890 in return for giving up interests in Zanzibar, and has used German stamps ever since.

• Lübeck
Before 1871

FIRST STAMPS ISSUED 1 January 1859

CURRENCY	
1859	16 schillings = 1 mark

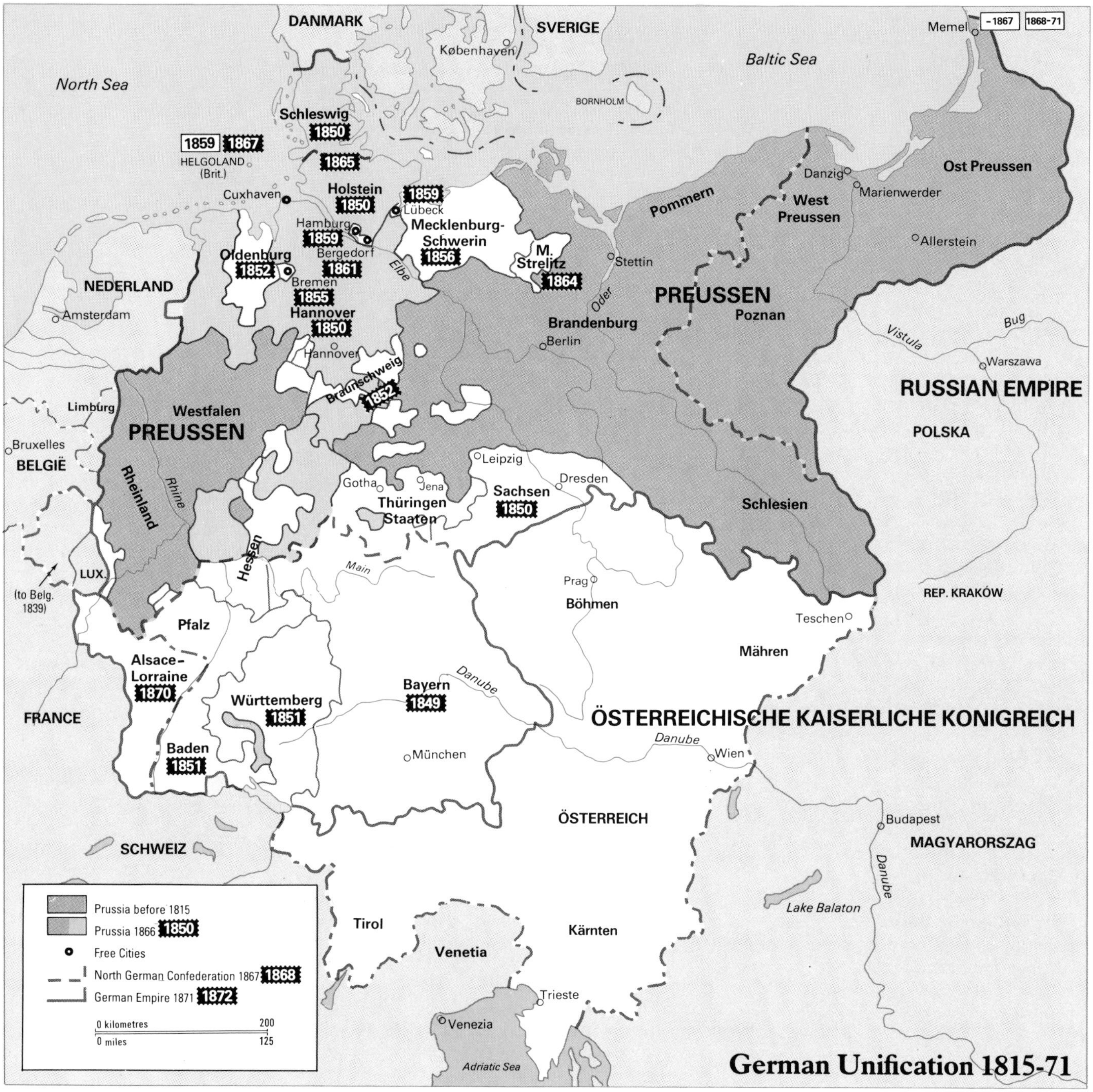
DANMARK
SVERIGE
København
North Sea
Baltic Sea
BORNHOLM
Memel
-1867
1868-71
Schleswig
1850
1865
1859
1867
HELGOLAND
(Brit.)
Cuxhaven
Holstein
1850
1859
Lübeck
Hamburg
1859
Mecklenburg-
Schwerin
1856
Bergedorf
1861
Oldenburg
1852
Bremen
1855
Hannover
1850
Elbe
M.
Strelitz
1864
Stettin
Danzig
Marienwerder
Ost Preussen
Pommern
West
Preussen
Allerstein
NEDERLAND
Amsterdam
PREUSSEN
Poznan
Oder
Brandenburg
Berlin
Hannover
Braunschweig
1852
Vistula
Bug
Warszawa
RUSSIAN EMPIRE
POLSKA
Limburg
Westfalen
PREUSSEN
Bruxelles
BELGIË
Rheinland
Rhine
Leipzig
Gotha
Jena
Thüringen
Staaten
Sachsen
1850
Dresden
Schlesien
Hessen
Main
LUX.
(to Belg.
1839)
Prag
Böhmen
REP. KRAKÓW
Teschen
Pfalz
Mähren
Alsace-
Lorraine
1870
Bayern
1849
Danube
Württemberg
1851
FRANCE
ÖSTERREICHISCHE KAISERLICHE KONIGREICH
Danube
Wien
Baden
1851
München
ÖSTERREICH
Budapest
MAGYARORSZAG
SCHWEIZ
Danube
Lake Balaton
Prussia before 1815
Prussia 1866
1850
Free Cities
North German Confederation 1867
1868
German Empire 1871
1872
0 kilometres
200
0 miles
125
Tirol
Venetia
Kärnten
Trieste
Venezia
Adriatic Sea
German Unification 1815-71

Important port on the Baltic between Mecklenburg and Hamburg. A free port in the Middle Ages, Lübeck became the chief city of the Hanseatic League as the League became less important. Occupied by the Danes in 1801, it was captured by the French in 1803 and became part of French Empire in 1810. Between 1806 and 1810 administered as part of the Duchy of Berg and a postal service with the postmark BGD [*Bureau Grand Ducal*] was in use until August 1808. Later the mark was altered to BJ de F [*Bureau Imperial de France*]. The city became independent again in 1815 and the importance of the area grew.

Lübeck joined the North German Confederation at the end of 1867. Following the incorporation of the Confederation into the German Empire in

1871, stamps of Germany were used throughout the region. Lübeck is now in West Germany.

• Marienwerder

FIRST STAMPS ISSUED 13 March 1920

CURRENCY

1920 As Germany

District of West Prussia which had used the stamps of Prussia, North German Confederation and Germany up to 1920. By the Treaty of Versailles, a plebiscite was to be held to determine whether it should be in Germany or Poland. The Inter-Allied Commission which was appointed to supervise this arranged for stamps to be issued.

Plebiscite was held on 11 July 1920 and 92 per cent of the votes were in favour of remaining in Germany. Marienwerder was returned to Germany on 16 August 1920 and special issues were withdrawn. German stamps were re-introduced and used until 1945, when the area was occupied by Soviet forces. It was handed to Poland and has been administered as Kwidzya since that date.

• Mecklenburg

FIRST STAMPS ISSUED
Mecklenburg-Schwerin 1 July 1856
Mecklenburg-Strelitz 1864

CURRENCY

1856 48 schillings = 1 thaler
1864 30 silbergroschen = 1 thaler

Area of eastern Germany on the south coast of the Baltic. In the 19th century extended from Lübeck to Stettin with two separate grand duchies inland — Mecklenburg-Schwerin and Mecklenburg-Strelitz.

Postal services in the area operated from 1810 and town postmarks were issued soon after this date. Mecklenburg-Schwerin maintained a PO in Hamburg and another at the railway station in Berlin.

Before the release of the Strelitz issues, the stamps of Schwerin were also used in part of this grand duchy. Both issues were withdrawn when both dukedoms joined the North German Confederation at the end of 1867. Following the incorporation of the Confederation into the German Empire in 1871, stamps of Germany were used throughout the region until 1945. (For later issues of Mecklenburg under Russian Occupation, *see* Germany 1945 to date).

• Oldenburg

CURRENCY

1852 72 grote = 1 thaler

Before 1850

Area of North Germany which was annexed to Denmark in the 15th century. Ceded to Russia by Christian VII in 1773, and a duchy was established soon afterwards. Ruled by the Bishops of Lübeck until overrun by the French and Dutch in 1806. However, the Bishop was reinstated the following year and joined the Confederation of the Rhine in support of Napoleon. In 1810 Oldenburg changed its allegiance and was made a grand duchy in 1815 at the Congress of Vienna.

First postmarks were used in 1811 and showed the name of the duchy and the date in two lines. It was included among the occupied *départements* by France and given the numbers 124, 129 and 130, which were included in the markings until 1815.

1850-71

FIRST STAMPS ISSUED 5 January 1852

Oldenburg joined the Austro-Prussian Postal Union on 1 January 1852 and issued stamps almost immediately.

Currency was the North German *thaler* divided into 72 *grote*. The initial stamps showed more than one currency so that they could be understood by the other members of the Union.

Oldenburg came increasingly under the control of Prussia, especially after the wars of 1864 and 1866. It joined the North German Confederation in 1867 and its issues were withdrawn. It became part of the German Empire from 1871 and issued no further stamps in its own name.

• Prussia

CURRENCY

1850 12 pfennig = 1 silbergroschen
30 silbergroschen = 1 thaler
1867 60 kreuzer = 1 gulden (in addition)

1815-50

Following the defeat of Napoleon and the Congress of Vienna in 1815, Prussia spent the next 30 years rebuilding its shattered economy. It made great material progress and began work to unify Germany into a single empire. In 1818 Prussia formed the 'Zollverein', a customs union of the North German states which foreshadowed an economic union.

In 1848 Berlin rioted and rose against the king. Martial law was declared and the rising was suppressed. In 1849 Prussia supported the German elements in Schleswig-Holstein.

1850-71

FIRST STAMPS ISSUED 15 November 1850

In April 1850 Prussia and Austria formed a postal union. This was joined by most of the independent German states, which then issued stamps. Prussia began to work more seriously towards unification in the late 1850s and the three wars with Denmark in 1864, Austria in 1866 and France in 1870-1 led to the achievement of this aim.

Following the Austrian war of 1866, the Prussians, who had acquired the postal interests of the Count of Thurn and Taxis in July 1867, formed the North German Confederation, which

A
B
PLEBISCIT
1. ZONE
75 SLESVIG Øre
SACHSEN
C
Neu 3 Grosch
Mark 10 Mark
D
SAARGEBIET
SAAR
6
F
FREIMARKE
SECHS PFENNIGE
G
E

A Schleswig-Hostein:Issued by Austria and Prussia 1865; **B** Schleswig:Plebiscite Issue 1920; **C** Saxony:King Johann 1854; **D** Saar:League of Nations Commission 1921; **E** Schleswig:Issued by Austria and Prussia 1864; **F** Saar:French Occupation 1947; **G** Prussia:King Friedrich Wilhelm IV 1850.

issued its own stamps in 1868. This provided a postal union of all the states north of the River Main.

However, although Prussia had a currency of silver *groschen* and *thaler* from 1857, with the acquisition of the POs of Thurn and Taxis it was necessary to issue stamps in *kreuzer* and *gulden*, for use in the southern region. These were released in July 1867.

Prussian stamps were withdrawn after 1867. It became part of the German Empire from 1871 and issued no further stamps of its own.

• Saar
Before 1939

FIRST STAMPS ISSUED Overprinted German issues 30 January 1920

CURRENCY

1920 onwards — French or German (see text)

Small but strategically important district of Germany on the frontier with France between Luxembourg and Alsace-Lorraine. By the treaty of Versailles in June 1919 the district was placed under the control of a League of Nations Commission for 15 years, when a plebiscite was to be held. During this period, France was to have ownership of the mines in the Saar. Stamps inscribed 'Saargebiet' continued until 1935 when the plebiscite was due. A British peacekeeping force was sent to the Saar. About 1500 men in all were involved and Field PO 10 was used from 4 January to 21 February 1935. The result of the vote was to return the district to Germany from 1 March 1935 and German stamps were used until 1945 when the area was captured by the Allies.

1945 to date

Saar was part of the French Zone of Germany and the general issue for the French Zone was used from 17 December 1945 until the issue of special stamps for Saar in January 1947. These were used until 1956. In 1955 a referendum of the population decided on a return to Germany, and from 1 January 1957 stamps were issued by the German Federal Republic inscribed 'Saarland' and valued in French currency. On 6 July 1959 stamps and currency of West Germany came into use in the district and have been used ever since.

• Saxony (Sachsen)

CURRENCY

1850	10 pfennig = 1 neugroschen
	30 neugroschen = 1 thaler

Before 1850

Kingdom in eastern Germany created in 1806 and including the cities of Leipzig and Dresden. An important and influential region in the 18th and 19th centuries. Leipzig was mentioned in the 1657 Act of Parliament for the British Post Office to which the rate was then 12*d* per single letter.

The King of Saxony supported Napoleon, and Saxony was the scene of the war of 1813, which led to the defeat of the French at the Battle of Leipzig in October that year. At the Congress of Vienna, Saxony lost territory to Prussia but the kingdom gradually regained its position and became one of the most highly industrialized areas of the German Empire.

The first postal markings were introduced at Dresden and Leipzig in 1817 and these were followed by marks at other towns from April 1818 onwards.

1850-71

FIRST STAMPS ISSUED 29 June 1850

Saxony joined the Austro-German Postal Union in July 1850. The first stamps issued were for the newspaper rate of 3 *pfennig*. Handstruck markings continued to be used for the other values until a more extensive range was issued in August 1851.

Saxony sided with Austria during the war of 1866 and the army was present at the Battle of Königgratz (Sadowa) on 3 July. The Prussians had entered Saxony on 18 June and peace was signed on 21 October. As a result, the army of Saxony was subjected to Prussia and the kingdom became part of the North German Confederation. Saxony ceased to have its own issues from 31 December 1867 when the stamps of the Confederation were introduced.

In 1871 Saxony became part of the German Empire and stamps of Germany were used from 1871 onwards. (For stamps of East and West Saxony issued under Russian control *see* Germany from 1945.)

• Schleswig-Holstein

CURRENCY	
1850	16 schilling = 1 mark

Before 1850

Two duchies on the Elbe peninsula south of Denmark and north of the River Elbe. The King of Denmark was also Duke of the territory. In 1839 Frederick VI died and under the Salic Law the inheritance should have passed to the Duke of Augustenburg as the nearest male heir. As the Salic Law did not apply in Denmark, when Frederick VII, the son of the previous king, inherited from his uncle, Christian VIII in 1848, he insisted that the duchies should remain as Danish provinces. The German population revolted, which led to the establishment of a provisional government on 24 March 1848.

During the period up to the issue of stamps in 1850, the duchies had used handstruck markings and most of the international mail was sent out through Hamburg.

1850-71

FIRST STAMPS ISSUED 15 November 1850

Stamps were issued by the provisional government to try to make sure that the western powers realized that they were independent from Denmark. Fighting between Denmark and Prussia was in danger of breaking out in the 1850s even though the Treaty of Berlin in 1850 had sided in favour of Denmark. The stamps of the provisional government were replaced by Danish stamps on 1 May 1851 in Schleswig and on 1 July 1853 in Holstein.

With Austria as ally, Prussia invaded Denmark in February 1864. This was followed by a truce in April, but a renewed invasion began on 26 June and Denmark sued for peace on 1 August. Denmark renounced its claim to the provinces and they were awarded to Prussia and Austria.

Danish stamps were withdrawn early in 1864 (Schleswig — 31 March, and Holstein — 29 February). At first, stamps were issued for each of the duchies. A joint issue by Austria and Prussia for Schleswig was released in 1864, and for Holstein an issue was released by the German Federal Commissioners on 1 March 1864. An issue for the combined duchies appeared under Austria and Prussia in 1865, but the individual duchies still issued their own stamps, Schleswig under Prussia and Holstein under Austria, although Prussia maintained a garrison in this area. Stamps were issued under the different authorities on 1 November 1865 but were again withdrawn in 1867 when Prussia gained the two duchies from Austria and incorporated them in the North German Confederation. Stamps of the Confederation were used until 1871, when Schleswig-Holstein became part of the German Empire.

A
B
C
D
E
F

A Württemberg: King 1869; **B** Thurn and Taxis: Northern Currency 1852; **C** Upper Silesia: Commission of Government 1920) **D** Württemberg: King Wilhelm I 1851; **E** North German Confederation 1868; **F** Thurn and Taxis: Southern Currency 1862.

1918 to date (Schleswig)

FIRST STAMPS ISSUED 25 January 1920

Under the Treaty of Versailles in 1919 Schleswig was divided into two zones and a plebiscite was held in each zone.

In northern zone 1 the voters elected to be included in Denmark, but southern zone 2 wished to remain in Germany. Zone 1 was incorporated in Denmark from 9 July 1920 and stamps were withdrawn at the same time.

• Thurn and Taxis

CURRENCY		
1852	N. District	30 silbergroschen = 1 thaler
	S. District	60 kreuzer = 1 gulden

Before 1815

The Counts of Thurn and Taxis orginated in northern Italy, and operated a postal service throughout the Holy Roman Empire and its successor states from the 16th to the 19th century. The first service began operation in the Tyrol about 1460 and quickly spread to cover Vienna and Brussels. By the mid-1500s the service of Thurn and Taxis covered Austria, Germany and the Low Countries. Later, the Counts became Princes of the Empire and were made Hereditary Postmasters of the Empire.

By the establishment of postal conventions with the independent states of Germany, the post operated by the Counts was maintained until the Napoleonic wars, but with the formation of the Kingdom of Italy and the Confederation of the Rhine, the French postal service gained the ascendancy; this was lost with the defeat of Napoleon in Russia and the re-alliance of the German states.

1815-50

The Counts of Thurn and Taxis re-established control of the German area after the Congress of Vienna. The first postal stationery was issued in Württemberg in 1846, and, although control was maintained in some of the northern states, the service which they had operated began to fall into disuse with the creation of the postal union of Prussia and Austria in 1850. At the same time, many of the independent states began to issue their own stamps.

1850-71

FIRST STAMPS ISSUED 29 January 1851

Counts of Thurn and Taxis continued to operate the postal services of those parts of Germany which did not have a postal administration of their own or issued stamps.

Because of the variation of currency throughout Germany, two issues were released on the same day. The first for the southern states in *kreuzer* and *gulden* and the northern in *silvergroschen* and *thaler*.

In the north the stamps were used in Bremen (until 1855), Camburg, Gotha, Hamburg (until 1859), Hesse-Kassel, Lippe Detmold, Lübeck (until 1859), Reuss, Saxe-Weimar-Eisenach, Schaumberg-Lippe and Schwarzburg-Sonderhausen. In the south: Coburg, Frankfurt-am-Main, Hesse-Darmstadt, Hesse-Homburg, Hohenzollern-Heckingen, Hohenzollern-Sigmaringen, Nassau, Saxe-Meiningen and Schwarzberg-Rudolstadt.

On 28 January 1867 the Count sold his postal service to the Prussian postal administration for three million *thaler*. At this time the postal service had 302 POs and services — although these had been disrupted by the Austrian war of 1866. Prussia had not issued stamps in *kreuzer* currency, and these were prepared and released for use in southern Germany on 1 July 1867. The Counts retained a franking privilege under the German Empire until 1918 and a special handstamp FRANCO TAXIS was applied to their letters until that date.

• Upper Silesia

FIRST STAMPS ISSUED 14 February 1920

CURRENCY	
1920	As Germany

This province of West Prussia bordering on Poland had to hold a plebiscite in 1921 under the terms of the Treaty of Versailles. First stamps were specially designed for the region and were inscribed in three languages, German, French and Polish. They were used concurrently with overprinted German stamps for the Inter-Allied Commission (C.G.H.S.). After the plebiscite on 20 March 1921, Upper Silesia was divided between Germany and Poland.

• Württemberg

CURRENCY	
1851	60 kreuzer = 1 gulden
1875	100 pfennig = 1 mark

Before 1850

Kingdom in southern Germany established in 1804, originally part of Swabia. Earliest postal service was established about 1750 and straight-line mark in French or German was introduced at that time. In November 1775 the Duke (Charles Eugene) concluded an agreement with the Counts of Thurn and Taxis allowing a 30-year concession for control of the posts within the dukedom. Agreement expired in 1805 and was replaced by a local service run by the government assisted by the French. System used in Germany by the French which computed the distances from the Rhine crossing was introduced. In 1819 the treaty with the Counts of Thurn and Taxis was reintroduced and carried on until 1851. Pre-stamped envelopes were introduced in 1846 but were for local use only.

1850-71

FIRST STAMPS ISSUED 15 October 1851

Kingdom assumed responsibility for its own postal affairs from Thurn and Taxis when it joined the Austro-Prussian Postal Union in September 1851. Württemberg sided with Austria against Prussia in the war of 1866, but made peace on the 13 August. In October 1867 Württemberg joined the Zollverein — the Prussian-sponsored customs union. In 1870 a contingent was sent to support the Prussians during the war with France.

1871-1914

Kingdom came increasingly under the control of Prussia and stamps for postage purposes were withdrawn in 1902 when German imperial stamps were issued on 1 April 1902. Stamps of Württemberg remained valid until the end of that year and official stamps continued to be issued until 1922.

1914-18

During World War I the forces of Württemberg played their part in the Germany army. As with other southern states of Germany, the collapse of the German government in 1918 was followed by abdication of the king. Provisional government was established on 30 November 1918 and a number of overprints on the official stamps were made.

1919-39

Provisional government of 30 November 1918 was replaced by a republic on 26 April 1919. In 1919 the earlier official issues were overprinted 'Volkstaat' (People's State). These municipal service stamps were used until 1924, the official stamps being replaced by overprints 'Deutches Reich' on 1 April 1920.

Thereafter, stamps of Germany were used throughout the former kingdom. (For issues for the French zone of occupation after World War II see Germany 1945 to date.)

• North German Confederation

FIRST STAMPS ISSUED 1 January 1868

CURRENCY

1868 30 groschen = 1 thaler = 60 kreuzer = 1 gulden

Political confederation of North German states established by Prussia following the defeat of Austria in 1866.

At the end of 1867 individual stamps of the member states were withdrawn and the new issues were used in Bremen, Brunswick, Hamburg, Lübeck, Mecklenburg-Schwerin, Mecklenburg-Strelitz, Oldenburg, Prussia and Saxony. By that date Prussia had also taken control of the postal services in Bergedorf, Hanover and Schleswig-Holstein and had acquired the postal interest of the Count of Thurn and Taxis. Thus the stamps of the Confederation were used universally in German territory north of the River Main. However, stamps were issued in the currency of the southern states for use in the region previously controlled by the Counts of Thurn and Taxis. Stamps of the Confederation were merged into the Imperial German service on 4 May 1871, and were withdrawn from 1 January 1872. Stamps of the Confederation were used in Constantinople in 1870 and 1871.

• Germany (before 1949)

CURRENCY

1872	Northern	30 groschen = 1 thaler
	Southern	90 kreuzer = 1 thaler
1875	100 pfennigs = 1 mark	
1923	100 reuten pfennig = 1 reuten mark	
1928	100 pfennig = 1 reichsmark	
1948	East and West marks were differentiated	

1850-71

Prussia's strength and the comparative weakness of the southern and Rhineland states which had tended to be used by Prussia as a buffer against France and Austria had prevented a full unification earlier in the century. However, economic, political and cultural forces which had always been present were now working towards unification. The realization of this dream of most Germans had been prevented by the jealousy of the many smaller states and the alliances with Prussia or Austria. The emergence of the German Empire in 1871 was also the triumph of the efforts of two Prussian aristocrats; the politician Bismarck, who was Chancellor of Prussia, and von Moltke, who was chief of the Prussian general staff.

Three wars were fought in this period which led to the creation of the German Empire. In 1864 Prussia and Austria settled by force the problem of Schleswig-Holstein which had troubled the major powers since the revolt in the province in 1848. The short war from 1 February to 1 August 1864 led to the inclusion of the disputed region in Germany with joint control by Prussia and Austria.

Bismarck now turned on Austria who had been the reluctant ally against Denmark. By exerting pressure and creating friction, Austria was forced to denounce Prussian power politics at the Diet of Frankfurt on 14 June 1866. In particular, the continuing occupation of Holstein and the secret treaty with France were cited as examples. Most German states including Bavaria, Hanover and Saxony, sided with Austria; Bismarck revoked the Germanic Confederation which had been formed after the Napoleonic wars. He had also concluded a treaty with Italy, and Austria was thus forced to fight a war on two fronts. Prussia having defeated the Austrians at Königgratz (or Sadowa) on 3 July 1866, the French were asked to mediate and, at the Treaty of Prague, Austria was excluded from German affairs. The German states north of the Main river were formed into the North German Confederation under Prussian leadership. The south German states remained nominally independent, but because of indemnities gradually became allied to Prussia.

Napoleon III of France believed his army to be invincible and the unexpected formation of the North German Confederation led to increasing friction between France and Prussia. When Bismarck tried to place a Hohenzollern prince on the Spanish throne, Napoleon realized that he might have to fight a war on both fronts, and declared war on Prussia. The result was a crushing defeat for France and the acquisition of Alsace and Lorraine by Prussia. Germany then became a reality as a unified territory and in December 1871 the King of Prussia became Emperor of Germany.

1871-1914

FIRST STAMPS see under individual states
FIRST STAMPS ISSUED 1 January 1872

The final unification of Germany took place after the fall of France in the Franco-Prussian War. The northern states had all been forced to join the North German Confederation in 1867 and the more independent southern states had all fought with Prussia against France.

First issues for the whole of Germany, excluding Bavaria and Württemberg, who still continued to issue their own stamps, were printed in both currencies — *groschen* and *thaler* for the former North German Confederation, and *kreuzer* and *gulden* for the incorporated southern states.

BADEN
PF.
30
10
10
DEUTSCHES REICH
Deutsches Reich
200
MILLIONEN
DEUTSCHE
3
PFENNIG
POST
DEUTSCHE REICHS-POST
1 GROSCHEN 1
A
B
C
D
E

A Germany:French Zone of Occupation, Baden 1948; **B** Germany:Germany under Hitler 1942; **C** Germany:German Inflation 1923; **D** Germany:British, American and Russian Zones 1946; **E** Germany:German Empire 1872.

In 1875, as a further step towards final integration, the currency for the whole Empire was changed to 100 *pfennig* to 1 *mark*. The new values were issued on 1 January in the Empire and Württemberg, but not until a year later in Bavaria.

During the next few years Bismarck, as Chancellor of the Empire, built a series of alliances and Germany began to spread its influence overseas. German stamps without overprints were used in Africa at Cameroun (1887), German East Africa (1888), German South-West Africa (1888) and Togo (1889); in Asia at Constantinople (1872), China (1887) and Kiaschow (1898) and in the Far East and Pacific in German New Guinea (1890), Marshall Islands (1889) and Samoa (1887).

In March 1890 Bismarck had completed his great work and was dismissed by the Kaiser. Germany then continued with its expansion in China, Africa and, by alliance with Turkey, in the Near East.

In 1874 the Postmaster of the German Empire, Heinrich von Stephan, had been largely responsible for the establishment of the General Postal Union (Universal Postal Union from 1878). The German Empire was one of the first 22 signatories.

1914-18

At the start of World War I Germany invaded Belgium on 3 August and the country was quickly overrun, except for some fortresses and the port of Antwerp. These eventually fell in October 1914. German stamps overprinted for use in Belgium were issued in 1914.

Throughout most of World War I Germany was not part of the battleground and German troops were in occupation of allied territories. Special issues appeared for the East and West Military Command areas in 1916. The East Area issues were used in the Russian Baltic Provinces after the conquest of Russian Poland. The West Area issues were used for line of communication troops in Belgium and northern France which were occupied by German forces. These issues were withdrawn late in 1918. Similar issues were also used in Russian Poland and Romania in 1915 and 1917 respectively.

The decisive factors in the latter stages of the war were the collapse of the Russian front after the Communist Revolution of 1917 and as a result Germany's ability to transfer substantial forces from the eastern to the western front. This led to the German offensive in March 1918, but with the support of the newly arrived American expeditionary force the Germans were held and then forced back in an Allied offensive. This began in August and led to the final collapse in October-November 1918.

Inspired by the Communists and sparked by mutiny in the German navy, civil disorder broke out in Germany and the Kaiser fled to Holland on 10 November 1918.

• Occupation of Germany 1918-30

At the end of World War I Alsace and Lorraine were returned to France, and the Rhineland was occupied by American, Belgian, British and French forces.

Belgium issued overprinted stamps for its area of the Rhineland, which were issued on 20 September 1919. They remained in use until the Belgian troops withdrew and stamps remained valid until 30 April 1931. At the same time, further overprints were issued for Eupen and Malmedy on 15 January 1920. These also used German currency. No referendum was held in these areas, but those who wished the territory to remain German were asked to sign a register. As few of the inhabitants took this opportunity, the League of Nations awarded the territory to Belgium and it has remained Belgian since 1920 when the decision became effective.

Britain did not issue special stamps, but normal stamps of Britain were available at the Field POs which were attached to the occupying forces. Initially, all items were handled as 'On Active Service' and no postage was charged except for special services such as registration. The situation was changed in 1921 and from then the forces were charged at the same rate as if they were in Britain.

In 1918, because roads and railways were severely damaged, mail was flown into Cologne, the British headquarters in Germany, by the RAF.

This service initially operated from Marquise near Boulogne, but later flew from Hawkinge near Folkestone to Cologne. This was the first British international airmail service. In October 1922 a regular airmail service was operated by Instone Airways to Cologne and the fee for mail carried was *2d*, a lower figure than for the rest of Germany. British forces gradually withdrew and the final army PO closed in December 1929.

French occupation was centred on Mainz and that of the Americans on Coblenz. These bridgeheads included a radius of 18 miles on the eastern bank of the Rhine. All occupying powers used Field POs for their troops in Germany. The Americans withdrew in 1923, but the occupation by the other Allies continued until 1929-30.

On 11 January 1923, because of Germany's failure to maintain payments of reparations, French and Belgian troops invaded and occupied the Rhur. The area was not evacuated until August 1925, and again military mail services were provided for the occupying forces.

The Rhineland was demilitarized on the withdrawal of the occupying powers but was re-occupied by the German army in March 1936.

• Germany 1918-39

Following the collapse of the German army and the victory of the Allied forces, the Kaiser was deposed and exiled to Holland. The Weimar Republic was formed on 9 November 1918 and issued its first stamps on 1 May 1919. Germany lost Alsace-Lorraine to France and had its eastern frontier re-organized to allow Poland access to the Baltic. West Prussia and Posen became part of Poland in 1918 and 1920 respectively. East Prussia still remained German but was separated from Germany by Polish territory. Bavaria and Württemberg ceased to issue their own stamps and became an integral part of Germany.

The rapid fall in the value of the *mark* in 1923 led to many overprints and frequent changes in the postal rates. On 1 December 1923, the currency was changed to the gold mark (1 gold *mark* was equivalent to x *marks* of the former devalued currency).

In 1923 Hitler made his first attempt to obtain control in Munich but failed and was imprisoned. In 1933 Hitler became Chancellor and the Third Reich was created. First stamps were issued on 12 April 1933.

Right
Sign for the Royal Great Britain Hanoverian Post Office in Hanover, 1825

KOENIGLICH GROSSBRITANNISCH-HANNOVERISCHES
NEC ASPERA TERRENT
POST AMT.

Post-box, Oberammergau, West Germany

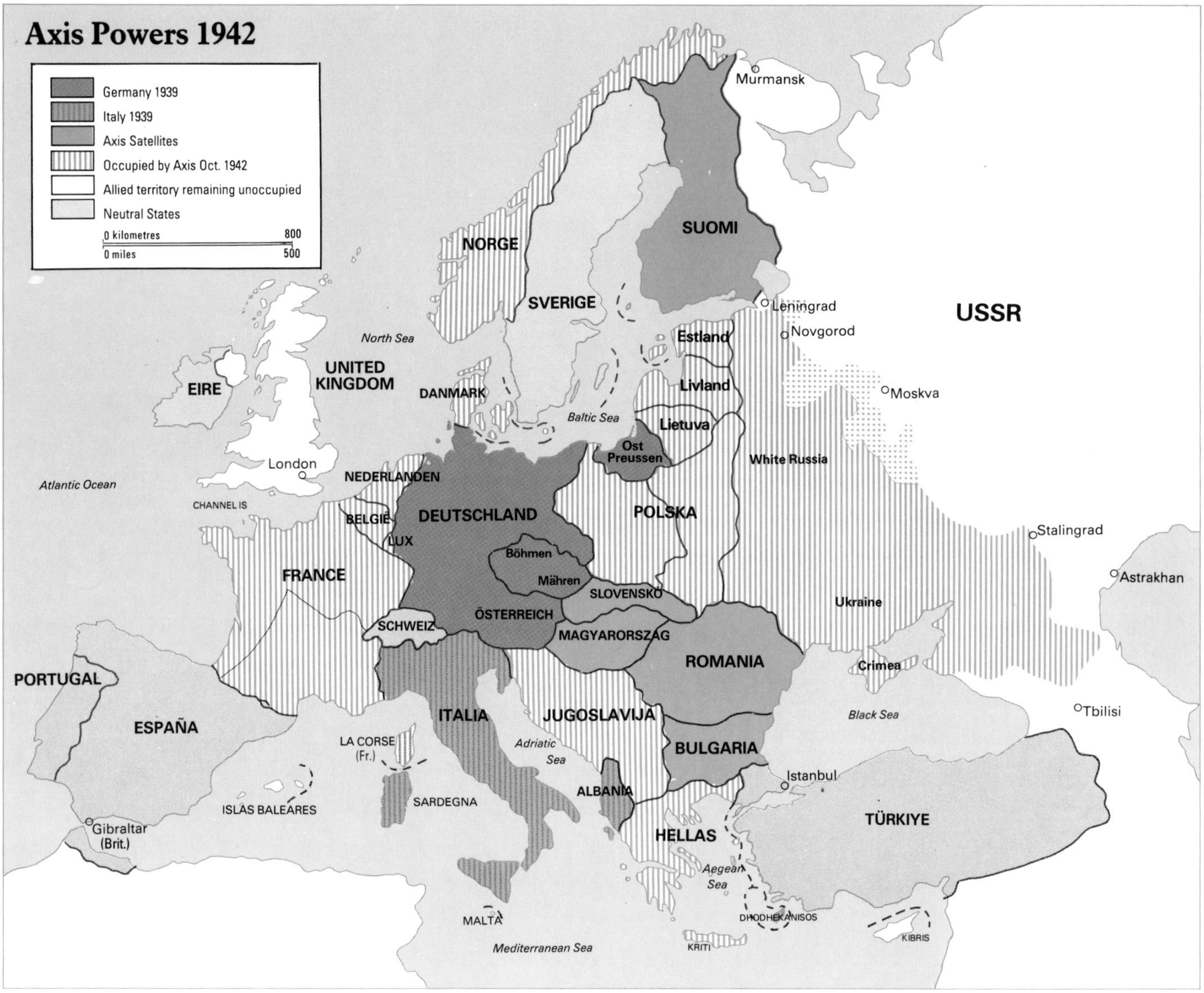
Axis Powers 1942
Germany 1939
Italy 1939
Axis Satellites
Occupied by Axis Oct. 1942
Allied territory remaining unoccupied
Neutral States
0 kilometres 800
0 miles 500
Murmansk
NORGE
SUOMI
SVERIGE
Leningrad
Novgorod
USSR
North Sea
Estland
UNITED KINGDOM
EIRE
DANMARK
Livland
Moskva
Baltic Sea
Lietuva
Ost Preussen
London
White Russia
NEDERLANDEN
Atlantic Ocean
CHANNEL IS
BELGIË
DEUTSCHLAND
POLSKA
Stalingrad
LUX
Böhmen
FRANCE
Mähren
Astrakhan
SLOVENSKO
Ukraine
ÖSTERREICH
SCHWEIZ
MAGYARORSZÁG
ROMANIA
Crimea
PORTUGAL
ITALIA
JUGOSLAVIJA
Black Sea
Tbilisi
ESPAÑA
LA CORSE (Fr.)
Adriatic Sea
BULGARIA
Istanbul
ISLAS BALEARES
SARDEGNA
ALBANIA
TÜRKIYE
Gibraltar (Brit.)
HELLAS
Aegean Sea
MALTA
DHODHEKÁNISOS
KIBRIS
Mediterranean Sea
KRITI

German forces re-occupied the Rhineland in 1936. Occupying forces had been withdrawn in 1926, but it had remained a demilitarized zone.

Austria was occupied on 13 March 1938; Sudetenland, part of Czechoslovakia, in October 1938; the balance of Czechoslovakia on 15 March 1939; and Memel on 23 March 1939. On 1 September 1939 Germany invaded Poland and World War II began.

1939-45

World War II began with the German invasion of Poland on 1 September 1939. On 17 September Russian troops invaded Poland from the east, and on 28 September Poland was divided. Germany annexed those parts of Poland which had been lost in 1919-21 and the remainder became a German protectorate called 'General Government'. Overprinted German stamps were used from December 1939 to April 1940, when the new definitive series appeared.

During 1940 to 1942 Germany continued to occupy territories until its control either by conquest or alliance stretched from the Pyrenees to the Caucasus and Volga River, and from El Alamein to the North Cape. Gradually during the succeeding years the Allies regained territory. For details of stamps issued in the conquered territories refer to individual countries.

Internally, there was little disruption initially; Germany had the tactical advantage of internal lines of communication and was not subject to the same problems as the Allies. However, the severe bombing which began in 1942 gradualy broke down the internal services. Railways and roads were severely damaged and not only strategic resources but mail was seriously affected.

German forces serving overseas were issued with letter forms and cards which did not require stamps and can only be recognized by the numbers in the 'Feldpost' marks. A similar system was used by British forces. By late 1944 the Allies in the west and east were beginning to enter Germany. The Rhine was crossed in March 1945 and from then until the surrender on 7-8 May 1945 Germany gradually disintegrated.

In the period following the surrender of Germany, the civil post was under continuous pressure. The road and rail systems were a shambles and little is recorded on the method by which letters were carried except on a local basis. However, an Allied Military Post was established in the area of Aachen, which had been captured by US forces in October 1944 and stamps were issued on 18 March 1945 (for further details see Allied Military Post below).

American
French
British
Russian
Occupied by Poland
0 kilometres 150
0 miles 100
DANMARK
Baltic Sea
RÜGEN
Danzig
Ost Preussen
Lübeck
Schleswig-Holstein
Mecklenburg
Pommern
Stettin
Hamburg
Bremen
Brandenburg
Berlin
POLSKA
Poznan
Frankfurt-on-Oder
Hannover
Hannover
NEDERLAND
Westfalen
Dusseldorf
Leipzig
DEUTSCHLAND
Dresden
Sachsen
Schlesien
Bonn
BELG.
Hesse
Rheinland
Frankfurt
Praha
LUX.
CESKOSLOVENSKÒ
Palatinate
Pfalz
Saarland
Nürnberg
Stuttgart
Württemberg
Bayern
FRANCE
Wien
Linz
Burgenland
Münich
Hohenzollern
Salzburg
Salzburg
Baden
Varalburg
ÖSTERREICH
Styria
Innsbruck
Tirol
Lake Balaton
Graz
SCHWEIZ
ITALIA
Kärnten
MAGYARORSZAG
Allied Zones of Occupation 1945

1945-49

Germany was divided into four zones; Russian, American, French and British. Berlin, the former capital, was inside the Russian zone and this was also divided into four sectors. The Russian zone became the German Democratic Republic on 7 October 1949, after the Allied zones had become the German Federal Republic on 21 September 1949. However, postally the period between 1945 and 1949 was complicated by the many issues which appeared in different areas.

At the Yalta Conference in February 1945 the division into zones of occupation had been agreed. Following the German surrender, stamps of the Allied Military Post which had been issued at Aachen in March 1945 came into use throughout the British and American zones, and by June local issues began to appear in the Russian zone.

• *Allied Military Post*

Stamps were used throughout the British and American zones from the surrender until they were replaced by a general issue in February 1946. There were three printings of the same design, one from America (Bureau of Engraving in Washington), one from Britain (Harrison & Sons Ltd of London) and one from Germany (G.Westermann of Brunswick).

• *American, British and Russian Zones*

Before the start of the Cold War and the Berlin Blockade from June 1948 to May 1949, a single issue was used throughout Germany except in the French zone. First stamps were issued in February 1946 and continued until June 1948. At that time, the British, American and French governments announced that they had introduced a reformed currency. The Russians reacted by introducing a reform of their own and from 24 June 1948 the combined issue was withdrawn.

• *British and American Zones*

Initially, the stamps of the combined zones were overprinted with a pattern of posthorns and these were used from July to September 1948, when the new definitives inscribed DEUTSCHE POST were issued. These remained in use until the formation of the Federal Government in September 1949.

• *French Zone*

A definitive issue for all sectors of the French zone was issued on 17 December 1945. It remained in use until 1947, when each of the sectors issued a set inscribed with the name of the area. Special issues appeared for

Baden, Rhineland-Palatinate (inscribed Rheinland-Pfalz), the Saar and Württemberg. This last included the area of Hohenzollern and the Kreis-Lindau district of Bavaria.

With the exception of the Saar district (q.v.), the French zone was incorporated into the Federal German Republic on 21 September 1949. The stamps of the zone then in use could be used throughout West Germany until the end of that year and commemorative stamps until 31 March 1950. A planned set for each of the districts, to commemorate the 75th anniversary of the UPU, was released on 4 October 1949, after the date when they joined the Federal Republic. These could be used throughout West Germany.

• *Russian Zone*
On first occupying the eastern part of Germany, the Russians organized the zone postally on the basis of O.P.D. (Oberpostdirektion or Higher Post Direction). These all issued stamps in 1945. The districts and dates were as follows:

Berlin – Brandenburg (OPD Berlin) – June 1945
Mecklenburg – Vonpommeru (OPD Schwerin) – 28 August 1945
Saxony (OPD Halls) – 10 October 1945
West Saxony (OPD Leipzig) – 28 September 1945
East Saxony (OPD Dresden) – 23 June 1945
Thuringia (OPD Erfurt) – 1 October 1945

From February 1946 the Soviet zone used the combined issue with the American and British Zones. However, when the Americans and British decided to reform the currency in June 1948, the Russians introduced a reform of their own on 24 June. As an emergency control, stamps were marked either by a handstamp or other means with the O.P.D. number. Many hundreds of different markings resulted, before a general overprint on the previous issue appeared on 3 July 1948. These were worded 'Sowjetische Besatzungs Zone'.

German Democratic Republic (DDR)

FIRST STAMPS ISSUED 9 October 1949

CURRENCY	
1949	100 pfennig = 1 East German mark

The Russian zone continued to issue stamps inscribed 'Deutsche Post' until the German Democratic Republic was created on 7 October 1949. The authorities released the first stamps inscribed for the new territory on 9 October 1949 and these were also valid for use in East Berlin.

German Federal Republic

FIRST STAMPS ISSUED 7 September 1949

CURRENCY	
1949	100 pfennig = 1 West German mark

Created by the Western Allies early in 1949, the Federal Republic came into formal existence on 21 September 1949. Pending the actual date, stamps for the new combined territory first appeared on 7 September to commemorate the opening of the new West German parliament at Bonn.

Berlin
During this complex period Berlin, which lay within the Russian zone, had gone through a number of similar changes. On 1 July 1948 the Russians withdrew from four-power control of the city as a result of the Berlin blockade and airlift, which had began on 22 June 1948. This continued until 12 May 1949. Stamps of the Allied occupation were issued on 1 September 1948 overprinted for use in the Western zone of Berlin. In January 1949 a further overprinted set was issued in the revised currency; these can be distinguished by the red overprint in place of the black which had appeared earlier. Issues for West Berlin have continued since that time.

Switzerland

FIRST STAMPS ISSUED Cantonal issues 1843-7
FIRST FEDERAL STAMPS ISSUED May 1850

CURRENCY	
1850	100 rappen = 1 franken 100 centimes = 1 franc 100 centimisi = 1 franko

to 1815
A republic of Western Europe set in the Alps. It now consists of 23 cantons but for many years had only 22. The first confederation in 1307 comprised three cantons — Uri, Schwyz and Unterwalden which declared Swiss independence from Austria. Lucerne joined the Confederacy in 1332 and, with four other cantons formed a 'perpetual league' in 1353.

Switzerland grew in size and importance during the following centuries and was established within its present borders by 1815. Postal markings were first used on Swiss mails in the middle of the 17th century. These were all in manuscript until 1689, when the Geneva post office began to use the single line handstamp DE GENEVE for letters to France. Similar handstamps appeared on letters sent to France from other offices during the 18th century, but other mail still had only manuscript markings. In the 1780s a more general range of town names began to appear notably at Aarau (1782), Basle (1783), Berne (1787), Fribourg (1787), Lausanne (1786), Lausanne (1786), St Blaise (1788), St Gallen (1784) and Vevey (1786).

Switzerland was invaded by the French in 1798 who then established the Helvetian Republic within the

EDWIN HOERNLE
1883-1952
DDR
10
A
20
DEUTSCHE DEMOKRATISCHE REPUBLIK
B
5 DM
REPUBLIK
DEUTSCHE DEMOKRATISCHE
C

A German Democratic Republic 1974;
B German Democratic Republic 1959;
C German Democratic Republic 1950.

DEUTSCHE BUNDESPOST
5
A
60 60
HELVETIA
B
TAG DER BRIEFMARKE 1972
20
DEUTSCHE BUNDESPOST BERLIN
C
PRO JUVENTUTE 1972
HELVETIA
40
+20
D
HELVETIA
5 5
FRANCO
E

A German Federal Republic 1951; **B** Switzerland 1918; **C** German Federal Republic 1972;
D Switzerland:Pro Juventute 1972; **E** Switzerland 1862.

French postal system. Until 1803, more town handstamps were introduced and cities used large oval handstamps with the insignia of the new republic.

Between 1798 and 1806, many handstamps of the French Military post were used in Switzerland. The Army of the Rhine was based at Basle in 1798 and the Army of the Danube at St Gallen. Handstamps of ARMEE DE GRISONS, ARMÊE D'ITALIE and ARMÊE DE SUISSE are also known.

After 1803, parts of Switzerland were incorporated into the French departmental system and numbers were allocated to Mont Blanc (84), Mont Terrible (87), Haut Rhin (66), Leman (Geneva) (99), and Simplon (127). In 1815, the Helvetian Confederation was reformed, and the boundaries of Switzerland have been generally respected ever since.

1815-50

By the Treaty of Vienna, Switzerland was increased to 22 cantons and the independence and neutrality of the Federation was guaranteed. There were religious problems related to the Jesuits in 1847-8 and the secularization of monastic property was agreed in November 1847.

The first stamps issued were the cantonal issues of Geneva (30 September 1843), Basle (1 July 1845) and Zürich (1 March 1847). These were only valid for postage within the individual cantons. Postage outside these areas had to be paid by the recipient.

So-called transitional issues for cantonal use, but worded 'Poste Local', were issued in 1849-50.

1850-71

Stamps for the Federal administration were issued in May 1850 and the famous 'Seated Helvetia' appeared in September 1854. These issues were accepted for postage by all countries with which Switzerland had postal conventions. In 1863 the Red Cross was formed based on the original idea of Henri Dunant. It was based in Switzerland and has remained so throughout its history.

Although Switzerland's neutrality had been guaranteed, the Swiss themselves protested over the annexation of Savoy by the French in 1860. In 1861 the French occupied the Valle de Dappes, and the problem was finally resolved by the Treaty of France in December 1862, when the area was demilitarized but ceded to Switzerland.

During the Franco-Prussian War Swiss neutrality was proclaimed. On 1 February 1871 a French army of 84,000 men entered Switzerland and was disarmed and interned. Postal services were provided for the prisoners until their return to France.

1871-1914

In 1874 Switzerland was home for the first meeting of the General Postal Union (Universal Postal Union from 1878). This body had been intended to meet in 1870, but the Franco-Prussian War delayed this. Although congresses of the new body were to be held every four to five years, the headquarters was based in Berne, where it still remains.

1914-1918

Switzerland's neutrality was preserved during World War I and the Red Cross used as the over-seeing body for prisoners-of-war throughout the world. In 1905 the Universal Postal Union had agreed that mail to and from prisoners-of-war should be without charge. Because of Switzerland's unique position, mail from the combatant nations was allowed to enter the country after censorship.

1918-39
Switzerland was declared the seat of the League of Nations, and overprinted Swiss stamps were issued from 1922-45. Overprints for the International Labour Office appeared in 1923.

1939-45
Again, Switzerland was the centre of the Red Cross and the link between prisoners-of-war and their home countries. Because of the extent of World War II, the problems were much greater, particularly in the Far East. The transfer of mail to Switzerland was much more difficult after the fall of France and the complete encirclement of the country. However, flights in and out were made and much worldwide mail is to be found addressed to the Red Cross International.

1945 onwards
With the end of the League of Nations, and the establishment of the United Nations, new overprinted stamps for the UN appeared on 1 February 1950. Special issues began to appear in 1955 and remained under Swiss administration until October 1969 when the issues came under control of the United Nations.

Issues have also appeared for the following international bodies: International Labour Office continued with special issues replacing the former overprinted stamps in February 1950. International Educational Office issued overprints in 1944 and special issues in 1958. These were withdrawn at the same time as Swiss UN stamps. World Health Organization issued overprints in 1948 and special issues in 1957. Although these were withdrawn in 1963, a further special issue appeared in 1975. International Refugee Organization issued overprinted stamps on 1 February 1950. World Meteorological Organization issued special stamps in October 1956. These were withdrawn in 1963, but there was a special issue for the centenary in 1973.

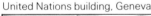

United Nations building, Geneva

Additionally, issues have appeared for the Universal Postal Union (1957 onwards) and the International Telecommunications Union (1958 onwards). These stamps are only used occasionally by these bodies and then concurrently with Swiss stamps.

In 1978, for the first time since 1815, the number of cantons was increased. The 23rd canton, Jura, was created by dividing the existing canton of Berne.

United Nations (Switzerland)

FIRST STAMPS Swiss Postal Administration 1950-69
FIRST STAMPS ISSUED 4 October 1969 (Swiss Currency)

CURRENCY

1951	As USA in New York
1969	As Switzerland in Geneva
1979	As Austria in Vienna

Initially this international organization with European headquarters in Geneva, Switzerland used Swiss stamps overprinted for the Palais des Nations. Swiss stamps were withdrawn on 4 October 1969 following a postal agreement between Switzerland and the United Nations.

Liechtenstein

CURRENCY

1912	100 heller = 1 krone
1921	100 rappen = 1 franc Swiss

Before 1850
Principality in Western Europe between Austria and Switzerland. As early as the 15th century it was on the mail route between Milan and Lindau and two postal stations were established, one at Balzers and the other at

Great St Bernard's Pass, Switzerland, a principal postal thoroughfare across the Alps

Schaan. The Austro-Hungarian government organized a state post in Tyrol and Vorarlburg in 1770, and an Austrian collecting office was opened at Balzers in 1819. However, this was closed after two years, owing to the competition with the carriers on the Milan route, who claimed a monopoly. Following a loss in importance of that service, the Austrian service was re-opened at Balzers on 1 January 1827 and a second office was opened at Vaduz in 1845.

1850-71

FIRST STAMPS Austria 1850-1912

Austrian stamps were issued on 1 June 1850 and were immediately valid for postage in the principality. Availability increased the number of letters being written and further POs were opened at Nendeln in 1864 and Schaan in 1872.

1871-1914

FIRST STAMPS ISSUED 1 February 1912

Further offices apart from the four which existed were opened at Triersena in 1890 and at Eschen in March 1912. At this time the office in Nendeln was closed.

First stamps were in designs and values stipulated by the Austrian government and showed a similar size and sheet layout to the existing Austrian adhesives. The values and colours used for the first three stamps were those stipulated by the UPU (5 *heller*, green; 10 *heller*, red; 25 *heller*, blue).

1914-18

Links with Austria were an embarrassment to the principality, especially in World War I, and the need to follow the increases in the Austrian postage rates led to problems in 1915. Although technically involved with Austria in the war, Liechtenstein took no open part and as it was not a fighting area managed to remain aloof.

1918 to date

With the collapse of the Habsburg Empire in 1918, the principality took over its own postal affairs. Austrian stamps became officially invalid from 1 March 1920. From July 1920 the principality began to issue its own adhesives and this has continued ever since. In the same year Liechtenstein became an independent postal administration within the postal territory of Switzerland. Under this agreement the principality continues to issue its own stamps but Swiss postal regulations apply. Liechtenstein was neutral during World War II.

• Austro-Hungarian Empire

FIRST STAMPS ISSUED 1 June 1850

CURRENCY

1850	60 kreuzer = 1 gulden
1858	100 kreuzer = 1 gulden
1899	100 heller = 1 krone

To 1815

A major power in central Europe until the end of the First World War when the Empire broke up. In the 19th century, Austro-Hungary contained the lands which are now Czechoslovakia and parts of Italy, Poland, Russia, Rumania and Yugoslavia as well as Austria and Hungary. This vast area made up of many nations, creeds and languages was ruled over by the Habsburgs from 1282. They became the

SCHWEIZERISCHE
ALPENPOSTEN

Above
Model of a PTT alpine bus, 1920

Left
Swiss poster (1929) showing a postbus carrying mail and passengers

hereditary Holy Roman Emperors in 1437 and continued until this title disappeared under Napoleon in 1806.

Until 1772, the only Austrian postal system, apart from the Court messengers and that of the Counts of Thurn and Taxis was the 'BIG MAIL' which handled the incoming foreign mail. In March 1772, Joseph Hardy started a local mail in Vienna. He collected and delivered mail within the capital at a charge of 2 *Kreuzers*, and outside the city limits for 3 *Kreuzers*. This service ran at a loss and was joined to the Supreme Court Post Office in 1785.

The Thurn and Taxis post had begún operations in Northern Italy in the 15th century and by the mid 1500s covered Austria and Germany, acting as a link between the many small states and the titular head in Vienna.

Hungary was linked to Austria and the Holy Roman Empire as a subject state from the mid-16th century.

During the Napoleonic Wars, Austria was allied with Britain and other countries against France. With Prussia and Russia, Austria bore the brunt of the land wars in Europe and was defeated on several occasions. In 1806, after the battle of Austerlitz, the Holy Roman Empire disappeared and in 1810, Napoleon married an Austrian princess.

After the final defeat of Napoleon, the Congress of the winning allies was held in Vienna and settled the future boundaries of Europe. Although Austria lost territory, principally to Prussia, the Emperor was firmly placed on the throne.

1815-50

The independence of Hungary has been guaranteed by Austria in 1790, but when it was not implemented, there was a popular uprising in 1848. This led to intervention by Russia and the embryo Hungarian government was suppressed. In 1815, Austria joined a German federation which was jointly promoted with Prussia. A customs union was formed in 1818 and in turn led to the Austro-German Postal Union in 1850. Stamps for use throughout the Austrian Empire were issued on 1 June 1850.

1850-71

In February 1867, a separate constitution was announced for Hungary. Stamps for the 'Dual Monarchy' were issued in 1867 and for Hungary as a separate area in 1868.

The Prussian attempt to gain control over Germany required the defeat of Austria and, after forcing the Austrian army to become reluctant allies in the war against Denmark in 1864, Prussia turned on Austria and defeated it in the Seven Weeks War of 1866. Having unwillingly gained a major power on its northern border, Austria increasingly turned to the Balkans to expand its sphere of influence.

1871-1914

In 1878, at the Congress of Berlin which followed the war between Turkey and Russia, the provinces of Bosnia and Herzegovina remained under

Turkish control but was occupied by an Austro-Hungarian Garrison. The Austrian Military Post was in operation until the area was annexed by Austria in 1908.

Austria-Hungary recognized the strength of the new Germany and was quick to form an alliance known as the Central Power. This was the basis of the structure which interlinked with other alliances in the early part of the 20th century and, in turn, led to the outbreak of World War I in June 1914 following the assassination of Archduke Franz Ferdinand at Sarajevo.

1914-18

Initiated World War I on 28 July 1914 by declaring war on Serbia, and against Russia on 6 August. Austria would never have been strong enough to wage war on both fronts without the support of Germany. However, Austria over-ran Serbia and later defeated the Italians at Caporetto. Details of the stamps issued for occupied territories are shown under each country.

The drain of the Eastern Front against Russia weakened the Austrian army and after the defeat of their Italian army by the Allies at Vittoria Veneto in 1918, the Empire began to disintegrate, as a result of internal as well as external pressures. Emperor Franz Joseph, who had reigned since 1848, was succeeded by Charles in November 1916, but the defeat in 1918 led to the formation of the first republic on 12 November 1918. Stamps were issued in December 1918 and were overprinted 'German Austria' in German, but this was forbidden by the Treaty of St Germain.

Austria

FIRST STAMPS USED Austrian Republic overprinted 'German Austria' December 1918
FIRST STAMPS ISSUED Unoverprinted July 1919

3KR.
TAG DER BRIEFMARKE
1972
4+1 S
REPUBLIK ÖSTERREICH
FÉDÉRATION MONDIALE DES ASSOCIATIONS POUR LES NATIONS UNIES
0,90 Nations Unies
THÉODORE CHAMPION
FÜRSTENTUM LIECHTENSTEIN
1873 1.20 1954
KAISERLICH KÖNIGLICH ÖSTERREICHISCHE POST
25 HELLER 25
FÜRSTENTUM LIECHTENSTEIN
K.K. ÖSTERR. POST
5 HELLER 5

Austria: Emperor Franz Joseph 1858; Austria: Republic 1972; United Nations: Swiss HQ 1976; Liechtenstein: Principality 1969; Austria: 60th Anniversary of the Emperor 1910; Liechtenstein: Austrian PO 1912.

CURRENCY

1925	100 groschen = 1 schilling
1938	As Germany
1945	100 groschen = 1 schilling

1919-39

At the end of World War I the Austro-Hungarian Empire was broken up. Hungary (q.v.) became totally independent; Bohemia and Moravia became part of Czechoslovakia; Silesia, part of Czechoslovakia and Poland; Galicia, part of Poland and Russia; Bukovina went to Romania; South Tyrol and Trieste to Italy and the provinces in Istria Dalmatia to Yugoslavia.

The republic issued its first definitive stamps in July 1919, when the 'German Austria' overprints were withdrawn.

The remaining German-speaking area was closely linked with Germany but the new republic remained independent despite an attempted Nazi uprising in 1934. On 13 March 1938 Austria was absorbed into the German Reich. German stamps were issued on 4 April 1938 but Austrian stamps remained valid until 31 October. Austria remained an integral part of Germany until May 1945.

1939-45

Occupied by Germany in 1938, Austria used German stamps throughout World War II. In 1945 the liberation of the country began and by the armistice in May 1945 the country was divided between the Western and Eastern Allies (Vienna had been liberated by the Russians).

1945 to date

FIRST STAMPS ISSUED Second Republic November 1945

On 28 April 1945 a provisional government was set up, later recognized by the Four Power Allied Control Council. The Second Republic was established on 14 May. First stamps were issued in November 1945, the Austrian government having taken the responsibility for the postal service from 1 October 1945.

The Russian zone, which comprised Lower Austria, part of Upper Austria on the left bank of the Danube and Burgenland, as well as a sector of

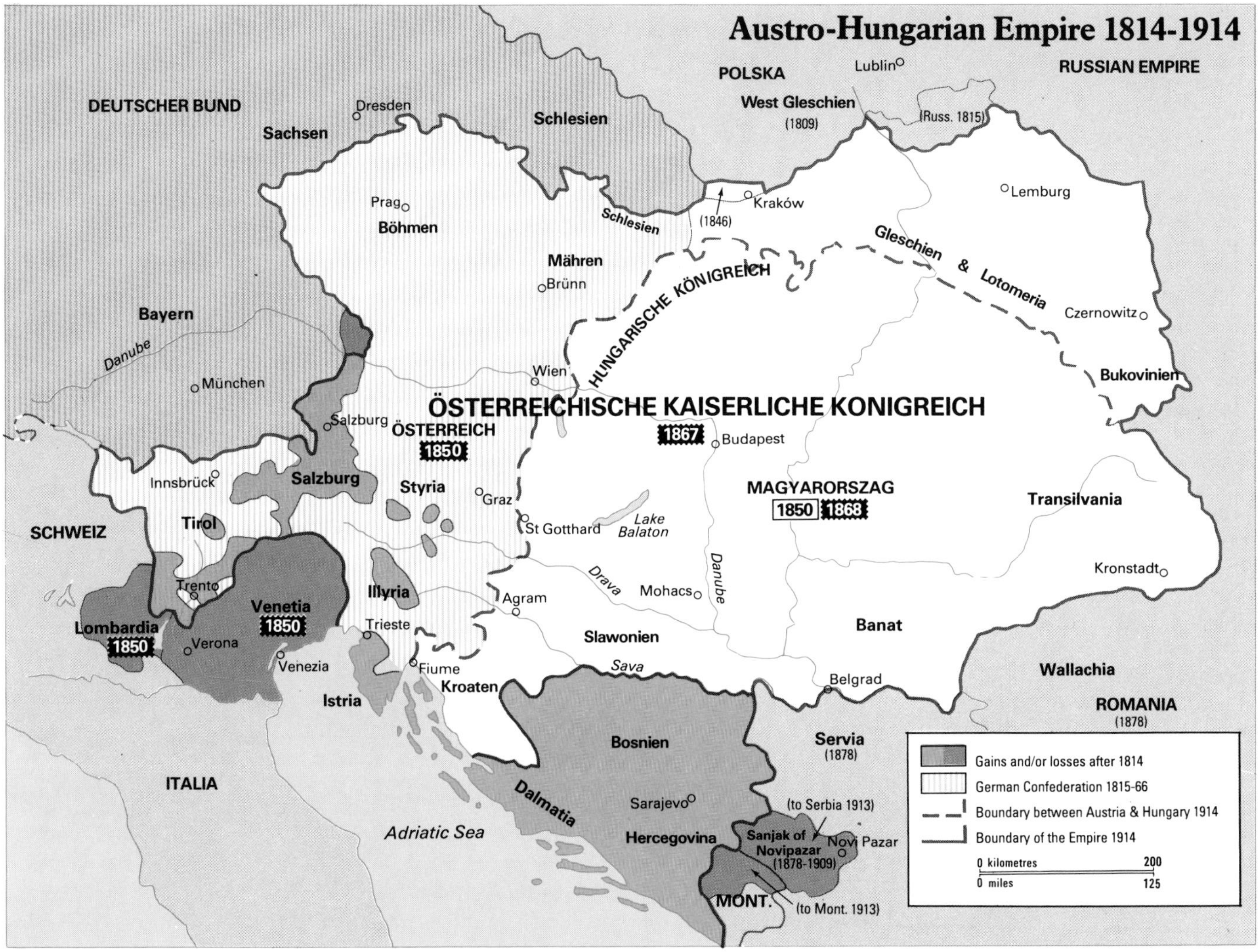
Austro-Hungarian Empire 1814-1914
POLSKA
Lublin
RUSSIAN EMPIRE
DEUTSCHER BUND
Dresden
Sachsen
Schlesien
West Gleschien
(1809)
(Russ. 1815)
Lemburg
Kraków
(1846)
Prag
Böhmen
Schlesien
Mähren
Brünn
Gleschien & Lotomeria
HUNGARISCHE KÖNIGREICH
Czernowitz
Bayern
Danube
München
Wien
Bukovinien
ÖSTERREICHISCHE KAISERLICHE KONIGREICH
Salzburg
ÖSTERREICH
1850
1867
Budapest
Innsbrück
Salzburg
Styria
Graz
MAGYARORSZAG
1850
1868
Transilvania
SCHWEIZ
Tirol
St Gotthard
Lake Balaton
Trento
Drava
Mohacs
Danube
Kronstadt
Illyria
Agram
Venetia
1850
Lombardia
1850
Verona
Trieste
Slawonien
Banat
Venezia
Fiume
Sava
Kroaten
Belgrad
Wallachia
Istria
ROMANIA
(1878)
Bosnien
Servia
(1878)
ITALIA
Dalmatia
Sarajevo
(to Serbia 1913)
Adriatic Sea
Hercegovina
Sanjak of Novipazar
(1878-1909)
Novi Pazar
MONT.
(to Mont. 1913)
Gains and/or losses after 1814
German Confederation 1815-66
Boundary between Austria & Hungary 1914
Boundary of the Empire 1914
0 kilometres 200
0 miles 125

Vienna, had restored a postal service in May 1945 but the overprinted stamps of Germany which were issued have many varieties, some bogus.

New definitives were issued for the Russian zone in July and August 1945. The remaining territories of Austria were divided between the Western Allies. The British occupied Carinthia, East Tyrol and Styria; the French, Tyrol and Vorarlburg; and the Americans, Salzburg and the section of Upper Austria on the right bank of the Danube. A special issue of stamps for these zones and the sectors of Vienna were made on 28 June 1945. They were withdrawn in October, but the occupying forces used their own Field POs.

A treaty was signed in May 1955 which restored the boundaries of 1938 and allowed for the withdrawal of the occupation forces. Austria has maintained neutrality ever since.

United Nations (Austria)

FIRST STAMPS 24 August 1979

Further series was produced in Austrian currency from 24 August 1979. These are for use on mail from Vienna International Centre for the United Nations or the International Atomic Energy Agency.

Hungary

Before 1871

FIRST STAMPS Austrian stamps 1 June 1850
FIRST STAMPS ISSUED for Austria and Hungary 1 June 1867
FIRST STAMPS ISSUED for Hungary alone 20 June 1868

CURRENCY

1858	100 krajczar = 1 forint
1900	100 filler (heller) = 1 korona (krone)
1919	Romanian and Serbian occupation 100 filler = 1 korona
1926	100 filler = 1 pengo
1946	100 filler = 1 forint

Part of Roman Dacia but settled by the Ungaru, a Scythian tribe, about AD800. For many centuries an independent state, but in 1393 the population invited the assistance of the Turks to overcome one of their kings — Sigismund of Brandenberg. In 1526 Turks again entered the country and overran a large part but, having captured Buda, the Turks were defeated at Mohatz and Hungary became a subject state of Austria.

Although the Hungarians were linked with Austria from then until the end of World War I, the population was constantly striving for independence. The independence of the state was guaranteed in 1790, but this undertaking was not implemented and a popular uprising began in 1848. The intervention of Russia in support of the Austrians led to the suppression of the Hungarian government and the state was assimilated into the Austrian Empire.

In February 1867 a separate constitution for Hungary was announced, and a separate government with limited self-governing rights came into existence. In November 1868 the Emperor Franz Joseph of Austria became King of Hungary and the Dual Monarchy was established.

An independent Hungarian postal administration was created in May 1867 and Austrian stamps were withdrawn on 31 May and demonetized on 15 June 1867. A joint issue was used throughout the Dual Monarchy for just over a year and the first stamps for Hungary alone were issued on 20 June 1868. In the meantime the Hungarian postal service had been extended and had taken control of the posts in Croatia-Slovenia on 1 April 1868.

1871-1914

The independence of Hungary within the Dual Monarchy was recognized by the other powers, and when the General Postal Union was formed in 1874 both administrations were included in the 22 signatories.

During the Balkan Wars, 1912-13, Hungary took no part but reinforced the borders to prevent invasion by the Serbian and Romanian forces.

POLSKA
DEUTSCH-LAND
Praha
Pilsen
Cracow
Lemburg (Lwow)
CZECHOSLOVAKIA
Brünn
Danube
Linz
Munchen
Wien
Bratislava
Innsbruck
ÖSTERREICH
Budapest
MAGYARORSZAG
Cluj
Lake Balaton
Danube
Szeged
ROMANIA
Trento
Ljubljana
Drava
Trieste
Zagreb
Veliki Kikinda
Temesvara
Fiume
JUGOSLAVIJA
Beograd
Danube
Austrian-Hungarian Empire 1914
New boundaries 1919
Railways
0 kilometres 200
0 miles 125
Disruption of railway communications 1919

1914-18

The Dual Monarchy entered World War I on 28 July 1914 when war was declared on Serbia in retaliation for the assassination of the Archduke Ferdinand at Sarajevo. Throughout the war, Hungarian forces fought with the Austrians on the eastern and southern fronts. All occupation stamps were overprinted on Austrian military post stamps.

The Austrian Emperor withdrew on 13 November 1918 and on 16 November a People's Republic was formed. Overprinted stamps were issued on 23 November 1918.

The break-up of the Austro-Hungarian Empire by the Allies led to the complete independence of Hungary, but the country was reduced to its ancient boundaries and the province of Transylvania was awarded to Romania (for details of stamps issued for the occupation of parts of Hungary *see* Romania and Serbia).

1919-39

Unrest continued in Hungary. The People's Republic of November 1918 was replaced by a Bolshevik régime under Bela Kun on 22 March 1919. Stamps for this government were issued on 14 June. At the same time a national government was formed in opposition under Admiral Horthy at Szeged and overprinted stamps for this party were issued on 28 June 1919. This area was under French occupation. The French were also in occupation of the region of Arad and issued overprinted stamps for this area in May 1919. It was awarded to Romania in 1920.

On 1 August 1919 Bela Kun fled to Vienna in the face of Romanian troops who had invaded Hungary in July. Under pressure from the Allies, the Romanians withdrew on 14 November, and a national republic was formed under Admiral Horthy on 16 November 1919. Overprinted stamps were issued the same day.

On 1 March 1920 Admiral Horthy was appointed Regent of Hungary after the National Assembly declared that Hungary was still a kingdom. The link with Austria was finally dissolved.

1939-45

Admiral Horthy continued as Regent of Hungary until October 1944 but, although he supported Germany's anti-Communist attitude, he favoured few other aspects of German policy. Hungary joined the Axis powers early in 1941 but had to be threatened with

1.80 Kčs
PRAHA
ČESKOSLOVENSKO
A
5 kr
B
MAGYAR POSTA
60f
C
40f
MAGYARORSZAG
D
ČESKOSLOVENSKO
1.50
V.I. LENIN
E
POSTA
ČESKO-SLOVENSKÁ
1
F

A Czechoslovakia 1970; **B** Hungary:Provisional Issue 1871; **C** Hungary:Republic 1971; **D** Hungary:Regency 1930; **E** Czechoslovakia 1949; **F** Czechoslovakia:Republic 1918.

invasion before any of its troops were released for action in Russia, though they did assist in the invasion of Yugoslavia in April 1941.

After Yugoslavia fell, Hungary was awarded certain portions of that country when it was broken into its constituent parts. These included the territory north of the Drava and west of the Tioja. Transylvania was returned to Hungary by Romania in 1940.

As Russia began the re-occupation of Eastern Europe, Hungary was included in the area under Russian dominance. In October 1944 Admiral Horthy offered an armistice to Russia and sought peace with the Allies. He was deported by the Germans to Austria. On 22 December 1944 a provisional government was formed at Debrecen under Soviet auspices. Overprinted stamps were issued on 1 May 1945.

Above
A rural postman in Hungary, 1872

Austro-Hungarian mail-coach making its appearance in recent Festival celebrations

1945 to date
On 1 February 1946 the kingdom, which had lasted without a king since 1918, was replaced by a republic. Stamps for the new constitution were issued on 12 February. In spite of the revolt in 1956, Hungary has remained a member of the Warsaw Pact and a Communist country ever since.

Teschen
POLSKA
(from Austria 1918)
USSR
(from 1939)
CESKO-SLOVENSKÒ
Brünn
Ruthenia
(Carpotho-Ukraine)
(Hungary 1938-45)
(Russia 1945)
Czernowitz
Danube
Wien
Bratislava
(Hungary 1938-45)
ÖSTERREICH
Sopron
Budapest
Debrecen
MAGYARORSZAG
1918
1919
1945
(Hungary 1941-5)
Cluj
Lake Balaton
Szeged
Drava
Arad
ITALIA
Ljubliana (Laibach)
Zagreb (Agram)
Mohacs
Subotica
Temesvar
Brasov
Trieste
Sombar
Vodjvodina
ROMANIA
Fiume
(Hungary 1941-5)
Novi Sad
Sava
Danube
Beograd
Hungary 1914
Territory lost 1918
New boundaries 1920
Hungary 1920 & 1945
Territory regained and lost 1938-45
(from Austria 1918)
Zara
JUGOSLAVIJA
Adriatic Sea
0 kilometres 250
0 miles 150
Hungary after 1914

Czechoslovakia

Before 1938

FIRST STAMPS Austria to 1918
FIRST STAMPS ISSUED October 1918

CURRENCY

1918 100 haleru = 1 koruna

Central European republic formed in 1918 from elements of the Austro-Hungarian Empire. It comprised Bohemia and Moravia, Slovakia, Austrian Silesia and the Sudetenland, which had a largely German population.

The early history of Czechoslovakia follows the fortunes of the Empire of which its components were part. Bohemia was absorbed into Austria after the Treaty of Westphalia in 1648. However, when the Czechs' agitation for limited independence was ignored by the Austrians, a major uprising took place in Prague in 1848. This was suppressed, but thereafter the Austrians took a more conciliatory attitude to the regions.

World War I provided an opportunity for the declaration of an independent republic. Many of the Czech and Slovak regiments in the Austrian army deserted and joined the allies. They fought in Russia, Italy and France. In February 1916 the Czechoslovak National Council was formed in Paris. On 28 October 1918 the Council declared its independence of Austria and two days later the Slovak National Council voted for union with the Czechs.

The failure of Austrian authority in 1918 affected all aspects of life in Czechoslovakia, including the postal service, which did not even operate in large cities. In Prague a local post was operated by scouts under the control of the Revolutionary Council. By 1919 the service began to return to normal and general issues appeared. Stocks of Austrian stamps found in the POs were overprinted for sale in Czechoslovakia and were sold at a premium of 50% over the face value to support various charities. These were purely local issues.

• Czechoslovak army in Siberia
During World War I many Czech and Slovak soldiers in the Austro-Hungarian Army surrendered to the Russians. After the war, 70,000 of these men were formed into the Czech Legion in Siberia, which joined the Allies against the Bolsheviks. Stamps for the military post were issued in 1919-20 and were also available on the Trans-Siberian Railway, though the latter were souvenirs which served no postal purpose.

1938-45
In 1938 Germany, which had absorbed Austria in March, demanded the cession of the German-speaking Sudetenland. For some time a propaganda campaign had been conducted by Germany mainly based on a German story that, following the Czech pact with Russia in 1935, Russian planes had been based in Czechoslovakia. Following a trip to Munich by the British Prime Minister in September 1938, Britain agreed to German demands and the Sudetenland was absorbed into the German Reich.

At the same time both Hungary and Poland made demands on the territory of Czechoslovakia. Polish troops occupied Tesin (Teschen) in early November 1938 and on 3 November Hungary was awarded the Komarno (Komaroma) district on the banks of the Danube. This was incorporated into Hungary from August 1939. The reduced area and population of the republic were now virtually defenceless and the name of the new territory was hyphenated, Czecho-slovakia, to emphasize the federal nature of the

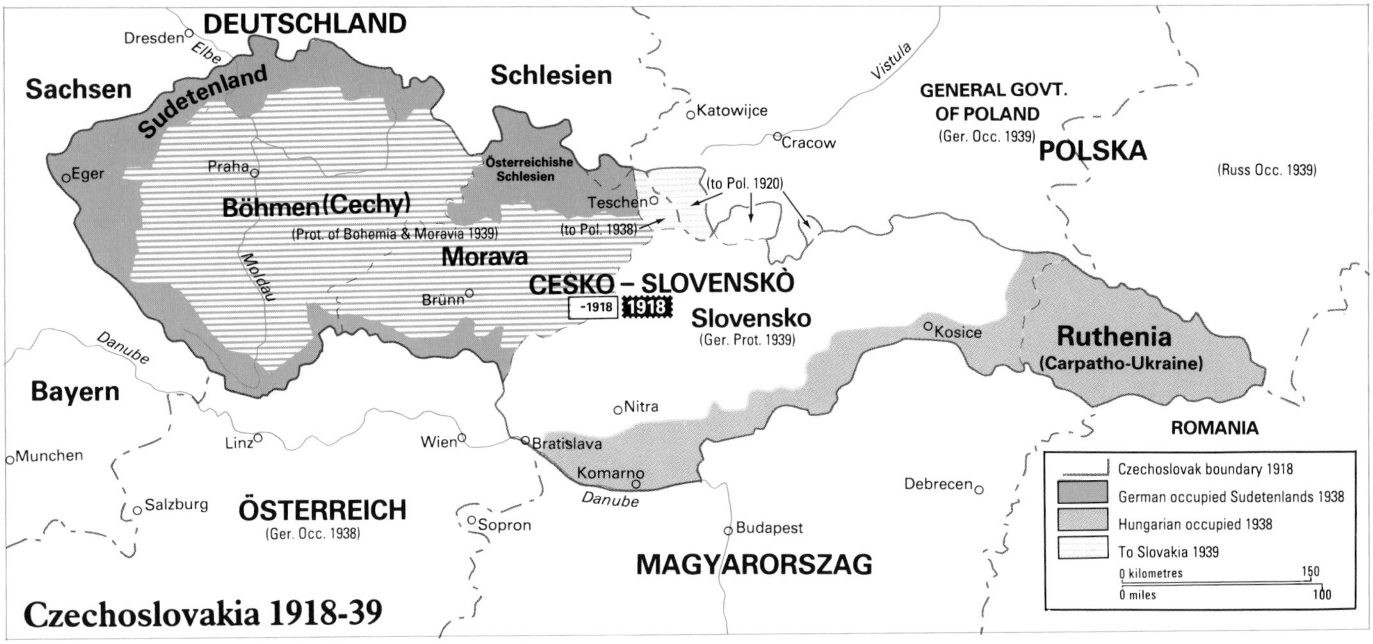
DEUTSCHLAND
Dresden
Elbe
Sachsen
Sudetenland
Schlesien
Vistula
Katowijce
Cracow
GENERAL GOVT. OF POLAND
(Ger. Occ. 1939)
POLSKA
(Russ Occ. 1939)
Eger
Praha
Österreichishe Schlesien
(to Pol. 1920)
Böhmen (Cechy)
Teschen
(Prot. of Bohemia & Moravia 1939)
(to Pol. 1938)
Morava
Moldau
CESKO - SLOVENSKÒ
Brünn
-1918
1918
Slovensko
(Ger. Prot. 1939)
Kosice
Ruthenia
(Carpatho-Ukraine)
Danube
Bayern
Nitra
ROMANIA
Munchen
Linz
Wien
Bratislava
Komarno
Danube
Debrecen
Salzburg
ÖSTERREICH
(Ger. Occ. 1938)
Sopron
Budapest
MAGYARORSZAG
Czechoslovak boundary 1918
German occupied Sudetenlands 1938
Hungarian occupied 1938
To Slovakia 1939
0 kilometres 150
0 miles 100

Czechoslovakia 1918-39

remaining area. Internal disorders were fomented by Germany and in January 1939 self-government was granted to Slovakia and Ruthenia within the federal area. The Slovak government met on 18 January and the Ruthenian (Carpatho-Ukraine) on 14 March 1939.

Slovakia also declared full independence on 14 March and, on the same day, Germany marched into Bohemia and Moravia. Slovakia remained an independent stamp-issuing territory under German dependence and control until 1945. Bohemia and Moravia used overprinted German stamps initially and remained a German protectorate until 1945.

Bohemia and Moravia, and Slovakia were German protectorates throughout World War II. The Czech government under President Benes established a government-in-exile in London during the war. Czech forces fought with the Allies and their special Field PO cancellations were used wherever the troops fought.

The territory was gradually regained by Russian forces in 1944 and 1945. After hostilities, Czechoslovakia regained all its original territory except Ruthenia (Carpo-Ukraine) which became Russian.

1945 to date

The reconstituted republic issued its first stamps after the war in 1945 and normal postal services were quickly resumed. However, many of the Czech partisan groups were pro-Russian and this is reflected in the early post-war stamps before the exiled government returned.

In 1948, with Russian backing, the Czech communist Party staged a *coup d'état*. The President was forced to retire and a People's Republic was established. This has continued except for a brief period in 1968 when a more liberal regime under Alexander Dubchek was instituted. Czechoslovakia remains a member of the Warsaw Pact.

Italy before and after unification

The early history of Italy is that of Rome and the Roman Empire, a martial and cultural administration which left its mark on the language and history of the Western World. This Empire was divided into two parts, Eastern and Western in the 4th century A.D. and began to break up the following century. Rome was taken by the Ostrogoths and the centralized government finally failed.

Throughout medieval times, the history of Italy followed no coherent form. It became a pattern of feudal states and fiefs which changed allegiances and led to many internal wars and tyrannic dynasties. From this nebulous grouping of dukedoms, emerged the Renaissance, a period of artistic and creative endeavour which led to the pre-eminence of Italian merchants throughout western Europe and the Levant. The need for these merchant princes to communicate throughout their areas of control led to the early establishment of regular messenger services which developed into an international European postal service.

The development of power of Venice into the control of the Adriatic and Aegean with services to many of the islands which they controlled saw the spread of Italian merchants towards the east, while the Florentines moved north. Merchant postal services in France, Britain and Germany were operating in the 16th century. Postal markings were not used, but letters which exist carry charge marks, sometimes in Italian or local currency and those which are marked with a Guild mark, do not appear to have been charged. An early example of Free Franking.

In the 17th and early 18th centuries, Italy became the battle grounds for the political interests of Spain, France and Austria. The War of the Spanish Succession began in Italy in 1701 and the country was divided into kingdoms and dukedoms at the Peace of Utrecht in 1713. In 1720, the Duke of Savoy became the King of Sardinia — a move which was to have far reaching results some 130 years later.

Postally, the states developed separately — in part because of the differences in currency which made the interchange of mail between them complicated. The use of handstamps developed during the 18th century and the spheres of influence were clearly defined by the outbreak of the French Revolutionary Wars.

In May 1796, Italy was invaded by France and gradually overrun until Rome was occupied. In 1797, at the Treaty of Campo Formi, the northern states of Italy were divided between France and Austria and the Cisalpine Republic was formed as a French puppet. The Roman Republic was formed soon afterwards. However, war continued between Austria and France and, after the Victory of Marengo in 1800, Bonaparte created the Italian Republic to replace the Cisalpine and Roman Republics. Italy became a kingdom within the French Empire in 1805.

Italy became incorporated into the French postal service and the provinces were given French style handstamps which were used until the collapse of the French control at the end of the Napoleonic Wars.

The Kingdom had taken over the Austrian provinces of North Italy in 1806 and they were returned in 1815 when the Lombardy-Venetia state was established. The boundaries of the dukedoms and kingdoms were ratified by the Congress of Vienna and the scene was set for the unification which finally began in the 1850s.

• Lombardy-Venetia

CURRENCY

1850	100 centesimi = 1 lira
1858	100 soldi = 1 florin
	100 kreuzer = 1 gulden

1815-50

After the Napoleonic Wars, Lombardy-Venetia was formed by the allied sovereigns and awarded to Austria to replace the Netherlands, which had been lost. This arrangement was not popular with the inhabitants and several minor uprisings took place. In March 1848 a major uprising took place and the kingdom joined Sardinia. However, defeated by Austria at Novara on 23 March 1849, the provinces were again subjected to Austria. The two states were administered postally as part of the Austrian Empire and normal postal markings were employed.

1850-71

FIRST STAMPS ISSUED 1 June 1850

These provinces issued their first stamps on the same day as the Austrian Empire. Different stamps were needed because the two currencies were different; Lombardy-Venetia used currency based on silver while those of the Empire used paper currency. The stamps were printed by the state printing works in Vienna.

Unrest continued to trouble the provinces and in 1856 an amnesty was proclaimed for political offences. However, Austria felt animosity towards Sardinia following the uprising of 1848-9. In 1857 diplomatic relations were suspended and in April 1859 Austrian forces crossed the River Ticino into Piedmont. The French Emperor, Napoleon III, declared war on Austria and sent troops to the help of Sardinia. Although the war is notable for the bravery of the troops and the incompetence of the general staff, the Piedmontese and French armies overwhelmed the Austrians in a series of battles — culminating in Solferino on 24 June 1859. Henri Dunant, a young Swiss banker, was present at the battle; observing the carnage and suffering of the wounded he called for a neutral body to care for the wounded. This led to the formation of the Red Cross in 1864. War was ended by the Peace of Villafranca on 11 July 1859 and most of Lombardy was awarded to France. It was immediately transferred to Sardinia in return for Savoy and Nice, which were incorporated into France.

Stamps for Lombardy-Venetia continued to be used in Venetia and the remainder of Lombardy until Venetia was incorporated into the kingdom of Italy in 1866. From that date these two provinces have remained part of Italy and have used Italian stamps.

• Modena

CURRENCY

1852	100 centesimi = 1 lira

Before 1850

Duchy in northern Italy which was part of the Cisalpine Republic set up by France in 1797. It became part of the Kingdom of Italy in 1805 but the archduke was restored in 1814. An invasion of his state by Murat in April 1815 was defeated. In 1831 the people rose against the duke but he was restored with the support of the Austrians. Although there was support for the people of Lombardy-Venetia in the rising against the Austrians in 1848-9, Modena did not become involved.

1850-71

FIRST STAMPS ISSUED 1 June 1852

First stamps were printed by the state stamp office in Modena and showed the arms of the ruling family of Este. Soon after the start of the war of 1859 between Austria and Piedmont with French support the duke was expelled and a provisional government established on 11 June 1859. Stamps were issued on 15 October.

On 16 March 1860, after a plebiscite, Modena became part of Sardinia, and stamps of Modena were replaced.

General Garibaldi (1807–1882) from a pastel drawing by James Luntley, 1864

• Naples

CURRENCY	
1858	100 grana = 200 tornesi = 1 ducato

1815-50

Port and continental division of the Kingdom of the Two Sicilies formed in 1816 by the union of Naples and Sicily. Because of the cruelty and tyrannical rule of the kings, several risings occurred and a major revolution took place in 1848. This lasted until 1850 and the liberals were virtually annihilated by royal troops. The precarious balance was retained by support from foreign powers but the scene was set for the beginning of the unification of Italy.

1850-71

FIRST STAMPS ISSUED 1 January 1858

Although Naples and Sicily were a joint kingdom, both parts issued their own stamps; Sicily (q.v.) followed in 1859.

Garibaldi landed in Sicily in May 1860 and defeated the Neapolitan army. On 30 July the Neapolitans withdrew from Sicily, but more internal unrest led to a further invasion by Garibaldi of the mainland and he occupied Naples on 7 September 1860.

Stamps were issued under control of the Garibaldi regime on 6 November 1860. These were produced by modifying the earlier design on the printing plates. A further modification was made in December 1860 when stamps showing the cross of Savoy were produced by excising the arms of Naples from the original plate.

On 21 October 1860 Naples and Sicily voted by plebiscite to join Sardinia and on 26 October Garibaldi, as a step towards the unification of Italy, acclaimed the King of Sardinia as King of the Neapolitan provinces.

On 15 February 1861 stamps were issued for the Neapolitan provinces (Naples and Sicily). Though similar in design to those of Sardinia they used the currency of Naples. These were superseded by the stamps of Italy in 1862.

• Papal States

CURRENCY	
1852	100 bajocchi = 1 scudo
1866	100 centesimi = 1 lira

Before 1850

Temporal sovereignty of the Popes began in the 8th century when the Lombards made a gift of the territory that they had gained from the Franks. From 1503 the area was fully administered.

In 1798-9 during the Napoleonic wars the region became the Republic of Rome and was regained by the Neapolitans for the Pope. It was retaken by the French in 1800 but was restored by them to the Pope. It was annexed by Napoleon as part of the Kingdom of Italy in May 1808. Rome was declared the second city in the Empire.

The States were returned to the Pope in 1814. The population wished to join with Sardinia against the Austrians in 1848 and the government was defeated by insurrection in the town. The Romans demanded a democratic ministry and the proclamation of Italian nationality. In November the Pope (Pius IX) escaped from the city and appealed to the Catholic powers.

After extensive fighting Rome surrendered to the French in June 1850 and was returned to the Pope.

1850-71

FIRST STAMPS ISSUED 1 January 1852

In 1850 the Papal States comprised Rome and the surrounding territory, the provinces of Romagna and the Marches and Umbria.

Romagna seceded from the States in 1859. During the war for the unification of Italy, Rome was garrisoned by French troops, who assisted in the defence until they were withdrawn during the Franco-Prussian War of 1870. Italian troops were in control of the city from 20 September and a plebiscite was held on 2 October 1870 which led to the incorporation of the states into Italy. The Pope lost all temporal power (see also Vatican City).

A
B
C
D
E
F

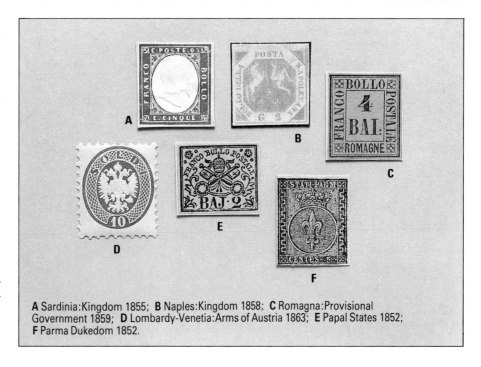

A Sardinia:Kingdom 1855; **B** Naples:Kingdom 1858; **C** Romagna:Provisional Government 1859; **D** Lombardy-Venetia:Arms of Austria 1863; **E** Papal States 1852; **F** Parma Dukedom 1852.

• Parma

CURRENCY	
1852	100 centesimi = 1 lira

Before 1850

Duchy in northern Italy which was a dependent state of France during the Napoleonic wars; the Duke of Parma was made King of Etruria in 1801. The dukedom was re-established but the area was occupied by the Austrians and Sardinians in the war of 1848. The Sardinians retired after the battle of Novara in April 1849.

1850-71

FIRST STAMPS ISSUED 1 June 1852

Stamps showing the coat-of-arms of the Bourbons were used until the duke was assassinated in 1854. His son was a minor and a regency was established. On 9 June 1859 the regent handed authority to a provisional government in order to prepare for union with Sardinia.

The dukedom of Parma with Piacenza became part of the Kingdom of Sardinia on 18 March 1860 following a plebiscite. As a result stamps of Parma were withdrawn and Sardinian stamps introduced until the first Italian general issue in 1862.

• Romagna

FIRST STAMPS Papal States from 1 January 1852
FIRST STAMPS ISSUED 12 June 1859

CURRENCY	
1852	100 centesimi = 1 lira

One of the Papal States; the Popes had full authority in the province after 1503 when it was regained from the Borgias. As with other Papal States it was part of the Kingdom of Italy during the Napoleonic Wars.

On 12 June 1859 a provisional government was formed to prepare for unification with Sardinia. A plebiscite was held and on 25 March 1860 Romagna became part of Sardinia, and stamps of Romagna were replaced by those of Sardinia until the Italian general issue in 1862. Romagna became part of the province of Emilia with Modena and Parma.

• Sardinia

CURRENCY	
1851	100 centesimi = 1 lira

Before 1815

Island in the Mediterranean south of Corsica. Acquired by the Duke of Savoy as King in 1720, it had previously been held by the Spaniards. The court of the combined territory was held in Turin until Piedmont was overrun by the French in 1792. Piedmont was annexed by the French to the Kingdom of Italy in 1805. The King of Sardinia resided in the island until 1814. At that time Piedmont was restored to the Kingdom, and Genoa, which had formed the Ligurian republic under the French, was also awarded to the Kingdom.

1815-50

Centre of the movement to unify Italy.

On 23 March 1848 the King openly began to support unification and an attack on the Austrians. After a successful campaign against the Austrians which led to the capture of Lombardy and Venetia (July 1848), the Sardinian army was defeated by the Austrians under Marshal Radetzky. The war ended with an armistice between Austria and Sardinia signed on 6 August 1849.

1850-71

FIRST STAMPS ISSUED 1 January 1851

To obtain support from the western powers, Sardinia supported Britain and France against Russia during the Crimean War. A convention was signed in April 1855 and 10,000 troops were sent to the Crimea.

In 1859 the war with Austria began again, this time with the support of France. Lombardy was gained in July, but Sardinia gave up Savoy and Nice to France in return. With the activities of Garibaldi and Cavour the states of Italy gradually came under the control of Sardinia.

Sardinian stamps were used in most of the states as they decided to join unified Italy, as follows:

MODENA 16 March 1860
PARMA 18 March 1860
TUSCANY 22 March 1860
ROMAGNA 25 March 1860

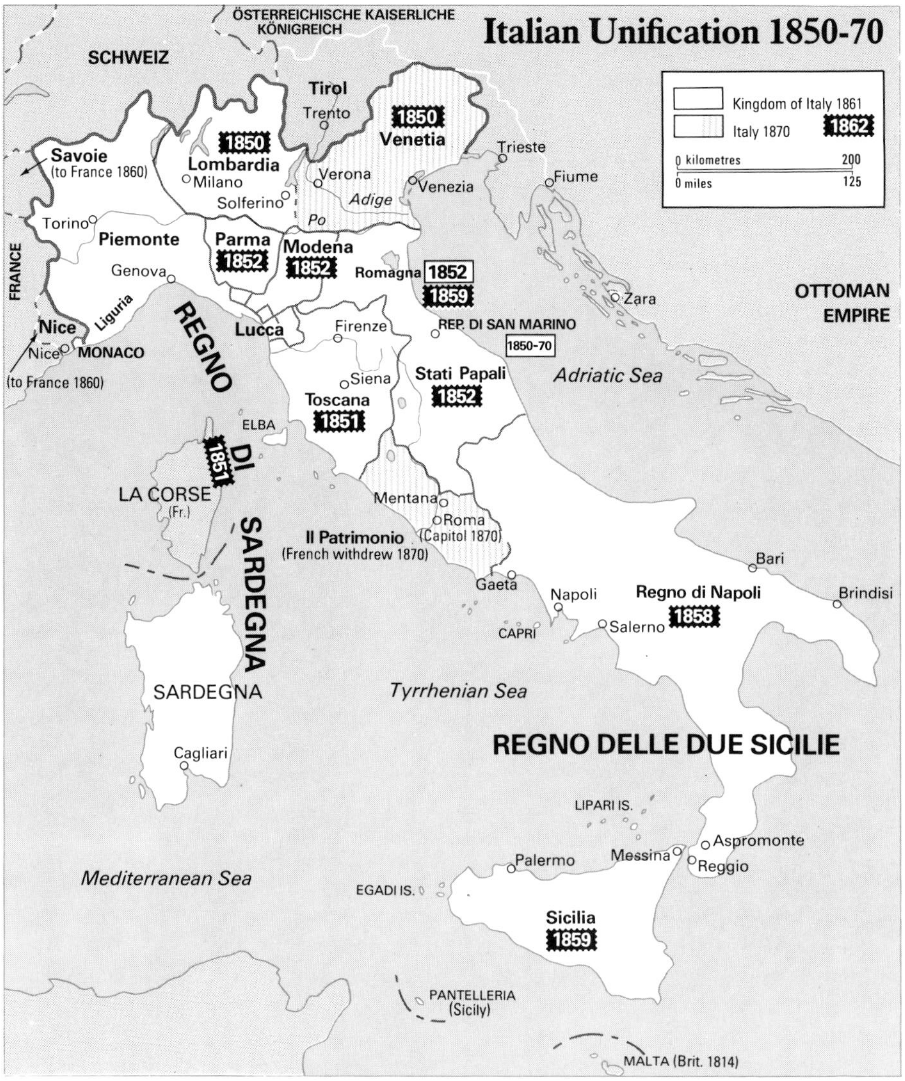
Italian Unification 1850-70
Kingdom of Italy 1861
Italy 1870
1862
0 kilometres 200
0 miles 125
ÖSTERREICHISCHE KAISERLICHE KÖNIGREICH
SCHWEIZ
Tirol
Trento
1850
Venetia
Trieste
Fiume
Savoie
(to France 1860)
1850
Lombardia
Milano
Verona
Venezia
Adige
Solferino
Po
Torino
Piemonte
Parma
1852
Modena
1852
Romagna
1852
1859
Genova
FRANCE
OTTOMAN EMPIRE
Zara
Liguria
Nice
Nice
MONACO
(to France 1860)
REGNO DI SARDEGNA
Lucca
Firenze
REP. DI SAN MARINO
1850-70
Siena
Toscana
1851
Stati Papali
1852
Adriatic Sea
ELBA
1851
LA CORSE
(Fr.)
Mentana
Roma
(Capitol 1870)
Il Patrimonio
(French withdrew 1870)
Bari
Gaeta
Napoli
Regno di Napoli
1858
Brindisi
Salerno
CAPRI
SARDEGNA
Tyrrhenian Sea
Cagliari
REGNO DELLE DUE SICILIE
LIPARI IS.
Aspromonte
Reggio
Messina
Palermo
Mediterranean Sea
EGADI IS.
Sicilia
1859
PANTELLERIA
(Sicily)
MALTA (Brit. 1814)

Venetia and the Papal States did not use the stamps of Sardinia as by the time they joined the kingdom Italian stamps had been issued. Naples and Sicily had a special issue because they had a different currency. The King of Sardinia was recognized as King of Italy in February 1861.

• Sicily

CURRENCY	
1859	100 grano = 1 ducato

1815-50

Island off southern Italy which was unified with Naples as the Kingdom of the Two Sicilies in 1816. All major cities in Sicily rose against the Bourbon king in 1848. A provisional government was proclaimed on 12 January but the Neapolitans attacked Messina and the rising collapsed in April 1850.

1850-71

FIRST STAMPS ISSUED 1 January 1859

The postal cancellation of Sicily was unusual; it took the form of a framework so that the head of the king would not be defaced.

Garibaldi landed in Sicily on 11 May 1860 and defeated the Neapolitan army which evacuated the island on 30 July. A new constitution was proclaimed in August but no new stamps appeared until the issue for the Neapolitan provinces on 15 February 1861. The Sicilians had voted to join Sardinia in October 1860 and stamps of Italy were issued in 1862.

• Tuscany

CURRENCY	
1851	60 quattrini = 20 soldi = 12 crazie = 1 Tuscan lira
1859	1 Tuscan lire = 1 Italian lira

Before 1850
Duchy in central Italy which was the chief base of the Medicis in the sixteenth century. When the Medicis died out in 1737, Tuscany was given to the Duke of Lorraine, who was married to Maria-Theresa of Austria. The French took Tuscany in the 1799 Italian campaign and the duke was dispossessed. The duchy was given to the Duke of Parma, who governed it as the King of Etruria.

Tuscany was incorporated into the French Empire in 1807 and was given as a grand-duchy to Eliza, sister of Napoleon. The Duke of Tuscany was reinstated in 1814. Lucca was united with Tuscany in 1847. After the insurrections of 1849 a provisional government was proclaimed but the duke was reinstated by the Austrians in July 1850.

1850-71

FIRST STAMPS ISSUED 1 April 1851

Stamps showing the arms of Tuscany were issued. These were printed at the Grand Ducal Printing Office in Florence.

The Tuscan army demanded alliance with the Sardinians in the war against Austria in April 1859. The duke refused and fled to Bologna. A provisional government was formed on 27 April and new stamps with the arms of Savoy were issued on 1 January 1860. On 22 March 1860, after a plebiscite, Tuscany became part of Sardinia, and the stamps of Tuscany were replaced. Sardinian stamps were used until the first Italian general issue in 1862.

Italy

CURRENCY

1862 100 centesimi = 1 lira

1850-71
Following the unrest of the preceding period, culminating in the unsuccessful War of Independence in 1848-9, the leading protagonist, Sardinia, made peace with Austria on 9 August 1849. However, the currents which had led to the earlier uprising still existed. They were aimed largely at the occupation of northern Italy by the Austro-Hungarian Empire (*see* Lombardy-Venetia), which in turn led to Austrian dominance of the Italian peninsula. The prime minster of Piedmont, part of Sardinia, was Count Cavour, whose interest was to increase the power of his small country, but who became the architect of the new state of Italy. He was ably supported by the Italian patriot Garibaldi.

Cavour joined with Britain and France in the Crimean War (1854-6). Having gained their good will, he secured a secret treaty which ensured that France would assist Piedmont in driving the Austrians out of Italy and support the federation of the Italian states. In return, France would receive Savoy and Nice.

In April-June 1859 war was fought in Lombardy-Venetia. As a result, Sardinia gained most of Lombardy but Venetia remained in Austrian hands.

Following the suppression of a major uprising in the Neapolitan states in 1860, Garibaldi invaded Sicily in May, and, having defeated the army of the king of Naples, crossed the Straits of Messina with British assistance. On 7 September 1860 Naples fell and Garibaldi prepared to march on Rome and to liberate Venetia.

Meanwhile, unrest in the Papal States gave Cavour the excuse he needed to assemble a Piedmontese army. It crossed the border on 10 September and marched south to link with Garibaldi, but the French occupied Rome and the French fleet took station off the coast to prevent any further Italian attack against the papal domains. The Neapolitan forces under their king made a last stand against the united Italian armies at Gaeta from 3 November 1860 to 13 February 1861. The withdrawal of the French fleet in January made bombardment from the sea possible and the final surrender of the Neapolitan army followed.

On 17 March 1861 the Kingdom of Italy was proclaimed with Victor Emmanuel as its first constitutional monarch. Unification was now complete except for Venetia and the papal territory around Rome. Occupation of these areas was foiled by the continued presence in Rome of French forces. In 1862 Garibaldi marched on Rome from Sicily but the Italian government could not allow a major act of war while the French were still in Rome, and defeated Garibaldi with government troops at Aspromonte on 29 August 1862.

In May 1866 Italy, with the approval of France, made an alliance with Prussia, and when the Austro-Prussian war broke out in June 1866, Italy declared war on the Austrians on 20 June 1866. After the defeat of the Italians by the Austrians there was a hiatus until the Austrians were withdrawn to defend Vienna against Prussian attack in July 1866. Venetia was annexed by the Italians later in July and this was ratified by the Treaty of Vienna on 12 October.

In December 1866 the French withdrew from Rome and Garibaldi attempted to seize the territory; he was defeated and the pressure by Italian forces to overthrow the Papal forces led to the return of the French in October 1867. Garibaldi renewed his invasion but was defeated at Mentana by a combined French and Papal force.

On 20 September 1870, French forces having been withdrawn to assist in the Franco-Prussian War, an Italian army bombarded Rome and Pope Pius IX surrendered. Following a plebiscite, the region was declared the capital of Italy and the area was formally annexed on 20 October 1870. The unification was complete.

FIRST STAMPS ISSUED 24 February 1862

The unification of Italy gradually assimilated the independent states which had been issuing stamps since 1850. The Kingdom of Italy was proclaimed on 17 March 1861 and the states of Lombardy, Sardinia, Naples,

B
POSTA
BOLLO DELLA
DI SICILIA
GR. 1
ENRICO
CARUSO
1873
1921
ITALIA L 50
C
POSTE ITALIANE
CENTESIMI
5 5
D
A
REPVBBLICA ITALIANA
POSTALE
FRANCO BOLLO
ITALIANO
C. QUINDICI
E
POSTALE
FRANCOBOLLO
TOSCANO
1 SOLDO
F

A Italy:Republic 1953; **B** Sicily:Kingdom 1855; **C** Italy:Republic 1973; **D** Italy:Kingdom 1906; **E** Italy:Kingdom 1863; **F** Tuscany:Grand Dukedom 1852.

Sicily, Modena, Romagna and Tuscany ceased to issue their own stamps. First Italian stamps were similar in design to those issued by Sardinia in 1855 but were perforated. The first complete issue inscribed 'Poste Italiane' was released on 1 December 1863. Venetia joined Italy in 1866 and the Papal States in 1870.

1871-1914

Having established the nation as a single entity, the govenment wished to establish its place among other Western nations. This led to the expansion of Italian interests in East and North Africa and the issue of overprinted stamps for various locations where other powers had offices.

In 1874 a general issue was made for POs in the Turkish Empire and POs were opened at Alexandria, Assab, La Goletta, Massowah, Susa, Tripoli and Tunis. The stamps were also used at the consular POs at Buenos Aires and Montevideo. On 10 July 1900 further overprints were issued for the Italian POs in Crete (q.v.). These were worded 'La Canea' and remained in use until the POs were closed on 30 December 1914.

Italian forces assisted in the relief of Peking during the Boxer Rising in China and unoverprinted Italian stamps were used from 21 January 1901. At the same time Italy was looking to increase its influence in the Levant area and further overprinted stamps for use in Albania were issued on 1 September 1902.

In 1908 Italy reorganized postal arrangements in the Levant. The Albanian surcharges were withdrawn and a general Levant surcharge replaced them. Further surcharges appeared for Constantinople and for other POs in Levant and Albania — Durazzo, Jamina, Jerusalem, Salonika, Scutari, Smyrna and Valona.

During the Italian-Turkish War of 1911-12 the Italians occupied the Dodecanese Islands (q.v.) in May 1912 and further overprinted stamps were issued for each of the 12 islands and Rhodes (Rodi). The islands were awarded to Italy, but this was not finally recognized until 1920.

1914-18

Italy did not enter the war immediately. In theory since 1882 it had been part of the Triple Alliance with Germany and Austria, but it wished to gain more territory in Trentino (South Tyrol). Italy entered the war on the side of the Allies on 23 May 1915.

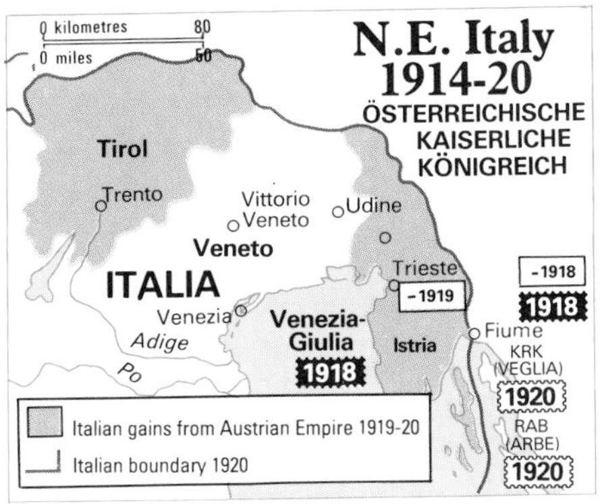
0 kilometres 80
0 miles 50
N.E. Italy
1914-20
ÖSTERREICHISCHE
KAISERLICHE
KÖNIGREICH
Tirol
Trento
Vittorio
Veneto
Udine
Veneto
ITALIA
Trieste
-1918
-1919
1918
Venezia
Adige
Po
Venezia-
Giulia
1918
Istria
Fiume
KRK
(VEGLIA)
1920
RAB
(ARBE)
1920
Italian gains from Austrian Empire 1919-20
Italian boundary 1920

After a series of minor offensives against the Austrians in the Trentino and Venezia Giulia areas, Italy was defeated by a combined German-Austrian force at Caporetto and its armies fell back to the line of the River Piave. The area north of this used stamps of Austria overprinted from 1 June 1918 to October that year.

British and other Allied forces were sent to assist, and in 1918 after the decisive victory of Vittorio Veneto the Allies occupied Trentino and Venezia Giulia (q.v.). Trentino was occupied by the Italians and overprinted stamps were used from 11 November 1918. A general issue for all occupied Austrian territory appeared in January 1919, but this was withdrawn in Trentino when the territory was awarded to Italy in September 1919, and Italian stamps were used thereafter. In September 1917 overprinted stamps were issued for use in China, at Peking and Tientsin.

1919-39

After World War I, Italy gained territory from Austria, particularly in the area of the Tyrol (Trentino) and Venezia Giulia. Stamps for these areas were issued on 11 November 1918. Trentino was awarded to Italy by the Treaty of St Germain on 10 September 1919 and Italian stamps were then used.

Italy closed its POs in China on 31

Alitalia
PRIMI VOLI AIRBUS FIRST FLIGHTS
ROMA AEROPORTO
-1.-7.80
ITALIA
ALITALIA
251, Regent Street
W1R 8AQ LONDON
Gran Bretagna

Above
Envelope and postmark specially issued to celebrate the first flight of Alitalia Airbus, 1 July 1980

Left
Post-box in a bell tower, Capri

December 1922.

Although a monarchy since unification in 1862, Italy was the first major European power to become a fascist dictatorship following the 'March on Rome' in October 1922.

In 1935, as part of plans for expansion in Africa, the Italians invaded Abyssinia (q.v). The war was successful but costly to Italian prestige, and in October 1936, after British pressure following Italy's action in Spain, the Italian-German Agreement was signed. Although this specifically related to Austria, it can be seen as the start of the Axis and, at this time, Germany recognized the conquest of Abyssinia.

On 7 April 1939 Italy invaded and captured Albania to consolidate control of the Adriatic Sea.

During the inter-war years Italy maintained control of the Dodecanese Islands and its occupation was recognized by the Greeks in August 1920. At the same time the island of Castelrosso was also transferred to Italy and overprinted stamps were issued on 11 July 1922.

1939-45

As Germany's ally, Italy declared war on 10 June 1940, just after France had retreated from the north-east of the country. Mussolini immediately attempted to gain control of the Mediterranean by an assault on Malta.

In October 1940 Italy invaded Greece from Albania and was driven back. As a result the Germans attacked through the Balkans and occupied Yugoslavia and Greece. Italy was given responsibility for part of this occupation and Italian overprints were issued for Slovenia, Fiume and Kupa, Brac and the Gulf of Kotor (q.v.). In Africa, Italian forces were gradually defeated and would have been destroyed but for German assistance in 1941. Following the collapse of the resistance in East Africa, the fall of Tunis and the invasion of Sicily and the mainland, Italy signed a secret armistice on 3 September 1943, which became effective on 8 September.

Italy was invaded by the Allies on 3 September 1943, but the Germans advanced south to meet their forces in the region of Naples and a prolonged action continued throughout the war. British, American and other Allied forces POs continued to operate until 1945.

On 17 September 1943 stamps for the Allied Military Government were issued in Sicily; further issues were released on 10 December 1943 for use in Naples. The Royal Italian Government was re-established at Brindisi in 1943 and moved to Salerno on 11 February 1944. At that time the control of the southern regions was transferred to them by the Allies. Stamps of Italy issued prior to this date were used.

On 23 September 1943 Mussolini proclaimed the Italian Social Republic at Salo on Lake Garda. The Republican government administered those parts of Italy north of the fighting zone which was occupied by Germany. Overprinted stamps were used from February 1944. Various overprints were used and these were withdrawn in April 1945 when the Royalist government was re-established.

• Campione 1939-52

A small town on the shores of Lake Lugano, surrounded by Swiss Territory. It declared for the royalists in 1943, but could not obtain stamps from the south. Stamps for the territory were issued in 1944. They were valid for use in Campione and Switzerland only. Withdrawn in 1952 and since then Campione has used Swiss or Italian stamps depending on the route which the letter is to take.

1945 to date

After the end of World War II, Italy lost some territory to France in the Savoy area and at the head of the Adriatic Sea (see Venezia Giulia and Trieste).

The Dodecanese Islands were transferred to Greece on 31 March 1947; Castelrosso was also transferred on 15 September the same year.

In June 1944 King Victor Emmanuel, who had reigned since 1900, abdicated in favour of his son Umberto, who became Regent and then King of Italy. On 10 June 1946 a republic was formed and Umberto abdicated. The first stamps of the republic were issued on 31 October 1946.

Italy is a member of NATO and of the EEC, which it joined on its formation.

• Italian issues for occupied Austrian territory 1919-39

FIRST STAMPS ISSUED 1 January 1919

CURRENCY	
1918	100 heller = 1 krone
1918	100 centesimi = 1 lira
1919	100 centesimi = 1 corona

Venezia Giulia, Dalmatia and Trentino, which had been occupied by the Italians in 1918, all used the same issue of overprinted Italian stamps from January 1919 until their allocation was decided by the Peace Treaties. These stamps were withdrawn from each territory in turn and the last were withdrawn in Dalmatia when it re-issued its own stamps in February 1921.

• Dalmatia

CURRENCY	
1919	100 centesimi = 1 corona

Before 1939

Province of the Austrian Empire occupied by the Italians in 1918. It included the port of Zara.

Stamps were issued for the Italian occupation in May 1919. These were replaced amost immediately by the general issue for the Italian occupation of Austrian territory (q.v.). In November 1920 Italy gave up the area except for Zara, and in February 1921 issued stamps for Zaro only, overprinted in local currency. These stamps were withdrawn in 1923, after which Italian stamps were used. The balance of the area was awarded to Yugoslavia. (*See also* Dalmatia *under* Yugoslavia).

• Venezia Giulia 1914-18

FIRST STAMPS Austria up to 1918
FIRST STAMPS ISSUED 14 November 1918

CURRENCY	
1945	As Italy

Area which includes the cities of Trieste, Gorizia, Fiume and the Istrian peninsula; it was part of the Austrian Empire and was occupied by the Italians after the defeat of the Austrians at the battle of Vittorio Veneto and the armistice of 3 November 1918. The area was awarded to Italy in 1919.

Overprinted Austrian stamps were used until 1919 and Italian stamps for the occupation of all occupied Austrian territory were issued in January 1919. From April 1919 until the end of World War II the area used Italian stamps.

1945 to date

Following the withdrawal of Yugoslav forces and the agreement of Belgrade on 9 June 1945, the area came under the control of the Supreme Allied Commanders and was administered by the Allied Military Government.

Overprinted stamps were issued on 22 September 1945 and remained in use until 10 February 1947, when the area, except Gorizia and the Free State of Trieste (q.v.), became part of Yugoslavia.

Further south, the area of Fiume and all the Istrian peninsula, excluding Pola, were placed under Yugoslav military control and special stamps for this region were released on 15 August 1945. The area was returned to Yugoslavia in February 1947 (*See also* Fiume and Kupa *under* Yugoslavia).

• Fiume 1914-18

FIRST STAMPS Austria to 1918
FIRST STAMPS ISSUED 3 December 1918, overprinted on stamps of Hungary

Above
Vatican City Guards

Left
P&O steamer westbound from Alexandria unloading mail at Brindisi, Italy, 1920s

CURRENCY

1918	100 filler = 1 krone
1919	100 centosmi = 1 corona
1920	100 centesimi = 1 lira

Austro-Hungarian seaport and naval base on the Istrian Peninsula. Occupied by Allied forces after the collapse of the Austrian Empire on 17 November 1918.

1919-39

Continued to issue overprinted stamps until seized by Italian volunteers on 12 September 1919 and declared the Italian Regency of Carnaro. Stamps issued on 20 September 1919.

By the Treaty of Rapallo between Italy and Yugoslavia, Fiume was declared a Free State and Italian troops entered the city on 24 December 1920. Stamps were again issued for the new political arrangement by overprinting the issues of the Regency on 2 February 1921.

Incorporated into Italy from 22 February 1924 and, to commemorate this, stamps of the Free State were overprinted and issued on the date of incorporation. After this set the stamps of Italy were used until July 1945.

During the Regency of Carnaro, stamps were also issued in November 1920 for the islands of Arbe and Veglia (now Rab and Krk). Withdrawn on 24 December 1920.

1939-45

FIRST STAMPS ISSUED 26 July 1945

Italian naval base captured by Yugoslav patriots in 1944-5

In July 1945 stamps of Italy were issued overprinted for use in Fiume.

Stamps withdrawn when the stamps of the Allied Military Government, Venezia Giulia, were issued in September.

• Istria
1939-45

FIRST STAMPS ISSUED 1 July 1945

CURRENCY

1945	As Italy

Italian province, formerly part of the Austrian Empire, largely occupied by Yugoslav partisans in 1943-4.

In June 1945 stamps of Italy were issued overprinted for use in this area, including Pola.

Withdrawn when the stamps for the Allied Military Government, Venezia Giulia were issued in September.

• Trieste
1939-45

FIRST STAMPS Austria to 1919 and Italian 1919-1945
FIRST STAMPS ISSUED Italy overprinted 15 June 1945
Used until stamps of Trieste were issued in 1947

CURRENCY

Zona A	1947	As Italy
Zone B	1948	As Italy
	1948	As Yugoslavia

Part of the Austrian Empire until after World War I. In 1919 the province of Istria, which included the town of Trieste, was ceded to Italy.

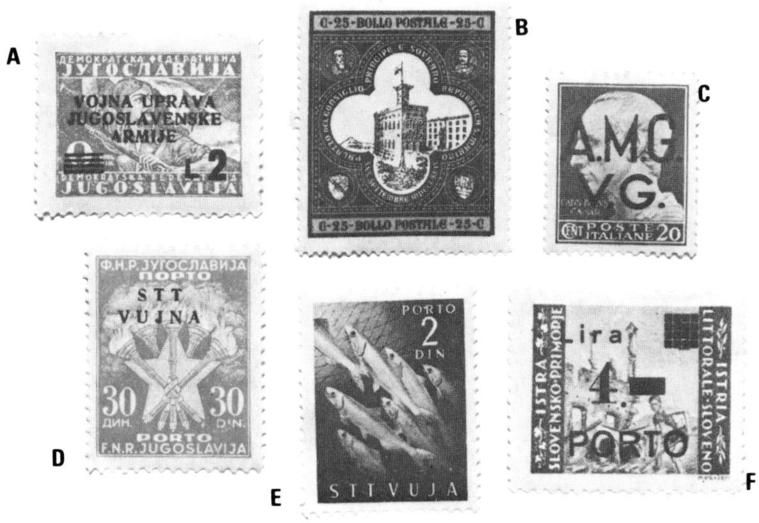
A
B
C
D
E
F
VOJNA UPRAVA JUGOSLAVENSKE ARMIJE
JUGOSLAVIJA
A.M.G. V.G.
POSTE ITALIANE 20
STT VUJNA
PORTO
F.N.R. JUGOSLAVIJA
PORTO 2 DIN
STT VUJA
ISTRA SLOVENSKO-PRIMORJE
ISTRIA LITTORALE SLOVENO
PORTO

A Venezia Giulia: Yugoslav Government 1947; **B** San Marino 1894; **C** Venezia Giulia Allied Government 1945; **D** Yugoslav Zone of Trieste 1949; **E** Yugoslav Zone of Trieste 1950: **F** Venezia Giulia: Yugoslav Government 1946.

Yugoslav partisans attacked cities in Venezia Giulia and Istria in the last days of the war. Trieste was captured on 30 April 1945 and was finally liberated for the Allies by the New Zealand Division on 2 May.

1945-75

Created a Free Territory by the Treaty of Paris in February 1947, it consisted of two zones.

Zone A included the City of Trieste and was administered by an Allied Military Government.

FIRST STAMPS Austrian to 1919, Italian 1919-45, Italian overprints 1945-6
FIRST STAMPS ISSUED 1 October 1947

Stamps of Italy overprinted AMG VG were used until the AMG FTT overprints were introduced on 1 October 1947. These were withdrawn in November 1954.

Zone B included the remainder of the region and was controlled by a Yugoslav Military Government. Initially in 1948 stamps with Italian currency were issued but overprinted Yugoslav stamps were introduced in 1949.

Trieste 1920-54
Italian-Yugoslav boundary 1920
Free City of Trieste 1947
Italian-Yugoslav boundary 1954
ÖSTERREICH
Lubiana
Udine
Gorizia
Vittoria Veneto
ITALIA
JUGOSLAVIJA
Hrvatska
Trieste
A 1947
B 1948
1949
1919-1945
1945
Venezia
1921
1924
Rijeka (Fiume)
(Free City 1920-4)
1945
Istria
1945
KRK
Pula (Pola)
CRES
RAB
Adriatic Sea
0 kilometres 80
0 miles 50

FIRST STAMPS Austrian to 1919 and Italian 1919-47
FIRST STAMPS ISSUED 1 May 1948

Yugoslav stamps were first issued on 15 August 1949. Use of these stamps ceased on 25 October 1954. The following day, under a Four Power Agreement, Zone A (except for three small villages) became Italian and Zone B (and the three villages) became Yugoslav. This final agreement was confirmed by Italy and Yugoslavia in 1974.

San Marino

FIRST STAMPS Papal States 1850 to 1870, Italy 1870-7
FIRST STAMPS ISSUED 1 August 1877

CURRENCY

1877 100 centesimi = 1 lira

According to tradition the oldest republic still in existence, San Marino is believed to have been founded in the 4th century by Marinus, an escaped stone-cutter who was avoiding religious persecution.

The republic was an enclave in the Papal States and used the stamps of that region from 1850.

San Marino has continued to issue stamps since 1877 and was not occupied during World War II.

Vatican City

FIRST STAMPS Italy from 1870 to 1929
FIRST STAMPS ISSUED 1 August 1929

CURRENCY

1929 100 centesimi = 1 lira

By the Lateran Treaty of 11 February 1929 the temporal power which the Pope had lost in 1870 was restored by the creation of the state of Vatican City in the heart of Rome.

The Vatican has continued to issue stamps throughout the ensuing years and has remained the temporal base of the Pope.

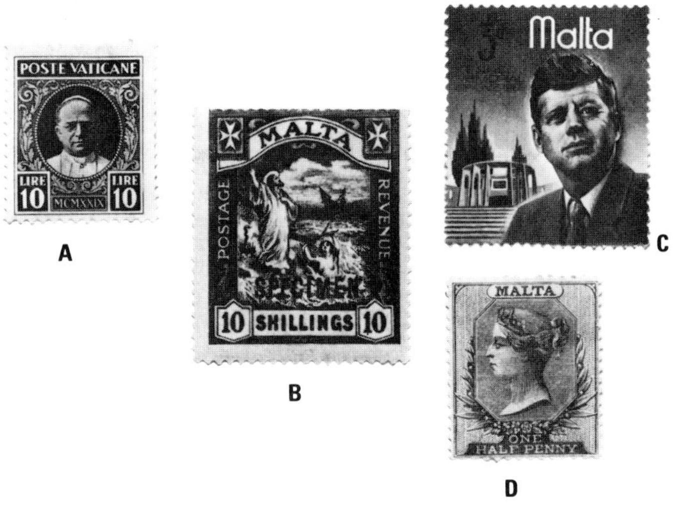
POSTE VATICANE
LIRE 10
MCMXXIX
LIRE 10
A
MALTA
POSTAGE
REVENUE
10 SHILLINGS 10
B
Malta
C
MALTA
ONE HALF PENNY
D

A Vatican 1929; **B** Malta:Crown Colony 1922; **C** Malta:Self-Governing 1966; **D** Malta:Crown Colony 1860.

Malta

CURRENCY

1860	sterling
1972	10 mils = 1 cent
	100 cents = £Maltese

Before 1650

Group of islands lying about 60 miles south of Sicily. In 1530 Charles V, Emperor of Germany and King of Spain, gave the islands to the Knights of St John after they had been driven from Rhodes. The Knights made a successful defence of the island against the Turks in 1551 and 1556. Letters of the 17th century are not uncommon and deal with supplies of material either to or from the island.

1793-1815

The Knights maintained control of the island for over 200 years and it was not until Napoleon was making his invasion of Egypt that the island fell to the French in 1798. Malta surrendered to the British in 1800.

By 1806 the British authorities had established a packet agency to deal with external mail, particularly for the garrison. This was operated by the government from Falmouth. Because of its location Malta was a centre of disinfection for mail carried through the Mediterranean.

1815-50

Continued to use handstruck marks even after Britain issued stamps in 1840.

Packet service from Falmouth was transferred from the government to the Peninsular Line in 1835, though this continued to operate from Falmouth until 1862. Special cancellations were introduced for disinfected mail including one which read 'Purifie au Lazaret, Malte'. By 1849 a local postal service had been introduced and was administered by the local authorities.

1850-71

FIRST STAMPS British stamps 1854
FIRST STAMPS ISSUED 1 December 1860

In 1854, and possibly earlier, British stamps were placed on sale in Malta and numeral 'A25' was allocated for the cancellation of adhesives as well as the letter 'M' in an oval of bars. The use of British adhesives continued until the PO was handed over to colonial administration in 1885. Although British stamps continued to be used for overseas mail, a *½d* stamp for the local post was introduced in 1860 and was used concurrently with British stamps.

The P & O service had continued to grow and Malta continued to be one of the main ports of call during the run through the Mediterranean.

1871-1914

Malta took control of its own postal affairs on 1 January 1885. The *½d* adhesive issued in 1860 and the British adhesives were withdrawn at that time and a new set was issued on 1 January 1885. The internal postal service within Malta increased and by 1914 there were 36 sub-offices.

1914-18

Malta was an important base for the Royal Navy during World War I. It continued to use its own stamps, but the size of the garrison led to a large increase in Forces' mail.

1919-39

Moved towards independence and in 1922 was granted self-government. However, the economic problems were such that this status was untenable and Malta reverted to a Crown Colony.

In 1928 Malta developed a feeder service to link into the London-Karachi service. In 1931 this was extended to provide services to Genoa and Tripoli.

Far left
Postmen at the Swedish post office in Hamburg, c.1840

Left
Norwegian postman and his carriole, c.1880

1939-45

During World War II Malta was under constant attack from mid-1940 to 1943. For the gallantry of the population and the garrison, the island was awarded the George Cross. To begin with the posts were very disrupted and it was difficult to maintain contact with Britain. About May 1943 Malta was included in the Middle East forces and troops were no longer allowed to use Maltese stamps. British stamps, unoverprinted, were used in Field POs.

1945 to date

FIRST STAMPS AS AN INDEPENDENT COUNTRY ISSUED
21 September 1964

After the first failure in the 1920s, Malta was again granted self-government in November 1948. This continued until 1964 when independence was granted.

Malta continues as an independent country within the Commonwealth.

Sweden

CURRENCY

1855	48 skilling banio = 1 riksdaler
1858	100 ore = 1 riksdaler
1875	100 ore = 1 krona

Before 1815

Kingdom in northern Europe which in the 17th and 18th centuries was the most powerful of the Scandinavian countries. Union of Sweden with Norway and Denmark, which had been created in the 14th century, was dissolved in 1523 when Gustavus Vasa became Gustavus I. Denmark retained control of some of the southern mainland and the island of Gotland, but, when Gustavus Adolphus came to the throne in 1611, the country quickly gained strength. During the Thirty Years War battles were won against Denmark, Russia and Poland. Sweden gained territory in Europe and its foundations as a major power in the Baltic area were laid.

Gustavus Adolphus was killed at the Battle of Lutzen in 1632 and was succeeded by his daughter. She abdicated in favour of her cousin Charles X in 1654. Swedish power grew over the next 50 years.

Postal service was established in 1636. At first, letters bore handstamps with the letter B or F for 'paid' or 'free'. By 1700 Stockholm had introduced a straight-line marking and this service was extended throughout the country with handstamps for all the major towns.

In the 18th century a system of attaching feathers to the seals of letters was introduced to indicate the need for speed in the carriage of letters. This method was unique to Sweden.

After the death of Charles XII in 1718 Sweden lost much of its German territory but this was regained by the end of the century. During the Napoleonic wars Sweden was neutral but in November 1807 a Swedish division was sent to Lübeck in support of Prussia; it was intercepted by Marshal Bernadotte and the First Corps of the Grande Armée and forced to return to

Sweden. During 1808 Bernadotte was elected Crown Prince of Sweden and was allowed to accept.

In 1813 a Swedish army entered Germany and assisted in the defeat of Napoleon at Leipzig. Bernadotte then entered Holstein and forced Denmark to cede Norway to Sweden under the Treaty of Kiel (14 January 1814).

1815-50

In 1818 Bernadotte became King of Sweden as Charles XIV and ruled until he died in 1844, the only one of Napoleon's marshals to have founded a dynasty which exists to this day.

The post office in Sweden continued to develop and as well as its control of Norway also maintained a PO in Hamburg, which provided the main transfer point for outgoing mails.

1850-71

FIRST STAMPS ISSUED 1 July 1855

First issue contained the rarest of all European stamps, the 3 *skilling* error of colour. This stamp, printed in yellow instead of green, resulted from the incorrect value of one stamp being included in a full sheet of the 8 *skilling* version. Only one copy of this variation is known to exist. A local stamp was issued in Stockholm in 1856 and was valued at 1 *skilling*, though this was not engraved in the design. On 1 July 1858 the currency was changed to 100 *ore* = 1 *riksdaler* and a new issue of stamps in the new currency appeared on that day.

1871 to date

In October 1905 the union with Norway was repealed and the latter became a separate nation. Although stamp issues had been separate, the two postal services had developed together and similarities existed. Sweden remained neutral throughout both world wars and has not joined either of the main alliances since that date.

Norway

Before 1871

FIRST STAMPS ISSUED 1 January 1855

CURRENCY	
1855	120 skilling = 1 speciedaler
1877	100 ore = 1 krone

Kingdom of Scandinavia united with Sweden from 1814 until 1905. There were many changes in the alignment and dependence of the Scandinavian countries in the Middle Ages. Norway was united with Denmark and Sweden under Queen Margaret in 1389. Sweden and Norway separated from Denmark in 1448 but reunited again about two years later. Denmark and Norway separated from Sweden in 1513 and remained thus until the Napoleonic period.

In 1814, as a result of the support given to the allies by Marshal Bernadotte after he became Crown Prince, Norway was awarded to Sweden by the Treaty of Kiel. However, the Norwegians declared their independence and the Swedes had to exert their control by military occupation. Order was restored in 1815 and Norway became a province under the Swedish crown.

Norway's first postal service had begun in 1647, but this was little more than a means for the different parts of the country to report to the central government. However, after 1814 the postal service was reorganized independently of Denmark or Sweden. Christiana (Oslo) had been built in 1624 and it now became the postal centre. In the following years a number of postal routes were established; these linked all the parts of the country together and also allowed for entry into other European postal systems.

Postal markings were first introduced in 1845 when a cancellation was used at Christiana. These markings were extended to other towns during the next few years.

When stamps were first issued, a series of numeral cancellations were introduced to indicate the office of use. Numbers up to 383 are known over the next few years, and make a study in themselves.

1871-1914

In 1905 the union with Sweden was dissolved and Norway became independent in October. King Haakon VII acceded to the throne on 18 November. At this time an early form of prepayment of letters by placing coins in a slot began at Christiana. This was successful and, although they were not used for mail overseas, it began a system which eventually led to meter mail being accepted by the UPU in 1922.

Norway remained neutral during World War I.

1919 to date

Norway maintained its neutrality and non-alignment during the period between the wars. Its postal service continued to develop on modern lines, a maritime coastal service was built up and an internal airmail service.

Despite the policy of neutrality, Norway was invaded by Germany early in April 1940 and a joint British and French force was sent to northern Norway. It was accompanied by Field POs. The Allied force was withdrawn in June 1940.

Stamps were issued during the German occupation, the first appearing on 4 October 1940. These were demonetized in May 1945 when the country was liberated.

The Norwegian government-in-exile in London issued stamps for use by the Norwegian navy and merchant service. They were also used in Jan Mayern Island, northern Norway, and from February 1945 at the Norwegian PO in Stockholm. This same set was released in Norway after liberation in June 1945.

Since World War II Norway has been a member of NATO, but elected not to join the EEC in 1973.

A Norway:King Oscar I 1856; **B** Sweden:King Gustav V 1919; **C** Sweden:First Issue 1855; **D** Sweden:King Gustav V 1921; **E** Norway:King Haakon VII 1937; **E** Norway:King Olav V 1978; **G** King Carl XVI Gustav 1974.

A
B
C
D
E
F
G
NORGE
SVERIGE
KUNGL.POST
25 öre
NORGE
KONG OLAV V
NORGE 1.00
75 SVERIGE

Denmark

CURRENCY

1857	96 rigsbank skilling = 1 rigsdaler
1875	100 ore = 1 krone

Before 1850

Smallest of the Scandinavian countries in modern times, Denmark holds a strategic position at the entrance to the Baltic Sea. Having exercised control over most of the British Isles in the 10th and 11th centuries, the exploring and raiding tendencies of the Danes were thereafter restricted. They fought several unprofitable European wars in the Middle Ages and from the 17th century the internal problems of the country became acute. From the 15th century Denmark, Sweden and Norway were linked under one sovereign until 1523, when Sweden separated from the other two. Denmark and Norway were a single kingdom until 1814, when Norway was annexed by Sweden.

A royal mail service was established in 1624. Postal markings began to appear in the 17th century. There were many different types of marking, including some which incorporated distances in miles used to calculate the charges.

In the early 18th century, under Frederick IV, Denmark occupied Schleswig-Holstein, Touringen and Stralsund on the south coast of the Baltic. This was extended to include most of Pomerania. Denmark held aloof from the later wars of the 18th century and formed the 'Armed Neutrality' in 1780 with Russia and Sweden. This lasted for one year only, and was designed as a confederation against Britain's claim to have the right to board ships at sea. The Armed Neutrality was re-formed in December 1800 against the British maritime system and breached the blockade of Napoleon's Europe. War broke out and the Danish fleet was destroyed by Admirals Parker and Nelson in 1801. Further wars led to the surrender of the Danish fleet in 1807, and in 1814, under the Treaty of Kiel, Pomerania and Ruger were gained by Denmark but were ceded to Prussia in 1815, in return for Lauenberg, a duchy in north Germany. At the same time Norway was ceded to Sweden.

In 1848 problems occurred over Schleswig-Holstein, with an uprising supported by the Prussians. War ensued, but an uncertain peace was agreed in 1850.

1850 to date

FIRST STAMPS ISSUED 1 April 1851

First Danish stamps were printed in a square format. The introduction of adhesives led to an expansion of the postal service; new values were required and a different design was released in 1854. The stamps were cancelled with numeral cancellations to indicate the town of origin.

The problems of Schleswig-Holstein (q.v.) continued during the 1850s, largely encouraged by Prussia. In 1864, with Austria as ally, Prussia invaded the twin duchies and after a short war both Schleswig and Holstein were annexed by Prussia.

In World War I Denmark remained neutral, but after the war the northern part of Schleswig voted to return to Denmark.

In World War II Denmark was invaded by Germany in April 1940 and was occupied until 1945. During the German occupation existing Danish stamps continued to be used and no special overprints were produced.

After the collapse of Germany, the Danish government quickly established control and normal postal services resumed. Denmark joined NATO in 1949 and the EEC in 1973.

Faroe Islands

FIRST STAMPS Danish from 1870
FIRST STAMPS ISSUED 30 January 1975

CURRENCY

1975	As Denmark

Group of islands between Scotland and Denmark which became part of the Danish kingdom in 1380.

ISLAND
16 AUR
PJONUSTU
POSTFRIM.
GRØNLAND
1 ØRE KGL·POST 1 ØRE
SURTSEY APRÍL 1964
ÍSLAND 2 00 KR
A
B
C

A Iceland: Danish Colony 1876; **B** Greenland: Danish Colony 1938; **C** Iceland: Republic 1965.

POSTVERK FØROYA
1. APRÍL 1976
FØROYAR 160
DANMARK 70
1941 SUOMI
MANNERHEIM
50p FINLAND
DANMARK
15
ØRE ØRE
POSTFRIMÆRKE
2 RIGSBANK SKILLING
20 PENNIÄ 20
SUOMI
FINLAND
A
B
C
D
E
F

A Denmark: Queen Margarethe 1974; **B** Faroe Island: Flag of the Faroes 1976; **C** Finland: Republic 1941; **D** Finland: Duchy of Russia 1875; **E** Denmark: King Christian X 1913; **F** Denmark: First Issue 1851.

Recognizable by the postmarks, Danish stamps were used until the British occupation in 1940. During 1919 bisected 4 *ore* value and a 2 *ore* on 5 *ore* surchage were issued during a temporary shortage of the 7 *ore* stamp.

In May 1940 occupied by British forces following the invasion of Denmark by the Germans. British Field POs were used until 1945 and some special surcharges on Danish stamps also appeared. From 1945 to 1975 Danish stamps were again used in the islands.

In 1948 the islands were given self-government within the Danish kingdom and stamps for the islands were issued in 1975.

Greenland

FIRST STAMPS ISSUED 1905

CURRENCY	
1938	As Denmark

A Danish colony formed from early missionary stations established in the 18th century. By 1900 the population was 10,000 and, although letters were carried free of charge, parcels were not and special stamps were issued in 1905.

Parcel post stamps continued to be used until 1 December 1938, when the first postage stamps were issued.

During World War II Greenland became a US protectorate while Denmark was occupied by the Germans. Following liberation, one set for Greenland was printed by the American Bank Note Co. but it was quickly replaced by the former definitive issue, when it became available from Denmark.

On 9 June 1953 Greenland became part of the Danish kingdom and has remained so ever since.

Iceland

FIRST STAMPS Denmark from March 1870

Numerals 236 and 237 were allocated to Reykjavik and Seydisfjordur respectively.

FIRST STAMPS ISSUED 1 January 1873

CURRENCY	
1873	96 skilling = 1 riksdaler
1876	100 aurar = 1 krone

An independent island republic in the North Atlantic. Iceland's parliament is the oldest in Europe having been formed in AD 930. The Tynwald in the Isle of Man (q.v) makes a similar claim, but the latter is not fully independent.

Came under the control of Denmark in the 13th century, but for many years its main contact with the outside world was through trade with Scotland and England. This became particularly important when the Danish coast was blockaded during the Napoleonic wars.

In 1776 a postal system was established in Iceland by royal decree. An annual mail-boat service between Reykjavik and Copenhagen was introduced two years later and gradually this service was extended. By 1858 sea trips were being made between April and November each year.

Internal mail in Iceland developed during the same period. However, the

KONGELIG
POSTGAARD

TROND ALBRIGTSEN
ANITA PEDERSEN
SKANSEGT 4
POST

Norwegian post-boxes

Royal Mail coach, Denmark, c.1850

terrain was too difficult to permit a service comparable to that in mainland Europe. By 1831 letters were delivered eight times a year on the west coast route, but it was not until 1849 that the demand for the service had generated a complete network.

The system was rapidly reorganized and 13 further POs were opened. In 1875 Iceland joined the UPU as a Danish possession. This was followed in 1876 by a new currency for Iceland alone. In 1918 Iceland became an independent constitutional monarchy under the Danish crown.

The first airmails in the island began in 1928. This was the easiest means of transporting mail internally and many small and local services were inaugurated.

During World War II, commencing in May 1940, British, and later American, forces garrisoned the island against possible German bases being established. Field POs of both countries were used. British FPOs were withdrawn in February 1943.

Iceland was declared an independent republic in May 1944, following a plebiscite. It has remained thus ever since and has maintained close links with Western Europe.

Finland (Suomi)

CURRENCY

1856	100 kopecks = 1 rouble
1865	100 penpi = 1 Finnish markka
1963	100 (old) marks = 1 (new) marks

Before 1850

Republic in northern Europe between Sweden and Russia, which had been under the control of one or other of its more powerful neighbours until the Bolshevik Revolution in Russia in 1917. Stamps of the country are inscribed 'Suomi' meaning 'The land of fens and lakes'.

Sweden conquered Finland in the 13th century. Under Swedish overlordship, Finland retained an autonomous government but was used as a buffer against the Russians, who, increasingly, harassed the Eastern frontier. In 1721 Peter the Great gained territory in the area of Vyborg. At the end of the Swedish-Russian War of 1808-9, Sweden ceded the rest of Finland to Russia and it became a grand duchy under the Tsar. The country retained its autonomous constitution.

A public postal service in Finland was introduced two years after the Swedish service, in 1638. The main route ran from Stockholm to Helsinki, and from there to the River Neva in Russia and south to the Baltic provinces. Eventually, the Finnish postal service was extended to all the ports round the Gulf of Bothnia.

After the formation of the grand duchy under Russia, foreign mail to and from Finland was routed through St Petersburg. In 1812 Finland's postal service was reorganized on Russian lines and the first handstruck postal markings were introduced. These were straight-line name stamps without a date and included the district name in Russian (Cyrillic) letters. Similar types but using the Roman alphabet were introduced in 1847. Stamped stationery was issued by Finland in 1845 and showed the coat-of-arms of the duchy on the back flap.

1850-71

FIRST STAMPS ISSUED 3 March 1856

First stamps were typographed in the Finnish Treasury and pre-dated the issue of Russian stamps by two years. The currency was Russian, but this was changed to Finnish currency in 1866. Printing of stamps continued in Finland until one issue of 1875, which for one value of a new design was printed in Copenhagen.

1871-1914
Increasing Russian influence in Finland was reflected by the new designs in 1889. These were similar to previous designs, but had the name in Russian instead of Finnish. In 1891 stamps were printed in Russia at St Petersburg and Russian currency was reintroduced. This move was short-lived and in 1895 Finnish currency was finally adopted.

1914-39
During World War I Finland supported Russia until the Bolshevik Revolution threatened. On 20 July 1917 Finland declared its independence from Russia, and this was confirmed by parliament on 6 December. First stamps for the independent country appeared on 1 October 1917. Finnish Communists or 'Red Guards' seized Helsinki on 23 January 1918 and a civil war broke out. The Communists were defeated following German intervention in April. Finnish independence was finally gained on 14 October 1920.

Finland remained uncommitted during the inter-war years and, with the rise of Hitler's power, tried to maintain a balance between Germany and Russia.

• Finnish occupation of Aunus
The Russian town of Olonetz, close to the Finnish border, was briefly occupied by Finland in 1919. Overprinted stamps of Finland were issued on 27 June 1919 but the area was soon recaptured by the Bolsheviks.

1939-45
Following the partition of Poland in September 1939, the Russians began to consolidate their position. Defence pacts and bases were negotiated with the Baltic states and in November the Russians demanded the occupation of the southern portion of the Karelian isthmus and other islands as a main base area. Finland refused and war broke out. After a successful defence for several months, Finland capitulated on 12 March 1940. Russia made peace on the acceptance of its original demands.

Following the invasion of Russia by Germany in June 1941, Finland allied itself with Germany and advanced down the Karelian isthmus to the original frontier. The Finnish army refused to advance further. However, when the Russians began their offensive to drive the Germans from their territory, they also attacked Finland. In September 1944 Finland made a truce with Russia and peace followed. As a result of its action on the side of Germany, at the end of the war Finland lost territory to Russia, in particular the Karelian isthmus and parts on the northern border.

Overprinted stamps were issued in 1943 for the military field post and these replaced an earlier imperforate issue of 1941.

• Finnish occupation of eastern Karelia
From 1941 to 1944 Finland occupied an area which had been lost during the war with Russia in 1939-40. Finnish stamps were overprinted and issued on 1 October 1941. Regained by Russia in 1945.

1945 to date
Finland has remained an independent republic since World War II. Its proximity to Russia has meant that it has been unable to be fully pro-western, but the Communist Party of Finland was banned in 1930 and it has not been allowed to take a major part in government.

However, Finland has not joined either of the main power organizations and still maintains its independence. It joined the European Free Trade Area (EFTA) in 1967.

• North Ingermanland
A Russian territory adjoining Finland between Lake Ludoga and the Gulf of Finland, which refused to accept the revolutionary government of Russia. It declared its independence and issued stamps. The revolt was quickly suppressed by Russian troops and has been part of Russia ever since.

Russia

CURRENCY

1858 100 kopeks = 1 rouble
German occupation of Russia 1941 As Germany

Before 1650
In early times an assembly of minor states under the central control of St Petersburg (now Leningrad), and then an empire until 1917. Had its beginnings with the establishment of the waterway between the Baltic and the Black Sea. This chain of lakes and rivers was the eastern defence of the Slav people against the incursions of Mongols and Tartars from the east. The Slavs were mainly settled in the areas of Novgorod in the north and Kiev in the south which both came under the control of the Vikings in the 9th century. By the 10th century a new nation based on these areas had arisen. Its people were Slavic but they were ruled by Varangian (Nordic) princes.

The first nation, based on Kiev, included most of what is now known as European Russia. Gradually the importance of Kiev waned and central control was dispersed by the growth of small states. This trend made invasion from the east much easier and, having

OH-CFW

Left
Seaplane delivering post in the Finnish lakelands

Middle
Collecting post by dog sleigh across a frozen lake in Finnmark, North Norway

YAMAHA

Right
Lapp collecting his post on a snowmobile

held the Mongols at bay for many centuries, Russia fell to the Mongol Empire in 1237-41. The only part to remain independent of the invaders was Novgorod.

The earliest postal service dates from the 11th century, which is much earlier than anywhere else in Europe. A number of letters written on birch bark have been found in and around Novgorod. These date from 1025 to 1055 and seem to carry messages of a largely personal or commercial nature. Although it is impossible to be certain, it would seem that an organized postal system existed and that literacy was at a much higher level than elsewhere in Europe. Letter carriers would have travelled by horse or cart or by boat on the rivers of the great waterway. Rules for the mail carriers were drawn up in the 13th century and those conveying military information were allowed to travel without limitation of cost or distance.

During the 15th century the power of the Mongol Empire began to wane and in south and east Russia it broke up into small territories. As the Mongols declined in power, so the Russians began to form themselves into a new nation based on Vladimir (now Moscow). Led by Ivan the Great, the Russians threw off the last remnants of Mongol control in 1481.

Russia's expansion continued during the following centuries. Eastward expansion into Siberia began in the 16th century. The colonization of Asian Russia continued in the 17th and 18th centuries. In the west, wars continued with Sweden and Poland, and in the south with the Turks and Persians.

The postal service in this period grew to meet the needs of the expanding territory. The Tartars did not interfere with the service which had already been established. They seem to have realized the importance of the link for the transfer of intelligence and commercial information. Post roads were established, and during the reign of Ivan the Great (1440-1505) the postal department was given its own centralized control and placed on an official basis. By 1526 it is reported that the mails could travel up to 125 miles per day. During the 16th century a new office was established which organized the post villages, and a tax was raised to pay for the service. This office, the Yamskoi Prikaz, or postcoachman's office, was also responsible for recruiting coachmen for the mail-coaches.

In the middle of the 17th century postmen were recruited from the literate coachmen. They wore a special uniform and were responsible for the delivery of mail. It is probable that during this period the Russian post was better organized than that elsewhere in Europe.

1650-1793

A period of extension and consolidation for Russia, much under the control of Peter the Great (ruled 1682-9 jointly with his brother and 1689-1725 by himself). He was the first Emperor of all the Russias and took his title in 1721. The early part of the 18th century was marred by a major war with Sweden which ended with defeat for the Swedes at Pultowa in 1709. This was followed by a war with Turkey, a near disaster, and thereafter Peter concentrated on extending Russian dominions in northern Europe, including Estonia, Lithuania and Finland.

In 1668 a statute of international postal communications was introduced. Initially this connected Moscow and Riga but was shortly extended to include Poland as well. As in Britain, this foreign service was maintained separately from the internal service. However, because of distance and hardship, the cost of the carriage of mail was high. It is reported that the cost of a letter from Moscow to Siberia in 1698 was 2 roubles.

The post was reorganized by Peter the Great, who closed down much of the earlier internal postal service, and a new main PO was opened in St Petersburg to which Peter had moved his capital.

In 1783, under the Empress Catherine II, a standard postage rate was established for the whole of Russia. The management of a single postal service was established at the same time.

The first Russian postal markings appeared in 1766. Initially they showed the name of the town with or without a frame and these were used only on mail abroad. Early letters were marked in French but, later, bilingual wording in German and Russian was introduced.

1793-1815

In 1772 the break-up of Poland had been initiated by the Russians, Prussians and Austrians. This was completed in 1795 when Russia moved its western boundary to the River Bug.

In 1798 Russia signed a treaty with Austria and Britain; an army was sent to Italy, which helped check the French advance. However, the French gained the upper hand and the troops were withdrawn. For a short period Russia was at war with Britain, but after the Peace of 1801 Tsar Alexander joined the coalition against France in 1805.

The Allies were defeated at Austerlitz and in 1807 the Russians signed the Treaty of Tilsit and withdrew from the war. In 1808-9 Russia gained control of Finland from Sweden. France invaded Russia in June 1812 and advanced to Moscow by September. The Russians burned Moscow on 14 September and the famous retreat began in October. The loss of the Grande Armée as a result of this campaign began the fall of Napoleon. The Russians advanced into Europe in 1813 and Tsar Alexander was present when the Allies entered Paris in March 1814.

By the beginning of the 19th century Russia had 458 POs and more than 5000 officials. Postal rates were reduced and the volume of letters increased — the same was to happen in Britain in 1840. The single service which had been introduced in the 1780s brought greater efficiency to the Russian mail system, but the enormous distances involved made it difficult for overall control to be maintained. Contracts were made with private concerns throughout the country for the establishment of additional local postal services where these were required.

The postmarks at this time began to show the date of acceptance into the postal service. Many shapes were used and colours varied.

1815-50

In the period following the Congress of Vienna, Russia consolidated its hold on the area gained. However, expansion still took place and war began with Persia in 1826. When this campaign was completed in 1828, war was declared on the Ottoman Empire. Both campaigns helped stabilize the southern frontier of the growing nation.

In 1830 Poland rose and tried to regain its independence but the uprising was suppressed by the Russian army in 1831. In 1849 Russia again

A
B
C
D
ПОЧТА
4к СССР

A Russia:USSR 1925; **B** Russia:Kingdom 1913; **C** Russia:USSR; **D** Russia:Kingdom 1883.

intervened in Europe and assisted the Austrians to put down the Hungarian revolt.

Postal services throughout Europe were beginning to take on their present form, and the Russian service was no exception. The old post roads fell into disuse following the construction of railways and the greater use of steamers on the rivers. Control of POs was transferred to a new ministry in 1819 but became independent in the 1830s. Prepaid envelopes appeared in Russia in 1845. They had first been used in Finland and were sufficiently successful for use to be extended to Moscow in 1846 and throughout the nation in 1848.

1850-71

> **FIRST STAMPS ISSUED** 1 January 1858

Russia began further agitations against Turkey in 1853. Though these revolved around the Orthodox and Ro-

Russian postmen loading mailbags onto sledges, 1905

man Catholic churches in Palestine and who should have control of the 'Holy Places', they were also a ruse to allow the Russians to give more support to the Slav people of the Balkans. The French and British sided with Turkey and, after war broke out in November 1853, an expeditionary force was sent to the Crimea. The Crimean War ended in 1856 and the Allied force, which by then included Sardinia (q.v.), evacuated the Crimea on 9 July 1856.

Printed in the state printing works at St Petersburg, the first issue of 1 January 1858 was imperforate. On 10 January 1858 perforated examples were issued. Preparatory work for the introduction of these stamps had started in 1850. In 1855 some suggested designs had been submitted, and the first essays appeared in 1856. These were approved by the Tsar in October 1857 after the department had made some major improvements in the production method. Although stamps were first issued on 1 January in European Russia and Siberia, they were not available in the Caucasus or Transcaucasia until two months later.

In 1865 the first Zemstvo, or local stamps, were issued (q.v.).

In the twenty years following the Crimean War there was a great surge in the building of railways and this speeded the transmission of mail. By 1876 the total length of Russia's railways was almost 11,800 miles.

1871-1914

The growth of railways led to the appointment of a special administrator for the transport of mail by rail. POs were established at the main terminals and TPOs were introduced on most of the lines. By 1917 there were 340 trains operating this service.

The construction of the Trans-Siberian Railway had been under way for some time and by 1903 was complete except for the section at Lake Baikal which still had to be crossed by steamer. A postal dispute arose between Russia, and Britain, France and Germany on the use of this line to transmit letters to and from the Far East. The latter conceded that the service was much quicker but considered the Russian charges too great. Eventually France and Germany accepted the charges and Britain fell into line. Some mail was then transported but the line closed in 1904 with the outbreak of the Russo-Japanese War.

In the meantime, Russia had its problems in the Balkans and with Turkey, and this was a period of almost constant border strife. Russian troops also fought in China during the Boxer Rebellion and Russian POs were opened in Peking, Kalgan, Tientsin and Urga in 1870, and at Shanghai and Chefoo in 1897. Stamps of Russia were used until special overprinted issues appeared in 1899.

In 1900 the Russians occupied Manchuria and held the area until 1907, when they were forced to give up the region after their defeat by the Japanese. Russian field and civilian POs were established and used either Russian or Russian 'China' stamps.

Russia became a signatory of the UPU in 1874.

1914-18

Following the assassination of Archduke Ferdinand at Sarajevo, the Russians were quick to support Serbia against Austria and were soon embroiled with German and Austrian armies along the whole front. The defeat of the Russians at Tannenberg allowed Germany to occupy vast areas along the Baltic. German stamps overprinted for use in these areas were issued in 1916.

The Russian military machine, which depended on a repressive bureaucracy to administer its needs, began to collapse in 1915-16. The minor revolts in the early part of the century had already weakened the Tsar's hold and, following a bloodless *coup* in March 1917, Tsar Nicholas II abdicated. A Provisional Government led by Kerensky was formed, but although new stamps were prepared they were never issued as the Provisional Government was overthrown by the Bolsheviks in October 1917. The capital was moved to Moscow, and the government became the Russian Socialist Federal Soviet Republic. Stamps were issued by the new government in January 1918, but no real mail service could operate during the civil war which ensued.

1918-39

FIRST STAMPS ISSUED USSR
19 August 1923

Postal services were seriously disrupted between 1918 and 1922. The Soviet authorities had no stamps of their own until 1921 and they used stamps of the earlier régimes as well as fiscal and savings bank stamps in the interim. During the period of the civil war many issues were prepared locally and an explanation of these appears in the following section.

The name of the country was changed in 1923 to the Union of Soviet Socialist Republics and first stamps were issued on 19 August 1923.

1939-45

Russia invaded Poland on 17 September 1939 and advanced to the River Bug. After a treaty with Germany, Russia absorbed eastern Poland into its own postal system. The war with Finland in the winter of 1939-40 eventually gained the Karelian isthmus for Russia and in the summer of 1940 the three Baltic states were absorbed. Bessarabia and Bukovina were gained from Romania, and Russia seemed to have built a buffer along almost the entire length of its western frontier. However, Germany invaded Russia in June 1941 and quickly advanced to establish a hold on the whole of western Russia. With its allies Finland, Romania, Hungary and Bulgaria all adding to the strength of its assault, Germany had reached the Volga and well into the Caucasus by the summer of 1942. However, the failure to capture Stalingrad led to a gradual withdrawal, which was accelerated by Russian pressure during 1943.

On 4 November 1941 German stamps overprinted 'Ostland' and 'Ukraine' were issued. The former was intended for use in the Baltic territories, part of Poland and northern occupied Russia, the latter in southern occupied Russia. Both were withdrawn when the territory was regained by Russia.

After the battle for Stalingrad in 1942, the Russians gradually regained their territory and by 1944 began to enter Poland and Romania. By the time the war finished in 1945 the Russians had captured Berlin itself.

1945 to date

When war ended, Russian troops occupied the east of Germany, part of Berlin, part of Vienna and a zone of Austria. Although the occupation of Austria ended in 1956, Communist governments were established in East Germany, Poland, Bulgaria, Romania and Hungary. Control spread to Czechoslovakia in 1948. The Baltic states, East Prussia, Poland east of the River Bug, and parts of the other states were included in Russia to extend the frontier further west. Russian stamps were used in all areas incorporated into the USSR.

• Russian Zemstvo posts

First Russian Zemstvo posts appeared in 1865. The Zemstvos were elected district councils which were set up as part of a general reform. Posts operated by these councils operated outside the state postal service. They had their own regulations and postage rates and each area had its own stamps. The carriers appointed by the district would take the mail from the district town to other local villages or to the nearest state PO.

These district services were approved originally in 1865 but official authorization was not received for five years. However, the demand for these local posts was sufficient to lead 30 districts to issue stamps in the first few years. Ultimately, 345 areas had their own posts, of which 162 used their own locally-produced stamps. The Zemstvo stamps were only valid within their own districts, and once a letter entered the state service the official Russian stamps had to be used in addition.

The need for the Zemstvos declined as the state service began to penetrate the rural areas with greater regularity. By the time of the Bolshevik uprising in October 1917 there were only 40 services left, and these were then quickly closed down. This ended the period of local posts but led to more complications during the Russian civil wars of 1918-22.

Russian Civil War 1918-20

The success of the Bolshevik Revolution of October 1917 led to a Civil War between the anti-Bolsheviks and the new central government. Many of the anti-Bolshevik groups issued stamps for the areas temporarily under their control.

• North West Russia

The Northern Army under General Rodzianko captured Pskov, Gdov and Yaurburg in May 1919. Stamps were issued in September 1919. These units were later incorporated in the North West Army, which comprised all the anti-Bolshevik forces in the Baltic area. On 1 August 1919, Russian stamps were overprinted for use in this area, but they were withdrawn in November 1919.

A Western Army attacked the Latvian forces defending Riga. Overprinted Latvian stamps were issued in October 1919 and these were followed by Russian overprints in November.

• South Russia

A Cossack Government had been set up at Kuban in October 1917 and issued overprinted stamps until 27 March 1920.

Another Cossack Government had been set up in the Don Republic. Stamps were issued in 1918 but the area fell to the Soviets in 1920.

The Provisional Government had issued its own stamps in January 1919, but these were followed in April by stamps issued by General Denikin, commander of the anti-Bolshevik force. General Denikin resigned his command to General Wrangel on 4 April 1920.

The forces, accompanied by many civilian refugees, were eventually forced to settle in Turkey. Until 1 July 1921, many stamps of Russia and Russian Levant were overprinted for use by this refugee body (*see* Wrangel Army Refugee Post *under* Asia).

• Wenden

A town in the former Russian province

of Livonia; later it became part of Latvia as Vidzeme and is now in Russia (Cesis). It issued stamps from 1863 to 1901 in its own name.

• Central Lithuania

Area between Russia, Lithuania and Poland which was claimed by all three. Bolshevik troops occupied Vilna, the chief town, on 5 January 1919 and set up a Communist government. Overprinted Russian stamps (100 *skatiku* = 1 *aukinsas*) were issued on 4 March. Vilna was retaken by the Polish army on 20 April 1919 and by treaty with Russia on 12 July 1920 Lithuanian rights to Vilna and Groduo were recognized. The Polish army again seized Vilna on 9 October 1920 and stamps (100 *fenigi* = 1 *mark*) were issued on 20 October 1920. Adhesives continued to be issued until 1922. After a plebiscite Central Lithuania was incorporated into Poland on 8 April 1922. The Russians returned the area to Lithuania in October 1939; in August 1940 it was incorporated into the Soviet Union and it has used Russian stamps ever since.

• Siberia

CURRENCY	
1919	As Russia

In November 1918, Admiral Kolchak assumed power as the ruler of Siberia, but he resigned on 4 January 1920 after the Bolsheviks captured Omsk. Stamps of Russia with surcharges of new values were issued during this period.

• Trans-Baikal Province

After the collapse of Admiral Kolchak, a local White Russian régime was established at Chita from 20 January to 21 October 1920.

Four stamps of Russia surcharged were used which are peculiar to the régime.

• Amur Province

FIRST STAMPS ISSUED 1920

In February 1920 a Communist administration was established at Blagoveschchensk which ended when the Far Eastern Republic was founded.

• Far Eastern Republic

FIRST STAMPS Russian overprinted September 1920

CURRENCY
1 gold rouble (zolotom) = 1 Japanese yen

A buffer state between the Soviet authorities and the Japanese set up on 6 April 1920. It extended from Lake Baikal to Vladivostok until 26 May 1921 when the Priamur and Maritime Provinces broke away. On 19 November 1922, after the Japanese evacuation of Vladivostok, it was annexed to Soviet Russia.

• Priamur and Maritime Provinces

FIRST STAMPS ISSUED July 1921

A Japanese-backed White Russian provisional government based on Vladivostok operated 26 May 1921 – 25 October 1922.

Stamps withdrawn in November 1922 when area was taken over by Soviet troops.

• Eastern Siberia

FIRST STAMPS ISSUED January 1923

Until gold currency was introduced throughout the Soviet Union, the annexed territories still needed specially surcharged stamps.

For later stamps valid and used throughout Soviet Asia, *see* Russia.

• Estonia

CURRENCY	
1918	100 kopecks = 1 rouble
1919	100 penni = 1 Estonian mark
1928	100 senti = 1 kroon
German occupation 1941	As Russia

Before 1918

Northernmost of three Baltic republics which were made independent after World War I. Estonia had a strategic importance in the eastern Baltic, and, as such, was seized in 1721 by Peter the Great, who wished to extend his maritime outlets. Apart from the period between the two World Wars, and conquest by the Germans, Estonia has always remained a Russian province.

During the latter part of the 19th century the Estonians were subject to severe victimization by the Russians and many of the peasants were moved. The uprising against the Tsar in 1905 started the demand for home rule in Estonia.

In World War I the Baltic states of Russia were occupied by German forces and stamps were issued overprinted for use by German troops in the area. In November 1917, following the Bolshevik uprising in Russia, the Estonian parliament declared independence. The Russians could not risk losing the naval base at Tallinn (Reval) and moved forces against the Estonians. In the spring of 1918 the Germans moved into the country at the request of parliament and drove the Bolsheviks out of the country. As a result, Russia renounced its rights to Estonia in April 1918. Germany tried to create a dependent duchy but when Germany collapsed in November 1918 the Estonian provisional government finally emerged. During this period Russian stamps were used except that German occupying forces used the issues of the Eastern Military Command Area.

1918 to date

FIRST STAMPS Russia, German Eastern Command overprints 1916-18
FIRST STAMPS ISSUED November 1918

First stamps were inscribed EESTI POST and were used concurrently with some Russian values overprinted for use in Estonia, though the provenance of these latter issues is questioned.

Estonia was sandwiched between

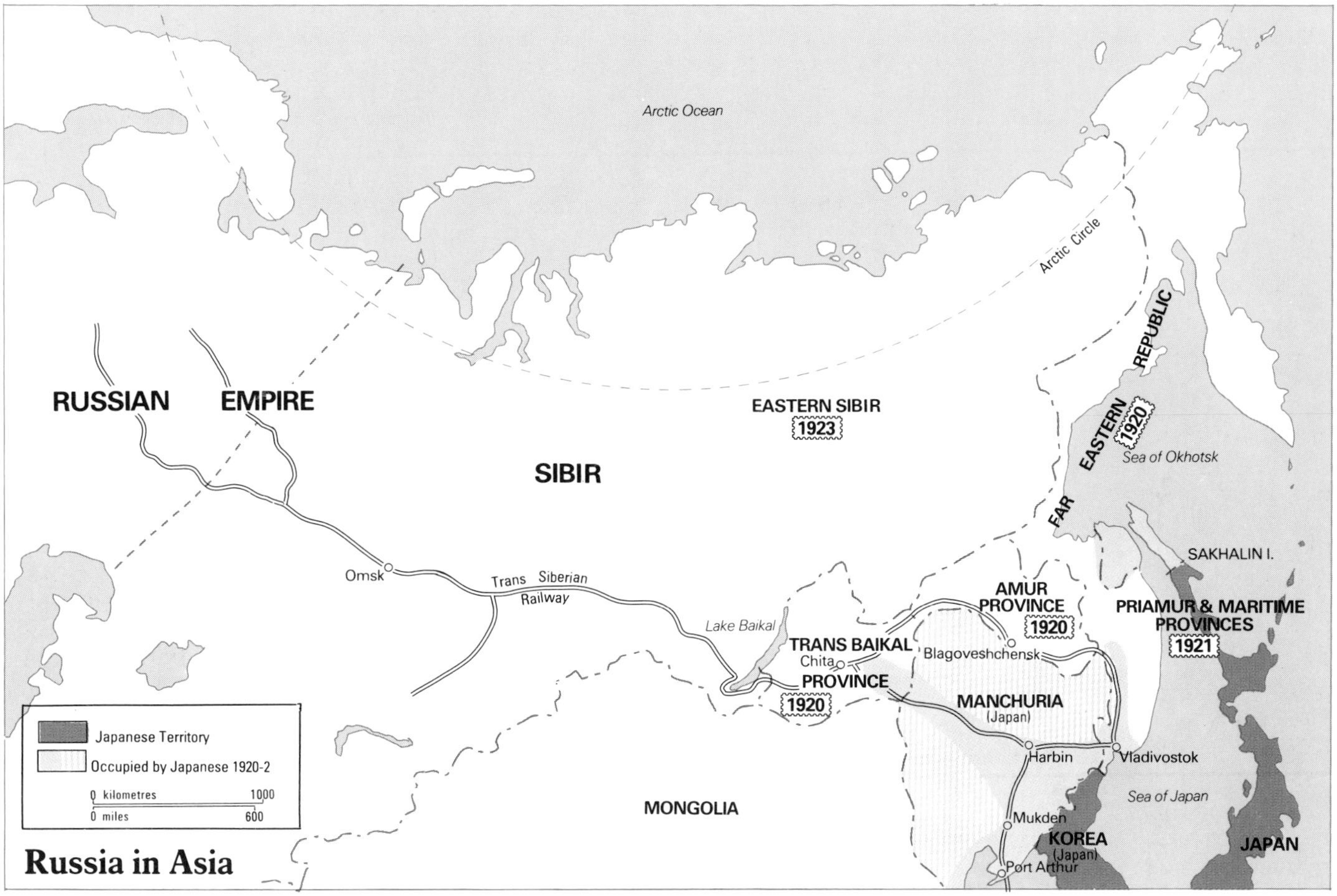
Arctic Ocean
Arctic Circle
RUSSIAN EMPIRE
SIBIR
EASTERN SIBIR
1923
FAR EASTERN REPUBLIC
1920
Sea of Okhotsk
SAKHALIN I.
Omsk
Trans Siberian Railway
Lake Baikal
TRANS BAIKAL PROVINCE
Chita
1920
AMUR PROVINCE
1920
Blagoveshchensk
PRIAMUR & MARITIME PROVINCES
1921
MANCHURIA
(Japan)
Harbin
Vladivostok
Sea of Japan
Mukden
KOREA
(Japan)
Port Arthur
JAPAN
MONGOLIA
Japanese Territory
Occupied by Japanese 1920-2
0 kilometres 1000
0 miles 600
Russia in Asia

the twin threats of fascism and communism, and in October 1934 martial law was declared. The Russo-German non-aggression pact of 1939 led to the partition of Poland, and Estonia was forced to accept Russian military bases on its territory. On 16 June 1940 Russia occupied Estonia and it was admitted into the USSR in August that year.

In June 1941 Germany invaded Russia and quickly overran the Baltic states. Stamps were issued by the Germans in 1941 and these were valid throughout Estonia from 29 September 1941 to 30 April 1942. The German OSTLAND overprints for occupied Russian territories were issued on 4 November 1941 and remained in use until the re-occupation of Estonia by the Russians in 1944-5. Russian stamps have been used ever since.

• Latvia

CURRENCY

1918 100 kopecks = 1 rouble
1923 100 santami = 1 lat
German occupation of Latvia 1941 As Russia

Before 1918

Middle of the three states on the Baltic Sea which were independent from 1918 to 1940. Area came under Russian control in 1795 and remained under Russian rule until the start of World War I. Latvia was occupied by the Germans and stamps of the Eastern Military Command were used from 1916 to 1918.

Following the Bolshevik revolution of 1917, fierce fighting took place in the Latvian area. Initially this was between the German and Russian armies, but was quickly followed by further fighting between Communist Lithuanian forces and the White Russians. Riga was liberated by a pro-German force in May 1918 and the national council was established. Britain was the first power to recognize Latvia's independence on 11 November 1918.

1918 to date

FIRST STAMPS Russia to 1916, German Eastern Military Command overprints 1916-18
FIRST STAMPS ISSUED 19 December 1918

First issue was printed on the back of captured German military maps and was in sheets of 228. In 1923 currency

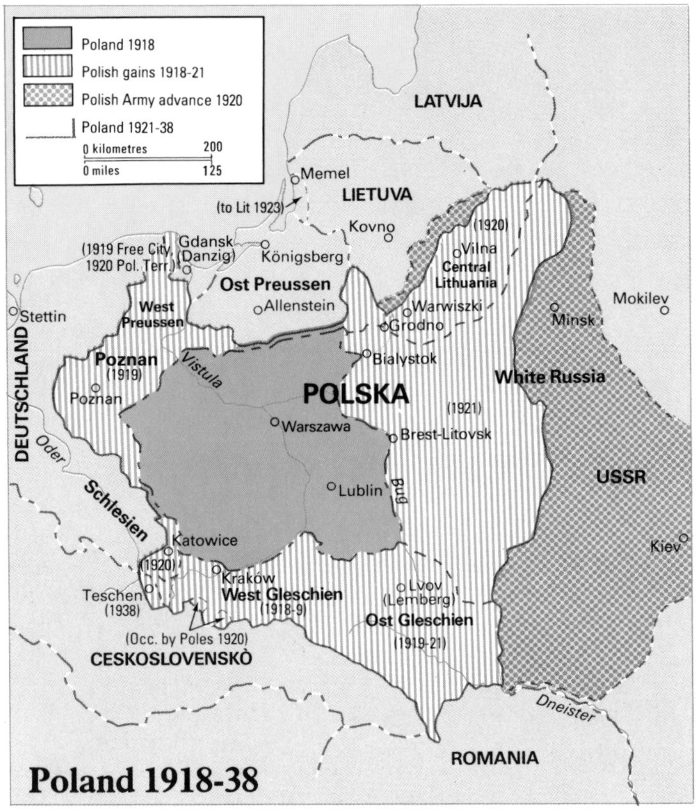
Poland 1918
Polish gains 1918-21
Polish Army advance 1920
Poland 1921-38
0 kilometres 200
0 miles 125
LATVIJA
Memel
(to Lit 1923)
LIETUVA
Kovno
(1920)
Vilna
Central Lithuania
(1919 Free City 1920 Pol. Terr.)
Gdansk (Danzig)
Königsberg
Ost Preussen
Allenstein
Warwiszki
Grodno
Stettin
West Preussen
Minsk
Mokilev
DEUTSCHLAND
Poznan (1919)
Poznan
Vistula
Bialystok
POLSKA
White Russia
(1921)
Warszawa
Brest-Litovsk
Oder
Lublin
Bug
USSR
Schlesien
Katowice
Kiev
(1920)
Kraków
West Gleschien (1918-9)
Teschen (1938)
Lvov (Lemberg)
Ost Gleschien (1919-21)
(Occ. by Poles 1920)
CESKOSLOVENSKÒ
Dneister
ROMANIA
Poland 1918-38

Poland 1938
Russo-German line Dec. 1939
Polish gains
Polish losses
Poland 1945
0 kilometres 200
0 miles 125
Latvija SSR
Memel
Lietuva SSR
(to Lith 1939)
Kaliningrad (Köningsberg)
Vilna
Gdansk
Szczecin (Stettin)
Grodno
Minsk
DEUTSCHLAND
Oder
Vistula
Bialystok
White Russia
Poznan
POLSKA
Warszawa
(Russ. Occ. 1939) (to Russ. 1945)
USSR
Breslau
Schlesien
Lublin
Bug
Praha
Katowice
Teschen
Kraków
Lvov
(to Czech. 1945)
CESKOSLOVENSKÒ
Dneister
ROMANIA
Poland 1938-45

was altered as the government wished to sever all links with Russia.

Attempts to remain neutral in 1939 were in vain. Non-aggression pacts were signed with both Russia and Germany, but the Latvians were forced to accept Russian bases in September 1939. In June 1940 Latvia was occupied by Soviet forces and was accepted into the USSR.

Germany invaded Latvia in June 1941 and captured Russian stamps were overprinted for use until the OSTLAND issue appeared in November 1941. In 1944 Latvia was liberated by the Russian army and Russian stamps have been used ever since.

• Lithuania

CURRENCY

1918	100 skatiku = 1 auksinas
1922	100 centu = 1 litas
German occupation of Lithuania 1941	As Russia

Before 1918

Southernmost of the three Baltic states which were independent from 1918 to 1940. Lithuania was independent in the Middle Ages, but joined with Poland in 1569 to form the Polish Commonwealth. When Poland was partitioned in 1795, Lithuania, as it is known today, was awarded to Russia, but part of the former territory was gained by Prussia.

Lithuania remained a province of Russia until World War I. At this time, the country was overrun by the German army, who tried to bring the area under German control. Stamps of the Eastern Military Command were used from 1916.

A nationalist movement began and in 1917 Lithuanian demands for independence were recognized. Initially, the provisional government sought to offer the crown to a Württemberg nobleman who claimed descent from a Lithuanian king. However, this offer was withdrawn when Germany was defeated in November 1918.

1918 to date

FIRST STAMPS Russia to 1916, German Eastern Military Command overprints 1916-18
FIRST STAMPS ISSUED 24 December 1918

In the development of eastern European airmail services, the Lithuanian airport of Kovno played an important part as the staging point for services further east. It was also linked with Finland and Scandinavia.

In 1922 Lithuania lost the town of Vilnius to the Poles and retaliated by seizing Memel (q.v) from the Allies. Lithuanian currency was changed in 1922. Hitler seized Memel in March 1939 and Lithuania formed an alliance with Russia. When Poland was partitioned in September, Vilnius was returned to Lithuania. The territory was incorporated into Russia on 21 July 1940.

Lithuania was invaded by Germany in June 1941 and various overprints on

Russian stamps were used before the OSTLAND overprints came into use in November 1941. Russian stamps were re-introduced in 1944, when Lithuania was regained, and these have been used ever since.

• Memel

FIRST STAMPS Prussia to 1867, North German Confederation 1868-71. German Empire 1871-1919
FIRST STAMPS ISSUED 1920

CURRENCY

1920	As Germany
1923	As Lithuania

City on the Baltic at the mouth of the River Niemen which had considerable importance as a trading centre. It was part of the Hanseatic League in the Middle Ages but passed to Swedish control and, subsequent to the Napoleonic wars, to Prussia. It remained a German city until 1919.

Memel and the country around it formed the eastern boundary of the German Empire and at the end of World War I was ceded to the Allies who wished to make it into a Free City. This was unacceptable to the government of the new Lithuania, which was immediately to the north. As a result, French troops garrisoned the town on behalf of the League of Nations from the end of 1918 to January 1923.

Stamps of France overprinted with Germany currency, and German stamps overprinted MEMEL GEBIET (first issued 1 August 1920) were used concurrently. On 10 January 1923 Memel was invaded by the Lithuanians and the French withdrew. After the introduction of Lithuanian currency in April, special stamps were issued by the new authority. On 8 March 1924 the Memel district became an autonomous part of Lithuania and no further issues were released. In March 1939 it was returned to Germany, and German stamps were issued without overprint. It used these issues until 1945, when it became part of Russia. Russian stamps have been used ever since.

Poland

CURRENCY

1860	100 kopecks = 1 rouble
German occupation of Poland 1915	As Germany
1918	100 pfennig = 1 mark
	100 hallerze = 1 krone
	100 fenigi = 1 mark
1924	100 groszy = 1 zloty
1950	100 old zloty = 1 new zloty

Before 1815

Area of northern central Europe between Russia and Germany which has changed its boundaries many times and has, on occasion, disappeared completely from the map of Europe.

Markings on letters date from the 17th century and, as in Russia, an organized message service was in operation at this time. By the Napoleonic wars named handstamps were in use in the large cities of Warsaw, Cracow and Lublin. Grande Armée cancellations were used during the period of the Duchy of Warsaw.

1815-50

After the Napoleonic Wars the part of Poland controlled by Russia was in a constant state of unrest. In 1830 there was a major uprising in Warsaw and the army declared its support for the people. In 1831 fighting took place and the Poles were largely successful until they were defeated in July; Warsaw was entered in September. As a result, the Tsar ruled in February 1832 that Poland should form an integral part of Russia. It became a Russian province in 1847. In 1846 there was a revolution in Austrian Poland and as a result Austria, Russia and Poland revoked the Treaty of 1815 and Cracow was declared an Austrian territory. During this period, in spite of civil disturbances, postal services were extended and handstamps were used in most of the large towns.

1850-71

FIRST STAMPS ISSUED 1 January 1860

In 1850 those parts of Poland which had been absorbed by Austria and Prussia used the newly-issued stamps of their parent territories, and in 1856 when Russia issued adhesives these were also used in the province of Poland. These can be recognized by postmarks and numerals which were issued by the respective authorities.

During a liberal régime under Tsar Alexander II, Poland was given a separate postal service in 1858. A 10 *kopek* value was issued in a design similar to Russian stamps. These stamps were printed in Warsaw but when the Poles again rose against the Russians in 1863 the freedom which the Poles had gained was lost, the printing works was closed down and Russian stamps were again introduced.

1871-1914

Poland continued as a province of Russia throughout this period and used Russian stamps. The postal service was dominated by the Russians and was also used as a means of censorship of the Polish liberals.

1914-39

As part of Russia, Poland was invaded in 1914 by both Germany and Austria-Hungary. By 1915 the country had been overrun and on 12 May 1915 German stamps overprinted RUSSISCH-POLEN were issued in their area. Further south, military post stamps of Austria-Hungary were brought into use. In 1916 the captured area became the 'General Gouvernement-Warsaw' and further overprnts were issued. Some areas of Poland also used overprinted stamps of the German Eastern Military Command — though these were originally intended for the Baltic states of Estonia, Latvia and Lithuania.

With the collapse of Austria and Germany, a Polish republic was proc-

LATVIJA
2 RUBLI 2
POMNIK ŻOŁNIERZA POLSKIEGO I ANTYFASZYSTY NIEMIECKIEGO W BERLINIE
POLSKA 60 GR
B
LIETUVA
25
C
EESTI 15s
D
A
MEMEL
30
pfennig
E
1K
POCZTA POLSKA
F
2½ 2½
Danzig
G

A Latvia 1921; **B** Poland:Republic 1972; **C** Lithuania 1926; **D** Estonia 1928; **E** Memel:French Occupation 1922; **F** Poland:Austrian Currency 1919; **G** Danzig:Free City 1920.

laimed on 3 November 1918. During 1919-20 Poland was awarded large areas from surrounding territories: Western Galicia from Austria (1919); Eastern Galicia for 25 years (1920); Posen, parts of West Prussia and Lower Silesia from Germany (1919); part of Upper Silesia after a plebiscite (1921). During all this period warfare had continued between Poland and Russia. The Treaty of Riga in March 1921 awarded parts of White Russia to Poland, and Central Lithuania (q.v.) was gained in 1922. In 1923 the agreement over Eastern Galicia was repealed and it became part of Poland. This set the boundaries for Poland until 1939.

• Polish POs abroad

In the period from May 1919 to 1923 a PO was operated in the Polish consulate in Constantinople. Overprinted Polish stamps in the north Polish currency of *fernigow* and *marka* were used. For details of the PO in Danzig, see that state. A further PO was opened in Odessa on the Black Sea in November 1919 during the civil war between the Bolsheviks and the White Russians. Normal postal routes were blocked and mail was carried from Odessa by sea to Poland on the Baltic.

1939-45

On 1 September 1939 German forces invaded Poland and precipitated World War II. On 17 September the Russians moved into Poland from the east. On 28 September Poland was divided between the two aggressors. Germany annexed those provinces which had been lost in 1918-19 and also parts of the provinces of Lodz, Warsaw, Cracow and Bialstok. These areas then used German stamps. The remaining German area was designated 'The General Government of Poland' and overprinted stamps were issued on 1 December 1939. East of the River Bug was annexed by Russia and used Russian stamps until the German invasion in 1941. The stamps for this second occupation by Germany, issued on 26 October 1941, were those of the General Government inscribed 'Deutsches Reich General Government', changed to 'Gross Deutsches' in August 1943.

In July 1944 a provisional government under Russian control was formed at Lublin and gradually assumed control of the liberated areas. On 26 June 1945 a government of national unity was formed. First stamps of the new government appeared on 7 September 1944 and were inscribed 'Poczta Polska'.

During the war a Polish government-in-exile was established in London and stamps were released on 15 December 1941. These were used on Polish seagoing vessels and on certain special days at Polish military camps. Polish troops fought in most theatres of war with Allied forces and special fixed PO markings were used for them.

1945 to date

Following World War II the shape of Poland changed again. Russia retained those areas east of the River Bug which had been occupied in 1939. To compensate, Poland was given large areas to the west in the former German provinces of East and West Prussia, Danzig, Silesia and Pomerania. This was followed by the transfer of the German-speaking population from the area and its resettlement by refugees from the Russian area.

On 28 October 1950 the currency was revalued and 100 old zloty became 1 new zloty. Overprints in the new currency were authorized and many local overprints were released.

Since the 1950s Poland has been a Communist state and a member of the Warsaw Pact. Over recent years Poland has issued many special stamps bearing non-political subjects.

• Danzig

CURRENCY

1920	As Germany
1923	100 pfennings = 1 Danzig gulden

Before 1871

Ancient Free City on the Baltic coast.

It was Polish in 1454, but was seized by the Prussians and annexed in 1793. Surrendered to the French in May 1807 but was restored to independence by the Treaty of Tilsit in July 1807. Came under the protection of Prussia and Saxony at this time but was besieged by the allies in 1812 and, although it surrendered in 1814, was awarded to the King of Prussia by the Treaty of Versailles.

Had commercial importance and was included in the list of towns in the British Post Office Act of 1657, at which time the postage rate was given as 12*d* per ounce. In general, Danzig followed the postal reforms of Prussia.

During the Crimean War of 1854-5 was the base of the British Baltic Fleet, which operated a postal service with three 1*d* stamps, which were cancelled on arrival in London, though many have a handstamp of Danzig on the face.

Danzig was incorporated into the German Empire with the rest of Prussia in 1872.

1918 to date

FIRST STAMPS ISSUED Overprinted Germany 14 June 1920

At the end of World War I Danzig was a German-speaking area in the centre of a region which was in the new territory of Poland. The Allied powers made it a Free State in an attempt to accommodate both parties. Before the new constitution was finally drawn up in November 1920, a British force was based in Danzig to keep the peace. This used a Field PO mark of H2 from March to November, when the troops were withdrawn.

Unoverprinted German stamps had continued to be used up to 13 June 1920, and new issues were prepared for the Free State and appeared in January 1921.

Danzig suffered from the post-war inflation which afflicted Germany and many surcharges were introduced to accommodate the ever-increasing rates of postage. A new currency was established in 1924.

A Polish PO operated in the harbour of Danzig. This used Polish stamps overprinted PORT GDANSK. The first issues were released on 5 January 1925 and the office remained open until the outbreak of World War II.

The government of the Free State became increasingly pro-Nazi in the years leading up to the war. It was occupied by the German army on 18 September 1939 and was re-absorbed into the German postal administration. After World War II Danzig was awarded to Poland and was renamed Gdansk. The German population was evacuated from the area and resettled west of the Oder-Niesse line, and displaced Poles from the Russian occupied provinces were allocated to the area.

• East Silesia

CURRENCY	
1920	Both Czech & Polish used

Area of the Austrian Empire round Teschen which was claimed by both Poland and Czechoslovakia following World War I. Although a plebiscite was decided upon, it was impossible to hold one owing to civil disturbances in the region. The area was divided between, and the respective sectors incorporated into, the two countries.

Early in 1920 the area was occupied by Polish and Czech forces and each region issued stamps overprinted SO [Silesie Orientale] 1920; the Czech region on 13 February 1920 in Czech currency and the Polish on 15 April 1920.

• Warwiszki

Small neutral zone between Lithuania and Poland occupied by the Poles in March 1923. Stamps of Poland overprinted SAMORZAD WARWISZKI were issued on 23-27 March 1923 but were quickly replaced when the area was incorporated into Poland.

• The Ottoman Empire in Europe

(*see also* Turkish (Ottoman) Empire p.214)

1815-50

The break-up of the Turkish European territories began in 1821 with a major revolt in the Danubian principalities in which Greece joined. The Greek War of Independence lasted from 1821 to 1828. There was much support from Britain, including volunteers one of whom, Lord Byron, died at Missolonghi in 1824. In July 1825 the provisional Greek government asked Britain for its protection. No immediate action was taken but when the Turks began to gain the upper hand by defeating the Greeks and capturing Athens, an Allied fleet was sent and this defeated the Turks at Navarino on 20 October 1827. The Treaty of London was signed by Britain, France and Russia on 6 July 1828, and marked the emergence of modern Greece. In addition, between 1830-40 Crete was administered from Egypt, and Serbia became an autonomous principality under Turkey in 1829.

Postal History

The first public post in the Turkish Empire was created by the announcement of the Director-General of the Imperial Post on 11 November 1840. This gave particulars of the service which was to be started and stated 'that offices were to be opened in all important places in the Empire'. This was slow to be introduced and by 1863 there were still only 58 POs in the entire Empire including Europe.

1850-71

FIRST STAMPS ISSUED 1863

The break-up of the European territories continued. Moldavia and Wallachia declared their independence in 1859, after the Russo-Turkish War of 1853-5. (Britain and France entered this war in support of Turkey and, after the Russians withdrew from modern Bulgaria, invaded the

Crimea.) The principalities united as Romania in December 1861.

Stamps were issued for the whole of the Empire, which extended from Europe to the tip of Arabia and westward to Libya, and were used at all POs. These can only be recognized by postmarks, but those for the foreign POs are much sought after and can be found for all countries, including Romania.

1871-1914

This period saw the final break-up of European Turkey and its restriction to the eastern part of Thrace. After the Russo-Turkish War, by the Treaty of San Stefano in 1878, Bulgaria became a principality, Serbia and Montenegro were made independent and Bosnia-Herzegovina was occupied by the Austrians. In 1881 Greece extended its territory by acquiring Thessaly. In 1899 Crete became autonomous. In 1908 Bulgaria became independent. In 1912 Italy seized the Dodecanese Islands. In 1913 Albania became independent, Crete joined Greece and, as a result of the first Balkan War, Turkey lost all European territory except eastern Thrace. Even this was yielded to Bulgaria in the first instance but was regained before the outbreak of World War I.

The postal effects of these many changes are reflected in the stamps of the different countries in the area. The Balkan Wars led to continuous disruption of civilian communication but the Turkish post continued to operate in each territory until it was replaced by that of the new government.

From 1914 the territory in eastern Thrace was administered by treaty and apart from postmarks is indistinguishable from Asian Turkey (q.v.). *See also* Turkish (Ottoman) Empire *under* Asia.

• The Danubian Principalities

Before 1871

FIRST STAMPS Turkish from 1853
FIRST STAMPS ISSUED 15 July 1858

CURRENCY

1858 40 parale = 1 piastre

The Danubian principalities of Moldavia and Wallachia were originally part of the Roman province of Dacia, hence the Latin language of this area. Until 1858 they were principalities under Turkish control forming the northernmost part of the Ottoman Empire.

There was a limited postal service after 1850 and Turkish POs operated in the territories. Stamps were handstruck on paper in Jassy (Moldavia), while the principalities were still under Turkey. In 1856 the southern part of Bessarabia was annexed and held until 1878. The principalities declared their independence in 1859 after the Russo-Turkish (Crimean) War. On 19 August 1858 a conference in Paris agreed the union of the two provinces. It was also agreed that each principality should have its own prince. In 1859 both principalities elected the same man, Alexander Cuza. On 23 December 1861 the union of the two principalities as the principality of Romania was agreed (*see* Romania).

Romania

Before 1871

FIRST STAMPS Turkey and the issues of Moldavia-Wallachia 1858
FIRST STAMPS ISSUED 26 June 1862

CURRENCY

1858 40 parale = 1 piastre
1867 100 bani = 1 leu
German occupation of Romania 1917
100 bani = 1 leu

Principality created on 23 December 1861 by the union of Moldavia and Wallachia. Alexander Cuza was elected the first prince, but a revolt in Bucharest forced his abdication in 1866. Prince Charles of Hohenzollern-Sigmaringen was elected in April of that year.

Stamps were produced by handstamping on to paper until 1865 when stamps printed in Bucharest were issued.

1871-1914

In 1896 overprinted Romanian stamps in Turkish currency were issued for the postal service on Romanian ships between Constanta and Constantinople (*See* Turkish Empire *under* Asia).

1914-18

During the occupation of Romanian territory Bulgarian troops occupied the Dobruja area and overprinted stamps were issued in 1916. These were for this area only. The rest of occupied Romania, all except Bukovina and north-eastern Moldavia, used overprinted German stamps or those of the Austro-Hungarian military post until November 1918.

1918-39

In 1919 Romania assisted in the occupation of European Turkey and a PO was established on board ship in Constantinople. This used overprinted Romanian stamps and was only open for a very short time (*See also* Romanian PO in the Turkish Empire *under* Asia).

On 1 December 1918 the union of Transylvania, the eastern portion of Hungary, with Romania was proclaimed, but the final frontiers were not finalized until the Treaty of Trianon in June 1920. Hungarian stamps which were in stock at the POs in this area were overprinted in Romanian currency, were then used throughout Transylvania and were valid for the rest of Romania.

Three other areas had overprinted stamps during the period before the Treaty of Trianon.

Banat Bacska: stamps issued in July 1919 after the withdrawal of Serbian troops. Subsequently divided between Romania and Yugoslavia.

Debrecen : Stamps issued on 20 November 1919; this area was retained

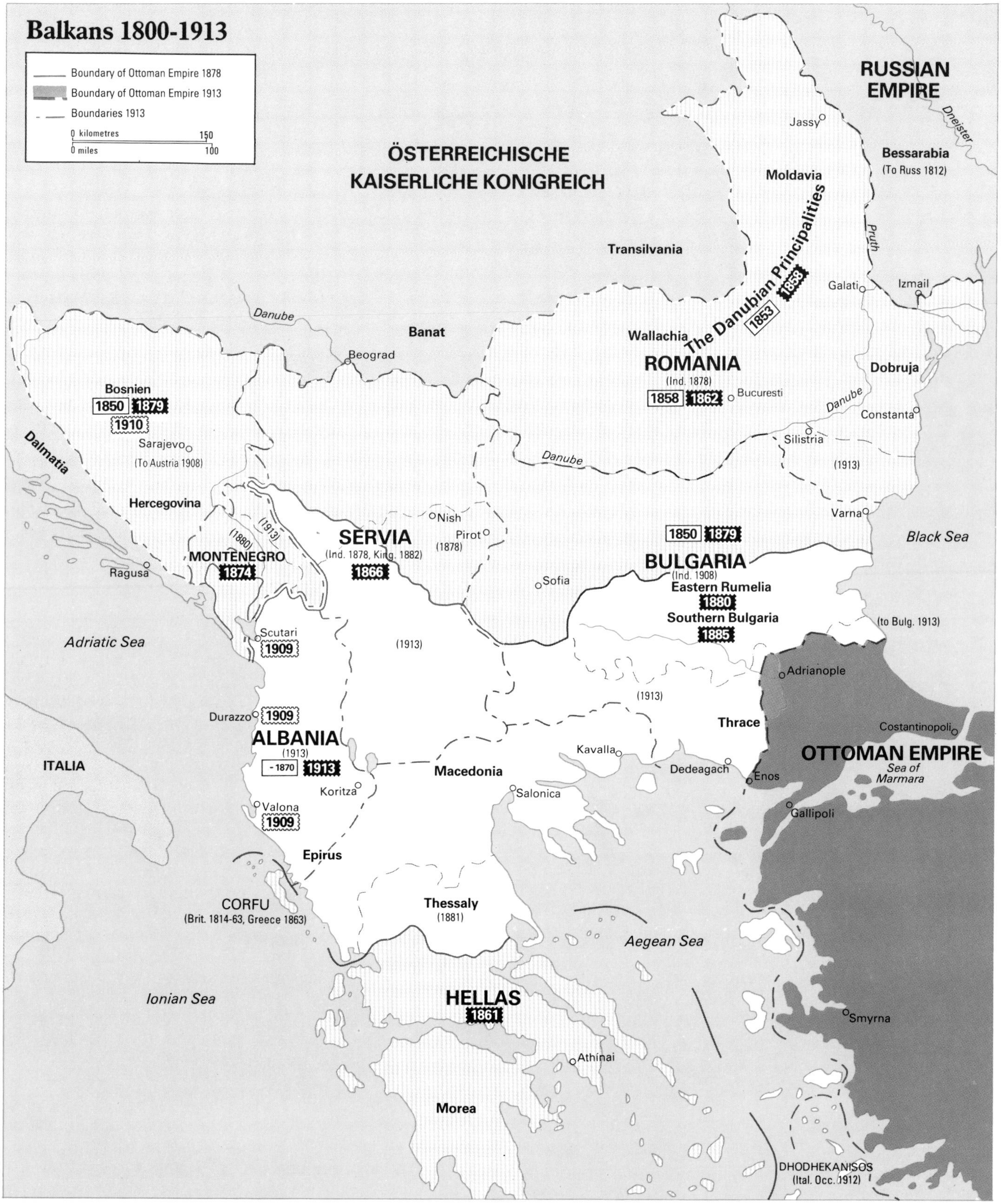
Balkans 1800-1913
Boundary of Ottoman Empire 1878
Boundary of Ottoman Empire 1913
Boundaries 1913
0 kilometres 150
0 miles 100
RUSSIAN EMPIRE
ÖSTERREICHISCHE KAISERLICHE KONIGREICH
Dneister
Jassy
Bessarabia
(To Russ 1812)
Moldavia
Pruth
Transilvania
The Danubian Principalities
1853
1858
Galati
Izmail
Danube
Banat
Wallachia
Beograd
ROMANIA
(Ind. 1878)
1858 1862
Bucuresti
Dobruja
Bosnien
1850 1879
1910
Danube
Constanta
Silistria
Dalmatia
Sarajevo
(To Austria 1908)
Danube
(1913)
Hercegovina
Nish
Varna
(1913)
(1880)
SERVIA
Pirot
(1878)
1850 1879
Black Sea
MONTENEGRO
(Ind. 1878, King. 1882)
BULGARIA
1874
1866
(Ind. 1908)
Ragusa
Sofia
Eastern Rumelia
1880
Southern Bulgaria
1885
(to Bulg. 1913)
Scutari
Adriatic Sea
1909
(1913)
Adrianople
(1913)
Durazzo
1909
Thrace
Costantinopoli
ALBANIA
(1913)
ITALIA
-1870 1913
Kavalla
OTTOMAN EMPIRE
Macedonia
Dedeagach
Sea of Marmara
Enos
Koritza
Salonica
Valona
1909
Gallipoli
Epirus
CORFU
(Brit. 1814-63, Greece 1863)
Thessaly
(1881)
Aegean Sea
Ionian Sea
HELLAS
1861
Smyrna
Athinai
Morea
DHODHEKANISOS
(Ital. Occ. 1912)

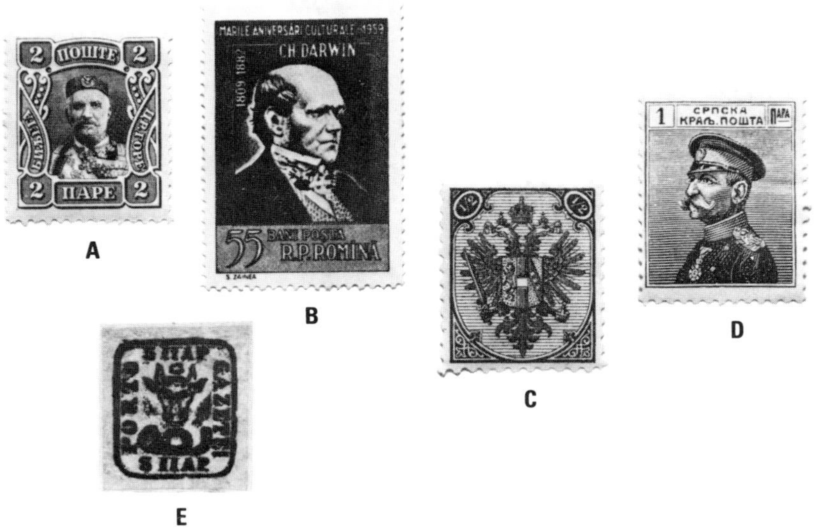
2 ПОШТЕ 2
2 ПАРЕ 2
CH DARWIN
1809 1882
55
R.P.ROMINA
1 СРПСКА КРАЉ. ПОШТА ПАРА

A Montenegro 1907; B Romania:Republic 1959; C Bosnia-Herzegovina 1900; D Serbia:King Peter I 1911; E Danubian Principalities 1858.

by Hungary and Romanian stamps were withdrawn in 1920.
Temesvar : Originally occupied by Serbian troops, who used their own overprinted stamps until August 1919. On 20 August overprinted Romanian stamps were issued until the area was a warded to Romania and renamed Timisoaro.

1939-45

Romania sided with the Axis powers in World War II. In April 1944 Russian troops entered Romania and gradually took over the country. On 23 August a *coup d'état* in Bucharest led by King Michael overthrew the pro-German government and the Romanians turned on their former allies. In October Russian dominance over Romania was recognized.

1945 to date

After World War II Transylvania and southern Dobruja were returned to Romania, but Bessarabia remained part of Russia. The country remained a kingdom until 30 December 1947, when it became a People's Republic, which it has remained ever since.

• Serbia

Before 1850

In 1829 a hereditary prince was recognized by the Turkish government and Serbia subsequently became an autonomous principality under Turkish suzerainty. A limited Turkish post operated after 1840, and several POs were in operation by 1866.

1850-71

FIRST STAMPS ISSUED 1866

CURRENCY

1866 100 paras = 1 dinar

Remained as an autonomous principality under Turkish control.

First stamps issued were printed locally at the state printing works in Belgrade but the higher values were produced in Vienna.

1871-1914

Serbia was one of the original signatories of the General Postal Union in 1874 and the principality became independent of Turkey in 1878. This was confirmed by Treaty of Berlin on 22 August 1878. At the same time Serbia gained further territory from Turkey including the towns of Nish and Pirot.

In 1882 the assembly elected Prince Milan to become king, and Serbia became a kingdom.

1914-18

When Archduke Ferdinand was assassinated in Sarajevo in Bosnia-Herzegovina on 28 June 1914, Austria accused Serbia of complicity. Because of the many interlocking alliances, this led to the outbreak of World War I.

During the occupation of Serbia, Austro-Hungarian military post stamps were issued from 1915 and were overprinted from 6 March 1916. Serbia continued to issue its stamps until 1920, when the kingdom of Yugoslavia was created.

During 1919 Serbia occupied the areas of Baranya and Temesvar in Hungary. Overprinted stamps were issued on 5 and 10 May respectively.

1939-45

FIRST STAMPS ISSUED 5 June 1941

Although part of Yugoslavia from 1920, Yugoslav stamps were issued in 1941 overprinted for use in the former territory of Serbia during the German occupation. These issues continued until 1944, when they were replaced by Yugoslav stamps after liberation by the Russians.

• Bosnia-Herzegovina

Before 1914

FIRST STAMPS Turkish and Austro-Hungarian
FIRST STAMPS ISSUED 1 July 1879

CURRENCY

1879 100 kreuzer (or novics) = 1 gulden
1900 100 heller = 1 krone

Two associated provinces of the Ottoman Empire in Europe. Came under Turkish control in the 15th century and remained part of the Empire until the end of the Russo-Turkish War in 1878.

A postal service had operated since the 1850s in this area and Turkish stamps were used.

During the Austrian occupation after 1878 military posts were in operation and in January 1879 a limited civilian service was introduced. At this time the stamps of Austria and Hungary were placed on sale but these were withdrawn when the stamps for the provinces were issued.

Bosnia-Herzegovina was annexed by Austria-Hungary on 6 October 1908. First stamps under the new regime were issued on 18 October 1910.

1914-18

At the end of the war, with the breakup of the Austro-Hungarian Empire, Bosnia-Herzegovina became part of the kingdom of the Serbs, Croats and Slovenes. For further history *see* Yugoslavia.

A
B
C
D
E
КРАЉЕВСТВО СРБА,ХРВАТА И СЛОВЕНАЦА
KRALJEVSTVO SRBA,HRVATA I SLOVENACA
25
ЈУГОСЛАВИЈА
1892 1962
10. IV. 1941
NEZAVISNA DRŽAVA HRVATSKA
FNRJUGOSLAVIJA
ФНРЈУГОСЛАВИЈА
12
ДРЖАВА СХС
5

A Yugoslavia:Kingdom 1921; **B** Yugoslavia:Marshal Tito 1962; **C** Yugoslavia:Croatia 1941; **D** Yugoslavia:Republic 1949; **E** Yugoslavia:Slovenia 1919.

• Montenegro
Before 1914

FIRST STAMPS ISSUED 1 May 1874

CURRENCY	
1847	100 novic = 1 florin
1902	100 heller = 1 krone
1907	100 para = 1 krone
1910	100 para = 1 perper

Independent principality in European Turkey. Conquered by the Turks in 1526, but established as an hereditary government in 1696. Declared independent of Turkey by the Treaty of San Stefano on 3 March 1878 at the end of the Russo-Turkish War.

Montenegro had had a limited postal service under Turkish suzerainty, and POs were open in the major towns of Cetina and Pet. Joined the UPU in 1874 but not a founder member, as it was not represented at the Berne Congress.

Fought with Serbia, Greece and Bulgaria against Turkey in the first Balkan War, and with Serbia and Greece against Bulgaria in the second. In 1913 Montenegro invaded the new state of Albania and besieged Scutari. Montenegrin stamps were used in northern Albania and are found postmarked SCUTARI SKADOR.

1914-18

Montenegro declared war on Austria-Hungary in support of Serbia. After the defeat of its ally in 1915, Montenegro was occupied by Austrian troops in January 1916. Overprinted stamps of Bosnia were issued by the Austrian military post, and the Montenegro government in exile at Bordeaux issued stamps in 1916, and, on 1 March 1917, four stamps were issued especially overprinted for Montenegro.

On 26 November 1918 the king was deposed because of his support of the Austrians, and the country was declared to be united with Serbia. No further stamps of Montenegro were issued and those of Serbia issued for the kingdom of Serbs, Croats and Slovenes were used. The union with Serbia was recognized on 13 July 1922 and Montenegro became part of Yugoslavia.

1939-45

FIRST STAMPS ISSUED 16 June 1941

Although part of Yugoslavia, overprinted stamps were issued during the Italian occupation of the former territory of Montenegro.

On 22 November 1943, after the surrender of Italy, further stamps were overprinted for the subsequent German occupation. These issues continued until the area was liberated by the Russians and they were replaced by Yugoslav issues.

Yugoslavia

Before 1939

FIRST STAMPS See individual countries
FIRST STAMPS ISSUED For individual provinces 1918-19
For unified country 16 January 1921
For stamps used in Serbia *see* Serbia

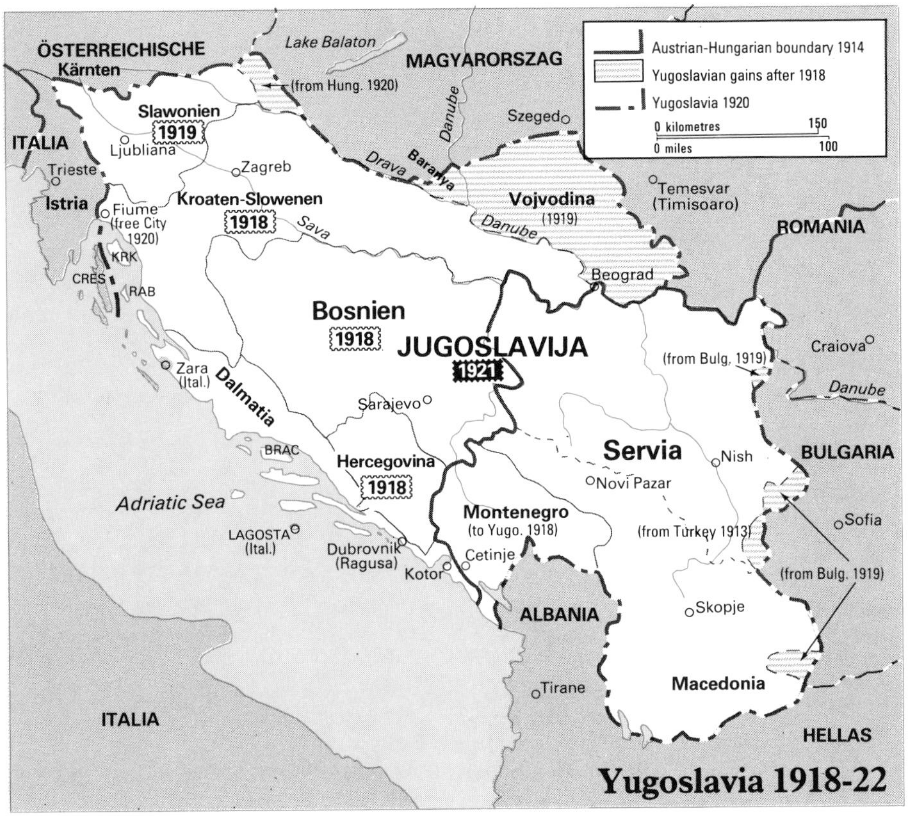
Austrian-Hungarian boundary 1914
Yugoslavian gains after 1918
Yugoslavia 1920
0 kilometres 150
0 miles 100
ÖSTERREICHISCHE
Kärnten
Lake Balaton
MAGYARORSZAG
(from Hung. 1920)
Slawonien
1919
ITALIA
Ljubliana
Trieste
Zagreb
Istria
Fiume
(free City 1920)
Kroaten-Slowenen
1918
Sava
Drava
Baranya
Danube
Szeged
Temesvar
(Timisoaro)
Vojvodina
(1919)
ROMANIA
KRK
CRES
RAB
Beograd
Bosnien
1918
JUGOSLAVIJA
1921
(from Bulg. 1919)
Craiova
Zara
(Ital.)
Dalmatia
Sarajevo
BRAC
Hercegovina
1918
Servia
Nish
BULGARIA
Novi Pazar
Adriatic Sea
Montenegro
(to Yugo. 1918)
(from Turkey 1913)
Sofia
LAGOSTA
(Ital.)
Dubrovnik
(Ragusa)
Cetinje
Kotor
(from Bulg. 1919)
ALBANIA
Skopje
Tirane
Macedonia
ITALIA
HELLAS
Yugoslavia 1918-22

CURRENCY

1918	100 filler (or heller) = 1 krone
1919	(Slovenia) 100 vinar = 1 krona
1920	100 para = 1 dinar

Formed in 1917 as a new country from the former territories of Serbia, Montenegro, Bosnia-Herzegovina, Slovenia and Croatia. The last three had been part of Austria-Hungary. Pact of Corfu in July 1917 had agreed the new state in principle, and the break-up of the Austrian Empire made the implementation possible.

On the establishment of the kingdom of the Serbs, Croats and Slovenes, overprinted or definitive stamps were issued for each of the individual provinces: Bosnia-Herzegovina in November 1918, Croatia on 18 November 1918 and Slovenia on 3 January 1919. These continued until the issue of the first combined stamps in 1921.

Stamps in Slovenia included a special issue for the plebiscite to be held in Carinthia, the province of Bavaria which subsequently became part of Austria, and the funds so raised were used to enable the Carinthians to travel to vote. Although Yugoslavia was ruled by a king it remained a loose association at first and only became a kingdom in 1929.

1939-45

In 1941 Yugoslavia was put under pressure by Germany to join the Axis powers. On 24 March the government agreed, but on 26 March General Simovic overthrew the government. On 6 April Germany invaded Yugoslavia and quickly overran the country. The government surrendered on 17 April but a guerrilla campaign began immediately against the occupying powers. On occupation, the Germans and Italians divided the country into its original constituent parts. Stamps were issued for each sector including Croatia, which became an autonomous state on 10 April 1941.

• Croatia

FIRST STAMPS ISSUED April 1941

CURRENCY

1941	100 paras = 1 dinar
	also 100 banicas = 1 kuna

Croatia comprised Bosnia-Herzegovina, the Dalmatian coast and all territory south of the river Drava. Further territory was added in 1943 when the Italians surrendered.

• Slovenia

FIRST STAMPS ISSUED April 1941

CURRENCY

1941	As Yugoslavia
1944	As Italy

Initially occupied by Italy, the stamps of Yugoslavia were issued with an Italian overprint. In May 1941 further overprints were produced when Slovenia became the Italian province of Lubiana. When Italy surrendered in 1943, stamps of Italy were overprinted for use in the territory which was then administered by the Germans.

• Fiume and Kupa

FIRST STAMPS ISSUED 16 May 1941

CURRENCY

1941	100 pares = 1 dinar

After initial overprints on Yugoslav stamps, Italian stamps were brought into use in this area after the territory was annexed by Italy. Re-occupied by Yugoslavia in 1945 and then administered as part of Venezia Giulia (q.v.). (*See also* Fiume *under* Italy).

• Dalmatia

FIRST STAMPS ISSUED 9 October 1943

Postal kiosks in Terazije Street, Belgrade

CURRENCY	
1919	100 centesimi = 1 corona

Areas in Dalmatia which had been under the control of Italy were occupied by Germany in September 1943. Issues of Italy were overprinted for use in this area, largely around Zara. (*See also* Dalmatia *under* Italy).

• Brac

FIRST STAMPS ISSUED May 1944

CURRENCY
100 banicas = 1 kuna

Island south of Split on the Dalmatian coast which issued one set while occupied by the Germans. It was a charity issue and similar issues were prepared for the islands of Hvar and Korcula but were never issued.

• Gulf of Kotor

FIRST STAMPS ISSUED 10 February 1944

CURRENCY	
1944	Italian or German currency

Part of Dalmatian coast first occupied by the Italians and then by the Germans after Italians surrendered in 1943. Since 1945 has been part of Yugoslavia, administered from Montenegro.

• Macedonia

FIRST STAMPS ISSUED 28 October 1944

Further occupation issues were produced for Serbia and Montenegro, and are listed under those countries.

In addition to occupation issues referred to above, other parts of Yugoslavia were controlled by other German allies. Hungary acquired all territory north of the river Drava, including the major town of Novi Sad. Albania was given a large area, including Uleinj on the coast and Pec, Dakovica, Pristina, Prizren and Kicevo. This part was officially annexed on 12 September 1942. Bulgaria gained Yugoslav Macedonia, which included the towns of Skopje, Pirot and Bitola, which had been part of Serbia. All these territories were returned to Yugoslavia after the war.

1945 to date

The guerrillas and partisans who had fought the Germans during their occupation of the country were themselves split by loyalties and political affiliation. Marshal Tito seized power in April 1945 and formed the territory into a democratic federation. Because of the general shortage of stamps, regional overprints were produced in Bosnia-Herzegovina, Croatia, Montenegro, Serbia and Slovenia. The first general issue, still an overprint, was released on 14 December 1944, but regular issues did not appear until February 1945.

Albania

Before 1914

FIRST STAMPS Turkish from 1870
FIRST STAMPS ISSUED 1913

CURRENCY	
1913	40 paras = 1 piastre or grosch
1913	100 qint = 1 franc
1947	100 qint = 1 lek
1965	100 oldler = 1 new lek

A Albania:Kingdom 1930; **B** Albania:Communist Republic 1960; **C** Albania:Regency 1923; **D** Bulgaria:Principality 1879; **E** Bulgaria:Communist Republic 1949; **F** Albania:Italian Occupation 1939; **G** Bulgaria:Independent Kingdom 1917.

A
B
C
D
E
F
G
POSTAT SHQIPTARE
R.P. E SHQIPERISE
Mbledhja Kushtetuese 12-IV-1939 XVII
Н.Р. БЪЛГАРИЯ
1915-1917

Province in European Turkey, formerly part of ancient Epirus. Had been defeated by the Turks in the 14th century, but a national hero, Scanderberg, rose up about 1443 and liberated Albania from Turkish control for a few years. Turkish control was re-established following the siege of Scutari in 1478.

During the period of Turkish control there were seven POs in Albania and each had its own special handstamp. Frequently the handstamps were only used as arrival marks, and stamps were applied at the office of delivery.

In 1902 Italy, as part of its policy of expansion in the Mediterranean opened POs in Albania which used Italian stamps overprinted ALBANIA and in Turkish currency. Offices were opened at Durazzo, Scutari and Valona. First issue was replaced in 1909 by a further issue overprinted for each of the towns.

Albania did not take part in the first Balkan War in 1912-13, but declared its independence on 28 November 1912. This was confirmed by the Treaty of London, which ended the war.

First stamps were issued in October and November 1913 with overprints on various Turkish adhesives. First permanent series was issued in December 1913. However, the new country was to suffer immediate problems. Albania was overrun by troops of Greece, Montenegro and Serbia. Essad Pasha set up his own regime and issued stamps for central Albania. The Greeks also issued stamps in 1914 for Epirus and Northern Epirus, which they had occupied. To try to bring peace, the Dutch were asked to send a detachment of police. These used their own special stamps at their headquarters in Koritza. The Montenegrins had occupied Scutari. Postmarks of SCUTARI-SKADOR are found on the stamps of Montenegro and Albania.

1914-18

During World War I Albania was a battleground and was occupied by different powers in different areas and by conflicting armies. However, some postal service was preserved and the central government continued to issue stamps throughout the period.

1918-39

Italy occupied most of the country as soon as World War I ended and tried to preserve its presence on the Greek side of the Adriatic. In 1920 the Albanians forced the Italians to recognize Albanian sovereignty and moved their capital from Durrazo to Tirane.

Albania was a republic until November 1928 when the president, Ahmed Zogu, declared a kingdom with himself as King Zog I. On 7 April 1939 Italy invaded and occupied Albania. Stamps were issued almost immediately and were overprinted 'Constituent Assembly 12 IV 1939 XVII'. This referred to the body who offered the crown of Albania to the King of Italy. The figure XVII refers to the 17th year of Fascist rule in Italy.

1939-45

Italy did not enter World War II until June 1940; after the fall of France it used Albania as its base for the invasion of Greece on 28 October 1940. The Greeks counterattacked and soon overran almost half of Albania. They issued stamps overprinted for southern Albania on 10 December 1940. When Germany invaded Yugoslavia and Greece in April 1941, it returned the control of Albania to Italy. However, when Italy surrendered in September 1943, Germany immediately assumed the occupation of Albania. Stamps were again issued. These were from the Italian occupation overprinted.

In 1944 a guerilla leader, General Hoxha, drove German forces from the country and proclaimed Albania to be a democratic republic on 22 November 1944. In January 1945 definitive stamps from the Italian occupation were further overprinted for the new republic.

1945 onwards

During this period, Albania has issued stamps regularly, mainly to acquire hard currency.

• Saseno

FIRST STAMPS ISSUED Italy overprinted Saseno — April 1923

CURRENCY

1923 As Italy

Island in the Gulf of Valona off the coast of Albania occupied by Italy on 30 October 1914. Remained an Italian possession until 1943 when it was occupied by the Germans. Returned to Albania by the Treaty of Paris in 1947.

A Greece: Centenary of Independence 1930; B Greece: Republic 1975; C Greece: Battle of Navarino 1932;

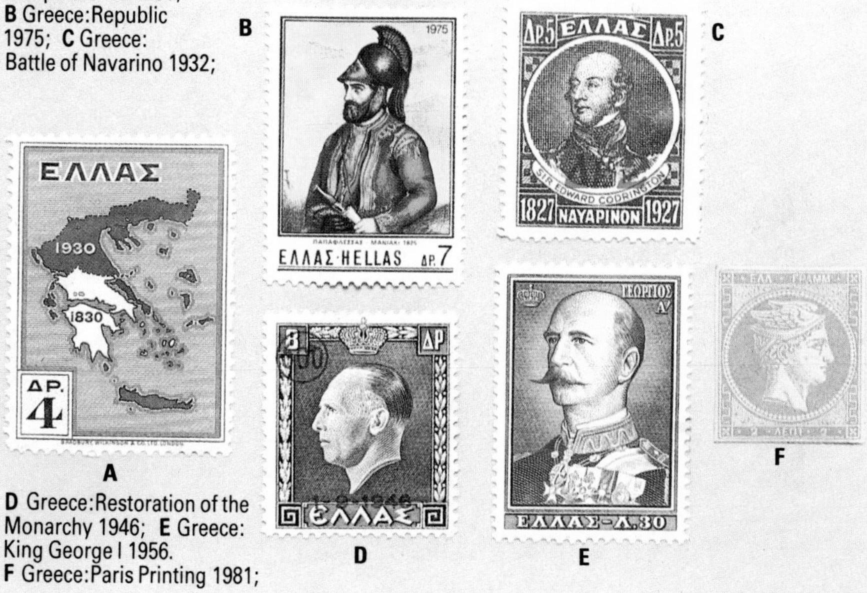

ΕΛΛΑΣ
1930
1830
ΔΡ.
4
1975
ΕΛΛΑΣ·HELLAS ΔΡ.7
ΔΡ.5 ΕΛΛΑΣ ΔΡ.5
1827 ΝΑΥΑΡΙΝΟΝ 1927
ΕΛΛΑΣ
A
B
C
D
E
F

D Greece: Restoration of the Monarchy 1946; E Greece: King George I 1956. F Greece: Paris Printing 1981;

Bulgaria

Before 1914

FIRST STAMPS Turkish Stamps from the 1850s
FIRST STAMPS ISSUED Bulgaria as a principality 1 March 1879

CURRENCY

1879 100 centimes = 1 franc
1881 100 stozinki = 1 lev

Bulgaria was conquered by the Turks in 1396 and was a province of the Ottoman Empire until 1877. It revolted in 1876 in support of Bosnia-Herzegovina when it was annexed by Austria-Hungary. This revolt was suppressed with great cruelty by the Turks, which drew the attention of the Great Powers to the area.

Bulgaria was the site of much of the fighting during the Russo-Turkish War 1877-8, and revolted again against Turkish control. Following intervention by Russia, a principality was established north of the Balkan mountains in 1878. This was confirmed by the Treaty of Berlin in the same year. The area south of the new territory, Eastern Rumelia, was granted a semi-autonomous administration, both regions remaining under Turkish suzerainty.

Postal service under direct Turkish control in both areas was well developed and at least 16 POs were in operation.

In 1880 Eastern Rumelia issued its own stamps overprinted on Turkish stamps. In 1885 there was a popular revolt in Rumelia in favour of union with Bulgaria and the name of the province was changed to Southern Bulgaria. This province then issued its own stamps from 10 September 1885 until Bulgarian stamps were introduced throughout the area from 1 October in the same year.

Bulgaria remained a principality under Turkey until it became an independent kingdom in 1908. Bulgaria supported the other Christian states, Serbia, Montenegro and Greece, in the first Balkan War in 1912. Bulgaria was keen to extend its boundary to the south into Thrace and to obtain a port on the northern Aegean Coast.

Britain and Germany restrained their allies to prevent a full-scale European war. Bulgaria was the most successful of the countries in the war and obtained much additional territory. However, an armistice was signed on 3 December 1912 and the London Peace Conference broke down because of the Bulgarian insistence that it should obtain Adrianople in Turkish Thrace. This could not be agreed and Bulgaria, underestimating the strength of the opposition, renewed the fighting. However, in face of attacks from Serbia and Greece, supported by Romania, who had held aloof from the first Balkan War, Bulgaria was defeated and the second Balkan War was concluded by the Treaty of Bucharest on 10 August 1913. By this, Bulgaria gained western Thrace and access to the Aegean.

1914-18

On 6 October 1915, after the British repulse at Gallipoli, Bulgaria entered the war on the side of the Central Powers and took part in the defeat of Serbia on the western border and Romania on the northern border. It acted in support of its Turkish allies in eastern Thrace and, after the defeat of Serbia, acted as the holding force in the Salonica area. The stalemate was broken in 1918 and Bulgaria was defeated by the Allies, who advanced through their territory into Romania and Russia. Bulgaria lost eastern Thrace to Greece and has remained largely within the same boundaries ever since.

1918-39

A kingdom under Boris III, Bulgaria

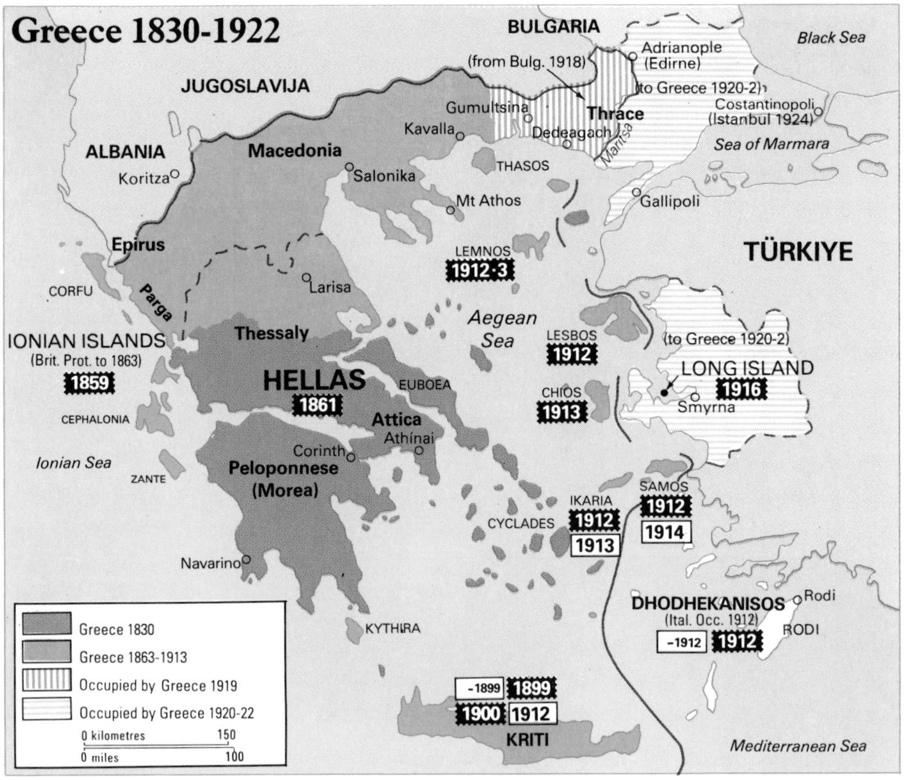
Greece 1830-1922
BULGARIA
Black Sea
Adrianople
(Edirne)
(from Bulg. 1918)
(to Greece 1920-2)
JUGOSLAVIJA
Gumultsina
Thrace
Costantinopoli
(Istanbul 1924)
Kavalla
Dedeagach
Maritsa
Sea of Marmara
ALBANIA
Macedonia
Koritza
Salonika
THASOS
Mt Athos
Gallipoli
Epirus
LEMNOS
1912-3
TÜRKIYE
CORFU
Larisa
Parga
Aegean
Sea
IONIAN ISLANDS
(Brit. Prot. to 1863)
1859
Thessaly
LESBOS
1912
(to Greece 1920-2)
HELLAS
1861
EUBOEA
LONG ISLAND
1916
CHIOS
1913
Smyrna
CEPHALONIA
Attica
Athínai
Corinth
Ionian Sea
ZANTE
Peloponnese
(Morea)
SAMOS
1912
1914
IKARIA
1912
CYCLADES
1913
Navarino
DHODHEKANISOS
Rodi
(Ital. Occ. 1912)
RODI
-1912
1912
KYTHIRA
Greece 1830
Greece 1863-1913
Occupied by Greece 1919
Occupied by Greece 1920-22
0 kilometres 150
0 miles 100
-1899
1899
1900
1912
KRITI
Mediterranean Sea

continued to develop a new national identity between the wars. The creation of the new Yugoslavia effectively contained the eastern frontier and after some fighting with Greece on the southern boundary in 1925-6, a period of comparative peace followed.

1939-45

World War II did not affect the Balkans immediately. However, the attack on Greece by Italy in October 1940 led to the need for German assistance in the area. German control was consolidated by forcing Bulgaria to join the Axis on 1 March 1941. German troops passed through Bulgaria to attack Greece on 6 April and Greece surrendered on 27 April.

As part of the Anglo-Russian discussions in 1944, Russian dominance in the Balkans and particularly Bulgaria was acknowledged. The advance from Russia into the Balkans led to the recapture of Sofia on 5 September 1944. Stamps of the kingdom of Bulgaria continued in use during the war.

1945 to date

As the result of a referendum, the king was deposed on 15 September 1946 and a People's Republic was declared on the same day. Stamps of the new regime replaced the previous royal issues.

Greece

CURRENCY

1861	100 lepta = 1 drachma
1944	1000 old drachma = 1 new drachma

Before 1850

Site of the first major European civilization. After the decline of Greek power in the 4th century BC, conquered first by the Macedonians and then by the Romans in 146 BC. Following invasion by the Crusaders in 1204, divided into small governments and then captured by the Turks in 1456, immediately after the fall of Constantinople. Greece remained a Turkish province until the War of Independence (1821-8), during which Greece held the Turks at bay, though in danger of being subdued, until the Allied fleet defeated the Turks at Navarino in 1827. The Turks evacuated Morea, the province of southern Greece, in October 1828, and independence was acknowledged by the Treaty of Adrianople in September 1829.

There was no public postal service under Turkish control, but by 1850 a limited civil post existed. Letters for overseas were carried by the captains of visiting ships.

1850-71

FIRST STAMPS ISSUED 1 October 1861

Greek territory was limited by the first treaty with Turkey and although this had been accepted when the kingdom was proclaimed, the boundaries paid no attention to similarities of race and language. As a result, many minor uprisings took place in Thessaly and Epirus.

First stamp issue was printed in Paris, but the plates were subsequently transferred to Athens, where printings were produced from November 1861.

Parts of present-day Greece, which were still under Turkish rule, used Turkish stamps until transferred.

1871-1914

Greece was not happy with the outcome of the Treaty of San Stefano, although it obtained southern Epirus. As a result of a further uprising the Turkish sultan proposed a rectification of the frontiers in July 1878. Eventually a convention was signed by Turkey and Greece at Constantinople in July 1881 and Thessaly was ceded to Greece. Greece supported the national uprising in Crete (q.v.) in the 1890s. Also supported the other Christian countries in the Balkans during the first Balkan War. As a result, Greece gained territory in Macedonia and western Thrace. In the second Balkan War, Greece occupied southern Albania and Thrace and issued overprinted stamps for these areas.

• Macedonia (before 1914)
The town of Kavalla was occupied by the Greeks in 1913 and stamps of Bulgaria were released overprinted in Greek on 1 July 1913. This area reverted to Greece in 1914 and Greek stamps were used.

• Western Thrace (before 1914)
Area on the northern edge of the Aegean Sea and west of the Maritsa river which had been administered by Turkey until the first Balkan War. It was occupied by Bulgarian troops and awarded to Bulgaria after the Treaty of London. However, in the second Balkan War the Greeks invaded the province and occupied Dedêagatz (now Alexandropoulos) and Gumultsina (now Komotini). In the former, Bulgarian stamps were issued overprinted, and in the latter, Turkish stamps. Overprints, in Greek, were issued in both places in July-August 1913 but were withdrawn when Greek troops withdrew at the end of September.

In October the Muslim inhabitants of western Thrace formed an autonomous republic and issued their own stamps. However, the area was awarded to Bulgaria by the Treaty of Bucharest, and Bulgarian stamps were used until 1918.

1914-18
Following the British repulse at Gallipoli in 1915, Allied forces were landed at Salonica and in August 1916 the line was stabilized on the Greek frontier. Although Allied forces were actually fighting on Greek soil. Greece entered the war on 30 June 1917 and assisted in the break-out from the Salonica front in 1918. During this period military posts of France and Britain operated in Salonica but the British PO in Salonica had been closed in 1914.

1918-39
After the defeat of Bulgaria, western Thrace was occupied by Allied troops and overprinted stamps were issued in January 1920. Under the terms of the Treaty of Sèvres in August 1920, Greece obtained western Thrace from Bulgaria and was given a mandate for the Turkish part of eastern Thrace except for Constantinople itself. This region was later incorporated into Greece. Overprinted stamps were issued in July 1920 and for the occupation of Adrianople (Edirne) in August.

The Greek-Turkish War broke out in May 1919 when the Allies landed a Greek Army at Smyrna (*see* Turkey). The Greek Army remained in Asia Minor until defeated by the Turkish Nationalists under Kemal Ataturk in September 1922. As a result of the Treaty of Lausanne, eastern Thrace was returned to Turkey.

1939-45
Greece remained neutral until invaded by Italy from Albania on 29 October 1940. The Greeks counter-attacked and occupied part of southern Albania including Koritza, until the German invasion in April 1941. Overprinted stamps were issued for this area on 10 December 1940.

British troops were sent to Greece to support the assault on the Italians in February 1941 and they brought their Field POs with them. More British forces arrived in March. The German assault came from Bulgaria on 6 April 1941 and quickly overran Greece. The last British troops were evacuated to Crete on 2 May, which was itself invaded by German paratroops on 20 May. The last Allied ships left southern Crete on 31 May when Greece fell under Axis control.

Greek stamps continued to be used throughout the territory until independence was regained in October 1944. First stamps with the new currency were issued on 11 November 1944. However, the transition to peace was difficult and Communist guerrilla leaders paid scant attention to the new government. Although Russian non-intervention had been agreed, once the last German troops left on 1 November 1944 internal disorder threatened and various partisan groups refused to hand over their weapons. The British troops quickly defeated the Communists once they were withdrawn from Athens and a truce was agreed on 11 January 1945. British Field POs were again used in Greece during this period.

1945 to date
By plebiscite, the Greek people voted for a return of the Greek monarchy in September 1946. However, King Constantine was deposed in June 1973 and the second republic was formed. Since that date there have been many changes of government control, but the postal service has remained intact and stamps have not reflected these changes.

• Mount Athos
An ecclesiastical centre on the most easterly promontory of the Khalkidhiki peninsula in Macedonia.

In 1915-16, the Allies were considering the occupation of this area to protect the eastern flank of the Salonica position, and, in anticipation, prepared a series of stamps intended for issue on 25 January. These were produced on board a naval vessel and are interesting in that they bear the language and currency of three different alphabets: English, Greek and Russian.

• Ionian Islands

CURRENCY	
1859	sterling
1941	Italian
1943	1000 centesimi = 1 lira = 8 drachma

1660-1793
Group of seven islands in the Ionian Sea off the west coast of Greece the largest of which is Corfu. For several centuries was under the rule of Venice and on the main trading route from Venice to the Levant. Under Venetian administration it was known as Cephalonia and at least one handstamp of 1714 is known.

1793-1815
In 1797 under the Treaty of Campo Formio islands were ceded to France.

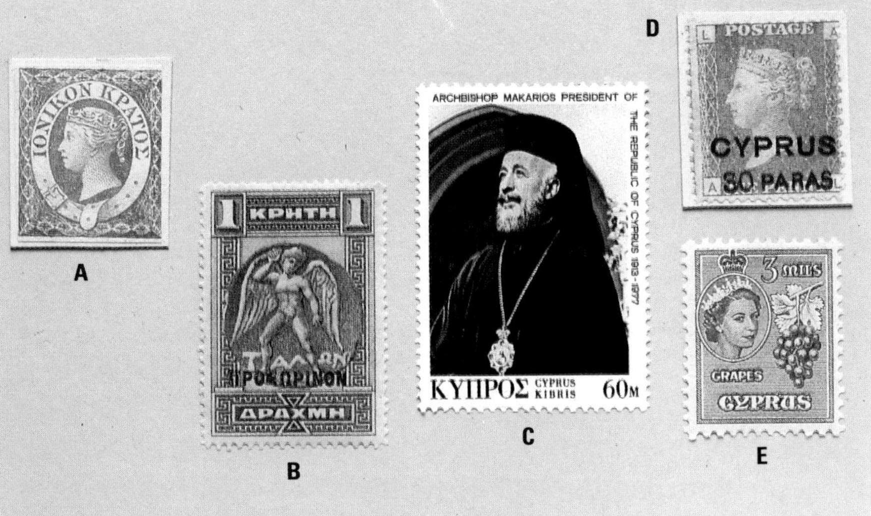
A
B
C
D
E
ΚΡΗΤΗ
ΔΡΑΧΜΗ
ARCHBISHOP MAKARIOS PRESIDENT OF
ΚΥΠΡΟΣ CYPRUS KIBRIS 60M
POSTAGE
CYPRUS
30 PARAS
GRAPES
CYPRUS

A Ionian Islands: United States of Ionia 1859; **B** Crete: Provisional Government 1900; **C** Cyprus: Republic 1977; **D** Cyprus: British Military administration 1881; **E** Cyprus: Crown Colony 1955.

After a blockade by the Russo-Turkish fleet, the islands were seized. Group was returned to France in 1807 and remained under its control until 1814. The French postal service had a number of handstamps in use.

In 1809 the British attacked and gradually occupied the islands until finally Corfu fell in 1814. The group was handed over to Britain in 1815 by the Treaty of Paris.

1815-50

Britain gave the islands a new constitution and they were entitled 'The United States of Ionia'. During this period the area also included the seaport and district of Parga on the Epirus coast, which was handed back to Greece in 1819. The British introduced a number of handstamps including the crowned circle types 'Paid at Zante', 'Paid at Cephalonia' and 'Paid at Corfu' from 1844 onwards. A British garrison was maintained in the group and soldiers' letters are known from this period.

1850-1919

FIRST STAMPS ISSUED 15 May 1859

Protection of the islands by Britain had been accepted for many years because of their strategic importance. However in the 1850s a more determined movement for union with Greece began. All the islands which had been Italian-speaking began to use Greek lettering. When stamps were issued these had lettering in Greek. The stamps became invalid when the islands were returned to Greece on 28 June 1864. During the transition period there were no Greek adhesives available, stamps of Austrian Italy and Austrian Levant were freely used and Austrian Lloyd steamers were used for the transport of mail. Greek stamps have been used since that time except for two short periods in 1921 and 1941.

1919-39

Following World War I, Italy occupied Corfu and Italian stamps were overprinted during a temporary dispute with Greece.

1939 to date

Italian forces invaded in 1941 and stocks of Greek stamps in the islands, mainly of 1937 issue, were overprinted. These were then replaced by Italian stamps overprinted ISOLE JONIE which were used until 1943. In that year the Italian regime collapsed and occupation was taken over by the Germans. They reissued some of the Italian overprints with the additional marking ELLAS [Greece] and 2-x-43 [the date of occupation]. These were used in Zante only. Since the recapture of the islands, Greek stamps have been used.

• Crete
1871-1914

FIRST STAMPS Turkey up to 1899
FIRST STAMPS ISSUED Joint occupying powers 1899
FIRST STAMPS ISSUED Crete March 1900

CURRENCY

1900 As Greece

Island in the Mediterranean about 60 miles south-east of Greece. It has a long and troubled history. Population is Greek but there is a Muslim minority. Under Venetian rule in the Middle Ages and up to 1669, when it fell to the Turks. Remained under direct control of Turkey until 1830, when it was ceded to Egypt, but was restored to Turkey in 1840. This was followed by a long period of civil war.

In 1898 an international occupation by British, French, Italian and Russian forces took place. The island was declared an autonomous republic in 1899 and was united with Greece in 1913. This was confirmed by the Treaty of London in the same year.

Before the arrival of joint occupying forces in 1898, there was a rudimentary postal service between Crete and the mainland. Turkish stamps were used. Before the issue of Cretan stamps in 1900, each of the occupying powers issued stamps for the use of their troops and the civilian population in their area of control. Britain and Russia issued stamps inscribed in Greek, but France and Italy used stamps overprinted with the name of the island. Austria also had specially overprinted stamps for use in its POs on the island. These stamps were used concurrently with Cretan issues, had a limited usage, and the British, in particular, may only have had local validity. The Austrian PO was not closed until 15 December 1914. Forces were withdrawn in 1909.

In 1908 stamps of Crete which had been issued in 1900 were overprinted HELLAS [Greece] when the local parliament declared unio with Greece, but these were suppressed in 1909. In 1912 Greek stamps began to be used in Crete and have been ever since.

View of Patmos, Dodecanese Islands, taken for official Greek postcard

• Dodecanese Islands 1871-1914

FIRST STAMPS Turkish up to 1912
FIRST STAMPS ISSUED Italy overprinted 1912

CURRENCY	
Up to 1912	As Turkey
1912	As Italy

Group of twelve islands in the eastern Aegean. Historically important group which formed part of the base for Venetian merchants in the area. Held by the Knights Hospitaller from 1309 to 1522, when the islands became part

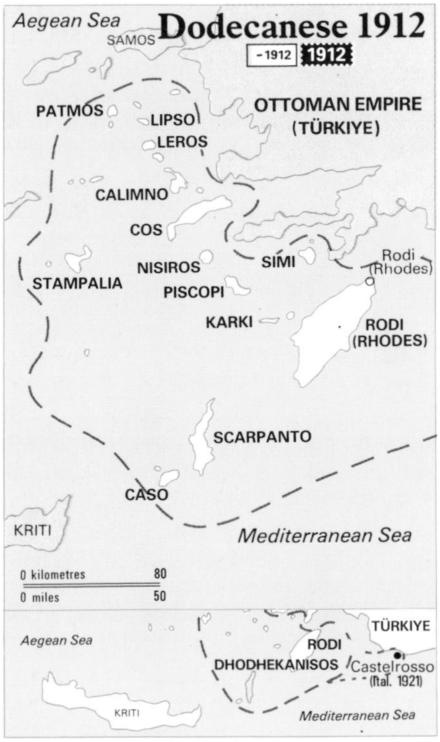
Aegean Sea
Dodecanese 1912
-1912
1912
SAMOS
PATMOS
LIPSO
LEROS
OTTOMAN EMPIRE
(TÜRKIYE)
CALIMNO
COS
NISIROS
SIMI
Rodi
(Rhodes)
STAMPALIA
PISCOPI
KARKI
RODI
(RHODES)
SCARPANTO
CASO
KRITI
Mediterranean Sea
0 kilometres 80
0 miles 50
Aegean Sea
TÜRKIYE
RODI
DHODHEKANISOS
Castelrosso
(Ital. 1921)
KRITI
Mediterranean Sea

of the Ottoman Empire. Seized by Italy in 1912 and remained under its control until 1943.

Before seizure by the Italians, islands had had a limited postal service under Turkish control. The first stamps issued were Italian stamps overprinted 'Egeo' and these were followed by a further series of overprints with the name of each of the islands. These were CALIMNO, CASO, COS, KARKI, LEROS, LIPSO, NISIROS, PATMOS, PISCOPI, RODI, SCARPANTO, SIMI and STAMPALIA.

1914-39

Continued as an Italian base during World War I. First stamps without overprints were issued in 1916. Turkey ceded the group to Italy in 1920.

1939-45

When Italy surrendered in September 1943, the Dodecanese Islands proclaimed union with Greece. Some of the islands were liberated by the Allied forces but they were quickly re-occupied by the Germans and were not finally freed until 1945.

1945 to date

Stamps of Britain overprinted MEF were used in the group from liberation in 1945 until 1947, when the islands were transferred to Greece. For a short period Greek stamps overprinted SDD [Dodecanese Military Occupation] were used but normal Greek stamps have been used since the summer of 1947.

• Aegean Islands

CURRENCY	
1912	As Italy

Before 1914

[All dates relate to the Julian Calendar; the Gregorian Calendar was 13 days ahead] During the first Balkan War, Greece occupied a number of islands which had previously been held by the Turks.

Overprinted stamps were issued as follows:
Khios (Chios) — occupied 11 November 1912, overprinted stamps issued in May 1913
Nesvos (Lesbos) — occupied 8 November 1912, overprinted stamps issued in November 1912
Limnos (Lemnos) — occupied 7 October 1912, overprinted stamps issued in 1912-13

Additionally, Ikaria (Icaria) declared its independence from Turkey as a free state at the end of July 1912, and stamps were issued on 8 October 1912. Island was occupied by Greece in support of the new state on 4 November 1912 and overprinted Greek stamps were issued in 1913. United with Greece in June 1913 and Greek stamps were used thereafter.

Samos was an independent principality under Turkish control with British, French and Russian protection. There was a French PO on the island from 1893 to 1914. Following a revolt in September 1912, the Turkish garrison was withdrawn and a provisional government was declared which sought union with Greece. Stamps were issued on 14 November 1912. Samos was united with Greece by the Treaty of London on 30 May 1913 and earlier stamps of Samos were overprinted 'Greece' in Greek letters. Although a later overprinted issue appeared on 17 January 1915, Greek stamps were generally used in Samos from 1914 onwards.

1914 to date

All the Aegean Islands except Castelrosso and the Dodecanese were unified with Greece following the second Balkan War. However, Castelrosso (Kastellorizo) was occupied by the French Navy on 27 December 1915. Initially it used stamps for the French POs in the Levant, which are recognizable by the postmarks. Special overprinted stamps were issued by the French administration on 19 June 1920. These remained in use until 21 August 1920 when French forces were withdrawn.

In accordance with the Treaty of Sèvres on 10 August 1920 Castelrosso was awarded to Italy. After a short transfer to Italian naval administration on 1 March 1921, it came under the rule of the governor of the Dodecanese in July 1922. Italian stamps overprinted for use in Castelrosso were issued on 11 July 1922. The island was transferred to Greece with the Dodecanese Islands by the Treaty of Paris in September 1947.

• Long Island

FIRST STAMPS ISSUED 7 May 1916

Small island, in the Gulf of Smyrna. Normally under Turkish rule, it was occupied by the British Navy in May 1916.

Local stamps were issued between 7 and 26 May 1916. They were typewritten and inscribed GRI LONG ISLAND. Turkish fiscal stamps were also overprinted GRI POSTAGE plus a new value in sterling. The status of these stamps is questionable as the British force would have had free postage.

Cyprus

Before 1914

FIRST STAMPS Turkish up to 1878 and British until 1880
FIRST STAMPS ISSUED 1 April 1880

CURRENCY

1881	40 paras = 1 piastre
	180 piastres = £ 1
1955	1000 mils = £ 1
1983	100 cents = £ 1

Island in eastern Mediterranean inhabited from earliest times. Captured by Richard I of England during the Third Crusade (1196), and handed to the Knights Templar, who controlled it until they sold it to Venice in 1487. Letters of the 15th and 16th century are known but did not represent an official postal service. Turkey conquered island in 1570 and it remained a Turkish possession, 'Kibris,' until handed over to the British administration on 12 July 1878.

A Turkish postal service operated before the British administration. There were three POs, at Larnaca, Limassol and Nicosia, but the use made of these can be gauged by the fact that only £14 worth of stamps were sold in the whole of Cyprus in 1871. Consular offices for the use of nationals were established by Britain, Austria, France, Naples and Spain. The Austrian office in Larnaca had a PO and Austrian adhesives were used there from 1864.

When the British military administration took over in 1878, a PO was opened at Larnaca on 27 July with British stamps on sale. After 1878, a number of British numeral obliterators were issued to offices in Cyprus as they opened:

942*	Larnaca	982*	Famagusta (Kyrenia)
969*	Nicosia	098*	Platres
974*	Kyrenia (Papho)	D47*	Polymedia Camp
975*	Limassol (Famagusta)	D48*	Headquarters Camp
981*	Papho (Limassol)		

Between 1854 and 1874 numbers marked with an asterisk had been issued to British towns and, unless the stamps are on pieces showing the datestamp, additional evidence that it was used in Cyprus is necessary. The names in brackets are those to which the numerals were officially allocated but evidence from covers indicate that the usage was different.

In 1880 postal administration was taken over by the island authorities and Cyprus overprints, which had been ordered by the military, were introduced. The Cypriot definitives were issued on 1 July 1881. In 1886 rural and parcel services were intro-

ISOLE ITALIANE
DELL'EGEO
1
ISOLE ITALIANE DELL'EGEO
2
B. N. F.
CASTELLORIZO
3
O. N. F.
Castellorizo
4
CASTELROSSO
5

Overprints: **1** & **2** Aegean Islands, 1930; **3** French occupation of Castelrosso, 1920; **4** Occupation Navale Française, 1920; **5** Italian Occupation.

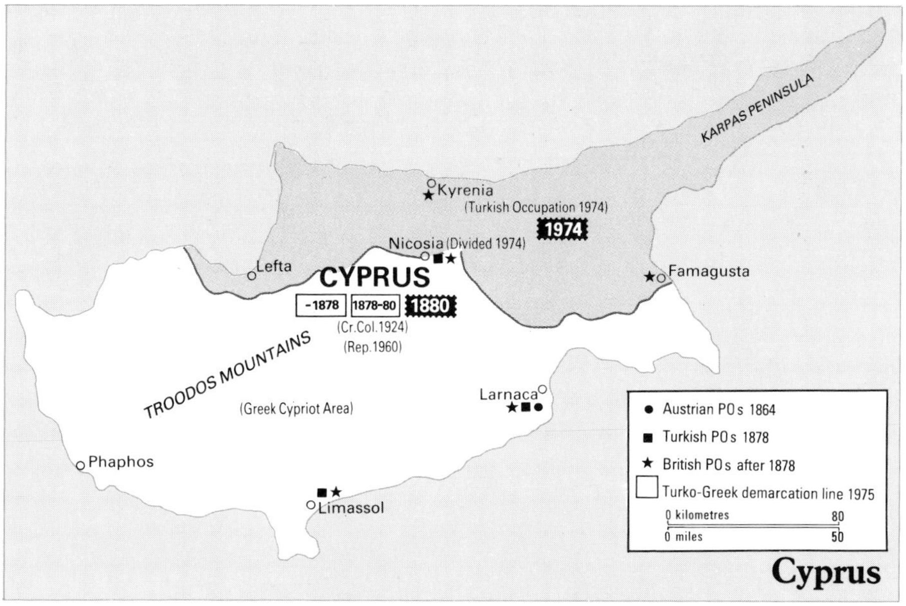
KARPAS PENINSULA
Kyrenia
(Turkish Occupation 1974)
1974
Nicosia (Divided 1974)
Lefta
CYPRUS
-1878
1878-80
1880
(Cr.Col.1924)
(Rep.1960)
Famagusta
TROODOS MOUNTAINS
(Greek Cypriot Area)
Larnaca
Phaphos
Limassol
● Austrian POs 1864
■ Turkish POs 1878
★ British POs after 1878
Turko-Greek demarcation line 1975
0 kilometres 80
0 miles 50
Cyprus

duced. First rural post was for POs on the Karpas peninsula and was served by a mounted postman. Service was further extended and by 1914 the whole island was covered. Cyprus joined the UPU in 1875 (under Turkey).

1914-18

Cyprus took little part in World War I, but was formally annexed by Britain after Turkey entered the war. Used as a transit base between Egypt and the Salonika area and also for rest and re-inforcement. Postal service continued to be expanded and by 1917 mule transport, which had been the traditional link between villages, was replaced by motor transport.

1918-39

Became a Crown Colony in 1924. External links in the eastern Mediterranean had traditionally been provided by steamship companies, and links existed with Turkey, Greece and Egypt. First flight from Famagusta to Egypt took place on 25 September 1930. In April 1932 flights were made to link with flights to England. Cyprus became part of the Empire 'All-up' service, via Alexandria, in 1937.

1939-45

During World War II Cyprus was a base for Allied forces and was garrisoned by British troops. Field PO markings were used. After the fall of France in June 1940, mail from Cyprus to Britain was carried by airmail via Singapore and Hong Kong to the USA. As in other colonies, there were some problems with the supply of stamps during the war, and unusual perforation varieties for the 1 *piastre* and 2 *piastre* stamps appeared in 1944.

1945 to date

During the 1950s agitation for Enosis — Union with Greece — began and resulted in a campaign against Britain by EOKA terrorists. As there was a large Turkish minority, Britain had to try to ensure an equitable solution to the problem, and for several years from 1956 there was a large British garrison, which was served by British Field POs. In August 1960 Cyprus became a republic within the British Commonwealth but with strong ties with Greece. A British presence was retained by bases on the south coast of the island, which continued to use British Field POs.

Clashes between the Greeks and Turks began in 1963 and a separated postal service was established in the Turkish Cypriot areas. A handstamp reading KIBRIS TURK POSTALAI was used and some local stamps were produced. During 1964 agreement was reached for the restoration of postal services and Turkish employees of the Cyprus Post Office staffed POs in the Turkish areas of Famagusta, Limassol, Lefka and Nicosia.

On 29 October 1973 stamps to commemorate the 50th Anniversary of the Turkish republic were issued by Turkish Cyprus, but these were not used for mail outside this area until after the Turkish invasion of Cyprus in July 1974. Following this intervention, an autonomous Turkish area was set up in the north-east of the island. On 13 February 1975 a Turkish Cypriot federated state was proclaimed in the area of Turkish occupation and 9000 Turkish inhabitants were moved from the southern area. Turkish Cyprus has continued to issue stamps since that date, but is not recognized by the UPU.

THE AMERICAS

NORTH, CENTRAL AND SOUTH AMERICA AND THE CARIBBEAN

The differences between the early postal histories of North and South America spring from the characteristics of their colonists. If these origins now seem too diverse to allow generalization, it is nonetheless no accident that English and French are officially spoken north and east of the Gulf of Mexico, Spanish and Portuguese west and south of it. Northern Europeans, with their independent and often nonconformist spirit, took their families with them and thus their whole way of life. The dominant theme of North American history is resistance to official and external interference.

Nevertheless North American ties with Europe remained cultural and racial as well as administrative and commercial; above all they remained personal.

The tradition of literacy and elementary schooling also ensured the development of widespread internal posts.

The Portuguese came as explorers, the Spanish as conquerors (*conquistadores*) bringing their despotic aristocracy and the Inquisition. The Spanish Indies were run as a vast royal estate rather than as open house for private enterprise. Settlers of Mediterranean origin tended to marry native women, which weakened European ties.

From 1514 the Spanish posts were farmed to the Galindez de Carvajal family for two and a half centuries. Services were operated by their private carriers and ships for the state and the nobility. A stream of edicts from Seville threatening penalties for interfering with the freedom to write letters had little effect; to Spanish administrators private correspondence smacked of subversion. Until the reforms of Philip V (1700-46), South Americans were lucky to see a mail once a year when the merchant fleet arrived from Seville. Only four ports were open in Spanish America; Havana, Vera Cruz, Cartagena and Portobello.

Though shipping was less rigidly controlled in the 18th century, not until Charles III took the posts back to the Crown in 1764 and introduced a packet boat was there a reliable regular service. But even this suffered from bureaucratic control and ceased in time of war.

The break-up of the Spanish Empire into a number of independent republics was fostered by Britain during the Napoleonic Wars for its own political ends ('calling the New World into existence to redress the balance of the Old'). In South America close relations with Spain did not survive the 19th-century wars of independence. Almost the only postal legacy was the series of handstruck town marks started after 1750.

Central and South American republics — and their US printers — were among the first to exploit collectors by issuing a steady stream of unnecessary stamps. The notorious Seebeck issues of Ecuador, El Salvador, Honduras and Nicaragua are the worst of many examples. Under contract, Seebeck (a director of Hamilton Bank Note Company, NY) supplied new stamps each year on condition that the demonetized remainders were returned for his exclusive sale to less sophisticated collectors. Though the practice endured only from 1892 to 1896, these countries have never recovered popularity for serious philatelists. Actual use of such stamps was small.

A characteristic of Latin America is the use for cancelling of violet and other coloured inks rather than black. This together with non-standard shapes (oval, rectangular, etc.) and sizes (often large) of the cancellers makes differentiation difficult between stamps used postally and fiscally.

The Americas from 1945

GRØNLAND
Baffin Bay
ALASKA (US)
CANADA
Hudson Bay
Gulf of Alaska
The Great Lakes
ST. PIERRE ET MIQUELON
1978
New York
UNITED NATIONS
(NEW YORK HQ)
1951
UNITED STATES OF AMERICA
BERMUDA
HAWAII (US)
Gulf of Mexico
1963
TURKS & CAICOS
1981
MEXICO
CUBA
DOMINICAN REP.
BELIZE
JAMAICA
Atlantic Ocean
GUATEMALA
1975
HAITI
HONDURAS
Caribbean Sea
West Indies
(see inset)
Pacific Ocean
EL SALVADOR
NICARAGUA
PANAMA
COSTA RICA
1966
VENEZUELA
GUYANA(BR.GUIANA)
CANAL ZONE
1977
SURINAME
1975
COLOMBIA
FRENCH GUIANA
GALAPAGOS ISLANDS
1957
ECUADOR
BRITISH VIRGIN IS.
1968
Atlantic Ocean
PUERTO RICO
ANGUILLA
1967
BARBUDA
1922
ST. CROIX
ST KITTS
ANTIGUA
1980
NEVIS
REDONDA
1979
1980
ST KITTS, NEVIS & ANGUILLA
MARTINIQUE
1947
1952
DOMINICA
GUADELOUPE
1947
ST. LUCIA
Caribbean Sea
ST. VINCENT
BARBADOS
1973
GRENADINES
(ST VINCENT)
1966
1973
GRENADINES
(GRENADA)
GRENADA
TOBAGO
TRINIDAD
Inset of West Indies for 1922 onwards
PERU
BRAZIL
BOLIVIA
PARAGUAY
CHILE
URUGUAY
ARGENTINA
FALKLAND IS.

NORTH AMERICA

Canada

FIRST STAMPS ISSUED April 1851

CURRENCY

1851 British, 'pegged' at 5s = 1 US silver dollar
1 July 1859 100 cents = 1 Canadian dollar

Canada now consists of ten provinces (from east to west, Newfoundland, Quebec, Nova Scotia, Prince Edward Island, New Brunswick, Ontario, Manitoba, Saskatchewan, Alberta and British Columbia) and two territories (Yukon and Northwest Territories). The vast region began as a number of colonies and settlements physically separated by virtually unexplored territory and its postal affairs developed accordingly.

• Canada (Colony)

Although Jacques Cartier sailed up the St Lawrence River in 1534, the first French settlement was made at Quebec in 1608. Conquered from the south by British troops during the Seven Years' War, 'New France' was ceded to Britain in 1763. In 1791 the British territory was divided into Upper Canada (English-speaking; now Ontario) and Lower Canada (French-speaking; now Quebec Province)). The provinces were reunited in 1840 as the self-governing colony of Canada.

Postal History

Under the French, New France had a single post road between Quebec and Montreal from 1734 and a packet service from La Rochelle. After 1763 the postal services of British North America were extended to Canada, and handstruck postal markings of British pattern are known from c.1776, about the time the American colonies seceded. In 1784 Canada was given its own postmaster-general. A regular overland service was established between Halifax (Nova Scotia) and Quebec. In 1791 there were only 11 POs (including Detroit and Machilimackinac, transferred to the United States in 1796); by 1800, there were 26. Stage-coaches (from 1808) and steamboats (from 1809) replaced couriers as the extension of postal services matched widespread government-sponsored immigration from Britain. By 1828 there were 151 POs. Standardized handstamps were introduced in 1829.

When stamps first appeared in 1851, there were in the colony of Canada about 600 POs to sell them. Railroads carried mail from 1853 as they came into service and a network of TPOs developed. Street letter boxes were introduced in 1859 (in Toronto).

First cancellations for stamps were in the form of a numeral with four concentric rings. They were issued on an alphabetical basis from 1 'Barrie' to 30 'Windsor'. Additional numerals were issued later and particularly 516 for Montreal and 627 for Ottawa Senate. In 1868 a new series appeared with two thick concentric circles. These were numbered from 1 to 60, and included allocation to some of the POs in the Maritime provinces (i.e. Nova Scotia, New Brunswick) which had joined the Confederation in 1867.

A further range of unofficial fancy cancellations and target obliterations also exist.

Duplex types of cancellation were introduced in 1860 and were in general use from 1880 onwards. Flag cancellations were used at Montreal and Ottawa in 1897.

• Nova Scotia

FIRST STAMPS ISSUED 1 September 1851

Nova Scotia was ceded to Britain in 1713 by the French, who had colonized it in 1598 under the name Acadia. Cape Breton Island had been assigned to France in 1632, but was united to Nova Scotia in October 1763. In 1784 it became separate, but was again joined in 1820. New Brunswick, which was gained from France in 1758, was part of Nova Scotia until 1784. Joined Canadian Federation on 1 July 1867.

The Nova Scotia PO was under control of GPO London from 1754 until 1851 and Halifax was an important link in the transatlantic service. Nova Scotia used many types of obliterations on the early stamps and by 1868 was included in the Canadian list (seven Nova Scotia and one Cape Breton POs).

• New Brunswick

FIRST STAMPS ISSUED September 1851

New Brunswick, formerly part of Nova Scotia, was won from the French in 1713. It became a separate colony in 1784 and remained thus until federation with Canada on 1 July 1867. A dispute over the boundary with Maine in the USA was not settled until the Ashburton Treaty on 9 August 1842.

The New Brunswick PO was under the control of GPO London from 1785 to 1851, by which time there were more than 20 POs in the colony. When issued, stamps were cancelled with an obliterator or with pen and ink. Initial allocation of numerals was alphabetic, except for number 1, which was St John. In all, 39 numerals were sent out. The 1868 Canadian list included five New Brunswick POs.

• Prince Edward Island

FIRST STAMPS ISSUED 1 January 1861

The island, ceded by France in 1763, was annexed to Nova Scotia until made a separate colony in 1769. Origi-

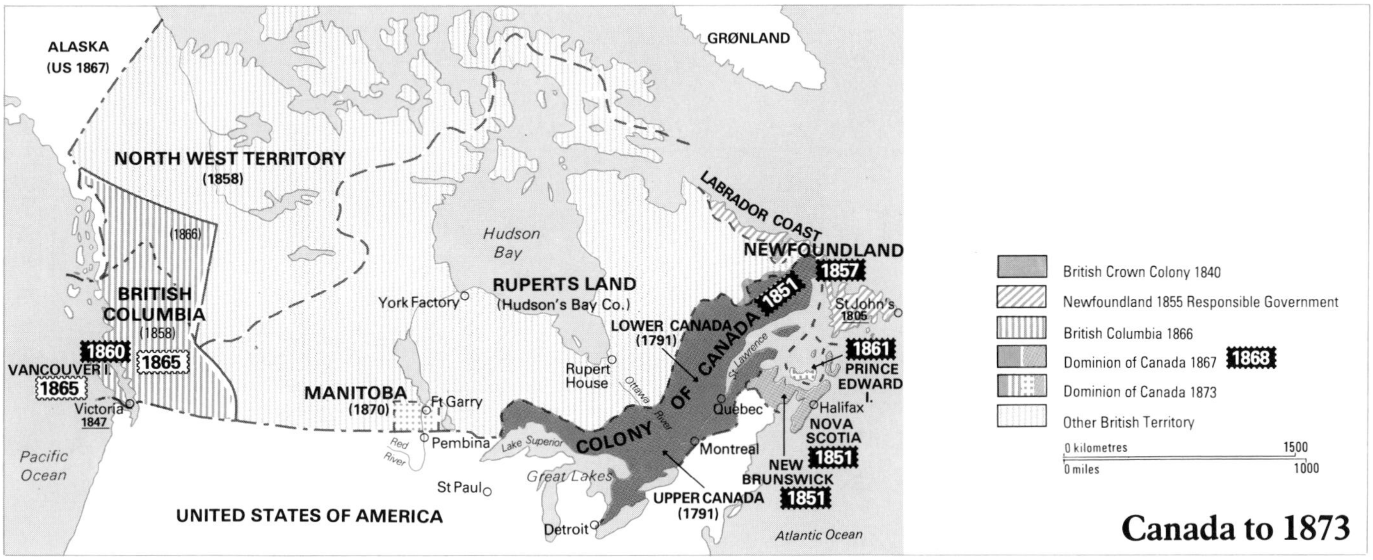
ALASKA
(US 1867)
GRØNLAND
NORTH WEST TERRITORY
(1858)
(1866)
Hudson Bay
LABRADOR COAST
NEWFOUNDLAND
1857
BRITISH COLUMBIA
(1858)
RUPERTS LAND
(Hudson's Bay Co.)
York Factory
1851
St John's
1805
LOWER CANADA
(1791)
1860
1865
VANCOUVER I.
1865
Victoria
1847
MANITOBA
(1870)
Ft Garry
Rupert House
Ottawa River
St Lawrence
COLONY OF CANADA
1861
PRINCE EDWARD I.
Quebec
Halifax
NOVA SCOTIA
1851
Red River
Pembina
Lake Superior
Montreal
NEW BRUNSWICK
1851
Pacific Ocean
Great Lakes
St Paul
UPPER CANADA
(1791)
1851
UNITED STATES OF AMERICA
Detroit
Atlantic Ocean
British Crown Colony 1840
Newfoundland 1855 Responsible Government
British Columbia 1866
Dominion of Canada 1867
1868
Dominion of Canada 1873
Other British Territory
0 kilometres 1500
0 miles 1000

Canada to 1873

nally called Ile St Jean (and St John's Isle) but renamed in 1799 after the Duke of Kent, Queen Victoria's father.

During the period of French rule there is reference to the fact that in 1705 the couriers of the governor's dispatches conveyed private letters for a fee. In 1816 administration of the post passed into the hands of the Postmaster of Nova Scotia but this was so infrequent that the islanders ran their own unofficial post. In 1851 control passed back to the islanders.

Stamps were obliterated with grids of bars until numerals were introduced in 1864 at Charlottetown. There were 32 POs on the island at this period. Stamps were withdrawn on 1 July 1873 when the colony became a province of Canada.

• British Columbia and Vancouver Island

> **FIRST STAMPS ISSUED** 1860
> Superseded by separate issues in 1865 after currency had been decimalized in Vancouver Island

Separate colonies originally with a joint stamp issue.

Vancouver Island, granted first to the Hudson's Bay Company, was made a colony in 1849. British Columbia (known until 1858 as New Caledonia) was surveyed by Vancouver 1792-4, had trading posts from 1805 and was sporadically settled from 1821 by the Hudson's Bay Company. The Fraser River gold rush of 1858 caused an influx of population via Vancouver Island, and British Columbia was made a separate colony. The two united in 1866 under the name of British Columbia, and in 1871 became a province of the Dominion.

Postal History
First PO was set up at Victoria in 1847, first mainland POs in 1858. External communications were via US expresses (Wells Fargo, etc.); internal mails beyond the small confines of the government service were also by private expresses. POs sold stamps of the USA to prepay external postage until 1870 (these were generally cancelled in transit at San Francisco). In 1871 there were 30 POs.

• Vancouver Island

> **FIRST SEPARATE STAMPS**
> 19 September 1865

• British Columbia

> **FIRST SEPARATE STAMPS**
> 1 November 1865

After 19 November 1866, when the colonies were united as British Columbia, their stamps (surcharged where necessary) were all valid throughout the region until withdrawn on 20 July 1871.

Canada (Dominion)

> **FIRST STAMPS** valid for use throughout original federation March 1868.
> Successive issues were made available over an ever-widening area as new provinces came into existence and as the settlements spread.

NEWFOUNDLAND
POSTAGE
FOURTEEN CENTS
ST. JOHN'S NEWFOUNDLAND
POSTAGE. THREE PENCE
CANADA
ROYAL WILLIAM
CENTS
NOVA SCOTIA
ONE SHILLING POSTAGE
A
B
C
D
E
F
A Canada 1859; **B** Newfoundland 1857; **C** Newfoundland 1937; **D** Canada 1858; **E** Canada 1933; **F** Nova Scotia 1851.

SAINT-PIERRE-ET-MIQUELON
POSTES
1 DOLLAR 1
A
B
C
D
E
A British Columbia 1860; **B** British Columbia 1869; **C** St Pierre et Miquelon 1909; **D** New Brunswick 1863; **E** Prince Edward Island 1862.

CURRENCY	
1867	100 cents = 1 Canadian dollar

In 1867 the provinces of Canada, New Brunswick and Nova Scotia federated as the Dominion of Canada. Prince Edward Island became a province in 1873. Though British Columbia joined the federation in 1871, it remained cut off geographically overland until the railway link was forged in 1886. The vast lands draining into Hudson's Bay had been assigned in 1670 to the Hudson's Bay Company, and after 1713 were recognized as a sphere of British influence. In 1763 the North West Company was formed to exploit the territories beyond. The two companies

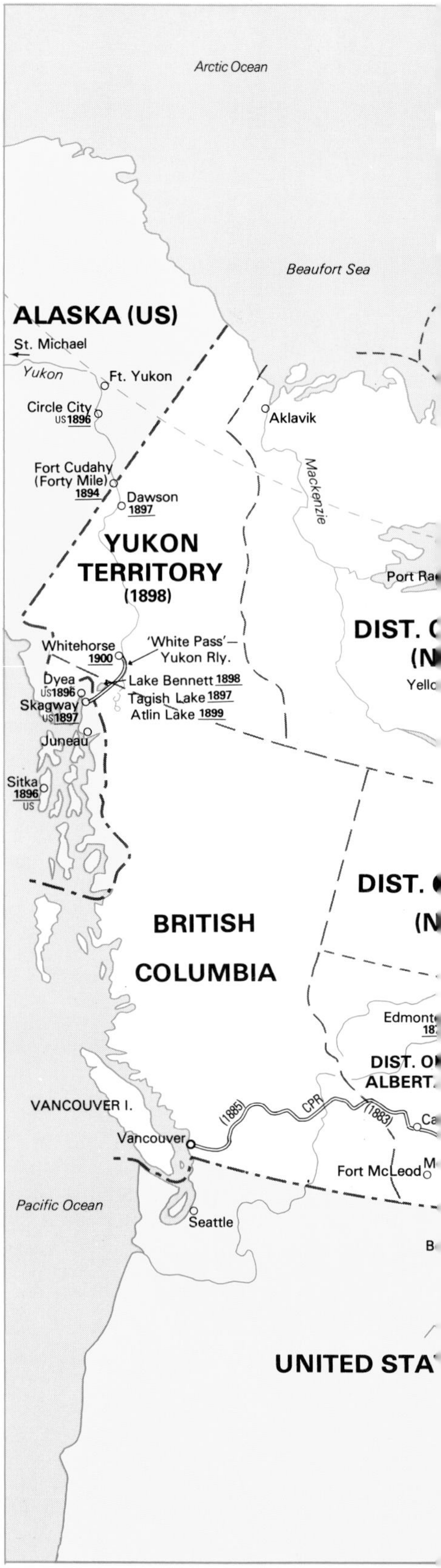
Arctic Ocean
Beaufort Sea
ALASKA (US)
St. Michael
Yukon
Ft. Yukon
Circle City
US1896
Aklavik
Mackenzie
Fort Cudahy
(Forty Mile)
1894
Dawson
1897
YUKON
TERRITORY
(1898)
Whitehorse
1900
'White Pass'–
Yukon Rly.
Dyea
US1896
Skagway
US1897
Lake Bennett 1898
Tagish Lake 1897
Atlin Lake 1899
Juneau
Sitka
1896
US
BRITISH
COLUMBIA
VANCOUVER I.
Vancouver
(1885)
CPR
(1883)
Fort McLeod
Pacific Ocean
Seattle
UNITED STA

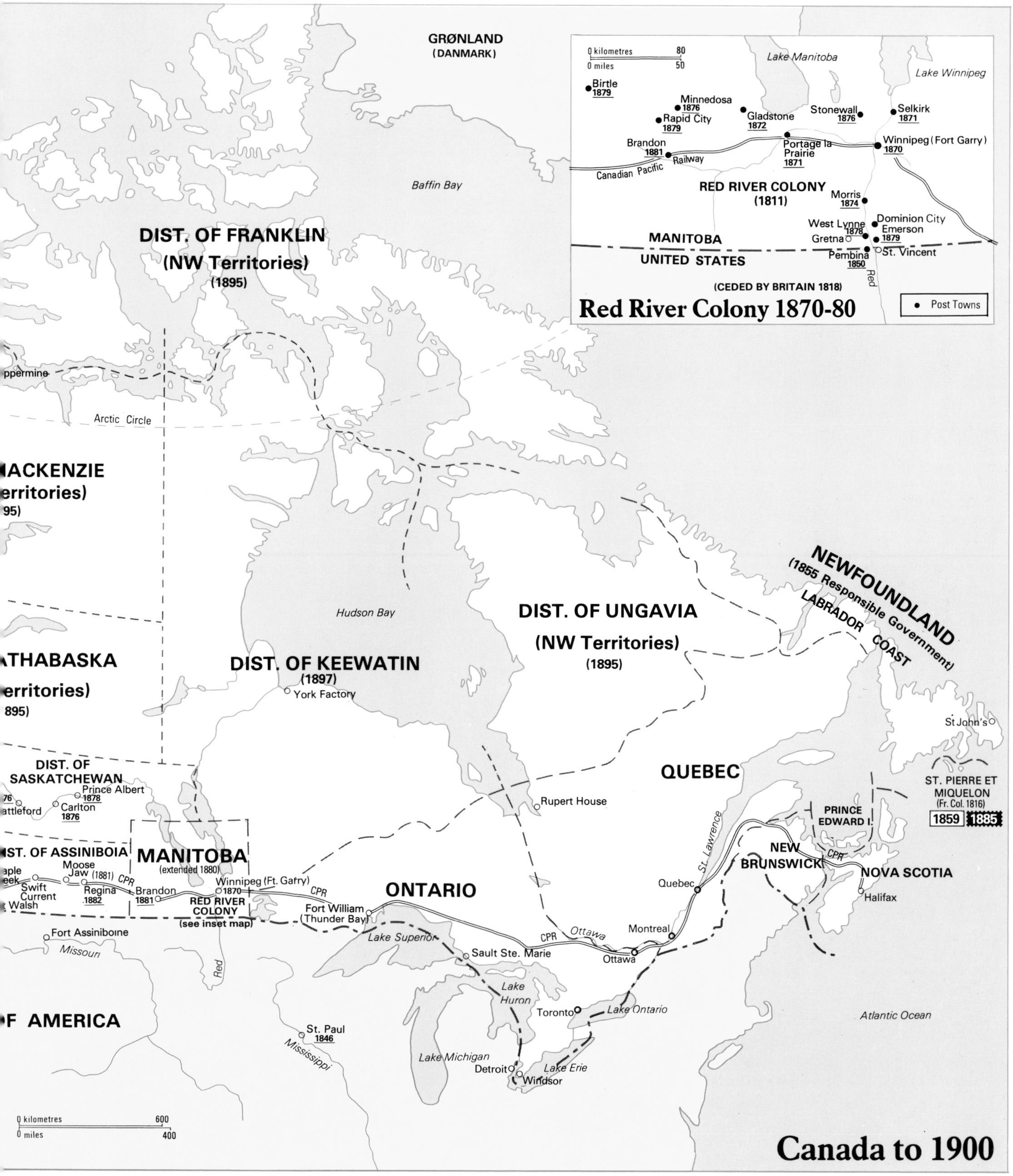
GRØNLAND
(DANMARK)
Baffin Bay
DIST. OF FRANKLIN
(NW Territories)
(1895)
Arctic Circle
Hudson Bay
DIST. OF UNGAVIA
(NW Territories)
(1895)
DIST. OF KEEWATIN
(1897)
York Factory
NEWFOUNDLAND
(1855 Responsible Government)
LABRADOR COAST
St John's
QUEBEC
Rupert House
ST. PIERRE ET MIQUELON
(Fr. Col. 1816)
1859
1885
PRINCE EDWARD I.
NEW BRUNSWICK
NOVA SCOTIA
Halifax
CPR
St. Lawrence
Quebec
Montreal
Ottawa
ONTARIO
Fort William
(Thunder Bay)
Lake Superior
Sault Ste. Marie
Lake Huron
Toronto
Lake Ontario
Lake Michigan
Detroit
Windsor
Lake Erie
Atlantic Ocean
St. Paul
1846
Mississippi
MANITOBA
(extended 1880)
Winnipeg (Ft. Garry)
1870
Brandon
1881
RED RIVER COLONY
(see inset map)
DIST. OF SASKATCHEWAN
Prince Albert
1878
Carlton
1876
Moose Jaw (1881)
Regina
1882
Swift Current
Fort Assiniboine
Missouri
Red
0 kilometres 600
0 miles 400
Canada to 1900
0 kilometres 80
0 miles 50
Lake Manitoba
Lake Winnipeg
Birtle
1879
Minnedosa
1876
Rapid City
1879
Gladstone
1872
Stonewall
1876
Selkirk
1871
Brandon
1881
Canadian Pacific Railway
Portage la Prairie
1871
Winnipeg (Fort Garry)
1870
RED RIVER COLONY
(1811)
Morris
1874
West Lynne
1878
Dominion City
Emerson
1879
Gretna
MANITOBA
UNITED STATES
Pembina
1850
St. Vincent
(CEDED BY BRITAIN 1818)
Post Towns
Red River Colony 1870-80

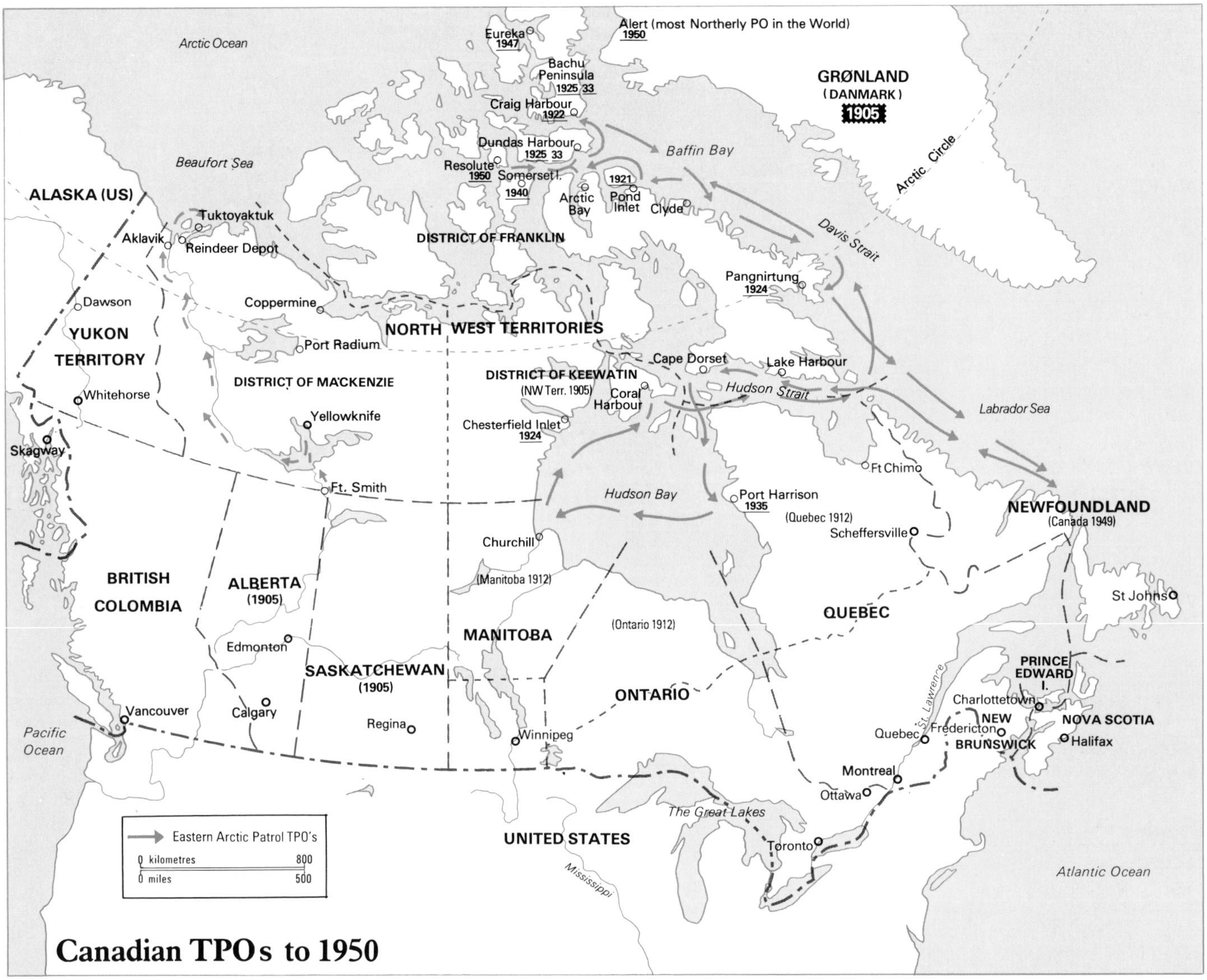
Arctic Ocean
Eureka
1947
Alert (most Northerly PO in the World)
1950
Bachu Peninsula
1925 33
Craig Harbour
1922
GRØNLAND
(DANMARK)
1905
Dundas Harbour
1925 33
Baffin Bay
Resolute
1950
Somerset I.
1940
Arctic Bay
1921
Pond Inlet
Clyde
Beaufort Sea
ALASKA (US)
Arctic Circle
Tuktoyaktuk
Aklavik
Reindeer Depot
DISTRICT OF FRANKLIN
Davis Strait
Pangnirtung
1924
Dawson
Coppermine
YUKON TERRITORY
NORTH WEST TERRITORIES
Port Radium
Cape Dorset
Lake Harbour
DISTRICT OF MACKENZIE
DISTRICT OF KEEWATIN
(NW Terr. 1905)
Coral Harbour
Hudson Strait
Whitehorse
Yellowknife
Chesterfield Inlet
1924
Labrador Sea
Skagway
Ft Chimo
Ft. Smith
Hudson Bay
Port Harrison
1935
(Quebec 1912)
Scheffersville
NEWFOUNDLAND
(Canada 1949)
Churchill
BRITISH COLOMBIA
ALBERTA
(1905)
(Manitoba 1912)
St Johns
QUEBEC
MANITOBA
(Ontario 1912)
Edmonton
SASKATCHEWAN
(1905)
PRINCE EDWARD I.
ONTARIO
Charlottetown
Vancouver
Calgary
Regina
Winnipeg
St Lawrence
Quebec
Fredericton
NEW BRUNSWICK
NOVA SCOTIA
Halifax
Pacific Ocean
Montreal
Ottawa
The Great Lakes
Eastern Arctic Patrol TPO's
0 kilometres 800
0 miles 500
UNITED STATES
Toronto
Mississippi
Atlantic Ocean

Canadian TPOs to 1950

amalgamated in 1821. In 1869 all territorial rights were sold to the Dominion government. As settlers moved in, Manitoba developed to become a new province. After British Columbia joined the federation, the Northwest Territories (so called after 1876) lost lands first to new 'districts' (some, such as Assiniboia and Athabaska, now only names), later to new provinces (Alberta and Saskatchewan, 1905).

Postal History

Before 1850 Fort Garry (Winnipeg) and the Red River Settlement of the Hudson's Bay Territory (Rupert's Land) exchanged one mail a year with Britain via York Factory and Rupert House, and two with Canada via Lake Superior and the Ottawa River. These were carried by canoe by the fur-trading *voyageurs*.

About 1853 a runner mail service was organized between Fort Garry and Pembina (just over the border in Minnesota), then the nearest US PO, for transmission via St Paul. Until 1871 US postage stamps were sold in Fort Garry to prepay the American postage. In 1870 Manitoba became Dominion territory and though mail was mainly carried via US territory until the Canadian railway reached Winnipeg in 1879, by agreement only Canadian stamps were necessary. Between 1870 and 1882 some 130 POs were opened in Manitoba.

In 1876 a mail was started between Winnipeg and Edmonton, serving five intermediate offices once every three weeks.

Farther west, though westbound mails to Fort Walsh, Fort McLeod, and Calgary were sent in closed bags from Windsor, Ontario via Montana office, the eastbound letters had to be put directly into the US system bearing US stamps via Fort Assiniboine or Benton. The arrival of the Canadian Pacific Railway and the opening of Western Terminus, a railhead distributing office, in 1883 rendered services via the USA unnecessary.

By 1900 there were c.120 POs in Alberta, c.180 in Assiniboia, 11 in Keewatin, c.50 in Northwest Territories, and c.50 in Saskatchewan. The last major territory to be reached was the Yukon, where a PO was established at Dawson in 1897 to cope with mail from the Klondyke gold rush. In the first year the mails were carried by the North-West Mounted Police, then by contractors.

Since 1921 scattered habitations in the Arctic north have been served as conditions permit by patrol boats, by aircraft fitted with skis and by snowcats.

Pony Express in the Rocky Mountains, 1880

• Newfoundland

FIRST STAMPS ISSUED 1 January 1857

CURRENCY	
1857	British
1865	100 cents = 1 dollar

Island discovered by the Cabots in the reign of Henry VII, administered as part of England from 1583, as a colony from 1713, and self-governing from 1855. Came to be treated as a dominion by 1917, but its constitution was suspended by request in 1934, and it joined Canada on 1 April 1949. Coast of Labrador was administered by Newfoundland from 1809 and from 1927 to 1944 a large area inland (formerly under Quebec Province) came under the island.

Postal History

First provincial PO opened 1805 (St John's); postal service came under the British Crown from 1840, when regular packets to Halifax were instituted (steam from 1844) for mails from Britain.

Has used stamps of Canada since 1 April 1949. The stamps were obliterated with a series of grids and fancy cancellations. One numeral, 235, is known, but this is fraudulent.

After World War I Newfoundland was the base for many attempts to cross the Atlantic by air. Although many of these failed, the technology that was developed in these trials enabled Imperial Airways to develop other overseas air routes after 1924. The first successful flight by Alcock and Brown was made in June 1919 and, as with other attempts to win the *Daily Mail* prize of £10,000, the stamps used were specially overprinted.

The long indented coastline of Labrador was served from 1896 to 1949 by Newfoundland steamer TPOs similar to those of Norway (and under Canada still is, though the railway and new town of Scheffersville opened up in 1950 a direct overland route from Quebec Province).

• St Pierre et Miquelon

FIRST STAMPS French Colonial General Issues from 1859
FIRST STAMPS ISSUED 5 January 1885
Used French stamps from 1978

CURRENCY
100 centimes = 1 franc

After periodic disputes between England and French settlers from 1713, these islands off the southern coast of Newfoundland became a French colony in 1816. Taken by a Free French naval force on 24 December 1941. Became a French overseas territory on 19 March 1946, and an overseas *département* of France on 1 July 1976.

The head PO is at St Pierre (handstamp from 1853); there are suboffices at Ile aux Chiens, Miquelon and Langlade.

Used French Colonies General Issues (oblit. SPM in lozenge). Since 1 April 1978 has used stamps of France.

United States of America

FIRST STAMPS ISSUED 1 July 1847

CURRENCY

100 cents = 1 dollar

A
B
C
D
E
F
G
U.S. POSTAGE
2¢
GADSDEN
PURCHASE
U. S. POSTAGE
NINETY CENTS
TEN 10 CENTS
YOSEMITE
ONE CENT
SPECIMEN

A USA:Roosevelt Memorial Stamp 1945; **B** USA:Pan American Exposition 1901; **C** USA: Centenary of the Gadsden Purchase 1953; **D** USA:President Washington 1857; **E** USA:Special Delivery Stamp 1888; **F** USA:National Parks Year 1934; **G** USA:Benjamin Franklin 1857.

Thirteen separate English colonies grew up on the North American seaboard between 1607 and 1775. Initially, parallel developments by Holland and Sweden had begun, particularly in the area of New York. This area was settled by the Dutch in 1625, who called it New Netherland and named the city on Manhattan Island, New Amsterdam. The British drove the Dutch and Swedes out in 1664 and it was named New York after the Duke of York, who was given the area by his brother, Charles II.

First combined action of the colonies against Britain was taken at the Congress of Philadelphia (1775), where Benjamin Franklin (*see below*) was elected to be postmaster-general to control inland mails. This was one of the first revolutionary acts of the colonies.

After the War of Independence (1775-83), Britain recognized the United States of America, and the country gradually expanded westwards. The permanent establishment of the northern frontier (between Maine and New Brunswick, 1842; 49th Parallel, 1846) and the absorption of Texas (1845) gave the United States the potential boundaries that enclose the 48 mainland states of today. Though steady progress was disrupted in 1861-5 by the secession of the Confederate States and the ensuing Civil War, the discovery of gold in California in 1849 started the first rush to the West.

Alaska (purchased from Russia, 1867) and Hawaii (annexed in 1898; territory of USA, 1900) had statehood conferred in 1959.

Postal History (Colonial period)

The earliest extant letter recorded is dated 8 August 1628 from Manhattan in New Netherland ('Manhates in

Above
Post office in Crystal, Estill Co. Kentucky, reputed to be the smallest post office in the USA

Left
Pony Express Memorial Statue, Sacramento, USA

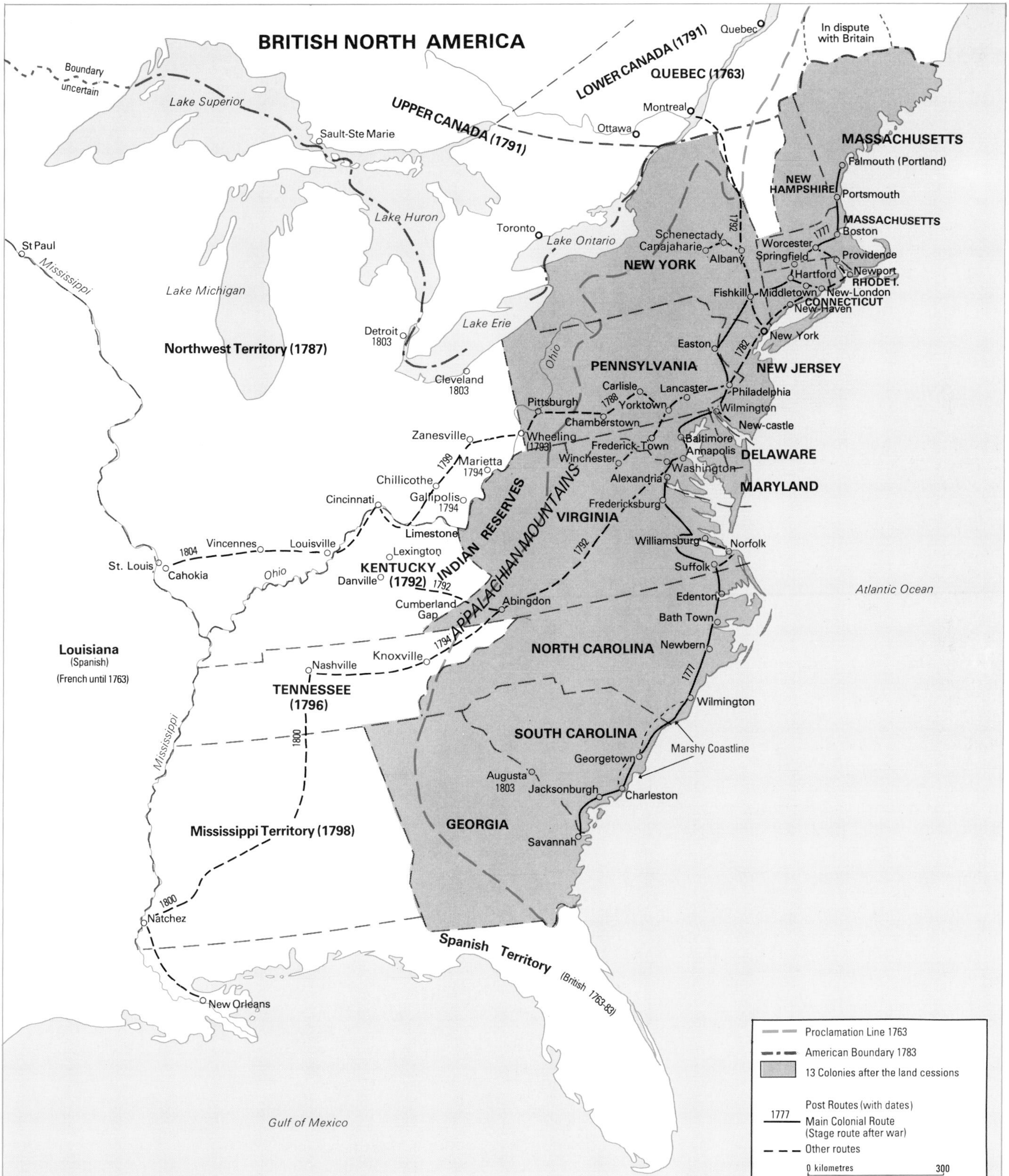
BRITISH NORTH AMERICA
Boundary uncertain
Lake Superior
Sault-Ste Marie
UPPER CANADA (1791)
LOWER CANADA (1791)
QUEBEC (1763)
Quebec
In dispute with Britain
Montreal
Ottawa
Lake Huron
Toronto
Lake Ontario
Lake Michigan
St Paul
Mississippi
Northwest Territory (1787)
Detroit 1803
Lake Erie
Cleveland 1803
MASSACHUSETTS
Falmouth (Portland)
NEW HAMPSHIRE
Portsmouth
MASSACHUSETTS
1777
Boston
Worcester
Providence
Springfield
Newport
RHODE I.
Hartford
New-London
Middletown
CONNECTICUT
New-Haven
Schenectady
Canajaharie
Albany
1792
NEW YORK
Fishkill
New York
Easton
1782
PENNSYLVANIA
NEW JERSEY
Ohio
Carlisle
Lancaster
Philadelphia
1788
Yorktown
Wilmington
Pittsburgh
Chamberstown
New-castle
Zanesville
Wheeling (1793)
Baltimore
Frederick-Town
Annapolis
DELAWARE
1798
Marietta 1794
Winchester
Washington
Chillicothe
Alexandria
MARYLAND
Gallipolis 1794
Cincinnati
Fredericksburg
VIRGINIA
INDIAN RESERVES
APPALACHIAN MOUNTAINS
Limestone
Lexington
Williamsburg
Norfolk
1804
Vincennes
Louisville
St. Louis
Cahokia
Ohio
KENTUCKY (1792)
Danville
1792
Suffolk
Edenton
Atlantic Ocean
Cumberland Gap
Abingdon
Bath Town
Louisiana (Spanish) (French until 1763)
Knoxville
1794
NORTH CAROLINA
Newbern
Nashville
TENNESSEE (1796)
1777
Wilmington
1800
SOUTH CAROLINA
Marshy Coastline
Georgetown
Augusta 1803
Jacksonburgh
Charleston
Mississippi
GEORGIA
Savannah
Mississippi Territory (1798)
1800
Natchez
Spanish Territory (British 1763-83)
New Orleans
Gulf of Mexico
Proclamation Line 1763
American Boundary 1783
13 Colonies after the land cessions
Post Routes (with dates)
1777 Main Colonial Route (Stage route after war)
Other routes
0 kilometres 300
0 miles 200

USA Postal Expansion 1763-1803

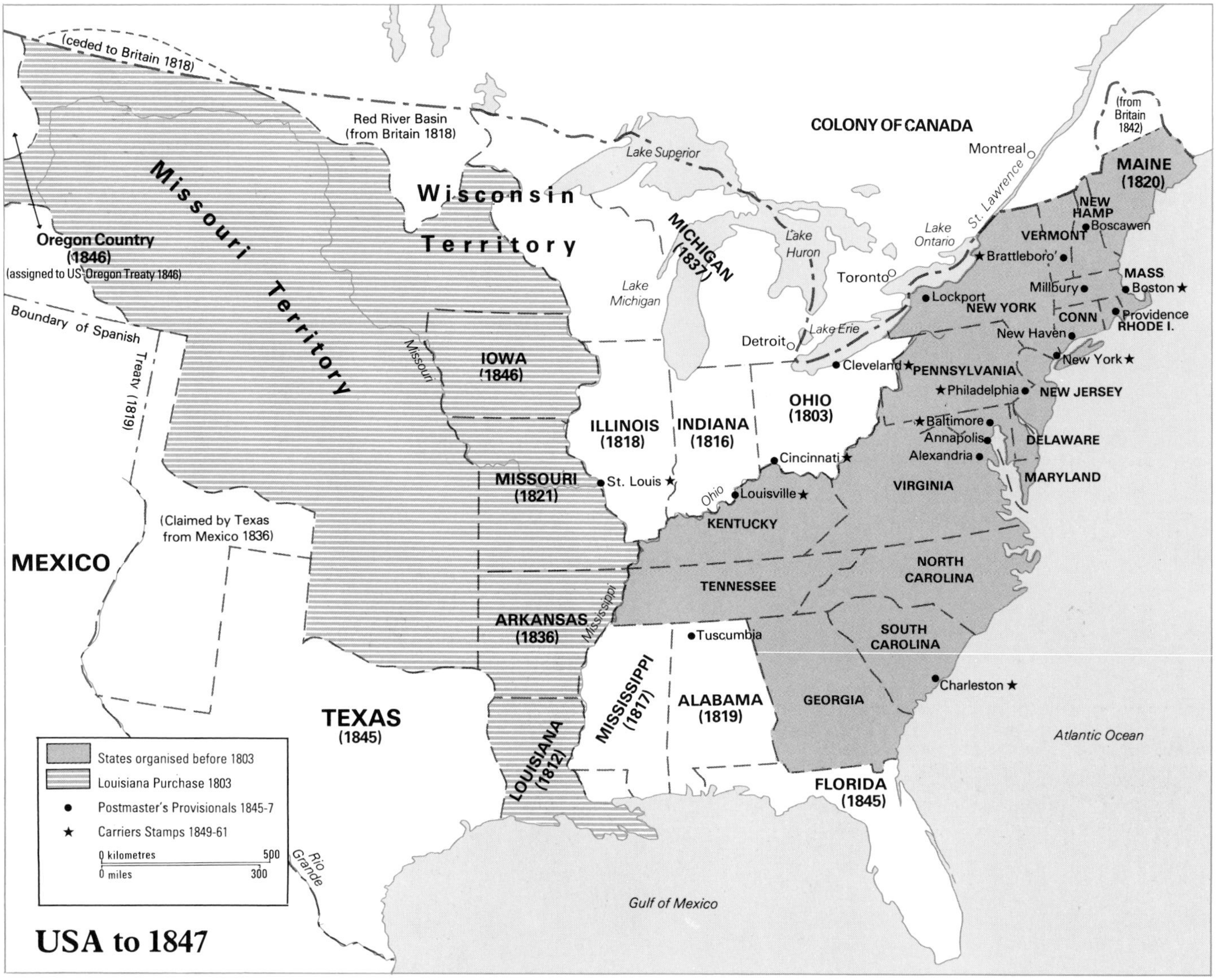
(ceded to Britain 1818)
Red River Basin (from Britain 1818)
COLONY OF CANADA
Montreal
(from Britain 1842)
MAINE (1820)
NEW HAMP
Boscawen
VERMONT
Brattleboro'
MASS
Millbury
Boston
Providence
RHODE I.
CONN
New Haven
NEW YORK
Lockport
New York
Lake Superior
Lake Huron
Lake Ontario
St. Lawrence
Toronto
Lake Michigan
Lake Erie
Detroit
Wisconsin Territory
Missouri Territory
MICHIGAN (1837)
Oregon Country (1846)
(assigned to US: Oregon Treaty 1846)
Boundary of Spanish Treaty (1819)
Missouri
IOWA (1846)
ILLINOIS (1818)
INDIANA (1816)
OHIO (1803)
Cleveland
PENNSYLVANIA
Philadelphia
NEW JERSEY
Baltimore
Annapolis
Alexandria
DELAWARE
MARYLAND
VIRGINIA
Cincinnati
St. Louis
Ohio
Louisville
KENTUCKY
MISSOURI (1821)
(Claimed by Texas from Mexico 1836)
MEXICO
TENNESSEE
NORTH CAROLINA
SOUTH CAROLINA
Charleston
GEORGIA
ARKANSAS (1836)
Mississippi
Tuscumbia
MISSISSIPPI (1817)
ALABAMA (1819)
TEXAS (1845)
LOUISIANA (1812)
FLORIDA (1845)
Atlantic Ocean
Gulf of Mexico
Rio Grande
States organised before 1803
Louisiana Purchase 1803
Postmaster's Provisionals 1845-7
Carriers Stamps 1849-61
0 kilometres 500
0 miles 300

USA to 1847

Nieuw Nederlandt') to Hoorn. Mail to Europe from Boston, Massachusetts was the subject of local legislation as early as 1639, and the first (short-lived) overland intercolonial service between New York City and Boston was established in 1673. Regular official posts date from 11 November 1692, at first under patent to Thomas Neale (the first serious attempt to organize an intercolonial system) and after the Act of Queen Anne in 1711 under the monopoly of the British crown directed from London. Post-riders carried the mail by land and private packets by sea between New York and Bristol. The appointment of Benjamin Franklin (jointly with William Hunter) as Crown Postmaster-General in North America in 1753 brought improvements. Admiralty mail packets between Falmouth and New York began on 18 September 1755. The first handstamps (town names, Bishop marks, etc.) date from this period. An overland mail from New York to Quebec was established in 1763 (*see* Canada). The high rates charged for letters were a cause of resentment in the colonies, though the Stamp Act of 1765, applying a revenue tax to newspapers, was a more immediate cause of the War of Independence. Franklin was dismissed from office in 1774, but William Goddard, a newspaper proprietor, started to usurp the Crown's prerogative to carry intercolonial mails.

Postal History (since Independence)
During the war North American packets served troops loyal to Britain, after the defeat at Saratoga terminating at Philadelphia (1778) and Charleston (1780). The states in rebellion maintained a packet service with France. In 1782 the US postal service was made the monopoly of the central govern-

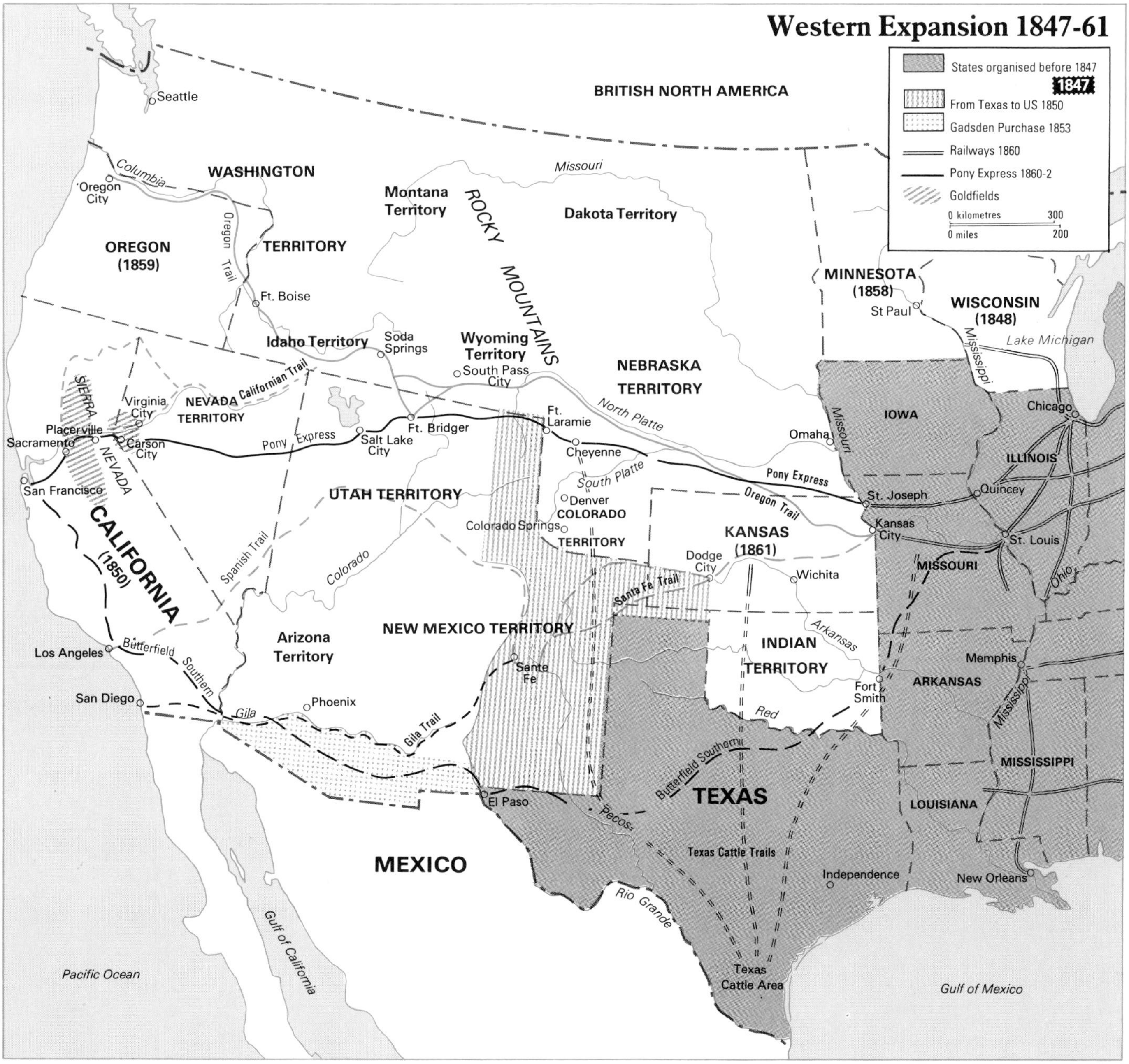
States organised before 1847
1847
From Texas to US 1850
Gadsden Purchase 1853
Railways 1860
Pony Express 1860-2
Goldfields
0 kilometres 300
0 miles 200
BRITISH NORTH AMERICA
Seattle
Columbia
Oregon City
WASHINGTON
TERRITORY
OREGON (1859)
Oregon Trail
Ft. Boise
Montana Territory
ROCKY MOUNTAINS
Missouri
Dakota Territory
MINNESOTA (1858)
St Paul
WISCONSIN (1848)
Lake Michigan
Mississippi
Idaho Territory
Soda Springs
Wyoming Territory
South Pass City
NEBRASKA TERRITORY
SIERRA NEVADA
Virginia City
NEVADA TERRITORY
Californian Trail
Placerville
Sacramento
Carson City
San Francisco
Pony Express
Salt Lake City
Ft. Bridger
Ft. Laramie
North Platte
Cheyenne
South Platte
Omaha
IOWA
Chicago
ILLINOIS
Quincey
St. Joseph
Kansas City
St. Louis
Pony Express
Oregon Trail
Denver
COLORADO TERRITORY
Colorado Springs
UTAH TERRITORY
KANSAS (1861)
Dodge City
Wichita
MISSOURI
Ohio
CALIFORNIA (1850)
Spanish Trail
Colorado
Santa Fe Trail
NEW MEXICO TERRITORY
Arizona Territory
Los Angeles
Butterfield Southern
Sante Fe
INDIAN TERRITORY
Arkansas
Memphis
ARKANSAS
Fort Smith
San Diego
Phoenix
Gila
Gila Trail
Red
Mississippi
MISSISSIPPI
Butterfield Southern
TEXAS
El Paso
Pecos
LOUISIANA
Texas Cattle Trails
Independence
New Orleans
MEXICO
Rio Grande
Gulf of California
Pacific Ocean
Texas Cattle Area
Gulf of Mexico

Western Expansion 1847-61

ment. In 1784 the Falmouth packet service was resumed with a British packet agent in New York. By 1789 there were 75 POs. Post-riders were used on most routes, though some stage-coaches were operated from 1782. The use of handstamps of origin increased after 1800.

All steamboat routes were declared 'post roads' from 1823 and all railroads from 1838, but from 1836 to 1839 the Eastern Pony Express still rode the Philadelphia-Mobile section of the New York to New Orleans mail service. The first (unofficial) adhesive stamps were issued by a local private carrier in New York on 1 February 1842. A reform of postal rates to a simplified system (on 1 July 1845) led to the general adoption of adhesive stamps. In 1845 there were 14,183 POs; an independent system with 119 POs in Texas was absorbed in 1846.

Some postmasters issued provisionals in 1845-7. US government stamps first issued 1 July 1847 (these were made available in 30 states, three territories and Panama.)

Prepayment of postage was made

compulsory on 1 April 1855, and prepayment by means of postage stamps on 1 January 1856.

Between 1849 and 1861 carriers in eight other cities followed New York's example of providing local delivery (issuing stamps for prepayment). By 1861 the total number of POs had doubled to 28,498 as settlers moved into the mid west.

Stage-coach and Pony Express

In 1849-58 the fastest route between New York City and San Francisco was provided by the packet via Panama, the isthmus being crossed at first by mule and after 1855 by the Panama Railroad (reducing the total time to three weeks). Overland it could take longer than this by stage-coach from Independence, Missouri, to Salt Lake City. Private 'express' companies were a natural feature of the pioneering movements westward (in particular the gold rushes), the government contracting only vital routes. Most private expresses used handstamps on printed envelopes already embossed with the obligatory US postage, but not separate adhesive stamps.

By 1858, however, a weekly mail had been established between St Joseph, Missouri, and Placerville, California, via Salt Lake City. Butterfield's overland stage service from St Louis to San Francisco by the southern route was inaugurated under government contract in 1858 and transferred in 1861 to the central route. The superiority of the latter had been proven by Russell, Majors and Waddell with their famous Pony Express. Though this ran for barely a year and a half (April 1860-October 1861) and carried a relatively small amount of mail (not surprising at $5 a half ounce, reduced latterly to $2), the exploits of its riders gave it immediate epic status.

The Pony Express carried mails for Wells, Fargo and Co., a successful security express outfit that specialized in transporting dust from successive gold rushes. By 1866 Wells Fargo had practically a monopoly of western stage lines. Three years later the first transcontinental railroad (Union Pacific) was completed. This did not immediately speed the mail from San Francisco to the east coast, as the contract for transport via Panama still had a number of years to run. The sea route was maintained until the mid-1870s.

The Civil War

FIRST CONFEDERATE STAMPS ISSUED 18 October 1861

When the Confederacy was proclaimed in February 1861, some 8500 POs lay in 'disloyal' territory. A rebel-appointed postmaster-general of the Confederate States maintained business as usual until 1 June when the US prohibited exchanges of mail and demonetized all existing stamps.

Various provisional stamps were prepared by postmasters of Confederate towns (many other towns used handstamps) 1 June–18 October 1861. These were used in a decreasing area until the end of secession in June 1865.

Characteristics of the period include the re-use of envelopes, bisected stamps, 'drop' letters (left at the local PO for collection at a reduced fee), and prisoner-of-war mail.

In the United States a uniform letter rate regardless of distance was introduced on 1 July 1863. The first Railway Post Office (RPO, as TPOs have always been designated in the USA) commenced operation on 28 August 1864 between Chicago and Clinton, Iowa. The service spread rapidly, reaching a peak about 1925. Fast mail trains were started between New York and Chicago on 16 September 1875 and led to widespread 'Limited Mail' trains over ever increasing distances. Coast-to-coast service from New York was achieved in November 1889 when the Omaha to San Francisco link was forged. In many cities posting boxes were placed on streetcars (trams) with a postal clerk who also collected from wayside boxes; this effected swift urban delivery and pouching (bagging) for despatch from main railway stations. On letters so posted the stamps received RPO cancellations. The cities involved were:

St Louis	1893-1915
Brooklyn	1894-1914
Boston	1895-1915
Chicago	1895-1915
Cincinnati	1895-1915
New York	1895-1900
Philadelphia	1895-1915
Washington	1895-1913
Rochester	1896-1908
San Francisco	1896-1905
Baltimore	1897-1929
Pittsburgh	1898-1917
Seattle	1905-1913
Cleveland	1908-1920
Omaha	1910-1921

A pneumatic post (already successful in Europe) gave an even faster service in Philadelphia (1893), New York (1897) and Boston (1897), and later in Chicago and St Louis. In New York the service extended to Brooklyn, the tubes being carried across the girders of the Brooklyn Bridge. The system was limited by size to letter post and was expensive; it lasted in Boston and New York until 1950.

Pictorial and commemorative stamps in the USA may be said to have started with the Columbus issue of 1893. They became a regular feature of policy from 1924. No living person may be depicted.

Rural free delivery service was inaugurated on 1 October 1896 in West Virginia. This is recorded as the most costly single extension of the postal service.

The number of POs reached a peak in 1901 (76,945), then started a long decline to about half, owing to improved sorting and delivery, a standard recently not maintained.

'Coil stamps' (Imperf. x Perf.) in rolls of 500 were made available for easier stamping of bulk mail on 29 December 1908. Another expedient was the widespread use of 'precancels', stamps officially cancelled before sale with the name of the issuing office (almost invariably Town/State in two lines between bars). These had come into use haphazardly since 1890, but were regularized by uniform procedures in 1911.

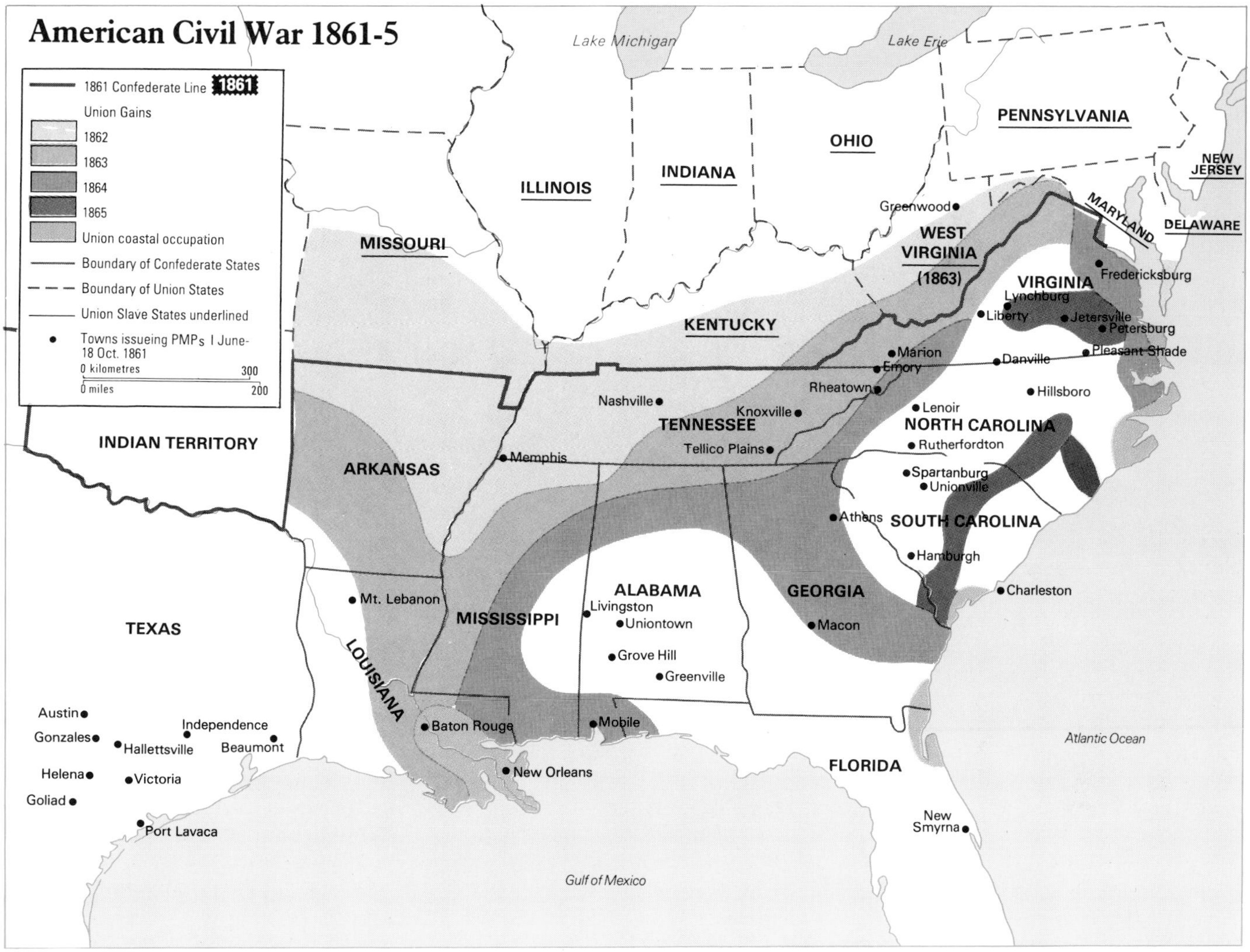
American Civil War 1861-5
1861 Confederate Line 1861
Union Gains
1862
1863
1864
1865
Union coastal occupation
Boundary of Confederate States
Boundary of Union States
Union Slave States underlined
Towns issueing PMPs I June-18 Oct. 1861
0 kilometres 300
0 miles 200
Lake Michigan
Lake Erie
PENNSYLVANIA
OHIO
INDIANA
ILLINOIS
NEW JERSEY
MARYLAND
DELAWARE
MISSOURI
WEST VIRGINIA (1863)
VIRGINIA
KENTUCKY
TENNESSEE
NORTH CAROLINA
SOUTH CAROLINA
INDIAN TERRITORY
ARKANSAS
MISSISSIPPI
ALABAMA
GEORGIA
LOUISIANA
TEXAS
FLORIDA
Greenwood
Fredericksburg
Lynchburg
Liberty
Jetersville
Petersburg
Pleasant Shade
Danville
Marion
Emory
Rheatown
Hillsboro
Lenoir
Nashville
Knoxville
Tellico Plains
Rutherfordton
Memphis
Spartanburg
Unionville
Athens
Hamburgh
Charleston
Mt. Lebanon
Livingston
Uniontown
Macon
Grove Hill
Greenville
Austin
Gonzales
Independence
Hallettsville
Beaumont
Helena
Victoria
Goliad
Baton Rouge
Mobile
New Orleans
Port Lavaca
New Smyrna
Atlantic Ocean
Gulf of Mexico

Though conventions had been signed as early as 1887 for exchange of parcels with foreign countries, the domestic transport of parcels was not taken out of the hands of private carriers until 1 January 1913. Parcel post stamps were issued, but their separate validity was ended after six months.

The first experimental airmail flight between US cities was made on 10 April 1912 between New Orleans and Baton Rouge. The first regular internal airmail service was inaugurated 15 May 1918 serving New York – Philadelphia – Washington. Special airmail stamps were issued two days earlier. From 1935 a regular transpacific clipper service connected San Francisco with Hawaii, Wake, Guam and Manila. It was extended in 1937 to Hong Kong, and in 1941 to Singapore. A regular transatlantic service flying New York – Bermuda – Lisbon began in 1939.

ALASKA

Though Alaska had no postal service under the Russians and has used only stamps of the USA, its geographical separation gives the stamps used there a particular interest.

Alaska had settlements of Russian fur traders from 1784, but was purchased from Russia by the USA in 1867. From 1884 it became a district of

A
HAWAII STATEHOOD 1959
U.S. AIR MAIL 7¢
B
U.S. AIR MAIL 7¢
ALASKA STATEHOOD 1959

A USA: Hawaii Statehood 1959;
B USA: Alaska Statehood 1959.

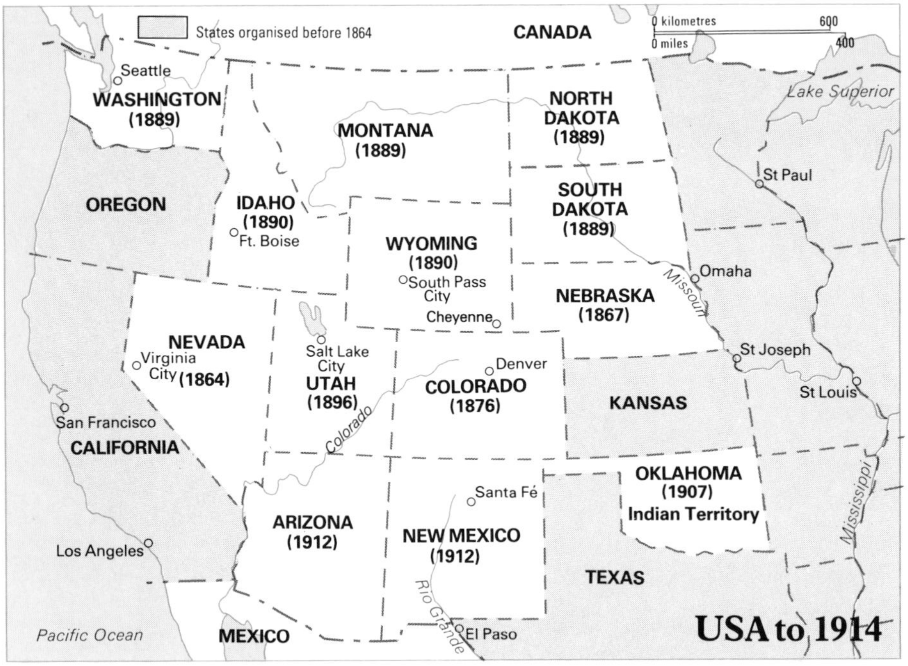
States organised before 1864
CANADA
0 kilometres 600
0 miles 400
Seattle
WASHINGTON (1889)
MONTANA (1889)
NORTH DAKOTA (1889)
Lake Superior
St Paul
OREGON
IDAHO (1890)
Ft. Boise
SOUTH DAKOTA (1889)
WYOMING (1890)
South Pass City
Cheyenne
Omaha
Missouri
NEBRASKA (1867)
NEVADA
Virginia City (1864)
Salt Lake City
UTAH (1896)
Denver
COLORADO (1876)
St Joseph
KANSAS
St Louis
San Francisco
CALIFORNIA
Colorado
OKLAHOMA (1907)
Indian Territory
Santa Fé
ARIZONA (1912)
NEW MEXICO (1912)
Mississippi
Los Angeles
TEXAS
Rio Grande
Pacific Ocean
MEXICO
El Paso

USA to 1914

Oregon, was made a territory on 24 August 1912, and gained statehood on 3 January 1959.

The first US PO in Alaska was at Sitka (1867) with a sea connection first to San Francisco, and after 1869 to Port Townsend, Washington Territory. After the Juneau gold strike, various expresses provided services until in 1896 a government service was attempted between Juneau and Circle City. In September 1897 an international exchange was put into operation between Dyea, Alaska, and Dawson City, Canada. By 1900 dog sleds were in use on inland routes.

• Hawaii

FIRST STAMPS ISSUED 1 October 1851
(stamps of Hawaii invalidated 14 June 1900) Used stamps of USA from 14 June 1900

Group of islands in the Pacific Ocean, comprising Hawaii, Oahu, Maui, Kauai, Molokai, Lanai, Niihau and Kahoolawe, 'discovered' in January 1778 by Captain James Cook and named Sandwich Islands after the fourth Earl of Sandwich. Here on his return Cook met his death. Hawaiian independence as a kingdom was recognized by Britain, USA and France in 1843. Foreign missionaries and American residents soon became numerous, and in 1887 white pressure forced a liberal constitution upon the Queen. The dynasty was overthrown in 1893 with the assistance of US marines, and a republic was declared. A US protectorate was proclaimed locally, but President Cleveland refused to ratify annexation. A short-lived republic ensued until on 12 August 1898 the islands were annexed to the USA. They were given territory status on 14 June 1900, and statehood on 21 August 1959.

First exchange of mails between Hawaii and the USA was established in 1849. Before that the merchants had relied on occasional visiting ships. Mail from a British naval force in 1846 was carried via Hong Kong. Until the islands joined the UPU in 1882, the stamps were valid only for local usage and US stamps were affixed as well to pay postage beyond San Francisco. The posts were absorbed into the US system on annexation.

United Nations (New York Headquarters)

FIRST STAMPS ISSUED 24 October 1951

The United Nations Organization superseded the League of Nations (*see* Switzerland) after World War II. Initiated at the Dumbarton Oaks Conference in 1944, it produced a charter signed by 50 nations at San Francisco on 26 June 1945, effective 24 October 1945. After an inaugural session in London, it was decided to locate the permanent seat in New York. Until the existing HQ was opened on the East River in 1952, sessions were held at Lake Success on Long Island.

Initially United Nations stamps were used only in New York, but as offices were established abroad, issues in other currencies became necessary. Stamps in Swiss francs were issued in Geneva (1969), and in Austrian currency in Vienna (1979) (*See also under* Switzerland and Austria).

Mexico

FIRST STAMPS ISSUED 1 August 1856

CURRENCY

100 centavos =1 peso

Mexico was under Spanish rule (Viceroyalty of New Spain) from 1521.

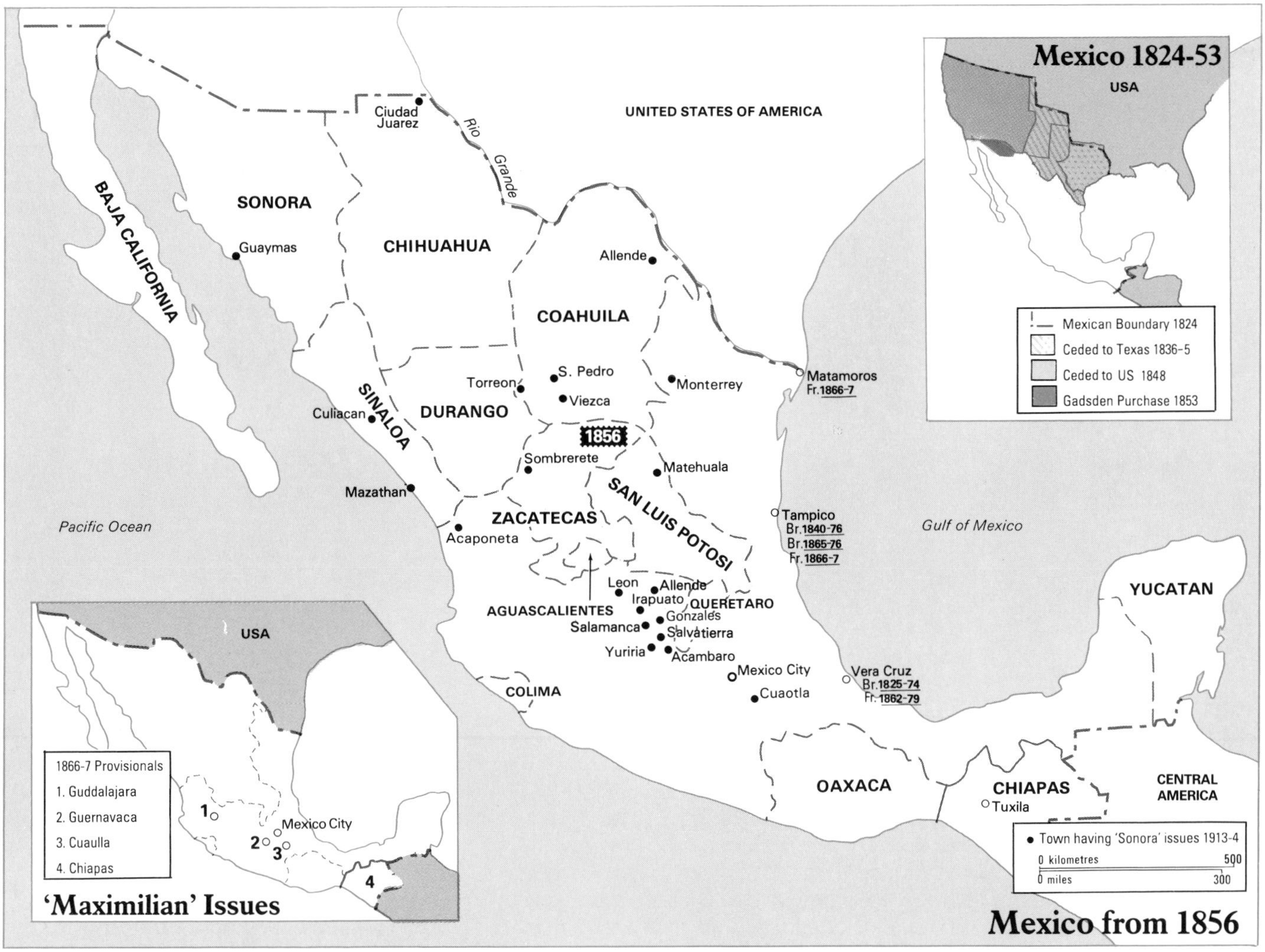
Mexico 1824-53
USA
Mexican Boundary 1824
Ceded to Texas 1836-5
Ceded to US 1848
Gadsden Purchase 1853
UNITED STATES OF AMERICA
Ciudad Juarez
Rio Grande
BAJA CALIFORNIA
SONORA
Guaymas
CHIHUAHUA
Allende
COAHUILA
S. Pedro
Torreon
Viezca
Monterrey
Matamoros
Fr.1866-7
SINALOA
Culiacan
DURANGO
1856
Sombrerete
Matehuala
Mazathan
SAN LUIS POTOSI
Pacific Ocean
ZACATECAS
Acaponeta
Tampico
Br.1840-76
Br.1865-76
Fr.1866-7
Gulf of Mexico
YUCATAN
Leon
Allende
Irapuato
QUERETARO
AGUASCALIENTES
Gonzales
Salamanca
Salvatierra
Yuriria
Acambaro
Mexico City
Cuaotla
Vera Cruz
Br.1825-74
Fr.1862-79
COLIMA
OAXACA
CHIAPAS
Tuxila
CENTRAL AMERICA
Town having 'Sonora' issues 1913-4
0 kilometres 500
0 miles 300
Mexico from 1856
USA
1866-7 Provisionals
1. Guddalajara
2. Guernavaca
3. Cuaulla
4. Chiapas
Mexico City
'Maximilian' Issues

California, New Mexico and Texas were colonized between 1769 and 1786. Mexico declared independence in 1821 and became a Federal Republic in 1824. It lost Texas in 1836. The area to the north (now California, New Mexico, Arizona, Nevada, Utah and part of Colorado) was lost to the USA a few years later. Since 1853 its international frontiers have remained substantially unchanged. A brief Anglo-French-Spanish occupation of Vera Cruz in 1861-2 (from which Britain and Spain soon withdrew) was followed by a French advance on Mexico City and the puppet empire of Maximilian (1864-67), overthrown by Juarez.

The usurpation by Huerta of the presidency led to civil war in 1913-15. 'Constitutionalist' forces set up the 'free' state of Sonora *(see below)* in opposition in March 1913, reached Mexico City in 1914, and controlled the whole country by 1917 after minor struggles for power had been resolved with several interventions by US forces.

Postal History

When Cortez conquered Mexico in 1521, he continued insofar as possible a system of messengers already well established by the Aztecs. From 1579 the postal rights were farmed to a succession of noble postmasters (Correo Mayor de la Nueva España). A law suit established that the Mexican posts were not part of the hereditary monopoly granted to the Galindez de Carvajal family in the Spanish Indies. The most important early route was between Mexico City and Vera Cruz. A calculation of distances for postal purposes was made in 1620.

After the administrator of posts in Madrid had been given a commission in 1742 to improve the Mexican system, a weekly post was established (1745) between Mexico City and Oaxaca, which made possible a monthly through communication with Guatemala three years later. In 1765 the

A
B
C
D
E
F
BERMUDA
CORREOS MEXICO
DIEZ CENTAVOS
CONSTITUYENTE DE 1857
CTS 60
CORREOS MEXICO
1879 1979
Rowland Hill
MEXICO AEREO 1.60
OCHO REALES
BERMUDA
1948
The PEROT STAMP
6D
CENTENARY OF FIRST POSTAGE STAMP

A Bermuda:First Issue 1865; **B** Mexico:Benito Juarez 1879; **C** Mexico:Centenary of the Constitution 1957; **D** Mexico:Centenary of Rowland Hill 1979; **E** Mexico:Republic 1856; **F** Bermuda: Centenary of Perot's Stamp 1948 (issued 1949).

Mexican posts were bought back by the Spanish crown.

Mexico was the pivot of Spanish control in the Americas; it was also the route for mail coming back from the East Indies. The galleons which carried intelligence, treasure and mail sailed annually from Acapulco to Manila. The returning mail was landed again at Acapulco, was carried overland to Vera Cruz and then returned to Spain via Havana. Earliest letters by this route have been recorded from 1783.

British packets began a service to Vera Cruz in 1825. British PAs existed at Vera Cruz 1825-74 and Tampico c.1840-76. Stamps of Britain were used in 1865-76 at Tampico (oblit. C63), but those supplied to Vera Cruz were never used. The British Mexican packet ran until 1914.

The French instituted a sailing packet in 1827 between Bordeaux and Vera Cruz, calling at Martinique and Haiti, which continued not very successfully until 1835. The Compagnie Générale Transatlantique restored the service in 1862 with a Ligne de Mexique from Saint-Nazaire to Vera Cruz, calling at Martinique and Santiago de Cuba. The packet-boats were reorganized in 1865, the Mexican packet becoming Ligne B until 1901, and continuing thereafter (although without PAs aboard) until 1939.

French consular agencies were established at Vera Cruz (1862-79), Tampico and Matamoros (1866-7), at which stamps of France were used.

The European packets carried not only Mexican mail to Europe brought down by mule from Mexico City, but also local mails between Vera Cruz and Tampico.

Intially stamps had to be validated before issue by a named handstamp on receipt at the district PO; this was to guard against theft of stamps in transit to postmasters. Stamps without overprint were invalid. From 1864 to 1867 stamps were overprinted in Mexico City with a London GPO invoice number and year date. From then until 1883, when the practice was discontinued as the railways started to supersede the vulnerable stage-coach, each main district was allotted a number which was overprinted on the stamps together with abbreviated year date.

Provisionals were issued in republican-held territories during the war against Maximilian 1866-7.

• Sonora

When the 'Constitutionalist' forces marched on Mexico City in 1914, they overprinted captured stocks of stamps. A map shows the areas in which local overprints were used, usually variants of E.C. or E.C. DE M. (Ejército Constitucional de Méjico) or GOBIERNO CONSTITUCIONALISTA.

Bermuda

FIRST STAMPS (local Postmaster's) 1848
FIRST STAMPS ISSUED 1865

CURRENCY

British to 1970
6 February 1970 100 cents = $1

Of 300 islands in the group, about 20 are inhabited and one important. They were all uninhabited before the first British settlement in 1612. A Crown Colony from 1684, Bermuda was given representative government on 2 July 1968.

Postal History

Lying c.850 miles north of St Thomas, c.700 miles from New York, and about the same distance from Halifax, Nova Scotia, Bermuda has depended at different times on all three for its sea communication by packet. A packet agent, appointed from London, dealt with external mails from 1818 (datestamps known from 1820) to 1859.

A domestic postal service, begun by the *Bermuda Gazette* in 1784, was continued officially from 1812. Daily services with delivery were established between 1835 and 1843. In 1859 control of all services was vested in the colony. The packet port and therefore the chief postmaster remained at St George's until 1879, though Hamilton had become the capital in 1815.

The first stamps were produced by the Postmaster in Hamilton, Mr Perot, in 1848 and these primitive strikes of a handstamp on gummed paper were used at Hamilton and St George's until 1861. The first issue of definitive stamps for Bermuda was released in 1865.

During the American Civil War, Confederate blockade runners passed letters through forwarding agents in Bermuda. During the Boer War, Boer prisoners were interned in the islands and their mail was censored. Bermuda played a major role in the censorship of Allied transatlantic mail in World War II.

Regular airmail services to New York were established by Imperial Airways on 16 June 1937 and to Baltimore by Pan American Airways on 6 March 1938.

THE CARIBBEAN

The West Indies saw the first landfall of Columbus, and by 1507 the Caribbean had attracted colonists from Spain. By the reign of Elizabeth I, Spanish sea power had become a threat to England, and Elizabeth's 'sea dogs' took the fight across the Atlantic, where the islands of the West Indies became pawns in attacks on the Spanish Main (i.e., mainland). The area soon teemed with pirates and privateers. The first British settlers, émigrés rather than colonists, appeared c.1620 as an offshoot from the North American mainland.

The earliest permanent British settlement was established on St Christopher in 1624. Barbados was founded in 1627. The idea of planting sugar as a staple crop, copied from Dutch settlers on the Guiana coast, led to the importing first of poor indentured servants from the British Isles and, later, to the wholesale shipment of slaves taken in Africa to work the plantations.

Permanent colonization for political as well as economic ends started with Cromwell (Jamaica, 1655). Various commissions and councils for foreign plantations sat from 1625, and the Lords of Trade and Plantations became the Board of Trade in 1696. For two centuries the West Indies figured as a commercial prize in all the wars of rivalry between Britain, France, Holland and Spain, disputed islands changing hands constantly. The indigenous peoples virtually disappeared.

The abolition of the British slave trade in 1807 cut off the plantations' supply of labour and the emancipation of slaves in 1833 made necessary the recruitment of indentured labour from India. Free Trade policies and cheap railway transport on larger islands altered the balance in favour of Cuba until, in the late 19th century, the success of the European sugar beet industry ruined the West Indian monopoly. The sugar industry gave place to bananas, cocoa and cotton. More recently tourism has become increasingly important.

The British islands have gone through the political gamut of unsuccessful federation. Up to 1671 the smaller islands were administered as a group. In 1671 the Leeward Islands, consisting of Antigua, St Kitts, Montserrat, the Virgin Islands and Nevis, were separated from Barbados and the Windward Islands (most of which were to be disputed with other powers until 1763) and given a governor-in-chief. A federal legislature existed until 1816, when the group broke in two; Antigua and Montserrat formed one division and St Kitts, Nevis and the Virgin Islands the other. In 1833 they were reunited and Dominica was added. In 1871 the Leewards became a federal colony, though each separate island retained its own institutions.

In 1763 Grenada, St Vincent, Dominica and Tobago were united under the Government of the Southern Caribee Islands. Dominica was detached in 1771, St Vincent in 1776, and Tobago perforce on its cession in 1783 to France. In 1833 Grenada, St Vincent, Tobago (now restored to Britain) and Barbados were grouped to form the Windward Islands under a governor-in-chief. St Lucia was added in 1838. Barbados was separated in 1885; Tobago was detached to Trinidad in 1889, and Dominica was attached from the Leeward Islands on 31 December 1939.

A Federation of the West Indies, comprising Leewards, Windwards, Jamaica and Trinidad, was established on 3 January 1958. Jamaica seceded by referendum in 1961, Trinidad followed, and the federation was dissolved in February 1962. In 1967 various islands became 'associated states' of Britain, a new status of self-government, rather less than full independence within the Commonwealth.

CURRENCY

With the exception of Trinidad and Tobago (which changed to a decimal 100¢ =$1 on 1 February 1935), all the British West Indies kept British currency until 1949.

Dates of changeover to a decimal currency (100¢ =1$):

1949, St Vincent, Dominica, St Lucia, Grenada, Montserrat, Antigua, Virgin Islands (the change was phased).

1 May 1950, Barbados

Early 1951, St Kitts Nevis

25 May 1966, Bahamas

8 September 1969, Turks and Caicos, and Jamaica.

Postal History

The earliest communications were with the respective mother country: Britain, France, Spain, and to a lesser extent Holland and Denmark. The British government relied even for official despatches on casual ships until, in 1702, Edmund Dummer, an ex-surveyor-general to the Navy, instituted a private packet service under government contract. The packets operated monthly from Falmouth (after 1705 Plymouth), serving Barbados, Antigua, Montserrat, Nevis, St Kitts and Jamaica. The round voyage took three to four months. The service ended in 1711.

COLONIAL
PENNY POST
SWAIN Sc.

Cartoon depicting Britannia and the colonial penny post, 1899

The postmaster-general authorized the use of British stamps for this purpose from 8 May 1858 not only in British islands but also at certain agencies on foreign soil. Stamps so used can be identified by cancellations. The practice was stopped on 1 May 1860 when the crowned circle handstamps were again used until colonial stamps were adopted in each colony.

In 1865 the French also set up postal packet agencies in connection with packet-boats of Compagnie Général Transatlantique plying between Saint-Nazaire and Mexico or Panama, which served Martinique and Guadeloupe. French stamps are known used either alone or in combination from Caribbean agencies between 1862 and 1881. The stamps can only rarely be identified off cover by named octagonal datestamps: more usually they were cancelled by an anchor in a lozenge of dots (proclaiming usage but not location) and the datestamps placed alongside on the envelope.

The greater part of the Caribbean area joined the UPU betwen 1877 and 1881.

The posts in the Spanish Indies were farmed to the Galindez de Carvajal family in 1514. Havana was one of the approved ports-of-call for Spanish merchantmen. Mail went mainly by casual ship until in 1764 Charles III decreed the *Correos Maritimos* (Maritime mail). A monthly packet was started in 1767 between Corunna and Havana, though the service was interrupted in time of war.

A British government packet service began in 1755, and postmasters in the main colonies were issued with handstamps. A monthly service was maintained despite hazards of war, piracy and mutiny. After 1783 packets left Falmouth on the first and third Wednesday of every month, and a system of inter-island schooners acted as mail distributors and collectors. Routes varied with changing conditions and fortunes of war. In 1820 all the postal services of the West Indies were overhauled.

British packet agents were required to collect prepaid postage on all letters despatched by British packet to foreign destinations, and were issued with 'Crowned circle' handstamps and datestamps. British packets also continued to serve islands which had become definitively French by the Congress of Vienna (1815), and British POs, PAs or packet agencies were set up wherever British consulates existed. Jacmel in Haiti, for example, had a British packet agency before 1830.

In 1840 the British packets were contracted out by the Admiralty to the Royal Mail Steam Packet Co. In 1842 the main RMS depot and coaling station was moved from Barbados to St Thomas in the Danish West Indies.

Prepayment of packet correspondence to British destinations was made compulsory in 1858. Accordingly various postmasters in the British West Indies urged the use of adhesives.

Bahamas

FIRST STAMPS Britain 1858-9 (oblit: A05 at Nassau)
FIRST STAMPS ISSUED 10 June 1859 inscribed 'Interinsular Postage'

CURRENCY

1859	sterling
1966	100 cents = 1 dollar

A group of about 700 islands of which only 30 are inhabited. They were the first point of discovery by Columbus. San Salvador was sighted on the night of 11 October 1492 and he landed there next day. New Providence was settled by the English in 1629 but they were driven out by the Spanish in 1641. The British returned in 1666 but the islands were again taken by Spanish forces in 1703. The Bahamas were finally ceded to Britain in 1783, after considerable fighting during the latter

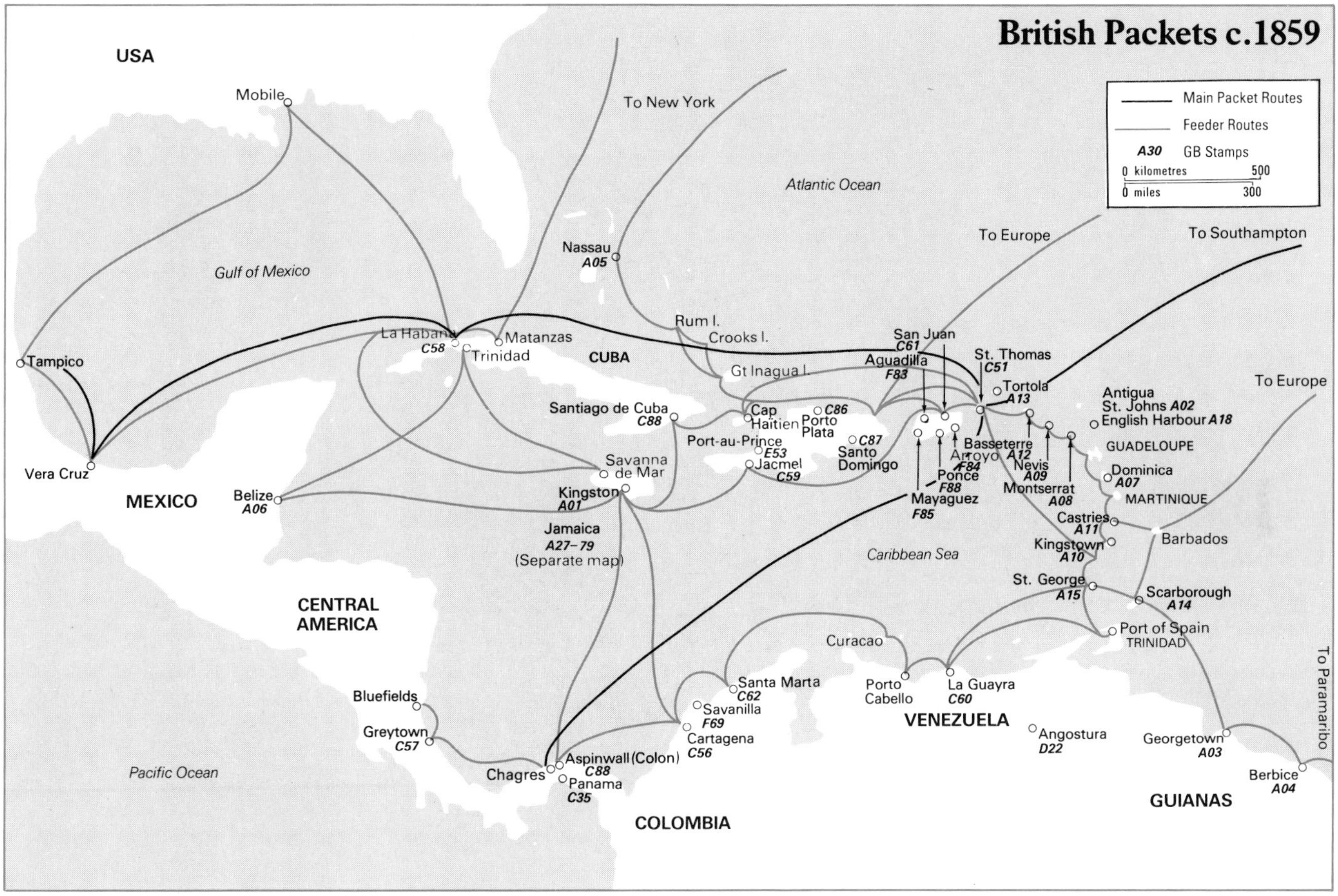

Main Packet Routes
Feeder Routes
A30 GB Stamps
0 kilometres 500
0 miles 300
USA
Mobile
To New York
Atlantic Ocean
To Europe
To Southampton
Nassau A05
Gulf of Mexico
Tampico
La Habana C58
Matanzas
Trinidad
CUBA
Rum I.
Crooks I.
Gt Inagua I.
San Juan C61
Aguadilla F83
St. Thomas C51
Tortola A13
Antigua St. Johns A02
English Harbour A18
To Europe
Santiago de Cuba C88
Cap Haitien
Porto Plata C86
Port-au-Prince E53
Jacmel C59
Santo Domingo C87
Basseterre A12
Arroyo F84
Ponce F88
Nevis A09
Montserrat A08
GUADELOUPE
Dominica A07
MARTINIQUE
Vera Cruz
MEXICO
Belize A06
Savanna de Mar
Kingston A01
Jamaica A27–79 (Separate map)
Mayaguez F85
Castries A11
Kingstown A10
Barbados
Caribbean Sea
St. George A15
Scarborough A14
CENTRAL AMERICA
Curacao
Port of Spain TRINIDAD
Santa Marta C62
Savanilla F69
Cartagena C56
Porto Cabello
La Guayra C60
VENEZUELA
Bluefields
Greytown C57
Angostura D22
Georgetown A03
To Paramaribo
Pacific Ocean
Chagres
Aspinwall (Colon) C88
Panama C35
Berbice A04
GUIANAS
COLOMBIA

British Packets c.1859

part of the American War of Independence.

Earliest letters from Bahamas are dated from the 1760s but there were no handstamps until 1804, when a straight line BAHAMAS was introduced. In 1841 a regular mail service was started by the Royal Mail Line and a 'Crown Paid' handstamp together with a dated postmark for New Providence was introduced in 1846.

The first British stamps were consigned to the colonies in April 1858, but the Bahamas PO became independent of London in 1859. The 'Interinsular' inscription was used because the external mails were still under the control of London until May 1860.

During the American Civil War (1861-65) the Bahamas enjoyed a financial boom as a base for Confederate blockade-runners.

The Bahamas remained a Crown Colony until gaining self-government on 7 January 1964. They became independent within the Commonwealth on 10 July 1973.

• Turks Islands

FIRST STAMPS ISSUED 4 April 1867

CURRENCY

1867 sterling

Uninhabited until 1678, when claimed as British. Permanent settlement was made from Bermuda in 1781. From 1799 to 1848 islands were attached to Bahamas. In 1848-73 they became a separate colony under the supervision of the Governor of Jamaica. From 1873 they were a dependency of Jamaica, but reverted to colonial rule on Jamaica's independence in 1962. Caicos Islands, which remained under Bahamas to 1900, then joined Turks.

Turks are said to have been issued with a Ship Letter stamp in 1840 and a datestamp in 1842, though the first PO was opened on 11 December 1854 and marks are known only from 1856.

Turks and Caicos Islands

FIRST COMBINED ISSUE 1900

CURRENCY

1900 sterling
1961 100 cents = 1 dollar (Bahamas)

BAHAMAS
1629 1729 1929
1d 1d
A
BAHAMAS
EIIR
ROSEATE SPOONBILLS
13c
15th. ANNIVERSARY of the BAHAMAS NATIONAL TRUST
B
TURKS ISLANDS
ONE SHILLING
C
TURKS & CAICOS ISLANDS
CAICOS BANK
6d
1848 1948
D
EIIR
Private, 1st West India Regiment, 1833
35c
TURKS & CAICOS ISLANDS
E

A Bahamas:Tercentenary of the Colony 1930; **B** Bahamas:Independent 1982; **C** Turks & Caicos Islands:First Issue 1867; **D** Turks & Caicos Islands:Centenary of Separation from Bahamas 1948; **E** Turks & Caicos Islands 1975.

Remained a dependency of Jamaica until 1962 when the islands became a Crown Colony. First issue in the new state was on 4 June 1963.

Caicos Islands
Although not politically independent, this group issued its own overprints on 24 July 1981. These overprints were inspired by a stamp marketing company and initially they were not accepted. However, they were subsequently used for postage. Their full status is questionable.

Cuba

CURRENCY

1855	8 reales plata fuerte = 1 peso
1866	100 centesimos = 1 escudo
1871	100 centesimos = 1 peseta
1881	1000 milesimas = 100 centavos=1peso
1898	100 cents =1 dollar
1899	100 centavos = 1 peso

FIRST STAMPS ISSUED April 1855

Discovered by Columbus on his first journey in 1492. He believed that it was the southern coast of China and it was not realized that it was an island until 1508. Spanish colony established c.1513. British captured Havana in 1762, but returned the island to Spain in 1763 in return for Florida. British PA reported to have been in operation in 1762 but no handstamps are recorded until 1840.

Cuba was one of the last outposts of the slave trade and suffered a civil war in 1868-78. Further insurrection occasioned an American naval presence to protect US interests and lives. An explosion aboard the USS *Maine* in Havana harbour on 15 February 1898 sparked the Spanish-American War.

Spanish PO in Havana first used handstamps in 1768 and perhaps earlier. Havana was on the main route for Spanish imperial packets from this time. By 1840 there were 28 offices using special handstruck markings.

About 1840 the British POs in Havana and St Jago de Cuba began to use crowned circle paid markings and these continued until British stamps were brought into use in 1866 (Havana — C58 and St Jago C88).
First stamps issued in April 1855; jointly valid in Puerto Rico but Cuba had its own separate issues from 1873. In 1862 there was a French PA in Santiago de Cuba and from 1865 in Havana. Both the British and French agencies were closed in 1877 when Spain's colonies joined the UPU.

Following the Spanish-American War, Cuba came under US control until 1902, though during this period an independent republic was declared which Spain was forced to recognize on 21 February 1901. It remained politically turbulent and was re-occupied by the Americans in 1906-9. By 1938 there were 634 POs.

Cuba became a Communist republic in 1959, but the US still maintains a base at Guantanamo which uses a Forces PO.

Jamaica

FIRST STAMPS Britain from 1858 (issued 8 May in Kingston, and November at other offices)
FIRST STAMPS ISSUED 23 November 1860

CURRENCY

1860	sterling
1869	100 cents = 1 Jamaican dollar

Discovered by Columbus in May 1493, it was originally named St Jago. Captured from the Spanish in 1655 and settled soon afterwards. British possession of the island was confirmed by the Treaty of Madrid in 1670.

Jamaica was the first British Colony to establish a PO. A postmaster was appointed on 31 October 1671. Originally overseas mail was carried by merchantmen but the British packet service was introduced in 1702. However, through piracy and shipwreck, the packet service went out of business in 1711 and letters once again were carried privately.

The British GPO assumed responsibility for Jamaica's external mails in 1755 and retained this until 1860. The

Jamaica 1859-60
Showing cancellers used on GB stamps

Key to towns with obliteration numbers

A27 Alexandria	*A54* May Hill
A28 Annotto Bay	*A55* Mile Gully
A29 Bath	*A56* Moneague
A30 Black River	*A57* Montego Bay
A31 Brown's Town	*A58* Montpelier
A32 Buff Bay	*A59* Morant Bay
A33 Chapleton	*A60* Ochos Rios
A34 Claremont	*A61* Old Harbour
A35 Clarendon	*A62* Plantain Garden River
A36 Dry Harbour	*A63* Pear Tree Grove
A37 Duncans	*A64* Port Antonio
A38 Ewarton	*A65* Port Morant
A39 Falmouth	*A66* Port Maria
A40 Flint River	*A67* Port Royal
A41 Gayle	*A68* Porus
A42 Golden Spring	*A69* Ramble
A43 Gordon Town	*A70* Rio Bueno
A44 Goshen	*A71* Rodney Hall
A45 Grange Hill	*A72* St David
A46 Green Island	*A73* St Ann's Bay
A47 Highgate	*A74* Saltgut
A48 Hope Bay	*A75* Savannah la Mar
A49 Lilliput	*A76* Spanish Town
A50 Little River	*A77* Stewart Town
A51 Lucea	*A78* Vere
A52 Manchioneal	*A79* Richmond
A53 Mandeville	

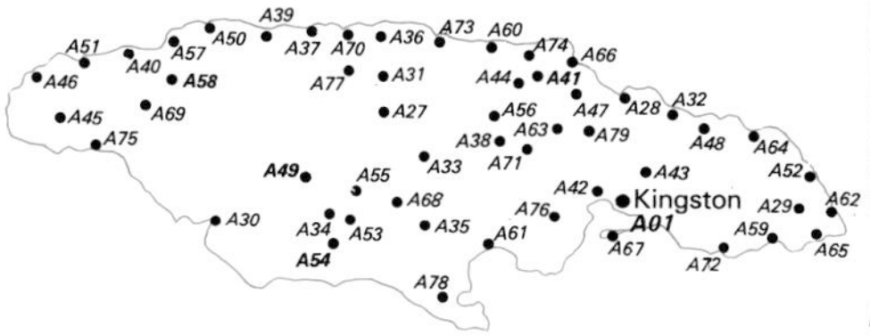
A39
A51
A57
A50
A37
A70
A36
A73
A60
A74
A66
A40
A46
A58
A77
A31
A44
A41
A45
A69
A27
A56
A47
A28
A32
A75
A38
A63
A79
A48
A64
A49
A55
A33
A71
A43
A52
A42
Kingston
A62
A30
A34
A68
A35
A76
A29
A53
A61
A01
A59
A65
A54
A67
A72
A78

CUBA CORREOS 3
1970
X ANIVERSARIO DE LA FEDERACION DE MUJERES CUBANAS
A
CUBA
CINCUENTA 50 CENTAVOS
C
2¢
CUBA-CORREOS
CENTENARIO NACIMIENTO MAYOR GENERAL JOSE MACEO 1849-1949
B

A Cuba:Independent 1970; **B** Cuba: Independent 1952; **C** Cuba:Independent 1907.

British packet service was restored but was closed down in 1840 when the service by the Royal Mail Steam Packet Co. was introduced.

Cancellation AO1 was used at Kingston and numerals A27 to A79 at other locations (*see* map). Post buses (introduced in 1881) are the main means of distribution.

Jamaica became self-governing in 1944 and was part of the short-lived Federation of the West Indies in 1958-62. Became an independent member of the British Commonwealth on 6 August 1962.

Cayman Islands

FIRST STAMPS Jamaica from April 1889

FIRST STAMPS ISSUED November 1900 (possibly not put into use before 19 February 1901)

Right
New General Post Office, Bridgetown, Barbados

Below right
Kingston, Jamaica

Below left
Sub-post office, Antigua

SUB POST OFFICE
STAMPS SOLD HERE

CURRENCY	
1900	sterling
1969	100 cents = 1 Jamaican dollar

Ceded by Spain to England in 1670 and colonized from Jamaica in the 18th century, they remained a dependency of Jamaica until granted a new constitution on 1 July 1959. Crown Colony on 28 November 1962.

Used stamps of Jamaica from April 1889, before which there were no regular postal facilities. Stamps so used are recognizable by cancellations: Grand Cayman (at Georgetown) and Cayman Brac (at Stake Bay).

There were initially 3 POs on Grand Cayman: Georgetown, Boddentown and East End (closed 1908). From 1908 a rural service was operated by mailcart between the two remaining offices with horseback messengers to East End and, after 1909, to West Bay. The driver and riders collected and cancelled mail until rural POs were re-opened in 1913.

Haiti

FIRST STAMPS Britain 1869
FIRST STAMPS ISSUED 1 July 1881

CURRENCY	
1881	100 centime = 1 gourde or piastre

Western part of the island of Santo Domingo (Hispaniola). For early history see under the Dominican Republic. Republic of Haiti was founded in 1804, but it was not until Jean-Pierre Boyer became president in 1818 that any stability resulted. In 1821 the island was consolidated and remained a single unit until 1844 when the Dominican Republic became independent.

Postal markings were introduced in the 1760s but these were largely undated. A public mail service did not operate until 1808-9. Britain and France recognized the sovereignty of Haiti in 1825. A packet agency was established at Jacmel before 1840. British PAs were established at Jacmel in March 1866 and Port-au-Prince in June 1869. Both closed in 1881. British stamps were authorized for use in 1869 and were obliterated E53 (Port-au-Prince) or C59 (Jacmel). French PAs at Cap Haïtien and Port-au-Prince used French stamps from 1865 and 1876 respectively. These were closed in June 1881. Haiti issued its own adhesive stamps on 1 July 1881, the day that the republic joined the UPU.

Republic was torn by political strife in the early part of the 20th century and in July 1915 American troops were sent to the island. American troops remained until August 1934 and the US maintained control of the revenue until 1947.

Postmarks have been recorded from less than 40 offices since Haiti took charge of its own affairs.

Dominican Republic

FIRST STAMPS Cuba/Puerto Rico 1861
FIRST STAMPS ISSUED 18 October 1865

CURRENCY	
1865	8 reales = 1 peso
1880	100 centavos = 1 peso
1883	100 centimos = 1 franco
1885	100 centavos = 1 peso

Comprises the eastern part of the island of Santo Domingo (Hispaniola). Discovered by Columbus in 1493, and came under French control in 1697. Under Haiti from 1804, but the area was reconquered by the Spanish after 1815. They were driven out by a popular uprising in 1821 and, again, the whole island was ruled by Haiti until 1844.

British PAs were opened at Porto Plata and San Domingo by 1866 and they used British stamps (oblit. C86 and C87) from 1867 to 1870, and again from 1876 to 1881 when the republic joined the UPU.

In 1861 the republic was annexed by Spain and first stamps used were the joint issue for Cuba and Puerto Rico. However, the unpopular Spanish government was expelled in 1865 and first stamps for the republic were issued on 19 October 1865.

The republic's political and economic instability led to American occupation in 1916. It remained under US military government until 1924 when, following a treaty, US troops withdrew. American forces used Army POs.

Politically, the Dominican Republic has remained unstable since the Trujillo dictatorship, which ended in 1961 with his assassination.

• Puerto Rico

FIRST STAMPS ISSUED with Cuba jointly 1855-56

CURRENCY	
1873	100 centimos = 1 peseta
1881	1000 milesimas = 100 centavos = 1 peso
1898	100 cents = 1 dollar

Most easterly of the islands in the Antilles archipelago, discovered in 1493 by Columbus. Not settled by the Spanish until 1508 when Ponce de Leon became governor. It remained Spanish until the Spanish–American War despite attempts by the English in 1595 and the Dutch in 1625 to occupy the island.

Handstruck markings began to be introduced early in the 19th century (1819 at San Juan de Puerto Rico) and by 1850 there were nine offices open. British PA was established on the island as early as 1844 at San Juan and this used a crowned circle handstamp until 1865. At that time British adhesives were introduced (oblit. C61), but were withdrawn the following year.

Further offices were opened in 1872 and stamps were re-introduced from 1873-7. Additional obliterations were issued as follows: Aguadilla (F83), Arroyo (F84), Mayaguez (F85) and Ponce (F88). A further office was opened in 1875 at Naguabo (582). There was a French PA at San Juan from 1865 and Mayaguez from 1876. Both offices used French stamps and were closed in 1877 when Spain joined the UPU.

First stamps issued were joint issues with Cuba which appeared in 1855 but were not generally used in Puerto Rico until 25 July 1856. First stamps with the name of the island appeared in 1873.

Spanish surrendered to American forces on 17 October 1898 and Puerto Rico was ceded to US on 10 December. Became a US Territory on 2 March 1917 and gained US Commonwealth status on 25 July 1952. American stamps overprinted PORTO RICO were used until April 1900 but unoverprinted American stamps have been used since 12 April 1900; US domestic postal rates apply.

• Virgin Islands

FIRST STAMPS Britain 1858-60 (oblit. A13 at Tortola)
FIRST STAMPS ISSUED 1866

CURRENCY

1866 sterling

After English buccaneers had ousted Dutch settlers in 1666-72, British possession of the 36 eastern islands of the archipelago was confirmed by the Treaty of Utrecht (1713). Part of the Leeward Islands until 1956.

The PO was controlled from London until 1860.

Individual stamps for the colony were replaced by the general issue for Leeward Islands in 1890. In 1899 separate issues were resumed and were used concurrently with those of the Leeward Islands until 1956.

The group had its own Legislative Council until 18 April 1967 when ministerial government was introduced.

British Virgin Islands

FIRST STAMPS ISSUED 2 January 1968

CURRENCY

1951 100 cents = 1 West Indian dollar
1962 100 cents = U.S. dollar

Successor to the Virgin Islands (*q.v.*) Stamps with the word 'British' added to the title were issued in 1968 to avoid confusion with the adjacent Virgin Islands of the United States.

One subsequent issue reverted to the former title but since 16 December 1968 all issues have been inscribed 'British'.

• Danish West Indies

FIRST STAMPS ISSUED November 1855
Also used British stamps on packet letters in 1865-79 (oblit. C51, St Thomas)

CURRENCY

1855 100 cents = 1 dollar = 5 Danish Kroner
1905 100 bit = 1 franc = 1 Danish Krone
1917 US

Group of 53 islands, some of which were occupied by the Danes in 1666 and declared a colony in 1674. St Thomas, St Croix and St John are the most important; St Croix became Danish in 1733 and St Thomas in 1754. A coaling station from 1841, St Thomas became the hub of the West Indies packet services in 1851 until 1885, when Barbados resumed its position of importance. The group was bought by and transferred to the USA as the US Virgin Islands on 1 April 1917.

Mail between St Thomas and Puerto Rico was carried by a Spanish mail packet until July 1867, when a contract was signed whereby all correspondence transported was to be sent via British agencies. A British mail clerk was put aboard each of its two vessels (oblit. D26 used on *Montezuma*).

United States Virgin Islands
Has used US stamps since 1 April 1917 (Danish West Indies stamps were valid to 30 September 1917 and are known from April to September in combination with those of the USA).

Nevis

FIRST STAMPS Britain from 1858 (oblit. A09).
FIRST STAMPS ISSUED 1861

CURRENCY

1861 sterling

A British possession since 1628. Captured by the French in 1782 but returned to British control by the Treaty of Versailles in 1783.

Nevis issued its own stamps until 31 October 1890 when the general issue for the Leeward Islands (q.v.) was released. Nevis was merged with St Christopher (St Kitts) in 1903. (For issues from 1903-79 *see* St Christopher).

Nevis as a dependency of St Christopher issued its own stamps again in June 1980.

• St Christopher (also known as St Kitts)

FIRST STAMPS Britain from 1858-60 (oblit. A12 at Basseterre)
FIRST STAMPS ISSUED 1 April 1870

JAMAICA
3d
BANANAS
JAMAICA POSTAGE
TWO SHILLINGS
3c TENTH ANNIVERSARY INDEPENDENCE 1962-1972
BAUXITE INDUSTRY
JAMAICA
CAYMAN ISLANDS
POSTAGE & REVENUE
CAT BOAT
HALF PENNY
1776-1976 BI-CENTENARY OF AMERICAN INDEPENDENCE
SEALS OF THE FIRST STATES
Georgia
Delaware
New Hampshire
CAYMAN ISLANDS
10c

A Jamaica 1938; B Jamaica 1875; C Jamaica:10th Anniversary of Independence 1972; D Cayman Islands 1935; E Cayman Islands 1979.

CORREOS
REPUBLICA DOMINICANA
SETENTA Y CINCO CENTS
REPUBLICA DOMINICANA
CORREOS
2c
Juan Pablo Duarte
FUNDADOR DE LA PATRIA
1981
PTO-RICO-1879
15 C^S PESETA
REPUBLIQUE D'HAITI
POSTE
CENT. 1 CENT.
PUERTO-RICO
6 C. DE PESO
REPUBLIQUE D'HAITI
COMMÉMORATION DU TRAITÉ DES FRONTIÈRES MCMXXIX
POSTES
10
CENTIMES DE GOURDE
LINCOLN 1959
1809 ABRAHAM
2.50 GOURDE
AVION
RÉPUBLIQUE D'HAÏTI

A Dominican Republic 1880; B Dominican Republic 1981; C Puerto Rico:Spanish Colony 1876; D Haiti:First Issue 1881; E Puerto Rico:Spanish Colony 1890; F Haiti:Frontier Agreement 1929; G Haiti:Commemoration of Lincoln 1959.

CURRENCY

1870 sterling

Settlement founded in 1624 by Sir Thomas Warner; island shared with the French as protection against the hostile Caribs. French area ceded to Britain in 1713 by the Treaty of Utrecht. Captured by the French in 1782, it was returned to British control the following year. First postmark was introduced in 1789. During the period 1860-70 various types of 'Paid' handstamps were used. St Christopher issued its own stamps until 31 October 1890 when the general issue for the Leeward Islands was released. For issues after 1903 see St Christopher–Nevis and St Christopher–Nevis and Anguilla.

• St Christopher–Nevis (St Kitts–Nevis)

FIRST STAMPS Britain 1858-60, Nevis 1861-90, St Christopher 1870-90 and Leeward Islands 1890-1903
FIRST STAMPS ISSUED inscribed St Kitts–Nevis 1903

CURRENCY

1903 sterling
1951 100 cents = 1 West Indian dollar

These two islands with Anguilla became a presidency of the Leeward Islands in 1882.

Stamps continued to be inscribed thus until 1952, but Anguilla appeared on a map stamp of St Kitts–Nevis in 1938.

Issues of the Leeward Islands were used concurrently until 1952 when, under a Legislative Council, the name of the colony was changed to St Christopher, Nevis and Anguilla.

• St Christopher, Nevis and Anguilla

FIRST STAMPS *see* St Christopher–Nevis
FIRST STAMPS ISSUED 2 June 1953

CURRENCY

1970 sterling

The successor of St Christopher–Nevis since 1952. Continued to use stamps of Leeward Islands concurrently until 1956.

Stages of self-government in 1952 and 1959 led to associated statehood in February 1967, when, by local referendum, Anguilla declared independence. Though the territories are still bound together and Anguilla's name continued to appear on the stamps until 1980, they were not accepted as valid in Anguilla after 1969. However, in June 1980 the stamp-issuing authorities changed and stamps were issued for St Kitts and Nevis separately.

St Kitts

CURRENCY

1980 100 cents = 1 West Indian dollar

The larger island of the St Christopher–Nevis group which issued stamps inscribed St Kitts on 23 June 1980.

VIRGIN ISLANDS
ONE PENNY
A
Centenary of Charles Dickens Death 1870-1970
5c
US.Cy
A TALE OF TWO CITIES
BRITISH VIRGIN ISLANDS
B
DANSK VESTINDIEN
8 8
POSTFRIM 8 CENTS
C
POST
K.G.L.
F.R.M.
3 CENTS
D
NEVIS
ONE SHILLING
E

A Virgin Islands 1883; **B** British Virgin Islands 1970; **C** Danish West Indies 1887; **D** Danish West Indies 1855; **E** Nevis 1866.

Anguilla

FIRST SEPARATE STAMPS
4 September 1967

First settled 1650 and later administered by St Christopher (*see above*). Having expelled the St Kitts police on 30 May 1967, Anguilla declared independence by referendum in July. Granted limited self-government on 12 February 1976.

Postal History

A St Kitts' sub-office on Anguilla was supplied with an A12 duplex canceller inscribed AN in 1900 (use not so far recorded). PO was opened at The Valley in 1904; in 1920 it appears to have been located at Crocus Hill. In 1927-31 there were sub-POs at The Forest, East End, The Road, and Blowing Point, replaced later by a motor TPO.

Used stamps of St Kitts-Nevis from 1904. In July-August 1967, during dispute with St Kitts, routed mail through US Virgin Islands.

Anguilla PO recognized by St Kitts 7 July 1969.

1/- ST KITTS-NEVIS 1/-
A
ST KITTS-NEVIS
ANGUILLA
TERCENTENARY
1650-1950
B
POSTAGE
REVENUE
5s ST KITTS-NEVIS 5s
C
SAINT CHRISTOPHER
POSTAGE
2½ PENNY
D
ST KITTS
Grey Kingbird
25c
E
SAINT CHRISTOPHER
NEVIS
ANGUILLA
SALT POND, ANGUILLA
POSTAGE
$1.20
REVENUE
F

A St Kitts-Nevis 1938; **B** Anguilla Tercentenary 1950; **C** St Kitts-Nevis 1920; **D** St Christopher 1870; **E** St Kitts 1981; **F** St Kitts, Nevis & Anguilla 1952.

Antigua

FIRST STAMPS Britain 1858-60 (oblit. A02 St Johns and A18 English Harbour)
FIRST STAMPS ISSUED August 1862

CURRENCY

1862 sterling
1951 100 cents = 1 West Indian dollar

Discovered by Columbus in November 1498, this island of the Leeward group was settled by the English in 1632 from St Christopher. Antigua was held for the Royalists during the English Civil War and was invaded by the French in 1666. It was returned to Britain by the Treaty of Breda in 1667. The British established English Harbour on the island as a naval dockyard in 1725 and it became the base for the Leewards Station throughout the French wars.

Postal communications between Antigua and Britain began early in the 19th century.

The first stamp was a 6*d* value to

prepay the letter rate to Britain. The general stamps of the Leeward Islands were used from 31 October 1890 until separate issues were again issued in 1903. These were used concurrently with the Leeward Island issues until 1956.

Antigua gained ministerial government on 1 January 1960 and associated statehood on 27 February 1967.

Barbuda

FIRST SEPARATE STAMPS 13 July 1922

CURRENCY	
1922	As Antigua

Dependency of Antigua. Presumably used stamps of Antigua from 1862. Overprinted stamps of Leeward Islands were issued in 1922. These were soon discontinued and stamps of Antigua were again used to 1968. Since 19 November 1968 has issued floods of unnecessary stamps (which are also valid in Antigua), except for a short period in 1972-3.

Redonda

A dependency of Antigua which is uninhabited. Stamps were issued in 1979 by overprinting stamps of Antigua. Philatelic mail was handled by a bureau in Antigua where, it is understood, the overprints are valid for postage. However, the stamps are not issued by a recognized postal authority.

Montserrat

FIRST STAMPS Britain 1858-60 (oblit.A08)
FIRST STAMPS ISSUED Antigua overprinted September 1876

CURRENCY	
1876	sterling
1951	100 cents = 1 West Indian dollar

Settled in 1632 from St Christopher, the island was captured several times by the French but was finally secured by Britain in 1783. It was a Crown Colony and part of the Leeward Group. From 1852 to 1879 there was a direct service to or from Montserrat, which was served twice monthly from St Christopher by sailing vessel.

Used British stamps in 1858-60 (oblit. A08) while the island was under the control of the GPO in London but reverted to local authority in 1860. Handstruck markings were used from 1860 until the first issue of stamps.

Montserrat used its own issues until the general issues of Leeward Islands were introduced in October 1890. In 1903 separate issues were resumed which were used concurrently with those from Leeward Islands until 1956.

• Leeward Islands

FIRST STAMPS ISSUED 1890

CURRENCY	
1890	sterling
1951	100 cents = 1 West Indian dollar

On 25 February 1890 the governor of the Leeward Islands requested a uniform issue and the stamps of Antigua, Dominica, Montserrat, Nevis, St Christopher and Virgin Islands were superseded by a general issue for all.

General issues were used concurrently with specific issues, which began again in 1903, until 30 June 1956 (in Dominica only until 31 December 1939 when it was transferred to the Windward Islands). General issues withdrawn and invalidated on 1 July 1956.

Netherlands Antilles (Curaçao)

CURRENCY
Dutch

FIRST STAMPS ISSUED (inscribed CURAÇAO) 23 May 1873
Little used before 1877, when Curaçao joined the UPU

Colony of the Dutch West India Company from 1634 to 1791 and of the United Netherlands in 1792-5. Under British occupation 1807-15. Dutch colony until made autonomous part of the Netherlands on 15 December 1954. Though known until 1948 as Curaçao, the colony consisted of six main islands, the others being Aruba, Bonaire, St Eustatius, St Martin and Saba.

Postal History

Though letters are known from earlier periods, they are mostly by casual ship until 1825, when the first official Dutch government PO was opened at Willemstad. A British PO operated during the occupation of 1807. In 1825-34 a Netherlands Royal packet operated between Hellevoetsluis and Willemstad. In 1842-54 mail was sent by feeder services into the British packet system. From 1854 to 1885 the Royal Mail Steam Packet Company operated a regular postal service: mails, bagged between Willemstad and Breda (1854) or Moerdijk (after 1855) in Holland, were routed via Southampton. Handstamps were issued in Willemstad and elsewhere.

First opening of other island POs were:
Philipsburg, St Martin 1 January 1882
Oranjestad, St Eustatius 1 March 1884
The Bottom, Saba 1 March 1884
Kralendijk, Bonaire 1886
Oranjestad, Aruba 1888

The name NED(ERLANDSE) ANTILLEN has appeared on all stamps since 1948.

• Guadeloupe

FIRST STAMPS France from 1851, and French Colonies General Issues from 1859. These can be recognized by the postmarks, including a lozenge of dots with the letters GPE
FIRST STAMPS ISSUED 20 November 1876

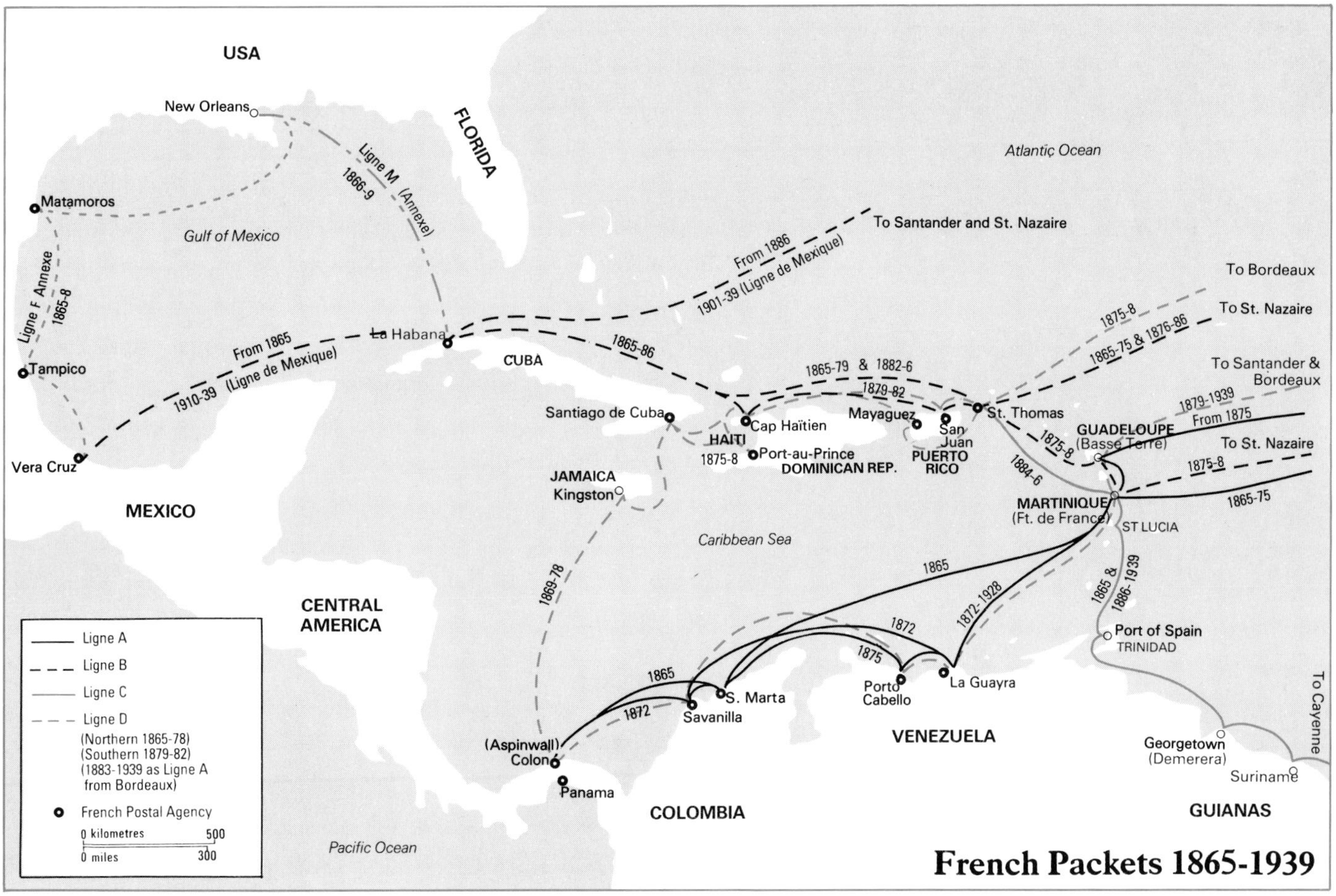
USA
New Orleans
FLORIDA
Ligne M (Annexe) 1866-9
Atlantic Ocean
Matamoros
Gulf of Mexico
Ligne F Annexe 1865-8
To Santander and St. Nazaire
From 1886
1901-39 (Ligne de Mexique)
To Bordeaux
To St. Nazaire
La Habana
From 1865
1910-39 (Ligne de Mexique)
Tampico
CUBA
1865-86
1875-8
1865-75 & 1876-86
To Santander & Bordeaux
1865-79 & 1882-6
1879-82
Santiago de Cuba
Cap Haïtien
Mayaguez
San Juan
St. Thomas
1879-1939
From 1875
GUADELOUPE (Basse Terre)
To St. Nazaire
HAITI
1875-8
Port-au-Prince
DOMINICAN REP.
PUERTO RICO
1875-8
Vera Cruz
JAMAICA
Kingston
1884-6
MARTINIQUE (Ft. de France)
1865-75
MEXICO
ST LUCIA
Caribbean Sea
1869-78
1865
1872-1928
1865 & 1886-1939
CENTRAL AMERICA
1872
Port of Spain
TRINIDAD
1875
1865
S. Marta
Porto Cabello
La Guayra
1872
Savanilla
To Cayenne
VENEZUELA
Georgetown (Demerera)
(Aspinwall) Colon
Surinam
Panama
COLOMBIA
GUIANAS
Pacific Ocean
Ligne A
Ligne B
Ligne C
Ligne D
(Northern 1865-78)
(Southern 1879-82)
(1883-1939 as Ligne A from Bordeaux)
French Postal Agency
0 kilometres 500
0 miles 300

French Packets 1865-1939

CURRENCY
As France

Discovered by Columbus in 1493, the French took possession in 1635 and colonized it in 1674. It was taken by the British in 1759, but returned in 1763. It was occupied again in 1779, 1794, and in 1810. It was offered as a colony to Sweden to encourage them to join the coalition against France but was returned to France again in 1814. It was seized once more in August 1815 but finally became French in July 1816. During their later occupations the British operated the island PO.

Handstamps are known from 1780 and datestamps from 1843, but there was no regular inland service until 1849.

During World War II the island sided with de Gaulle and used Free French stamps during 1940-4. It became an overseas *département* of France on 19 March 1946 and has used the stamps of France since 1947.

• Martinique

FIRST STAMPS France from 1851, and French Colonies General Issues from 1859 (oblit. MQE in lozenge of dots)

FIRST STAMPS ISSUED 18 July 1886

CURRENCY	
1886	As France

Discovered by Columbus in 1502; the French settled the island in 1635. Taken by the British in 1762, it was restored in the following year. It was captured again in 1794 and held until 1802 and again during 1809-15. On this latter occasion a British PO was established.

Posts were set up on 4 March 1766 with four main offices : Saint Pierre, Fort-de-France, La Trinité and Le Marin. The first handstamp was used from 1816 and datestamps from 1832. In 1865 Fort-de-France was the main port of call on the French Ligne A, between St Nazaire and Panama.

During World War II the island sided with de Gaulle. It became a French overseas *département* on 1 January 1947 and has used French stamps since that date.

LEEWARD ISLANDS
SPECIMEN
BARBUDA
3s
POSTAGE
REVENUE
A
ANTIGUA
ONE PENNY
B
Antigua
EIIR
5
cents
Measled Cowrie
C
EIIR
55c
MONTSERRAT
Cereus hexagonus
D
MONTSERRAT
ONE PENNY
E

A Barbuda 1922; **B** Antigua:Crown Colony 1863; **C** Antigua:Associated Statehood 1972; **D** Montserrat 1977; **E** Montserrat:Crown Colony 1876.

LEEWARD ISLANDS
A
20 C
NED-ANTILLEN
B
4F
RF
GUADELOUPE
C
LEEWARD ISLANDS
POSTAGE
& REVENUE
60c
D
POSTES
45
GUADELOUPE
E
CURAÇAO
2½
CENT
F

A Leeward Islands:Diamond Jubilee 1897; **B** Netherlands Antilles 1950; **C** Guadeloupe 1947; **D** Leeward Islands 1954; **E** Guadeloupe 1928; **F** Curaçao 1943.

Dominica

FIRST STAMPS Britain 1858-60 (oblit. A07 at Roseau)
FIRST STAMPS ISSUED 4 May 1874

CURRENCY

1874	sterling
1949	100 cents = 1 West Indian dollar

Discovered by Columbus on 3 November 1493, it was originally settled by the French. It was captured by the British in 1761 and awarded to them by the Peace of Paris which followed. The French took Dominica again in 1778 but it was again restored to Britain in 1783. A French attack in 1805 was repulsed.

Dominica became a Crown Colony and was initially part of the Leeward Islands. Branch of the GPO in London was established at Roseau in 1845 and a handstruck mark 'Paid at Dominica' was used.

Colonial authorities assumed control of postal affairs and used handstruck postal markings until stamps were again issued in 1874. These were replaced by the stamps of Leeward Islands from 31 October 1890 until 1903. At that time separate issues were resumed and these were used concurrently with the Leeward Islands stamps until 31 December 1939 when Dominica joined the Windward Islands.

Dominica was given associated statehood in November 1967 and independence within the Commonwealth on 3 November 1978.

St Lucia

FIRST STAMPS Britain 1858-60 (oblit. A11 at Castries)
FIRST STAMPS ISSUED
18 December 1860

CURRENCY

1860	sterling
1949	100 cents = 1 West Indian dollar

Discovered by Columbus in 1502, this island was long disputed by Britain and France. It changed hands 16 times between 1605 and 1803, but was finally ceded to the occupying British in 1814.

Branch of the British GPO was established at Castries in 1844 and handstruck marks were introduced. St Lucia joined the UPU in 1881. Because of the long connection with France, the French Ligne C visited St Lucia between 1865 and 1887. From the 1880s an internal post operated with individual villages having index letters in the postmarks. Some of these were used up to the reign of King George V.

The island became a member of the British Caribbean Federation 1956-62, an associated state on 1 March 1967 and independent within the Commonwealth on 22 February 1979.

FIRST ANNIVERSARY of INDEPENDENCE
50 CENTS 1967
BARBADOS
Parliament Building
BARBADOS
BARBADOS

A Barbados:Independent 1967; **B** Barbados:Crown Colony 1852; **C** Barbados:Crown Colony 1938.

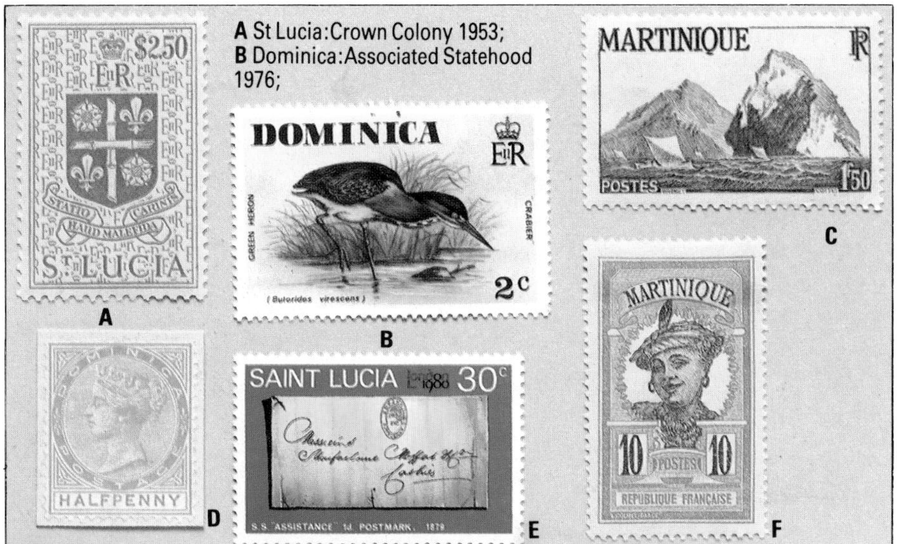
$2.50
ST LUCIA
DOMINICA
2c
MARTINIQUE
POSTES
HALFPENNY
SAINT LUCIA 30c
MARTINIQUE
10
10
REPUBLIQUE FRANCAISE

A St Lucia:Crown Colony 1953; **B** Dominica:Associated Statehood 1976; **C** Martinique:French Colony 1908; **D** Dominica:Crown Colony 1877; **E** Saint Lucia:Associated Statehood 1980; **F** Martinique:French Département 1947.

ST VINCENT
PAX ET JUSTITIA
$1.20
GRENADINES of St. VINCENT
Bequia Island
5c
GRENADA
TWELVE CENTS
5c
GRENADA

A St Vincent:Crown Colony 1938; **B** St Vincent:Ministerial Government 1974; **C** Grenada:Crown Colony 1951; **D** Grenada:Independent 1978.

St Vincent

FIRST STAMPS Britain 1858-60 (oblit. A10 at Kingston)
FIRST STAMPS ISSUED 8 May 1861

CURRENCY	
1861	sterling
1949	100 cents = 1 West Indian dollar

Discovered by Columbus 28 January 1498; was declared neutral in 1600 and its native Carib population was left undisturbed. Agreed to be awarded to Britain in 1763, but France captured the island in 1779. It was returned in 1783.

In 1795 the French again landed on the island and, with Carib support, captured it. They were driven out in 1796 and the Caribs were re-settled on the island of Roatan in the Bay of Honduras. Village postmarks of St Vincent were issued in the 1880s. The island joined the UPU in 1881.

Ministerial government was introduced in 1963 and associated statehood in 1969.

Grenadines of St Vincent

FIRST STAMPS ISSUED 14 November 1973

A group of islands south of St Vincent comprising Bequia, Mustique, Canouan and Union Islands.

Used the stamps of St Vincent until 1973. In 1984 issues for Bequia and Union Is. were prepared and issued. However, there is no genuine philatelic need for these stamps as the mail from these islands is minimal.

Grenada

FIRST STAMPS Britain 1858-60 (oblit. A15 St Georges)
FIRST STAMPS ISSUED 1861

CURRENCY	
1861	sterling
1949	100 cents = 1 West Indian dollar

Discovered by Columbus in 1498, it was settled by the French in 1650. Captured by Britain in April 1762 and held by them until July 1779. Grenada was finally awarded to Britain by the Treaty of Versailles in 1783.

Like the other Windward Islands, Grenada was under control of the British GPO in London, especially for overseas mail, and British stamps were introduced in 1858.

Grenada was granted responsible government in 1951, ministerial government and then associated statehood in 1967. It became independent within the Commonwealth on 7 December 1974. A left-wing government became established and there was an internal revolt in November 1983, which was followed by invasion by US troops. The occupying force left early in 1984 and no special stamps were issued. However, mail from American forces can be recognized by special Army PO numbers.

Grenadines of Grenada

FIRST STAMPS ISSUED 29 December 1973

Group of islands south of Grenada, the largest of which is Carriacou. Used the stamps of Grenada until 1973.

Some issues have been remaindered, cancelled to order, to the philatelic trade, for which most of them were designed. Their necessity for postal purposes is minimal.

Barbados

FIRST STAMPS ISSUED 1 August 1851

CURRENCY	
1852	sterling
1950	100 cents = 1 West Indian dollar

The most easterly island of the Caribbean group which was discovered by the Portuguese in about 1600. It was uninhabited when occupied by the British in 1605. The colony was founded in 1627. As many Royalists settled here after the English Civil War, it was seized by Cromwell in 1652.

Regular mail service to England began with a mail packet agency early in the 18th century. First postal markings appeared on mail in the 1760s. The spelling of the name of the colony was Barbadoes until the 1850s.

Barbados was the chief transfer station for mail to and from the West Indies from 1885 to 1911.

Barbados joined the UPU in 1881, gained self-governing status in 1962 and became independent within the Commonwealth on 30 November 1966. First stamps after independence were issued on 2 December 1966.

• Tobago

FIRST STAMPS Britain 1858-60 (oblit. A14 at Scarborough)
FIRST STAMPS ISSUED 1 August 1879

CURRENCY	
1879	sterling

Discovered by Columbus in 1498, it was settled by the Dutch in 1642. Taken by the British in 1672 but regained by Holland two years later. In 1748 it was declared a neutral island, but in 1763 was ceded to the British. Tobago was taken by the French in 1781 and confirmed to them in 1783. It was taken again by the British in 1793 but was restored to France at the Peace of Amiens in 1802. Taken once more by the British in 1803 and finally confirmed as British in 1814.

One of the Windward Islands from 1833. PO was opened in 1805, but a branch of the GPO in London was established at Scarborough, the capital, in 1841.

Control of the postal system reverted to the colony in 1860 and a handstamp, crowned circle '*Paid at Tobago*', was used until stamps were reissued.

A coastal steamer, used as a TPO, called round the island's coast taking

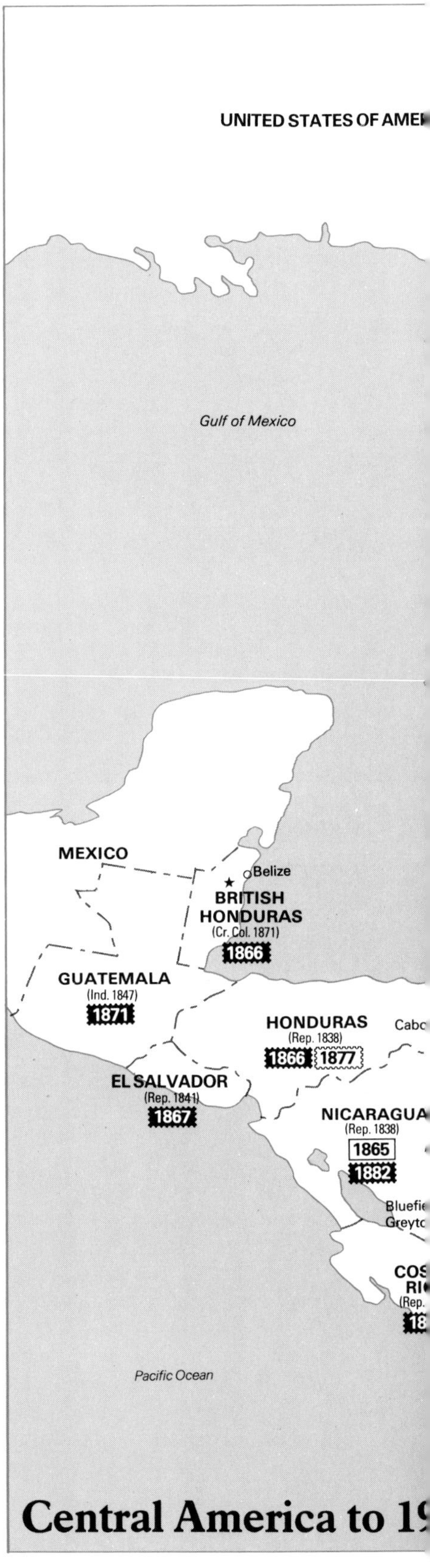

UNITED STATES OF AME
Gulf of Mexico
MEXICO
Belize
BRITISH HONDURAS
(Cr. Col. 1871)
1866
GUATEMALA
(Ind. 1847)
1871
HONDURAS
(Rep. 1838)
1866
1877
EL SALVADOR
(Rep. 1841)
1867
NICARAGUA
(Rep. 1838)
1865
1882
Pacific Ocean
Central America to 1

BERMUDA
(Cr. Col. 1684)
1848 1865
Atlantic Ocean
BAHAMA ISLANDS
(Cr.Col.1670)
1858 1859
Nassau
Havana
CUBA
(Rep. 1898 US admin. to 1902)
1855 1873
CAICOS IS.
1900
TURKS IS.
(Br. 1678)
1867
VIRGIN IS.
Br. 1866 US 1917
DANSK VESTINDIEN
1855 1865-79
ST. THOMAS
NEDERLANDSE ANTILLEN
1873
ANGUILLA
1904
BARBUDA
Santiago de Cuba
HAITI
(Rep. 1859)
1869 1881
DOMINICAN REPUBLIC
1861 1865
Porto Plata
Port au Prince
Jacmel
Santo Domingo
Mayaguez
San Juan
ST. CROIX
ST KITTS
1870
ANTIGUA
1862 1903
1903
NEVIS
1861
CAYMAN
(Brit. 1670)
1889 1900
PUERTO RICO
(US 1898)
1855 1873
1900
GUADELOUPE
(Fr. 1674) 1851 1876
MONTSERRAT
1876 1903
DOMINICA
(Cr. Colony 1771) 1874 1903
JAMAICA
(Cr. Colony 1655)
1858 1860
Kingston
Hispaniola
MARTINIQUE
(Fr. 1674) 1851 1886
LEEWARD ISLANDS
(1871)
1890
ST. LUCIA 1860
(Brit. 1814)
BARBADOS 1851
(Brit. 1852)
Caribbean Sea
ST. VINCENT
(Brit. 1783)
1861
WINDWARD ISLANDS
(1890)
GRENADA
(Brit.1783)
1861
NEDERLANDSE ANTILLEN
(CURACAO)
1873
ARUBA
BONAIRE
CURAÇAO
TOBAGO
(Brit. 1814)
1879
TRINIDAD
(Brit. 1802)
1851
1913
S. Marta
Savanilla
La Guarya
CANAL ZONE
(US)(1903)
1904
Cartagena
Used GB Stamps 1858-60
ocas
l Toro
Chagres
Aspinwall
(Colon)
VENEZUELA
Demerara
(Georgetown)
PANAMA
1878
(Ind. 1903)
1904
Panama City
Panama Canal
COLOMBIA
GUIANA
0 kilometres 500
0 miles 300

Caribbean to 1917

Tobago:Crown Colony 1879; Guatemala:Republic 1978; Guatemala: Republic 1875; Trinidad & Tobago 1938; British Honduras:Crown Colony 1866; British Honduras 1949.

Belize 1979; Salvador:General Ezeta 1893; Honduras:4th Centenary of Discovery of America 1891; Honduras 1958; Nicaragua: Seebeck Issue 1894; Nicaragua:President Somoza 1940; Nicaragua 1970.

Stamps are 80 percent actual size

mail to Port of Spain. On 4 January 1892 an inland postal service began with a PO at Roxborough and, in 1896, at Pembroke and Moriah.

In 1887 Tobago was joined with Trinidad and used the stamps of Trinidad after 1896. Stamps inscribed Trinidad and Tobago were introduced in 1913 when the two islands were combined postally.

• Trinidad

FIRST STAMPS ISSUED 14 August 1851

CURRENCY

1851	sterling

Discovered by Columbus in 1498, it was taken from the Spanish in 1595 by Sir Walter Raleigh. Captured by the French in 1676, but seized by the British in February 1797; their occupation was confirmed at the Peace of Amiens in 1802.

A British PO was opened in 1801 but dealt only with overseas mail and no internal deliveries were made outside Port of Spain until 1816. A local stamp, 'The Lady Macleod', was released in 1847 to prepay postage on letters carried by a Trinidad shipping company.

A postal system was proposed in 1847, but its introduction was delayed for four years because the British government anticipated it would run at a loss. In 1851, on the day of issue of stamps, POs for internal mail were opened at San Fernando and Port of Spain.

In 1887 Trinidad was linked with Tobago by vote of Parliament, and the stamps of Trinidad were used in Tobago until 1913, when stamps inscribed Trinidad and Tobago were issued.

Trinidad and Tobago

FIRST STAMPS ISSUED 1913

CURRENCY

1913	sterling
1935	100 cents = 1 West Indian dollar

Crown Colony which became part of the shortlived British Caribbean Federation from 3 January 1958 until 31 August 1962. Became independent within the Commonwealth on 31 August 1962.

CENTRAL AMERICA

Guatemala

CURRENCY

1871	100 centavos = 8 reales = 1 peso
1927	100 centavos de quetzal = 1 quetzal

FIRST STAMPS ISSUED 1 March 1871

A Spanish dominion until 1821, Guatemala was conquered by Pedro de Alvarado in 1523. The postal service was originally directed from Mexico but in 1620 the postal concession was formally auctioned to Pedro Crespo Suarez, who became the Guatemalan Postmaster. A monthly postal route was started to Oaxaca in 1748, and the posts returned to the Spanish Crown in 1767. First postal markings were introduced in 1770 at the former capital of Guatemala, now known as Antigua.

Guatemala's independence from Spain in 1821 made little difference to the postal service. A network of agents who forwarded the international mail was created before the formation of the UPU in 1874. A mailboat service on a monthly basis was introduced on the east coast in 1851 and on the west coast in cooperation with other nations. This service ran down the coast to connect with the railway at Panama.

On 1 July 1823 Guatemala, after a brief union with Mexico, became part of the United Provinces of Central America, which comprised all of modern Central America except the Mosquito Coast of Nicaragua; the capital was Guatemala City. The union broke up in 1838. Full independence was declared in March 1847.

Guatemala still lays claim to Belize (q.v.), where a small British garrison is stationed.

GUANACASTE
PANAMA
unesco
CORREOS DE COLOMBIA
DIEZ CENTAVOS
COSTA RICA
COLONES

A Panama:Colombia 1892; B Costa Rica 1889; C Panama 1970; D Costa Rica 1949; E Colombia 1948; F Colombia 1859.

EE.UU.DE VENEZUELA
20 CENTIMOS 20
FEDERACION
UN REAL
BRITISH GUIANA
FOUR CENTS
POSTAGE & REVENUE
CANAL ZONE POSTAGE
AIR MAIL

A Venezuela 1948; B Venezuela 1863; C British Guiana 1860; D British Guiana:Centenary of Colony 1931; E Canal Zone 1949.

• British Honduras

FIRST STAMPS Britain 1858-May 1860 (oblit. A06 at Belize)
FIRST STAMPS ISSUED January 1866

CURRENCY

1866	sterling
1888	100 cents = 1 dollar

British settlements began in 1638 after shipwreck, and were followed by a regular colony in 1662, which was established from Jamaica to exploit the mahogany and timber industry. The area was disputed by Spain and the rights to the area were only accepted in 1763, though the Spanish insisted on the destruction of all fortifications. The settlement was seized by Spain in 1779, but was returned to Britain in 1783. Although it was recognized internationally in 1786, with the area as well as the town known as Belize from 1788, it was again attacked by Spain during the revolutionary wars, but on this occasion the colonials defeated the invaders.

Letters via Jamaica are known from 1786. The first local PO was established on 31 October 1809 but a handstamp reading 'Belize' was used on foreign mail as early as 1800. The first regular packet service ('Mexican Packet') called on the run from Jamaica to Vera Cruz in 1829. A branch PO directly under London was opened in 1857. The colony took over the posts on 1 April 1860. From 1860-66 used only handstamps.

British Honduras was declared a colony in 1862 under Jamaica and a Crown Colony in 1871. Became independent of Jamaica in 1884. In 1933 Guatemala repudiated a long-standing treaty of friendship and has since threatened to invade. A small British force supported by a Field PO has been in operations since the 1960s.

British Honduras changed its name on 1 June 1973 to Belize (*see below*), and became self-governing within the Commonwealth on 1 January 1984.

Caribbean Sea
Atlantic Ocean
Pacific Ocean
St. Marta
C62
Barranquilla
Savanilla
Cartagena
F69
C56
Chagres
Colon E88
(Aspinwall)
Panama
C35
Panama
1878
Bolivar
1863
Antioquoia
1868
Santander
1884
Cúcuta
Medellin
Boyacá
1899
Cauca
1902
Tolima
1870
Cundinamarca
1870
Bógota
COLOMBIA
(Rep. 1886)
1859
VENEZUELA
British
Guiana
Tumaco
Quito
ECUADOR
(Rep. 1830)
1865
Guayaquil
C41
Amazon
BRAZIL
Republic of Gt. Colombia 1830
Ecuador 1880
Civil War Provisionals 1902-3
C56 GB Stamps 1865-84
French Stamps 1865-81
0 kilometres 500
0 miles 300

Colombia & Ecuador to 1902

Belize

FIRST STAMPS ISSUED June 1973

CURRENCY

1973 100 cents = 1 dollar

Formerly British Honduras, changed its name in 1973. First stamps released in the colony on 11 June 1973 but available in London on 1 June.

Became independent member of the Commonwealth in 1981. Britain has retained a military presence in the territory against threatened invasion from Guatemala. British Forces' PO is in operation.

Cayes of Belize

Islands off the coast of Belize which are part of that territory. Issued stamps in 1984 which were sponsored by a stamp dealer. They had little postal usage.

El Salvador

FIRST STAMPS ISSUED May 1867

CURRENCY

1867 8 reales = 100 centavos = 1 peso
1912 100 centavos = 1 colon

Invaded by the Spaniards in 1524 and the capital was established at San Salvador. Six POs were in operation before the collapse of the Spanish Empire. Became independent of Spain on 22 September 1822. The country fought to prevent annexation by Mexico and joined the United Provinces of Central America in 1823. It became independent and assumed the name of El Salvador on 30 January 1841.

Seebeck held the contract for the supply of Salvador's stamps from 1890 to 1898. In recent years Salvador has been involved in a major civil war between the Government and left-wing forces. This has caused serious disruption of the postal service, though government issues are still circulated regularly through the UPU.

Honduras

FIRST STAMPS ISSUED 1 January 1866 (but it is probable that these were never in fact issued. Second series issued 1877-8)

CURRENCY

1866 8 reales = 1 peso
1878 100 centavos = 1 peso
1933 100 centavos = 1 lempiru

Honduras was discovered by Columbus in 1502 during his last voyage to the West Indies. It was colonized by Spain soon after and was governed as part of the Captain-Generalcy of New Granada. Like other Spanish colonies in Central America, Honduras rebelled in the aftermath of the Napoleonic Wars and became independent in 1821. It was part of the United Provinces of Central America 1823-38, but following the dissolution became involved in a series of wars and revolutions.

In 1866 a series of stamps appeared inscribed *'Correos de Honduras'*, but it is probable that these were never issued. A further attempt to establish a postal service was made in 1877 and the stamps of 1866 were overprinted with new values. In 1878 a new series inscribed *'Republica de Honduras'* was released.

Honduras was the first country to issue the notorious Seebeck stamps, which were available for reprint in New York for collectors in return for the right to issue a new series each year. This contract was terminated by Honduras in 1895.

Honduras joined the UPU in 1879.

Caribbean Sea
PANAMA
VENEZUELA
BRITISH GUIANA
SURINAME (Dutch)
GUYANE FRANCAIS
Atlantic Ocean
COLOMBIA
Inini
1932
(1905)
(1905)
(1922)
Amazon
ECUADOR
(1904)
(1934)
(1942)
(1903)
BRAZIL
PERU
(1927)
BOLIVIA
CHACO
(1938)
PARAGUAY
(1927)
Pacific Ocean
ARGENTINA
URUGUAY
CHILE
Atlantic Ocean
(1902)
FALKLAND ISLANDS
(Brit.)
0 kilometres 800
0 miles 500
South America 1939

Nicaragua

FIRST STAMPS British from 1865
FIRST STAMPS ISSUED 1882

CURRENCY

1862	100 centavos = 1 peso (paper currency)
1912	100 centavos de Cordoba = 1 peso de Cordoba (gold currency)
1925	100 centavos = 1 cordoba

First explored by the Spanish under Gonzales de Avila in 1522. Established as a Spanish province which was administered as part of Guatemala. It was a section of the province of Leon which included most of Costa Rica and Guanacaste. There were five offices in the area from 1806 to 1820.

Nicaragua became independent of Spain in 1821 and initially became part of the short-lived Mexican Empire in 1822. In 1823 joined the United Provinces of Central America, then, in 1838, became an independent republic.

British POs were opened at Bluefields on the Mosquito Coast and Greytown in 1857. British stamps were used from Greytown with cancellation C57 from 1865-82. The Bluefields office was closed in 1863. Nicaragua entered into an agreement with Seebeck in 1890 for the regular issue of new stamps each year. This followed until 1900 when the agreement was revoked. In 1904-12 separate stamps were overprinted locally for use in Bluefields (Zelaya) and Cabo Gracias a Dios. These were in a different currency because the value of the *peso* in these areas was higher than in the remainder of the country. A further general issue was made in February 1912 for six months.

In January 1937 General Somoza became president and his family controlled the country until defeated by left-wing guerillas.

Costa Rica

FIRST STAMPS ISSUED March 1863

CURRENCY

1863 8 reales = 1 peso
1881 100 centavos = 1 peso
1901 100 centavos = 1 colon

Visited by Columbus in 1502, this was the first place in America where the Spaniards found gold, hence its name 'Rich Coast'. After three centuries of Spanish rule the province revolted in 1821 and joined the United Provinces of Central America until 1838, when Costa Rica became an independent republic.

Postal service was coastal in most of its routes. Postal markings of only five offices are recorded between 1800 and 1821. These were at Alajuela, Cartago, San Jose, Villa Nueve and Villa Vieja.

Independent Costa Rica had some difficulty in establishing boundaries with its neighbouring countries. A dispute with Nicaragua over the sovereignty of Guanacaste was resolved in 1896. Area had been annexed by Costa Rica in 1821 and led to the War of 1856-7, which had been won by Costa Rica. Stamps were issued with 'Guanacaste' overprinted on Costa Rican stamps in 1885-9.

Boundary with Panama was not finally settled until May 1941.

SOUTH AMERICA & PANAMA

Colombia

FIRST STAMPS Granadine Confederation August 1859

CURRENCY

100 centavos = 1 peso

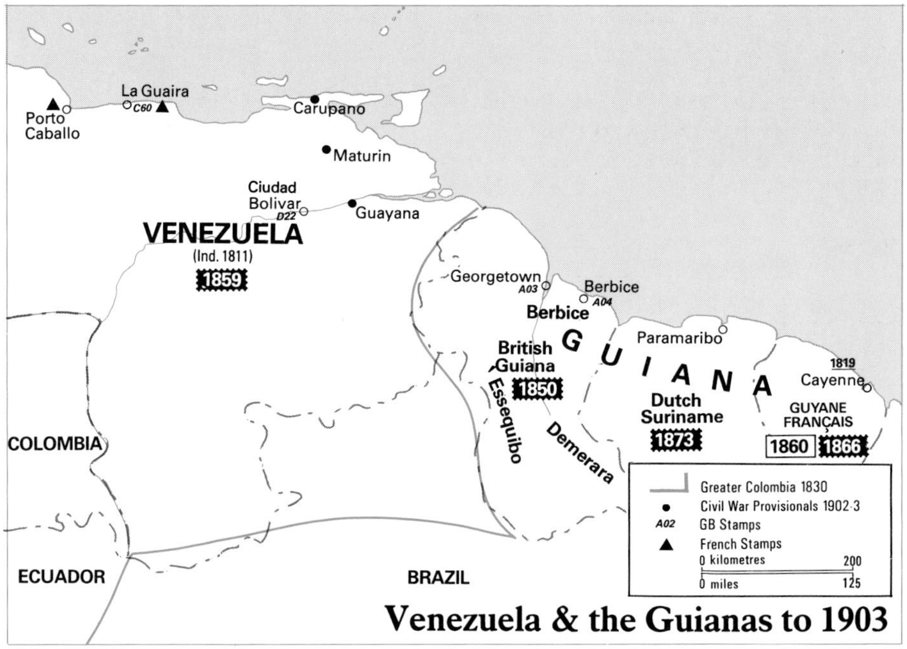
La Guaira
C60
Porto Caballo
Carupano
Maturin
Ciudad Bolivar
D22
Guayana
VENEZUELA
(Ind. 1811)
1859
Georgetown
A03
Berbice
A04
Berbice
British Guiana
1850
Essequibo
Demerara
G U I A N A
Paramaribo
Dutch Suriname
1873
1819
Cayenne
GUYANE FRANÇAIS
1860
1866
COLOMBIA
ECUADOR
BRAZIL
Greater Colombia 1830
Civil War Provisionals 1902-3
A02 GB Stamps
French Stamps
0 kilometres 200
0 miles 125

Venezuela & the Guianas to 1903

Conquered by Spaniards in 1525-50. From 1770, with Venezuela and Ecuador, formed the Viceroyalty of New Granada. Republic of Colombia proclaimed in 1819. After breakaway of Venezuela and Ecuador in 1830, was known until 1858 as the Republic of New Granada, then as the Granadine Confederation, the United States of New Granada, and in late 1861 the United States of Colombia. The nine sovereign states constituted in 1858 became departments in 1886 and the country became the Republic of Colombia. The department of Panama became an independent country in 1903 (*see* Panama).

The earliest identifiable mail of the Spanish period dates from after 1750 when handstamps of origin came into use in main towns. Spanish mails to Europe went by casual ship. Interest centres on the Isthmus of Panama, where numerous forwarding agents dealt with the transmission of mail: their cachets are known from 1834.

In 1842 British packet agents were appointed at Panama and Chagres to control transfer of mails between the Royal Mail Steam Packet Co. and the Pacific Steam Navigation Co.; they were issued with handstamps.

A US Mail Despatch Agency was in existence in 1847 and used stamps of the USA (oblit. red grid). Additional offices at Cartagena and Santa Martha were opened by the British in the 1840s.

Later, British and French packet agents exercised mail facilities with obliterators and datestamps and stamps of Britain or France, as follows:

Panama
- British 1865-84 (oblit. C35)
- French 1872-4 (datestamps not known)

Cartagena
- British 1865-81 (oblit. C56; also in error C65)

Santa Martha
- British 1865-81 (oblit. C62)
- French 1865-72 and 1875 (datestamps from 1866)

Colon-Aspinwall
- British 1870-81 (oblit. E88)
- French 1865-81 (datestamps from 1875)

Savanilla
- British 1872-81 (oblit. F69)
- French 1872-81 (datestamps 1872-81)

Owing to the country's poor natural communications, but also in pursuance of their sovereign rights, the states of the republic had their own posts, which operated concurrently with (but were separate from) the national post. From 1863 until various dates between 1886 and 1906 they issued their own stamps; the last such stamps were withdrawn by decree of 28 July 1906.

Bolivar

FIRST STAMPS 1863

Antioquoia

FIRST STAMPS 1868

Cundinamarca

FIRST STAMPS 1870

Tolima

FIRST STAMPS 1870

Santander

FIRST STAMPS 1884

Boyacá

FIRST STAMPS 1899

Cauca

FIRST STAMPS 1902

During the civil war of 1899-1902 a series of provisional issues was made in parts of the country cut off from Bogotá:
Cartagena, Cúcuta, Tumaco, Barranquilla, Medellin.

Private air companies under government contract had their own stamps to show the airmail fee as follows:

COMPANIA COLOMBIANA DE NAVEGACIÓN AÉREA in 1920

SCADTA (Sociedad Colombo-Alemana de Transportes Aéreos) 4 October 1920 – 30 April 1932;

LANSA (Lineas Aéreas Nacionales S.A.) 22 June 1950, use ceased when merged with AVIANCA 1952;

AVIANCA (Aerovias Nacionales de Colombia S.A.) 12 July 1950, use no longer necessary after merger with LANSA.

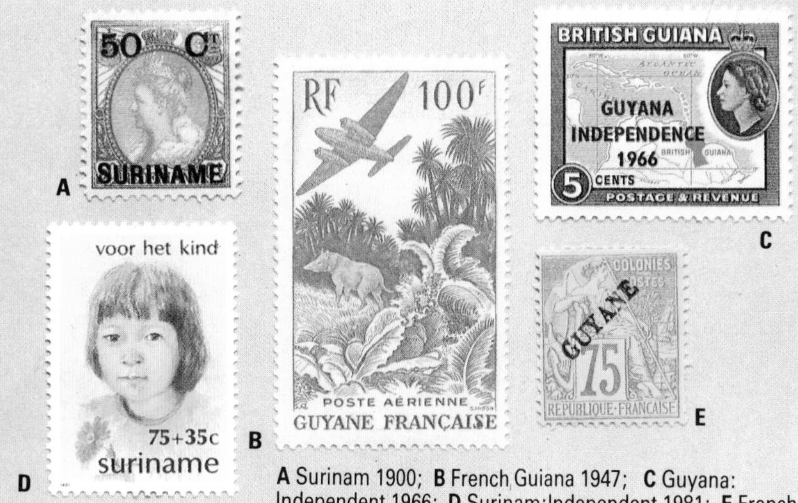
A
50 C
SURINAME
B
RF 100F
POSTE AÉRIENNE
GUYANE FRANÇAISE
C
BRITISH GUIANA
GUYANA
INDEPENDENCE
1966
5 CENTS
POSTAGE & REVENUE
D
voor het kind
75+35c
suriname
E
COLONIES POSTES
GUYANE
75
REPUBLIQUE·FRANCAISE

A Surinam 1900; **B** French Guiana 1947; **C** Guyana: Independent 1966; **D** Surinam:Independent 1981; **E** French Guiana 1892.

A
20
B
BRAZIL
80
OITENTA REIS
C
Brasil 83
30,00
TUCANUCU
D
S/.2.00
AEREO
ECUADOR
DR.VICTOR MANUEL PEÑAHERRERA
1884-1984
IBARRA
E
ECUADOR CORREOS
MEDIO REAL

A Brazil:Empire 1850; **B** Brazil:Empire 1879; **C** Brazil:Republic 1983; **D** Ecuador 1967; **E** Ecuador:Printed in Paris 1872.

Panama

FIRST STAMPS 1878
FIRST STAMPS ISSUED August 1904

CURRENCY

1878	100 centavos = 1 peso
1906	100 centesimos = 1 balboa

Former state and department of Colombia whose history is bound up with the need of the European powers and the USA for efficient transport across the isthmus. This was maintained from 1849 by mule train until the Panama Railroad was completed in 1855. When the Colombian senate refused to ratify a Colombian-USA treaty leasing territory for the construction of a canal, Panama declared its independence (3 November 1903) and concluded the treaty granting the Canal Zone (*see below*) to the USA.

For use of stamps of USA, Britain

and France, *see* Colombia.

Provisionals issued 1903 in Panama City, Colón and Bocas del Toro.

• Canal Zone

FIRST STAMPS 24 June 1904

CURRENCY

1904	100 centavos = 1 peso
1906	100 centesimos = 1 balboa
1924	US

A territory five miles either side of Panama Canal (excluding Panama City and Colón), leased in perpetuity to the USA on 18 November 1903 but under a treaty of 1977 control will revert to Panama in the year 2000, and the territory already has. Canal opened 15 August 1914. The administration was a government agency of the USA, its governor being appointed by the president.

Postal system was run by the USA but independent of the US postal system. It was not a member of the UPU, and its domestic postal rates apply on mail to Mexico and Canada as well as Panama and all US possessions. Panama protested against the use in July 1904 of US stamps overprinted (the second issue).

By the Taft Agreement (1904) between the USA and Panama, stamps of Panama were supplied for overprinting CANAL ZONE. Panamanian currency was maintained until the abrogation of the agreement (1924) when the Canal Zone adopted the US dollar and USA stamps overprinted. After 1928, distinctive stamps were issued until the change of status in 1977, when Panamanian stamps were used.

Venezuela

FIRST STAMPS 1 January 1859

CURRENCY

1859	100 centavos = 8 reales = 1 peso
1879	100 centesimos = 1 venezolano
1880	100 centimos = 1 bolivar

Discovered by Columbus and colonized by the Spanish c.1550, Venezuela formed part of the Viceroyalty of New Granada. Independence was proclaimed on 5 July 1811, and after a 10-year war Venezuela became part of Greater Colombia. From this it withdrew in 1830. In the 19th and early 20th centuries, Venezuela was one of the most turbulent of all South American republics, with civil wars in 1863-70 and 1899-1903 and many revolutions. However, since the discovery of oil (1922) and the exploitation of iron resources, it has become one of the richest and most stable of South American republics, with a parliamentary constitution dating from 1958.

Mail from the colonial period bore straight-line postal markings. In the period under Greater Colombia, markings took the form of a large oval. In 1842-59 they were circular.

Stamps inscribed ESCUELAS and INSTRUCCION were revenue stamps showing payment of a tax to finance state primary schools. They were also valid for postage until 1911 and were so used, more especially during the chaos of March 1871-August 1873 and in 1879-80.

Since at least 1818 outgoing Venezuelan mail has been sent from La Guaira to St Thomas for onward transmission to Europe.

La Guaira

In 1863 a private concession was granted to Captain Robert Todd to carry mail between La Guaira, Porto Caballo, and St Thomas. After many changes of hands the service eventually succumbed to the superiority of its rivals.

Non-governmental stamps issued July 1864-73. Stamps with the same face value but in different colours were necessary for sale in Venezuelan ports and in St Thomas as the island *real* was worth more than the mainland *real*.

Stamps of Britain were used at La Guaira in 1865-80 (oblit. C60) and at Ciudad Bolivar in 1868-80 (oblit. D22).

Stamps of France were used in 1866-79 at La Guaira and Porto Cabello in connection with Ligne L to Fort-de-France (Martinique).

During the civil war of 1899-1903, provisionals were issued as follows:

• Carupano

FIRST ISSUE November 1902 during hostilities
SECOND ISSUE January 1903 during blockade by European powers

• Guayana

STAMPS ISSUED March 1903

• Marino

STAMPS ISSUED 1903

• Maturin

STAMPS ISSUED 1903

• British Guiana

FIRST STAMPS ('cottonreels') 1 July 1850 (these were produced locally pending arrival of definitive from London)

CURRENCY

1850	100 cents = 1 dollar

The three Dutch counties of Demerara, Essequibo and Berbice, settled by the Dutch West Indies Company c.1620, were captured in 1796 by Britain, ceded to it in 1814, and united as British Guiana in 1831. The colony became an independent member of the Commonwealth on 26 May 1966 as Guyana.

A packet office existed in Demerara from 1796 and in Berbice somewhat later. A local boat met the Falmouth packet at Barbados. Datestamps are known from soon after. From 1842 the service changed to steam and British Guiana shared the services of the West Indies packet until World War I. An inland PO was established by London on 1 July 1850. In 1856 a crowned circle 'PAID' mark was supplied. Prepayment of letters to Britain was made compulsory in 1858. In 1860 the colony took control of the PO. Difficult terrain and broad rivers with rapids impeded communications until regular airmails started in 1944. In 1880 there were 49 POs and even by 1938 only 73.

British Guiana boasts the world's highest-priced stamp in the one cent black on magenta of 1856 (of which only one copy is known).

Stamps of Britain were used on mail to Britain in 1858-60 (oblit. A03, Georgetown; A04, Berbice).

Guyana

FIRST STAMPS 26 May 1966

CURRENCY

100 cents = 1 dollar

Formerly British Guiana, this country became independent within the British Commonwealth on 26 May 1966. A member of the Caribbean Free Trade Area (CARIFTA) and since 23 February 1970 a 'co-operative republic'. In 1975 there were 170 POs and PAs.

Suriname

CURRENCY

1873 Dutch

FIRST STAMPS ISSUED 1 October 1873
FIRST STAMPS ISSUED AS INDEPENDENT COUNTRY 25 November 1975

Disputed between Dutch, French and British until confirmed as a Dutch colony in 1816. The labour shortage caused by the abolition of slavery in 1863 was solved by immigration from Asia. An autonomous part of the Netherlands from 15 December 1954 until 25 November 1975 when it became independent.

Postal History

Between 1706 and 1804 mail from the Dutch West Indies, carried by ships of the Geostroyeerde Westindische Compagnie, received a characteristic 'Postage Due' mark in Amsterdam; from Suriname three examples are recorded in 1757-69. During the British period, mail bearing handstamps is known from 1805 and 1813. Dutch markings were authorized in 1828; dated stamps exist from 1847 (Paramaribo). In 1825-34 mail was sent by casual schooner to Curaçao to catch the Royal Dutch packets. After 1834 mail between the Netherlands and Suriname was generally routed by British packet via Southampton (later Plymouth) or (after 1865) by French packet (Ligne C) via Saint-Nazaire. A French packet agent was placed at Suriname in 1865. Route instruction marks were applied to letters after 1877. A Dutch packet, restarted in 1883, became fortnightly in 1904 (handstamps were used on board to cancel stamps). Until 1930 the majority of inland letters were also carried by water.

• French Guiana

FIRST STAMPS French Colonies General Issues from 1860
FIRST STAMPS ISSUED December 1886

CURRENCY

100 centimes = 1 franc

Settled by the French in 1626, it became a colony in 1674 and achieved

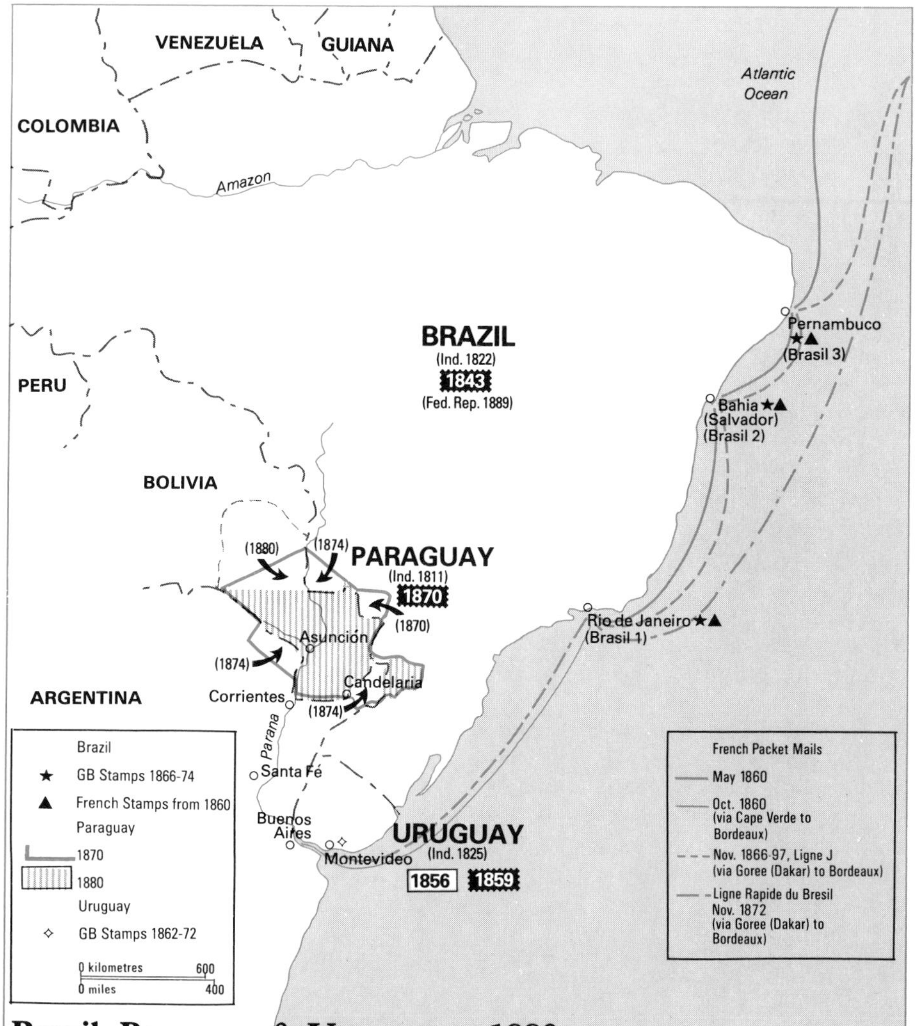

VENEZUELA
GUIANA
COLOMBIA
Amazon
Atlantic Ocean
BRAZIL
(Ind. 1822)
1843
(Fed. Rep. 1889)
PERU
BOLIVIA
Pernambuco
(Brasil 3)
Bahia
(Salvador)
(Brasil 2)
(1880)
(1874)
PARAGUAY
(Ind. 1811)
1870
(1870)
Asunción
(1874)
Candelaria
ARGENTINA
Corrientes
(1874)
Rio de Janeiro
(Brasil 1)
Paraná
Santa Fé
Buenos Aires
Montevideo
URUGUAY
(Ind. 1825)
1856
1859
Brazil
GB Stamps 1866-74
French Stamps from 1860
Paraguay
1870
1880
Uruguay
GB Stamps 1862-72
0 kilometres 600
0 miles 400
French Packet Mails
May 1860
Oct. 1860 (via Cape Verde to Bordeaux)
Nov. 1866-97, Ligne J (via Goree (Dakar) to Bordeaux)
Ligne Rapide du Bresil Nov. 1872 (via Goree (Dakar) to Bordeaux)

Brazil, Paraguay & Uruguay to 1880

Above
Ecuador Army plane delivering post to soldiers at Teisha in the middle of the Amazon jungle

Left
Swimming couriers, Peru, 1834

notoriety as a penal settlement in 1854-1938. Successively under Vichy and Free French administration in 1941 and 1944, it became an overseas *département* of France from 19 March 1946.

Postal History
Cayenne had the only post office (opened 11 August 1819) until 1888. Internal mail was passed free. External mail was handstamped from 1833. Cayenne was served from 1865 to 1939 by packets of the French Ligne C, a branch line from Martinique, connecting at Fort-de-France with Ligne A for Saint-Nazaire (in 1884-6 at St Thomas with Ligne B, from 1933 with Ligne D for Bordeaux). Used French Colonies General Issues from 1860.

Local stamps of Compagnie des Transports Aeriens Guyanais issued July-October 1921 to prepay the internal airmail fee.

• Inini

FIRST SEPARATE STAMPS ISSUED
7 April 1932

An inland territory of French Guiana, administered separately from 6 July 1930 to 19 March 1946, when it was reunited.

Brazil

FIRST STAMPS ISSUED ('bullseyes')
1 August 1843

CURRENCY

1843	1000 reis = 1 milreis
1942	100 centavos = 1 cruzeiro

Discovered in 1500 by the Portuguese and became their principal colony. When Napoleon invaded Portugal in 1807, the Portuguese court went into exile in Brazil. Britain's many connections with its oldest ally were moved from Lisbon to Rio de Janeiro, Brazil was declared a kingdom in 1815 and on 7 September 1822 an empire, independent of Portugal. The Federal Republic of the United States of Brazil was proclaimed 15 November 1889, when Pedro II was overthrown. In 1969 the official title reverted simply to Brazil.

Postal History
Before 1798 letters to and from Portugal were carried by favour of travellers or by special messenger aboard official vessels; those arriving in Rio were thrown to claimants from a window of the governor's palace. A royal postal service between Portugal

and Brazil was founded by decree of 20 January 1798. Government packets (*paquetes*) plied on alternate months from Lisbon to Assu and Salinas or to Bahia and Rio de Janeiro. Provision was made for internal communication between provincial capitals. Postal rates were fixed. The Rio PO was installed in the Plaza 15 de Novembre (and remained in the same building for a century and a half). With the arrival of the Portuguese court in Brazil (1808), a monthly sailing packet service was started between Falmouth and Rio via Madeira, Pernambuco, and Bahia.

Internal services were improved. Paid (FRANCA) marks were introduced c.1829 to mark prepaid letters. Brazil became second only to Britain in issuing adhesive stamps. Urban collection and delivery were started in 1849 (after an abortive attempt in 1845). From Falmouth, steam replaced sail in 1851 when the Royal Mail Steam Packet was given the contract. British PAs were placed at ports of call. After 1860 other connections were made from Rio to Bordeaux (Ligne du Brésil, later Ligne J), Marseille, and Liverpool (Pacific Steam Navigation Co.). French PAs were placed at the ports of call and provided with datestamps. The Brazilian PO was subordinate to various ministries until December 1931.

Stamps of France were used at Rio, Bahia and Pernambuco from 1860 (usually oblit. anchor in lozenge of dots).

Stamps of Britain were used at British packet ports in 1866-74:

Bahia (oblit. C81)
Pernambuco (oblit. C82)
Rio de Janeiro (oblit. C83).

CORREOS DE CHILE
40 CTS
PERU
TRAJES TIPICOS
8.50 AEREO
CHILE 5 CENTAVOS
CHILE $10
D/SN°20
BOLIVIA
Bs 1200
PEDRO DE LA GASCA PACIFICADOR DEL PERU
CORREO AEREO BOLIVIA
A
B
C
D
E
F
G

A Chile:Centenary of Santiago 1941; B Peru:Provincial Costume 1874; C Chile:First Issue 1853; D Peru:Republic 1866; E Chile:Republic 1982; F Bolivia:First Issue 1867; G Bolivia:Explorer 1962.

Ecuador

FIRST STAMPS 1 January 1865

CURRENCY	
1865	8 reales = 1 peso
1881	100 centavos = 1 sucre

Under Spanish rule part of the Viceroyalty of New Granada, it was freed in 1822 and became part of Greater Colombia. It became an independent republic on 13 May 1830. Few heads of state or constitutions have lasted any time; a military junta assumed power in 1976.

Handstamps were in use from 1779, including the 'beaded oval' type (1819-30). A British PO at Guayaquil handled external mail from 1849 to 1880, with handstamps from 1849.

Stamps of Britain used at Guayaquil (oblit. C41) 26 January 1865-1874.

Stamps of France used at Guayaquil 25 April 1872-4 March 1874 in connection with Pacific Ligne F.

• Scadta

STAMPS ISSUED 28 August 1928-27 December 1930

Colombian company which established internal air routes in Ecuador with external services to Colombia and Peru (*see also* Colombia).

Galapagos Islands

FIRST STAMPS ISSUED 15 July 1957. These are found used also on the mainland

Territory, and since 1973 a province, of Ecuador.

Peru

FIRST STAMPS (originally printed for Pacific Steam Navigation Co.) 1 December 1857
FIRST STAMPS ISSUED 10 March 1858

CURRENCY	
1857	8 reales = 1 peso
1858	100 centavos = 10 dineros = 5 pesetas = 1 peso
1874	100 centavos = 1 sol

Spanish adventurers under Pizarro landed in 1532 and quickly subjugated

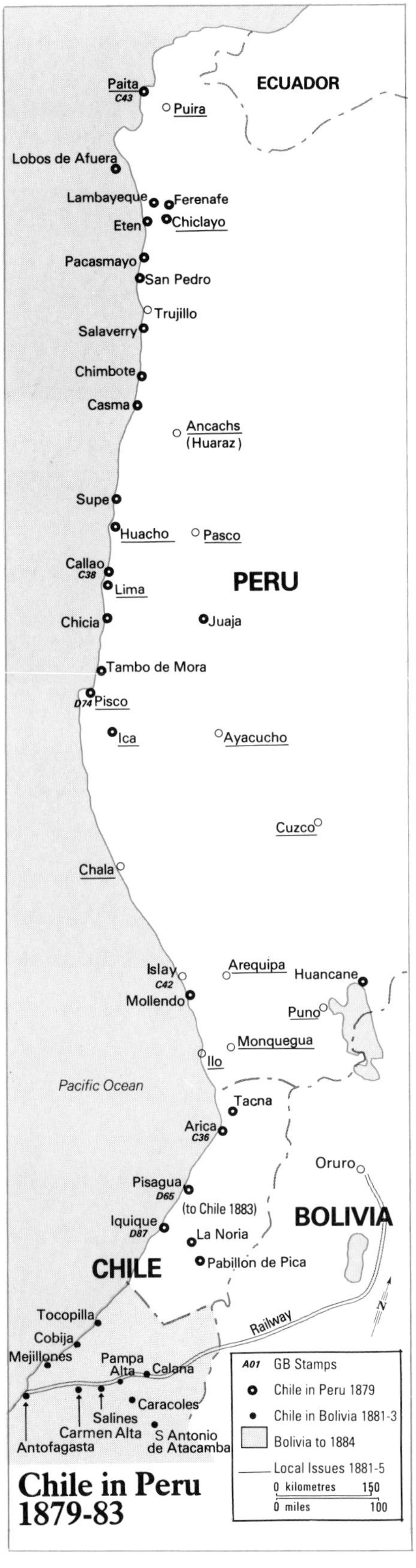
ECUADOR
Paita
C43
Puira
Lobos de Afuera
Lambayeque
Ferenafe
Eten
Chiclayo
Pacasmayo
San Pedro
Trujillo
Salaverry
Chimbote
Casma
Ancachs
(Huaraz)
Supe
Huacho
Pasco
Callao
C38
Lima
PERU
Chicia
Juaja
Tambo de Mora
D74 Pisco
Ica
Ayacucho
Cuzco
Chala
Islay
C42
Arequipa
Huancane
Mollendo
Puno
Monquegua
Ilo
Pacific Ocean
Tacna
Arica
C36
Oruro
Pisagua
D65
(to Chile 1883)
Iquique
D87
La Noria
BOLIVIA
CHILE
Pabillon de Pica
Tocopilla
Railway
Cobija
Mejillones
Pampa Alta
Calama
Caracoles
Salines
Carmen Alta
S Antonio de Atacamba
Antofagasta
A01 GB Stamps
Chile in Peru 1879
Chile in Bolivia 1881-3
Bolivia to 1884
Local Issues 1881-5
0 kilometres 150
0 miles 100

Chile in Peru 1879-83

the Incas. From 1542 the Viceroyalty of Peru was governed from Lima, a city founded by Pizarro on the old Inca highway. Until 1717 this comprised the whole of Spanish South America, including Panama, Ecuador, Colombia and Venezuela, and even until 1776 included Argentina, Uruguay and Paraguay. Peru declared its independence on 28 July 1821; this became reality in 1824 after the ensuing war.

The War of the Pacific (1879-83) was waged over nitrate rights, Bolivia and Peru against Chile. By using its much stronger navy, Chile soon had the upper hand and most of the fighting was on Peruvian soil. The consequent boundary dispute between Peru and Chile was only finally settled on 28 July 1929, Tacna returning to Peru and Arica being ceded to Chile. Boundary disputes with Ecuador were settled in 1948.

Postal History

Before the Spanish landed in 1532, the Incas employed state runners (*chasquis*) between Quito and Cuzco, verbal messages being memorized and passed on from one relay station to the next. Lima became the headquarters of the posts of the Spanish Indies in 1561. Runner services to Potosí are recorded in 1599. A service to Buenos Aires via Tucumán was started in 1748. Marks of origin struck in black or red and 'Paid' (FRANCA) marks are known from 1766. Posts then extended to Santiago de Chile. In 1840 the Pacific Steam Navigation Co. opened a route from Panama to Valparaiso. From 12 August 1851 mail to Europe was permitted through British consular offices. In 1867 the PSNCo started a service to Valparaiso from Liverpool via Cape Horn. In 1870 Peru had only 166 POs.

Stamps of Britain used at packet agencies: in 1861-79 at Paita (oblit. C43); in 1865-79 at Arica (oblit. C36), Callao (oblit. C38) and Islay (oblit. C42); in 1868-78 at Iquique (oblit. D87); in 1868-70 at Pisco (oblit. D74); and (dates not known) at Pisagua (oblit. D65).

A Peruvian stamp depicting a railway engine issued in 1871 on the occasion of the 20th anniversary of the first South American railway is generally considered to be the world's first commemorative stamp.

During the War of the Pacific, stamps of Chile used in occupied Peru 5 April 1879 or later until 11 October 1883 can be identified by dated postmarks of 34 towns (*see map*). Local issues were made in various towns in 1881-5 (*see map*).

Bolivia

FIRST STAMPS ISSUED 1867

CURRENCY

1867	100 centavos = 1 boliviano
1963	100 centavos = 1 peso boliviano

Formerly known as Upper Peru, and until 1776 under the Viceroyalty of Peru, the region became part of the Viceroyalty of La Plata. On becoming an independent republic on 6 August 1825, it took its name from Simon Bolivar. The nitrates of the coastal provinces attracted the envy first of Peru and later of Chile, being lost to Chile by the War of the Pacific (1879-83).

In 1895 internal post routes consisted of the Oruro-Antofagasta railroad, post riders on horseback, and river boats. Routes remained primitive until the start of airmails in the 1920s. In 1974 there were 418 POs.

Stamps of Britain used in 1865-78 at Cobija, an important port town which no longer exists (oblit. C39).

Stamps of Chile were used in occupied areas of Bolivia with special postmarks 1 December 1881-11 October 1883.

The issue of politically provocative stamps by both Bolivia and Paraguay in 1932 was a contributory factor to the Gran Chaco War between the two countries (1932-5).

Chile

FIRST STAMPS ISSUED 1 July 1853

CURRENCY

1853	100 centavos = 1 peso
1960	1000 milesimos = 100 centesimos = 1 escudo
1975	100 centavos = 1 peso

Between 1535 and 1541 the Spanish gained a foothold in northern Chile and founded Santiago. Opposition from southern tribes continued for another century. A first attempt at independence in 1810 was frustrated soon after by the intervention of Royalist forces of the Spanish viceroy of Peru. Independence was formally gained in 1818 with the help of San Martin, the liberator of Argentina, who joined forces with the Chilean patriot Bernard O'Higgins and led an army over the Andes to defeat the Spaniards at the battle of Maipu.

Postal History
Posts first achieved a measure of efficiency when a regular monthly service between Buenos Aires and Santiago (which took 15 days) started in 1748. This became an extension of the royal packet from Spain after 1772. MS markings are known from 1762 and handstamps from 1770. Inland services began in 1762, Santiago being linked with Concepción and Valparaiso.

First regular coastal mail services were started in 1840 by the Pacific Steam Navigation Co., and a contract to carry mail from Valparaiso to Panama via intermediate ports was signed with the British government in 1845. Such mail was conveyed over the isthmus to Chagres to be transferred to ships of the Royal Mail Steam Packet Co. for Britain and Europe.

Chile was briefly served in 1872-4 by French packets of Ligne F, by which Valparaiso, Coquimbo, Huasco and Caldera were linked with ports northward to Panama. There were 138 POs in 1861 and 1486 in 1975.

First issue was printed by Perkins, Bacon & Co. of London by the same process and in the same colours as their current stamps for Britain (1*d* red and 2*d* blue); also in inappropriate sheets of 240 (Chile having a decimal currency).

Stamps of Britain were used in 1865-81 at Valparaiso (oblit. C30), Caldera (oblit. C37) and Coquimbo (oblit. C40).

During the War of the Pacific, revenue stamps were authorized for postal use:
5 *centavos* 3 July 1880-15 January 1881; 1 *centavo* and 2 *centavo* 27 November 1880-8 August 1881.

During the revolution of 1891, when northern POs were cut off from Santiago, revenue and telegraph stamps were used for postage from 21 April 1891 until exhausted; thereafter (10 July-5 September 1891) internal mail was allowed to go free.

Revenue stamps are known used postally during further shortages in 1900, 1901 and 1913.

Paraguay

FIRST STAMPS ISSUED 1 August 1870

CURRENCY

1870	8 reales = 1 peso
1878	100 centavos = 1 peso
1944	100 centimos = 1 guarani

Declared independence from Spain and Buenos Aires in 1811. At war with Argentina, Brazil and Uruguay in 1864-70 when between two-thirds and nine-tenths of the population and much territory were lost. Occupied by Brazilian army 1870-6. Fought Bolivia in the Gran Chaco War 1932-5, and kept the territory won by arms. The current president has been re-elected five times since 1954.

Internal postal service begun in 1769 functioned until 1811. The mail route ran from Buenos Aires via Santa Fé and Corrientes to Candelaria and Asunción.

Argentina, Bolivia, Chile & Peru pre1900

ECUADOR
Confederation of Peru & Bolivia 1836-9
B33 GB Stamps in Argentina 1860-73
in Chile 1865-81
French Stamps 1860-78
Provisional Issues (with dates)
0 kilometres 800
0 miles 500
BRAZIL
Lima
PERU
(Ind. 1821)
1857
1858
Pacific Ocean
Oruro
BOLIVIA
(Ind. 1825)
1867
(to Chile 1883)
Railway
Cobija
C39
(to Chile 1884)
Antofagasta
PARAGUAY
Caldera
C37
Puquois
Huasco
Tucumán
Corrientes
1856
Coquimbo
C40
Cordoba
1858
Valparaiso
C30
Santiago
URUGUAY
Buenos Aires
B32
1858
Montevideo
Concepción
ARGENTINA
Confederation 1858
Republic 1862
CHILE
(Ind. 1818)
1853
Atlantic Ocean
Porto Gallegos
FALKLAND ISLANDS
(Crown Colony 1842)
1878

A
B
C
D
E
F
G
ISLAS MALVINAS
REPUBLICA ARGENTINA
PARAGUAY
MUESTRA
SERVICIO AEREO
SOBRETASA
URUGUAY

A Uruguay: Government Issue 1864; B Paraguay: Republic 1879; C Argentina: San Martin 1867; D Argentina: Republic 1928; E Argentina: Antarctic Claim 1964; F Paraguay: Re-Election of President 1958; G Uruguay: Republic 1945.

Uruguay

FIRST STAMPS (private mail coach routes) 1 October 1856
FIRST PERMANENT STAMPS|ISSUED 1 July 1859)

CURRENCY

1856 120 centavos = 1 real
1859 1000 milesimos = 100 centesimos = 1 peso

Early attempts at colonization were frustrated by the fierce natives. The territory was disputed between Spain and Portugal until the end of the 18th century. A British expedition to the Rio de la Plata in 1806-7 weakened Spanish power but the independence of Uruguay (25 August 1825) from both Argentina and the Portuguese in Brazil was not guaranteed until 1830. The country suffered constant internal strife through the remainder of the 19th century, with civil wars in 1843-52, 1896 and 1904.

Montevideo was a port of call on both British and French packet services to Buenos Aires and enjoyed similar facilities.

Stamps of Britain used in 1862-72 at Montevideo (oblit. C28).

Argentina

CURRENCY

8 reales = 1 peso (= 5 centavos Federation)

Discovered in 1515, the lands of the River Plate (Rio de la Plata) were annexed by Spain in 1534. Buenos Aires was founded in 1536. The Viceroy of La Plata, who ruled Argentina, Paraguay, Uruguay and Bolivia, was deposed by a junta on 25 May 1810. Paraguay had already broken away (1811) when the United Provinces of Rio de la Plata declared themselves independent on 9 July 1816. Bolivia broke away in 1825 and Uruguay in 1828. The early history of independent Argentina concerns the struggle between the centralists and federalists. The Confederation of General Rosas expended its energies in trying to reincorporate Uruguay. In 1854 Buenos Aires drew up its own constitution and in 1859 briefly waged war with the provinces of the federation. The Republic was formed under General Mitre, who led the Buenos Aires army to victory at the battle of Pravon in September 1861. The terms of reunion were not finally settled until 1862.

Postal History

Even after Charles III's reforms in 1767, Argentina seems to have had only a quarterly extension from Havana (via Montevideo) of the royal packet service from Corunna. Some postal connections between the Viceroyalty of La Plata and that of Peru seem to have begun earlier in the 18th century, but the earliest known postal markings appear in Buenos Aires c.1771. First independent posts were set up by decree in 1814, but under the dictatorship of General Rosas (1829-52) posts were all but suppressed. In 1853 rural mails in the province of Buenos Aires were made up only once a month.

To serve the newly appointed British consuls to the independent South American republics, a monthly packet was started from Falmouth to Buenos Aires in 1824. This became a branch of the Rio packet (*see* Brazil) in 1832. After 1869 the service was combined, the Rio packet continuing to Buenos Aires. In 1860 a French packet was started from Bordeaux to Brazil with an extension to Buenos Aires. The extension became Ligne K in 1866-9, while from 1869 Ligne J took over the through service. In various guises the service continued till superseded by airmails.

From 1867 another service was based on Marseille.

Stamps of Britain were used in 1860-73 at Buenos Aires (oblit. B32) on mail sent by British packet.

Stamps of France were used at Buenos Aires 1860-78.

Buenos Aires

CURRENCY

1858 8 reales = 1 peso

Province seceded from Confederation; independent 1852-62.

Corrientes

FIRST STAMPS 21 August 1856
Stamps suppressed 11 September 1880

CURRENCY	
1856	1 real moneda corriente = 12½ centimos moneda corriente
1860	500 centimos = 100 centavos fuerte = 1 peso fuerte

A remote state that went its own way for many years.

Cordoba

CURRENCY
100 centavos = 1 peso fuerte

FIRST STAMPS 28 October 1858

Argentine Confederation

FIRST STAMPS ISSUED 1 May 1858

Argentine Republic

CURRENCY	
1858	100 centavos = 1 peso
1970	100 old peso = 1 new peso
1985	(devaluation) 1000 pesos = 1 austral

1st PARTICIPATION
COMMONWEALTH GAMES 1982
25p FALKLAND ISLANDS
A
1833–1933
3d POSTAGE REVENUE
SOUTH ATLANTIC
3d FALKLAND ISLANDS 3d
B
C
FALKLAND ISLANDS
ONE PENNY

Falkland Islands
A 1982; **B** 1933;
C 1878.

Left
RAF Hercules transport aircraft delivering mail to the Falkland Islands 1982

Official postcard to celebrate the maritime exploration of Argentina

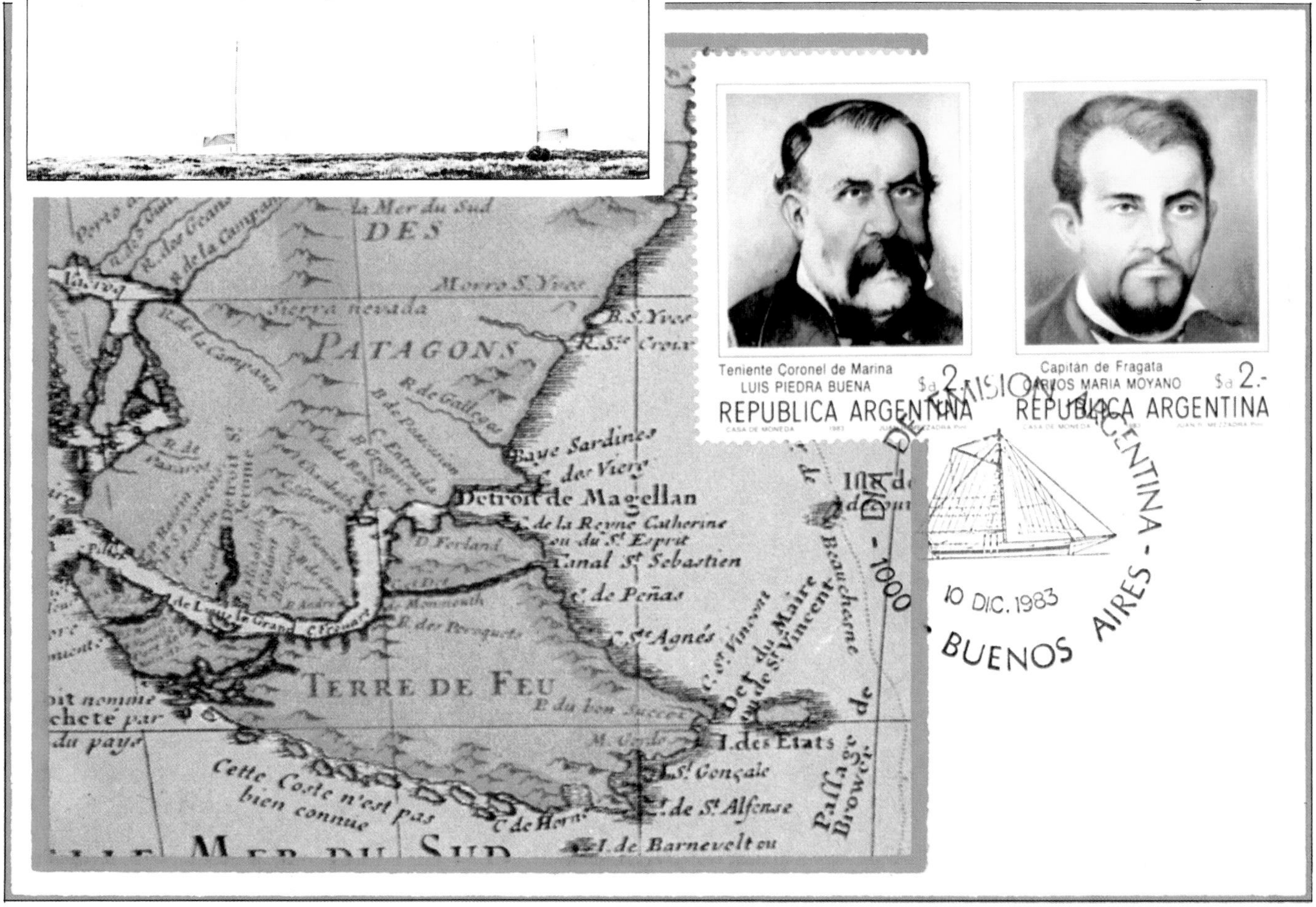
Teniente Coronel de Marina
LUIS PIEDRA BUENA
REPUBLICA ARGENTINA
Capitán de Fragata
CARLOS MARIA MOYANO
REPUBLICA ARGENTINA
10 DIC. 1983
BUENOS AIRES
PATAGONS
Detroit de Magellan
TERRE DE FEU
I. des Etats
Cette Coste n'est pas bien connue

FIRST STAMPS ISSUED of Argentine Republic 11 January 1858

In 1913-38 as a security measure stamps used by government departments were overprinted with the initials of the ministry concerned.

After World War II Argentina suffered a series of repressive military governments following the defeat of the Peronists. Problems of internal inflation and general unrest led the military junta to attack the Falkland Islands and South Georgia in April 1982. After issuing stamps for use in the Falklands (Malvinas), the Argentinians were defeated by the British Task force. The junta collapsed and a civil government took over.

Falkland Islands

FIRST STAMPS 19 June 1878

CURRENCY

1878 sterling
1971 decimal currency

Islands were disputed between Britain and Spain between 1765 and 1771. An Argentinian settlement of 1828 was destroyed by the USA in 1831. Reoccupied by the British in 1833, the Falkland Islands and all dependent territories have been claimed ever since by either Argentina or Chile. Naval administration gave place to civil government in 1842 as a British Crown Colony. A Falkland Islands Company was chartered in 1852.

On 21 July 1908 South Georgia, South Orkneys, South Shetlands, South Sandwich Islands and Graham Land were made dependencies of the colony An extensive whaling and fishing industry existed, mainly based on Norway. The whaling industry declined in the 1950s and 1960s. Scientific bases in the area became permanent in 1943-4 with a meteorological station on South Georgia.

In 1962 all dependencies (except South Georgia and South Sandwich Islands) were constituted a separate colony as British Antarctic Territory (*see* Antarctica).

The population of the Falklands rose from c.500 in 1856 to a peak of 2,350 in 1910 and has since fallen slightly. Consistently about half the total has lived in Stanley.

Postal History

Earliest mails were dependent upon casual ships connecting with the Brazil packet via Montevideo. The earliest recorded letter is dated 28 January 1827. From 1852 to 1880 a service between Stanley and Montevideo was maintained about every two months by contract or government schooner (except in 1854-6 and 1861-3, when *ad hoc* arrangements had to be made). In 1880 carriage of mail both in and out was made a statutory duty for any ship's master calling at Stanley. From 1880 to 1900 the mail was contracted to German steamships of the Kosmos Line operating a route Hamburg-Antwerp-Dartmouth (later Tilbury)-St Vincent - Montevideo - Stanley - Punta Arenas-Callão. This was superseded (1900-14) by a monthly service of the Pacific Steam Navigation Co. operating between Liverpool and Valparaiso. The opening of the Panama Canal in 1914 removed most shipping routes from the passage of Cape Horn and a regular service (via Montevideo) was not resumed until 1927. Occasional mail is known via Porto Gallegos, the nearest Argentinian port. From 1944 letters could be sent to Montevideo for onward transmission by air.

Before the 1982 war, there was a quarterly mail service by chartered ship direct to London. External airmail was carried weekly by Argentinian aircraft to Comodoro Rivadavia and thence to Buenos Aires (British mail by this route in sealed bags between Stanley and London.

Irregular internal mails were carried by local boats between East Falkland and West Falkland, where a PO was opened in 1899 at Fox Bay. Regular internal services between Stanley, Fox Bay and New Island (PO 1909-17) operated from 1910. These were taken over by air in 1948. Internal distribution is now made by Land Rover over peat tracks or by float planes of the Government Air Service. In Stanley there is no house delivery, but collections are made from pillar boxes.

From 1861 until 31 December 1933 the office of postmaster was doubled by one government official or another. Prepayment of mail was not possible before 17 July 1861; PAID franks are known from 1868. There was no actual PO at Stanley until 1887 When the government offices were moved in 1891 to the very edge of Stanley, the PO went with them; central stores were then licensed to sell stamps and a letterbox erected.

In the dependencies, South Georgia has had a PO since 20 November 1909. South Shetlands had a PO from 1912 to 1931. Mails went via Buenos Aires (and, after 1912, also direct to Norway). The volume of mail from South Georgia was as great as that from Stanley. Not until 1924 were there any direct posts between the dependencies and Stanley.

The claims of sovereignty by Argentina came to a head in 1982 when the islands were invaded by a combined naval and military force on 2 April. A British Task Force was hastily formed and sailed to the South Atlantic. Ascension Island became an essential staging post and a Field PO was established in May.

The Argentinians were defeated in June 1982 and a British garrison has been maintained ever since. British Field POs operate on the island and much of the mail is carried by British air transport via Ascension Island (q.v). A new airfield was constructed and opened in May 1985.

AUSTRALASIA

AUSTRALIA, NEW ZEALAND AND THE PACIFIC ISLANDS

This section deals with the continent of Australia, New Zealand and the Pacific Islands. Australia was the last continent to be discovered and explored. It was not until 1519 that Magellan first crossed the Pacific and even in the 19th century the whole area was not fully mapped. In the 16th century, frequent services across the Atlantic maintained links between the Americas and Europe, initially between Spain and South America but shortly after between the North American colonists and Britain. At the time that the American colonies were breaking away, Australia was being explored by Cook and many of the Pacific islands were still unknown or underdeveloped.

In the 19th century, the Western powers began to create the spheres of influence which were to form the basis of their colonial empires in the Pacific. No regular postal service existed between the Philippines and America until the late 18th century and China was not linked postally with the outside world until the 1840s.

The vast area of the Pacific with its myriad small islands and its many different ethnic groups is difficult to treat in a logical fashion whether from the point of view of geography or postal history. The method used has been to deal first with Australia and New Zealand, followed by New Guinea. The Pacific islands have been grouped into three segments. The dividing lines employed are the Equator between north and south, and the International Dateline between south-east and south-west, giving south-eastern, south-western and northern groups which are treated in turn. Two sections have also been included on the mailboats of France and Germany and of America to show how these routes were developed in line with the colonial interests of the nations involved.

Although there was little fighting in the Pacific during World War I, it did change the map of the area. The German colonies were taken over by the Australians and the New Zealanders in the south and by the Japanese in the north. This, in turn, laid the foundation for the Japanese hold on the Pacific which gave them some of the bases they needed for the attack on American, Dutch and British territories in 1941.

Since World War II, the gradual change from territories dependent on or protected by the European powers has accelerated and, now, with the exception of some of the French islands, the Pacific islands are largely independent.

JAPAN
China Sea
30°
CHINA
WAKE I.
(US)
1951
MARIANA
ISLANDS
1945
15° North
Manila
PILIPINAS
INDO-CHINE
GUAM I. (US)
MARSHALL
ISLANDS
1945
MICRONESIA
(US Trust Territory)
1984
(Ind. 1983)
CAROLINE ISLANDS
PALAU
1945
1983
MALAYSIA
GILBERT ISLANDS
(Cr. Col. 1976)
1976
KIRIBATI
(Ind. 1979)
1979
0° Equator
NAURU
1968
(UN Trust. 1945)
(Ind. 1968)
INDONESIA
PAPUA-
NEW GUINEA
Bismarck
Archipelago
SOLOMON ISLANDS
1975
1976
(Self Govt. 1976)
ELLICE ISL
TUVAL
(Cr. Col. 19
197
(Ind. 197
Arafura Sea
1952
1972
1973
1975
Timor Sea
Darwin
Coral Sea
15° South
1980
VANUATU
(NEW HEBRIDES)
(Brit. & Fr.)
FI
ISLAN
197
NORTHERN
TERRITORY
QUEENSLAND
AUSTRALIA
NOUVELLE CALEDONIE
(Fr.)
WESTERN AUSTRALIA
Brisbane
30°
SOUTH AUSTRALIA
NORFOLK I.
1947
Perth
LORD HOWE I.
NEW SOUTH WALES
Adelaide
Canberra
Sydney
Great Australian Bight
Tasman Sea
VICTORIA
Melbourne
NORTH ISLAND
Auc
NEW ZEALAND
TASMANIA
Hobart
SOUTH ISLAND
Wellin
Christchu
45°
Southern Ocean
AUCKLAND I.
105°
120°
135°
150°
MACQUARIE I.
165° East

Australia, New Zealand & Pacific Islands from 1945

MIDWAY I.
(US)
USA
MEXICO
OAHU
Honolulu
HAWAIIAN ISLANDS
HAWAII
Pacific Ocean
Equator
TOKELAU ISLANDS
(UNION ISLANDS)
1948
PENRHYN
1952
1973
WESTERN SAMOA
1962
SAMOA SISIFO
SAMOA
(US)
COOK ISLANDS
(NZ)
TONGA ISLANDS
NIUE
1974
AITUTAKI
1932-72
1972
SOCIETY ISLANDS
ETS FRANÇAIS DE L'OCEANIE
(FRENCH POLYNESIA)
1958
PITCAIRN I. (Brit.)
KERMADEC IS.
INTERNATIONAL DATE LINE
HATHAM I.
165° West
150°
135°
120°
105°

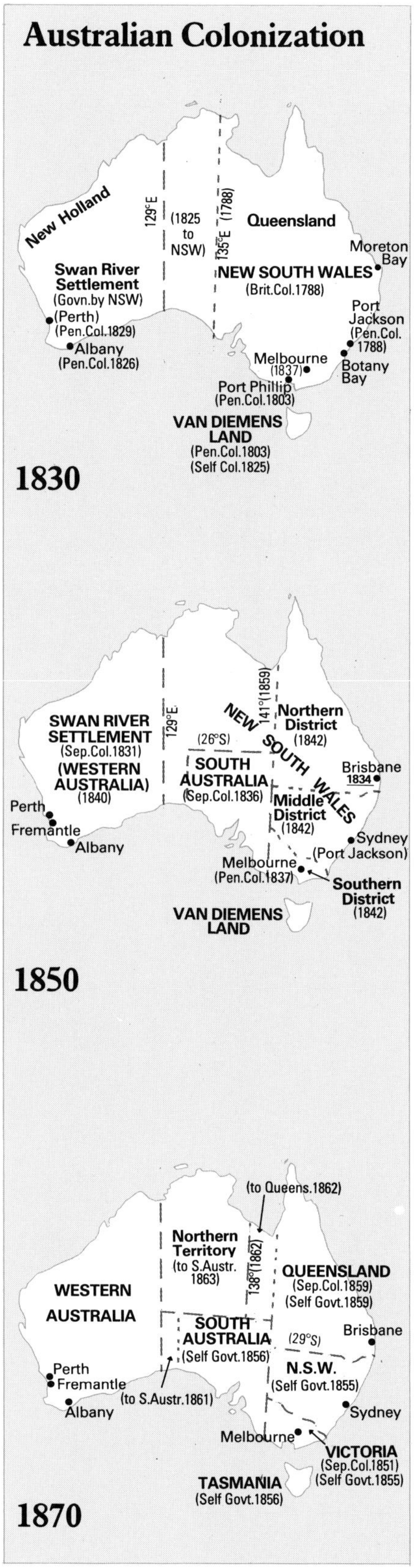
Australian Colonization
New Holland
129°E
(1825
to
NSW)
135°E (1788)
Queensland
Moreton
Bay
Swan River
Settlement
(Govn.by NSW)
NEW SOUTH WALES
(Brit.Col.1788)
(Perth)
(Pen.Col.1829)
Albany
(Pen.Col.1826)
Port
Jackson
(Pen.Col.
1788)
Melbourne
(1837)
Botany
Bay
Port Phillip
(Pen.Col.1803)
VAN DIEMENS
LAND
(Pen.Col.1803)
(Self Col.1825)
1830
SWAN RIVER
SETTLEMENT
(Sep.Col.1831)
(WESTERN
AUSTRALIA)
(1840)
129°E
141°(1859)
NEW SOUTH WALES
Northern
District
(1842)
(26°S)
SOUTH
AUSTRALIA
(Sep.Col.1836)
Brisbane
1834
Middle
District
(1842)
Perth
Fremantle
Albany
Sydney
(Port Jackson)
Melbourne
(Pen.Col.1837)
Southern
District
(1842)
VAN DIEMENS
LAND
1850
(to Queens.1862)
Northern
Territory
(to S.Austr.
1863)
138°(1862)
141°E
QUEENSLAND
(Sep.Col.1859)
(Self Govt.1859)
WESTERN
AUSTRALIA
SOUTH
AUSTRALIA
(Self Govt.1856)
(29°S)
Brisbane
Perth
Fremantle
N.S.W.
(Self Govt.1855)
(to S.Austr.1861)
Albany
Sydney
Melbourne
VICTORIA
(Sep.Col.1851)
(Self Govt.1855)
TASMANIA
(Self Govt.1856)
1870

Australia

The Spaniard Torres sailed through the strait between what is now Queensland and New Guinea in 1606. It is not clear whether he actually sighted the continent but its presence had been reported as early as the 13th century when Marco Polo learned that the Chinese already knew of its existence. Dutch navigators named the continent 'New Holland' in the 17th century. On his voyages in 1642-4 the Dutchman Tasman discovered Van Diemens Land (now Tasmania) and New Zealand, and in 1688 the Englishman Dampier explored the Australian coast.

In the later part of the 18th century Cook and Bass began accurately to survey the coast. Cook landed at Botany Bay in April 1770, and in 1797 Bass sailed through the strait which now bears his name and discovered that Van Diemens Land was not part of the mainland. A fleet sailed from England carrying about 750 convicts and the first settlement was established at Port Jackson (Sydney) on 26 January 1788. This was followed by further settlements in Van Diemens Land (1803), Port Phillip (1803) and Melbourne (1837); Western Australia was settled at Albany (1826) and the Swan River Settlement (Perth) in 1829. Queensland was settled from Sydney in 1825 and South Australia in 1836.

All these initial attempts at colonization were based on the coast and were quickly followed by internal explorations. In 1813 Blaxland crossed the Blue Mountains, an exploration which was instrumental in opening up the interior. At that time New South Wales was described as including all the territory east of longitude 135°E, roughly half the continent. The balance, to the west, was not administered. Western Australia (originally the Swan River Settlement) was settled and was bounded by longitude 129°E, and this has remained so to the present day. South Australia was originally within the area allocated to New South Wales but became a separate colony in 1836. The final change was in 1859 when the western boundary of New South Wales and Victoria was moved back to longitude 141°E.

Contact with the home country had always been difficult because of distance and the time taken for messages to reach Britain and return. Mail could travel in either direction via the Cape of Good Hope or Cape Horn. By 1845 the P & O Line was beginning to operate in the Far East and in 1852 a service was introduced from Singapore to Sydney via Batavia, King George's Sound (near Albany), Adelaide, Melbourne and Sydney. This two-monthly service operated for three years and was then discontinued, but the regularity of the mails had led to stimulation of commercial interest. P & O had refused the new terms offered for the Australian contract and the European and Australian Royal Mail Co. began a service in October 1856. However, it failed in 1858 and a new contract was awarded to P & O in March 1859. With a few minor alterations in routes and frequency of sailings, P & O maintained the contract up to World War I.

In the meantime, self-government had been granted to New South Wales and Victoria in 1855, South Australia and Van Diemens Land (renamed Tasmania, 1853) in 1856, Queensland in 1859. The Swan River Settlement had been renamed Western Australia in 1840, and became self-governing in 1890. In 1901 the six colonies were federated as the Commonwealth of Australia, although Commonwealth postage stamps were not issued until 1 January 1913. The Postage Due issues, common to all states, were issued in 1902.

The distances to be covered in carrying the mails in Australia led to many travelling post offices (TPOs) on the railways (see separate section) and an early interest in airmail.

• New South Wales

FIRST STAMPS ISSUED 1 January 1850

CURRENCY

1850 sterling

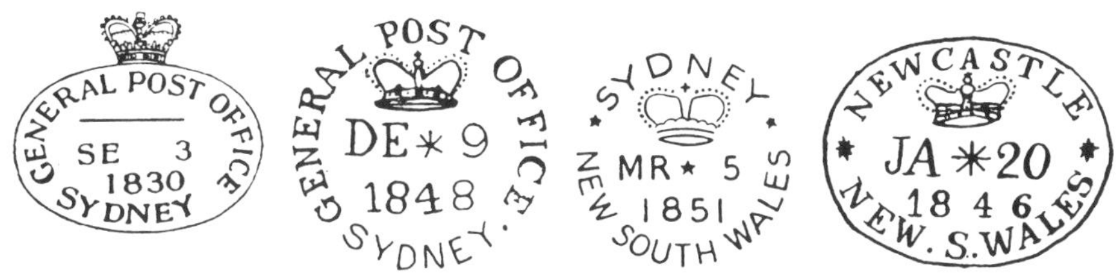
GENERAL POST OFFICE
SE 3
1830
SYDNEY
GENERAL POST OFFICE
DE*9
1848
SYDNEY.
SYDNEY
MR*5
1851
NEW SOUTH WALES
NEWCASTLE
JA*20
1846
NEW. S. WALES
A selection of New South Wales postmarks

The first state of Australia to have been settled. In 1788, it was proclaimed that it was to administer all the land east of longitude 135°E. This meant that all settlements in what are now Queensland, South Australia, Tasmania and Victoria came under the control of New South Wales.

In May 1787 the first settlers and convicts left Britain for Botany Bay, an area which had been discovered earlier by Captain Cook. On arrival in 1788, the site was found to be unsuitable and the party disembarked further north at Port Jackson, which became Sydney.

Over the years the dependent settlements gradually broke away and gained self-government. New South Wales itself became self-governing in 1855, and continued to exercise control over Queensland until 1859. The Northern Territory was transferred to South Australia in 1863, but New South Wales remained the most influential colony and also provided the base for much of the trading within the Pacific Islands.

In 1901 New South Wales was federated into the Commonwealth of Australia.

Postal History

As early as 1803 there was a postal service operating between Sydney and Parramatta, at a cost of 2d per letter. At this time most of the mail was coming in by private ship and to prevent this being handled privately a 'collecting office' was set up in 1809. This was intended to be solely a distribution centre and it was not until 1825 that an Act was passed which was designed to expand the postal service.

By 1830 a mail-coach service was started from Sydney and this was quickly followed by the establishment of a local twopenny post which operated in the Sydney area.

A new Postage Act was passed by the Governor in 1835 which repealed the 1825 Act and set the rates on the basis of weight and distance travelled. The postmaster, James Raymond, had been pressing for cheaper postage for some time, and had been in correspondence with Rowland Hill to try to make the prepayment of letters between New South Wales and Britain compulsory. This was not approved and, in fact, when he tried to introduce stamps in 1841, after they had been issued in Britain, official objections were raised against the use of stamps in the colonies.

Earlier, in 1838, Raymond had the permission of the Governor to introduce cheaper postage in the local Sydney area. To this end, he produced envelopes with a prepaid embossed stamp showing the seal of the colony. These were considered locally to be the first postage stamps and were commemorated by the colony in 1889 with two special postcards. However, as they were of purely local significance, they have not been accepted as such by philatelists. The usage of these envelopes appears to have been very sparse. They were sold at 1s 3d per dozen as against 2d each for private letters. The public were also allowed to provide their own paper and this could be stamped at a charge of 1s 8d per 25 impressions. All these showed a marked reduction in cost but the demand remained small. In 1848 stamped covers were recorded as just 15,000 in the year.

By 1838 there were 40 POs in the colony and the 'Ship Letter' Office had been opened in the early 1830s. In 1842 a steamer service was set up between Sydney and Melbourne and in 1844 the first contract mail packet arrived from Britain.

In December 1848 the new Act to reform postage was passed and the first stamps, 'The Sydney Views', were issued on 1 January 1850. The stamps were also available in Victoria until 1853 and Queensland until 1860. At this time there were 97 country POs in addition to Sydney. These were issued with numeral cancellations of two types and the numbers were allocated to the offices as they were opened. By 1852 there were 109 POs.

Stamps of New South Wales were also used in New Hebrides and New Caledonia (q.v.).

New South Wales became a member of the UPU in 1891. It continued to use its own stamps until 1913.

NORTHERN TERRITORY

The large area in the north and centre of the continent, now administered from Alice Springs, was originally placed under the control of New South Wales. The area was expanded even further in 1829 when the boundary of the Swan River Settlement was established. In 1863 the administration was transferred to South Australia. This created the strange anomaly that Darwin, the most northerly city in Australia, used a postmark describing it as part of South Australia. In 1911 control passed to the Commonwealth of Australia. Northern Territory has never issued stamps, but items from this area can be identified by postmarks.

POSTAGE
NEW SOUTH WALES
7
Australia
AUSTRALIA
50c
DAMPIER
ONE HUNDRED YEARS
NEW SOUTH WALES POSTAGE
ONE SHILLING
AUSTRALIA
POSTAGE
1½d
SPECIMEN
10/-
TEN SHILLINGS

A New South Wales:Colony 1863; **B** Australia:Cricket 1974; **C** Australia:Explorer 1964; **D** New South Wales:Centenary of Colony 1888; **E** Australia:King George VI 1937; **F** Australia:first design of the Commonwealth 1913.

• Queensland

FIRST STAMPS New South Wales 1851
FIRST STAMPS ISSUED 1 November 1860

CURRENCY

1860 sterling

Occupies the north-east of the Australian continent; visited by the Spanish in the 17th century. Captain Cook explored the east coast. In 1825 a penal colony, Moreton Bay, was established and administered from New South Wales (until 1859). The last convicts were withdrawn in 1842 and the area was allocated for free persons only.

In the early 1850s there was agitation to separate the settlement from

BRIEF HISTORY
CONSERVATION COMMISSION OF THE NORTHERN TERRITORY
ALICE SPRINGS TELEGRAPH STATION HISTORICAL RESERVE.
PLAN OF HISTORIC AREA

Left
Post and Telegraph station, Alice Springs, Australia

Below
Typical terrain in Northern Queensland showing dirt-track road over which post must be delivered

81
QL
59
37
V
1
2
3
4

1 & **2** Postmarks of Queensland
3 Numeral Postmark of Van Diemens Land
4 First type cancellation of Victoria

A
B
C
D
E
F
TWO PENCE
QUEENSLAND
ONE HALFPENNY
POSTAGE
WESTERN
AUSTRALIA
FOUR PENCE
TASMANIA
SPECIMEN

A Victoria 1865; **B** Van Diemens Land 1855; **C** Queensland 1899; **D** Western Australia 1861; **E** Queensland 1860; **F** Tasmania 1899.

New South Wales. The area was granted self-government against strong opposition on 13 May 1859 and became the colony of Queensland on 10 December 1859.

Postal History

First POs opened at Brisbane in 1834, and White in 1842 (closed soon after). Handstruck markings similar to New South Wales types were issued and stamps of that colony introduced at Queensland POs as they opened until 1860. By that time there were 15 POs in the colony. Each was allocated a numeral canceller in the New South Wales series, which they retained. Brisbane was still using the 95 numeral in 1895. As new POs were opened, numerals were allocated and these remained in use until 1915, when they were withdrawn by federal directive.

The Queensland dependency of Thursday Island, north of Cape York, was the first point of call for vessels leaving British New Guinea (q.v.) and for several of the Japanese and other shipping lines operating between South-east Asia and Australasia. Its numerals (51 [1871], 136, 148 and 336) can be found on the stamps of many countries, probably as a transit marking or 'posted on board'.

Stamps of Queensland were used in British New Guinea in 1884-91. Queensland provided the main trading link with South-east Asia and in 1882 signed a postal treaty with Hong Kong. Stamps of both countries can be found with each other's postmarks when letters were posted on board ship.

The colony joined the UPU in 1891, and continued to issue its own stamps until the first Australian stamps were released in 1913.

• Victoria

FIRST STAMPS ISSUED 5 January 1850

CURRENCY	
1850	sterling

State of Australia which joined the Commonwealth of Australia in 1901. Known in the 1790s to whalers and sealing parties, and visited by Bass on his explorations in 1796 and 1798. A limited exploration in the area of Western Port and Port Phillip was made in 1802. An early attempt to colonize followed, mainly to discourage any French approaches, but many of the convicts who were landed escaped and the party was withdrawn to Van Diemens Land (q.v.) in 1804.

In 1824 two explorers from New South Wales, Hinne and Howell, reached the area overland and discovered the vast pasturage areas in the country between Sydney and the south coast. As a result, two parties arrived from Van Diemens Land and founded the first permanent settlement in 1834. However, because of problems in trading with the aboriginals and an attempt to establish independence, the Governor of New South Wales proclaimed on 26 August 1835, that 'the Settlement (called Port Phillip)' was 'in the Colony of New South Wales'. In 1836 the control of the new settlement was further strengthened by another proclamation which introduced the New South Wales Crown Land Regulations into Port Phillip. At that time there were only about 200 settlers in the area, but there was a considerable growth over the next few years and the population had reached 77,000 in 1851.

Not unnaturally, the settlers resented this remote control from Sydney and the traditional competition between the two great cities of Sydney and Melbourne dates from this period. Numerous petitions were sent to London to try to arrange for separate government for Victoria. The Australian Colonies Government Act was passed in August 1849 and the separation came into being, though it was not effected until a further Act was passed by the New South Wales Assembly on 1 July 1851. Self-government was finally achieved in 1855.

Postal History

The first PO was not opened until April 1837 when Melbourne began operation. This was followed by Geelong and Portland. By 1850 forty-five POs were open. During the period of control from New South Wales, only two or three of the cancellations included the correct description of the colony. The majority either simply used the name of the town or the words 'Port Phillip'.

When the first stamps were issued, Victoria was still part of the colony of New South Wales and for the first few months the stamps of both colonies appear to have been accepted as valid in the whole area. These stamps can be recognized by individual postmarks, but after mid-1851 these usages can be accounted for by 'arrival cancellations' on ships to or from Sydney.

Victoria used three quite distinctive series of numbered postmarks. The first, or 'butterfly' type, was used in 1850-1 and allocated to the first 45 POs. In July 1851 the second series — the 'barred oval' — was delivered and numbers are known up to 50. From 1856 a further range — the 'barred numerals' — were issued with numbers up to 87. These types were used up to 1906, and after that date new POs received only a circular datestamp.

Between 1858 and 1875 it was easier for some offices in southern New South Wales to send their mail overland to Melbourne and thence to Britain by P & O steamer rather than route letters via Sydney. For this purpose, Victorian adhesives were available in some New South Wales POs.

Victoria joined the UPU in 1891 at the same time as the other Australian colonies and, following the federation in 1901, continued to issue its own adhesives until 1913.

• Van Diemens Land

FIRST STAMPS ISSUED 1 November 1853

CURRENCY

1853 sterling

Later known as Tasmania (q.v.), this island 120 miles off the southern coast of the continent was a colony until it joined the Commonwealth of Australia in 1901. It was discovered by Tasman, the Dutch explorer, on 25 November 1642. He named it after the Governor-General of Batavia who had commissioned him.

The first settlement was made as a penal colony in 1803. By 1817 the population was more than 3000, and martial law was proclaimed in 1828 because of the aggressiveness of the local aborigines.

In 1825 the island became independent of New South Wales, and was renamed Tasmania in August 1853.

Postal History

Internally, there was little post before 1816 when a government messenger carried mail fortnightly between Hobart and Port Dalrymple (Launceston). The land conditions were such that the 120-mile journey took 7 days. Mail for overseas was also infrequent and no regular service existed, even to Sydney which was responsible for the administration of the island.

In September 1822 the first PO town markings appeared. These were the earliest markings in Australia. In 1828 a new Act was passed to establish a regular service in the island. However, no attempt was made to implement this until 1832, when a principal postmaster was apointed. In 1824 there were 9 POs, and 26 by 1833.

By 1835 deliveries were made weekly throughout the island by mail cart and stage-coach and, 15 years later, the system of deliveries had been established on a weekly or, in some cases, twice weekly basis.

In August 1853 the colony was renamed Tasmania but stamps with the former name had been ordered and these were issued three months later. They continued in use until stamps with the revised colony name appeared in 1858.

• Tasmania

FIRST STAMPS ISSUED January 1858

CURRENCY

1853 sterling

Island state of the Commonwealth originally known as Van Diemens Land (q.v.). Renamed in August 1853, it became a self-governing colony in 1856, and was federated with the other colonies as the Commonwealth of Australia in 1901.

Postal History

Stamps of Van Diemens Land had been issued in 1853, after the name of the colony had already been changed. A second issue was made in a new design in August 1855 and the first issue with the corrected name was only released at the start of 1858.

In 1853 to coincide with the issue of stamps, a series of barred numeral cancellations was issued to the most important POs. These were similar in style to the New South Wales type and both were based on the British design which had been introduced in 1844. Numerals from 10 to 75 are recorded.

In 1861 a second series of numbers was issued and the first series was withdrawn. Generally, the numbers in the second series were shorter by

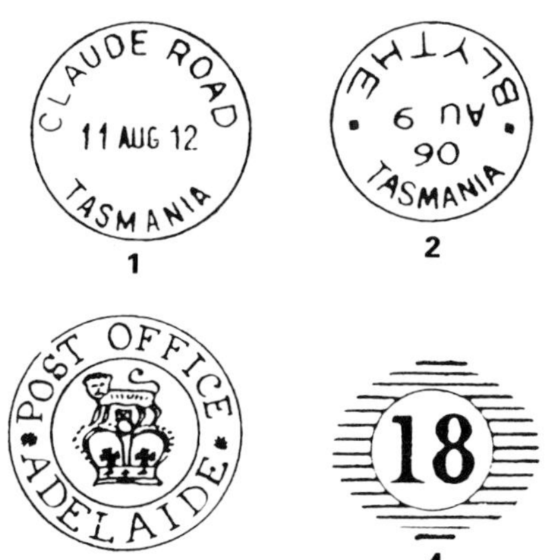
CLAUDE ROAD
11 AUG 12
TASMANIA
BLYTHE
6 AU
90
TASMANIA
POST OFFICE
ADELAIDE
18
1 2
3 4

1 & **2** Postmarks of Tasmania
3 Pre-adhesive mark of Adelaide, South Australia
4 Numeral cancellation of Western Australia

2mm. As the need grew for new POs, each was provided with the new type of cancellation. By 1899, 382 numbers had been issued.

Tasmania joined the UPU in 1891. It continued to issue its own stamps until 1913.

• South Australia

FIRST STAMPS ISSUED 1 January 1855

CURRENCY	
1855	sterling

State of the Commonwealth of Australia between longitudes 129°E and 141°E. Originally part of New South Wales under the Act of 1788, which set the boundary at 135°E. However, when the first settlements began in the area of Adelaide, there was no allegiance to Sydney and the area was declared a British colony in December 1836. The boundary was moved to its present location in 1859.

South Australia became self-governing in 1856 and was given control of the Northern Territory in 1863. It was federated into the Commonwealth in 1901 and continued to administer Northern Territory until 1911.

Postal History

Upon the foundation of the colony in 1836, the first postmaster, Thomas Gilbert of Adelaide, was appointed. Handstamps were introduced at Adelaide at about the same time. In 1839 the expansion of the service began and POs were opened at Port Adelaide and Port Lincoln, with smaller offices at Willunga and Encounter Bay. Unusually, the first inland mails were carried by the Mounted Police.

In 1840 there were 6 POs, and 41,000 letters and 50,000 newspapers were mailed. By 1860 the corresponding figures were 146 POs, 1,360,000 letters and 1,000,000 newspapers. South Australia was served by P & O steamers 1852-5 and again from 1859 onwards, thus providing a link to Britain and Europe.

Seventy-five POs were open when stamps were issued in 1855, and they were equipped with a numeral cancellation which had a number in a diamond set within a series of bars. Within two years circular datestamps began to be introduced and from 1858 they were used almost exclusively.

In 1891 the colony joined the UPU and in 1901 it was federated into the Commonwealth, but continued to use its own stamps until 1913.

• Western Australia

FIRST STAMPS ISSUED 1 August 1854

CURRENCY	
1854	sterling

State of Australia occupying that part of the continent west of longitude 129°E. It was first known to the Dutch in the 17th century as 'New Holland'. The first British settlement was in 1826 at King George's Sound, close to what is now Albany. This was a military post initially and the first settlers who arrived in 1829 founded the towns of Fremantle and Perth on the Swan River. In 1850 Swan River Settlement, which had been proclaimed the colony of Western Australia in 1840, was made a penal settlement and continued to use convict labour until 1868. The colony was given self-government in 1890 and joined with the other colonies to form the Commonwealth of Australia on 1 January 1901.

Postal History

In December 1829 the harbourmaster of Fremantle was appointed to act as postmaster for the settlers. At this time the masters of ships were forbidden to accept letters 'unless stamped with the Post Office stamp'. Because it was nearer to the ocean, Fremantle was the site of the main PO until 14 February 1835, when Mr Macfaull was made the principal postmaster at Perth. In 1834 the route to Albany was surveyed and a PO was opened there on 14 October that year. This led to the establishment of a monthly overland service in 1841.

When postage stamps were issued in 1854 prepayment was compulsory and unstamped letters were detained. At this time there were 16 POs, each issued with a barred numeral for cancelling stamps.

All mail to and from overseas was carried by private ship until the P & O service began to visit King George's Sound regularly in 1852. This service made the overland service from Albany to Perth even more important.

By 1880 the number of POs had increased to 59 and a new type of cancellation which included letters instead of numerals was introduced. In 1891 Western Australia joined the UPU and, after joining the Commonwealth, continued to issue its own stamps until 1913.

AUSTRALIAN CAPITAL TERRITORY (ACT)

Apart from the six states which federated into the Commonwealth of Australia, it is also necessary to consider the Australian Capital Territory, although it never issued its own stamps.

In 1900 the Australian Parliament was given the task of establishing a national capital. In 1901-3, 23 out of 40 proposed sites were examined and in 1904 Dalgety in New South Wales was nominated. However, the New

TERRITORY OF PAPUA
TIMOR
Arafura Sea
THURSDAY I.
Port Moresby
Darwin
Gulf of Carpentaria
Timor Sea
Coral Sea
Cooktown
NORTHERN TERRITORY
Townsville
COMMONWEALTH OF AUSTRALIA
(Fed. Rep. 1901) 1913
QUEENSLAND
1851
1860
Alice Springs
Rockhampton
WESTERN AUSTRALIA
1854
(Self Govt.1890)
Moreton Bay
Toowoomba
Brisbane
1834
SOUTH AUSTRALIA
1855
Kalgoorlie
NEW SOUTH WALES
1850
Terowie
Perth
Fremantle
Port Lincoln
Port Adelaide 1839
Adelaide
Great Australian Bight
Parramatta
Sydney
Albany
1834
Willunga
Encounter Bay
Bendigo
Canberra
King George's Sound
Ballarat
Dalgety 1837
Indian Ocean
Melbourne
Portland
Geelong
Port Phillip
Western Port
VICTORIA
1850
Bass Strait
Port Dalrymple (Devonport)
• Places served by early TPO's
VAN DIEMENS LAND
1853
Launceston
TASMANIA
1858
Hobart
1822
Tasman Sea
0 kilometres 800
0 miles 500

Australian Commonwealth to 1913

THE NATIONAL CAPITAL G.P.O. CANBERRA A.C.T.
22 FEB 1984
FIRST DAY OF ISSUE

A postmark of Canberra, 1984

South Wales Government could not agree and confusion continued until 1908 when the Canberra-Yass district was finally accepted. The land was transferred by the New South Wales Government in 1911, but delays in the building continued and it was not until 1927 that Parliament was opened there by the Duke of York (later King George VI). The first government departments were also transferred from Melbourne to Canberra in that year.

Postal History

Stamps for ACT are only distinguishable by their postmarks. The stamps of New South Wales were used up until 1913 and since then Australian issues have been used.

The Commonwealth of Australia

FIRST STAMPS see individual states
FIRST STAMPS ISSUED 1 January 1913

CURRENCY	
1913	sterling
1966	100 cents = 1 Australian dollar

Formed on 1 January 1901 by the federation of the six self-governing colonies. In 1885 a Federal Council had been formed which was used as forum for discussion between the states. In 1897 delegates of all the states except Victoria met to try to frame a constitution. In 1900 Victoria having by then joined in, the constitution was agreed and the Commonwealth became law.

The first Federal Parliament met in Melbourne and the seat of government remained there until the Federal Capital was established at Canberra in 1927.

The Commonwealth started as a Dominion of Great Britain; gradually, over the years, direct control from Britain was relaxed and Australia became fully independent after World War II.

Postal History

The problems of aligning the individual needs of each of the states presented many difficulties. An initial start was made with the Post and Telegraph Act of 1902, which agreed similar rates for telegrams and newspapers.

The first stamps of a common design were the Postage Due stamps issued in July 1902, but no postage stamps were issued until 1913. In May 1911 the rates throughout Australia were made uniform by the Postal Rates Act of 1910. At the same time, stamps of each state could be used throughout the Commonwealth.

The great distances involved in the carriage of mail in Australia led to the early use of travelling post offices (TPOs) on the railways (see separate section), and this was followed by intense interest in air transport. In July 1914 a flight from Melbourne to

Sydney carried 2500 cards, and towards the end of World War I a number of trial flights were started. From these early beginnings, internal services quickly developed and before the end of the 1930s a regular service between Perth and Adelaide was in operation. This enabled mail to be landed in Western Australia and flown to the east coast. The first experimental through mail via Karachi was carried from Adelaide to London in December 1929 and this was followed by a special Christmas mail in 1931 between Sydney and London. A regular service was introduced in December 1934 when the London-Singapore service of Imperial Airways joined with Qantas to complete the link to Sydney.

During both World Wars, Australia supplied troops to many theatres of operation. Special postmarks were used for the forces though letters from active service were carried free of charge.

Since World War II, mails have gradually moved from seamail to airmail. Speed has increased until the schedule for mail between London and Sydney is now down to about 24 hours elapsed time.

Travelling Post Offices

Because of the vast distances involved in Australia, the sorting of mail on trains became very important. This was particularly true of the more commercially oriented eastern states.

A
POSTAGE
1½d
FOUNDED 1788
NORFOLK ISLAND
B
FIRST AIRCRAFT TO VISIT - 28 MARCH, 1931
SIR FRANCIS CHICHESTER 1901-1972
14¢
NORFOLK ISLAND

A Norfolk Island 1947; **B** Norfolk Island 1972.

LETTER

Postman emptying Australian pillar-box, 1891

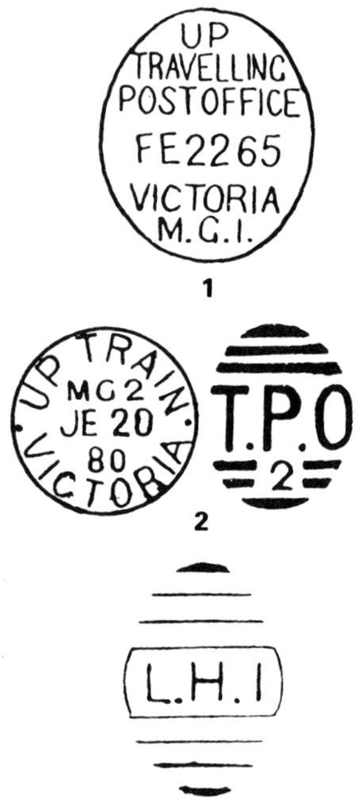
UP
TRAVELLING
POST OFFICE
FE2265
VICTORIA
M.G.I.
1
UP TRAIN
MG2
JE 20
80
VICTORIA
T.P.O
2
2
L.H.I
3

1 & 2 Travelling Post Office marks of Victoria
3 Cancellation of Lord Howe Island

Western Australia and Tasmania, the latter because of its size, did not start a service until 1889-90. However, in all other states the need to link centres of population led in the 1860s to the introduction of railway services and travelling post offices (TPOs).

Victoria began the system on eight different lines in 1865. The coaches were owned by the railways, but, as in Britain, they were staffed by postal clerks. The number of TPOs rose to 19 by early in this century, but by 1932 all the TPOs had been withdrawn. The most important Victorian TPOs were those which served the goldfields at Ballarat (TPOs 1 and 2) and Bendigo (TPOs 3 and 4).

Queensland followed the lead of Victoria in 1867 with the establishment of a service from Ipswich near Brisbane to Toowoomba. This expanded into four systems, two based on Brisbane and one each from Rockhampton and Townsville. A fifth line was opened in 1911. The TPOs were withdrawn in 1932.

In South Australia the sorting clerks accompanied the mail trains from 1868. By 1883 ten sorters were employed, and there was a widespread service operating out of Adelaide, mostly on the northern routes towards Terowie. In October 1917 South Australian services began to decline and by 1932 all TPOs had been withdrawn.

New South Wales was the last of the eastern states to introduce TPOs, but it also kept them running much later. The service began in 1869 on the Northern, Western and Southern lines operating out of Sydney. In 1872 a Late Fee of 3d was proposed, but owing to public opposition it appears to have been dropped. Special handstamps for each of the lines were used up to 1954 and later. At that time the TPO service in the state covered some 3000 miles in the most eastern area.

Western Australia relied on the overland route from Perth to Albany for all its foreign mail service but it was not until 1889 that the railway system between these two centres was completed. TPOs began to run in 1895 and continued to expand until 1900. This service was particularly important for the new goldfields in and around Kalgoorlie. The TPOs were discontinued gradually during the first years of this century and had vanished by 1917-20.

The first TPO service in Tasmania was not introduced until the government took over the main line between Hobart and Launceston in 1890. The second or Western Line came into operation in 1903. Extension followed until a peak in the early 1920s.

LORD HOWE ISLAND Island in the Tasman Sea. Discovered in 1788, first settled in 1834 and administered from New South Wales. It was handed over to the Commonwealth of Australia in 1914.

No stamps have been issued, but New South Wales and Australian stamps have been used. A postmaster was appointed in 1878; the receiving office became a PO in 1882 and an obliterator lettered LHI was introduced. This continued to be used until the 1920s. Current styles of datestamps have been used since then.

Norfolk Island

FIRST STAMPS Van Diemens Land (?) 1853; New South Wales; and Commonwealth of Australia
FIRST STAMPS ISSUED 10 June 1947

CURRENCY

1947 As Australia

Island in the Tasman Sea between Australia and New Zealand. It was discovered by Cook on his voyage in 1774, and was first settled as part of New South Wales in 1788. It was abandoned in 1805 and the original settlers were provided with land in Van Diemens Land (Tasmania).

In 1826 it became a penal settlement under New South Wales administration, but was transferred to Van Diemens Land from 1844 to 1856 because the convicts had been removed from New South Wales at that time. It reverted in 1856, was incorporated into New South Wales in 1896, and became part of the Commonwealth of Australia in 1914.

Postal History
In 1832 the commandant's clerk was acting as postmaster for the garrison of the island. In 1840 a civil postmaster was appointed and the first handstamps were provided. These were two line marks reading 'Free/Norfolk Island' for official mail and 'Paid at/Norfolk Island' for general correspondence .

In 1853, while under the administration of Van Diemens Land, a numeral obliterator '102' was allocated to Norfolk Island and stamps were sent, but none have been recorded. After 1856 the mail was irregular and few examples have survived, but stamps of New South Wales were available from 1896. The island was transferred to the Commonwealth of Australia on 1 July 1914, though

POST OFFICE
POST OFFICE

Post office, Taihape, North Island, New Zealand

stamps of Australia may have been used in the preceding 18 months.

During World War II New Zealand Forces POs were established on the island.

New Zealand

FIRST STAMPS ISSUED 18 July 1855

CURRENCY

1855	sterling
1967	100 cents = 1 NZ dollar

British Dominion situated 1600 miles east and south of Australia. It comprises two main islands, North and South Islands, and a number of smaller territories. It was first discovered in December 1642 by the Dutch explorer, Tasman, who landed and named it Staaten Island. It was again visited by Cook in 1769-70 when he circumnavigated the islands. He returned in 1773-7 and formally annexed the islands in the name of King George III but this was not ratified by the British Government. However, in spite of this, British missionaries and whalers began to settle the area in the early 19th century.

In 1839 the New Zealand Company was formed and began to acquire land from the Maoris. In 1840, because it was feared that the islands might be annexed by the French, a British party under Captain Hobson was sent, with instructions to conclude treaties with the Maori chiefs. In 1854 the island was granted self-government and this became effective in 1856.

There had been intermittent armed strife with the natives during the 1840s, mainly over land disputes. In March 1860 there was a major insurrection against the colony and it was only brought under control when troops were brought from Australia and Britain. Peace was signed in July 1866 but, when 150 Maoris escaped from Chatham Island where they were imprisoned, war broke out again in July 1868. Fighting continued for some time and it was not until December 1870 that the main body was finally dispersed. The Maori King, Tawihiao, finally submitted in February 1875. The British troops which had been engaged in the wars left in 1876.

Gold had been discovered in 1853 and 1861 leading to an influx in population which rose from 84,000 in 1860 to 490,000 in 1881.

On 26 September 1907 the colony was constituted as the Dominion of New Zealand. During World War I New Zealand forces were involved in most theatres of war but especially in the Dardanelles campaign.

After the war, Western Samoa (q.v.) was entrusted to New Zealand as a mandate under the League of Nations.

5c
New Zealand
CLASS "Ab"
NEW ZEALAND
POSTAGE
SIX PENCE

A New Zealand 1973;
B New Zealand 1858.

Pacific Ocean
NOUVELLE CALEDONIE
AUSTRALIA
NORFOLK
(Van Diemen 1844-56)
1853
(NSW 1896)
LORD HOWE
1882 (NSW 1834)
Sydney
Tasman Sea
Kororarika
1840
GT. BARRIER I.
Auckland
1840
NORTH ISLAND
NEW ZEALAND
(Self Govt.1854 (Domin. 1907)
1855
Wellington 1840
(Port Nicholson)
TASMANIA
(VAN DIEMENS LAND)
Nelson
1842
SOUTH ISLAND
Christchurch
Akaroa
1842
CHATHAM IS.
1856
Dunedin
STEWART I.
0 kilometres 300
0 miles 200

New Zealand to 1907

The Cook Islands (q.v.) and Tokalau Islands (q.v.) are also included in the Dominion, together with the Ross Dependency (q.v.) in the Antarctic.

Postal History

As is the case with many of the Pacific areas, the first correspondence emanated from British missionaries. Few ships arrived at the islands and these carried the mail in both directions.

In 1831 regular communication was established with Sydney, but there was no official PO. A charge of 4d was made for mail in either direction. This was followed, in 1840, by the first PO which was established in Kororarika. Later in the same year five other POs were opened, including Port Nicholson (subsequently Wellington) and Auckland.

Overseas mail was still controlled by Sydney, which acted as the forwarding office for mail to and from New Zealand. As the letters were held for the first available ship, many delays occurred and the New South Wales PO was unfairly blamed for this.

The Post Office was under control of the GPO in Britain until 1848, but after that date the colony took control of its own affairs. The first POs on the South Island were opened at Nelson and Akaroa in 1842. By 1843 there were nine POs and three receiving houses and the Controlling Office had been moved to Auckland. During the 1840s a series of overland routes were established but the difficulty of the terrain and the state of relations with the natives meant that the sea route from Auckland to Wellington via Sydney, which could take three months, was more reliable. This use of seaborne carriage continued for many years and it was not until 1878 that the first main railway link between Wellington and Auckland was completed.

When stamps were first issued there were 16 POs and sub-offices and four receiving houses where letters could be received but no charges were collected. By 1858 the New Zealand Post Office Act was passed and this regularized rates throughout the colony.

Circular barred numerals were issued to each of the major POs in 1855. These were numbered 1 to 18. In 1860 this series was extended with additional numbers up to 24. Further types were issued, and during the Maori Wars cancellations with the name of the POs in an oval of bars were also used. These include 'Headquarters' and 'Queens Redoubt'.

In 1858 a short-lived service to Britain via Panama was established. There was no additional charge for this service, but there was insufficient mail from New Zealand alone to sustain the route. Subsequently, other services were established and until World War I and later it was possible for letters to be carried in either direction.

Between the wars there was a demand for the establishment of an air connection with Australia to connect with the service to Britain. There were many early attempts to connect the towns in New Zealand by air. These started in 1919. By 1930 mail was being carried by sea to Karachi to connect with the London flight. This was followed in July of that year by a quicker route connecting with the Adelaide-Perth flight and then by sea to Karachi. The Trans-Tasman service began in 1934 and by 1938 New Zealand was included in the Empire 'all-up' service.

New Zealand forces served in the South African War of 1899-1902, but used the British Forces Postal Service. In World War I there were special postmarks in Egypt and on the Western Front. In World War II New Zealand forces had Field POs in the Middle East, Italy, Fiji, Norfolk Island, Tonga, New Caledonia and the Solomon Islands.

B
C
A
D
E
PAPUA
ONE PENNY
Deutsch-Neu-Guinea
TERRITORY OF NEW GUINEA
DEUTSCH-NEU-GUINEA
25 PFENNIG 25
AIR MAIL POSTAGE

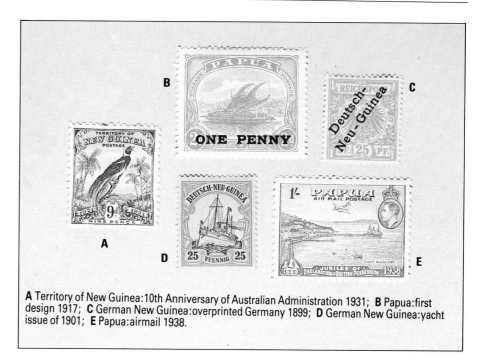

A Territory of New Guinea: 10th Anniversary of Australian Administration 1931; **B** Papua: first design 1917; **C** German New Guinea: overprinted Germany 1899; **D** German New Guinea: yacht issue of 1901; **E** Papua: airmail 1938.

AUCKLAND ISLANDS

Group of uninhabited islands 300 miles south of New Zealand. In 1866 the *General Grant* was wrecked there. Several unsuccessful attempts have been made to salvage her. In 1915 a major attempt was made and two stamps were issued. These were unauthorized and, although some were accepted without surcharge in New Zealand, they had no postal validity.

CHATHAM ISLANDS

Small group of islands 500 miles east of Christchurch. They were discovered in 1790. A PO was established in 1856 and the group was used as a prison for Maori insurgents after the war of 1860-6.

New Zealand stamps were used and are still current. These can only be recognized by their postmark. In December 1970 two stamps were issued inscribed 'Chatham Islands', but these were for use throughout New Zealand and not specifically for the islands.

GREAT BARRIER ISLAND

Island situated 50 miles north-east of Auckland. First PO was established as 'Port Fitzroy'. In October 1892 the Union steamer *Wairarapa* en route from Sydney to Auckland was wrecked with the loss of 125 lives. Mail was salvaged and marked with a cachet before delivery. Until 1897 there was no regular communication with the mainland and in May of that year a pigeon post was established. This operated until 1908, when cable communication was established by the Government. Several POs now exist on the island but these can only be recognized by their postmarks.

• British New Guinea

FIRST STAMPS Queensland from 1885 onwards
FIRST STAMPS ISSUED 1 July 1901

CURRENCY	
1901	sterling

New Guinea lies to the north of Australia. The western part was annexed by the Dutch in 1828 (*see under* Asia). Britain and Germany established protectorates over the eastern part in 1884.

Was visited by the Spanish and Portuguese in the 16th century. In 1606 Torres explored the southern coast and the strait between the island and Australia. Visits by Dutch, French and British explorers took place in the following two centuries. The East India Company annexed the island in 1793, but the Dutch claim to the area west of 141°E was upheld in 1828.

Many surveys of the eastern area were carried out by the British in the middle of the 19th century; the last of these, by John Moresby in 1873, pointed out the danger to Queensland if the island was occupied by a foreign power. With popular support, the area in question was annexed by Queensland on 4 April 1883. Although this move was not ratified by the British government, when Germany proclaimed a protectorate over the northern coast and several other island groups in November 1884, the annexed area in the south was made the protectorate of British New Guinea by proclamation in 1888.

The boundaries were set by a commission in 1885. The government of the British area was managed by Queensland on behalf of that colony, New South Wales and Victoria. In 1902, this responsibility was transferred to the Government of Australia. Federal control was regulated by the

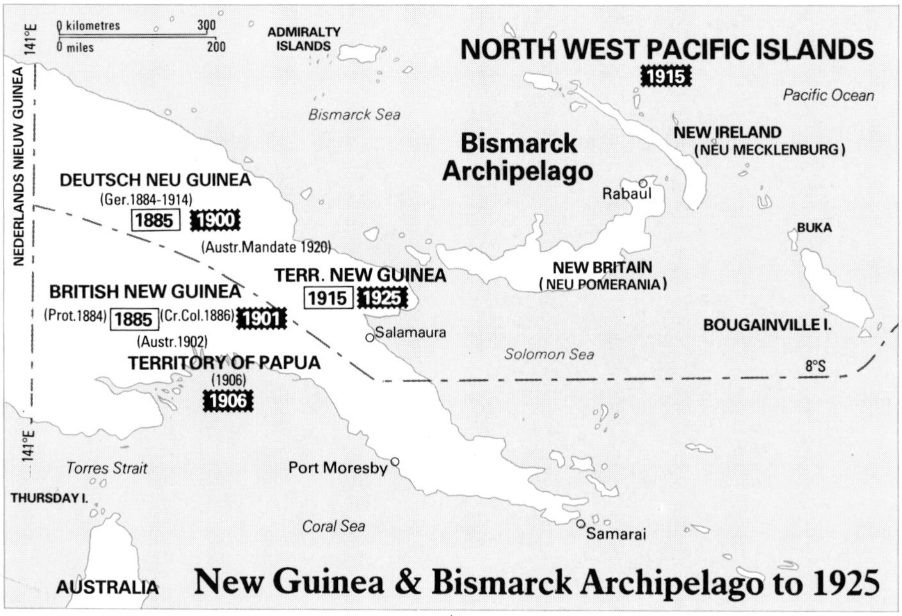
0 kilometres 300
0 miles 200
141°E
ADMIRALTY ISLANDS
NORTH WEST PACIFIC ISLANDS
1915
Pacific Ocean
Bismarck Sea
NEW IRELAND
(NEU MECKLENBURG)
Bismarck Archipelago
Rabaul
NEDERLANDS NIEUW GUINEA
DEUTSCH NEU GUINEA
(Ger.1884-1914)
1885 1900
(Austr.Mandate 1920)
BUKA
TERR. NEW GUINEA
1915 1925
NEW BRITAIN
(NEU POMERANIA)
BRITISH NEW GUINEA
(Prot.1884) 1885 (Cr.Col.1886) 1901
(Austr.1902)
Salamaura
BOUGAINVILLE I.
TERRITORY OF PAPUA
(1906)
1906
Solomon Sea
8°S
141°E
Torres Strait
Port Moresby
THURSDAY I.
Coral Sea
Samarai
AUSTRALIA
New Guinea & Bismarck Archipelago to 1925

Papua Act of 15 November 1905, which came into effect the following year when the name was changed to the Territory of Papua.

Postal History

When a protectorate was proclaimed outright on 4 September 1888, POs were opened at Port Moresby and Samarai, but there is evidence that postal arrangements, possibly only for official mail, existed immediately after the arrival of the Special Commission in 1884.

From 1886 a monthly steamer service was under contract to carry mails and supplies to and from the protectorate. This sailed from Sydney or Cooktown and may have stopped on the return journey at Thursday Island to collect other southbound mail.

First cancellations for stamps were barred ovals with the letters NG or BNG, accompanied by a dated stamp. The island joined the UPU in 1892 and by 1905 there were eight POs in operation.

• Territory of Papua

CURRENCY	
1901	sterling

FIRST STAMPS Queensland and British New Guinea
FIRST STAMPS ISSUED BNG stamps overprinted — 8 November 1906

Created by the Papua Act of 1905, this territory was administered by the Federal Government of Australia. It changed its name from British New Guinea on 1 September 1906.

Used as a base for operations against German New Guinea (q.v.) during World War I, but continued to use its own stamps even when the occupied German territory was using overprinted Australian adhesives.

In January 1942 the Japanese invaded the north-west and landed in the mandated territory of New Guinea. The Government of Australia suspended civil government throughout the island on 14 February 1942 and it came under military control. Civil administration recommenced in October 1945 and the territory was then administered as Papua New Guinea.

Postal History

First stamps were quickly produced by overprinting existing issue of British New Guinea. The new definitive issue began to appear in 1907.

Postmarks were gradually changed and the new Papua type included letters which indicated the district in which the PO was situated (W.D. is Western, C.D. is Central and so on).

Internal air connections began in 1928 with flights from Port Moresby to Salamaua. Because of the terrain, this provided great advantages and was used increasingly during the 1930s. By 1938 there was a regular service on a weekly basis to Australia to connect with the London flight.

By the outbreak of the Japanese War in 1941 there were 31 POs on the mainland.

• German New Guinea

FIRST STAMPS German standard stamps from 1885
FIRST STAMPS ISSUED 1900

CURRENCY	
1898	German
1915	sterling

Germany annexed the northern area of the island of New Guinea in 1884, together with islands in the Bismarck Archipelago (New Britain and New Ireland). In 1885 the boundaries of the Dutch, German and British spheres were settled. When war broke out in 1914, German New Guinea was quickly occupied by Imperial Forces and the whole area was placed under Australian administration in October 1914. At the end of the World War I German New Guinea became an Australian mandate under the League of Nations as the territory of New Guinea.

Postal History

When Germany annexed the northern part of the island in 1884, POs were opened quickly and began to use German adhesives, which were replaced by the standard German colonial design in 1900. These stamps were used throughout the German colonies in the area including New Britain (then New Pomerania), New Ireland (then New Mecklenburg) and Western Solomon Islands. At the out-

PAPUA
NEW
GUINEA
15t
COMMONWEALTH DAY
14 MARCH 1983

Above
Stamp illustration for Papua New Guinea taken from a poster issued to commemorate Commonwealth Day, 14 March 1983

Left
Postal van and travellers, Papua New Guinea

break of World War I there were 17 POs. Stock of the colonial stamps were seized when the islands were occupied, and overprinted GRI with a value. They were first introduced in October 1914 and were used concurrently with the overprinted stamps of the Marshall Islands in December. The two issues were replaced by the issue 'North West Pacific Islands' (q.v.) in March 1915.

• Territory of New Guinea

FIRST STAMPS German issues from 1885
FIRST STAMPS ISSUED 1925

CURRENCY

1925 sterling

Mandated territory administered by Australia under the League of Nations. Formerly German New Guinea and the associated islands of the Bismarck Archipelago. Until World War II Nauru (q.v.) was included in this area for administrative purposes, but it had a separate postal service.

With the Japanese invasion in January 1942, the area of Papua and the territory of New Guinea were combined under the Australian New Guinea Administrative Unit (ANGAU), a military control. Civil administration was re-established, commencing on 30 October 1945 and completed by July 1946. The new trust territory combined Papua (q.v.) and the territory of New Guinea.

Postal History
Stamps of North West Pacific Islands continued to be used until the special stamps for the new territory were issued in 1925. By the outbreak of the Japanese war in 1942 there were 20 POs operating, including three in the Solomon Islands. All offices closed early in that year. Forces POs of Australia and New Zealand were used in New Guinea during World War II.

Papua New Guinea

CURRENCY

1952 sterling
1966 100 cents = 1 dollar Australian
1975 100 toea = 1 kina

FIRST STAMPS Queensland, British New Guinea, German New Guinea and Territory of New Guinea
FIRST STAMPS ISSUED As a trust territory: 30 October 1952. As Papua New Guinea: 26 January 1972. As a self-governing territory: 5 December 1973. As an independent country: 10 September 1975

The former territory of New Guinea and the colony of Papua were consolidated as an Australian trust territory under the United Nations in 1946. The civil administration was resumed earlier than this and was completely operative from July 1946. The name was changed to Papua New Guinea in 1972 and the territory became self-governing on 5 December 1973. Independence was granted on 10 September 1975.

Postal History
Used the stamps of Australia from 1945 to 1952. Stocks of the former adhesives were destroyed in 1945-6 but were accepted within the boundaries of the former territories until 1954. In 1945-6, three Australian commemorative issues were made avail-

A
N. W.
PACIFIC
ISLANDS.
B
7
DENDROBIUM BRACTEOSUM
PAPUA NEW GUINEA
C
35c
Canoe protector spirit
Nguzu-nguzu
Solomon Islands
D
PAPUA &
NEW GUINEA
AMBLYORNIS SUBALARIS
1d
E
2/6
NATIVE HOUSE REEF ISLANDS
BRITISH
SOLOMON ISLANDS
F
SPECIMEN
1d
POSTAGE
1d

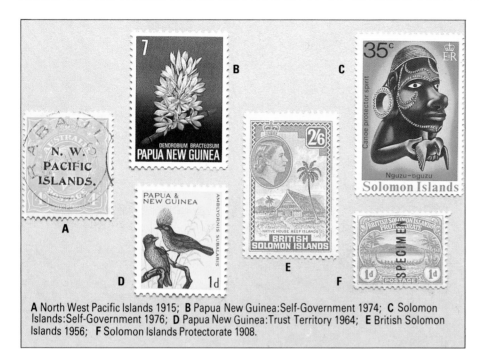

A North West Pacific Islands 1915; **B** Papua New Guinea:Self-Government 1974; **C** Solomon Islands:Self-Government 1976; **D** Papua New Guinea:Trust Territory 1964; **E** British Solomon Islands 1956; **F** Solomon Islands Protectorate 1908.

able, including the Victory issue, but thereafter only the definitive issues were used.

• North West Pacific Islands

FIRST STAMPS see under individual territories
FIRST STAMPS ISSUED 15 March 1915

CURRENCY

sterling

General term for the occupied German territories during World War I. It included the area which subsequently became the territory of New Guinea, the Bismarck Archipelago, the Admiralty Group, the westernmost Solomon Islands of Bougainville and Buka and Nauru. The intention to use these issues in the smaller island groups — the Carolines, Marshall and Mariana Islands — was not implemented as they were occupied by Japanese and not Australian forces.

Postal History
Stamps from the individual islands and territories can be recognized from the postmarks. These stamps were issued until 1922, when they were replaced by the adhesives of the Australian manadate.

• British Solomon Islands

FIRST STAMPS New South Wales from 1896
FIRST STAMPS ISSUED 14 February 1907

CURRENCY

1907 sterling

Group of islands stretching east and south of New Guinea, first discovered by the Spaniards in the 16th century. Some of the islands still have the original Spanish names — San Cristobal, Guadalcanal and Santa Isabel. They were charted by the English and French towards the end of the 18th century. In 1893 Britain declared the southern islands to be a British protectorate and Germany laid claim to the northern area.

In 1898 some further islands, Santa Cruz to the south and the Lord Howe Atolls to the north-east, were annexed. Two years later in return for concessions in Samoa, Germany ceded all its possessions in the group to Britain except Bougainville and Buka. These two islands were subsequently captured during World War I and remained part of the territory of New Guinea or Papua-New Guinea (q.v.).

In World War II the group was overrun by the Japanese in 1942, but was recaptured by the Americans and Australians. The area was returned to civil control in 1945. A new constitution was enacted in 1960 and the islands were governed by a Legislative Council. A further constitution was agreed in 1974 and 'British' was dropped from the name of the group.

Postal History
All early mail was carried by private ship to Sydney where mail was franked with the stamps of New South Wales. A resident commissioner was appointed in 1896 and he applied a postmark to covers alongside the New South Wales stamps of which he held a small stock. These items were cancelled in Sydney on arrival.

First stamps were issued in 1907, in part to assist in the cost of the resettlement of labourers who had returned from Queensland. The British Solomons joined the UPU in 1907 as a British protectorate, but ceased to be a member from 1976-83 after gaining independence.

The first PO in the British protectorate was opened at Tulagi in 1907, followed by four other POs before World War I. After the capture of the German islands in 1914, they were placed under the control of New Guinea, and remained an Australian mandate. They now form part of Papua-New Guinea.

In 1939 there were four POs in operation but these closed when the Japanese invaded and stamps were taken to Fiji. The first PO was reopened at Lunga on Guadalcanal in July 1943, but this was closed in 1946 when Honiara, the new head PO for the group, was opened.

In 1952 airmail services started and were increasingly used to link the islands. All stamps bore the name 'British Solomon Islands' until August 1975, when the group was renamed 'Solomon Islands'.

Solomon Islands

FIRST STAMPS New South Wales to 1907 and British Solomon Islands
FIRST STAMPS ISSUED 4 August 1975
FIRST STAMPS ISSUED AS A SELF-GOVERNING TERRITORY 12 January 1976

CURRENCY	
1966	100 cents = 1 Australian dollar

This successor of the British Solomon Islands attained self-government on 2 January 1976. The two northern islands of Bougainville and Buka remained part of Papua-New Guinea.

Postal History
Stamps inscribed 'British Solomon Islands' continued to be used after the change of name, though a new set was introduced in November 1975 with an overprint to obliterate 'British'.

On achievement of self-government, membership of the UPU lapsed, though stamps continued to be circulated to other member countries. The islands became a member of the UPU in their own right in 1983.

• New Hebrides

FIRST STAMPS New South Wales from 1888
FIRST STAMPS ISSUED October 1908

CURRENCY	
1908	sterling & French
1938	100 gold centimes = 1 gold franc
1977	100 centimes = 1 franc (New Hebrides)

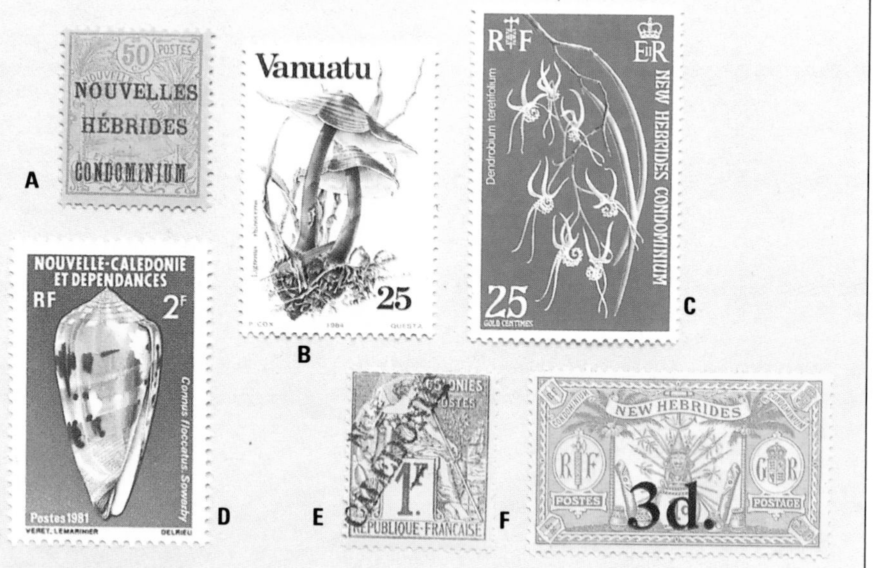

A
NOUVELLES HÉBRIDES CONDOMINIUM
B
Vanuatu
25
C
RF
EIIR
NEW HEBRIDES CONDOMINIUM
Dendrobium teretifolium
25
D
NOUVELLE-CALEDONIE ET DEPENDANCES
RF
2F
Conus floccatus Sowerby
Postes 1981
E
1F
REPUBLIQUE FRANÇAISE
F
NEW HEBRIDES
3d.

A New Hebrides:Condominium 1908; B Vanuatu 1984; C New Hebrides:Condominium 1973; D New Caledonia 1981; E New Caledonia 1892; F New Hebrides:Condominium 1924.

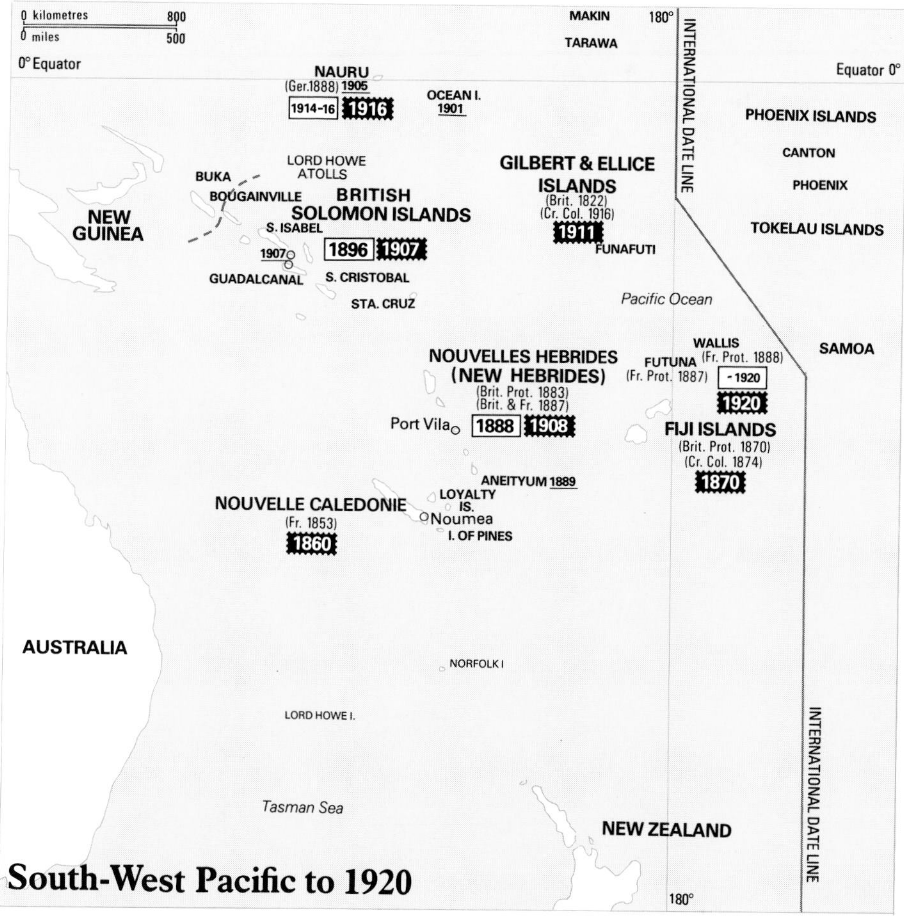

0 kilometres 800
0 miles 500
0° Equator
Equator 0°
MAKIN
TARAWA
180°
INTERNATIONAL DATE LINE
NAURU
(Ger.1888) 1905
1914-16 1916
OCEAN I.
1901
PHOENIX ISLANDS
CANTON
PHOENIX
TOKELAU ISLANDS
LORD HOWE ATOLLS
BUKA
BOUGAINVILLE
BRITISH SOLOMON ISLANDS
S. ISABEL
NEW GUINEA
1907
1896 1907
GUADALCANAL
S. CRISTOBAL
STA. CRUZ
GILBERT & ELLICE ISLANDS
(Brit. 1822)
(Cr. Col. 1916)
1911
FUNAFUTI
Pacific Ocean
WALLIS
FUTUNA
(Fr. Prot. 1888)
(Fr. Prot. 1887)
-1920
1920
SAMOA
NOUVELLES HEBRIDES (NEW HEBRIDES)
(Brit. Prot. 1883)
(Brit. & Fr. 1887)
Port Vila
1888 1908
FIJI ISLANDS
(Brit. Prot. 1870)
(Cr. Col. 1874)
1870
ANEITYUM 1889
LOYALTY IS.
NOUVELLE CALEDONIE
(Fr. 1853)
1860
Noumea
I. OF PINES
AUSTRALIA
NORFOLK I
LORD HOWE I.
Tasman Sea
NEW ZEALAND
180°

South-West Pacific to 1920

Discovered by the Portuguese explorer Quiros in 1606; he believed it to be part of Australia and it was named Espiritu Santo. The French discovered they were islands in 1768; named by Captain Cook in 1774.

On appeal to the British government, became a protectorate in 1883. Although the British and French had agreed not to occupy the islands in 1878, the Australian colonies protested against French aggression in 1887 and, as a result, an Anglo-French Convention was signed in November of that year which placed the islands under a joint commission of French and English naval officers on the Pacific Station.

A further agreement in 1904 provided for jurisdiction over the islands and set up a commission to settle disputes between the English and French colonists. In 1906 a special convention bestowed equal rights on British and French citizens and this situation remained until the islands became independent on 30 June 1980 as Vanuatu (q.v.).

During World War II, New Hebrides was a base for Allied forces and at one time in early 1942 was threatened with invasion by the Japanese.

Postal History

The islands had no regular contact with Australia or other Pacific colonies before 1888. In that year a feeder line was established between the group and Sydney, which connected with both the French and British services to Europe. Stamps of New South Wales and, occasionally, France were used to prepay mail and these were postmarked either Sydney or Noumea.

A New South Wales PA was opened on Aneityum in 1889 but this was short-lived. The mail was re-routed via Port Vila and a canceller was introduced in 1892.

In the same year the contract for the carriage of mail to Australia lapsed and the Australian New Hebrides Company and its French counterpart took over responsibility for the postal service. However, the companies, which had issued their own stamps, soon went into liquidation and PAs for New Caledonia were opened in 1903 and 1905. Stamps of both New South Wales and New Caledonia continued to be used until the PO of the Condominium was established in October 1908. The former PAs were closed soon afterwards.

The struggle for independence in the 1970s led to a minor revolt and some islands declared their own independence. Although this led to some disruption of mail, no special stamps were issued, the revolts were suppressed by a joint French and British force and the islands became Vanuatu on 30 June 1980.

Vanuatu

FIRST STAMPS ISSUED 1980

CURRENCY

1980 100 centimes = 1 franc (Vanuatu)
1981 Vatus

Name given to former Anglo-French Condominium of New Hebrides when it became independent on 30 June 1980.

New Caledonia

FIRST STAMPS ISSUED 1 January 1860

CURRENCY

1881 As France
French (franc) and
CFP (Colonial franc pacifique)

Island discovered by Captain Cook on 4 September 1774. Seized by the French in 1853 and colonized by them. This followed a dispute between the natives and the French traders who had begun to settle the island in the early part of the 19th century.

New Caledonia remained a French colony throughout this century. In 1940 it initially supported Vichy France, but declared for de Gaulle soon afterwards. During the Pacific war, the island was used as a base by Allied troops. It became a French overseas territory in 1946 and has remained such ever since.

Postal History

Early letters are uncommon and, although primitive local stamps were produced in 1860, New Caledonia had no regular mail service until Ligne T of the Messageries Maritimes was extended to Noumea in 1882–3. The first steamer left Marseille on 23 November 1882 and arrived on 13 January 1883.

When the first stamps were issued, they were not valid for postage outside the island, and, on mail for Europe, stamps of New South Wales had to be added as well. The stamps were suppressed in 1862 and French colonial stamps were used instead.

In 1876 the supply of stamps became exhausted and special cachets were applied to outgoing mail.

Stamps of New Caledonia were used in the dependencies of the colony; the Loyalty Islands to the north-east and the Isle of Pines to the south. They were also used in Wallis and Futuna Islands (q.v.) until 1920. In 1915 there were 54 POs, including 3 in the Loyalty group and 1 in the Isle of Pines.

During World War II some stamps were prepared for use under the short-lived Vichy regime but these were never issued. American and Australian Forces POs operated in the island during the war.

Fiji

FIRST STAMPS ISSUED 1 November 1870
FIRST STAMPS ISSUED AS AN INDEPENDENT TERRITORY 10 October 1970

CURRENCY

1870	sterling
1964	100 cents = 1 dollar

Group of islands in the Pacific situated on the international dateline, which deviates to ensure that the date remains the same throughout the islands. Although the group was known to the Dutch in the 17th century, it was not explored until visited by Cook in 1773. Escaped convicts from Australia helped to settle parts of the group in the early 19th century.

Although there was an attempt to gain British protection in the middle of the 19th century, it was not until 1874 that Britain accepted unconditional cession of the group and it became a Crown Colony, having been a protectorate for four years.

In 1966 the move towards independence began with the creation of a Legislative Assembly. Full independence followed on 10 October 1970.

Postal History

Before the establishment of the British protectorate, mail was carried by trading vessels to Sydney and placed in the post there. In 1870 the proprietors of the *Fiji Times* instituted an efficient letter and parcel service. This was not accepted by the British Consul, who tried to close it in 1871, and appointed an official postmaster. The government postal service was more expensive, but on 8 May 1872 the *Fiji Times* closed its service stating that it had '. . . received notice from the Fiji Government to discontinue the receipt and despatch of inter-island correspondence'.

On 3 December 1871 the government issued the first stamps with the cypher of King Kakobau and established their own service. The first Post Office Act was passed soon afterwards, and the stamps were overprinted with VR in 1874 when Fiji became a Crown Colony.

Fiji joined the UPU in 1891 at the same time as the Australian colonies. The currency of Fiji was complicated by the fact that the stamps and postage rates were in sterling while the locals used dollars and cents. The two different currencies had to be quoted on Post Office notices.

Before Fiji became a member of the UPU, stamps were not accepted for prepayment outside the colony, though a special agreement must have existed between the islands and Australia and New Zealand.

During World War II Fiji was used as a base and in 1940 the Local Defence Force was strengthened by the addition of New Zealand troops. Forces PO marks were used in the islands. Mails of the Fijian forces were also active in the Solomons with the New Zealand forces.

In 1950 there 57 POs in Fiji. The first stamps of the newly independent country were issued on independence day, 10 October 1970.

• Gilbert and Ellice Islands

FIRST STAMPS ISSUED 1 January 1911

CURRENCY

to February 1966	British (sterling)
14 February 1966	Australian (dollar)

COMMONWEALTH DAY 1983
VANUATU
25
Kiribati
TUVALU
FIRST CONTAINER SHIP "MORNING STAR"
50c
COMMONWEALTH DAY 14th MARCH 1983
Bure in Traditional Village
8c FIJI

Stamp illustrations for Vanuatu, Kiribati, Tuvalu and Fiji taken from a poster issued to commemorate Commonwealth Day, 14 March 1983

fiji
Sacred Heart Cathedral Suva
30c
A
Kiribati
POSTAGE & REVENUE
TWO SHILLINGS & SIX PENCE
B
1c
CUTTING TODDY
GILBERT & ELLICE ISLANDS
C
GILBERT & ELLICE ISLANDS PROTECTORATE
SPECIMEN
POSTAGE
D
TIMES
1
PENNY.
FIJI
EXPRESS.
E
FIJI
2/6
F

A Fiji:Independent 1979; **B** Kiribati 1979; **C** Gilbert & Ellice Islands 1971; **D** Gilbert & Ellice Islands:Protectorate 1911; **E** Fiji Times Issue 1870; **F** Fiji:Crown Colony 1954.

These groups of islands cover an area of 2 million square miles and straddle both the Equator and the International Date Line. Spanish explorers in the 16th century first sighted some of the islands, but they were not fully explored until early in the 19th century. First rediscovered by Captain Byron in the *Dolphin*; Captain Cook also visited the area in 1777 when he discovered Christmas Island. In the 1790s the Americans discovered Washington and Fanning Islands and the Phoenix Group. Ocean Island was named after the ship that called there in 1804. The groups were annexed by the British in 1822.

The Pacific Islands Protection Act of 1857 established them as a British protectorate and a High Commissioner was appointed in 1893. The status of the groups was changed in 1916 when they became a Crown Colony. Christ-

Above
Captain James Cook who discovered the Cook Islands (originally known as the Hervey Islands), 1773–5

HOTEL METROPOLE HOTEL METROPOLE

Left
Post-box outside Hotel Metropole, Fiji

mas Island joined the group in 1919.

Early in World War II the northern part of the groups was captured by the Japanese (Tarawa on 10 December 1941). The European population was withdrawn but some control was maintained at Funafuti in the Ellice Islands until Tarawa was recaptured by the Americans in November 1943. Ocean Island was held by the Japanese until August 1945.

Postal History
Before 1911 all mail services were of a limited nature and depended on the ships that called at the islands. As a result, almost any stamps that were available were used. A New South Wales PA was established on Ocean Island in 1901, but no postmarks were issued to this office. At Fanning Island, a New Zealand PO was opened and the stamps of that dominion were used there until the island was incorporated in the colony in February 1939. No PO was opened on Christmas Island until 14 February 1939.

Washington Island relied on its contacts with Fanning Island, some 80 miles away, but as the authorities insisted that mail was returned to Fanning, considerable delays resulted. As a result the New Zealand PO opened an agency on Washington Island on 1 February 1921. This was short-lived as the slump in prices for copra caused the island to be evacuated in 1922. It was resettled in 1925 but finally evacuated in March 1934.

The United States maintains an air base on Canton Island and American stamps are used by the troops there.

During World War II Field POs of both the Australian and American forces were in use on the island. The political changes since 1976 have been reflected in the stamps and postmarks of these groups.

• Gilbert Islands

FIRST STAMPS ISSUED 1 January 1976

CURRENCY	
1976	As Australia

A
B
C
D
COOK
ISLANDS
BICENTENARY OF FIRST VOYAGE OF DISCOVERY · CAPTAIN JAMES COOK
4c
COOK ISLANDS
ONE SHILLING
POSTAGE
AITUTAKI
ONE PENNY

A Cook Islands:British Protectorate 1893; **B** Cook Islands:Self-Government 1968; **C** Cook Islands:New Zealand Territory 1932; **D** Aitutaki:New Zealand Dependency 1920.

The Gilbert Islands became a separate Crown Colony on 1 January 1976.

Kiribati

FIRST STAMPS ISSUED 12 July 1979

CURRENCY	
1979	100 cents = 1 Australian dollar

On 12 July 1979, the former Gilbert Islands became the independent republic of Kiribati.

Tuvalu

FIRST STAMPS ISSUED 1 January 1976

CURRENCY	
1976	100 cents = 1 Australian dollar

The Ellice Islands became the Crown Colony of Tuvalu on 1 January 1976 and fully independent on 1 October 1978.

Cook Islands

FIRST STAMPS ISSUED 7 May 1892

CURRENCY	
1892	sterling
1967	New Zealand dollar

Group of islands about 1600 miles north-east of New Zealand. It comprises eight islands, the most important of which are Rarotonga and Aitutaki. For administrative purposes, Niue and Penrhyn are also included in the group.

Islands were discovered by Captain Cook in 1773-5; he named them the Hervey Islands after the then First Lord of the Admiralty. The group was proclaimed a British protectorate in April 1888 and formal possession was taken in 1900. By Order in Council of 13 May 1901 Cook Islands were placed under New Zealand control and they have remained so ever since. Rarotonga is the principal island and the administrative centre of the group.

Postal History
As with many of the Pacific islands,

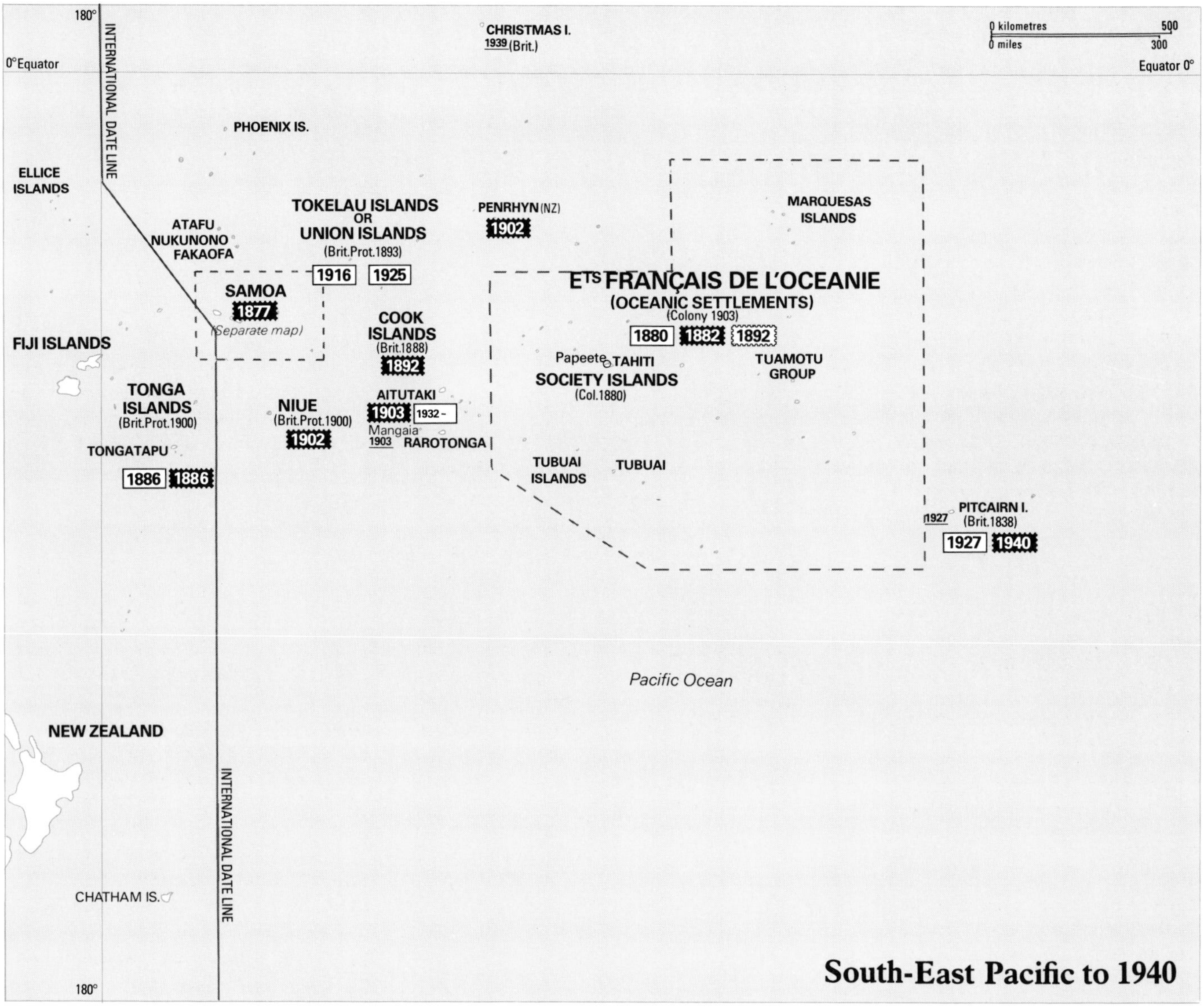
180°
INTERNATIONAL DATE LINE
0°Equator
CHRISTMAS I.
1939 (Brit.)
0 kilometres 500
0 miles 300
Equator 0°
PHOENIX IS.
ELLICE ISLANDS
ATAFU
NUKUNONO
FAKAOFA
TOKELAU ISLANDS
OR
UNION ISLANDS
(Brit.Prot.1893)
1916
1925
PENRHYN (NZ)
1902
MARQUESAS ISLANDS
ETS FRANÇAIS DE L'OCEANIE
(OCEANIC SETTLEMENTS)
(Colony 1903)
1880
1882
1892
SAMOA
1877
(Separate map)
COOK ISLANDS
(Brit.1888)
1892
FIJI ISLANDS
Papeete
TAHITI
SOCIETY ISLANDS
(Col.1880)
TUAMOTU GROUP
TONGA ISLANDS
(Brit.Prot.1900)
NIUE
(Brit.Prot.1900)
1902
AITUTAKI
1903
1932 -
Mangaia
1903
RAROTONGA
TONGATAPU
1886
1886
TUBUAI ISLANDS
TUBUAI
PITCAIRN I.
(Brit.1838)
1927
1927
1940
Pacific Ocean
NEW ZEALAND
CHATHAM IS.
INTERNATIONAL DATE LINE
180°
South-East Pacific to 1940

contact with the outside world was originally maintained by missionaries who first started missions in the islands in 1821. At that time, letters were carried by the few ships which called occasionally at the islands, but there is evidence that these were coordinated by the British consulate.

Under the British protectorate, stamps were issued and these were used at Rarotonga, which was the only PO open at that time. Mangaia PO on a neighbouring island was opened in 1903.

Stamps of Cook Islands were inscribed 'Rarotonga' from 1919 to 1932, but reverted to 'Cook Islands' when Aitutaki and Penrhyn were included in the group and their separate issues withdrawn (*see also* Aitutaki, Niue and Penrhyn islands). Eight POs within the group were operating by 1935.

Aitutaki

CURRENCY

1903 As Cook Islands

FIRST STAMPS ISSUED New Zealand stamps overprinted January 1903

FIRST STAMPS RE-ISSUED Cook Islands stamps overprinted 7 August 1972

One of the Cook Islands group, discovered by Captain Bligh shortly before the mutiny on the *Bounty*.

It was annexed at about the same time as the rest of the group — though the islanders claim it was in 1891, after the group was a protectorate but before the official annexation. Administered as a separate unit from the Cook Islands by New Zealand from 1900 to 1932 when it became a part of the group. In 1972 Aitutaki became a port of entry into the Cook Islands and it is a separate postal entity.

Postal History
There was no PO on the island prior to New Zealand control in 1903. New Zealand stamps were used with suitable overprint until 1932 when the island was included in the Cook Islands for postal purposes. Cook Islands stamps were used from 1932 to 1972. On 1 April 1972, Cook Islands stamps were withdrawn because the island had become postally independent and it has continued to issue its own stamps.

Niue

FIRST STAMPS ISSUED 4 January 1902
FIRST STAMPS ISSUED ON SELF-GOVERNMENT 19 October 1974

CURRENCY	
1902	As New Zealand

Geographically part of the Cook Islands, but the natives continually resented any control from Rarotonga. Discovered by Captain Cook in June 1774, it was originally called 'Savage Island'. Became a British protectorate in April 1900 and a New Zealand dependency in October the same year. It was at this time that it was placed under the Cook Islands, but because of local resentment it was separated in 1903. Granted self-government in October 1974.

Postal History
Prior to the establishment of a New Zealand PO in November 1901, there were no official postal arrangements from the island. When stamps were provided, they were overprinted New Zealand stamps; there was no handstamp for the first week and all cancellations were in manuscript. The island continued to use either New Zealand or Cook Islands stamps overprinted NIUE, or of the same design with NIUE added, until July 1950.

Penrhyn Island

FIRST STAMPS Cook Islands
FIRST STAMPS ISSUED New Zealand overprinted May 1902
FIRST STAMPS RE-ISSUED Cook Islands overprinted 24 October 1973

CURRENCY	
1902	As New Zealand

Most northerly of the Cook Islands group. It was proclaimed a New Zealand dependency and administered as part of the Cook Islands from 1901.

Postal History
There was no issue of stamps for the island when it became a dependency so the stamps of Cook Islands were used until the first special issue in 1902. The island continued to use overprinted stamps until 1932 when the Cook Islands issues were reintroduced.

The northern Cook Islands began to issue their own stamps again in 1973 and since then Penrhyn has used issues inscribed 'Penrhyn Northern Cook Islands'. It still remains a New Zealand dependency.

Tonga

FIRST STAMPS Fiji in 1886
FIRST STAMPS ISSUED 1886

CURRENCY	
1886	sterling
1967	100 seniti = 1 pa'anga

Kingdom in the Pacific between New Zealand and Samoa comprising many islands of which about 20 are inhabited. Islands were discovered by the Dutch in 1616 and were visited by Cook in both 1773 and 1777. He was so impressed with the hospitality of the natives that they were called the 'Friendly Islands'. Despite this name, the islanders remained at war with the Fijians and, in the first half of the 19th century, fought a civil war among themselves.

At the end of this period, a strong chief was proclaimed king as George I and reigned until 1893. After his death, he was succeeded by his son, George II. In 1880 treaties had been signed with Britain and the USA and in 1900 the group became a British protectorate, in part to counteract the German attempts to increase their influence in the area. Tonga has remained a protectorate kingdom ever since.

Postal History
Early covers all emanate from the Wesleyan missionaries who had arrived in 1822. A postal service was organized by the Collector of Customs for Fiji in 1886 at Nukualofa, the capital, on Tongatapu the largest island. Before stamps were issued, a small number of Fijian stamps were made available, though these were not cancelled until they arrived at Suva. At the same time, by agreement with the British consulate, Germany opened a PA which handled parcels only.

POs exist on four islands and occasional mail also operates from Niuatobutabu and Niuafoou. The latter has no harbour, and mail for the islanders used to be floated ashore in a tin can and picked up by swimmers who would come out one or two miles. Mail for despatch was brought out by the swimmers. In later years canoes replaced the swimmers after one was attacked by a shark.

Tonga adopted the UPU rates in 1893 and many overprints resulted between 1897 and 1904. The name of the islands appears on the stamps as Toga; this is the native name for the islands, and is not a separate stamp-issuing country.

In October 1942 New Zealand troops landed on Tonga and Army PO No. 100 opened the following month. This was closed in January 1944.

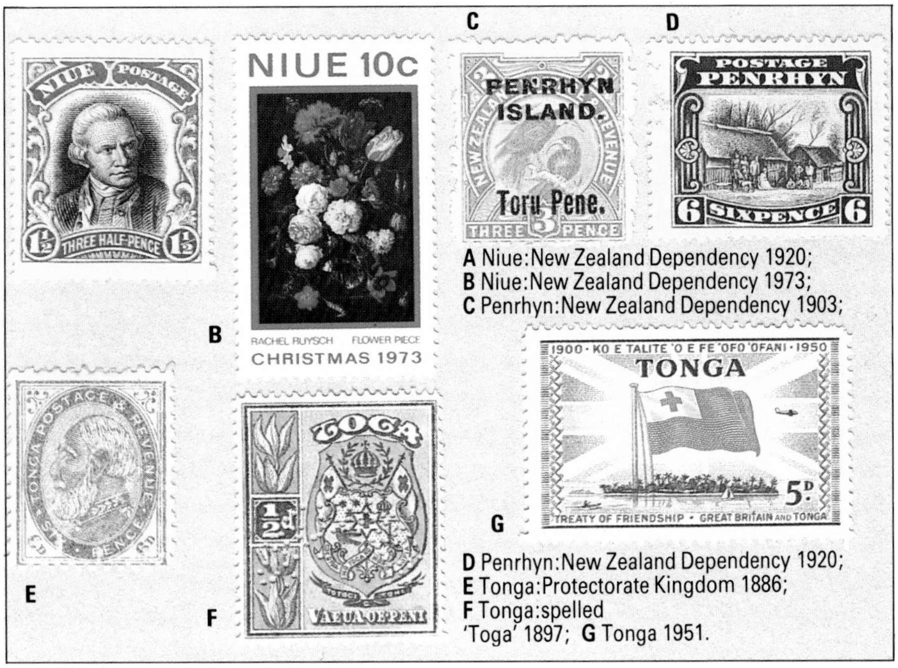
NIUE POSTAGE
THREE HALF-PENCE
NIUE 10c
RACHEL RUYSCH FLOWER PIECE
CHRISTMAS 1973
PENRHYN ISLAND.
Toru Pene.
THREE PENCE
POSTAGE PENRHYN
SIXPENCE
1900 · KO E TALITE 'O E FE'OFO'OFANI · 1950
TONGA
5D
TREATY OF FRIENDSHIP · GREAT BRITAIN AND TONGA
TOGA
B
C
D
E
F
G

A Niue:New Zealand Dependency 1920; **B** Niue:New Zealand Dependency 1973; **C** Penrhyn:New Zealand Dependency 1903; **D** Penrhyn:New Zealand Dependency 1920; **E** Tonga:Protectorate Kingdom 1886; **F** Tonga:spelled 'Toga' 1897; **G** Tonga 1951.

• Samoa

FIRST STAMPS ISSUED 1877

CURRENCY	
1877	sterling
1900	German currency
1914	As New Zealand
1967	100 sene = 1 Samoan dollar

Group of 14 islands which lies about 1600 miles north-east of New Zealand on the main route from Australia to America. The islands were known to the Dutch and French in the 18th century. American interest began in the 1830s and Britain appointed a missionary as consular agent in 1847. As part of its expansion into the Pacific, Germany was officially represented in 1861.

Although there were numerous requests for annexation by Britain, strongly supported by New Zealand, the government refused to act until 1887 when civil war broke out between rival factions led by Malietoa and Tamasese. Britain supported the

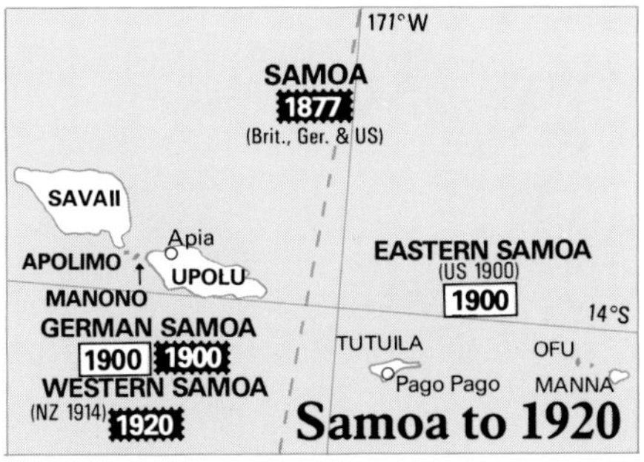
171°W
SAMOA
1877
(Brit., Ger. & US)
SAVAII
Apia
APOLIMO
UPOLU
MANONO
GERMAN SAMOA
1900
1900
WESTERN SAMOA
(NZ 1914)
1920
EASTERN SAMOA
(US 1900)
1900
14°S
TUTUILA
OFU
Pago Pago
MANNA
Samoa to 1920

former, and following the Berlin Agreement in 1889, he was reinstated and a three-power protectorate was established.

In 1898 Malietoa died and civil war broke out again. By 1900 the situation had become so serious that a new agreement was signed. As a result, Britain withdrew from the area and Germany gained control of the westernmost group in return for other concessions, including the Solomon Islands (q.v.). The USA were granted control of the eastern group.

Postal History

As in Fiji, the first postal service was organized by a local newspaper, the *Samoan Times*. The Samoan Express PO was opened in 1877, but the operation was a failure and it closed in 1881. The earlier system was reverted to and letters, usually franked with New Zealand stamps, were forwarded by the first available ship. In 1886, another PO was established and further stamps were issued.

In 1891 New Zealand joined the UPU and the question of the validity of Samoan stamps for overseas postage was raised. Although mail to New Zealand and Australia was accepted without surcharge by those authorities, letters to the USA needed an additional 5 cent American adhesive to pay for inland delivery. In 1895 Apia PO in the capital was destroyed by fire.

After the convention of 1900 the stamps of Samoa were withdrawn and replaced by German or USA issues.

• German Samoa

FIRST STAMPS Samoa and Germany in 1900
FIRST STAMPS ISSUED 1900

CURRENCY	
1900	As Germany

Created from the western part of the kingdom of Samoa by the three-power convention of 1900. Germany controlled Savaii, Upolu and the smaller islands of Apolimo and Manono.

When World War I started, the German authorities surrendered to the New Zealand Expeditionary Force on 29 August 1914. Military administration was maintained until 1920, when the western islands were placed under New Zealand mandate by the League of Nations.

Postal History

When Germany took control in 1900, German stamps without overprints were issued. These were quickly replaced by the standard German colonial design in the same year. Before World War I there were nine POs.

On the evening of the invasion by New Zealand forces in 1914, the German issues were demonetized, and the confiscated stocks were overprinted GRI with a sterling value.

During the military administration, New Zealand stamps were used overprinted SAMOA.

Western Samoa (Samoa I Sisifo)

FIRST STAMPS Samoa and German Samoa
FIRST STAMPS ISSUED New Zealand overprinted July 1920
FIRST STAMPS AS AN INDEPENDENT NATION 2 July 1962

Comprising the four islands of Savaii, Upolu, Apolimo, and Manono, this New Zealand mandated territory replaced German Samoa after its capture in 1914. In 1920 the islands were placed under New Zealand civil control.

With American Samoa, the group was an important base during World War II, and subsequently became a trust territory of the United Nations under New Zealand. Samoa was the first territory in the Western Pacific to become independent on 1 January 1962. It then became known by its native name of Samoa I Sisifo.

Postal History
First stamps issued continued the pattern of New Zealand overprints which had started in 1914. The main mail link with New Zealand continued and a range of cancellations was used between the wars. The first 'Western Samoa' postmark was introduced at Apia in 1931.

At the time of independence there were 17 POs on the islands.

DOMINION OF NEW ZEALAND
SAMOA.
ONE SHILLING
REICHSPOST
Samoa
SAMOA
5 PFENNIG 5
CORONATION 1953
WESTERN SAMOA
25th. ANNIVERSARY SOUTH PACIFIC COMMISSION
7 SENE
SAMOA I SISIFO
A
B
C
D
E

A Samoa:New Zealand overprint 1914; **B** German Samoa:overprinted Germany 1900; **C** German Samoa:yacht issue of 1900; **D** Western Samoa:New Zealand Dependency 1953; **E** Samoa:Independent 1984.

Tokelau or Union Islands

FIRST STAMPS Gilbert and Ellice Islands from 1916, Western Samoa from 1925
FIRST STAMPS ISSUED 22 June 1948

CURRENCY

1948	sterling
1967	100 cents = 1 New Zealand dollar
1982	100 sene = 1 Samoan tola

Group of three islands between the Gilbert and Ellice Islands and Samoa. Discovered towards the end of the 18th century, they were declared a British protectorate in 1893 under the administration of the Gilbert and Ellice Islands. They were incorporated into that colony in 1916, but in 1925 they became a New Zealand dependency and were administered from Western Samoa. The name of Tokelau was adopted on 7 May 1946.

Postal History
Early mail is very rare and was carried by local traders and stamped on arrival at the first port of call. When the group was incorporated into the Gilbert and Ellice Islands in 1916, the recently issued stamps of that colony were used until 1925 when the issues of Western Samoa were released.

There was a PO on each of the three islands, Atafu, Fakaofa, and Nukunono. The group was not occupied by the Japanese in World War II.

AMERICAN OR EASTERN SAMOA

When the three-power protectorate was established in 1889, the Americans formally started to exercise some control in the area. In 1900, following the agreement of the British and Germans over Western Samoa, the USA accepted control over the eastern islands. There were ten of these with a capital at Pago Pago.

It has continued as a US overseas territory since then and was one of the main American bases in the southern pacific during World War II.

No stamps have been issued. USA issues, without overprint, have been used since 1900. Mail from the islands can only be recognized by the postmarks. During World War II the civi-

Above
Busy street scene, Papeete, Tahiti

Right
Steamer at Morea, Tahiti

lian mail became much scarcer as most correspondents used the military mail service.

Wallis and Futuna Islands

FIRST STAMPS New Caledonia until 1920
FIRST STAMPS ISSUED May 1920

CURRENCY
French (franc) and
CFP (Colonial franc pacifique)

Two small islands to the west of Samoa; though geographically closer to New Hebrides than New Caledonia, they were administered by the latter.

Wallis Island, or Uvea, was discovered by the English explorer Samuel Wallis in 1767; the Futuna (or Horne) Island to the south was discovered in 1616 by the Dutch explorers Willem Schouten and La Maine. French influence began in 1837 when the islands were settled by missionaries. In 1842 France would not accept the islands as a protectorate, but they had a French adviser from 1843 onwards.

On 5 April 1887 Wallis became a French protectorate and this was followed by a further decree on 16 February 1888, when it was joined by Futuna. The islands declared for de Gaulle in 1940 and stamps prepared by Vichy France were not issued.

The islands were administered from New Caledonia until a local referendum in 1959, and became a French overseas territory on 24 July 1961. This they have remained ever since.

Postal History
Early postal links were established through New Hebrides and New Caledonia. The postal vessels from Sydney came via Noumea to Port Vila, New Hebrides and a feeder service operated from Wallis Island in 1935. The mail before this had depended on occasional schooners.

Stamps were released in 1920 and the issues of New Caledonia continued to be overprinted for use in the islands until 1944. The first issue as an overseas territory was on 18 July 1962.

• Oceanic Settlements (Etablissements Français de l'Oceanie *or* Oceanie)

FIRST STAMPS
French Colonial General issues from 1880
FIRST STAMPS ISSUED
Locally overprinted June 1882

CURRENCY
1892 As France

Groups of islands in the South Pacific, now known as French Polynesia (Polynesie Francais). The most important are the Society Islands, named after the Royal Society by Captain Cook in 1759; Tuamotu Islands, Tubuai and the Marquesas.

Known to the early explorers from the 16th century, they were not colonized until 1774, when the Spaniards made an attempt to convert the natives to Catholicism. British missionaries followed in 1797 but had no greater success and were driven out by a civil war. They returned in 1812 with the King, who had gone into exile with them, but after he died in 1824, their influence waned and they left the islands.

French missionaries and traders returned in the 1830s and in 1843 the Society Islands became a protectorate and, in 1880, a colony. The other islands were added in 1903.

The Oceanic Settlements declared for de Gaulle in 1940 and the name was changed to French Polynesia in 1958.

French Polynesia

FIRST STAMPS ISSUED November 1958

CURRENCY

French (franc) and
CFP (Colonial franc pacifique)

Name for the former Oceanic Settlements. In 1957 the new name was agreed, and, following a referendum in November 1958, the inhabitants voted to become an overseas territory of the French Republic.

• Tahiti

The principal island of the French Oceanic Settlements. The first stamps issued specifically for the Settlements were overprinted TAHITI. These were replaced in 1893 with special stamps for the full colony, but further overprints for Tahiti appeared in 1903 and 1915.

Postal History

Letters can be found from Tahiti in the middle of the 19th century, usually carried privately to the nearest port – either in Australia or South America. The first stamps were local overprints on the French General issue, but these were replaced by a permanent issue in 1893.

From 1870–5 the local government, at its own cost, established a regular monthly service, first by sailing vessel and later by steamer, to send the mail from Tahiti via San Francisco to France.

In 1915 there were 14 POs in the group; 2 on Tahiti, Papeete and Taravao, and the rest spread among the other islands.

French steamers of the Messageries Maritimes did not reach as far as Tahiti until 1923 when a new service was introduced from New Caledonia to Marseille via New Hebrides, Oceanie and Panama. The first of these left Noumea for the return run on 15 August 1923 and arrived in Marseille on 27 October.

In 1928 a regular inter-island service was established by the government.

After 1958 the name of the colony was changed to French Polynesia.

Pitcairn Island

FIRST STAMPS New Zealand from June 1927
FIRST STAMPS ISSUED 15 October 1940

CURRENCY

1940	sterling
1968	100 cents = 1 New Zealand dollar

Island to the south-east of French Polynesia, discovered by Carteret in 1767. The first settlers were the Bounty mutineers who landed there in 1790. Their presence was not suspected until 1808. The island was formally annexed by Britain in 1838.

In 1856 a number of the inhabitants were moved to Norfolk Island because of the risk of famine but returned to Pitcairn between 1858 and 1864.

In 1898 the island was placed under the jurisdiction of the High Commissioner for the Western Pacific. Responsibility for administration was transferred to Fiji in 1952, but the island remained a Crown Colony. At its peak, the population reached about 250 but was down to 100 in the 1970s.

Postal History

With such a small and largely illiterate population, early letters are very uncommon. In the 1880s letters were sent by visiting ships, often American whalers and the missionary steamer *Pitcairn*. These are known with a straight line 'Pitcairn Island' usually struck in the lower left-hand corner. However, this was discontinued in 1900 when the service by the *Pitcairn* was withdrawn.

In 1921-6, Britain and New Zealand agreed to accept mail from the island. Handstamps were used inscribed 'Posted at Pitcairn Island — No stamps available'. In 1927 a New Zealand PA was opened and current New Zealand stamps were used until the stamps of the island were issued in 1940.

Palau Islands

FIRST STAMPS under Caroline Islands 12 October 1899
FIRST STAMPS ISSUED 1983

CURRENCY

up to 1899	Spanish (peseta)
1899–1914	German (mark)
1914–1945	Japanese (yen)
1945 to date	American (dollar)

Also known as the Pelew Islands, they were discovered by the Spaniards in the 17th century. It is recorded that an East India Company's packet, the *Antelope*, was wrecked there in 1783. Originally under Spanish control, they were administered as part of the Caroline Islands (q.v.). Sold to Germany in 1899 and occupied by Japan in 1914. Became a Japanese

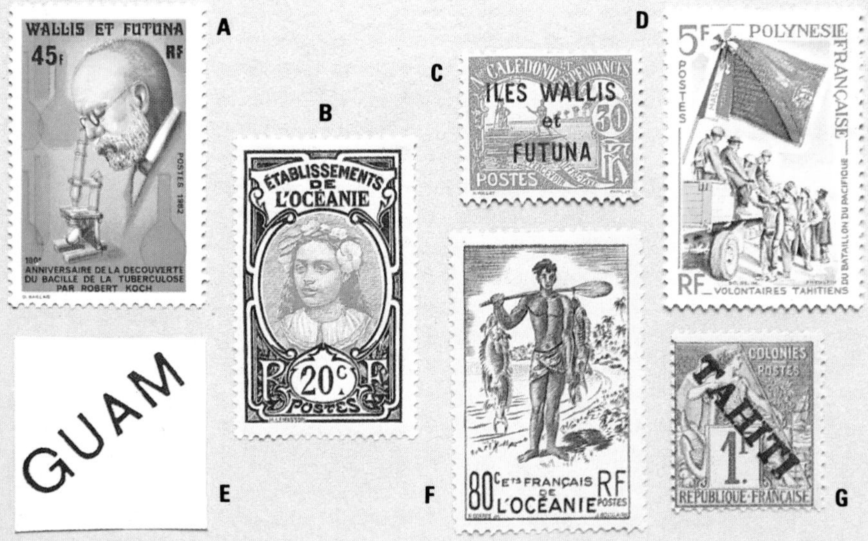
A
WALLIS ET FUTUNA
45F RF
100e ANNIVERSAIRE DE LA DECOUVERTE DU BACILLE DE LA TUBERCULOSE PAR ROBERT KOCH
B
ÉTABLISSEMENTS DE L'OCÉANIE
20c
POSTES
C
ILES WALLIS et FUTUNA
30
POSTES
D
5F POLYNESIE FRANÇAISE
RF VOLONTAIRES TAHITIENS
E
GUAM
F
80 Cts FRANÇAIS DE L'OCÉANIE RF POSTES
G
COLONIES POSTES
TAHITI
RÉPUBLIQUE FRANÇAISE

A Wallis & Futuna 1982; **B** Oceanic Settlements 1913; **C** Wallis & Futuna 1922; **D** French Polynesia 1964; **E** Guam: overprint 1899; **F** Oceanic Settlements 1948; **G** Tahiti 1893.

mandate in 1919 and captured by the Americans in September 1944. Became a trusteeship territory under the United Nations, administered by the USA. Gained independence in 1983.

Postal History
Very few early letters are recorded. It was not until German control that a regular mail service was introduced in 1901 by the Jaluit Company. This connected with Jaluit, Ponape and Yap in the Caroline and Marshall Islands (q.v.). Japanese stamps were used from 1914 to 1945 and American stamps from 1945 until the issue of their own adhesives in 1983.

• Mariana Islands

FIRST STAMPS ISSUED
German Colonial type overprinted 18 November 1899

CURRENCY	
up to 1899	Spanish (peseta)
1899–1914	German (mark)
1914–1944	Japanese (yen)
1944 to date	American (dollar)

Group of islands in the north Pacific, also known as the Ladrone. They were discovered by Magellan in his first crossing of the Pacific in 1519. The name Ladrone, or Thief, Islands was given because the inhabitants stole some of Magellan's goods, but they were renamed after the Spanish queen in the 17th century. Islands were administered by the Spaniards as part of the Philippine Islands until they were occupied by the USA during the Spanish-American War in 1898. The largest and most southerly island — Guam (q.v.) — was ceded to the USA after that and the remainder were occupied by the Americans until the islands were sold to Germany in 1899.

They remained German until occupied by the Japanese in 1914, and they were then a Japanese mandate until 1944, when they were re-occupied by the USA. Since World War II they have been administered by the USA as a trusteeship territory of the United Nations.

Postal History
All mail of the Spanish period is rare but there was a Spanish PO on Guam (q.v.). After the US occupation in 1898 some values of the stamps of the Spanish Philippines were overprinted MARIANAS ESPANOLAS. Germany introduced stamps on the day it took over administration and these are known cancelled with Spanish seals.

German stamps continued to be used until 1914, and two of the later issues (3 *pfennig* and 5 *mark*) are known on watermarked paper. These were never used in the islands but were sold in Berlin, after the Japanese had occupied. The Jaluit Company established mail lines throughout the northern Pacific in the early years of the 20th century and one of these, opened in 1904, was routed via Saipan in the Marianas. Service operated until July 1914. Adhesives of the Marianas are known cancelled with postmarks of the Sydney-Hong Kong Line and the Jaluit Line.

Japanese stamps were used from 1914 to 1944 and American stamps from 1945 until the present day.

• Guam

FIRST STAMPS Spanish Philippines until 1899
US stamps overprinted 7 July 1899

CURRENCY	
up to 1899	Spanish (peseta)
1899 to date	American (dollar)

Most southerly and largest of the Mariana or Ladrone Islands (q.v.). It was the administrative centre of the group when under Spanish control. In 1899 ceded to USA under the Treaty of Paris, at the end of the Spanish-American War.

Remained under USA control until occupied by the Japanese in 1941. Regained by the USA in 1945, and remains a US dependency.

Postal History
Until 1899 stamps of Spanish Philippines were used and a rare postmark MARIANAS was used on outgoing mail. After USA takeover in 1899, USA stamps overprinted GUAM were used for almost two years while the island was still under control of the Navy

Department. Thereafter USA stamps have been used, except during period of Japanese Occupation (1941-4). Local post was set up in 1930 to carry letters between some of the small towns on the island. Contemporary 2 cent and 4 cent stamps of the Philippine Islands were overprinted GUAM GUARD MAIL. This local post was discontinued in 1931 after a year.

• Caroline Islands

FIRST STAMPS ISSUED
German Colonial type overprinted 12 October 1899

CURRENCY	
1899–1914	German (mark)
1914–1945	Japanese (yen)
1945 onwards	American (dollar)

Pitcairn Islands
8d
SCHOOL 1949
A
POLYNESIAN STONE DEITY
20c
PITCAIRN ISLANDS
B
KAROLINEN
10 PFENNIG 10
C
REICHSPOST
Marianen
PF. 10 PF.
D

A Pitcairn Islands 1951; **B** Pitcairn Islands 1971; **C** Caroline Islands: German Colony 1901; **D** Mariana Islands: German Colony 1899.

Below
Gigantic stone money, Yap

Right
Native girl, Ngulu, Yap

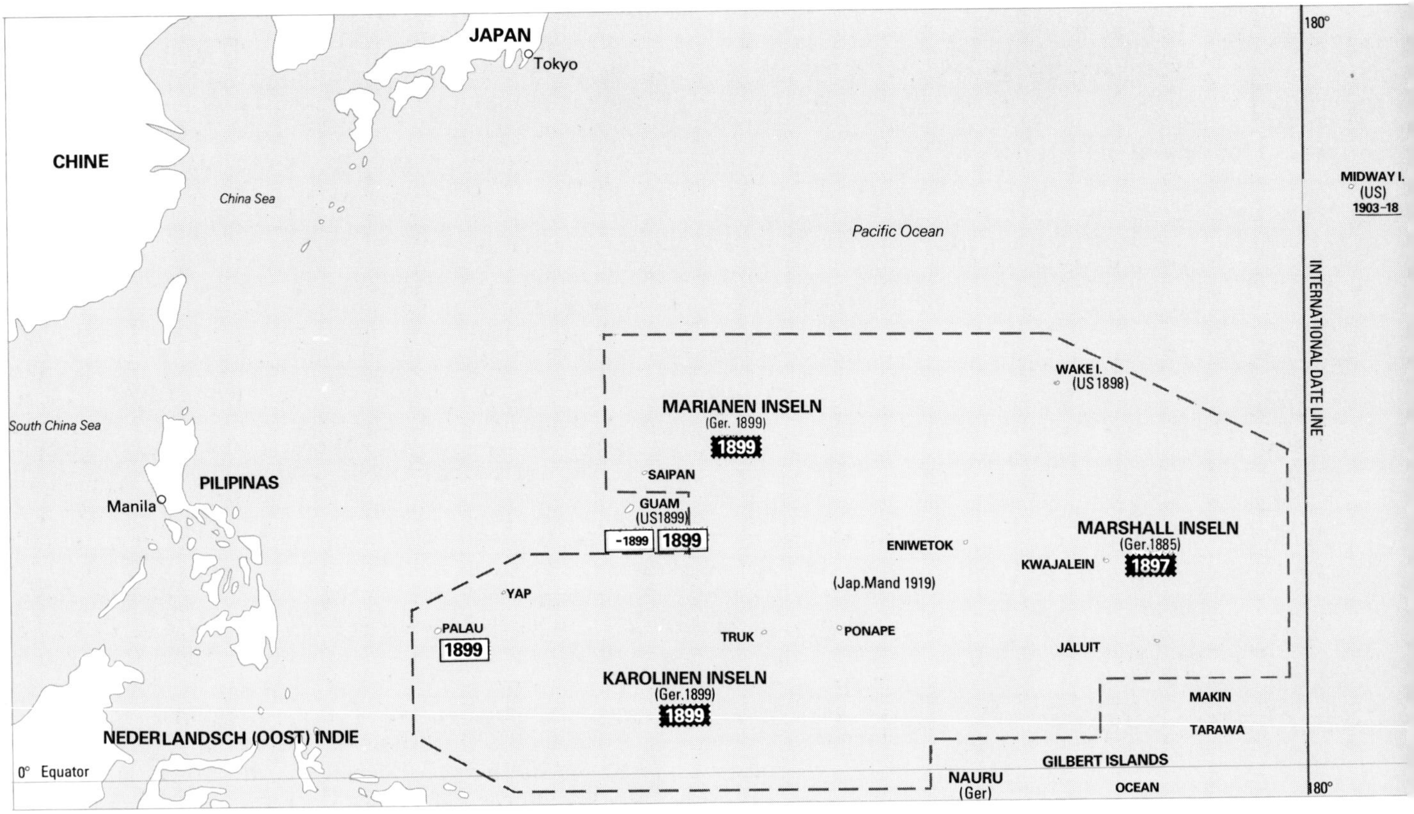
JAPAN
Tokyo
CHINE
China Sea
Pacific Ocean
180°
MIDWAY I.
(US)
1903–18
INTERNATIONAL DATE LINE
South China Sea
WAKE I.
(US 1898)
MARIANEN INSELN
(Ger. 1899)
1899
SAIPAN
PILIPINAS
Manila
GUAM
(US1899)
-1899
1899
ENIWETOK
MARSHALL INSELN
(Ger.1885)
KWAJALEIN
1897
(Jap.Mand 1919)
YAP
PALAU
1899
TRUK
PONAPE
JALUIT
KAROLINEN INSELN
(Ger.1899)
1899
MAKIN
TARAWA
NEDERLANDSCH (OOST) INDIE
GILBERT ISLANDS
0° Equator
NAURU
(Ger)
OCEAN
180°

Group of islands in the Pacific north of New Guinea including, among many others, Yap, Truk and Ponape. Palau (q.v.), administratively the most westerly of the group, is ethnically different. Islands first discovered by the Spanish and Portuguese in the 16th century and named after Charles II of Spain in 1686. Attempts in the 18th century to establish the Roman Catholic church there failed, but Spain maintained its claim to the group until 1875, when Britain protested because of its sphere of influence. Spain allowed its claim to lapse until the Germans occupied some of the islands in 1885. The resulting dispute was referred to the Pope, who awarded sovereignty to Spain, but with commercial concessions for Germany and Britain. The inhabitants did not accept European control and, during the 1890s, frequently attacked the Spanish garrison. The islands were ceded to Germany in June 1899 and the Spanish left in December that year.

Germany remained in control until invasion by Japan in October 1914. After the war it remained as a Japanese mandate until the end of World War II, when the group was handed over to the United Nations. In July 1947 the USA took over trusteeship for the UN and the islands achieved independence as Micronesia in 1983.

Postal History

All early covers were dependent on occasional vessels that visited the islands. No stamps were issued during the Spanish period and, although some Spanish military marks may exist, no postmark was issued.

Germany established a number of mail routes in the Pacific and, by the end of 1900, Yap and Ponape were on a regular route from German New Guinea to Hong Kong that connected with the European mail. Initially subsidized by the government as Reich Mail Steamer Lines, they were superseded in 1902 by a service operated by the Jaluit Company from the Marshall Islands (q.v.).

During 1905 and 1910 stamps of the Carolines were bisected owing to local shortages. That of 1905 was caused by a typhoon in which all 5 *pfennig* stamps were destroyed. From German surrender in 1914 until the end of World War II Japanese stamps were used; replaced by USA stamps in 1946.

Philatelically, the group began to break up in 1983, when Palau issued its first stamps. Stamps for the new state of Micronesia were issued in 1984.

Micronesia

FIRST STAMPS ISSUED 1984

CURRENCY

1984 US dollar

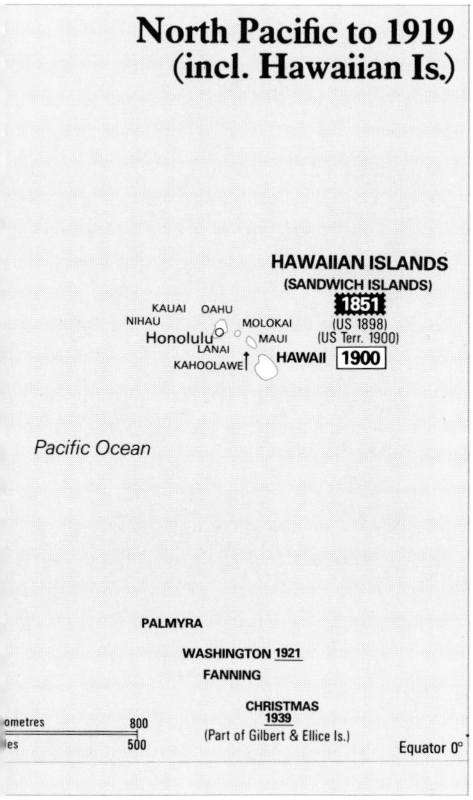
North Pacific to 1919
(incl. Hawaiian Is.)
HAWAIIAN ISLANDS
(SANDWICH ISLANDS)
1851
KAUAI
OAHU
NIHAU
MOLOKAI
(US 1898)
Honolulu
MAUI
(US Terr. 1900)
LANAI
KAHOOLAWE
HAWAII
1900
Pacific Ocean
PALMYRA
WASHINGTON 1921
FANNING
CHRISTMAS
1939
(Part of Gilbert & Ellice Is.)
800
500
Equator 0°

Name given to Caroline Islands when they became independent in 1983.

Nauru

> **FIRST STAMPS**
> NW Pacific Islands overprinted 1914–16
> **FIRST STAMPS ISSUED** 1916

CURRENCY

1889–1914	German (mark)
1914–1941	British (sterling)
1941–1945	Japanese (yen)
1945–1966	British (sterling)
1966 to date	Australian (dollar)

Island in the Pacific just south of the Equator, famous for its phosphate deposits. Discovered by Captain Fearn of the Royal Navy in 1798 but in the 1880s annexed by Germany and administered as part of the Marshall Islands (q.v.). Captured by the Australians in September 1914. Granted a temporary British mandate in 1916 and became a mandate under the League of Nations in 1919. Was placed jointly under Australian, British and New Zealand control because of its importance as a supplier of phosphates, but was administered by Australia until 1968. Occupied by Japan during World War II. Nauru became a United Nations trusteeship territory in 1945 and became independent on 1 February 1968.

Postal History
No PO on the island until 1905 when the stamps of Marshall Islands were released. When the Australians conquered the island in 1914, stocks of stamps were sent to New Guinea to be overprinted GRI. None of these were returned to the island and Australian stamps overprinted 'North West Pacific Islands' were used until 1916. Then control passed to the British government and stamps overprinted NAURU were issued in October 1916. They remained in use until 1924 when a series of stamps produced in Australia was issued.

Special stamps have been used in Nauru ever since and overprints for the Republic of Nauru were issued a day before the actual date of independence on 1 February 1968.

• Marshall Islands

> **FIRST STAMPS ISSUED**
> German Colonial Type overprinted 1897

CURRENCY

up to 1914	German (mark)
1914–1945	Japanese (yen)
1945–to date	American (dollar)

Group of islands in the North Pacific, including Jaluit, Kwajalein, and Eniwetok. Discovered in the 17th century by the Spaniards, but not developed as they were too far from the Philippines, the main administrative centre. Constituted a German colony on 15 October 1885 and administered from the capital on Jaluit.

Invaded by a Japanese force in September 1914. Became a mandated territory under the League of Nations, and a UN trusteeship territory in 1945.

Postal History
First Germany PO opened on 1 October 1888 but initially no stamps were available. Contemporary German stamps were placed on sale in March 1889, but can only be distinguished by their postmarks. In 1897 German colonial stamps were issued overprinted, and these together with later German issues were used until 1914. In 1901 the Jaluit company operated a mail service from the Marshall Islands to Sydney, and the following year extended the service to Hong Kong. Both of these lines connected with the main lines to Europe.

Japanese stamps were used from 1914 to 1944 and USA stamps since then. These can only be distinguished by the postmarks.

WAKE ISLAND

CURRENCY

American dollar

Small group in the mid-Pacific, north of the Marshall Islands. Placed under the jurisdiction of the US Navy Department in December 1934, having been annexed in 1898.

Wake Island had been selected by Pan American Airways as a port of call on their Clipper Service to the Philippines, and their first plane landed on 9 August 1935. It was the site of a heroic defence by American Marines against Japanese invasion. Group was finally occupied on 24 December 1941, and recaptured in 1945.

No special stamps issued.

Postal History
Although there was a hotel on one of the smaller islands, the mail was normally handled through Pan American

NAURU
POSTAGE & REVENUE
HIS MAJESTY'S JUBILEE.
1910-1935
2 TWO PENCE 2
A
UNION 1874-1974
CENTENARY OF THE UNIVERSAL POSTAL
REPUBLIC OF NAURU $1
B
MARSHALL-INSELN
20 PFENNIG 20
C
POSTAGE REVENUE
NAURU
1 ONE PENNY 1
D
NAURU 5/
POSTAGE
FIVE SHILLINGS
E

A Nauru: Australian Mandate 1935; B Nauru: Independent 1974; C Marshall Islands: German Colony 1901; D Nauru: British Mandate 1915; E Nauru: Australian Mandate 1954.

Airways to Honolulu or Guam. A civil PO was established on 1 May 1961, and USA stamps used. Single PO handles both civil and military mail.

MIDWAY ISLANDS

CURRENCY

American dollar

Small group of islands in the mid-Pacific area to the west of the Hawaiian Islands. Discovered by the Royal Navy in 1859 and occupied by the USA in 1903, when a station for the Transpacific cable was built there. In 1936 became a stopping-point on the Pan American Airways Clipper Service from Hawaii to Manila. Attacked by the Japanese in December 1941, but held out and was the site of a major naval action in June 1942 in

POST OFFICE

Child outside post office, Nauru

Mailboat, 1850s

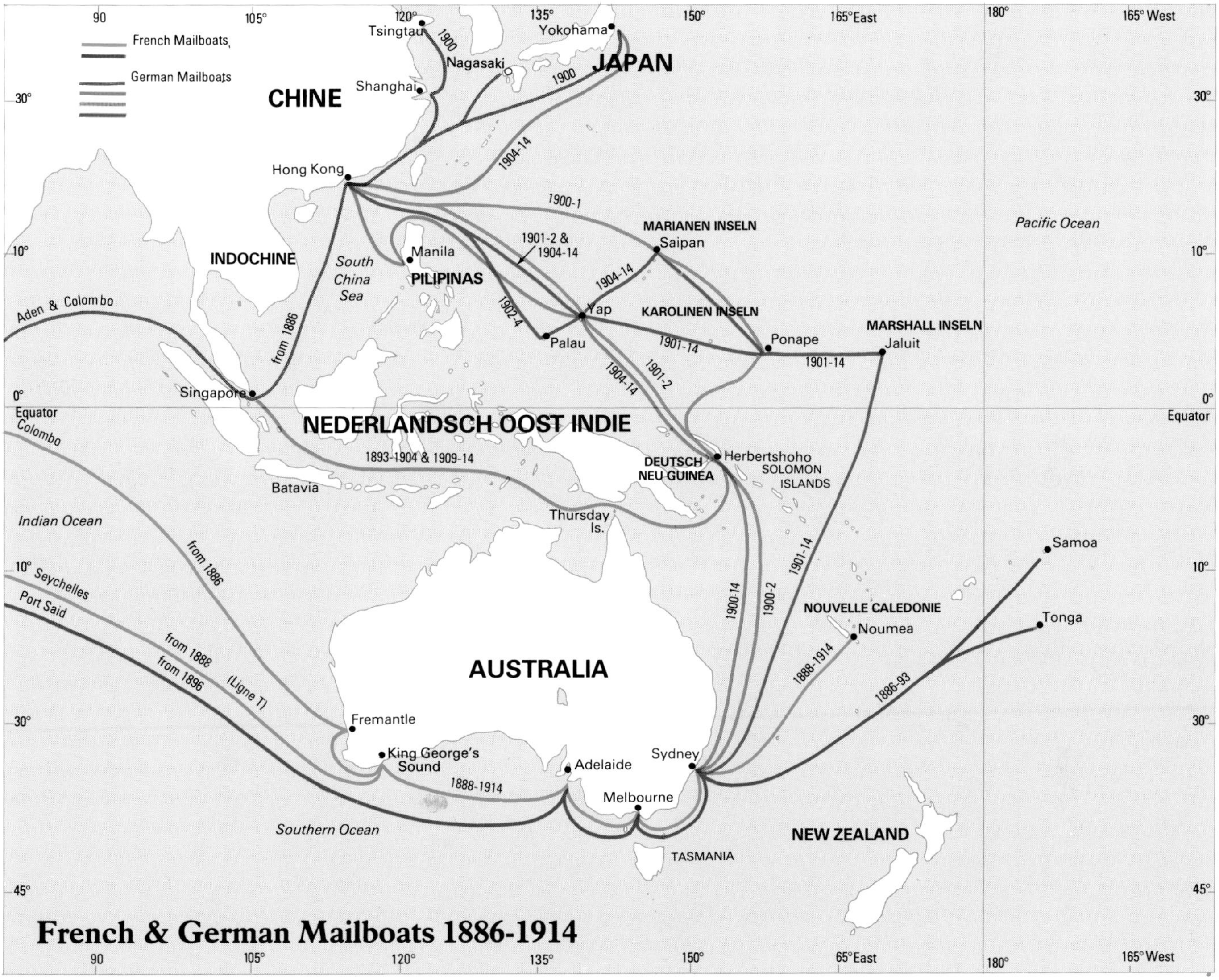
French Mailboats
German Mailboats
CHINE
JAPAN
Tsingtau
Yokohama
Nagasaki
Shanghai
Hong Kong
INDOCHINE
South China Sea
Manila
PILIPINAS
MARIANEN INSELN
Saipan
KAROLINEN INSELN
Yap
Palau
Ponape
MARSHALL INSELN
Jaluit
Pacific Ocean
Aden & Colombo
from 1886
Singapore
Equator
Colombo
NEDERLANDSCH OOST INDIE
1893-1904 & 1909-14
Batavia
DEUTSCH NEU GUINEA
Herbertshoho
SOLOMON ISLANDS
Thursday Is.
Indian Ocean
Seychelles
Port Said
from 1888
from 1896
(Ligne T)
AUSTRALIA
Fremantle
King George's Sound
1888-1914
Adelaide
Sydney
Melbourne
TASMANIA
Southern Ocean
NEW ZEALAND
NOUVELLE CALEDONIE
Noumea
Samoa
Tonga
1886-93
1888-1914
1900-14
1900-2
1901-14
1900-1
1901-2 & 1904-14
1904-14
1902-4
1901-2
1900
French & German Mailboats 1886-1914

which the Japanese carrier fleet was largely destroyed.

No special stamps issued.

Postal History

A USA civil PO was in operation between 1903 and 1918; administered as part of the Hawaiian Postal Sector. There was no PO on the island between the wars, though unofficial cachets were placed on mail by Pan American Airways. The military took over in November 1940. After the war, and up to the present day, Midway has remained a military station and there is no civil PO.

French and German Mailboats in the Pacific

The French shipping line Messageries Maritimes was operating in the Indian Ocean to service Mauritius and Réunion as early as 1864. This became Ligne T in 1867 and was extended to Australia and New Caledonia in 1888.

The first service was routed via Seychelles and Mauritius, but in 1888 the ships passed direct from Seychelles to King George's Sound. In 1896 the service was altered again and sailed direct from Colombo to Fremantle in Western Australia. Throughout this period, the shipping points in Eastern Australia remained the same — Adelaide, Melbourne, Sydney — and thence to Noumea in New Caledonia.

In 1903 the pressure of the German service from Singapore to New Guinea and on to the Marshall and Mariana Islands caused the French to reorganize their service. The regularity of the mail trips increased but the ships did not carry PAs on board. This service ended with the outbreak of war in 1914.

In 1886 Norddeutsche Lloyd of Bremen began a service to Singapore and China via Aden, Colombo, Singapore, Hong Kong and Shanghai. It

Via California
Mr. Augustine Heard
Boston
Massatts
U.S.A.
HONGKONG
FOUR CENTS

Letter carried by Pacific Mail Steamship Company from Hong Kong to San Francisco postmarked 15 July 1868

was extended to Japan in 1900. Later on, every other steamer on a monthly service went to Tsingtao. In the period between 1886 and 1900 there was a feeder line from Hong Kong to Nagasaki.

Also in 1886 a service was opened to Australia via Port Said, Adelaide, Melbourne and Sydney and a feeder service was initiated between Sydney, Tonga and Samoa. This was closed in 1893 because it was unprofitable.

Other branch lines were established as follows:

Singapore to German New Guinea in 1893–1900 and in 1909–14
Hong Kong to Sydney via Saipan, Ponape and German New Guinea 1900–01
Hong Kong to Sydney via Yap and German New Guinea 1901–02
Singapore to Sydney via German New Guinea 1900–04
Yokohama to Sydney via Hong Kong, Manila, Yap, and New Guinea 1904-14

In 1901, the Jaluit Company began services in the Marshall, Mariana and Caroline Islands, as follows:

Sydney to Palau via Jaluit, Ponape and Yap 1901–02
Sydney to Hong Kong via Jaluit, Ponape, Yap and Palau 1902–04
Sydney to Hong Kong via Jaluit, Ponape, Saipan and Yap 1904–14

All German lines closed in 1914 and did not reopen.

After the war, the French service was reorganized again and from 1920 to 1923 operated only to Australia and Noumea, but in 1923 the line to Noumea began to sail via the Panama Canal and the Australian route was extended to terminate at Brisbane. This service continued until 1940. The New Caledonia (Noumea) line was routed via Tahiti and New Hebrides. It continued until World War II. This was the only French service which was 'Transpacific' and linked with local services in all three island groups.

Transpacific mail

No regular subsidised mail contract existed for a service from China and Japan before 1867. In 1866, the Pacific Mail Steam Navigation Co. gained a contract from the US Government for a regular fortnightly service from San Francisco to Hong Kong via Hawaii and Yokohama. Four ships were built for this route and they were the largest wooden coal-burning ships ever built. As they were not ready by the start of 1867, on 1 January that year the *Colorado* made the inaugural voyage to Hong Kong. This was successfully completed but it was not until 1868 that there were sufficient ships to fulfil the contract.

In 1867, Hong Kong and the USA signed a convention to establish the rates of postage at 8 cents (Hong Kong) or 10 cents (USA). These rates were introduced after ratification in 1868. At the same time the American POs in Shanghai and Japan were opened and a feeder service was introduced to carry mail to Japan and connect with the main service to Hong Kong.

PMSNC retained the monopoly of this service until 1877. At that time, Hong Kong joined the UPU, the convention on postal rates was no longer necessary and the Oriental and Oceanic Steamship Co. began an alternative service.

In 1892, a further service from Hong Kong to Vancouver was opened by the Canadian Pacific Railway to connect with their newly completed transcontinental service. Mail was routed from Vancouver to Toronto and thence via Buffalo to New York to connect with the Atlantic service.

ASIA

'The mysterious East' has been a magnet to explorers, traders and tourists over the centuries. It stretches from the Middle East, the seat of modern civilization, to the Far East which was hardly explored by Westerners until the 18th and 19th centuries.

Encompassing a wide range of cultures, from the Sumerian civilization, and its clay tablets on which messages were written, to the early Chinese dynasties and the Mongol armies which marched through Russia into eastern Europe, it is probably one of the more difficult continents in which to provide a balanced account of the various territories. The waxing and waning of power over the centuries and the generally loose control which the centralized governments were able to exert meant that teams of messengers had to be employed at a very early stage. Coupled with this, the European demand for products such as silk and spices led to the establishment of overland merchant links even before the Portuguese gained the route to the East by sea in the 15th and 16th centuries.

Because of the Levant's involvement in trade from earliest times and Turkish strength in Europe in the Middle Ages, and up to the end of the Balkan Wars, the continent of Asia has been dealt with by means of a general south-easterly sweep from Turkey, through the Middle East to India and south-east Asia. From modern Indonesia, the progress turns north and finally covers China and Japan.

Russia in Asia, one of the greatest land areas in the world, has followed the postal development of that nation as a whole and is dealt with under Russia in Europe. The special stamps issued in eastern Russia during the Revolution have also been treated under Europe where all the issues of that period are dealt with in one section.

To the south of the continent spreads the expanse of the Indian Ocean, one of the earliest trading routes after the Mediterranean. This section is dealt with after Africa, but in many ways the history of the development of these routes is a subject in itself. Europeans needed to develop under their own control a sea route to the trading centres of south and south-east Asia and this led to the colonial development of southern Africa and the Indian coast. This, in turn, led to the postal development of the region and philatelic issues which are depicted and explained.

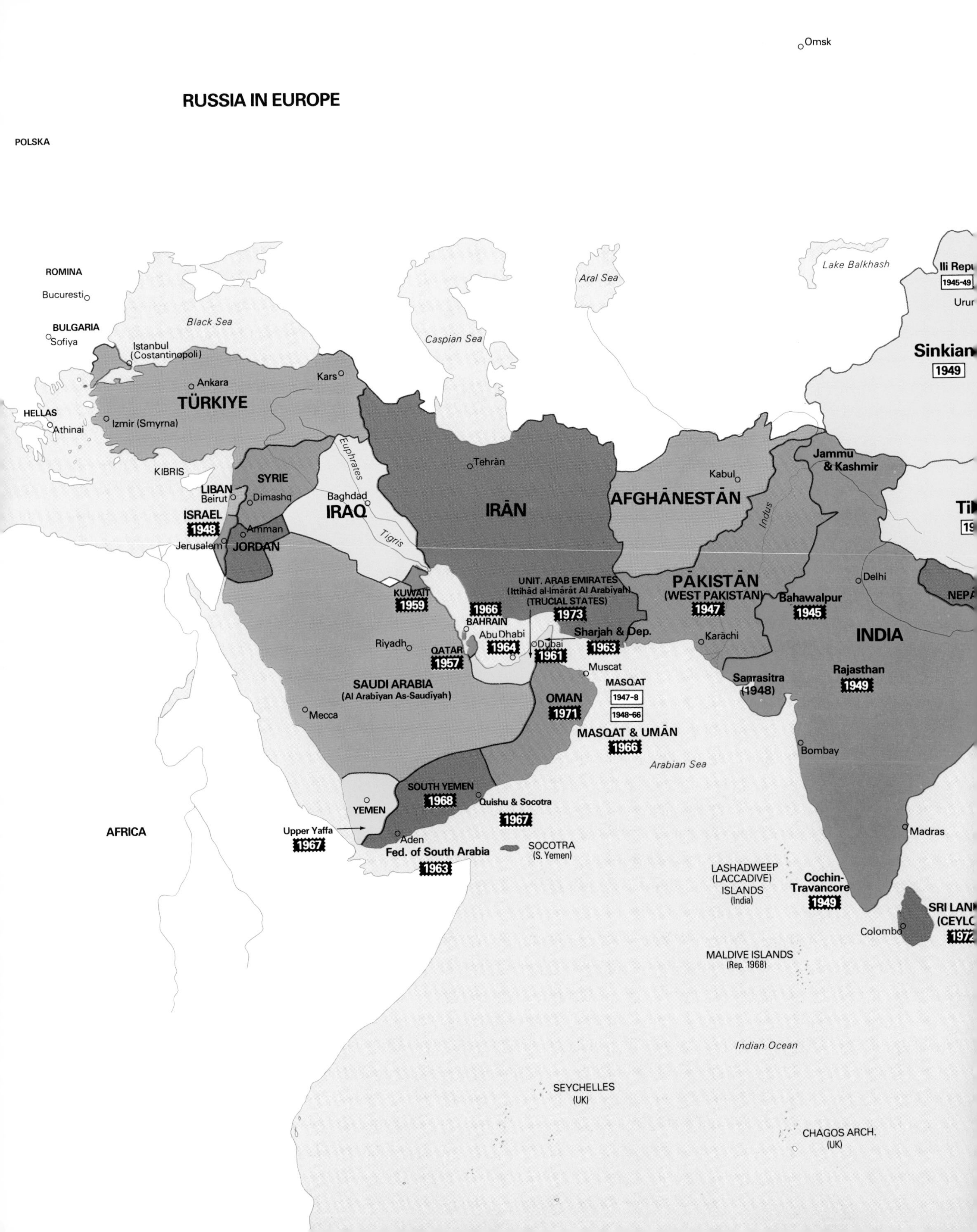

Omsk
RUSSIA IN EUROPE
POLSKA
ROMINA
Bucuresti
BULGARIA
Sofiya
Black Sea
Aral Sea
Lake Balkhash
Caspian Sea
Ili Repu
1945-49
Urur
Sinkian
1949
Istanbul
(Costantinopoli)
Ankara
Kars
TÜRKIYE
HELLAS
Athinai
Izmir (Smyrna)
Euphrates
Tehrān
Kabul
Jammu
& Kashmir
KIBRIS
SYRIE
LIBAN
Beirut
Dimashq
Baghdad
IRAQ
IRĀN
AFGHĀNESTĀN
Indus
ISRAEL
1948
Amman
Tigris
Jerusalem
JORDAN
Delhi
UNIT. ARAB EMIRATES
(Ittihād al-Imārāt Al Arabiyah)
(TRUCIAL STATES)
1973
PĀKISTĀN
(WEST PAKISTAN)
1947
Bahawalpur
1945
NEPA
KUWAIT
1959
1966
BAHRAIN
Sharjah & Dep.
1963
Karāchi
INDIA
Riyadh
QATAR
1957
Abu Dhabi
1964
Dubai
1961
Muscat
Sanrasitra
(1948)
Rajasthan
1949
SAUDI ARABIA
(Al Arabīyan As-Saudīyah)
MASQAT
1947-8
1948-66
OMAN
1971
Mecca
MASQAT & UMĀN
1966
Bombay
Arabian Sea
SOUTH YEMEN
1968
Quishu & Socotra
1967
YEMEN
AFRICA
Upper Yaffa
1967
Aden
Fed. of South Arabia
1963
SOCOTRA
(S. Yemen)
Madras
LASHADWEEP
(LACCADIVE)
ISLANDS
(India)
Cochin-
Travancore
1949
SRI LAN
(CEYLO
1972
Colombo
MALDIVE ISLANDS
(Rep. 1968)
Indian Ocean
SEYCHELLES
(UK)
CHAGOS ARCH.
(UK)

Asia from 1945

RUSSIA IN ASIA
Lake Baikal
Asia from 1945
SAKHALIN
KURIL IS.
Ulan Bator
MONGOLIA
1951
NE Provinces (Nats.)
1946-48
NE Provinces (Comms.)
1946-51
Harbin
MANCHURIA
1951
Inner Mongolia
Vladivostok
HOKKAIDO
Mukden
Beijing (Peking)
CHINESE REPUBLIC
1949
Lyao-Tung
1946
1950
NORTH KOREA
1946
P'yongyang
Sea of Japan
HONSHU
JAPAN
Seoul
SOUTH KOREA
1946
Tokyo
Yellow Sea
Osaka
Hwang Ho
KYUSHU
Shanghai
Yangtse-Kiang
RYUKYU IS.
1948
1972
OKINAWA
BHUTAN
1955
Dacca
BURMA
Canton
Macao (Port.)
Hong Kong (UK)
TAIWAN (FORMOSA)
1949
Pacific Ocean
Ha-noi
VIETNAM (VIET MINH)
1945
NORTH VIETNAM
1954
Vientiene
LAOS
1951
Mekong
THAILAND (SIAM)
Rangoon
VIETNAM 1951
SOC REP OF VIETNAM
1976
LUZON
Manila
PILIPINAS
Bangkok
SOUTH VIETNAM
1955
SOUTH VIETNAM (VIET CONG)
1963
KĀMPUCHEA (CAMBODGE)
1951
Th-Pho-Ho Chei Minh (Saigon)
South China Sea
GUAM
YAP
MINDANAO
PALAU
TRUK IS.
NICOBAR ISLANDS (India)
Sabah
1964
FEDERATION OF MALAYA
1957
MALAYSIA
1963
Brunei
Kuala Lumpur
Sarawak
Malacca (Melaka)
Penang (Palau Pinang)
Johore Negri Sembilan
Pahang Selangon
Trengganu
Kedah
Perak
Kelantan
Perlis
SINGAPORE
1948
Riau-Lingga Arch.
1954
Kalimantan (Borneo)
SUMATERA
Sulawesi (Celebes)
South Maluku
1950
NEDERLANDS NIEUW GUINEA
1950
West New Guinea
1962
West Irian
1963
Irian Jaya
1973
REPUBLIK INDONESIA
1950
INDONESIA
1950
Java Sea
Jakarta(Batavia)
Banda Sea
JAWA
TIMOR
Timor Sea
AUSTRALIA
COCOS OR KEELING IS.
1963
(Australia)
1966-9
1969
CHRISTMAS I. (UK)
1946 8
1948-58
1958

Turkish (Ottoman) Empire

(*see also* the Ottoman Empire in Europe p.113)

The Ottoman Empire reached its furthest extent in 1648 when its sultan ruled from the gates of Vienna to the Persian Gulf and included within his dominions the coasts of North Africa and the Black Sea. Only a decisive defeat in Malta had blocked the way still further west. After defeat at the hands of Catherine the Great of Russia decline was continuous from 1774 to the end of World War I. By the time of the first stamp issue (1863) the Ottoman Empire still comprised most of the Balkans (except southern Greece) as far as the Danube, and much of the Near East. Successive issues, therefore, were used in an ever-contracting area as territories were lost.

Postal History

The earliest Turkish handstamps known date from 1840 and it is probable that only an official service operated between provincial capitals before this time. The right to organize services of couriers was granted to Russia in 1720 and to Austria in 1739. Both set up a PO in Constantinople in 1748. Britain, France and Italy had all established posts in the Turkish Empire before 1840. Until 1914 most mail leaving the Empire was sent by one or the other.

The right of resident foreigners to run their own postal services grew from the 'Capitulations'. These were extra-territorial rights negotiated by treaties for the purposes of trade since 1535. Capitulations were abrogated on 9 September 1914 and foreign POs were closed down. Capitulations were restored between 10 August 1920 and 24 July 1923 and some foreign POs were re-opened.

Turkey

FIRST STAMPS ISSUED May 1863

CURRENCY

1863	40 paras = 1 piastre
1929	40 paras = 1 kurus
	100 kurus = 1 lira (TD)
1942	100 paras = 1 Kurus
1947	100 kurus = 1 lira

The gradual erosion of the Ottoman Empire was hastened by World War I. By 1919, Turkey in Asia was reduced to its present boundaries, except for some difficulties in the establishment of the Syrian border, which was not finalised until 1939. The collapse of internal government allowed Greece to invade through Izmir (Smyrna) in 1919, but the Greeks were repulsed by a reconstituted Turkish Army led by Kemal Ataturk. A confrontation with the Western Allies at Charnak in 1923 was avoided and Ataturk welded the factions of the nation into a single unit. Turkey remained neutral for most of World War II, but took part in the Korean War and subsequently became part of NATO.

• Austrian POs in Turkish Empire

FIRST STAMPS Turkish 1863
FIRST STAMPS ISSUED 1 June 1867

CURRENCY

1863	100 Soldi = 1 Florin
1886	Turkish

An overland courier service established after the Peace of Passarowitz (1721) was recognized in 1739. In 1748 an Austrian PO was set up in Galata separately from the Constantinople embassy, and the service extended to Smyrna. For POs with dates *see* map. After 1836 mail was carried by the Austrian Lloyd Steam Navigation Company, based in Trieste, which operated TPOs and whose agents acted as postmasters.

Used stamps of Lombardy-Venetia ('Austrian Italy') in 1863-7: dates of issue:

Constantinople 1 December 1863
Danubian Provinces 17 February 1864
Other Levant offices 14 April 1864

• ROPiT (Russian POs in Turkish Empire)

FIRST STAMPS Russian November 1862
FIRST STAMPS ISSUED 1 January 1863

CURRENCY

1863	As Russia
1900	40 paras = 1 piastre

Though Russian consular couriers carried despatches between Constantinople and St Petersburg from 1721, a regular Russian postal service was a consequence of the Treaty of Kutchkuk Kainarji (1774). A consular PO was opened in Constantinople (Pera; used handstamps from c.1830), a mailboat plied between Constantinople and Kherson from 1779, and an overland mail route was opened in 1781 (Constantinople - Giurgiu - Bucharest - Focsani-Jassy-Bratzlav). This was suspended during various wars: 1787-92, 1806-12, 1828-9, and 1854-6. In 1856, after the Crimean War, the Russian service was entrusted to RUSSKOE OBSHCHESTVO PAROKHODSTVA i TORGOVLI (ROPiT; Russian Company of Trade and Navigation) with a PO at Constantinople (Galata) and PAs at every port-of-call. Handstamps were used from 1859 at Constantinople and from 1862 on ROPiT ships. There was direct transmission between POs; all external mail was routed via Odessa into the Imperial Russian PO. Numeral cancellers were allocated to ports in 1862: Batum, 777; Trebizond, 778; Mytilene, 779; Smyrna, 780; Merson, 781; Alexandretta, 782; Beirut, 783; Jaffa, 784; Alexandria, 785; Salonica, 787; and to many others in later periods. From May 1868 the ROPiT agencies were given the status of Russian POs abroad and surviving consular POs were closed.

Individually overprinted stamps were issued in 1909 for the following POs: Galata, Kerassunde, Trebizond, Rizeh, Dardanelles, Smyrna, Beirut, Jaffa, Jerusalem, Mytilene, Salonica, Mount Athos.

All Russian POs on Turkish soil

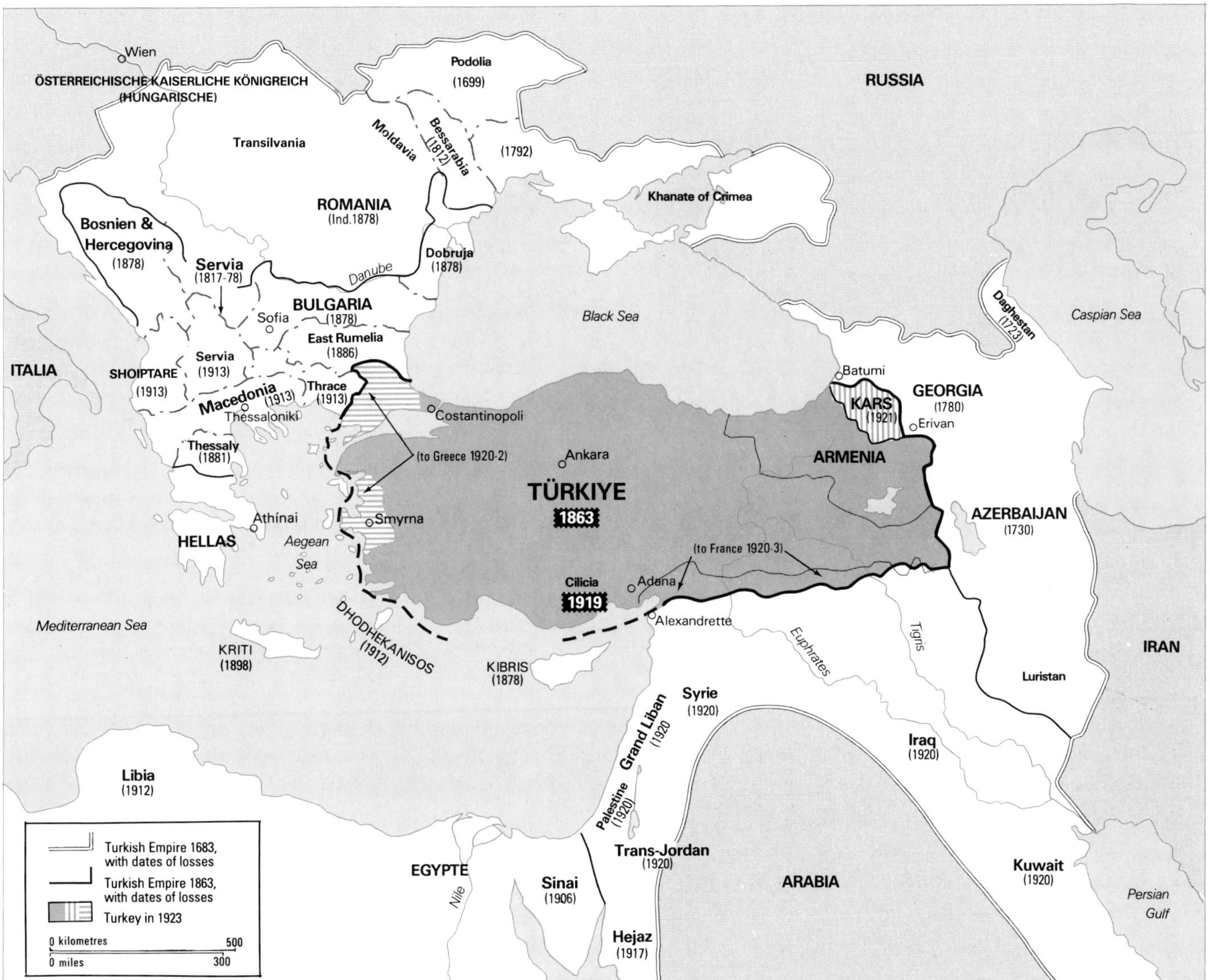
Wien
ÖSTERREICHISCHE KAISERLICHE KÖNIGREICH
(HUNGARISCHE)
Podolia
(1699)
RUSSIA
Transilvania
Moldavia
Bessarabia
(1812)
(1792)
Khanate of Crimea
ROMANIA
(Ind.1878)
Bosnien &
Hercegovina
(1878)
Servia
(1817-78)
Danube
Dobruja
(1878)
BULGARIA
(1878)
Sofia
East Rumelia
(1886)
Black Sea
Daghestan
(1723)
Caspian Sea
ITALIA
SHOIPTARE
(1913)
Servia
(1913)
Macedonia
(1913)
Thrace
(1913)
Thessaloniki
Costantinopoli
Batumi
KARS
(1921)
GEORGIA
(1780)
Erivan
Thessaly
(1881)
(to Greece 1920-2)
Ankara
ARMENIA
TÜRKIYE
1863
Athínai
Smyrna
AZERBAIJAN
(1730)
HELLAS
Aegean
Sea
(to France 1920-3)
Cilicia
1919
Adana
Alexandrette
Mediterranean Sea
DHODHEKANISOS
(1912)
KRITI
(1898)
KIBRIS
(1878)
Euphrates
Tigris
IRAN
Luristan
Syrie
(1920)
Grand Liban
(1920)
Iraq
(1920)
Libia
(1912)
Palestine
(1920)
Trans-Jordan
(1920)
Turkish Empire 1683, with dates of losses
Turkish Empire 1863, with dates of losses
Turkey in 1923
0 kilometres 500
0 miles 300
EGYPTE
Nile
Sinai
(1906)
ARABIA
Kuwait
(1920)
Persian
Gulf
Hejaz
(1917)
Red Sea

Turkish Empire 1683-1923

were closed on or before 30 September 1914 (though those in places ceded to Greece in 1913 may have remained open later). Though some ROPiT agencies re-opened briefly in 1919, the postal service failed for lack of ships in White Russian hands; stamps were sold to collectors rather than used for postage.

• Wrangel Army Refugee Post

FIRST STAMPS late November 1920 (suppressed 31 May 1921)

CURRENCY

Depreciated Wrangel roubles

Post organized by General Wrangel to serve White Russian refugees (military and civilian) from the Crimea, lodged in camps mainly round Constantinople. There were in addition camps on Lemnos, in Belgrade, at Cattaro (Kotor in Yugoslavia) and Bizerta. (*See also* South Russia *under* Europe).

• French Levant (POs in Turkish Empire)

FIRST STAMPS ISSUED 5 August 1885

CURRENCY

1885 25 centimes = 1 piastre
1921 Turkish

French PO was opened in Constantinople in 1812. Suspended in 1827-35 as a consequence of the Greek War of

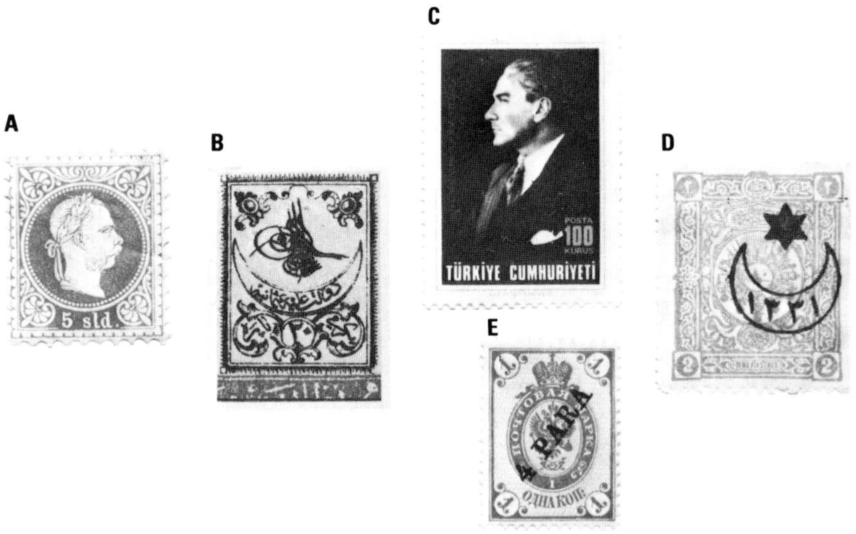
A
B
C
D
E
5 sld
POSTA
100
KURUŞ
TÜRKIYE CUMHURIYETI
4 PARA

A Austrian POs in Turkey 1867; **B** Turkey 1863;
C Turkey 1973; **D** Turkey 1915. **E** Russian POs in Turkey 1863;

Independence. After the closures of 13 October 1914, only Constantinople reopened August 1921 – July 1923.

Used stamps of France 1857-85 (identifiable by various diamond-of-dots obliterations).

• British POs in Turkish Empire (British Levant)

FIRST STAMPS British 1854
FIRST STAMPS ISSUED 1 April 1885

CURRENCY

1885 40 paras = 1 piastre
1886 Turkish

British Embassy mail started in 1832. In November 1854 an Army PO was established in Constantinople as a sorting and forwarding office for forces in the Crimea. The PO was opened for public service (oblit. 'C' in oval of bars) in September 1857; further POs were opened in Smyrna in 1872 (oblit. F87) and Beirut in 1873 (oblit. G 06). A second office was opened at Stamboul (oblit. S in oval bars) in 1884 but this was closed in the 1890s and did not reopen until 1908.

Because of speculation with Turkish currency, stamps overprinted in Turkish currency were issued on 1 April 1885. These were used concurrently with British adhesives and, later, stamps in British currency overprinted LEVANT. The latter were used for prepayment of parcels where the value of the contents was expressed in sterling.

An office was opened at Salonica in 1900 but only circular postmarks were used. All offices were closed on 30 September 1914, but the Smyrna office was reopened during 1919-22 and used unoverprinted adhesives.

Constantinople had a British Army PO in 1918-20 and a civilian PO with overprinted stamps was open from 1920 to 1923.

• German POs in Turkish Empire

FIRST STAMPS North German Confederation 1 March 1870; Germany 1872
FIRST STAMPS ISSUED 1884

A Constantinople office was opened at Pera on 1 March 1870, but moved to Galata on 1 October 1877; a branch office was placed at Stamboul on 1 January 1876. Short-lived branches operated at Büyükdere 1880-4 and Therapia 1884-8. Later offices: Jaffa (1 October 1898), Jerusalem, Smyrna, Beirut, Pera (all 1 March 1900), were closed on 30 September 1914.

• Italian POs in Turkish Empire

FIRST STAMPS Italy 1873
FIRST STAMPS ISSUED 1908 (Constantinople)

CURRENCY

1908 As Turkey

Both Venice and Naples maintained postal connections with the Levant in the 18th century but these had lapsed before Unification. In 1873 Italian PAs were established in Constantinople, Smyrna, and Beirut. These were suppressed in 1883. From 1901 in Albania (q.v.) and 1908 elsewhere, Italian POs were opened (some by threat of force): Constantinople (Galata, Pera, Stamboul) 1 June 1908; Smyrna, Jerusalem, Salonica, and Valona.

Used stamps of Italian POs Abroad (ESTERO overprints) 1 January 1874-December 1883.

Stamps of Italy were used in Constantinople because of shortages caused by collectors. Aegean Islands issues, *see* Greece.

• Constantinople

First separately overprinted (COSTANTINOPOLI) stamps February 1909.

• Jerusalem

First separately overprinted (GERUSALEMME) stamps February 1909.

• Salonica

First separately overprinted (SALONICCO) stamps February 1909.

• Romanian POs in the Turkish Empire

FIRST STAMPS 16 March 1896

CURRENCY

As Turkey

TPO was placed aboard a Romanian Steamship Company vessel to carry

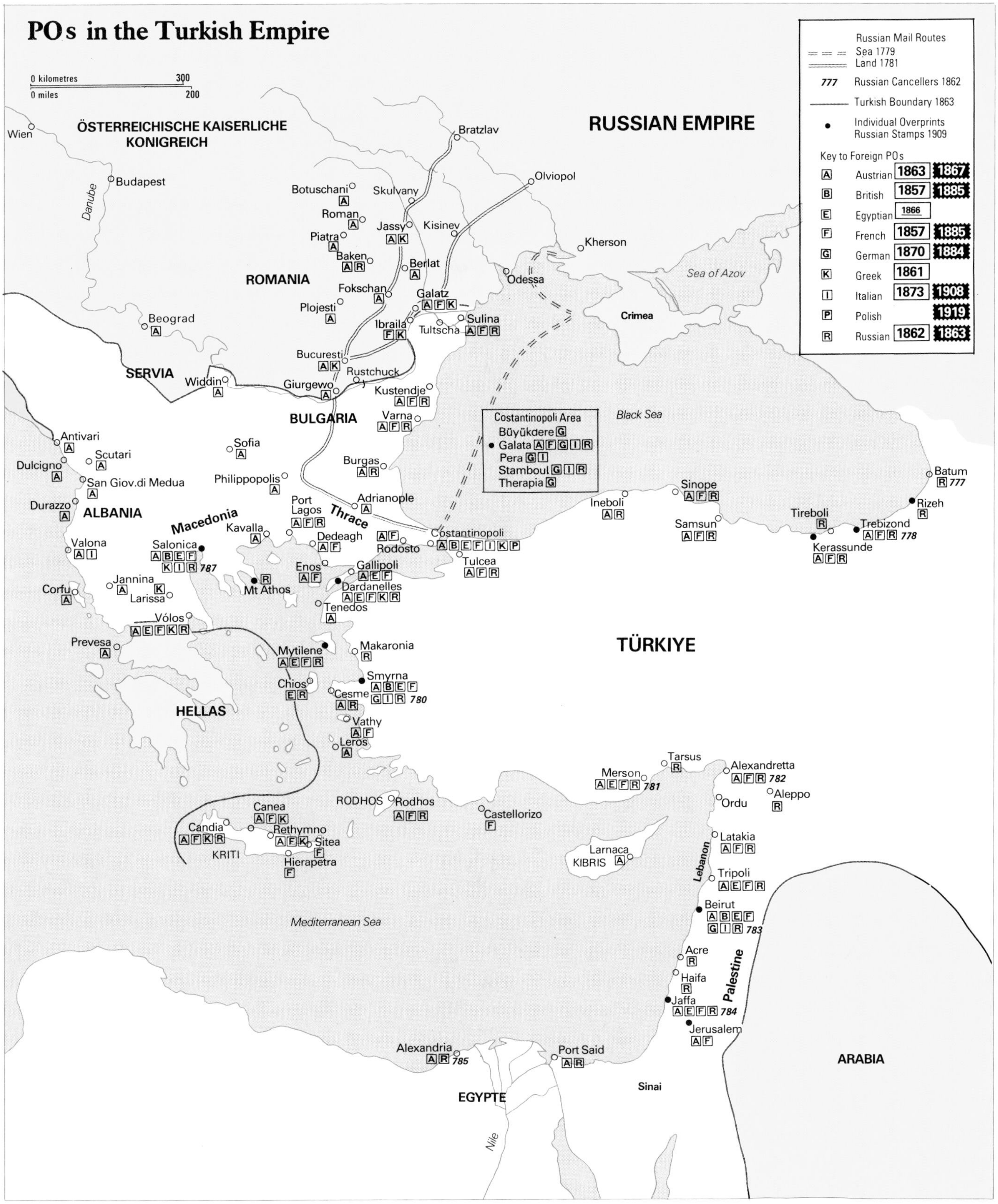
POs in the Turkish Empire
0 kilometres 300
0 miles 200
Russian Mail Routes
Sea 1779
Land 1781
777 Russian Cancellers 1862
Turkish Boundary 1863
Individual Overprints Russian Stamps 1909
Key to Foreign POs
A Austrian 1863 1867
B British 1857 1885
E Egyptian 1866
F French 1857 1885
G German 1870 1884
K Greek 1861
I Italian 1873 1908
P Polish 1919
R Russian 1862 1863
RUSSIAN EMPIRE
ÖSTERREICHISCHE KAISERLICHE KONIGREICH
Wien
Budapest
Danube
Bratzlav
Olviopol
Kherson
Odessa
Crimea
Sea of Azov
Botuschani A
Skulvany
Roman A
Jassy AK
Kisinev
Piatra A
Baken AR
Berlat A
ROMANIA
Fokschan A
Galatz AFK
Plojesti A
Ibraila FK
Sulina
Tultscha AFR
Beograd A
SERVIA
Widdin A
Bucuresti AK
Rustchuck
Giurgewo A
Kustendje AFR
BULGARIA
Varna AFR
Black Sea
Costantinopoli Area
Büyükdere G
Galata AFGIR
Pera GI
Stamboul GIR
Therapia G
Antivari A
Scutari A
Dulcigno A
Sofia A
Burgas AR
San Giov.di Medua A
Philippopolis A
Durazzo A
ALBANIA
Port Lagos AFR
Thrace
Adrianople A
Macedonia
Kavalla A
Dedeagh AF
AF Rodosto
Costantinopoli ABEFIKP
Valona AI
Salonica ABEF KIR 787
Enos AF
Gallipoli AEF
Tulcea AFR
Ineboli AR
Sinope AFR
Samsun AFR
Tireboli R
Trebizond AFR 778
Kerassunde AFR
Rizeh R
Batum R 777
Jannina A
K Larissa
Mt Athos R
Dardanelles AEFKR
Corfu A
Tenedos A
Vólos AEFKR
Prevesa A
Mytilene AEFR
Makaronia R
TÜRKIYE
Chios ER
Smyrna ABEF GIR 780
Cesme AR
HELLAS
Vathy AF
Leros A
Tarsus R
Merson AEFR 781
Alexandretta AFR 782
Ordu
Aleppo R
RODHOS Rodhos AFR
Castellorizo F
Canea AFK
Candia AFKR
Rethymno AFK
Sitea F
KRITI
Hierapetra F
Larnaca
KIBRIS A
Lebanon
Latakia AFR
Tripoli AEFR
Beirut ABEF GIR 783
Mediterranean Sea
Acre R
Palestine
Haifa R
Jaffa AEFR 784
Jerusalem AF
Alexandria AR 785
Port Said AR
ARABIA
Sinai
EGYPTE
Nile

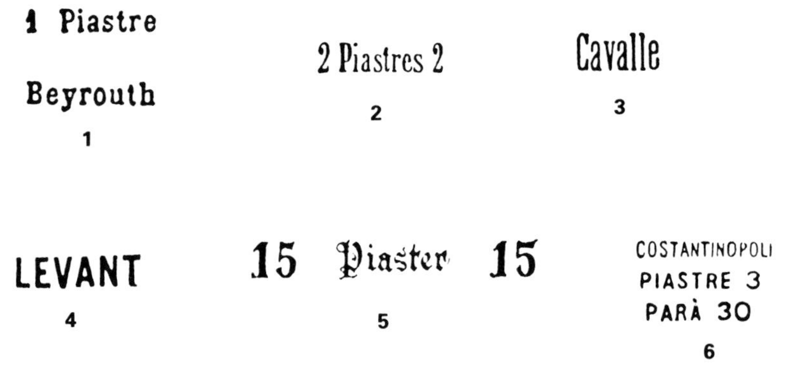
1 Piastre
Beyrouth
1
2 Piastres 2
2
Cavalle
3
LEVANT
4
15 Piaster 15
5
COSTANTINOPOLI
PIASTRE 3
PARÀ 30
6

1 French overprint for Beirut, 1905 **2** & **3** French overprints for Kavalla, 1893 **4** British overprint for Levant, 1905 **5** German overprint for Levant, 1905 **6** Italian overprint for Constantinople, 1922

consular mails from Constantinople. This used special stamps. (*See also* Romania). In 1919 an attempt was made to restart the service. While the ship was moored at Constantinople, mails and stamps were seized by Turkish police on 25 May and the PO closed.

• Polish PO in Constantinople

FIRST STAMPS ISSUED May 1919

CURRENCY

1919 As Poland 100 fenigi = 1 marka

Polish consulate opened a PO in May 1919, which closed in 1923.

• Egyptian POs in Turkish Empire

POs were established at Constantinople (1866), and in 1870 at Beirut, Chios, Jaffa, Mersin, Mytilene, Salonica, Smyrna, Tripoli, Volós, Dardanelles and Gallipoli.

Used stamps of Egypt (distinguishable by cancellations).

• Greek POs in Turkish Empire

Greek consular PAs were established at Constantinople (1834); Salonica and Dardanelles (1835); Bucharest, Ibraila, and Jassy (1857); Galatz and Larissa (January 1860); also at Volós, and at Candia, Canea and Rethymno in Crete. POs at Constantinople (1849) and at Smyrna (1857) were separated from the consulates and handled the mail of Greek citizens.

Used stamps of Greece 13 October 1861 – 25 April 1881 (cancellations bear the name of the town transliterated into Greek with TOYPKIA in brackets in the lower segment).

• Cilicia

FIRST STAMPS ISSUED 4 March 1919 (inscriptions TEO and OMF, *see* Syria)

CURRENCY

1919 As Turkey

An area between the Taurus Mountains and the Gulf of Alexandretta corresponding roughly to the Turkish *vilayet* of Adana, occupied by French troops 1918 – 20 October 1921.

• Hatay

FIRST STAMPS Syria 1918
FIRST SEPARATE STAMPS 16 April 1938

CURRENCY

1938 100 centimes = 1 piastre
1939 100 santims = 40 paras = 1 kurus

The northern part of the former Turkish province of Syria round Antioch, given autonomy by the French on 4 March 1923 as the Sanjak of Alexandretta. After some rioting against reincorporation into French Syria, an election on 2 September 1938 voted for an autonomous republic. This was incorporated into Turkey on 30 June 1939 (the province and chief town are now known as Antakya, and Alexandretta has been renamed Iskenderun).

Used stamps of Syria in 1918-38.

Used stamps of Turkey from 1939.

Syria

FIRST STAMPS Turkish 1883
FIRST STAMPS ISSUED French Military Occupation 21 February 1919

CURRENCY

1919 40 paras = 10 milliemes = 1 piastre
1920 100 centimes = 1 piastre

Part of the Turkish Empire between 1516 and 1918. Damascus was taken in 1918 from the south by Allied (Arab and Australian) forces and Beirut from the sea by a French naval landing. In 1919 Syria was divided into a French occupation zone based on Beirut and an Arab administration based on Damascus. By the end of the year fighting broke out between the two. In March 1920 the Emir Faisal was proclaimed king of Syria. With the approval of the Allies, French troops took Damascus (25 July 1920) and dethroned Faisal, who became King of Iraq in 1921. On 1 September 1920 the French divided Syria into three autonomous states: Aleppo, Damascus, and the Alaouites (q.v.). A French mandate was approved by the League of Nations in 1922, the Christian Lebanon was given separate status, and civil rule was established on 29 September 1923. In 1925 Damascus and Aleppo were reunited as Syria.

To forestall the infiltration of German forces into Vichy-held territory, British and Free French forces invaded both countries on 8 June 1941 and (in honour of a pledge made in 1936) a Syrian Republic was proclaimed on 16 September 1941. All British and French troops left before 15 April 1946. On 1 February 1958 Syria federated with Egypt as the United Arab Republic, from which Syria broke away on 28 September 1961.

Used stamps of Turkey up to 1919. Note inscriptions:

TEO Territoires Ennemis Occupés
OMF Occupation Militaire Française

Stamps were issued in the Arab kingdom March – July 1920.

Mandate stamps (inscribed for and valid throughout Syria and in Lebanon) were used September-December 1923 (no postal distinction being made between Aleppo and Damascus). Since 1 January 1924 the stamps of Syria have simply reflected each change of government.

• Alaouites

FIRST STAMPS ISSUED 1 January 1925

CURRENCY	
1925	100 centimes = 1 piastre

The state of the Alawi or Alaouites between Hatay and the Lebanon. A geographical part of Syria, it had a separate existence as a French mandate in 1920-30 and as a republic in 1930-6. On 22 September 1930 it took the name of its chief town, Latakia (*see below*).

Before 31 December 1924, *see* Syria.

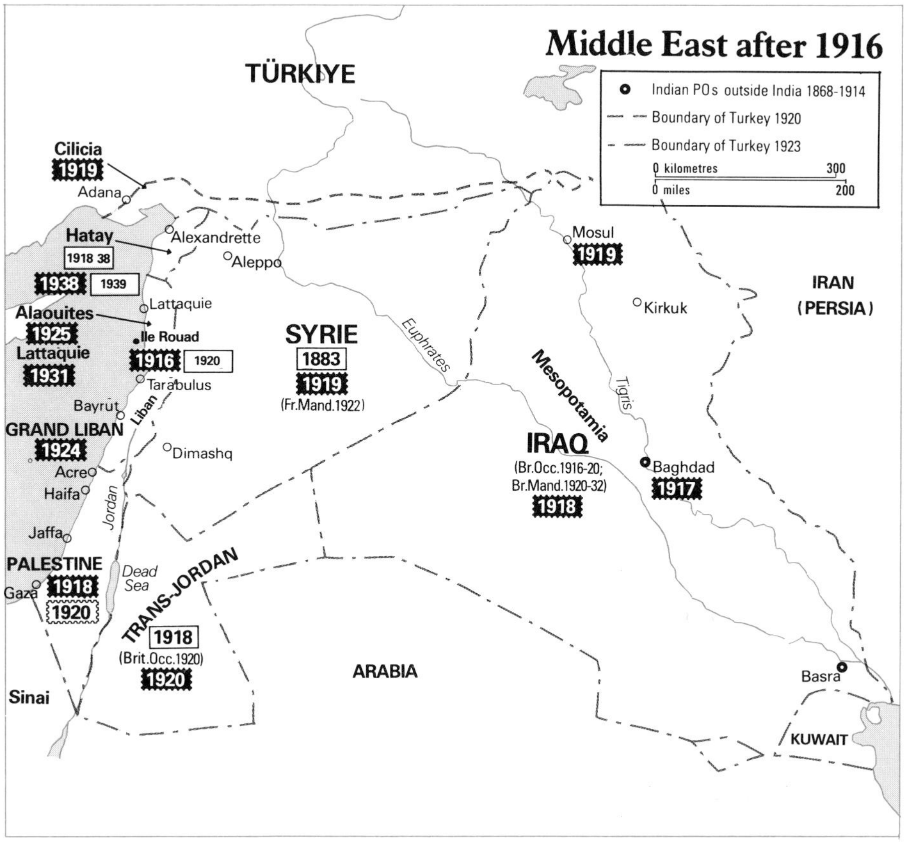

Middle East after 1916
Indian POs outside India 1868-1914
Boundary of Turkey 1920
Boundary of Turkey 1923
0 kilometres 300
0 miles 200
TÜRKIYE
Cilicia
1919
Adana
Hatay
1918 38
1938
1939
Alexandrette
Aleppo
Alaouites
1925
Lattaquie
Ile Rouad
Lattaquie
1931
1916
1920
Tarabulus
Bayrut
Liban
GRAND LIBAN
1924
Dimashq
Acre
Haifa
Jordan
Jaffa
PALESTINE
1918
1920
Gaza
Dead Sea
TRANS-JORDAN
1918
(Brit.Occ.1920)
1920
Sinai
SYRIE
1883
1919
(Fr.Mand.1922)
Euphrates
Mesopotamia
Tigris
Mosul
1919
Kirkuk
IRAQ
(Br.Occ.1916-20;
Br.Mand.1920-32)
1918
Baghdad
1917
IRAN
(PERSIA)
ARABIA
Basra
KUWAIT

Above left
Inside new post office in Jeddah, Saudi Arabia

Above right
Post office, Abu Dhabi

Below right
Post office, capital area, Oman

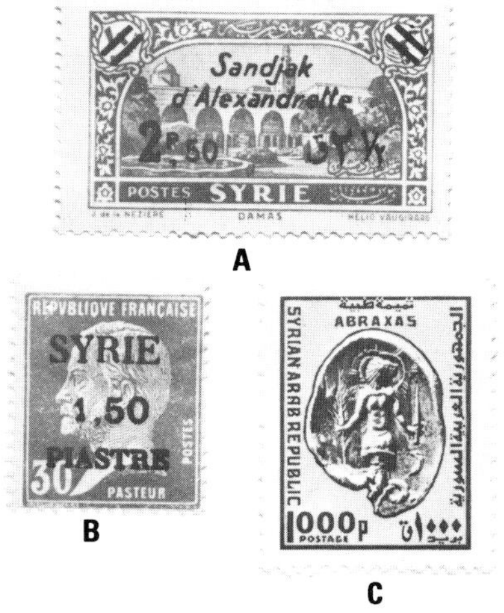
Sandjak d'Alexandrette
2P,50
POSTES SYRIE
A
REPUBLIQUE FRANCAISE
SYRIE
1,50
PIASTRE
PASTEUR
B
ABRAXAS
SYRIAN ARAB REPUBLIC
1000P
C

A Hatay 1938; **B** Syria 1920; **C** Syria 1976.

• Latakia

FIRST STAMPS ISSUED July 1931

CURRENCY	
1931	100 centimes = 1 piastre

Formerly Alaouites, *see above*.

Stamps withdrawn 28 February 1937, after which stamps of Syria were used.

• Ile Rouad

FIRST STAMPS ISSUED 12 January 1916

CURRENCY	
1916	100 centimes = 1 piastre

An island south of Latakia occupied in 1916 by the French navy as a base from which to supply Christian Syrians hostile to the Turks. Later part of the Alaouites. Military PO opened 12 January 1916; civil PO 12 May 1916, closed 1922.

After 1920 used stamps of Syria.

• Free French Forces in the Levant

CURRENCY	
1942	As France

Special stamps for use in Free French FPOs in Syria and Lebanon were issued in 1942-6.

Lebanon (Liban)

FIRST STAMPS Turkish from 1883 **FIRST STAMPS ISSUED** 1 January 1924

CURRENCY	
1924	100 centimes = 1 piastre

Emirate under Turkish rule from 1516 to 1842. After a civil war between Muslims and Christians, the Powers intervened in 1861 to insist that a Christian governor be appointed by the Sultan. A period of French military administration (1918) was followed by a French mandate in 1920, initially as part of Syria, after 29 September 1923 as Greater Lebanon (Grand Liban). Republic was proclaimed on 23 May 1926. Vichy régime was overthrown by British and Free French troops in June 1941. The country gradually assumed independence.

• French PO in Beirut

Particular provisional issued 17 January 1905

CURRENCY	
1859	As France

Opened c. 1840, closed 1914.

Used stamps of France c. 1858?-85 (oblit.3706, small figures; 5082, large figures). 1885-1914, *see* French POs in Turkish Empire.

• British PO in Beirut

Particular provisional issued 2 July 1906

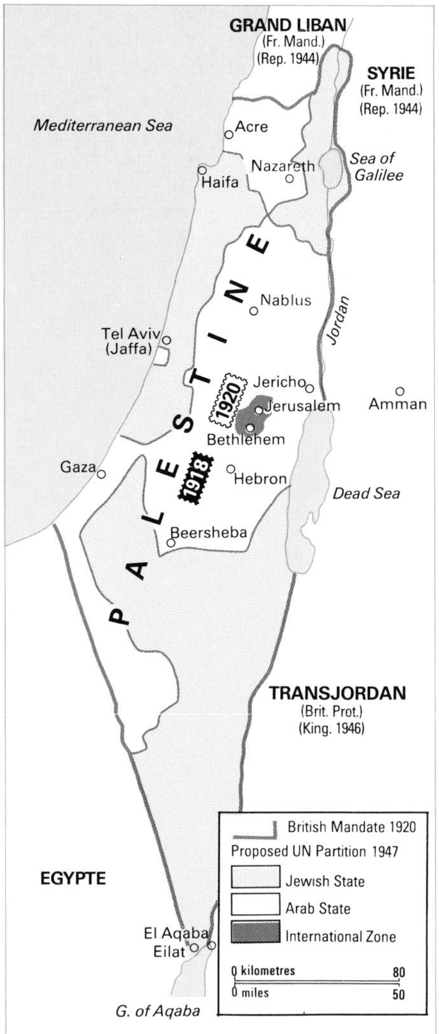
GRAND LIBAN
(Fr. Mand.)
(Rep. 1944)
SYRIE
(Fr. Mand.)
(Rep. 1944)
Mediterranean Sea
Acre
Haifa
Nazareth
Sea of Galilee
PALESTINE
Nablus
Jordan
Tel Aviv
(Jaffa)
Jericho
Jerusalem
Amman
1920
Bethlehem
Gaza
1918
Hebron
Dead Sea
Beersheba
TRANSJORDAN
(Brit. Prot.)
(King. 1946)
British Mandate 1920
Proposed UN Partition 1947
Jewish State
Arab State
International Zone
EGYPTE
El Aqaba
Eilat
0 kilometres 80
0 miles 50
G. of Aqaba

Palestine 1918-48

CURRENCY
As British Levant

Opened c. 1873, closed 1914.

Used stamps of Britain (oblit.G06) and British Levant.

• Russian PO in Beirut

An agency of ROPiT was opened in 1857, closed in 1914.

Used stamps of Russia 1863-5 (oblit. 783).

Used stamps of ROPiT 1865-8. 1868-1914, *see* Russian POs in Turkish Empire. Particular stamps were issued in 1879 and 1909-10.

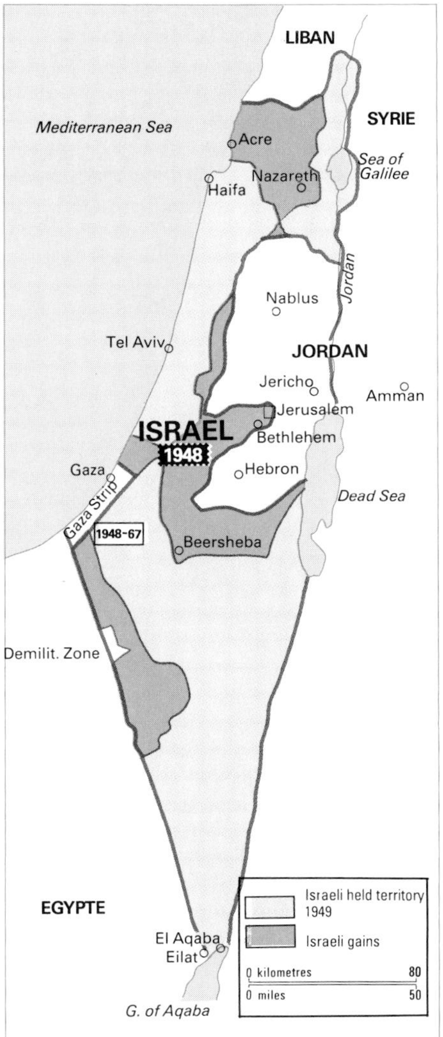
LIBAN
SYRIE
Mediterranean Sea
Acre
Haifa
Nazareth
Sea of Galilee
Jordan
Nablus
Tel Aviv
JORDAN
Jericho
Amman
Jerusalem
ISRAEL
1948
Bethlehem
Gaza
Hebron
Gaza Strip
1948-67
Dead Sea
Beersheba
Demilit. Zone
EGYPTE
Israeli held territory 1949
Israeli gains
0 kilometres 80
0 miles 50
El Aqaba
Eilat
G. of Aqaba

Israel 1948-50

GRAND LIBAN 1,50 PIASTRE
1 PIASTRE 30 PARAS
4 PIASTRES 4
POSTE
REPUBLIQUE FRANÇAISE
LIBAN
300P.
ILE ROUAD
LEVANT

A Lebanon 1924; **B** British Levant 1885; **C** French Levant 1885; **D** Lebanon 1924; **E** Ile Rouad 1916.

For the Austrian PO and German PO in Beirut *see* Austrian and German POs in the Turkish Empire (they issued no particular stamps).

• Palestine

FIRST STAMPS ISSUED 1 February 1918
First stamps specifically overprinted PALESTINE 1 September 1920

CURRENCY

1918 Egyptian
1927 1000 mills = 1 Palestine pound

Part of Turkish Syria between the Mediterranean Sea and the Jordan Valley, taken from the Turks 31 October – 9 December 1917, was under British military occupation to 1 July 1920. A British civil administration was followed on 23 September 1923 by a League of Nations mandate until 15 May 1948, to which Muslim 'Palestinians' and Zionist settlers alike became increasingly hostile.

Forerunners
(For further details, *see* Turkish Empire): Turkish Empire mail before 1863 is so rare that little is known about the service. A weekly Turkish courier service was inaugurated between Beirut and Jerusalem, via Sour-Acre-Haifa-Jaffa, in the 1840s. Early POs existed at Jerusalem, Jaffa, Acre, Bethlehem, Gaza, Hebron, Nablus, and Tiberias. Stamps of Turkey were used 1863-1917. Until 1874 when Turkey joined the UPU, all external mail was probably sent via one of the foreign powers' POs.

First stamps of February 1918 were inscribed E.E.F. and were valid in territories occupied by the British 'Egyptian Expeditionary Force', which included Transjordan, Cilicia, Sinai, and Syria; they are, however, generally treated by collectors as the first issue of Palestine.

Israel

FIRST STAMPS ISSUED 16 May 1948

CURRENCY

1948 1000 prutot = 1 Israeli pound
1960 100 agorot = 1 Israeli pound
1980 1 sheqel (=10 pounds) = 100 agorot
1986 1 new sheqel (=1000 sheqel) = 100 new agorot

Independent republic was proclaimed on 14 May 1948 and invaded the following day by combined forces of Iraq, Transjordan, Lebanon and Syria. These were driven back and an armistice agreed in 1949. Israel supported Anglo-French action at Suez in 1956 by invading the Sinai penisula but was forced by diplomatic pressure to reliquish its gains. By the 'Six-day War' (6-11 June 1967) the Israelis forestalled Arab action by taking the initiative against Egypt, Jordan and Syria simultaneously, occupying the

Gaza strip and Sinai, part of Jordan, and the Golan Heights. The 'Yom Kippur' war in October 1973 was halted by UN intervention. A separate peace was signed with Egypt.

British postal services in Palestine were suspended by decree of 13 April 1948 and most POs were closed 15 April – 5 May. Local personnel were instructed by the Jewish National Council to maintain services where possible until full Israeli services started. Some unofficial provisional stamps were produced. Post buses are a feature of modern postal transport.

• Gaza Strip

On 15 May 1948 at the close of the British mandate over Palestine, Egyptian troops seized Gaza; by the armistice terms of 24 February 1949 a smaller area remained under Egypt. The area was occupied by Israeli troops from 29 October 1956 to 7 March 1957 and again from June 1967 to January 1980.

Used stamps of Egypt overprinted PALESTINE 1 June 1948 – June 1967.

During Israeli occupation used stamps of Israel.

In 1965 a special stamp (issued 15 January) was used by the Indian contingent of the UN forces in Gaza.

Iraq

FIRST STAMPS Turkish 1863
FIRST STAMPS ISSUED 1 September 1918

CURRENCY

1917	16 annas = 1 rupee
1931	1000 fils = 1 dinar

Known also in the West as Mesopotamia, the land between the rivers (Tigris and Euphrates), Iraq was part of the Turkish Empire from 1638 to 1918, when it comprised the *vilayets* of Baghdad and Mosul. During World War I Basra was occupied on 22 November 1914 by British and Indian forces who fought their way, with many reverses, to the capture of Baghdad on 11 March 1917. An Indian Expeditionary Force occupied Mosul on 10 November 1918.

The British occupation was succeeded by a mandate under the League of Nations and, on 23 August 1921, the Emir Faisal was proclaimed king. Mosul *vilayet* was transferred to Iraq by the League of Nations in December 1925. The mandate was given up on 3 October 1932 in favour of an independent kingdom, though Britain retained rights of transit and air bases at Habbaniya and Shaibah. In 1941 a pro-German government posed a threat countered by British military action in May-June. King Faisal II was assassinated on 14 July 1958 and a republic declared. A further military *coup d'état* occured in 1963.

Postal History

An efficient Assyrian postal service carrying merchants' letters written in cuneiform on clay tablets and enclosed in addressed (clay) envelopes is known by finds on many sites over a wide area. In the 8th and 9th centuries BC the Assyrian royal post reached to the capitals of subject states.

Turkish POs operated from (?) 1863 at Baghdad, Basra, Kirkuk, Mosul and elsewhere. Indian POs were open in Baghdad and Basra in 1868-1914. Troops in Iraq in World War I used stamps of India overprinted I.E.F. (*see* India) in their FPOs.

Stamps of Turkey used in 1863-1917 have town cancellations in Arabic script.

Stamps of India can be identified by cancellations of Baghdad (alternative spelling Bagdad) or Basra (Bussorah or Busreh).

• Baghdad

Special stamps for British occupation forces September 1917.

CURRENCY

1917	As India

• Mosul

Special stamps for I.E.F. 'D' Force from February 1919.

The RAF operated a desert airmail in 1921-27 between Baghdad and Cairo which was taken over by Imperial Airways in 1927 and extended to Basra as the first regular stage of the service planned for India and Australia. In 1923 Nairn Transport Company ran a motorized 'Overland Mail': Baghdad-Damascus-Haifa. There were 352 POs in 1973.

Jordan

FIRST STAMPS E.E.F. stamps (Palestine) 10 February 1918
FIRST STAMPS ISSUED November 1920

CURRENCY

1920	1000 milliemes = 100 piastres = £1 Egyptian
1927	1000 milliemes = £ 1 Palestine
1950	1000 fils = 1 Jordanian dinar

Part of the Turkish province of Syria lying east of the Jordan captured by Colonel Lawrence's irregular forces in 1918. It was administered from Syria until 25 April 1920 when it was mandated with Palestine to Britain under the name Transjordan. In 1921 Abdullah, a son of the King of the Hejaz, was made Emir and on 26 May 1923 Transjordan was recognized as an autonomous Arab state with British advisers. Abdullah assumed the title of King of Transjordan on 25 May 1946 and the country's independence from Britain was acknowledged. It was renamed the Hashemite Kingdom of Jordan on 2 June 1949. Its boundaries have been in dispute with Israel ever since. An attempt at federation with Iraq in 1958 was upset by revolution in Iraq.

In the Turkish period the region was virtually without posts.

Until 1927 stamps of Palestine or Hejaz were overprinted in Arabic 'East of Jordan' or 'Arab Government of the East'. From 1927 to 1947 they were inscribed TRANSJORDAN.

• Jordanian Occupation of Palestine

In 1948 the Arab Legion occupied

areas within the boundaries allocated to the newly proclaimed state of Israel. These were incorporated into Jordan on 24 April 1950, but lost again in the 'Six-day War' of 1967.

Stamps of Transjordan overprinted PALESTINE in English and Arabic were used 2 December 1948 – 24 April 1950.

• Aden

FIRST STAMPS	India from 1854
FIRST STAMPS ISSUED	1 April 1937

CURRENCY

1937	16 annas = 1 rupee
1951	100 cents = 1 shilling

Breakdown of an attempt to lease Aden from the Sultan of Lahej as a coaling station for the steamship route from Suez to India led to its capture on 19 January 1839 by a combined British and East India Company force. The Kuria Muria Islands, presented to Britain by the Sultan of Muscat in 1854, were placed under Aden in 1868, and various protective treaties were made with local rulers south of the 'Empty Quarter' of Arabia. The opening of the Suez Canal in 1869 and the arrival of the telegraph (1870) increased Aden's importance and it became the port of exchange for East Africa (1872).

Aden itself, administered for nearly a century by the Bombay Presidency, was made a Crown Colony on 1 April 1937.

Postal History

A residency PO was opened under Indian administration in 1839 and mail is known from 15 June 1839. Handstamps came into use very quickly, though a postmaster was not appointed until 1857. The original PO at Crater was called Aden Cantonment or Aden Camp after the main office moved c. 1858 to Steamer Point. Aden became the exchange port for mail between the packets of four or more nations operating through the Red Sea to the Indian Ocean and Far East. Sub-POs were opened at Sheikh Othman (1891); Khormaksar (1892); Dthali (1903-7); and Maalla (1924).

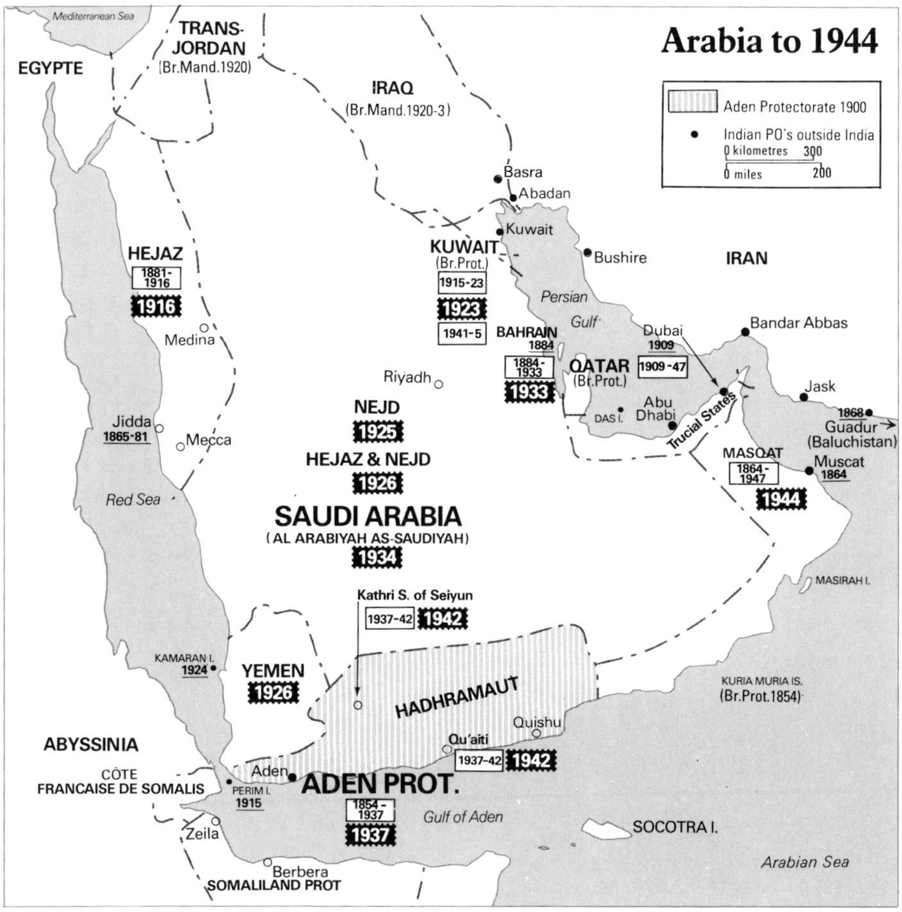
Arabia to 1944
Aden Protectorate 1900
Indian PO's outside India
0 kilometres 300
0 miles 200
Mediterranean Sea
TRANS-JORDAN
(Br.Mand.1920)
EGYPTE
IRAQ
(Br.Mand.1920-3)
Basra
Abadan
Kuwait
KUWAIT
(Br.Prot.)
1915-23
1923
1941-5
Bushire
IRAN
HEJAZ
1881-1916
1916
Medina
Persian Gulf
BAHRAIN
1884
1884-1933
1933
QATAR
(Br.Prot.)
1909-47
Dubai
1909
Bandar Abbas
Riyadh
NEJD
1925
Jidda
1865-81
Mecca
HEJAZ & NEJD
1926
Abu Dhabi
DAS I.
Trucial States
Jask
1868
Guadur
(Baluchistan)
MASQAT
1864-1947
Muscat
1864
1944
Red Sea
SAUDI ARABIA
(AL ARABIYAH AS-SAUDIYAH)
1934
Kathri S. of Seiyun
1937-42
1942
MASIRAH I.
KAMARAN I.
1924
YEMEN
1926
HADHRAMAUT
KURIA MURIA IS.
(Br.Prot.1854)
Quishu
Qu'aiti
1937-42
1942
ABYSSINIA
CÔTE FRANCAISE DE SOMALIS
PERIM I.
1915
Aden
ADEN PROT.
1854-1937
1937
Gulf of Aden
SOCOTRA I.
Zeila
Berbera
SOMALILAND PROT
Arabian Sea

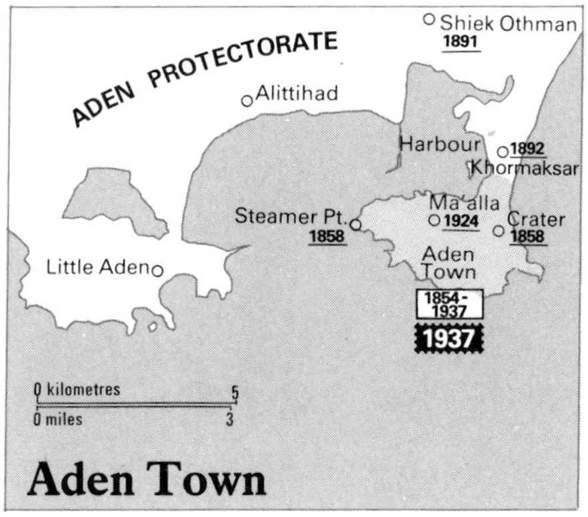
ADEN PROTECTORATE
Shiek Othman
1891
Alittihad
Harbour
1892
Khormaksar
Steamer Pt.
1858
Ma'alla
1924
Crater
1858
Aden Town
1854-1937
1937
Little Aden
0 kilometres 5
0 miles 3
Aden Town

Aden controlled POs at Berbera and Zaila 1887-1902 (*see* British Somaliland).

PERIM ISLAND

Though never a separate postal entity, Perim has for collectors the interest of any island. Its mail was transported by camel dak and small boat. Postcards are known from Perim in the 19th century; its PO was open 1915-36.

Used stamps of India 1 October 1854 – 31 March 1937 (Early oblit. 124 in diamond of bars).

All Aden stamps withdrawn 31 March 1965.

• Qu'aiti State in Hadhramaut

FIRST STAMPS	Aden 1937-42
FIRST STAMPS ISSUED	July 1942

CURRENCY

1937	16 annas = 1 rupee
1951	100 cents = 1 shilling
1966	1000 fils = 1 dinar

An Arab sultanate bordering on the Gulf of Aden under British protection from 1886.

Mails were passed through forward-

A
B
C
D
E
EGYPT
GAZA PART OF ARAB NATION
10 M
ISRAEL 1887-1944
BERL KATZENELSON
2.00
PALESTINE
POSTAGE
PAID
5

A Palestine:Civil Administration 1920; **B** Gaza:Egypt overprinted 1957; **C** Israel 1978; **D** Israel:First Issue 1948; **E** Palestine:British Mandate 1942.

A
B
C
D
E
SPECIMEN
200 FILS
IRAQ POSTAGE
POSTAGE
I.E.F. 'D'
3 Annas
VINGT PARAS
IRAQ
IN BRITISH OCCUPATION
3 An.
REPUBLIC OF IRAQ
POSTAGE
75 FILS
SADDAM'S BATTLE OF QADISIYA
1 ANNA 2
IRAQ
SPECIMEN

A Iraq:Kingdom 1954; **B** Mosul:British Occupation 1919; **C** Baghdad:British Occupation 1918; **D** Iraq: Mandate 1923; **E** Iraq: Republic 1980.

ing agents in Aden from 1891. On 22 April 1937 at the request of the sultan a PO dependent on Aden was opened at Mukalla. Separate stamps became desirable after King George VI's head was added to the stamps of Aden, but were delayed by World War II. A postal union between Aden and the protected states was signed in 1939 by which any stamps were inter-valid.

Inscriptions: 1942 QU'AITI STATE OF SHIHR AND MUKALLA.

Became HADHRAMAUT in 1955.

• Mahra Sultanate of Qishu and Socotra

CURRENCY	
1937	16 annas = 1 rupee
1951	100 cents = 1 shilling
1966	1000 fils = 1 dinar

FIRST STAMPS 12 March 1967

Before independence from Britain could be granted to this and the two preceding Eastern Aden Protectorate sultanates on 30 November 1967, they had already fallen to Communist insurgents and were quickly swallowed up by the People's Republic of Southern Yemen.

• Federation of South Arabia

FIRST STAMPS 25 November 1963 (withdrawn 1967)

CURRENCY	
1963	100 cents = 1 shilling
1965	1000 fils = 1 dinar

Six sheikhdoms of the Aden Western Protectorate were federated on 11 February 1959; four more joined in 1960. The Federation of South Arabia was planned as a free entity within the British Commonwealth sufficiently strong to stand against subversion and against Yemeni attacks fostered by Egypt. Aden Colony was forced into it against local wishes on 18 January 1963.

The postal history is an extension of that of Aden.

KAMARAN ISLAND had a Turkish PO until its capture by British forces in 1915. It had a sub-PO of Aden from 1924. The island became part of Southern Yemen in 1967 but was occupied by Yemen Arab Republic in 1972.

• Kathiri State of Seiyun

FIRST STAMPS Aden 1937–42
FIRST STAMPS ISSUED August 1942

CURRENCY	
1937	16 annas = 1 rupee
1951	000 cents = 1 shilling
1966	1000 fils = 1 dinar

Another Arab sultanate with a similar history.

On 25 May 1937 a PO was opened at Seiyun, and several PAs followed.

(Southern) Yemen

FIRST STAMPS ISSUED 1 April 1968

CURRENCY

1967 1000 fils = 1 dinar

The seventeen sultans of the Federation of South Arabia were deposed in 1967 by rival 'liberation fronts', who then fought each other. Before the end of the year the three Eastern Aden Protectorate states had been absorbed into the People's Republic of Southern Yemen. An agreement in 1972 for union with Yemen Arab Republic within a year has not been implemented.

PEOPLE'S REPUBLIC OF SOUTHERN YEMEN
75 FILS
POSTAGE
CENTENARY OF THE BIRTH OF LENIN
POSTAGE
U.P.U. CENTENARY 1874-1974
40 FILS
PEOPLE'S DEMOCRATIC REPUBLIC OF YEMEN
Y.A.R.
4 B.
POSTAGE 1963
1ST ANNIV. OF REVOLUTION

A Southern Yemen;
B Democratic Republic of Yemen 1974;
C Hejaz:Kingdom 1917;
D Yemen Arab Republic 1963;
E Hejaz-Nejd:Kingdom 1927.

Yemen Arab Republic

FIRST STAMPS ISSUED 1926

CURRENCY

1926 40 bogaches = 1 imadi
1964 40 bogaches = 1 rial
1975 100 fils = 1 rial

An independent Imamate of the Zaidi sect of Shia Muslims set up in 897, Yemen was incorporated into the Turkish Empire in 1517-1630 and 1872-1918, but regained independence. The Imam escaped from a republican *coup d'état* on 26 September 1962 and, although a Yemen Arab Republic was recognized by the UN and supported by Egypt, he held out in the northwest with Saudi Arabian aid until 1970.

Royalist Forces
The Royalist forces operated a postal service in the area they held and externally via Saudi Arabia.

Stamps were issued 7 November 1962-70, though many (supplied by contract agents on their own initiative) were neither necessary nor appropriate, and have been declared undesirable.

ADEN 5RS
FILS THE HASHEMITE KINGDOM OF
100 JORDAN
ADEN 3AS 3AS
ADEN 2RS
2 SHILLINGS
3 PALESTINE
TRANSJORDAN POSTAGE

Aden 1939; Jordan:a Modern Issue; Aden 1937; Aden 1951; Jordan: Occupation of Palestine 1948; Transjordan 1933.

• Upper Yafa

FIRST STAMPS ISSUED 1967

CURRENCY

1967 1000 fils = 1 dinar

A Sultanate of South Arabia, formerly part of the Western Aden Protectorate. Independent from September to December 1967, then part of the People's Democratic Republic of Yemen.

• Hejaz

FIRST STAMPS Turkey from 1881
FIRST STAMPS ISSUED 20 August 1916

CURRENCY

1916 40 paras = 1 piastre

The western part of Arabia, including Mecca and Medina, came under Turkish power in 1517 but was not directly administered until 1845. The building of the Damascus-Medina railway (1900-8) brought central government closer. When on 27 June 1916 Hussein proclaimed an Arab state and later took the title King of the Hejaz, the destruction of the railway became the goal of Col. T.E. Lawrence. The country was conquered by Nejd in 1925 (*see below*).

At Jeddah an Egyptian PO operated c.1865 – 30 October 1881 and used stamps of Egypt.

Used stamps of Turkey from 1881 to 1916.

All stamps were withdrawn or overprinted by Nejd authorities by the end of 1925.

• Nejd

FIRST STAMPS ISSUED 23 March 1925

CURRENCY

1926	As Hejaz

A sultanate of the Muslim Wahabi in central Arabia with a capital at Riyadh founded in 1824. The rise of Ibn Saud as leader in 1923 heralded rapid expansion, including the conquest of the Hejaz by 23 December 1925.

First stamp issue superseded in 1926 by joint issues for Hejaz and Nejd (*see below*).

• Hejaz and Nejd

FIRST STAMPS ISSUED February 1926

CURRENCY

1926	40 paras = 1 piastre
1929	110 guerche = 10 riyal = 1 gold sovereign

Ibn Saud, sultan of Nejd, took the title King of the Hejaz in 1926 and in 1927 adopted the kingship of Nejd also. The kingdom was renamed Saudi Arabia on 22 September 1932.

Saudi Arabia

FIRST STAMPS ISSUED 1 January 1934

CURRENCY

1916	40 paras = 1 piastre
1923	As Hejaz Nejd
1929	110 guerche = 10 riyal = 1 gold sovereign
1952	440 guerche = 40 riyal = 1 gold sovereign
1960	100 hululch = 20 guerche = 1 riyal
1976	100 halalas = 1 rial

Kingdom comprising the greater part of the Arabian peninsula.

Initially a little known traditional Arab nation, the wealth provided by the oil has enabled the country to act as a stabilising influence in the Middle East. Internal mail services were dependent on camel transport until roads became established. More recently internal mail has been carried by air. Overseas mail was dependent on British services from the Gulf and Aden until after World War II when the Saudis developed their own air service.

The Persian (Arabian) Gulf

• Muscat and Oman

FIRST STAMPS India 1864
FIRST STAMPS ISSUED inscribed MUSCAT & OMAN 30 April 1966

CURRENCY

1944	Indian to 1966
1966	64 baizas = 1 rupee
1970	1000 baizas = 1 Saidi rial

The powerful sultanate of Muscat and Oman became fully independent of Persia in 1744 and signed a treaty of friendship with the East India Company in 1798. A political agency was established in Muscat in 1800 and the friendliest relations established during the rule of Seyyid Sa'id (1807-56). In 1854 the Kuria Muria Islands were presented to the British Crown (*see* Aden). On the death of Seyyid Sa'id in 1856, Zanzibar (occupied from Muscat since 1720) became a separate sultanate.

In 1970 the territory was renamed the Sultanate of Oman (*see below*).

Postal History
PO was opened in the port of Muscat on 1 May 1864 under the Bombay circle. After transfer to the Sind circle (Karachi) in April 1869, it returned to Bombay in 1879. There was only one PO until 1970. On the partition of India, postal control passed for a time to Pakistan and then to Britain. The Sultan's government took over the posts on 30 April 1966.

Used stamps of India 1 May 1864 – 19 December 1947 (initial oblit. 309 in diamond of bars; after c. 1873 named datestamps were used). Special stamps were issued in 1944 to mark 200 years of the Al bu-Said dynasty.

Used stamps of Pakistan 20 December 1947 – 31 March 1948.

Used stamps of British PAs in Eastern Arabia 1 April 1948 – 29 April 1966.

Oman

FIRST STAMPS ISSUED inscribed SULTANATE OF OMAN 16 January 1971

CURRENCY

1971	1000 diazas = 1 rial Saudi

The former Muscat and Oman under a new sultan. Britain supplies financial aid, officers the Oman levies, and has by treaty an RAF staging post on Masirah Island.

Guadur
A dependency of Muscat on the Mekran coast of Baluchistan from 1792 until 8 September 1958 when it was sold to Pakistan. A port-of-call of the British India Steam Navigation Co. from 1862, it became an important

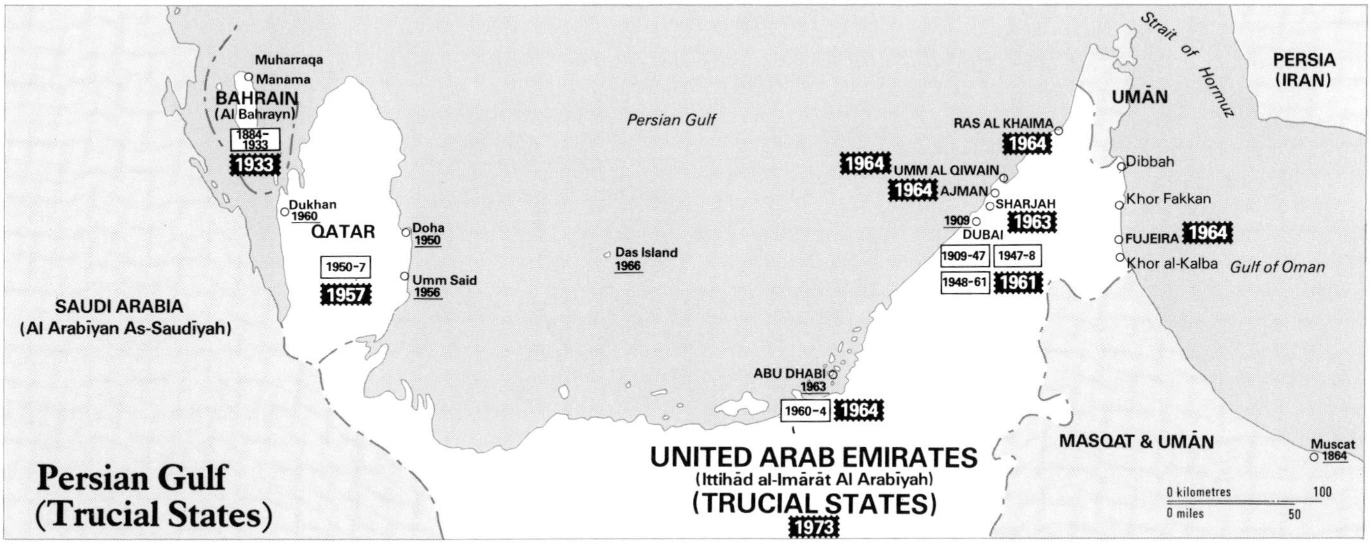
Muharraqa
Manama
BAHRAIN
(Al Bahrayn)
1884–1933
1933
Dukhan
1960
QATAR
Doha
1950
1950-7
1957
Umm Said
1956
SAUDI ARABIA
(Al Arabīyan As-Saudīyah)
Persian Gulf
Das Island
1966
Strait of Hormuz
PERSIA
(IRAN)
UMĀN
RAS AL KHAIMA
1964
1964
UMM AL QIWAIN
1964
AJMAN
SHARJAH
1963
1909
DUBAI
1909-47
1947-8
1948-61
1961
Dibbah
Khor Fakkan
FUJEIRA
1964
Khor al-Kalba
Gulf of Oman
ABU DHABI
1963
1960-4
1964
MASQAT & UMĀN
Muscat
1864
UNITED ARAB EMIRATES
(Ittihād al-Imārāt Al Arabīyah)
(TRUCIAL STATES)
1973
0 kilometres 100
0 miles 50

Persian Gulf (Trucial States)

telegraph station (with an undersea cable to the Persian Gulf) in 1865.

An experimental Indian PO, opened from Bombay 12 April 1868, became permanent on 30 January 1869. Transferred to Sind in April 1869. It was never controlled postally by Muscat.

Used stamps of India 1868-1947 (distinguishable by cancellation).

Has used stamps of Pakistan since Ocober 1947 (not, as might be expected, those used in Muscat in 1948-58).

Bahrain

FIRST STAMPS India 1 August 1883
FIRST STAMPS ISSUED 10 August 1933

CURRENCY

1933 As India
Indian to 1966
1966 1000 fils = 1 Bahrain dinar

An island sheikhdom with dependent islets in the Arabian Gulf, protected by treaty of 1861 with Britain until its independence 15 August 1971. Exclusive agreements were signed in 1880 and 1892, and a British Political Agent was appointed in 1902.

Postal History
Sub-PO of Bushire under the Indian postal administration was opened in the island capital, Manama, on 1 August 1884. A second PO at Muarraq was opened in 1946. After the independence of India, a British postal administration operated from 1 April 1948 until the Bahrain post department took over on 1 January 1966.

Used stamps of India 1 August 1884-1933 (distinguishable by named datestamps).

• Dubai

FIRST STAMPS India 1909
FIRST STAMPS ISSUED (inscribed TRUCIAL STATES) 7 January 1961 (these were on sale only in Dubai).

CURRENCY

1963 100 naye paise = 1 rupee
1966 100 dirhams = 1 riyal
Indian external rupees to 1966
1966 100 dirhams = 1 Gulf riyal

The sheikh of Dubai, one of the parties to the 1820 peace treaty, renounced allegiance to Abu Dhabi in 1833. In 1853 Dubai became one of the Trucial States.

Indian PO under Karachi was opened on 19 August 1909.

Used stamps of India 1909-47 (cancellations 'Dubai Persian Gulf').

Used stamps of Pakistan October 1947 – 31 March 1948.

Used stamps of British PAs in Eastern Arabia 1948-61. Now part of the U.A.E.

Kuwait

FIRST STAMPS India 1915
FIRST STAMPS ISSUED 1 April 1923

CURRENCY

Indian to 1961
1961 1000 fils = 1 Kuwait dinar

An independent Arab sheikhdom, having a dynasty founded in 1756. Fearing Turkish attack, it sought a treaty of protection with Britain in 1899, reaffirmed in 1914 and again by treaty in 1961. It is the richest oil state in the Gulf.

Postal service of the East India Company operated in 1775-95 when a desert express camel service was maintained to Aleppo and Constantinople. A PO was planned in 1904 under Indian administration but not opened until 21 January 1915 (postal business was previously done in the Consul's

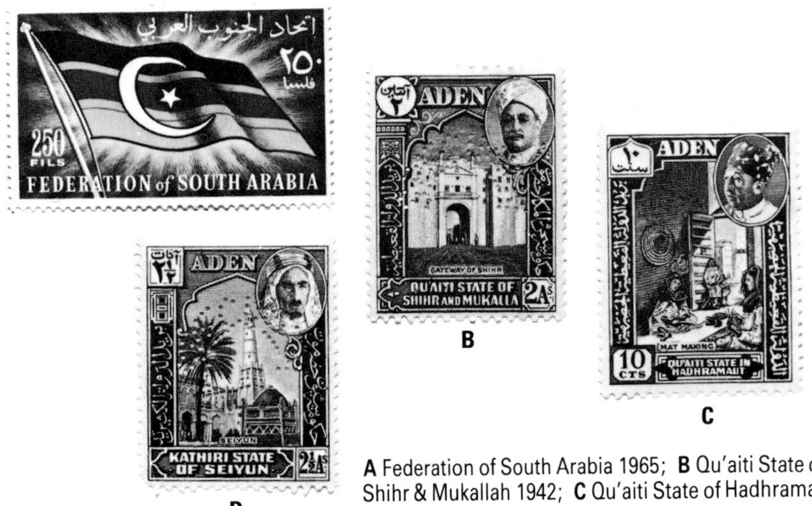
FEDERATION of SOUTH ARABIA
250 FILS
ADEN
QU'AITI STATE OF SHIHR AND MUKALLA
ADEN
QU'AITI STATE IN HADHRAMAUT
ADEN
KATHIRI STATE OF SEIYUN
B
C
D

A Federation of South Arabia 1965; **B** Qu'aiti State of Shihr & Mukallah 1942; **C** Qu'aiti State of Hadhramaut 1963; **D** Kathiri State of Seiyun 1942.

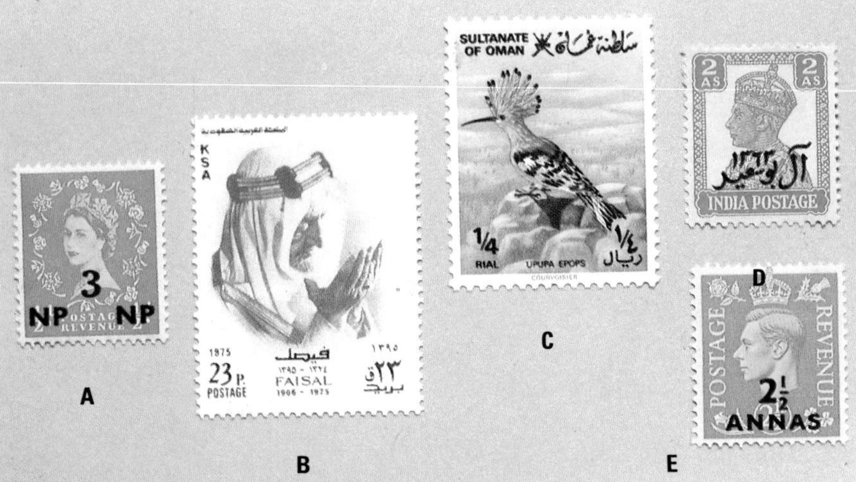
SULTANATE OF OMAN
1/4 RIAL
INDIA POSTAGE
3 NP NP
23 P. POSTAGE
FAISAL
POSTAGE REVENUE
2½ ANNAS
A
B
C
D
E

A British POs in Eastern Arabia 1957; **B** Saudi Arabia:Kingdom 1975; **C** Oman:Sultanate 1982; **D** Muscat:Indian Administration 1944; **E** British POs in Eastern Arabia 1951.

office, using stamps obtained from Bushire, letters being sent via Bushire or put direct on to steamers). PO was administered from Iraq (sub-office of Basra) 1 August 1921 – April 1941 when, owing to the Franco-British invasion of Iraq, it was closed. Mail was sent by diplomatic bag via London 1 April – mid-May until the PO could be re-opened under Indian administration. It was under Pakistan administration 1947-8, under British from 1 April 1948 and under Kuwaiti from 31 January 1959.

Used stamps of India without overprint May 1941-5.

Qatar

FIRST STAMPS Bahrain 1950
FIRST STAMPS ISSUED 1 April 1957

CURRENCY

1957	100 naye paise
1966	100 dirhams = 1 riyal

Arab sheikhdom under Turkish suzerainty in 1871-1915. Doha, the capital, fell to the British navy in August 1915 and the sheikh signed an exclusive agreement with Britain on 3 November 1916. Oil was found in 1940. A British Political Officer was appointed to Doha in August 1949. Qatar chose full independence on 3 September 1971.

The small amount of mail prior to 1950 was fed privately into the PO at Bahrain. A British postal administration set up in Doha (May 1950) was extended to Umm Said (1 February 1956) and Dukhan (3 January 1960); it was transferred to Qatar post department on 23 May 1963.

Used stamps of British PAs in Eastern Arabia August 1950-7 (these continued to be valid but were not on sale after 1957).

• Abu Dhabi

FIRST STAMPS British PAs in Eastern Arabia 1963
FIRST STAMPS ISSUED 30 March 1964

CURRENCY

1964	100 naye paise = 1 rupee
1966	100 fils = 1 dinar

The largest and — in the 19th century — most influential of the Trucial States. The town, on an offshore island, was first settled in 1761. After lapsing into obscurity, its fortunes soared with the successful prospecting for oil off Das Island in 1956-60.

Mail from Das Island construction workers before 1963 was channelled through the office of the British Postal Superintendent Bahrain; after 1960 stamps of British PAs in Eastern Arabia were supplied to the island. Das Island PO remained in Bahrain until removed to the island itself on 6 January 1966. It was then administered as agency by the oil company until taken over by Abu Dhabi on 1 January 1967.

The first British Agency PO was opened in Abu Dhabi on 30 March

1963. The service was taken over locally on 1 January 1967.

Used stamps of British PAs in Eastern Arabia 30 March 1963 – 29 March 1964.

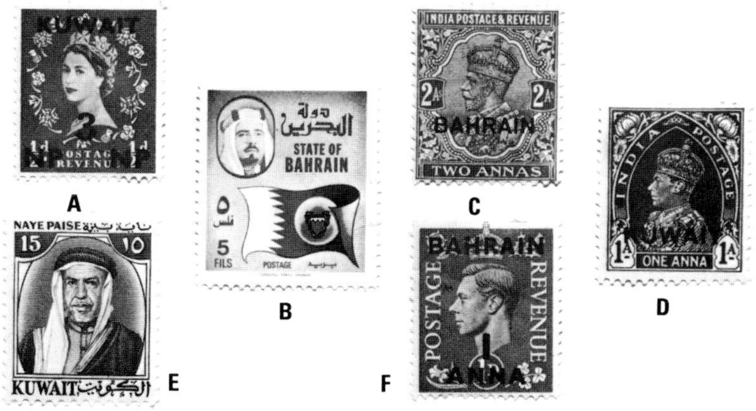

A Kuwait:British Administration 1957; B Bahrain:Independent 1976; C Bahrain:Indian Administration 1933; D Kuwait:Indian Administration 1939; E Kuwait:Independent 1959; F Bahrain:British Administration 1951.

• British PAs in Eastern Arabia

After the partition of India, the British postal administrations in independent states of the Persian Gulf were organized from Britain. Some had particular stamps. Stamps of Britain were also surcharged in Indian currency (with no other distinguishing marks) for general use in:

Muscat 1 April 1948 – 29 April 1966
Dubai 1 April 1948 – 6 January 1961
Qatar August 1950-7
Abu Dhabi (incl. Das Island) December 1960 – 29 March 1964. They were also sold in Kuwait during shortages in 1951 and 1953 and are known used from Bahrain.

• Sharjah and Dependencies

FIRST STAMPS ISSUED 1963

CURRENCY

1963 100 naye paise = 1 rupee
1966 100 dirhams = 1 riyal

Former Trucial State dependencies Dibbah, Khor Fakkan and Khor al-Kalba, to the east on the Gulf of Oman). Although the office of the Political Officer for the Trucial Coast was here 1948-54 and the airport, Sharjah had no PO nearer than Dubai until 1963.

Stamps unnecessarily inscribed or overprinted KHOR FAKKAN were doubtfully used postally.

A United Arab Emirates 1973; B Iran:Kingdom 1951; C Iran:Islamic Republic 1983; D Persia: Kingdom 1885.

• Ras al Khaima

FIRST STAMPS ISSUED 21 December 1964

CURRENCY

1964 100 naye paise = 1 rupee
1966 100 dirhams = 1 riyal

Former Trucial State with a tiny population recognized as a separate sheikhdom.

• Fujeira

FIRST STAMPS ISSUED 22 September 1964

CURRENCY

1964 100 naye paise = 1 rupee
1968 100 dirhams = 1 riyal

Former Trucial State relying mainly on its fishing industry. Its independence was recognized in 1952.

• Ajman

FIRST STAMPS ISSUED 1964

CURRENCY

1964 100 naye paise = 1 rupee
1967 100 dirhams = 1 riyal

Former tiny Trucial State.

Some stamps were unnecessarily overprinted MANAMA supposedly for an even smaller enclave.

• Umm al Qiwain

FIRST STAMPS ISSUED 29 June 1964

CURRENCY

1964	100 naye paise = 1 rupee
1967	100 dirhams = 1 riyal

Former Trucial State with a tiny population.

Note
Most of the stamp issues made by agencies on behalf of Sharjah, Ras al Khaima, Umm al Qiwain, Fujeira, and Ajman were inappropriate and speculative; few were used postally. All used stamps of United Arab Emirates from 1 January 1973.

United Arab Emirates

FIRST STAMPS ISSUED 1 January 1973

CURRENCY

1973	100 fils = 1 dirham

Six of the former Trucial States formed a union on 2 December 1971: Abu Dhabi, Ajman, Dubai, Fujeira, Sharjah, and Umm al Qiwain. Ras al Khaima joined in February 1972. All continued to use their own stamps until after the adoption of a common currency and postal administration on 1 August 1972.

Some stamps inscribed UAE.

Iran (Persia)

CURRENCY

1868	20 shahis = 1 kran
	10 kran = 1 toman
1881	100 centimes = 1 franc
1885	as 1868
1932	100 dinars = 1 rial
	20 rials = 1 pahlavi

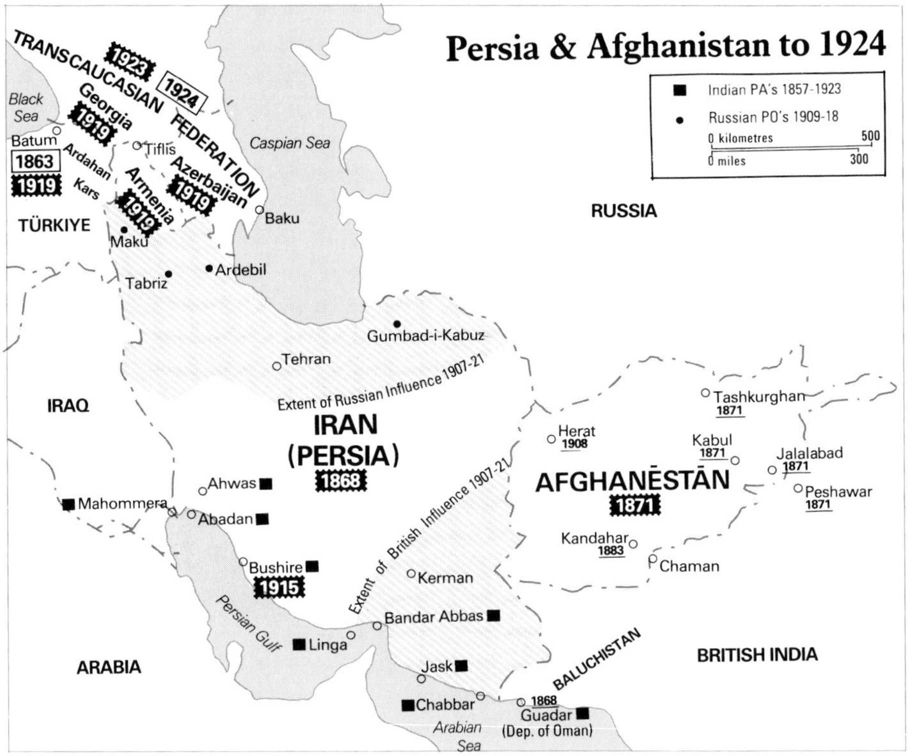
Persia & Afghanistan to 1924
Indian PA's 1857-1923
Russian PO's 1909-18
0 kilometres 500
0 miles 300
TRANSCAUCASIAN FEDERATION
1923
1924
Georgia
1919
Black Sea
Batum
1863
1919
Ardahan
Kars
Tiflis
Armenia
1919
Azerbaijan
1919
Caspian Sea
Baku
TÜRKIYE
Maku
Tabriz
Ardebil
RUSSIA
Gumbad-i-Kabuz
Tehran
Extent of Russian Influence 1907-21
IRAQ
IRAN
(PERSIA)
1868
Herat
1908
Kabul
1871
Tashkurghan
1871
Jalalabad
1871
Peshawar
1871
AFGHANISTAN
1871
Ahwas
Mahommera
Abadan
Extent of British Influence 1907-21
Kandahar
1883
Chaman
Bushire
1915
Kerman
Persian Gulf
Bandar Abbas
Linga
ARABIA
Jask
BALUCHISTAN
BRITISH INDIA
Chabbar
1868
Guadar
(Dep. of Oman)
Arabian Sea

FIRST STAMPS ISSUED 1868

Independent kingdom down the ages, subject in the 19th century to pressure from Russia and Britain. Absolute rule gave place to constitutional government in 1906. Iran was adopted as the official name of the country on 21 March 1935. The former Anglo-Iranian Oil Company was nationalized in 1951 and the supply of oil became an international issue. In 1979 revolution led by Ayatollah Khomeini forced the Shah into exile.

Postal History
The swift courier posts of the ancient Persian Empire were praised by Herodotus. These were an improvement on an earlier Assyrian model and inspired those of the Romans.

Indian PAs were established in Persia from 1857 to 1923 at Bushire, Bandar Abbas (1867), Linga (1867), Jask (1880), Mahommera (1892), Chabbar (1913-20), Henjam (1913), Abadan (1914), Ahwaz (1914). These used stamps of India from 1864.

Russian POs operated in 1909-18 in northern Persia, using stamps of Russia. All are rare; cancellations have been identified from Ardebil, Tabriz, Gumbad-i-Kabuz, and Maku.

• Bushire

CURRENCY

As Iran

While under British occupation had separate stamps 15 August – 16 October 1915.

• Armenia

FIRST STAMPS ISSUED 1919

CURRENCY

1919	As Russia

Once a kingdom with a dynasty claiming descent from Solomon, Armenia has been in turn subject to Persians, Seljuks, Byzantines, Mongols, Turks and Russians. Russia extended its hold at the expense of Turkey in 1878. The Armenians proclaimed their inde-

Right
Mail escort in the Khyber Pass, North West Frontier, during the Afghan Wars, 1879

Above
Postman, Muscat

pendence on 28 May 1918, were ruthlessly attacked by the Turks, but regained independence after the Allied victory. Batum (*see below*) was placed under British occupation, but Kars and Ardahan were again lost to Turkish arms. National and Communist governments succeeded one another until on 2 April 1921 Communist forces entered Erivan and set up a Soviet republic.

On 12 March 1922 Armenia, Azerbaijan and Georgia were federated, but each continued to have separate stamps until, on 1 October 1923, these were replaced by a general issue for the Transcaucasian Federation.

• Batum

CURRENCY

As Russia

Armenian port on the Black Sea and the gateway to Transcaucasia. Turkish before 1878, it was ceded to Russia, who extended to it the Transcaucasian Railway from Baku and Tiflis. Became an important oil pipe terminal in 1903. Was recaptured by the Turks in April 1918 and came under British occupation December 1918 – 6 July 1920. Handed to the Republic of Georgia, it was again seized by the Turks for a few days in March 1921. The Georgians retook it and surrendered it to the invading Bolsheviks. It is now part of the Georgian SSR.

Batum seems never to have had a Turkish PO; a PA of ROPiT was in existence from before 1862 to 1877.

Used stamps of Russia 1863-4.

Used stamps of Russian Levant (ROPiT) 1865-77.

Used stamps of Russia 1878-1918.

Separate stamps (during British occupation) 1919 – July 1920.

• Azerbaijan

FIRST STAMPS ISSUED 1919

CURRENCY

1919 As Russia

A once independent princedom split between Russia and Persia. The October Revolution in Russia occasioned a new bid for independence on 27 May 1918. Soviet troops invaded on 27 April 1920 and set up a Communist régime. *See also* Armenia.

• Georgia

FIRST STAMPS 26 May 1919

CURRENCY

1919 As Russia

Once a kingdom with a history similar to that of Armenia, Georgia came under the Turks and Russians in turn. On 26 May 1918 it declared independence but was occupied by the Red Army in 1921. *See also* Armenia.

• Transcaucasian Federation

FIRST GENERAL STAMPS ISSUED
15 September 1923

CURRENCY

1923 As Russia

Federation of the Soviet republics of Armenia, Azerbaijan and Georgia, established on 12 March 1922, but absorbed into the USSR on 6 July 1923.

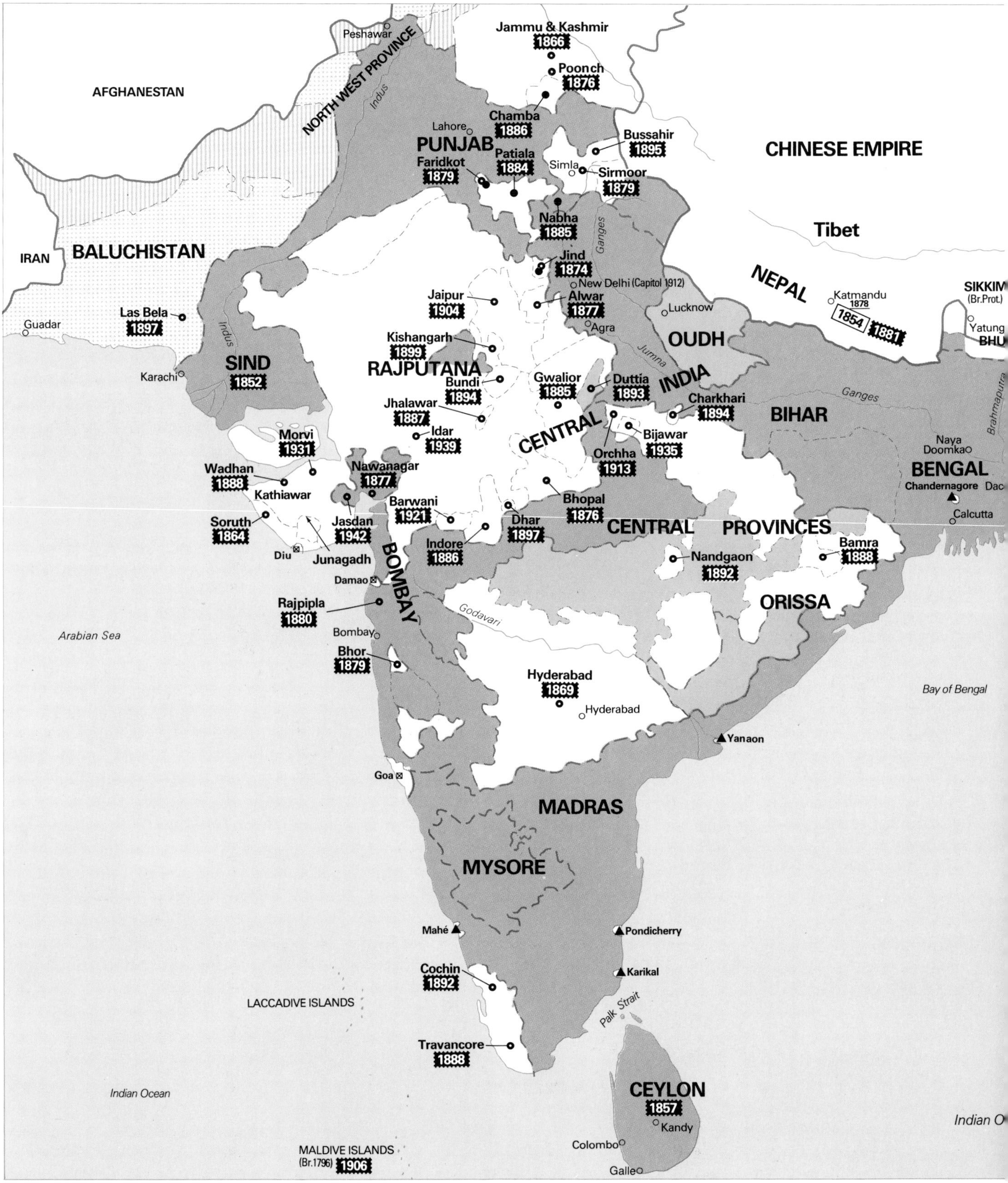
Peshawar
NORTH WEST PROVINCE
Indus
AFGHANESTAN
Jammu & Kashmir
1866
Poonch
1876
Chamba
1886
Lahore
PUNJAB
Patiala
1884
Faridkot
1879
Bussahir
1895
Simla
Sirmoor
1879
CHINESE EMPIRE
Nabha
1885
Tibet
Ganges
IRAN
BALUCHISTAN
Jind
1874
New Delhi (Capitol 1912)
NEPAL
Katmandu
1878
1854
1881
SIKKIM
(Br.Prot.)
Jaipur
1904
Alwar
1877
Lucknow
Yatung
Las Bela
1897
Guadar
Agra
OUDH
Kishangarh
1899
Indus
Jumna
SIND
1852
RAJPUTANA
Karachi
Bundi
1894
Gwalior
1885
Duttia
1893
INDIA
Charkhari
1894
Ganges
BIHAR
Brahmaputra
Jhalawar
1887
Idar
1939
CENTRAL
Bijawar
1935
Morvi
1931
Orchha
1913
Naya
Doomka
Wadhan
1888
Nawanagar
1877
BENGAL
Chandernagore
Kathiawar
Barwani
1921
Bhopal
1876
Soruth
1864
Jasdan
1942
Dhar
1897
CENTRAL
PROVINCES
Calcutta
Indore
1886
Bamra
1888
Diu
Junagadh
BOMBAY
Nandgaon
1892
Damao
ORISSA
Rajpipla
1880
Godavari
Arabian Sea
Bombay
Bhor
1879
Hyderabad
1869
Hyderabad
Bay of Bengal
Yanaon
Goa
MADRAS
MYSORE
Mahé
Pondicherry
Cochin
1892
Karikal
LACCADIVE ISLANDS
Palk Strait
Travancore
1888
CEYLON
1857
Indian Ocean
Kandy
Colombo
MALDIVE ISLANDS
(Br.1796)
1906
Galle

dia & Burma 1852-1942
British India 1852 1852
British acquisitions to 1858
British acquisitions after 1858
Native States 1858
Native States added after 1858
British India 1937
Burma-India Boundary 1937
French Stamps 1859-92 1892
Portuguese Stamps 1871
Convention State
Feudatory State
ASSAM
Bhamo
Upper Burma
BURMA
(Br.Prot.1886)
1854
(Separated from India 1937)
1937
Mandalay
Irawaddy
Salween
Arakan
Akyab
1827
Kyouk Phyoo
Thyetmyo
Ramree
Prome
(Namayan)
Toungnoo
Sandoway
Shoay Coyen
Pegu
SIAM
(THAILAND)
Pegu
Sittang
Sarawah
Rangoon
1862
Bassein
Moulmein
Tovoy
Tanasserim
Mergui
ANDAMAN ISLANDS
(Brit. 1864)
Port Blair
1860
MALAY
STATES
NICOBAR ISLANDS
(Brit. 1868)
0 kilometres 500
0 miles 300

INDIA POSTAGE
SILVER JUBILEE
COMMEMORATION
6th May 1935
A
INDIA
ONE ANNA
B
भारत INDIA
PBG
20
1773-1973
राष्ट्रपति अंगरक्षक PRESIDENT'S BODY GUARD
C
1981
9 AFS
POSTES AFGHANES
D
E

A Empire of India 1931; **B** East India Company 1854; **C** Republic of India 1973; **D** Arghanistan:Republic 1981. **E** Afghanistan:Kingdom 1871;

Postal services were centralized on 1 October 1922.

Used stamps of USSR from 1924.

Afghanistan

FIRST STAMPS ISSUED 1871

CURRENCY

1871	12 shahi = 6 sanar = 3 abasi = 1 rupee
1920	60 paisa = 2 kran = 1 rupee
1926	100 poul = 1 afgani (rupee)

Independent kingdom (Kingdom of Kabul until 1890) from 1747 to 1973 when the king was deposed and a republic declared. In 1978 a Russian-inspired *coup* set up a puppet Soviet régime. Following opposition by Muslim loyalists, the Russians occupied the country by force in December 1979.

Postal History

Four POs were opened in 1871: Kabul, Peshawar, Jalalabad, and Tashkurghan. Mail to India was routed via Chaman. The route via Kandahar, where a PO was opened c. 1883, was started in 1906. Herat was opened 1908.

The method of cancelling stamps was generally by tearing off a corner!

In 1961-4 many 'undesirable' issues appeared with face values that could pay no rate of postage.

India

FIRST STAMPS ISSUED 1 July 1852 (the so-called 'Scinde Dawk' issue, made by the commissioner of Sind province, the first adhesive postage stamps in Asia)

CURRENCY

1852	12 pies = 1 annas : 16 annas = 1 rupee
1957	100 naye paise = 1 rupee
1964	100 paisa = 1 rupee

The sea route to India via the Cape of Good Hope was pioneered in 1498 by the Portuguese, who founded a colony at Goa. By 1580 the Portuguese had settled much of the coast belonging to the sub-continent of the Moghul empire. These possessions, with few exceptions, were lost in the early 17th century to Dutch and British merchants.

The East India Company received a royal charter from Elizabeth I on 31 December 1600. The city of Madras was founded in 1639 on land purchased; Bombay came to the English Crown in 1660; Calcutta was founded in 1668. The Seven Years War (1756-63) gave Britain mastery over the French and Dutch, and the control of the East India Company was extended to the innumerable separate states, large and small, by successive governors and governors-general. A general rising ('Indian Mutiny') in 1857 was suppressed and on 1 November 1858 the government of India was transferred to the Crown under a viceroy.

In 1947 India was partitioned into a predominantly Hindu India and a Muslim Pakistan and both were granted independence within the British Commonwealth. In May 1949 India became a republic, but remained a member of the Commonwealth while acknowledging non-allegiance to the British throne.

Postal History

Though an overland route operated in the 17th and 18th centuries (most successfully in 1636-68 and 1769-83) through various consular forwarding agencies in Marseille, Leghorn, Venice, Aleppo and Basra, the principal mails to India were carried via the Cape. An organized system regulating carriage of letters by sea between England and the presidencies of Bombay, Madras and Calcutta, with POs at those places, was established in 1688. Regular overland communication between Madras and Calcutta began in 1720 and to Bombay in 1775. Handstruck marks are known on mail from the 1770s.

When the British GPO extended its steam packet from Malta to Alexandria in 1835, Thomas Waghorn operated an overland mail service by camel to Suez to connect with an East India Company's steamer. On 1 October 1837 the Indian Post Office was established under the governor-general, the East India posts and the former official King's Post being combined. The Bombay-Suez packet became regular (British India Steam Navigation Co.); the Alexandria packet passed in 1842 to the Peninsular and Orient line, which also took over the Egyptian overland mail.

Use was made from 1839 of European mail routes to the Mediterranean (Marseille, Trieste or Brindisi) which improved as coach and river-steamer gave place to the railway. The Egyptian section was improved by successive rail openings in 1856, 1859 and 1868. Though the Suez Canal was opened in 1869, mail was not passed through without transhipment until 1888 (though it was often put back on the same steamer). The P & O and BISN shipping lines amalgamated in 1914.

Airmails reached India on a weekly basis from Croydon in 1929, though experimental flights started in India in 1911.

The vast scope of India has always been a challenge to collectors. The basic stamps are common and have never attracted advanced specialist interest beyond the first issue. The catalogue listings have remained simple. The existence of 114,000 POs, including many rail and river steamer TPOs using only numbered cancellers, make a daunting challenge for collectors of postmarks. Certain aspects of the postal history have a large following, particularly letters to Britain stamped INDIA LETTER and the place of landing, military campaign mail, and 'India Used Abroad'.

• Indian Native States

CURRENCY

1886 As India

Many native feudatory states (some with their own currencies) set up or continued local postal systems which carried mail within the state. Certain states signed a 'convention' with British India which allowed them to difference the stamps and postal stationery of India by an overprint bearing their name (unlike the feudatory states' issues, these stamps were valid throughout the Indian Empire). Faridkot and Jind had periods as both feudatory and convention states. All surviving separate issues were replaced by stamps of the Republic of India on 1 April 1950, though convention stamps remained valid to 31 December 1950 (others 30 April).

• Chamba

FIRST STAMPS 1886

A convention state.

• Gwalior

FIRST STAMPS 1885
Hindi inscription:

Largest convention state, with 120 POs.

• Nabha

FIRST STAMPS 1885

A convention state.

• Patiala

FIRST STAMPS 1884
Overprinted variously PUTTIALLA, PATIALA

A convention state.

• Alwar

FIRST STAMPS ISSUED 1877

A feudatory state in Rajputana.

Separate stamps discontinued in 1902.

• Bamra

FIRST STAMPS ISSUED 1888

A feudatory state of the Central Provinces.

Separate stamps discontinued in 1894.

• Barwani

FIRST STAMPS ISSUED 1921

A feudatory state.

Separate stamps discontinued on 1 July 1948.

• Bhopal

FIRST STAMPS ISSUED 1876

A Muslim feudatory state.

Separate stamps went out of use in 1903, but after 1 July 1908 further issues were made for use on official mail. These continued to 30 April 1950.

Inscription until 1903: H. H. NAWAB SHAH JAHAN BEGAM.

• Bhor

FIRST STAMPS ISSUED 1879

A feudatory state south-east of Bombay.

The state POs were closed in 1895, but a stamp 'issued' in 1901 was supplied to collectors (mint or used!).

• Bijawar

FIRST STAMPS ISSUED 1935

A feudatory state in Central India. Separate stamps discontinued in 1939.

• Bundi

FIRST STAMPS ISSUED May 1894

A feudatory state in Rajputana. In 1948 joined Rajasthan.

Separate stamps discontinued in 1948.

• Bussahir

FIRST STAMPS ISSUED 20 June 1895

A feudatory state of the Punjab.

There were three POs: Rampur, Rorhu, and Chini. Stamps were declared obsolete on 31 March 1901 and remainders (cancelled Rampur 19 MA 1900) sold to the stamp trade. There are also later clandestine reprints.

• Charkhari

FIRST STAMPS ISSUED 1894

A feudatory state in Central India.

Separate stamps discontinued on 30 April 1950.

• Cochin

FIRST STAMPS ISSUED 1 April 1892. Most have characteristic Umbrella watermark.
Note: ANCHAL = Postage

CURRENCY	
1892	6 puttans = 5 annas
1911	as in British India

A feudatory state in south-west India, united with Travancore on 1 July 1949.

• Dhar

FIRST STAMPS ISSUED 1897

A feudatory state of Central India.

Separate stamps discontinued on 31 March 1901.

• Duttia (Datia)

FIRST STAMPS ISSUED 1893

A feudatory state in Bundelkhand.

The last stamp appears to have been issued c. 1920.

• Faridkot

FIRST STAMPS ISSUED 1879

A Cis-Sutlej Sikh feudatory state, which in 1887 signed the convention.

Used convention issues 1 January 1887 – 31 March 1901.

• Hyderabad (Deccan)

FIRST STAMPS ISSUED 1869
Stamps inscribed in native script or H.E.H. THE NIZAM'S GOVERNMENT

A large feudatory state in south central India. (occ. Indian troops 1948).

Separate stamps discontinued on 30 April 1950.

• Idar

FIRST STAMPS ISSUED 21 February 1939

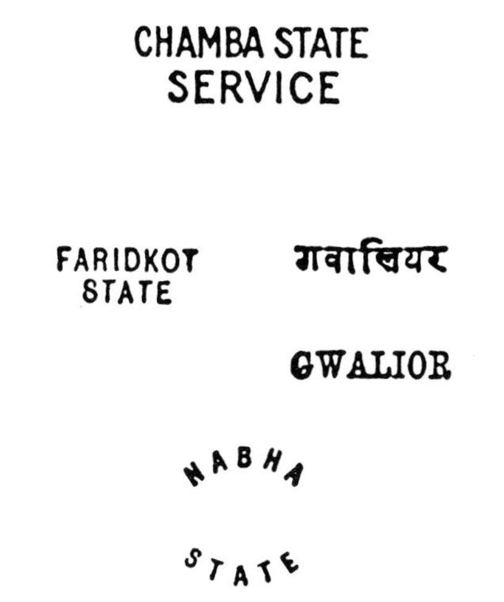
CHAMBA STATE
SERVICE
FARIDKOT
STATE
GWALIOR
NABHA
STATE

A selection of overprints of India for the Convention States, 1885-1947

A feudatory state in western India.

Separate stamps discontinued on 30 April 1950.

• Indore (Holkar)

FIRST STAMPS ISSUED 1886

A feudatory state in central India, known as Holkar before 1904.

Separate stamps discontinued on 30 April 1950.

• Jaipur

FIRST STAMPS ISSUED 1904

A feudatory state in Rajputana. In 1948 it joined with other states (including Bundi and Kishangarh) to form Rajasthan.

Separate stamps discontinued in 1949.

• Jammu and Kashmir

FIRST STAMPS ISSUED March 1866

A feudatory state of two provinces in north-west India.

PAKISTAN
POSTAGE
20P
FRANCAIS
DANS L'INDE
ETABLISSEMENTS
POSTES
2 fa. 2 ca.
PAKISTAN
13 PAISA
POSTAGE
MOHENJODARO
REPVBLICA PORTVGVESA
8 T.
CORREIO
INDIA
10c
POSTES
ETABLISSEMENTS FRANCAIS DANS L'INDE

A Pakistan: Modern Adhesive; B French India 1948; C Pakistan: Dominion 1948; D Portuguese India 1922; E French India 1914; F Pakistan: New Currency 1963.

TEA PLUCKING
BANGLADESH 75P
4CH
1874
1974
CENTENARY OF THE UNIVERSAL POSTAL UNION
BHUTAN
BURMA POSTAGE
1½AS
BURMA
POSTAGE
NEPAL
UNION OF BURMA
15P

A Bangladesh: Independent 1973; B Bhutan: Kingdom 1974; C Burma: British Administration 1938; D Burma: Independent 1948; E Burma: Union of Burma 1967; F Nepal: Kingdom 1957.

A post existed as early as 1820. This was carried by runners. The provinces had both joint and separate stamps on issue concurrently in 1866-77. All issues are inscribed in native scripts only.

Separate stamps discontinued on 1 November 1894.

• Jasdan

FIRST STAMPS ISSUED 1942

A feudatory state merged on 15 February 1948 with Kathiawar.

Used stamps of Soruth 1948-50.

• Jhalawar

FIRST STAMPS ISSUED 1887

A feudatory state of Rajputana.

Separate stamps discontinued on 1 November 1900 when the state PO was taken over by the Imperial government.

• Jind

FIRST STAMPS ISSUED 1874

A Sikh feudatory state and from 1885 a convention state.

Convention stamps overprinted variously JEEND, JHIND, JIND, and (in error) JEIND. Stamps invalidated on 1 January 1951.

• Kishangarh

FIRST STAMPS ISSUED 1899

A feudatory state in Rajputana. In 1948 it joined Bundi and Jaipur to form Rajasthan.

Separate stamps discontinued in 1949.

• Las Bela

FIRST STAMPS ISSUED 1897

A feudatory state in Baluchistan.

Separate stamps discontinued in March 1907.

• Morvi

FIRST STAMPS ISSUED 1 April 1931

A feudatory state, incorporated into Saurashtra on 15 February 1948.

After 1948 used stamps of Soruth.

• Nandgaon

FIRST STAMPS ISSUED February 1892

A feudatory state in central India.

Separate stamps discontinued in July 1895.

• Nawanagar

FIRST STAMPS ISSUED 1877

CURRENCY

1877 6 docra = 1 anna

A feudatory state.

Separate stamps discontinued in 1895.

• Orchha

FIRST STAMPS ISSUED 1913

A feudatory state in central India.
Stamps were prepared for use in 1897 but never issued.
Separate stamps discontinued on 30 April 1950.

• Poonch

FIRST STAMPS ISSUED 1876

A feudatory state tributary to Jammu and Kashmir.
Separate stamps discontinued in 1894.

• Rajasthan

FIRST STAMPS ISSUED 1949

A union of several Rajputanan states.
Separate stamps discontinued on 30 April 1950.

P&O vessel *Caledonia,* the fastest mail-carrying vessel to Bombay, India, 1894

• Rajpipla

FIRST STAMPS ISSUED 1880

A feudatory state near Bombay.
Separate stamps discontinued in 1886.

• Sirmoor

FIRST STAMPS ISSUED 1879

A feudatory state in the Simla hills.
Separate stamps discontinued on 30 March 1902.

• Soruth

FIRST STAMPS ISSUED November 1864

CURRENCY

1864	Before 1913: 40 docras = 16 annas = 1 koree.

A feudatory state, otherwise Saurashtra, which with Junagadh forms part of Kathiawar. Early stamps were inscribed in Hindi or English SORUTH and the name continues in use by philatelists. Later stamps are inscribed SAURASHTRA. The state became part of the Indian union on 9 November 1947. On 15 February 1948 the United State of Saurashtra was formed from 201 Kathiawar states, including Jasdan, Morvi, Nawanagar and Wadhwan, though Junagadh, where the majority of stamps have always been used, did not join until 20 January 1949.
Separate stamps discontinued on 30 April 1950.

• Travancore

FIRST STAMPS ISSUED 16 October 1888. Most have characteristic conch shell watermark.
Note: ANCHEL = Postage

CURRENCY

1888	16 cash = 1 chuckram 28 chuckrams = 1 rupee

A feudatory state, united with Cochin on 1 July 1949.

• Travancore-Cochin

FIRST STAMPS ISSUED 1 July 1949

The united states of Cochin and Travancore after 1 July 1949.
Separate stamps discontinued on 30 June 1951.

• Wadhwan

FIRST STAMPS ISSUED 1888

A tiny feudatory state on the Bombay-Baroda Railway.
Separate stamps discontinued c. 1894.

• Indian Army POs

Stamps of India have been used by troops of the Indian Army serving abroad all over the world where these have not been specially differenced by surcharges. Those differenced for particular locations will be found under the appropriate country. General surcharged issues, *see below*.

• Indian Expeditionary Forces
Indian troops serving abroad in 1914-22 used stamps of India overprinted I.E.F. Places of use in Near East, Egypt, East Africa, etc. can be located only by the FPO cancellation numbers.

• China Expeditionary Force

CURRENCY
As India

The international Chinese Expeditionary Force sent to relieve Peking in 1900 suppressed the Boxer Rebellion and policed northern China until 1906. Thereafter a smaller contingent remained.

FPOs maintained in China used stamps of India overprinted C.E.F. from c. August 1900 to 25 November 1923.

• India Used Abroad
Stamps of India have also been used at civil POs outside India. See particularly: Burma, Aden, British Somaliland, Zanzibar, Persian Gulf, Persia, Iraq, and Straits Settlements.

• French Indian Settlements (Établissements Français dans l'Inde)

FIRST STAMPS ISSUED November 1892

CURRENCY	
1892	100 centimes = 1 franc
1923	24 caches = 1 fanou ; 8 fanous = 1 rupee

Of the large French Empire in India, which opposed the British in the Seven Years War, only five settlements remained after 1814: Pondicherry and Karikal, Chandernagore, Mahé, and Yanaon (Orissa). After referenda, Chandernagore was transferred to India on 2 May 1950; the other four on 1 November 1954.

Possibly used stamps of France from 1849.

Used French Colonies General issues 1859-92 (oblit. various lozenges of dots with or without indication of place, e.g. INDE).

There were also British Indian POs and sub-POs in the settlements in which stamps of India were used 1854-1947.

• Portuguese India (India Portugueza)

FIRST STAMPS ISSUED 1 October 1871 (after 1877 these were valid for overseas postage via Bombay)

CURRENCY	
1871	1000 reis = 1 milreis
1882	12 reis = 1 tanga; 16 tanga = 1 rupee
1959	100 centavos = 1 escudo

Three settlements, Goa, Damao (Damaon), and Diu, flourished from the 16th century until 17 December 1961, when they were invaded by Indian troops and annexed to India.

Little is known of an early Portuguese post, though regular mails were exchanged with Lisbon from 1825. The Portuguese had mail conventions with Britain and probably used British packets. In the 19th century mail seems to have been routed mainly via Bombay, both before and after Portuguese colonial stamps were available. From 1854, Portuguese handstamps and in 1871-7 stamps were used in combination with stamps of British India, which were sold at the Portuguese POs.

Used stamps of India from 29 December 1961.

Pakistan

FIRST STAMPS India to 1947
FIRST STAMPS ISSUED 1 October 1947

CURRENCY	
1947	As India
1961	100 paisa = 1 rupee

Until partition in 1947 all British India shared the same fortunes (*see* India). As established as a British dominion on 14 August 1947, Pakistan consisted of two geographically separate parts: Western, comprising Baluchistan, the Western Punjab and Sind, and the North West Frontier Provinces; Eastern, comprising Assam and North and East Bengal. The former stamp-issuing states of Las Bela and Soruth came within its borders. On 29 February 1956 an Islamic republic was declared within the British Commonwealth. Military dictatorships and new constitutions have alternated ever since. In 1959 the capital was moved from Karachi to Islamabad (near Rawalpindi). Following a civil war between East and West Pakistan, the Eastern province declared itself independent as Bangladesh. On 30 January 1972 Pakistan withdrew from the Commonwealth.

• Bahawalpur

FIRST STAMPS ISSUED 1 January 1945 (official only)

CURRENCY	
1945	As India

A native state of Pakistan.

Separate stamps, which were valid only locally within the state, were discontinued at the end of 1949.

Bangladesh

FIRST STAMPS ISSUED 29 July 1971

CURRENCY	
1971	100 paisa = 1 rupee
1972	100 paisa = 1 taka

Once part of India, then of Pakistan, Bangladesh was proclaimed an independent state within the British Commonwealth in 1972.

Various Pakistan stamps were overprinted locally during the war that preceded independence.

Bhutan

FIRST STAMPS 1 January 1955 (fiscal stamps validated for internal postal use)

CURRENCY

1955	16 annas = 1 rupee
1957	100 chetrum = 1 ngultrum
1962	100 chetrum = 1 ngultrum (or rupee)

A Buddhist kingdom in the Eastern Himalayas, having treaty relations with India which continue those formerly made with Britain. It changed from absolute to democratic monarchy in 1969.

Postal History
Runner routes between lamaseries existed in the 19th century. External mails (such as there were) were sent at least from 1920 by a regular route to Yatung in Tibet. The modern posts with 51 POs date from 1962.

Until Bhutan joined the UPU (7 March 1969), external mails usually bore in addition stamps of India, Tibet or China.

• Sikkim
Independent state in the Himalayas.

Stamps inscribed SIKKIM STATE may or may not have had postal validity in the 1920s; they are not generally listed in catalogues. Experiments were apparently made in 1935 with mail-carrying rockets!

Nepal

FIRST STAMPS India 1854
FIRST STAMPS ISSUED May 1881

CURRENCY

1881	16 annas = 1 rupee
1907	64 pke = 1 rupee
1954	100 paisa = 1 rupee

A Gurkha kingdom in the Himalayas with capital at Katmandu. After fighting the British in India in 1814-6, the Gurkhas aided the government during the Indian Mutiny. Gurkha regiments have formed part of the British Army ever since, though Nepal was never part of the Empire. A treaty of friendship was signed in 1923.

A PO was opened at the British Residency in 1816 with a dated handstamp; it was finally closed by the Indian government in 1966. A PO was established at Katmandu in 1878 and some 40 offices followed in Nepal. Mails were carried by runner until the first motor transport in 1948. Nepal joined the UPU in 1957 and established exchange offices on the Indian border in 1960. Since 1954, when there were 124 POs, the number has risen to c.1000.

Used stamps of India from 1854. External letters were usually sent through British residency/legation or Indian embassy bearing Indian stamps.

• Ceylon

FIRST STAMPS ISSUED 1 April 1857

CURRENCY

1857	12 pence = 1 shilling
1872	100 cents = 1 rupee

The coasts of Ceylon were subject to the Portuguese until 1656 and then to the Dutch, though neither subdued the native kings in Kandy. The island was taken by the British in 1796 and after two years under the Madras presidency was made a Crown Colony. The king was deposed and exiled.

Ceylon became independent within the British Commonwealth on 4 February 1948. On 22 May 1972 it became the republic of Sri Lanka.

Postal History
A postmaster-general was appointed in 1802 and handstamps supplied in 1813. Internal posts grew with the building of roads 1820-45. Mail for Europe was routed overland and across the Palk Strait via India until packets started calling at Galle c.1845. Mail coaches connected Galle with Colombo, Colombo with Kandy. Ceylon joined the UPU in 1877. The first railway TPO started 11 April 1892.

Sri Lanka

FIRST STAMPS ISSUED 22 May 1972

Formerly Ceylon (*see above*).

Maldive Islands

FIRST STAMPS ISSUED 1906

CURRENCY

1906	100 cents = 1 rupee
as Ceylon to 1950	
1950	100 larees = 1 rupee
1951	100 larees = 1 rupee

A group of c.2000 coral islands in the Indian Ocean, of which 220 are inhabited. The sultanate was part of the Ceylon possessions ceded to Britain by the Dutch in 1796, but made a separate protectorate in 1887 administered by the Governor of Ceylon. It became an independent sovereign state on 26 July 1965 and was declared a republic on 11 November 1968.

Burma

FIRST STAMPS India October 1854
FIRST STAMPS ISSUED 1 April 1937

CURRENCY

Indian to 1942 and in 1945-53	
15 October 1942	100 cents = 1 rupee
1953	100 pyas = 1 kyat

The kings of Ava broke free of the Chinese in 1765-9 and extended their rule until in 1785 Burma had a common frontier with India. Assam was annexed in 1816 but designs upon the Ganges delta precipitated the First Burmese War (1824-7) with Britain. Arakan and Tenasserim were annexed to Bengal in February 1826. War again broke out in 1852 and resulted in the annexation to India of the province of Pegu. British Burma was made a separate administration on 31 January 1862. Control of the Andaman Islands was added in 1864 and of the Nicobar Islands on their annexation in 1868.

The discovery of secret intrigues betwen Ava and France led to the Third Burmese War (1885), in which Mandalay was quickly occupied. The suppression of dacoity and piracy in Upper Burma took several years, but on 1 January 1886 Burma became the largest province of the Indian Empire.

On 1 April 1937 Burma was transferred to direct British rule. Largely occupied in 1942 by Japanese forces, who encouraged independence as a puppet on 1 November 1942, it was recaptured before the end of World War II. A period under British Military Administration was followed by rapid moves towards real independence (4 January 1948), upon which Burma left the British Commonwealth. It fell to a military revolutionary council in 1962. After a referendum in 1973, it became a one-party socialist republic.

Postal History

A postal service developed from the military needs of the First Burmese War. It depended on Bengal. By 1827 Akyab PO was established and by 1837 there were four sub-offices (Kyouk Phyoo, Ramree, Sandway and Moulmein). Handstamps are known from 1838. A postmaster was appointed at Rangoon soon after its capture in 1852, and the posts extended to Pegu province. There were 22 POs with numbered cancellers of the Bengal circle, including Port Blair in the Andaman Islands (opened February 1860).

A separate Pegu circle in 1861 gave place to the British Burma circle in 1862. The posts were hardly used except by foreign residents, and district posts proved unnecessary until 1874. Internal communication by runner and riverboat remained slow and difficult for many years. Mail to Europe was routed via Calcutta into the Indian posts. Residency PAs were opened intermittently between 1869 and 1885 at Mandalay and Bhamo while they were still in the kingdom of Ava.

TPOs on river steamers and railways were operated from 1887. The regular Indian airmail from England reached Akyab and Rangoon in October 1933 and soon extended to Singapore.

In World War II the Burma Independence Army reopened the postal service in May 1942 with the authority of the Japanese. The Japanese directorate-general took over in August, but returned control in November 1942. There were 1094 POs in 1975.

Imperial troops operating in Burma in 1941-5 used stamps of India.

Japanese occupation stamps (from May 1942) bear peacock overprints or are inscribed in Japanese or in Burmese.

A
75+25
THAILAND
REPUBLIC of MALDIVES
MALDIVES
15c
5R
B
CEYLON
TEN PENCE
C
TICAL 1
D
CEYLON
10
E
WORLD FOOD DAY
3.00
SRI LANKA
F

A Thailand:Kingdom 1979; B Maldive Islands:Republic 1979; C Ceylon:Crown Colony 1857; D Siam:Kingdom 1905; E Ceylon:Dominion 1968; F Sri Lanka:Independent 1984.

Thailand (Siam)

FIRST STAMPS ISSUED 4 August 1883

CURRENCY

1883	32 solot = 16 atts = 8 pelnung = 4 songpy = 2 fuang = 1 sulung
1909	100 satangs = 1 tical
1912	100 satangs = 1 baht

Now properly called Thai Muang (Land of the Free People), though the people were called Siamese before they were free, and Siam and Thailand have been almost equally used. Siam became a strong kingdom in the 13th century occasionally succumbing to Burmese domination. The Chakri dynasty has ruled since 1782 with Bangkok as capital. Laos was ceded to France in 1893 and other provinces in 1907. Claims to the unfederated Malay states (Kedah, Kelantan, Perlis and Trengganu) were relinquished to Britain in 1909. The name of the country was changed officially to Thailand in

June 1939. Between September 1945 and 10 May 1949 the name reverted to Siam.

Postal History

Even the Court had no communications outside the country until King Mongkut started a voluminous correspondence with European countries.

A British consular PO was opened in Bangkok in 1858 which exchanged mails by steamer through Singapore.

Stamps of Hong Kong are known on mail from Bangkok.

From 1882 to 1 July 1885 used stamps of Straits Settlements overprinted 'B'.

An internal mail started in Bangkok in 1881. Siam joined the UPU in 1885.

A
B
C
D
E
F
S.UJONG
SPECIMEN
MALAYA
PAHANG
PERAK
EIGHT CENTS
STRAITS SETTLEMENTS

A Pahang 1941; **B** Sungei Ujong 1893; **C** Perak 1939; **D** Straits Settlements 1938; **E** Straits Settlements on India 1867; **F** Selangor 1935.

Malaysia

CURRENCY

1867 100 cents = 1 Straits dollar
(conversion rate at its inception was R1 = 45½c or 1 anna = 3 cents)

Left
Posting a letter in Malacca, Malaysia

Below
Kuala Lumpur, Malaysia

Peninsular Malaya has attracted European attention since 1511 when the Portuguese took Malacca. The Dutch East India Company became dominant in South-east Asia from 1623 to 1785. The British acquired Penang in 1785 to prevent it falling to the French, Singapore in 1819 from the Sultan of Johore, and Malacca by cession from the Dutch in 1824. Province Wellesley on the mainland was administered by Penang. Penang superseded Malacca in importance between 1800 and 1820, being made a presidency of the East India Company in 1805, and when all three were incorporated in 1826 as the Straits settlements, Penang became the seat of government. In 1836 this was transferred to Singapore. The Straits Settlements were ruled from India until made a Crown Colony in 1867. To them were added the Dindings in 1874 (part of Perak since 1935), Christmas Island in 1900, the Cocos Islands in 1903, and Labuan in 1906.

The British pursued a policy of non-intervention in the independent sultantates of Malaya until 1873, after which the sultanates gradually accepted British Residents and protection. In 1896 Selangor, Negri Sembilan, Pahang and Perak became the Federated Malay States with the centre of administration at Kuala Lumpur. Johore accepted a British advisor but remained outside the Federation. In 1909 Siam ceded the disputed northern states (Kedah, Perlis, Kelantan and Trengganu) to British control. In 1941 the whole region was attacked and occupied by Japan.

In 1946 Singapore became a Crown Colony. The two other Straits Settlements and the nine states formed the Malayan Union and in 1948 the Federation of Malaya, which on 31 August 1957 became a full independent member of the British Commonwealth. Singapore lost the Cocos Islands and Christmas Island in 1955 and became self-governing in 1958. On 16 September 1963 the Federation joined with North Borneo and Sarawak to form the Federation of Malaysia. Singapore joined the Federation on 26 September 1963 but seceded on 9 August 1965 to become an independent republic within the Commonwealth.

Postal History
Early mail connections with British traders in Malaya and the East Indies were made by casual ship as an extension of the services to India; Dutch mails were routed through Batavia. These exist from at least 1688 but letters are rare outside Duch archives before 1799. The earliest postal markings date from c.1806 when a PO existed at Prince of Wales Island (Penang). For later development, *see below*.

Terms in Malay:
PERSEKUTUAN TANAH MELAYU Federation of Malaya
MEL UDARA By Airmail
PEJABAT POS BERGERAK Mobile PO
WAKIL POS BERGERAK River PO
KEMBALIKAN KAPADA PENGIRIM Return to Sender
DI-TOLAK Refused

• Straits Settlements

FIRST STAMPS India 22 October 1854-31 March 1867
FIRST STAMPS ISSUED 1 April 1867

CURRENCY
1867 96 cents = 1 silver dollar
1880 100 cents = 1 Straits dollar

The Indian Post Office Act of 1837 was applied to the Straits Settlements as part of the Bengal circle (1854-61) or the Burma circle (1861-7). The Settlements joined the UPU on 1 April 1877, and until 1899 operated a local postal union with other Malayan territories under British influence. This was renewed in 1946.

When stamps were first issued, the cancellations of the main offices were B109 Malacca, B147 Penang and B172 Singapore. Stamps were also available in Manila until 1862 and were cancelled in transit at Singapore.

Successive issues remained valid in the three main settlements until the Japanese occupation of 1942, also in Province Wellesley, the Dindings (from 1874), Christmas Island (from 1900), Cocos Islands (from 1903), and Labuan (from 1906).

Perak

FIRST STAMPS Straits Settlements 1874-8
FIRST STAMPS ISSUED 1878

CURRENCY
1878 100 cents = 1 dollar Malayan

A Malay state, later one of the Federated Malay States. Initially stamps were for local postage only and these were used in combination with those of Straits Settlements for overseas mail until 1892. Used stamps of Federated Malay States from 1900-35.

Separate stamps resumed 2 December 1935 (for period 1942-8 *see below*).

Although commemoratives were issued in 1948 and 1949, the definitive issue was not released again until 17 August 1950. From 1957, stamps for the Malayan Federation were used concurrently with those of Perak.

In September 1963, Perak became part of the new Federation of Malaysia, since when only low values have been issued by Perak itself.

• Dindings

Small enclave on the coast of Perak which was administered by the Straits Settlements from the Treaty of Pangchor in 1874 until it was returned to Perak in February 1935.

Used the stamps of Straits Settlements at the offices of Lumut, Pangchor Islands, Peng Kalur Bharu.

• Sungei Ujong

FIRST STAMPS ISSUED 1878

CURRENCY
1878 100 cents = 1 dollar (Malay)

A Malay state later incorporated with other smaller states in Negri Sembilan; separate issues ceased in 1895.

Selangor

FIRST STAMPS Straits Settlements 1874-81
FIRST STAMPS ISSUED 1881

CURRENCY
1881 100 cents = 1 Malay dollar

A Malay state, later one of the Federated Malay States. Initially stamps were for local postage only and these were used in combination with those of Straits Settlements for overseas mail until 1891. Used stamps of the Federated Malay States from 1900-35.

Separate stamps resumed 2 December 1935.

In 1941, owing to shortages of local values, some stamps of Selangor were used in other states (for period 1942-8 *see below*).

Although a commemorative issue was released in 1948, the definitive issue was not released again until 12 September 1949. From 1957, stamps for the Malayan Federation were used concurrently with those of Selangor.

In September 1963, Selangor became part of the new Federation of Malaysia, since when only low values have been issued by Selangor itself.

Pahang

FIRST STAMPS ISSUED January 1889

CURRENCY	
1889	100 cents = 1 dollar Malayan

A Malay state, later one of the Federated Malay States.

Used stamps of the Federated Malay states from 1900-35.

Separate stamps resumed on 2 December 1935 (for period 1942-8 *see below*). Although commemoratives were issued in 1948 and 1949, the definitive issue was not released again until 1 June 1950. From 1957, stamps of the Malayan Federation were used concurrently with those of Pahang.

In September 1963, Pahang became part of the new Federation of Malaysia, since when only low values have been issued by Pahang itself.

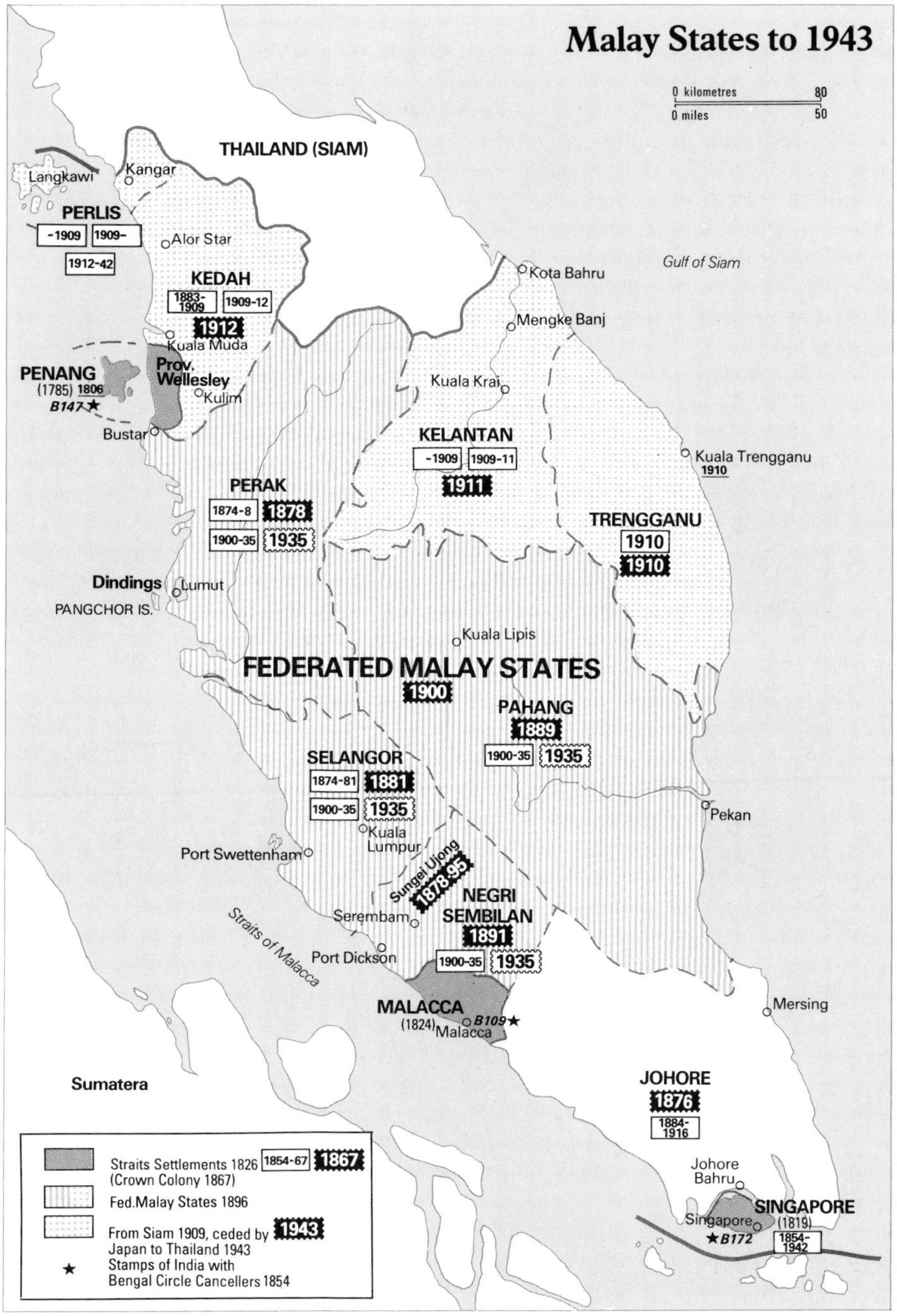
Malay States to 1943
0 kilometres 80
0 miles 50
THAILAND (SIAM)
Langkawi
Kangar
PERLIS
-1909
1909-
1912-42
Alor Star
KEDAH
1883-1909
1909-12
1912
Kuala Muda
PENANG
(1785) 1806
B147★
Prov. Wellesley
Kulim
Bustar
Kota Bahru
Gulf of Siam
Mengke Banj
Kuala Krai
KELANTAN
-1909
1909-11
1911
Kuala Trengganu
1910
PERAK
1874-8
1878
1900-35
1935
TRENGGANU
1910
1910
Dindings
Lumut
PANGCHOR IS.
Kuala Lipis
FEDERATED MALAY STATES
1900
PAHANG
1889
1900-35
1935
SELANGOR
1874-81
1881
1900-35
1935
Kuala Lumpur
Pekan
Port Swettenham
Sungei Ujong
1878-95
NEGRI SEMBILAN
1891
1900-35
1935
Seremban
Straits of Malacca
Port Dickson
MALACCA
(1824)
Malacca
B109★
Mersing
Sumatera
JOHORE
1876
1884-1916
Johore Bahru
SINGAPORE
(1819)
Singapore
★B172
1854-1942
Straits Settlements 1826
1854-67
1867
(Crown Colony 1867)
Fed.Malay States 1896
From Siam 1909, ceded by Japan to Thailand 1943
1943
Stamps of India with Bengal Circle Cancellers 1854

Negri Sembilan

FIRST STAMPS ISSUED 1891

CURRENCY	
1891	100 cents = 1 Malayan dollar

A Malay state, later one of the Federated Malay States.

Used stamps of the Federated Malay states from 1900-35.

Separate stamps resumed on 2 December 1935 (for period 1942-8 *see below*). Although a commemorative issue was released in 1948, the definitive issue was not released again until 1 April 1949. From 1957, the stamps of the Malayan Federation were used concurrently with those of Negri Sembilan.

In September 1963, Negri Sembilan became part of the new Federation of Malaysia, since when only low values have been issued by Negri Sembilan itself.

• Federated Malay States

FIRST STAMPS individual states from 1878
FIRST STAMPS ISSUED 1900

CURRENCY	
1900	100 cents = 1 Malay dollar

Consisted of the protected states of Negri Sembilan, Perak, Pahang and Selangor which federated on 1 July 1896. Owing to shortages before the introduction of the new stamps, cer-

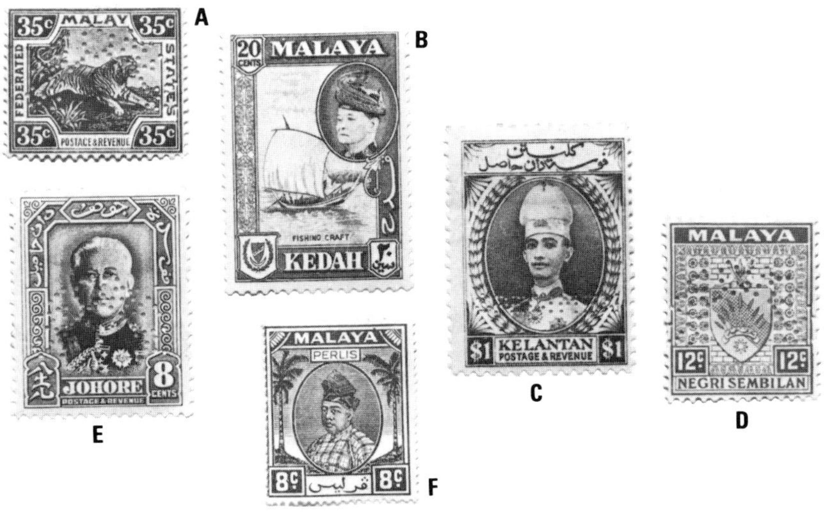
A
MALAY
FEDERATED
STATES
POSTAGE & REVENUE
B
MALAYA
FISHING CRAFT
KEDAH
C
KELANTAN
POSTAGE & REVENUE
D
MALAYA
NEGRI SEMBILAN
E
JOHORE
F
MALAYA
PERLIS

A Federated Malay States 1922; **B** Kedah 1957; **C** Kelantan 1928; **D** Negri Sembilan 1935; **E** Johore 1940; **F** Perlis 1951.

tain values were interchanged between states. In 1935, the Malayan Postal Union was formed and the states reverted to separate issues.

Johore

FIRST STAMPS ISSUED July 1876

CURRENCY	
1876	100 cents = 1 Malay dollar

An unfederated Malay state.

Used stamps of Straits Settlements on overseas mail either alone or in combination 1884-1916 (for period 1942-8 *see below*).

Although a commemorative issue was released in 1948, the definitive issue was not released again until 2 May 1949. From 1957 the stamps of the Malayan Federation were used concurrently with those of Johore.

In September 1963, Johore became part of the new Federation of Malayasia, since when only low values have been issued by Johore itself.

Kedah

CURRENCY	
1912	100 cents = 1 Malay dollar

FIRST STAMPS Siam to 1909, Federated Malay States 1909-12
FIRST STAMPS ISSUED 1 July 1912

An unfederated Malay state which was ceded to British protection by Siam in 1909. At that time there were four POs; Alor Star (postmarked KEDAH), Kuala Muda, Kulim and Langkawi which can be found with their Siamese postmark on Federated Malay State stamps.

Alor Star was an airmail transfer point for both Imperial Airways and KLM (for period 1942-8 *see below*).

Although commemoratives were issued in 1948 and 1949, the definitive issued was not released again until 1 June 1950. From 1957 stamps for the Malayan Federation were used concurrently with those of Kedah.

In September 1963, Kedah became part of the new Federation of Malayasia, since when only low values have been issued by Kedah itself.

Kelantan

CURRENCY	
1911	100 cents = 1 Malay dollar

FIRST STAMPS Siam to 1909, Federated Malay States 1909-11
FIRST STAMPS ISSUED January 1911

An unfederated Malay state which was ceded to British protection by Siam in 1909. At that time, there were two POs; Kota Bharu and Batu Mengkebang. The latter was transferred to Kuala Krai in 1913 (for period 1942-8 *see below*).

Although commemoratives were issued in 1948 and 1949, the definitive issued was not released again until 11 July 1951. From 1957, stamps for the Malayan Federation were used concurrently with those of Kelantan.

In September 1963, Kelantan became part of the new Federation of Malayasia, since when only low values have been issued by Kelantan itself.

Perlis

FIRST STAMPS Siam to 1909, then as Kedah to 1948
FIRST STAMPS ISSUED 1 December 1948

CURRENCY	
1948	100 cents = 1 dollar Malayan

An unfederated Malay state which was ceded to British protection by Siam in 1909. At that time there was one PO at Kangar which used a postmark PERLIS. Used the same stamps as Kedah until 1948 (for period 1942-8 *see below*).

Although the first commemorative was issued in 1948 and another in 1949, the first definitive issue was not released until 26 March 1951. From 1957, stamps of the Malayan Federation were used concurrently with those of Perlis.

In September 1963, Perlis became part of the new Federation of Malayasia, since when only low values have been issued by Perlis itself.

Trengganu

FIRST STAMPS Straits Settlements 1910
FIRST STAMPS ISSUED 1910

CURRENCY

1910 100 cents = 1 Straits or Malay dollar

An unfederated Malay state which was ceded to British protection by Siam in 1909. There was no postal service prior to 1910 because the Sultan refused to allow stamps to be used without his head on them. The new PO at Kuala Trengganu (postmarked TRENGGANU) was opened in 1910 (for period 1942-8 *see below*).

Although commemoratives were issued in 1948 and 1949, the definitive issue was not released again until 27 December 1949. From 1957, stamps of the Malayan Federation were used concurrently with those of Trengganu.

In September 1963, Trengganu became part of the new Federation of Malayasia, since when only low values have been issued by Trengganu itself.

TRENGGANU POSTAGE & REVENUE
5 DOLLARS
A
4 CENTS
1959 STATE OF SINGAPORE
B
MALAYAN POSTAL UNION
8 cents
POSTAGE DUE
C
MALAYA
35c MALACCA 35c
D
pulau pinang
malaysia
5c
E

A Trengganu 1910; **B** Singapore:Self-Governing 1959; **C** Malaya Union:Postage Due 1938; **D** Malacca 1949; **E** Penang:Pulau Pinang 1971.

• Japanese occupation of Malaya

FIRST STAMPS Stamps of all states and Straits Settlements overprinted 1942-3
FIRST STAMPS ISSUED 1943

CURRENCY

1942 As Straits Settlements

Invaded in December 1941, the Malayan pensinsula was quickly overrun and Singapore fell in February 1942. All the stocks of stamps captured were handstamped with seals (chops) in Japanese or overprinted DAI NIPPON 2602 (the Japanese Year equivalent to 1942).

Many of these were made and sold locally, but they could be used throughout Malaya. The four northern states were ceded to Thailand in 1943. Definitive stamps for the rest of Malaya were issued in the same year.

• Thai occupation of Northern States (Syburi)

FIRST STAMPS ISSUED November 1943 in Kelantan December 1943 (general issue)

CURRENCY

1943 As Straits Settlements

Kedah, Kelantan, Perlis and Trengganu were ceded by Japan to Thailand on 19 October 1943. Initially Japanese occupation stamps of Kelantan were overprinted for use in that state. The general issue was released in December 1943. Perlis was placed postally under Kedah and a postmark 'Kangar/ Kedah' was introduced. The area was named Syburi by the Thais but it seems that only Kedah used postmarks with this name. In 1944, Japanese occupation stamps were again overprinted — this time for use in Trengganu.

In September 1945, all four states were returned to British protection.

軍政部
マラッカ州
政廳之印
DAI NIPPON
2602
MALAYA
2 Cents
DAI NIPPON
2602
PENANG

Overprints by Japan for occupation of Malaya, 1942-45

• Malaya (British Military Administration)

FIRST STAMPS See above
FIRST STAMPS ISSUED (?) 19 October 1945

CURRENCY

1946 100 cents = 1 Malayan dollar

In 1945-8 while under British Military Administration the whole of Malaya used stamps of Straits Settlements overprinted BMA MALAYA. Some of the values were issued in different colours and were specially printed to be overprinted. Gradually from 1948 the states reissued their own stamps, but the BMA stamps continued to be used until 1951 (Kelantan).

Singapore

FIRST STAMPS See Straits Settlements above
FIRST STAMPS ISSUED 1 September 1948

CURRENCY

1948 100 cents = 1 Malayan dollar
1965 100 cents = 1 Singapore dollar

One of the Straits Settlements until 1946, then a separate British Crown Colony until 1957. When the Federation of Malaya became independent on 1 August 1958, Singapore became the State of Singapore, and used the stamps of the Federation which were used concurrently with those of Singapore.

On 16 September 1963 it joined the Federation of Malaysia but seceded on 9 August 1965 to become an independent republic within the British Commonwealth.

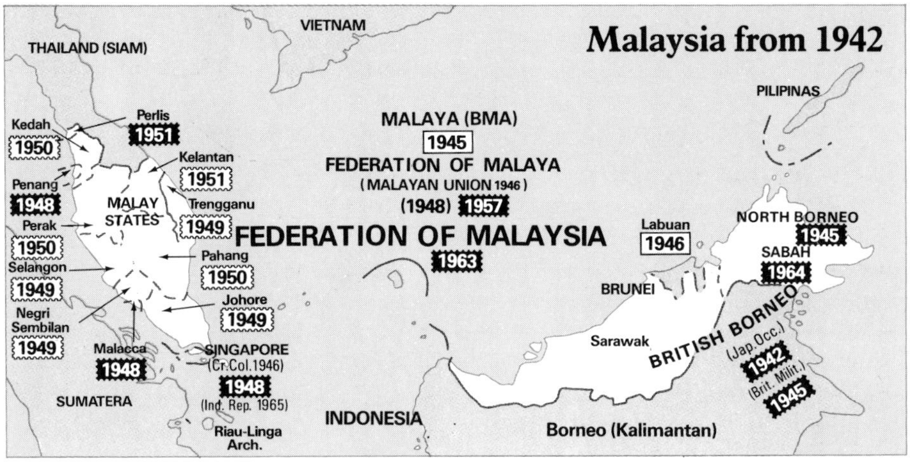
Malaysia from 1942
VIETNAM
THAILAND (SIAM)
PILIPINAS
Perlis 1951
Kedah 1950
MALAYA (BMA) 1945
FEDERATION OF MALAYA
(MALAYAN UNION 1946)
(1948) 1957
Kelantan 1951
Penang 1948
MALAY STATES
Trengganu 1949
Perak 1950
FEDERATION OF MALAYSIA 1963
Labuan 1946
NORTH BORNEO 1945
SABAH 1964
Selangon 1949
Pahang 1950
BRUNEI
Johore 1949
Negri Sembilan 1949
Sarawak
BRITISH BORNEO
(Jap.Occ.) 1942
(Brit. Milit.) 1945
Malacca 1948
SINGAPORE (Cr.Col.1946) 1948 (Ind. Rep. 1965)
SUMATERA
Riau-Linga Arch.
INDONESIA
Borneo (Kalimantan)

Melaka (Malacca)

FIRST STAMPS See Straits Settlements above
FIRST STAMPS ISSUED 1 December 1948

CURRENCY

1948 100 cents = 1 Malayan dollar

One of the Straits Settlements until 1946. Issued commemorative in December 1948 but the first definitive issued appeared on 1 March 1949. From 1957 stamps for the Malayan Federation were used concurrently with those of Malacca.

In September 1963, Malacca became part of the new Federation of Malayasia. The first issue after the formation was on 15 November 1965 and the wording was changed to 'Melaka'. Since that date, only low values have been issued.

Pulau Pinang (Penang)

CURRENCY

1948 100 cents = 1 dollar Malayan

FIRST STAMPS See Straits Settlements above
FIRST STAMPS ISSUED 1 December 1948

One of the Straits Settlements, an island which also administered Province Wellesley on the mainland. Issued commemoratives in December 1948, but the first definitives were released on 21 February 1949. From 1957 stamps for the Malayan Federation were used with those of Penang.

In September 1963, Penang became part of the new Federation of Malayasia. The first issue after the formation was on 18 November 1965 and the wording was changed to 'Pulau Pinang'. Since that date, only low values have been issued.

• Malayan Postal Union

FIRST STAMPS ISSUED Postage Due only 1936

CURRENCY

1936 100 cents = 1 Malayan dollar

The formation of the Union in 1935 led to the reissue of individual stamps for the four Federated Malay States. The Postage Due stamps were in use as follows:

1936–42 Straits Settlements, Negri Sembilan, Pahang, Perak and Selangor
1945–63 Singapore and the Federation of Malaya
1963–15 August 1966 Singapore and the Federation of Malaysia (incl. the territories in Borneo)
15 August 1966–31 January 1968, Singapore only

In 1946, Victory stamps of the Colonial omnibus design were prepared but were never issued. A few of these were, however, released on the market.

• Federation of Malaya

FIRST STAMPS See individual territories
FIRST STAMPS ISSUED 5 May 1957

CURRENCY

1957 100 cents = 1 Malayan dollar

In 1946, Penang, Malacca and the nine Malay States formed the Malay Union and, in 1948, the Federation of Malaya. This achieved independence on 31 August 1957. From 1948-63 each of the 11 territories issued their own stamps (*see above*) which were valid in each other's territories. In 1957, general issues for the Federation were introduced which could be used throughout the Federation and were used concurrently with the stamps of the states. All stamps were superseded on 15 November 1965 by the stamps of Malaysia.

Federation of Malaysia

FIRST STAMPS See individual territories
FIRST STAMPS ISSUED 16 September 1963

CURRENCY

1963 100 cents = 1 Malaysian dollar

A Federation comprising the 11 peninsular Malayan territories with the addition of Sarawak and Sabah (formerly North Borneo).

Each constituent territory has its own 'omnibus' issue up to 25 cent value. For values above that, the stamps of the Federation are used.

1963-5 Singapore was also a member.

Christmas Island

FIRST STAMPS Straits Settlements from 1900
FIRST STAMPS ISSUED 15 October 1958

CURRENCY

1958 100 cents = 1 dollar Malaysian
1968 100 cents = 1 dollar Australian

Previously uninhabited island in the Indian Ocean, south of Java, known since the 17th century but annexed by the British only in 1888. A settlement was established from the Cocos Islands and administration passed to the Straits Settlements in 1900. The island was occupied by the Japanese navy 31 March 1942. In 1946 the island was administered from Singapore until 1 January 1958 when, for 10 months, it was treated as a Crown Colony before being handed over to Australia.

In 1891-1900 mail was passed by visiting ships usually via Fremantle (Western Australia). PO was opened in 1900.

Used stamps of Straits Settlements 1900-42.

No civil mails known under Japanese occupation.

Used stamps of B.M.A. Malaya 1946-8.

Used stamps of Singapore 1948 – 14 October 1958.

Cocos Islands

FIRST STAMPS Straits Settlements 1903
FIRST STAMPS ISSUED 1963

CURRENCY

1963 sterling
1966 as Australia

The islands, discovered by Captain Keeling in 1609, were settled in 1827 by a British subject, John Clunies-Ross, who was adopted as local ruler. In 1857 they were declared a British possession. Placed under the Ceylon government in 1876, they were transferred to the Straits Settlements in 1886 and incorporated with Singapore in 1903. From July 1942 to 3 April 1946 (with Singapore in Japanese hands) they were placed under Ceylon and a military administration. When Singapore became independent in 1955, they were transferred to Australia.

Used stamps of Straits Settlements 1933-7.

Used stamps of Singapore 1952-5.

Used stamps of Australia 1955-63.

Used stamps of Australia 14 February 1966 – 8 July 1969 owing to change to decimal currency.

Separate stamps resumed 9 July 1969.

• Labuan

FIRST STAMPS Straits Settlements 1867
FIRST STAMPS ISSUED May 1879

CURRENCY

1879 100 cents = 1 Straits dollar

Previously uninhabited island off the north coast of Borneo used from 1840 as a British naval base for anti-piracy patrols and as a station on the Singapore-Hong Kong cable, Labuan was ceded to Britain by the Sultan of Brunei in 1846. Became a Crown Colony in 1848. Placed under North Borneo on 1 January 1890, but on 30 October 1906 joined the Straits Settlements. After occupation by Japanese forces (December 1941-June 1945), it came under military administration until rejoined on 15 July 1946 to North Borneo. With North Borneo, Labuan is now part of Malaysia.

A PO existed in 1864 and used a circular date stamp, passing mail through Singapore. Labuan joined the UPU in 1889.

Used stamps of Straits Settlements from 1867. (Stamps of India and Hong Kong exist on mail from Labuan in 1864, but were probably not on sale there.)

Used stamps of Straits Settlements October 1906.

(For period 1941-6, *see below*).

After 1946 used stamps of North Borneo.

• North Borneo

FIRST STAMPS ISSUED June 1883

CURRENCY

1883 100 cents = 1 Malaysian dollar

James Brooke, appointed Consul-General to the Sultan of Sulu in 1849, signed a treaty of friendship in 1849 leading to trade and eventually to the formation in 1882 of the British North Borneo Company. The settlements were made a British Protectorate in 1888 and Labuan attached to it in 1890-1906. After Japanese occupation (January 1942 – 10 June 1945) and British military administration, North Borneo had colonial status restored on 15 July 1946. On 16 September 1963 it became part of the Federation of Malaysia and changed its name to Sabah.

From 1882 channelled mail either through Labuan or Singapore using stamps of Straits Settlements in combination with local stamps. North Borneo joined the UPU in February 1891.

From 1892 several beautiful but unnecessary issues were designed with

MALAYA
12 CENTS
FEDERATION OF MALAYA
MALAYSIA
10¢
COCOS (KEELING) ISLANDS
8d
LABUAN POSTAGE
2 CENTS
NORTH BORNEO
POSTAGE & REVENUE
ONE CENT
NORTH BORNEO
CLOUDED LEOPARD
5 CENTS

Stamps are 90 percent actual size

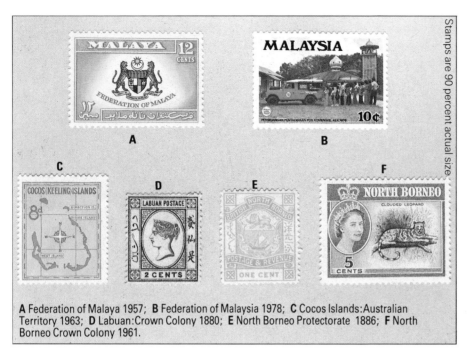

A Federation of Malaya 1957; **B** Federation of Malaysia 1978; **C** Cocos Islands: Australian Territory 1963; **D** Labuan: Crown Colony 1880; **E** North Borneo Protectorate 1886; **F** North Borneo Crown Colony 1961.

NED-NIEUW-GUINEA
10c+5
LEPRABESTRIJDING
4 RUPIAH 4
REPUBLIK INDONESIA
400,-
REPUBLIK INDONESIA

A Netherlands New Guinea 1955;
B Indonesia: Republic 1951;
C Indonesia: Republic 1981.

the philatelic market in mind; when, cancelled by bars, these stamps were remaindered in huge quantities, serious philatelic interest in the country was impaired.

(For period 1941-6, *see below*).

All stamps inscribed North Borneo were withdrawn on 30 June 1964.

Sabah

FIRST STAMPS ISSUED inscribed SABAH 1 July 1964

CURRENCY

1964 100 cents = 1 Malaysian dollar

State of the Federation of Malaysia, formerly North Borneo.

Also uses stamps of Malaysia and no values above 25 cents issued for the territory since 1964.

Sarawak

FIRST STAMPS ISSUED 1 March 1869

CURRENCY

1964 100 cents = 1 Malaysian dollar

In 1839 James Brooke, then a young British merchant-adventurer, helped the Sultan of Brunei to quell a rebellion; in reward he was made Rajah of Sarawak in 1841. In 1846 the British government authorized him to accept from Brunei the island of Labuan as a coaling station on the China route. Sarawak was recognized as independent and from 1888 assured of British protection.

After occupation by the Japanese 17 December 1941 – 11 September 1945, it came under British military administration from 1 November 1945. Civil government was restored on 15 April 1946 and Sarawak was ceded to the British Crown on 1 July 1946. It joined the Federation of Malaysia in 1963.

Postal History

Casual mail was sent by ship via Singapore from 1839, and by a monthly service after 1842. The earliest recorded postal marking from Sarawak dates from 1858. A local Postal Union was set up with Straits Settlements; until Sarawak joined the UPU on 1 July 1897, letters for destinations beyond Singapore needed stamps of India or Straits Settlements.

(For period 1942-5, *see below*).

Japanese PO closed down and destroyed its stocks on 4 September 1945. Mail was accepted by FPOs of liberating Australian forces, at first free, then (29 October – 17 December 1945) franked with stamps of Australia.

(For period 17 December 1945 – 25 April 1946, *see* BMA *below*).

Uses both separate issues and stamps of Malaysia but no values above 25 cents issued for the territory since 1963.

• Japanese Occupation of British Borneo

FIRST STAMPS ISSUED June 1942

CURRENCY

1869 100 cents = 1 dollar Malayan

The four territories (Brunei, Labuan, North Borneo and Sarawak) were administered as an entity and had general issues of stamps. Various stamps of the territories were overprinted in Japanese.

• British Military Administration of North Borneo

FIRST STAMPS ISSUED 17 December 1945

CURRENCY	
1946	As North Borneo

The four territories liberated from the Japanese continued to be administered together.

Only stamps of North Borneo and Sarawak were available for overprinting B.M.A., and both series were sold throughout Brunei, Labuan, North Borneo and Sarawak.

TROIDES BROOKIANA
1 CENT
SARAWAK
A
SABAH
PAYAU
1 CENT
B
8c BRUNEI 8c
POSTAGE & REVENUE
8c EIGHT CENTS 8c
C
NEDERLANDSCH-INDIE
30 CENT 30
D
50 Ct
NED.-INDIE
E
10 sen
BRUNEI
F
SARAWAK
TWELVE CENTS
G

A Sarawak:Crown Colony 1950; **B** Sabah:Malaysia 1964; **C** Brunei:Protectorate 1933; **D** Netherlands Indies 1945; **E** Netherlands Indies 1900; **F** Brunei:Protectorate 1974; **G** Sarawak: Brooke Family Administration 1875.

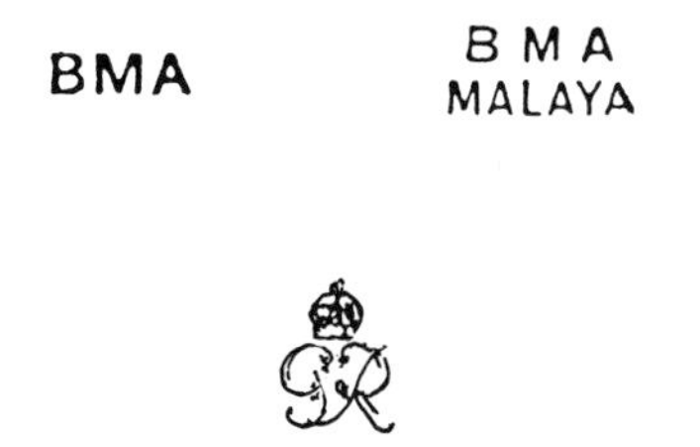
BMA
B M A
MALAYA

Overprinted for British Military Administration of Malaya, North Borneo & Sarawak, together with the cypher used when North Borneo became a crown colony in 1947.

Above and left
Letter-writers in Chinatown, Singapore

Brunei

FIRST STAMPS ISSUED 11 October 1906

CURRENCY

1906 100 cents = 1 dollar (Straits)

After exercising power over all Borneo in the 16th century the sultanate of Brunei declined to a seaboard state beset by pirates. Much of its territory was ceded during the 19th century to form Sarawak and British North Borneo. What survived remained independent under British protection after 1888, though a British Resident was not appointed until 1906. Brunei decided to remain independent rather than join Malaysia, and invoked British aid against invasion from Indonesia in 1962-6. Became fully independent in 1985.

Any postal connections were via Labuan until a Sarawak PO was opened at Brooketon c.1888. The first Brunei PO opened in Brunei Town on 11 October 1906. Brunei joined the UPU on 1 January 1916, but Brunei stamps had been accepted as valid since 1906.

Changes of town names in Brunei:
Brooketon, *later* Muara
Belait, *later* Kuala Belait
Temburong, *later* Bangar
Brunei Town, *later* Bandar Seri Begawan

Local stamps of 1895 are not accepted by all authorities as genuinely issued, though some accept that they paid postage on mail via the Sultan's yacht to Labuan.

• Netherlands Indies (Nederlandsch-Indie)

FIRST STAMPS ISSUED 1 April 1864

CURRENCY

1864 As Netherlands

Six years after the first Dutch merchants landed in Java, the Dutch East India Company was founded in 1602. A British trading post at Amboina was eliminated by massacre in 1623. The Company was taken over in 1799 by the Batavian Republic. When Napoleon seized Holland, a British force took Java and Sir Stamford Raffles held it as governor in 1811-16. In 1816 Java was restored to the Netherlands and in 1824 a former British trading post in Sumatra was exchanged for Malacca. The Dutch subdued one island after another by force, but never changed the region's character or eliminated nationalism. The Japanese invaded Borneo and Celebes on 11 January 1942 and after winning the Battle of the Java Sea took Java (1-8 March 1942) and occupied the remaining islands. In 1945-8 some islands were restored to Dutch rule.

Postal History
Packets plied between Amsterdam and Batavia via the Cape from 1786. Handstamped postal markings are known from 1789 and datestamps from 1811 (British period). An airmail service of KLM started in 1928.

Japanese occupation of 1941-5, *see below*.

Stamps resumed 1945-8 (in those areas restored by US forces to Dutch rule or recaptured from the Indonesian Republic).

Stamps inscribed INDONESIA 1948-9.

• Japanese Occupation of Java

FIRST STAMPS 9 March 1943

• Japanese Occupation of Sumatra

FIRST STAMPS 1 August 1943

Administered from Malaya until 1943.

• Japanese Naval Control Area

FIRST STAMPS 1942

This comprised all the eastern islands of the group.

Various available stamps were overprinted locally at island centres with an anchor and Japanese inscription (DAI NIPPON); many types exist.

• Indonesian Republic (Repoeblik Indonesie)

Java, Madura and Sumatra were still in Japanese hands when the Japanese surrendered to Allied forces on 17 August 1945, marking the end of World War II. No Dutch troops were available to re-occupy their territory and before British Indian troops were landed to receive the surrender in September-October 1945, a local republic had been proclaimed. Fighting ensued. Dutch troops took over in 1946. On 27 March 1947 the Dutch recognized the Indonesian Republic as part of the United States of Indonesia under the Dutch Crown, but disagreements led to further fighting. UN intervention brought a temporary truce, but in 1948 a new Dutch offensive captured the capital and the president. After further UN intervention in 1949 the war ended.

There were no general issues, stamps being locally produced in each main island.

• Java and Madura

FIRST STAMPS October 1945

• Sumatra

FIRST STAMPS 1945

Many bogus propaganda stamps were produced in the USA.

• United States of Indonesia (Republik Indonesia Serikat)

FIRST STAMPS ISSUED 1950

CURRENCY

1950 As Indonesia

The former Netherlands East Indies except New Guinea became independent on 27 December 1949 within the Netherlands-Indonesian Union. In 1950 federation was the *de facto* Indonesian Republic (Jave and Sumatra) was accomplished and a unitary state proclaimed.

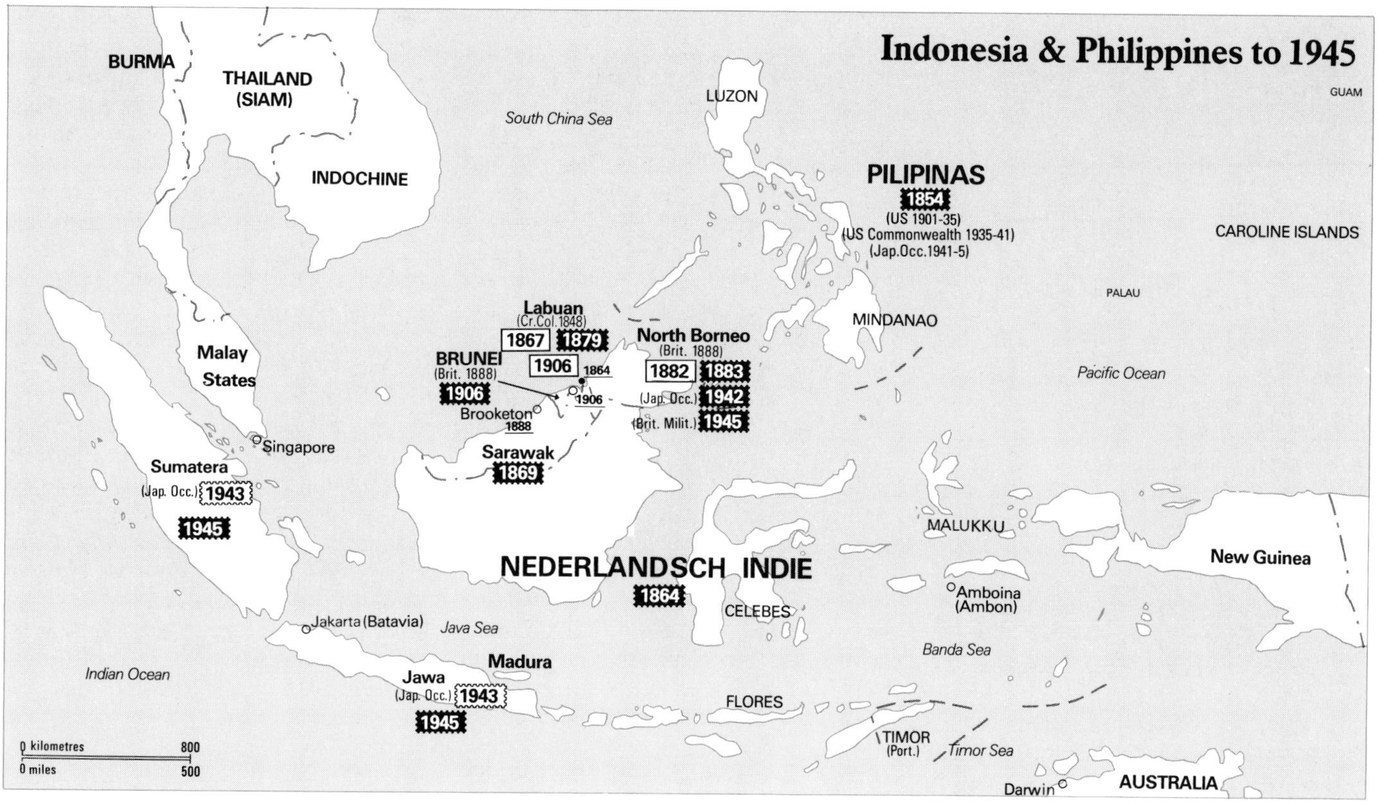
Indonesia & Philippines to 1945
BURMA
THAILAND (SIAM)
INDOCHINE
South China Sea
LUZON
GUAM
PILIPINAS
1854
(US 1901-35)
(US Commonwealth 1935-41)
(Jap.Occ.1941-5)
CAROLINE ISLANDS
PALAU
MINDANAO
Labuan
(Cr.Col.1848)
1867
1879
North Borneo
(Brit. 1888)
1882
1883
(Jap. Occ.)
1942
(Brit. Milit.)
1945
BRUNEI
(Brit. 1888)
1906
1906
1864
1906
Brooketon
1888
Sarawak
1869
Malay States
Singapore
Sumatera
(Jap. Occ.)
1943
1945
Pacific Ocean
MALUKKU
New Guinea
NEDERLANDSCH INDIE
1864
CELEBES
Amboina (Ambon)
Banda Sea
Jakarta (Batavia)
Java Sea
Madura
Jawa
(Jap. Occ.)
1943
1945
Indian Ocean
FLORES
TIMOR (Port.)
Timor Sea
Darwin
AUSTRALIA
0 kilometres 800
0 miles 500

Indonesia (Republik Indonesia)

FIRST STAMPS ISSUED 17 August 1950

CURRENCY

1950 100 cents (or seu) = 1 gulden (or rupiah)

On 15 August 1950 a unitary Republic of Indonesia came into being which remained within the Netherlands-Indonesia Union until this was dissolved on 10 August 1954.

• South Moluccas (Republik Maluku Sélatan)

CURRENCY

As Indonesia

Part of the ex-Dutch United States of Indonesia, the South Moluccas revolted against the unitary state in 1950 and declared independence. Some islands held out until 1955.

Stamps overprinted REPUBLIK MALUKU SELATAN were issued in 1950. (Pictorial stamps bearing a similar inscription were produced spuriously in the USA.

• Riau-Lingga Archipelago

FIRST STAMPS 1 January 1954

CURRENCY

1954 As Indonesia

Stamps specially overprinted RIAU were necessitated owing to currency differences (the islands being off the Malayan coast).

All stamps withdrawn after revaluation of the *rupiah*, December 1965.

• Netherlands New Guinea

FIRST STAMPS ISSUED 1 January 1950

CURRENCY

1950 As Netherlands

A Dutch possession from 1828, with boundaries set at longitude 141°E. in 1885, it was administered from the Moluccas until 1949. Indonesian claims were supported by the UN, which took over the territory on 1 October 1962 and transferred it to Indonesia on 1 May 1963.

• West New Guinea

FIRST STAMPS ISSUED 1 October 1962

CURRENCY

1962 As Holland

Formerly Netherlands New Guinea, from 1 October 1962 – 1 May 1963 under United Nations Administration.

• West Irian (Irian Barat)

FIRST STAMPS ISSUED 1 May 1963

PILIPINAS
6s
KOREO
JOSE RIZAL
KARET
IRIAN BARAT
30 s
REPUBLIK INDONESIA
FILIPINAS
2 4/8 C.DE PESO
PHILIPPINES
A
B
C
D

A Philippines:Independent 1962;
B West Irian 1963;
C Philippines:American Occupation 1900;
D Philippines:Spanish Colony 1890.

INDOCHINE
POSTE AERIENNE 66c
RF
BUU CHÍNH 20đ
VIỆT NAM CỘNG HÒA
25c +10c
POSTES
INDOCHINE
REPUBLIQUE FRANÇAISE
10
INDO-CHINE
VIỆT NAM CỘNG HÒA
Tem phạt
Bưu-chính
2đ
S.M. BAO.DAI
ANNAM
15 CENTS
POSTES
INDOCHINE
A
B
C
D
E
F

A Indo-China 1933; **B** Vietnam 1974; **C** Indo-China 1936; **D** Indo-China 1946; **E** Indo-China 1892; **F** Vietnam:a Modern Adhesive.

CURRENCY

1963	As Indonesia

Formerly West New Guinea. A province of Indonesia from 1 May 1963.

Has used stamps of Indonesia since 1973.

Note: For Eastern New Guinea *see under* Australia, New Zealand and the Pacific.

Philippines (Filipinas)

FIRST STAMPS ISSUED 1 February 1854

CURRENCY

1854	20 cuartos = 1 real ; 8 reals = 1 peso plata fuerte
1864	100 centimos = 1 peso plata fuerta
1871	100 centimos = 1 escudo (½ peso)
1872	100 centimos = 1 peseta (½ peso)
1876	1000 milesimas = 100 centavos = 1 peso
1899	100 cents = 1 dollar
1906	100 centavos = 1 peso
1962	100 sentimos = 1 piso

The scene of Magellan's death in 1521, the islands were named in 1542 and settled by the Spaniards in 1565, though resistance by the Muslim inhabitants of Mindanao continued until 1878. The population is mainly Roman Catholic of mixed native, Spanish and Chinese descent.

A Filipino revolt had already had some success when the Spanish-American War broke out in 1898. The Philippine president cooperated with the Americans to expel the Spanish, then fought the Americans until his capture in 1901. Ceded to the USA by Spain (in exchange for $20m), the Philippines were ruled militarily until 4 July 1901, then as a colony. They were granted US commonwealth status in 1935. Captured by the Japanese between 10 December 1941 and 6 May 1942 (Battle of Corregidor), the Philippines were declared a republic on 14 October 1943. They were recaptured by US forces under Macarthur between 24 October 1944 (Battle of Leyte) and 2 September 1945, and became an independent republic on 4 July 1946.

Postal History

Early mails to Manila were carried by the Acapulco galleon from Mexico. This service was interrupted by the rebellions in Central and South America and the route via Asia and Africa was run on a casual basis. When Hong Kong was ceded to Britain in 1841 mail was routed through that colony. From 1854, stamps of India were available in Manila and were used to pre-pay postage by the merchants. In 1863 these were replaced by stamps of Hong Kong which were available until 1873 when Straits Settlements adhesives were available, except for mail to the USA for which Hong Kong stamps continued to be used. The use of foreign stamps ceased in 1877 when the Spanish colonies joined the UPU.

Under the USA, Manila played a prominent part in the Transpacific clipper airmail service.

Stamps show the characteristics of each phase of government, including Spanish, US, and Japanese.

• Cochin China

FIRST STAMPS France 1862
FIRST (differenced) STAMPS 16 May 1886

CURRENCY	
1892	6 puttans = 5 annas
1911	As India

After a French punitive expedition against Saigon in 1859, the eastern provinces were ceded to France in 1862. A protectorate was established over Cambodia in 1863 and the remaining area occupied by 1874.

Used French Colonies General Issues 1863-92 (oblit. lozenges of dots with CCH or CCN and a figure, etc).

• Annam and Tongking

FIRST STAMPS French Colonies General Issues 1885-92
FIRST (differenced) STAMPS 21 January 1888

CURRENCY	
1888	As France

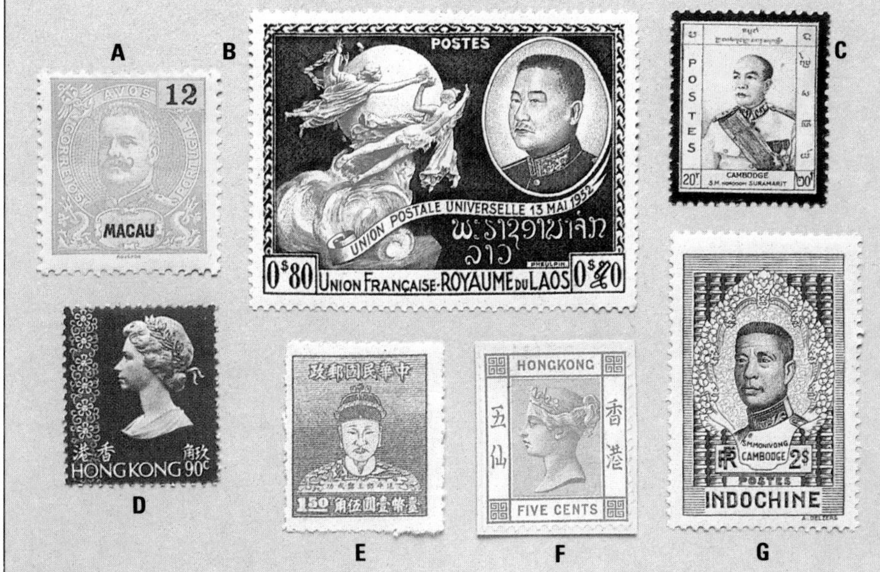
A
B
C
D
E
F
G
12
MACAU
POSTES
UNION POSTALE UNIVERSELLE 13 MAI 1952
0$80 UNION FRANÇAISE·ROYAUME DU LAOS 0$80
POSTES
CAMBODGE
HONG KONG 90c
HONGKONG
FIVE CENTS
CAMBODGE 2$
POSTES
INDOCHINE

A Macao 1898; **B** Laos 1952; **C** Cambodia 1960; **D** Hong Kong 1973· **E** Taiwan 1950; **F** Hong Kong 1880; **G** Cambodia 1936.

A French protectorate (1883) was established after war with China (1884-5)

• Indo-China (Indochine)

FIRST STAMPS 1889

CURRENCY	
1889	100 centimes = 1 franc
1918	100 cents = 1 piastre

A union of Cambodia, Cochin China, Annam and Tongking decreed on 17 October 1887 with the addition of Laos after 1893. It also included after 1898 Kouang Tcheou Wau, an enclave of China between Pakhoi and Hoihow, in the area of the Lui-Chow peninsula The constituent parts continued to be identified by name on their cancellers. After the fall of France in 1940, the Japanese controlled the country through a puppet Vichy regime (though the Chinese supported movements in the north resistant to both French and Japanese). The rulers the Japanese set up in 1944-5 in Cambodia and 'Vietnam' and the rival insurgent armies in the north set the scene for future conflicts, though French authority was re-established in 1945-9. On 14 June 1949 Cochin China, with Annam and Tongking, became independent within the French Community as Vietnam. Laos and Cambodia followed as independent states on 19 July and 8 November.

• Vietnam (Viet Minh)

FIRST STAMPS 1945

CURRENCY	
1945	100 cents = 1 piastre
1945	100 xu = 10 hao = 1 dong
NB	Viet Ming = 30 xu = 10 Hao = 1 dong

A 'Democratic Republic' was proclaimed by Ho Chi Minh in Hanoi on 2 September 1945. It was recognized by France on 6 March 1946 as a *de facto* free state within Indo-China. When its forces refused to give up Haiphong to the French, hostilities flared. From 1946, with fluctuating boundaries, it made war on the French and the rival independent state set up by them under Bao Dai on 14 June 1949.

Stamps inscribed DAN CHU KONG HOA.

• North Vietnam

FIRST STAMPS ISSUED October 1954 (a continuation of the issues of the Viet Minh)

CURRENCY	
1946	100 cents = 1 dong
1959	100 xu = 1 dong

After the French defeat at Dien Bien Phu, Vietnam was partitioned on 21 July 1954 near the 17th parallel. North Vietnam became a recognized Communist republic.

• Vietnam

FIRST STAMPS ISSUED 6 June 1951

An independent state within the French Indo-Chinese Union, under pressure from Viet Minh forces in the north.

• South Vietnam

FIRST STAMPS 6 June 1955

CURRENCY	
1959	100 cents = 1 piastre

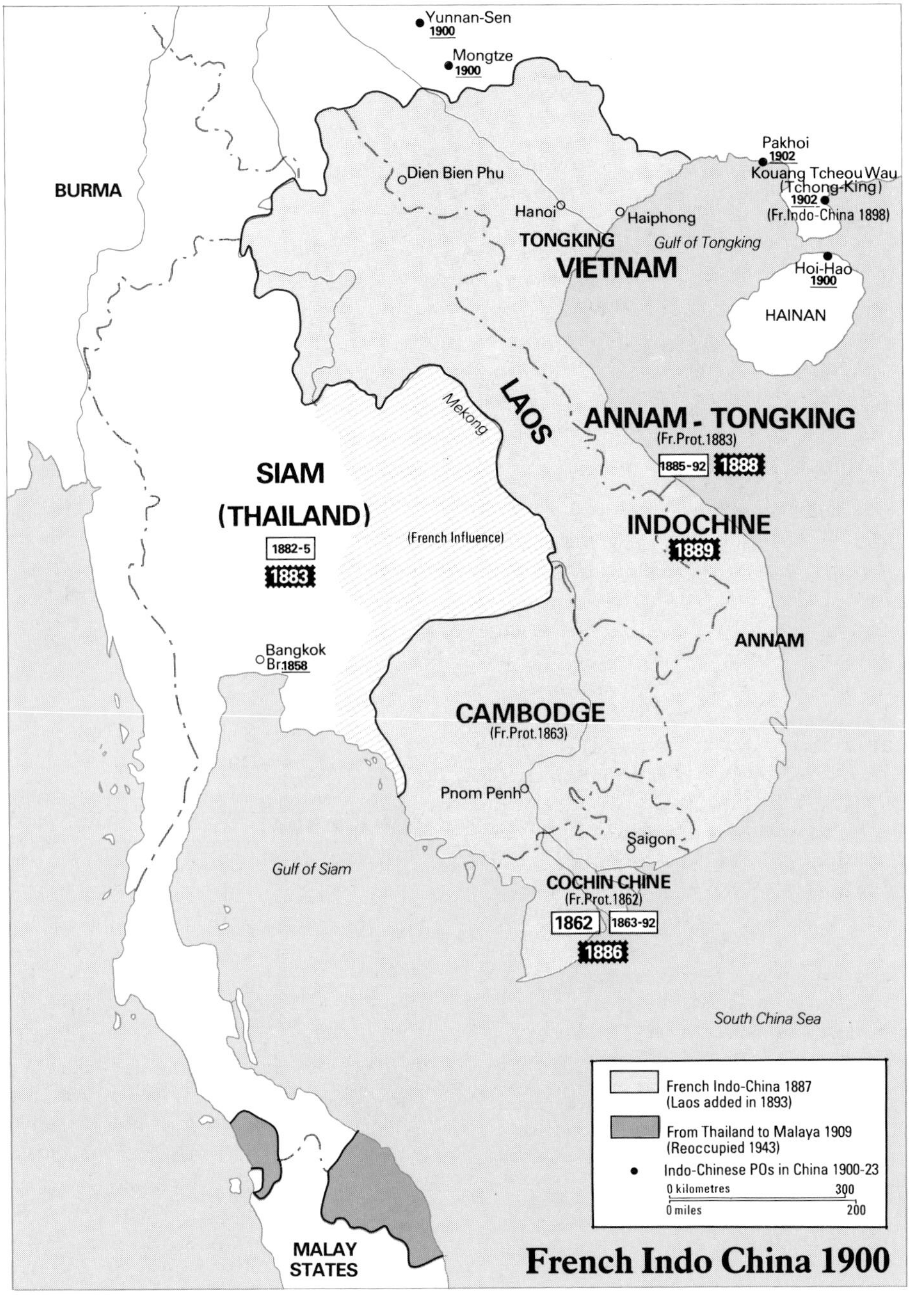
Yunnan-Sen
1900
Mongtze
1900
Pakhoi
1902
Kouang Tcheou Wau
(Tchong-King)
1902
(Fr.Indo-China 1898)
Dien Bien Phu
Hanoi
Haiphong
TONGKING
Gulf of Tongking
VIETNAM
Hoi-Hao
1900
HAINAN
BURMA
LAOS
Mekong
ANNAM - TONGKING
(Fr.Prot.1883)
1885-92
1888
SIAM
(THAILAND)
1882-5
1883
(French Influence)
INDOCHINE
1889
ANNAM
Bangkok
Br1858
CAMBODGE
(Fr.Prot.1863)
Pnom Penh
Saigon
Gulf of Siam
COCHIN-CHINE
(Fr.Prot.1862)
1862
1863-92
1886
South China Sea
French Indo-China 1887
(Laos added in 1893)
From Thailand to Malaya 1909
(Reoccupied 1943)
Indo-Chinese POs in China 1900-23
0 kilometres 300
0 miles 200
MALAY
STATES

French Indo China 1900

After the French defeat at Dien Bien Phu, Vietnam was partitioned on 21 July 1954 near the 17th parallel. South Vietnam remained an independent state within the French Union for a year, then after a referendum became an independent republic.

Stamps inscribed DAN CHU KONG HOA.

• International Commission in Indo-China

FIRST STAMPS 1 December 1954

CURRENCY	
1954	As India

Various stamps of India were overprinted in Hindi characters for use in Vietnam, Laos or Cambodia between 1954 and 1968.

• National Front for the Liberation of South Vietnam (Viet Cong)

FIRST STAMPS 5 October 1963

CURRENCY	
1963	100 xu = 1 dong

Communists in South Vietnam fighting with support from North Vietnam and China against the established South Vietnamese government supported by the USA.

Stamps inscribed MAT TRAN DAN TOC GIAI.

Socialist Republic of Vietnam

FIRST STAMPS ISSUED 27 July 1976

CURRENCY	
1976	100 xu = 1 dong

After the American withdrawal from South Vietnam, the south was completely overrun and on 2 July 1976 incorporated into a unified Communist state.

Laos

FIRST STAMPS ISSUED 13 November 1951

1951	100 cents = 1 piastre
1955	100 cents = 1 kip

When the constituent parts of French Indo-China broke up in 1949, Laos became an independent kingdom and associate state within the French Union. On 22 October 1953 it became fully independent within the Union and on 7 December 1956 left the Union. From 1953 the Pathet Lao (Laos People's Front) backed by North Vietnam fought the established régime. In 1975 the king was deposed and a People's Democratic Republic ruled.

Kampuchea (formerly Cambodia)

FIRST STAMPS ISSUED 3 November 1951

CURRENCY

1951	100 cents = 1 piastre
1955	100 cents = 1 rial

Khmer kingdom centred until 1432 on Angkor was weakened by constant wars with the Siamese until on 11 August 1863 it became a French protectorate. Incorporated into a united Indo-China in 1887. During the Japanese occupation in March 1944 the king proclaimed independence. French rule was restored in 1945 but Cambodia became an autonomous kingdom within the French Union on 7 January 1946. Left the French Union on 25 September 1955. From 1960 the king ruled as head of state without accepting the crown. He was deposed on 18 March 1970 and a Communist Khmer Republic was proclaimed on 9 October 1970. Insurgent Khmer Rouge forces gradually became dominant and in 1975 took Pnomh Penh. Ideological struggles continue and Kampuchea was invaded by Vietnam.

Hong Kong

FIRST STAMPS ISSUED 8 December 1862 (their use was not compulsory until 15 October 1864). Oblit. B 62.

CURRENCY

1862	96 cents = 1 dollar (Mexican)
1880	100 cents = 1 Hong Kong dollar

Taken by an East India Company naval force on 26 January 1841 to provide a base for 2000 British subjects expelled from Canton, Hong Kong has been a British colony ever since. Extended in 1861 by the acquisition of Kowloon on the mainland opposite and in 1898 by the lease of the New Territories for 99 years. Occupied by the Japanese 25 December 1941 – 14 August 1945.

Postal History

PO was opened at Victoria before the end of 1841 using locally-made handstamps. Crowned circle marks followed. The service was under the London GPO until 1 May 1860, when it passed to the colony. Prepayment of mail to Britain became compulsory on 1 May 1858. Other POs were opened after 1898. Owing to its deep harbour Hong Kong became a transfer point for European mailboat services.

Stamps of Hong Kong are found used in Bangkok (1885), Labuan (1864), Macao (1865-84), Manila (1865-77), Anping (Formosa) in 1889-92, Chinese treaty ports (1862-1917), *see* British POs in China, Japan (*see* Japan).

• Japanese Occupation of Hong Kong

FIRST PARTICULAR STAMPS 16 April 1945

CURRENCY

1942	As Japan

After the attack of 6 December 1941, little if any mail seems to have left the island; the PO was re-opened by the Japanese on 22 January 1942.

Used stamps of Japan 22 January 1942 – April 1945.

The Japanese POs remained open until 28 August; British POs were re-opened on 5 September and used POSTAGE PAID handstamps until supplies of stamps became available on 28 September 1945.

Macao (Macau)

FIRST STAMPS ISSUED 1 March 1884

CURRENCY

1884	1000 reis = 1 milreis
1894	78 avos = 1 rupee
1913	100 avos = 1 pataca

Portuguese trading post in 1557, leased from China until 1849 and later made a colony. Since 11 June 1951 a Portuguese overseas province.

Used stamps of Hong Kong in 1863 – 29 February 1884.

Taiwan (Formosa)

FIRST STAMPS ISSUED August 1886
FIRST STAMPS as Chinese province 4 November 1945
FIRST STAMPS as Republic of China 1 December 1949

CURRENCY

1946	100 sen = 1 dollar

Dutch and Spanish trading settlements and a Taiwan dynasty were short-lived and in 1683 the island became a province of Manchu China. In 1895 China ceded the island to Japan, whereupon the governor declared a republic. This lasted in the south of the island until 21 October. Formosa then formed part of the Japanese Empire until 1945, when on 25 October it was returned to Chinese rule. As the last Nationalist stronghold it received Chiang Kai-shek and became the Republic of China, being recognized as such by the United Nations until 25 October 1971. When the UN recognized the People's Republic of China, Taiwan lost its status but remains precariously independent.

The first postal service was set up by the governor in 1886.

Stamps of 'Black Flag Republic' August-September 1895.

Used stamps of Japan 1895-1945.

Used separate stamps (locally printed) in October 1945.

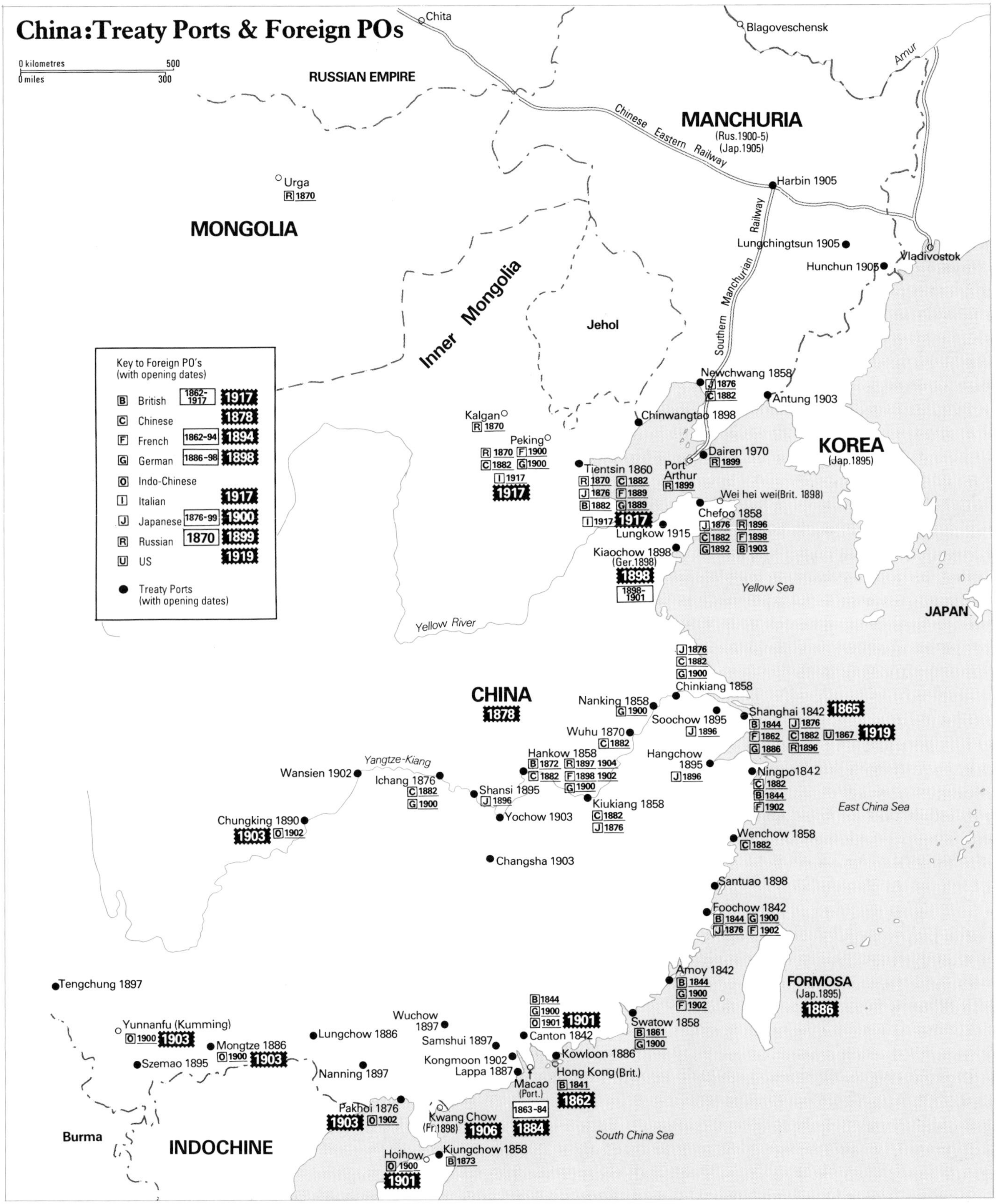
China: Treaty Ports & Foreign POs
0 kilometres 500
0 miles 300
RUSSIAN EMPIRE
Chita
Blagoveschensk
Amur
Chinese Eastern Railway
MANCHURIA
(Rus.1900-5)
(Jap.1905)
Harbin 1905
Urga
R 1870
MONGOLIA
Lungchingtsun 1905
Hunchun 1905
Vladivostok
Southern Manchurian Railway
Inner Mongolia
Jehol
Key to Foreign PO's
(with opening dates)
B British 1862-1917 1917
C Chinese 1878
F French 1862-94 1894
G German 1886-98 1898
O Indo-Chinese
I Italian 1917
J Japanese 1876-99 1900
R Russian 1870 1899
U US 1919
Treaty Ports
(with opening dates)
Newchwang 1858
J 1876
C 1882
Antung 1903
Kalgan
R 1870
Chinwangtao 1898
Peking
R 1870 F 1900
C 1882 G 1900
I 1917
1917
Dairen 1970
R 1899
Port Arthur
R 1899
KOREA
(Jap.1895)
Tientsin 1860
R 1870 C 1882
J 1876 F 1889
B 1882 G 1889
I 1917 1917
Wei hei wei (Brit. 1898)
Chefoo 1858
J 1876 R 1896
C 1882 F 1898
G 1892 B 1903
Lungkow 1915
Kiaochow 1898
(Ger.1898)
1898
1898-1901
Yellow Sea
Yellow River
JAPAN
J 1876
C 1882
G 1900
Chinkiang 1858
CHINA
1878
Nanking 1858
G 1900
Soochow 1895
J 1896
Shanghai 1842 1865
B 1844 J 1876
F 1862 C 1882 U 1867 1919
G 1886 R 1896
Wuhu 1870
C 1882
Hankow 1858
B 1872 R 1897 1904
C 1882 F 1898 1902
G 1900
Hangchow 1895
J 1896
Ningpo 1842
C 1882
B 1844
F 1902
Yangtze-Kiang
Wansien 1902
Ichang 1876
C 1882
G 1900
Shansi 1895
J 1896
Kiukiang 1858
C 1882
J 1876
Yochow 1903
Chungking 1890
1903 O 1902
East China Sea
Wenchow 1858
C 1882
Changsha 1903
Santuao 1898
Foochow 1842
B 1844 G 1900
J 1876 F 1902
Amoy 1842
B 1844
G 1900
F 1902
FORMOSA
(Jap.1895)
1886
Tengchung 1897
B 1844
G 1900
O 1901 1901
Swatow 1858
B 1861
G 1900
Yunnanfu (Kumming)
O 1900 1903
Wuchow 1897
Lungchow 1886
Samshui 1897
Canton 1842
Mongtze 1886
O 1900 1903
Szemao 1895
Kowloon 1886
Kongmoon 1902
Lappa 1887
Hong Kong (Brit.)
B 1841
1862
Nanning 1897
Macao
(Port.)
1863-84
1884
Pakhoi 1876
1903 O 1902
Kwang Chow
(Fr.1898) 1906
South China Sea
Burma
INDOCHINE
Hoihow
O 1900
1901
Kiungchow 1858
B 1873

China

China under the Ch'ing (or Manchu) dynasty (1644-1912) followed an expansionist policy westward in Asia while discouraging European interference. By 1720 the Chinese Empire comprised China proper, Jehol, Inner Mongolia and Manchuria, while vassal states owing suzerainty extended from Trans-Amur and Outer Mongolia in the north to Tibet, Burma and Indo-China in the south. Foreign missionaries were expelled in the 18th century. Trade with European powers was confined to Canton and a foothold at Macao held by the Portuguese since 1557.

The 'Opium War' of 1840-2 forced trading concessions from the Chinese and the opening to foreign residents of five 'treaty' ports: Canton, Amoy, Foochow, Ningpo, and Shanghai. The uninhabited island of Hong Kong, taken by a naval force in 1841, was ceded to Britain. Kowloon was taken by Britain in 1861 and China recognized the principle of 'extraterritorial' settlements virtually ruled by foreign consuls.

At the same time the Russians were beginning to encroach on all the northern and western borders of Mongolia and Turkestan. In 1861 they moved into Vladivostok. Non-Chinese areas which had previously paid allegiance to China were lost: Annam to France, Burma to Britain.

War in 1894-5 between Japan and China for possession of Korea weakened the Chinese. Formosa passed to Japan and as a result of European intervention in the treaty of peace, Russia acquired a foothold at Port Arthur. In 1898 Kiaochao was leased to Germany, the 'New Territories' (adjacent to Kowloon) and Wei-Hai-Wei to Britain (the latter handed back to China in 1930), both for 99 years, and Port Arthur to Russia for 25 (though it passed to Japan after seven).

The Boxer Rebellion in 1900, during which foreign nationals were besieged in the legations of Peking, occasioned an international relief force and further occupations of key places.

Revolution broke out in 1911. The deposition of the Empress broke the only unifying bond between provinces. Rival republics in Peking and Canton gave Japan the opportunity in 1915 to enforce its 'Twenty-one Demands', the most fateful of which gave the Japanese freedom of residence in Manchuria and extended their control of the South Manchurian Railway. Soviet Russia's designs focused on Outer Mongolia and on the Chinese Eastern Railway, which passed through Northern Manchuria to Vladivostok. Communist influence spread rapidly through China.

Following the death of Sun-Yat-Sen in 1925, Chiang Kai-Shek, his successor as president, defeated the northern war lords in 1928.

After the outlawing of the Communist Party by Chiang Kai-Shek in 1927, Mao Tse-tung and Chu Teh fought the Nationalists from the Ching Kang mountains, setting up a 'Chinese Soviet Republic' in south-eastern Kiangsi in November 1931. After five campaigns in 1930-4, the Communists were forced to make the Long March to north-west China, the survivors setting up HQ at Yenan in Shensi.

The seizure of Manchuria in 1931-2 by Japan was condemned by the League of Nations, from which organization Japan then withdrew. On 7 July 1937 the Japanese launched an invasion into China proper. The Communists and Nationalists made common cause against the enemy, but after the surrender of Japan to the Allies in 1945 resumed fighting each other until the defeat of the Nationalists in 1949. A People's Republic was set up in October 1949, while the old regime continued on Formosa. Communist China was admitted to the United Nations in 1971, and the USA was the last country to transfer recognition from the Nationalists to the Communists.

Postal History

The ancient Chinese had a postal system from the Chou Dynasty (1122-255 BC) onwards. Although the government service (I-Chan) had by the 13th century AD, according to Marco Polo, some 10,000 post stages, the Min Hsin Chu, comprised of letter guilds, or *hongs*, carried unofficial mails. The Treaty of Kyakhta (1727) provided for the first regular exchanges of mails between China and Russia (*see* Mongolia). Diplomatic couriers were permitted to foreigners by treaty in 1858. An internal service of the Imperial Maritime Customs, developed by an Englishman, Robert Hart, in the 1860s, grew into an Imperial Postal Service by 1896, which put the Min Hsin Chu out of business and absorbed an earlier Shanghai local service. Until China joined the UPU in 1914 all mail for foreign destinations had to pass through one or other foreign PO; for this purpose supplies of appropriate foreign stamps were held for sale at Imperial Chinese POs and used in combination with Chinese stamps (or with a Chinese handstamp where the internal postage was paid in cash). The foreign stamps were not date-cancelled until the letter reached the national PO, but (perhaps to obviate pilfering) they were usually tied to the envelope at source by an official IPO in rectangle (1899-1904).

The great powers maintained their own systems for sending mail abroad until 1922.

See also China (modern) on page 260.

• British POs in China

FIRST STAMPS Hong Kong 1862-1917
FIRST (overprinted) STAMPS ISSUED 1917 (after 1922 these were valid only at Wei-Hei-Wei; withdrawn 1930)

CURRENCY

1917 100 cents = 1 dollar (Hong Kong)

Consular POs were opened in treaty ports from 1844. Handstamps were in use before the issue of stamps.

From 1862 until obliterators were issued, all mail was bagged for cancelling B62 at Hong Kong; even after their issue only 'loose letters' were cancelled at source. Later the treaty ports had their own named datestamps.

The POs were:

	opened	Oblit.	in use from
Amoy	1844	A1	1866
		D27	1876
Canton	1844	C1	1866
Foochow	1844	F1	1866
Ningpo	1844	N1	1866
Shanghai	1844	S1	1866
Swatow	1861	S2	1866
Hankow	1872	D29	1879
Kiungchow	1873	D28	1876
Tientsin	1882		
Chefoo	1903		

All the above were closed on 30 November 1922.

Other offices using a similar system were placed in the colony of Wei-Hei-Wei which was handed back to China in 1930 (Liu Kung Tau 1 September 1899 – 1 October 1930 and Port Edward 1904 – 1 October 1930); in Portuguese Macao 1838- 84 and in Japan 1859-79 (*see* Japan).

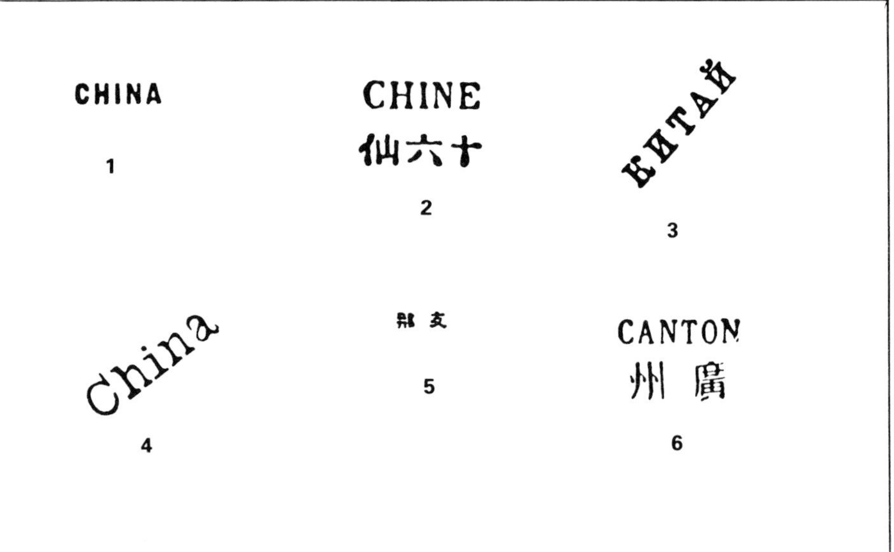
CHINA
1
CHINE
2
КИТАЙ
3
China
4
5
CANTON
6

Overprints: **1** China Agencies in Hong Kong, 1917; **2** French Agencies in China, 1902; **3** Russian Agencies, 1899; **4** German Agencies, 1900; **5** Japanese Agencies, 1900 and **6** Indo-Chinese Agency in Canton, 1901

• French POs in China

FIRST STAMPS ISSUED 1894

CURRENCY

1894 100 centimes = 1 franc
1907 100 cents = 1 piastre

These comprised Shanghai (November 1862); Tientsin (16 March 1889); Chefoo (November 1898); Hankow (agency, November 1898; PO, October 1902); Peking (December 1900); Amoy (January 1902); Foochow (1902); Ningpo (1902). All were closed on 31 December 1922.

Used stamps of France 1862-94.

• Kwang Chow

FIRST STAMPS ISSUED October 1906

CURRENCY

1906 As France
1919 100 cents = 1 piastre

Territory leased by China to France as a naval base and coaling station in April 1898 and placed under the Governor-General of French Indo-China in January 1900. Returned to China in February 1943 and immediately occupied by the Japanese until returned to China 18 August 1945.

• Russian POs in China

FIRST STAMPS Russia from 1870
FIRST STAMPS ISSUED 1899

CURRENCY

1899 Russian
1917 Chinese

These comprised *Peking, Kalgan, *Tientsin, Urga (*see* Mongolia), opened 1870; *Shanghai, *Chefoo, before 1897; *Hankow, agency 1897, PO 1904; Port Arthur, Dairen (Talienwan, *later* Dalny) in 1899-1904. Closed 1920.

First stamps issued (1899) surcharged in Cyrillic КИТАЙ, were supplied only to main offices (**above*), but were valid in the remainder, as were Russian stamps without overprint in the main offices. They were all inscribed in Russian currency, but Russian POs accepted Chinese currency in payment for them at par (1 Chinese cent = 1 Russian kopek).

• Japanese POs in China

FIRST STAMPS ISSUED January 1900

CURRENCY

1900 As Japan

Comprising Shanghai (15 April 1876), and agencies at Chefoo, Chinkiang, Foochow, Hangchow, Kiukiang, Newchwang (*now* Yingkow), Mingoo, and Tientsin. From 1896 Hangchow, Shansi, and Soochow.

Used stamps of Japan 15 April 1876 – 31 December 1899.

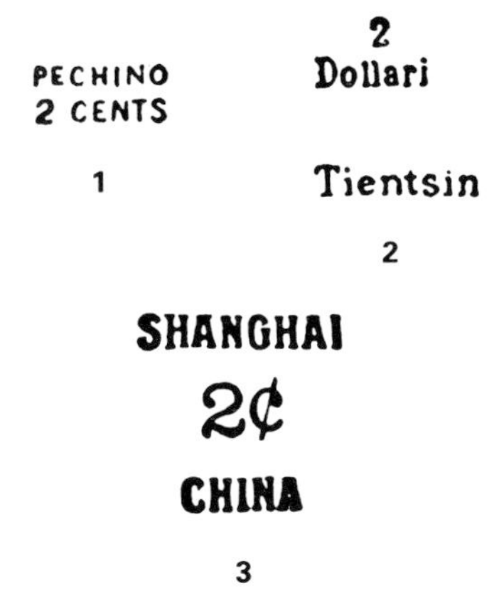
PECHINO
2 CENTS
1
2
Dollari
Tientsin
2
SHANGHAI
2¢
CHINA
3

Overprints: **1** Italian Agency in Peking, 1917; **2** Italian Agency in Tientsin, 1918; **3** United States Agency in Shanghai, 1919

• German POs in China

FIRST STAMPS ISSUED 1898

CURRENCY

1898	As Germany
1905	100 cents = 1 dollar

Comprising Shanghai (16 August 1886); Tientsin (October 1889); Chefoo (1 June 1892); after 1 January 1900: Amoy, Canton, Foochow, Hankow, Ichang, Nanking, Peking, Swatow, Chinkiang. All closed on 17 March 1917.

Used stamps of Germany 1886-98.

• Kiaochow (Kiautschou)

FIRST STAMPS ISSUED 26 January 1898

CURRENCY

1900	German
1905	Chinese

Tsingtao on the Kiaochow Bay was occupied on 14 November 1897 by the German navy after the murder of two German missionaries. The surrounding territory was leased to Germany for 99 years on 6 March 1898. It surrendered on 7 November 1914 to Japanese forces after a three months' siege.

PO was opened at Tsingtao 26 January 1898 and various others on the Shantung Railway (Schantungbahn) from 1900, including a TPO (1901).

Also used stamps of Germany 26 January 1898 – 31 December 1901.

• Indo-Chinese POs in China

CURRENCY

1903	100 centimes = 1 franc
1919	100 cents = 1 piastre

• Mongtze (*now* Mengtsze)

Opened 25 January 1900; closed 31 December 1922.

• Yunnanfu (*now* Kunming)

FIRST STAMPS ISSUED 1903

First issue was inscribed YUNNANSEN.

• Hoihow

FIRST STAMPS ISSUED 1901 (overprinted HOI HAU)

Opened 15 May 1900; closed 31 December 1922.

• Canton

FIRST STAMPS ISSUED 15 June 1901

Opened 15 June 1901; closed 31 December 1922.

• Pakhoi

FIRST STAMPS ISSUED April 1903

Opened 1 February 1902; closed 31 December 1922.

• Chungking

FIRST STAMPS ISSUED 1903 (overprinted TCHONGKING)

Opened 7 February 1902; closed 31 December 1922.

• Italian POs in China

CURRENCY

1917	100 centesimi = 1 lira 100 cents = 1 dollar

Two POs were opened from September 1917 to 31 December 1922 for diplomatic staff and troops.

• Peking

FIRST STAMPS ISSUED September 1917

• Tientsin

FIRST STAMPS ISSUED September 1917

• United States PA in Shanghai

FIRST STAMPS ISSUED 1 July 1919

CURRENCY

1919	As China

Opened 3 August 1867; closed 31 December 1922.

Stamps (in Chinese currency) were used only on mail to USA. Sea connection was made at Yokohama with the Pacific Mail Steamship Company.

• Shanghai

FIRST STAMPS ISSUED 1865

CURRENCY

1865	10 casn = 1 candareen : 100 candareen = 1 tael
1890	100 cents = 1 dollar (Chinese)

Although part of Imperial China, Shanghai was locally governed by an international Municipal Council. As the national services were inefficient and charges high, in 1864 the municipality organized a postal service with agencies in 16 cities. This was merged in the Imperial service in 1898.

China (modern)

FIRST STAMPS ISSUED ('Large Dragons') 1878

CURRENCY

1878 100 candarins = 1 tael
1897 100 cents = 1 dollar
Chinese Peoples Republic
1955 100 feu = 1 yuan

CHINA.
1 CANDARIN. 1
A
限吉黑貼用
REPUBLIC OF CHINA POSTAGE
B
中国人民邮政
C
D
E
FEN
F
G

A China:Imperial Customs Post 1878; **B** Yunnan Province 1926; **C** China:Communist Republic 1976; **D** Szechwan Province 1933; **E** Manchuria:Kirin 1927; **F** Manchukuo 1932; **G** China:Republic 1938.

Postal History

More generally, *see above*. From 1865 foreign consular mails were entrusted to the Maritime Customs postal service, which for the first time accepted also private mails. These were pouched weekly between Shanghai, Peking and Tientsin. The service was given a postmaster and opened to the public on 1 May 1878. Until 1882 all outward Chinese mail for foreign des-

Left
Posting a letter in Guilin, China

Below
P&O paddle-steamer *Braganza*, which sailed to Hong Kong, extending the mail route from Ceylon in the middle of the nineteenth century

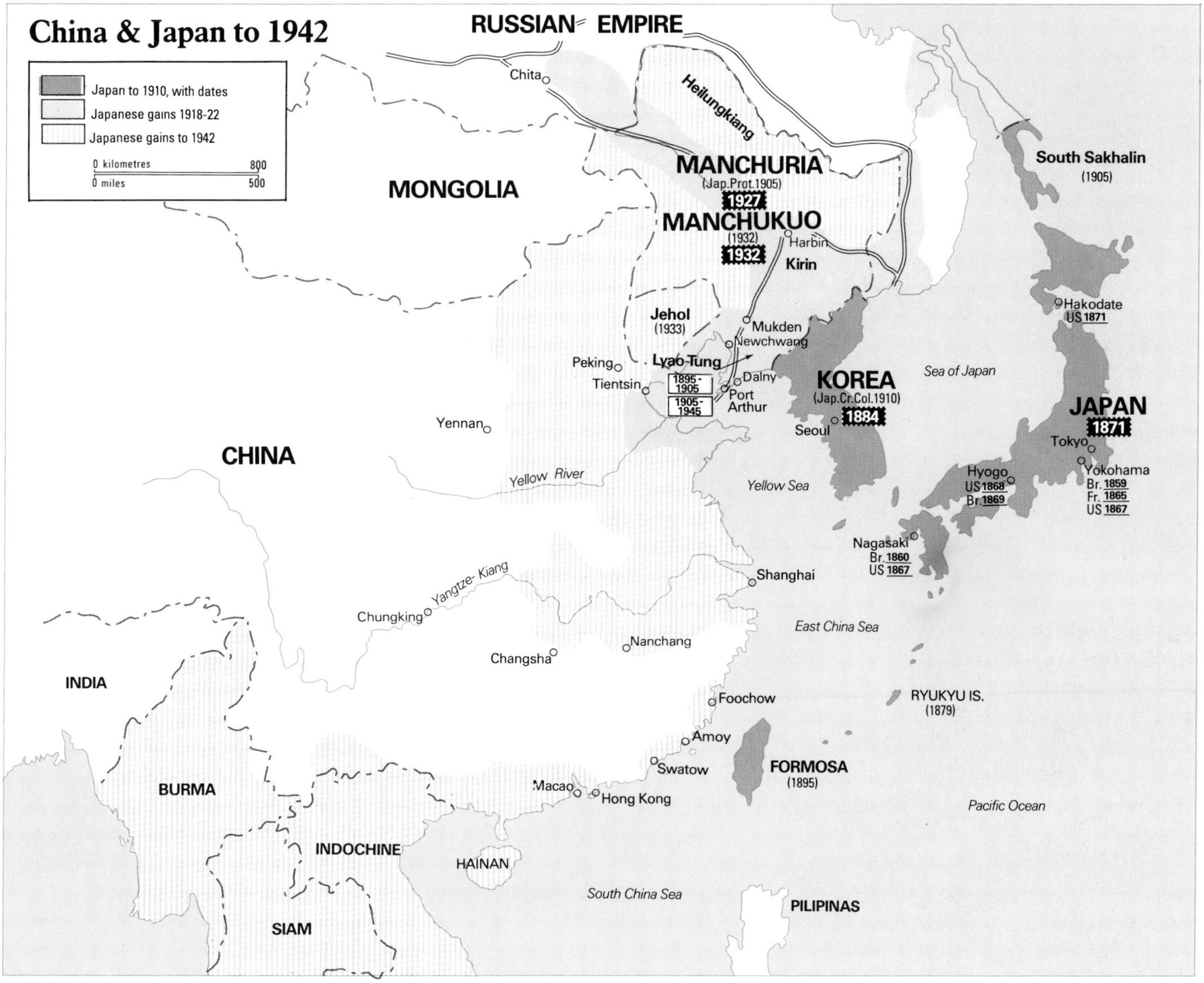
China & Japan to 1942
Japan to 1910, with dates
Japanese gains 1918-22
Japanese gains to 1942
0 kilometres 800
0 miles 500
RUSSIAN EMPIRE
Chita
Heilungkiang
MONGOLIA
MANCHURIA
(Jap.Prot.1905)
1927
MANCHUKUO
(1932)
1932
Harbin
Kirin
South Sakhalin
(1905)
Hakodate
US 1871
Jehol
(1933)
Mukden
Newchwang
Lyao-Tung
Peking
Tientsin
1895-1905
1905-1945
Dalny
Port Arthur
KOREA
(Jap.Cr.Col.1910)
1884
Seoul
Sea of Japan
JAPAN
1871
Tokyo
Yokohama
Br. 1859
Fr. 1865
US 1867
Hyogo
US 1868
Br. 1869
Yennan
CHINA
Yellow River
Yellow Sea
Nagasaki
Br. 1860
US 1867
Shanghai
Yangtze-Kiang
Chungking
East China Sea
Nanchang
Changsha
INDIA
Foochow
RYUKYU IS.
(1879)
Amoy
Swatow
FORMOSA
(1895)
BURMA
Macao
Hong Kong
Pacific Ocean
INDOCHINE
HAINAN
South China Sea
PILIPINAS
SIAM

tinations was routed via Shanghai (*see also* Foreign POs, *above*). In 1882 there were 12 POs (Chefoo, Chinkiang, Hankow, Ichang, Kiukiang, Ningpo, Newchwang, Peking, Shanghai, Tientsin, Wenchow and Wuhu). By 1896 the system had become the Imperial Postal Service.

Various stamp issues had only local validity owing to problems of distribution, divided rule, and foreign invasion. The general pattern is illustrated by maps; precise details for individual stamps must be sought in specialized works.

Alterations in postal rates in 1940-3 made necessary the surcharging of stocks held.

This was done by provincial authorities. The stamps of each province are identifiable by different typefaces. In the 'Border Areas' the Communists issued their own stamps area by area.

The years 1945-9 were characterized in both Nationalist and Communist areas by inflation provisionals. In January-October 1949 'Regional Issues' were made for each 'Liberation Area' until the first general issue for the Chinese People's Republic (8 October 1949). In north-east China, where the currency had a lower value, separate issues continued until May 1951.

• Szechwan

FIRST STAMPS 1933; withdrawn 31 October 1936 (necessitated by local currency devaluation)

• Yunnan

FIRST STAMPS 15 August 1926; withdrawn 31 July 1935 (necessitated by local currency devaluation)

• Japanese Occupation of China

CURRENCY	
1946	As China

• Kwangtung

Special stamps issued 13 June 1942-c.9 September 1945.

• Mengkiang (Inner Mongolia)

Special stamps issued 1 July 1941-1945.

• North China

Special stamps issued 5 June 1941-1945.

• Nanking and Shanghai

Special stamps issued 23 December 1941-1945.

• Manchuria

FIRST STAMPS China and Russia in their respective POs (until 1920)
FIRST STAMPS ISSUED 18 March 1927 (overprints on stamps of China, necessitated by currency depreciation in Kirin and Heilungkiang provinces). These issues are sometimes so designated, though they were also used elsewhere in Manchuria.

CURRENCY	
1946	As China

The huge domain from which the Manchu conquered the Ming dynasty (1643-51) soon became a mere province of China proper. The northern half was ceded to Russia in 1858-60; the southern half became more Chinese through mass immigration from the south. Russian support against Japanese aggression in 1895 earned Russia the right to build the Chinese Eastern Railway. Provocation by the Boxers led to Russian occupation in 1900 to protect the unfinished railway (opened 1901). Manchuria fell to Japan in 1905, but Chinese rule was restored in 1907.

In the closing years of World War I, when a huge number of White Russian refugees arrived from the west.

In 1931 the Japanese took the whole country and set up Pu Yi as Emperor Kang-teh of Manchukuo. This was overrun after 8 August 1945 by Soviet troops, who withdrew in April-May 1946 leaving Communist forces opposing Nationalist troops.

Postal History
The town of Newchwang may have had a Japanese PA 1876-81 dependent upon Shanghai. An Imperial Chinese PO operated from 1897. Russian POs operated from 1900 throughout Manchuria (probably earlier in Kharbin and Newchwang), also along the Chinese Eastern Railway; including TPOs they form the largest single group of Russian POs abroad.

Manchuria used stamps of China (Chinese People's Republic) from May 1951.

• Manchukuo

FIRST STAMPS 26 July 1932

CURRENCY	
1932	100 fen = 1 yuan

The name was changed from Manchuria by the Japanese invaders. Jehol was annexed in 1933.

• North Eastern Provinces (Nationalist)

Stamps issued February 1946-October 1948.

• North Eastern Provinces (Communist)

Stamps issued February 1946-May 1951.

• Lyao-Tung

FIRST STAMPS Russia 1895-1905
Japan 1905-45
FIRST STAMPS ISSUED (stamps of Japan overprinted) 15 March 1946 (until 1950) (these are listed in some catalogues as China-Provinces-Manchuria-Port Arthur and Dairen)

An eastern maritime province, leased to Russia by China 1895-1905, in which Port Arthur became a base for the Russian fleet. It was surrendered

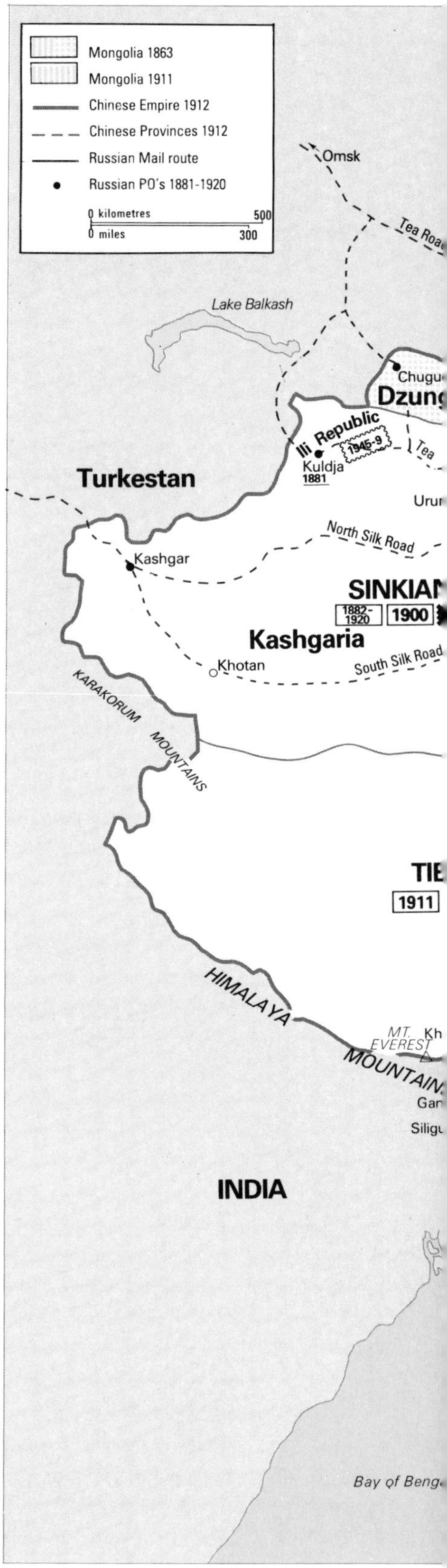
Mongolia 1863
Mongolia 1911
Chinese Empire 1912
Chinese Provinces 1912
Russian Mail route
Russian PO's 1881-1920
0 kilometres 500
0 miles 300
Omsk
Lake Balkash
Ili Republic
1945-9
Kuldja
1881
Turkestan
North Silk Road
Kashgar
1882-1920
1900
Kashgaria
Khotan
South Silk Road
KARAKORUM MOUNTAINS
1911
HIMALAYA
MT. EVEREST
INDIA

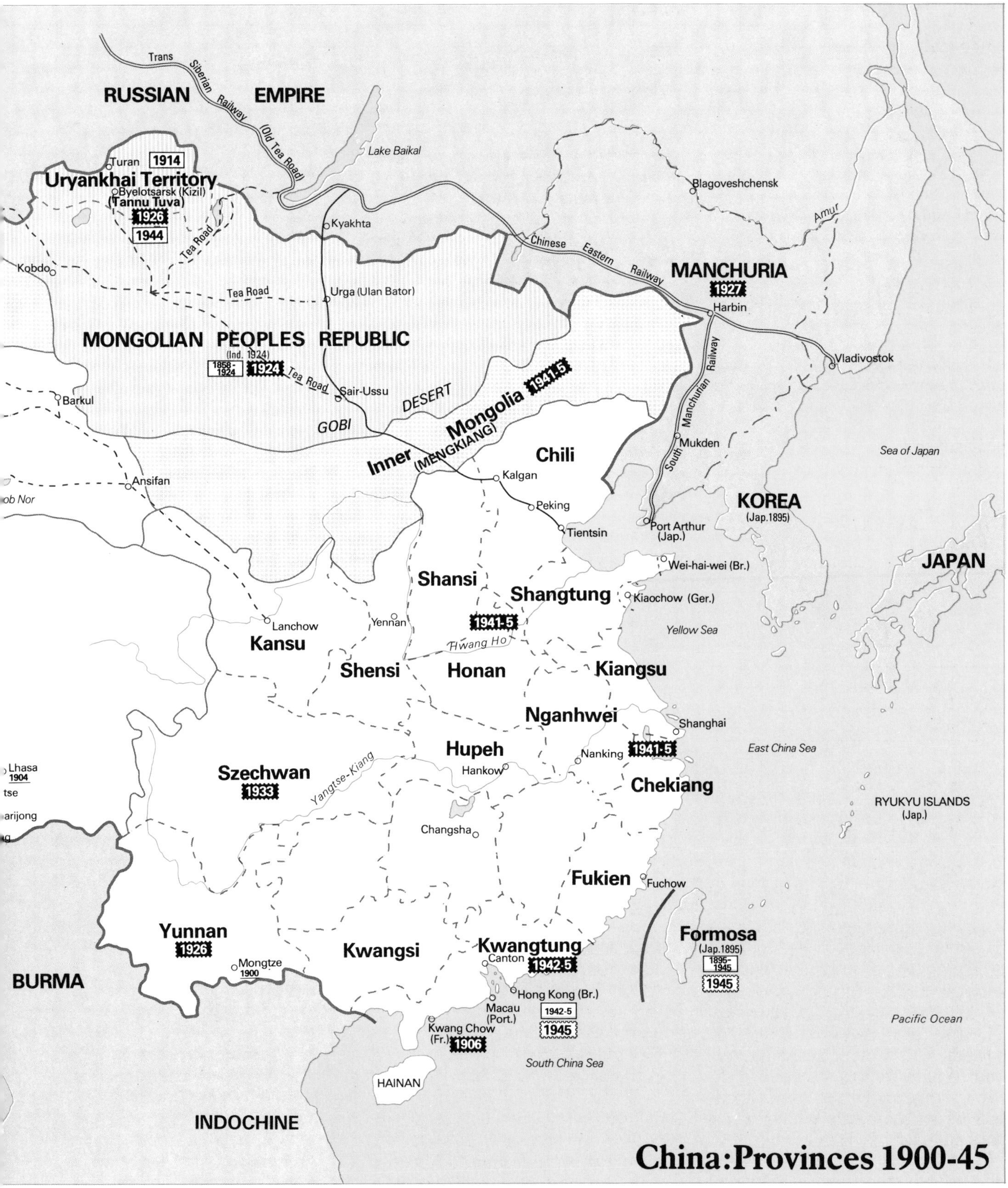
RUSSIAN EMPIRE
Trans Siberian Railway (Old Tea Road)
Lake Baikal
Turan 1914
Uryankhai Territory
Byelotsarsk (Kizil)
(Tannu Tuva)
1926
1944
Tea Road
Kyakhta
Blagoveshchensk
Amur
Chinese Eastern Railway
MANCHURIA
1927
Harbin
Kobdo
Tea Road
Urga (Ulan Bator)
MONGOLIAN PEOPLES REPUBLIC
(Ind. 1924)
1858-1924
1924
Tea Road
Sair-Ussu
Vladivostok
South Manchurian Railway
Barkul
GOBI
DESERT
Inner Mongolia
(MENGKIANG)
1941-5
Chili
Mukden
Sea of Japan
Ansifan
ob Nor
Kalgan
Peking
Tientsin
KOREA
(Jap.1895)
Port Arthur
(Jap.)
Wei-hai-wei (Br.)
JAPAN
Shansi
Shangtung
Kiaochow (Ger.)
Lanchow
Yennan
1941-5
Yellow Sea
Kansu
Hwang Ho
Shensi
Honan
Kiangsu
Nganhwei
Shanghai
Hupeh
1941-5
East China Sea
Lhasa
1904
tse
arijong
Szechwan
1933
Yangtse-Kiang
Hankow
Nanking
Chekiang
RYUKYU ISLANDS
(Jap.)
Changsha
Fukien
Fuchow
Yunnan
1926
Kwangsi
Kwangtung
Canton
1942-5
Formosa
(Jap.1895)
1895-1945
1945
Mongtze
1900
BURMA
Hong Kong (Br.)
Macau
(Port.)
1942-5
1945
Kwang Chow
(Fr.)
1906
Pacific Ocean
South China Sea
HAINAN
INDOCHINE
China: Provinces 1900-45

KOREA
10 POON
조선은
하나이다
DPRK 1979
REPUBLIC OF KOREA
30
A
B
C
D

A Korea Empire 1895; **B** North Korea 1979; **C** Imperial Korea 1901; **D** South Korea 1960.

to Japan in 1905 and, after reversion to China in 1945, again leased to Russia until 1955 when (26 May) all Russian forces were withdrawn.

The main POs were Port Arthur (*Jap.* Ryojun; *Chin.* Lyu-Shun) and Dalny (*Jap.* Dairen; *Chin.* Te Lien).

Used stamps of Chinese People's Republic from 1950 (though in 1950-5 cancellers were inscribed bilingually in Chinese and Russian).

• Tibet

FIRST STAMPS China, March 1911
FIRST STAMPS ISSUED December 1912

CURRENCY

1911	As India
1912	6 ⅔ trangka = 1 sang

Buddhist state ruled by the Dalai Lama. Chinese influence, intermittent in the 18th century, was dormant in the 19th when Russian ambitions were in the ascendant. The Chinese gradually re-occupied Tibet in 1950-9, and the land is now ruled as an autonomous region of China.

Postal History
The Tibetan Frontier Commission set up temporary POs in 1903 using Indian stamps from Khamba Jong and elsewhere, and passing mail over their supply lines via Gangtok (in Sikkim). The Younghusband Expedition set up FPOs on its 1904 mission to Lhasa, passing their mail over a 16,000 ft pass via Gyantse to Siliguri, their Indian base. Indian PAs were later set up in Gantok, Gyantse, Pharijong (reputedly the highest permanent PO in the world) and Yatung. These have functioned until recent times. Various special cachets have been used on mail from Mount Everest expeditions (1924, 1933, etc). Some Chinese POs were opened in 1909.

Used stamps of China overprinted in Chinese and Tibetan with value in *annas* and *rupees*, March 1911.

Has used stamps of China since 1951-60.

• Sinkiang

FIRST STAMPS Russia 1882-1920; China c.1900
SEPARATE STAMPS ISSUED 1915-49 (Chinese stamps bearing surcharged values because of currency difficulties).

CURRENCY

1915	As China

A region somewhat larger in area than Spain and Portugal. Through it passed the western 'Tea Road' to Russia and the 'Silk Road' to the west, the main caravan highways of Central Asia until the completion of the Trans-Siberian Railway. It was annexed in 1759 to form, once again, the north-west province of the Chinese Empire. The province was virtually independent after the Chinese revolution of 1912. The Soviet Russians never gained a foothold.

Postal History
Russian consulate POs, opened in Kuldja and elsewhere by 1881, were the only postal system until c.1900 when the first Chinese PO opened. The Chinese system only became efficient c.1909, but the Russian PO in Kashgar remained important. Russian POs were closed in October 1920.

Stamps of Russia were used in Russian POs 1882-1920 (Kuldja, Chuguchak, Kashgar, and Urumchi are known from cancellations); also (at Urumchi) stamps of Russian POs in China.

Stamps of China were in use in Chinese POs from c.1900.

Has used stamps of China (Chinese People's Republic) since 20 October 1949.

• Ili Republic

A short-lived Uighur republic in the Ili valley (north-west Sinkiang) declared independent in 1945, and which rejoined China in 1949.

Separate stamps issued August 1945-1949.

Mongolia

FIRST STAMPS Russia 1858-1924
FIRST STAMPS ISSUED August 1924

CURRENCY

1924	100 cents = 1 Chinese dollar
1926	100 mung = 1 tugrik

The Mongols had carried their banners of empire under Genghis Khan (1206-27) to the gates of Vienna and under Kublai Khan (1260-94) to Peking. Their empire soon broke up into various khanates. Russian influence, however, remained dominant. The Mongolian People's Republic was proclaimed on 26 November 1924.

Postal History
A frontier PO was opened for government mails at Kyakhta before 1898. A Russian consular post began in 1863 at Urga, while Russian merchant guilds at Kyakhta, Urga and Sair-Ussu on the 'Tea Road' operated posts across the Gobi Desert to Kalgan (Peking) until these were taken over in 1870 by the Russian postal administration. A Chinese PO operated also at Urga in 1909-12 and 1919-21. The Russian offices became the basis of the Mongolian posts in 1924.

• Tannu Tuva

FIRST STAMPS Russia from 1914
FIRST STAMPS ISSUED October 1926 (occasionally found in combination with stamps of Russia).

CURRENCY

1926	As Russia
1935	100 kopecks = 1 tugrik
1936	100 kopecks = 1 aksha

Uryankhai, or Wu-Lyang-Hai, a nomadic area ringed by mountains, was first recognized as Chinese in 1864, though by this time Russian traders were established. The region was cut off geographically from China by Mongolia's declaration of independence in 1911. A Russian protectorate in 1914 moved the capital to Byelotsarsk, and though Chinese rule was re-established for a short time following the Russian Revolution, the Red Army re-occupied the territory in 1921. It is now an autonomous republic of the Soviet Union.

Postal History
There were no organized posts before 1914. A Russian PO at Byelotsarsk from about this time remained after 1921 when the town's name changed to Kizil. The country never joined the UPU so that its stamps were valid only internally or to Russia and Mongolia.

Inscriptions: POSTA TOUVA or TUBA. Only post town known: Kizil and Turan. Has used only stamps of USSR since 1944.

• Korea

FIRST STAMPS ISSUED 18 November 1884 (these were shortlived as the PO was burned down during a revolt in December 1884; new stamps were not issued until 1895)

CURRENCY

1884	100 mon = 1 tempo
1895	5 poon = 1 cheun
1900	19 rin = 1 cheun (sen)
	100 cheun = 1 weun (yen)

A closed kingdom owing suzerainty to China in 1637-1895. Opened diplomatic relations with Japan in 1876, was annexed by Japan in 1910 and, as its colony, was known as Chosen. In November 1942 was declared part of the Japanese Empire. In August 1945 it was divided at the 38th Parallel between Soviet and US administrations, a situation which exploded into war as soon as North Korea and South Korea became independent republics.

Used stamps of Japan in 1905-46.

• Japanese POs in Korea

FIRST STAMPS Japan 1876-99
PARTICULAR STAMPS ISSUED 1 January 1900-1 April 1901

POs opened at Pusan, 10 November 1876; Wonsan, April 1880; Chemulpo (*now* Inchon), December 1883; Seoul, July 1888; Mokpo, October 1897. After 1905 these POs became indistinguishable from any others in Korea.

Used stamps of Japan 1876-99 and from 1 April 1901.

NIPPON
60
A
B
15
C
A Japan 1983; **B** Japan 1871; **C** Japan 1942.

North Korea

FIRST STAMPS Japan
FIRST STAMPS ISSUED 12 March 1946

CURRENCY

1959	Old won = 1 chon ; 100 chon = 1 new won

The area north of the 38th Parallel wrested from the Japanese by the USSR after 10 August 1945, occupied until 30 December 1948 after a People's Democratic Republic had been proclaimed (9 September).

Used stamps of Japan until 1946.

South Korea

FIRST STAMPS Japan
FIRST STAMPS 1 February 1946

CURRENCY

1946	100 cheun = 1 weun
1953	100 weun = 1 hwan
1962	100 chon = 1 won

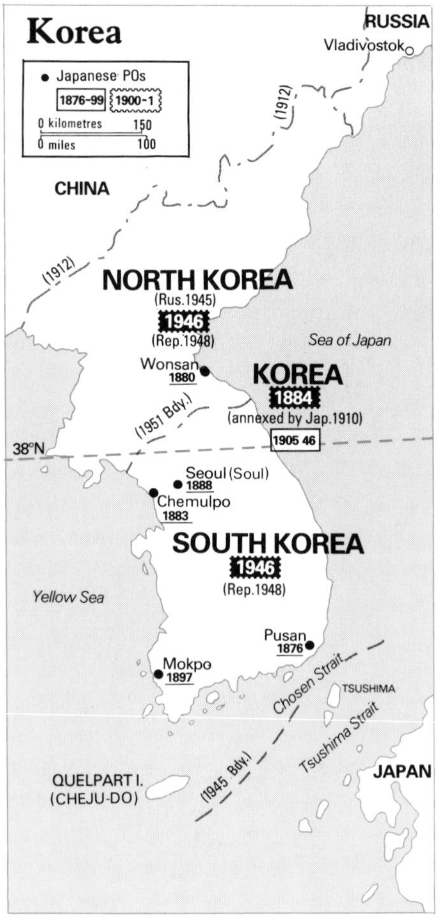
Korea
RUSSIA
Vladivostok
Japanese POs
1876-99
1900-1
0 kilometres 150
0 miles 100
CHINA
(1912)
(1912)
NORTH KOREA
(Rus.1945)
1946
(Rep.1948)
Sea of Japan
Wonsan
1880
KOREA
1884
(annexed by Jap.1910)
(1951 Bdy.)
1905 46
38°N
Seoul (Soul)
1888
Chemulpo
1883
SOUTH KOREA
1946
(Rep.1948)
Yellow Sea
Pusan
1876
Mokpo
1897
Chosen Strait
TSUSHIMA
Tsushima Strait
QUELPART I.
(CHEJU-DO)
(1945 Bdy.)
JAPAN

Came under US military government on 8 September 1945. It was proclaimed a republic on 15 August 1948. US forces were withdrawn on 29 June 1949. When North Korean troops crossed the 38th Parallel on 25 June 1950, the United Nations (whose mission had been in Korea since 1948) condemned the act and called for a UN force to aid the South Koreans. The nations involved in the ensuing war were Australia, Belgium, Britain, Canada, Colombia, Denmark, Ethiopia, France, Greece, India, Italy, Luxembourg, Netherlands, New Zealand, Norway, Philippines, Sweden, Thailand, Turkey, South Africa and the USA most of which were served by their own Field POs.

Used stamps of Japan until 30 June 1946.

Japan

FIRST STAMPS ISSUED 20 April 1871

CURRENCY

1871	100 mon = 1 sen
1872	10 rin = 1 sen; 100 sen = 1 yen

A policy of isolation was pursued by the Japanese until 1854, all foreigners being unwelcome. Imperial rule replaced that of the shoguns in 1867. The Japanese occupied the Ryukyu Islands in 1879, Formosa in 1895 and Southern Sakhalin after defeating the Russians in 1905. They annexed Korea in 1910. Fighting on the Allied side in World War I, Japan received under mandate the former German colonies lying north of the Equator (Marianas, Carolines, and Marshall Islands, *see* Australia, New Zealand and the Pacific).

After seizing Manchuria in 1931, Japan began the invasion of China, capturing both Peking and Shanghai by 1937 and penetrating coastal areas beyond the River Yangtze. French Indo-China was attacked after the fall of France in July 1941. A treacherous attack without declaration of war on 7 December 1941 upon the US, British and Dutch possessions in South-east Asia extended Japanese dominion by 1942 to the borders of India and Australia. After defeat and unconditional surrender on 14 August 1945, Japan was reduced to its original islands. A constitutional monarchy was decreed on 3 May 1947.

Postal History

Official government posts, reformed in 1630, were not open to the public. Private couriers carried some letters, but in general there was no public service before 1871.

Foreign POs were established in Japan soon after the first merchants were allowed in.

British POs were opened at Yokohama (1859), Nagasaki (1860) and Hyogo (Kobe) in 1869. All closed in December 1879.

Used stamps of Hong Kong from 1864 (Yokohama, oblit. Y1 from 1866; Nagasaki, oblit. N2 from 1866; Hyogo, oblit. D30 from 1876).

French PO opened at Yokohama in 1865 (closed in March 1880).

Used stamps of France (oblit. 5118 in diamond of dots to 1876; then datestamps).

United States POs were opened at Yokohama and Nagasaki in 1867; at Hyogo in 1868; and at Hakodate in 1871. All closed in December 1874.

Used stamps of USA with named cancellers.

Japan joined the UPU in 1877.

Until 1947 all Japanese stamps incorporated a symbolic representation of the chrysanthemum in their designs.

Stamps of Japan without distinguishing overprint were used in many places in the Japanese Empire. The general issue of 1942-5 was used in conquered territories.

BCOF

Australian stamps overprinted BCOF JAPAN 1946 were issued for the Commonwealth Occupation Forces on 11 October. They were withdrawn on 12 February 1943.

• Ryukyu Islands

FIRST STAMPS Japanese until 1945
FIRST STAMPS ISSUED 1948

CURRENCY

1948	Japanese
1958-72	US

Okinawa was captured by US forces 1 April – 21 June 1945 and the group was occupied by the USA until restored to Japan on 15 May 1972.

A US military PO was established in August 1945 and, later, civilian mail passed free.

Has used stamps of Japan since 15 May 1972.

AFRICA

AFRICA, THE INDIAN OCEAN, THE SOUTH ATLANTIC AND ANTARCTICA

Though North Africa shared the communication systems of the ancient empires – Egyptian, Phoenician and Roman (which included the transmission of official, and to a lesser extent private, correspondence) – in modern times the postal systems of Africa have been almost without exception European in conception.

The reasons are self-evident: with the exception of the Arabs, Copts and Ethiopians in the north-eastern quarter, few people could write; in many areas language and experience were so localized that correspondence was in any case impossible or unnecessary. The little that was needed, mostly warnings of danger, could be better accomplished by talking drums.

Where culture reached a high level, as in the Lake kingdoms of Central Africa, runners were trained in accurate delivery of verbal messages well before the penetration of European explorers. It was from places such as Uganda (after Stanley had brought to King Mtesa a freed slave who could take dictation, translate and write) that the few letters of genuinely African origin are known.

The introduction of adhesive stamps, here as everywhere, is a wholly European-inspired development. Europeans at first used their own. With the exception of Liberia, where the impetus came (1860) via the United States, no truly independent state followed suit until Ethiopia (1894).

The colonial era in Africa set a pattern that is probably reversible only at the price of reverting to tribalism. European languages are well rooted and provide the only *lingua franca* in areas with tongues without a common root. Thus English remains necessary to Kenya, not only for converse in the UN but in order to avoid a choice between giving preference to Swahili, Kikuyu or Masai.

The destinations of overseas mail have probably not changed dramatically since independence. Habits break very slowly, so that a population reared on Fiats is more likely to continue to import them than to change to Peugeots; this, combined again with the language barrier, ensures that commercial correspondence from Somalia will more likely be in Italian to Turin than in French to Brussels. In general, French-speaking tourists are more easily attracted to Dakar, English to Mombasa, and German still to Dar-es-Salaam.

The routing of mail, on the other hand, was internationalized in the 19th century by the UPU. Though in colonial times railways tended to cross boundaries only if both territories were under the same flag (exceptions were the Beira-Mashonaland and the Franco-Ethiopian railways), shipping routes were less parochial (being less susceptible to military misuse). Even air routes tend to the conservative, so that European services to the Congo (Zaire) are still predominantly Belgian, those to West Africa mainly French.

Stamp-collecting habits will therefore tend the same way, since stamp printing also has linguistic and stylistic traditions.

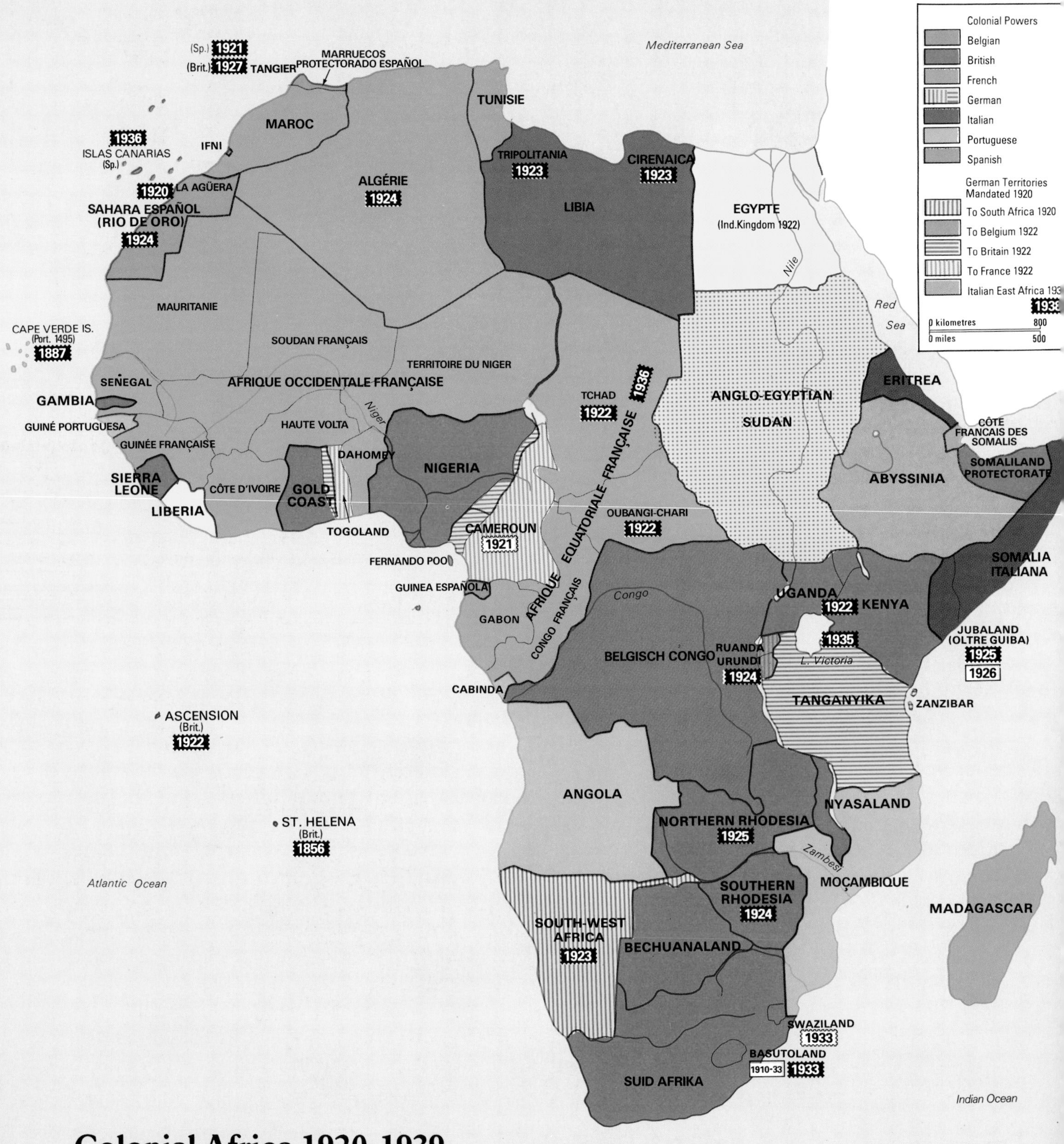
Colonial Powers
Belgian
British
French
German
Italian
Portuguese
Spanish
German Territories Mandated 1920
To South Africa 1920
To Belgium 1922
To Britain 1922
To France 1922
Italian East Africa 1936
0 kilometres 800
0 miles 500
Mediterranean Sea
(Sp.) 1921
(Brit.) 1927 TANGIER
MARRUECOS PROTECTORADO ESPAÑOL
TUNISIE
MAROC
1936
ISLAS CANARIAS (Sp.)
IFNI
ALGÉRIE 1924
TRIPOLITANIA 1923
CIRENAICA 1923
LIBIA
1920 LA AGÜERA
SAHARA ESPAÑOL (RIO DE ORO) 1924
EGYPTE (Ind.Kingdom 1922)
Nile
Red Sea
MAURITANIE
CAPE VERDE IS. (Port. 1495) 1887
SOUDAN FRANÇAIS
TERRITOIRE DU NIGER
SENEGAL
AFRIQUE OCCIDENTALE FRANÇAISE
TCHAD 1922
1936
ANGLO-EGYPTIAN SUDAN
ERITREA
GAMBIA
Niger
GUINÉ PORTUGUESA
HAUTE VOLTA
GUINÉE FRANÇAISE
DAHOMEY
NIGERIA
CÔTE FRANCAIS DES SOMALIS
SOMALILAND PROTECTORATE
ABYSSINIA
SIERRA LEONE
CÔTE D'IVOIRE
GOLD COAST
LIBERIA
TOGOLAND
AFRIQUE EQUATORIALE FRANÇAISE
OUBANGI-CHARI 1922
CAMEROUN 1921
FERNANDO POO
SOMALIA ITALIANA
GUINEA ESPAÑOLA
Congo
UGANDA
1922 KENYA
GABON
CONGO FRANÇAIS
1935
JUBALAND (OLTRE GUIBA) 1925 1926
RUANDA URUNDI 1924
BELGISCH CONGO
L. Victoria
CABINDA
TANGANYIKA
ZANZIBAR
ASCENSION (Brit.) 1922
ANGOLA
NYASALAND
NORTHERN RHODESIA 1925
ST. HELENA (Brit.) 1856
Zambesi
MOÇAMBIQUE
Atlantic Ocean
SOUTHERN RHODESIA 1924
MADAGASCAR
SOUTH-WEST AFRICA 1923
BECHUANALAND
SWAZILAND 1933
BASUTOLAND 1910-33 1933
SUID AFRIKA
Indian Ocean

Colonial Africa 1920-1939

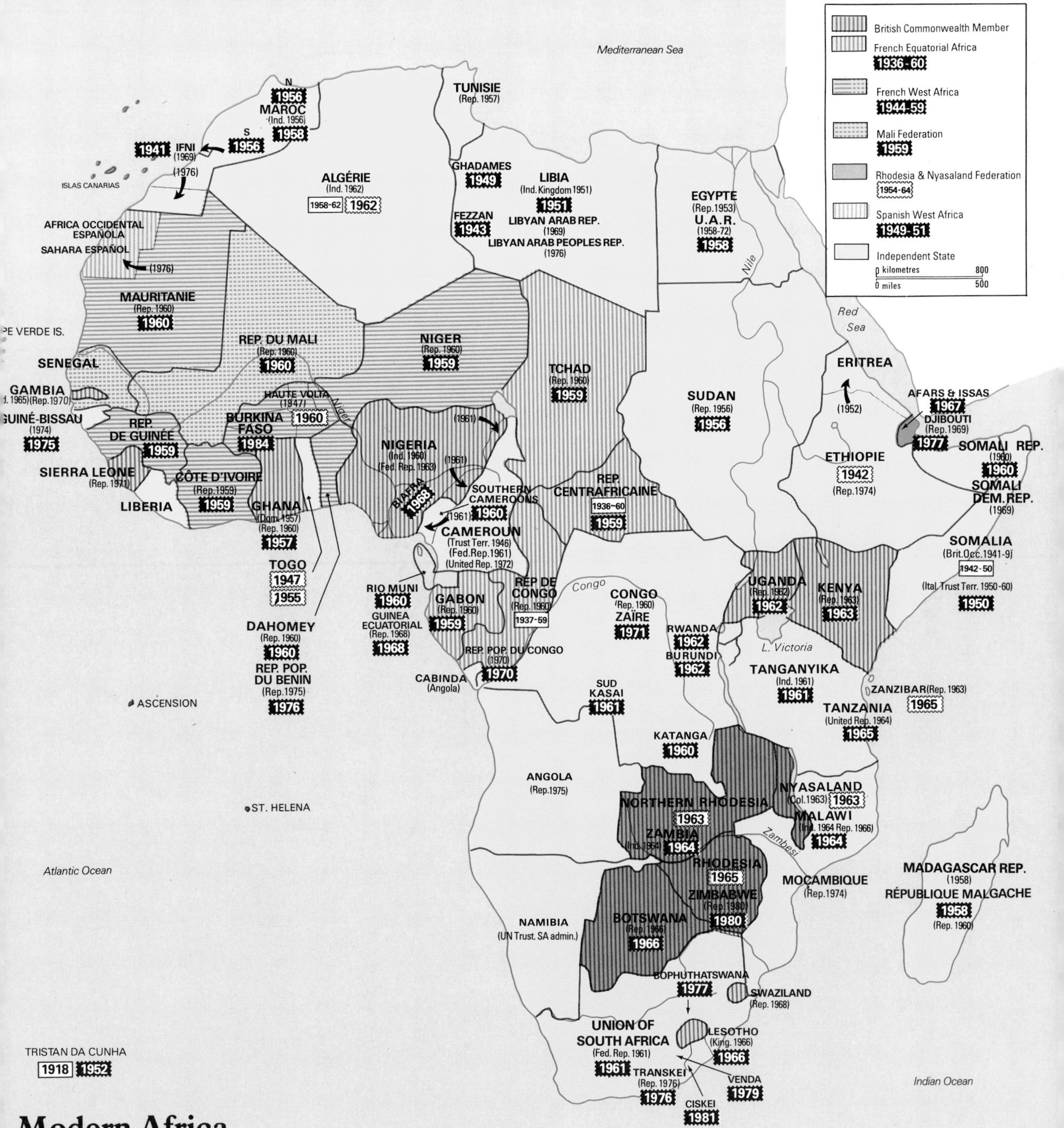
British Commonwealth Member
French Equatorial Africa
1936-60
French West Africa
1944-59
Mali Federation
1959
Rhodesia & Nyasaland Federation
1954-64
Spanish West Africa
1949-51
Independent State
0 kilometres 800
0 miles 500
Mediterranean Sea
N
1956
MAROC
(Ind. 1956)
1958
S
1956
1941
IFNI
(1969)
(1976)
ISLAS CANARIAS
TUNISIE
(Rep. 1957)
ALGÉRIE
(Ind. 1962)
1958-62
1962
GHADAMES
1949
FEZZAN
1943
LIBIA
(Ind. Kingdom 1951)
1951
LIBYAN ARAB REP.
(1969)
LIBYAN ARAB PEOPLES REP.
(1976)
EGYPTE
(Rep.1953)
U.A.R.
(1958-72)
1958
Nile
AFRICA OCCIDENTAL ESPAÑOLA
SAHARA ESPAÑOL
(1976)
MAURITANIE
(Rep. 1960)
1960
PE VERDE IS.
SENEGAL
GAMBIA
(Ind. 1965)(Rep.1970)
GUINÉ-BISSAU
(1974)
1975
REP. DU MALI
(Rep. 1960)
1960
NIGER
(Rep. 1960)
1959
TCHAD
(Rep. 1960)
1959
Red Sea
ERITREA
(1952)
SUDAN
(Rep. 1956)
1956
AFARS & ISSAS
1967
DJIBOUTI
(Rep.1969)
1977
SOMALI REP.
(1960)
1960
SOMALI DEM. REP.
(1969)
ETHIOPIE
1942
(Rep.1974)
HAUTE VOLTA
(1947)
1960
BURKINA FASO
1984
Niger
REP. DE GUINÉE
1959
SIERRA LEONE
(Rep. 1971)
LIBERIA
CÔTE D'IVOIRE
(Rep.1959)
1959
GHANA
(Dom. 1957)
(Rep. 1960)
1957
TOGO
1947
1955
DAHOMEY
(Rep. 1960)
1960
REP. POP. DU BENIN
(Rep.1975)
1976
NIGERIA
(Ind. 1960)
(Fed. Rep. 1963)
(1961)
(1961)
BIAFRA
1968
SOUTHERN CAMEROONS
1960
(1961)
CAMEROUN
(Trust Terr. 1946)
(Fed.Rep.1961)
(United Rep. 1972)
REP. CENTRAFRICAINE
1936-60
1959
RIO MUNI
1960
GUINEA ECUATORIAL
(Rep. 1968)
1968
GABON
(Rep. 1960)
1959
REP DE CONGO
(Rep. 1960)
1937-59
Congo
CONGO
(Rep. 1960)
ZAÏRE
1971
REP. POP. DU CONGO
(1970)
1970
CABINDA
(Angola)
SOMALIA
(Brit.Occ.1941-9)
1942-50
(Ital. Trust Terr. 1950-60)
1950
UGANDA
(Rep. 1962)
1962
KENYA
(Rep. 1963)
1963
RWANDA
1962
BURUNDI
1962
L. Victoria
TANGANYIKA
(Ind. 1961)
1961
ZANZIBAR(Rep. 1963)
1965
TANZANIA
(United Rep. 1964)
1965
ASCENSION
SUD KASAI
1961
KATANGA
1960
ANGOLA
(Rep.1975)
ST. HELENA
NORTHERN RHODESIA
1963
ZAMBIA
(Ind. 1964)
1964
NYASALAND
(Col.1963)
1963
MALAWI
(Ind. 1964 Rep. 1966)
1964
Zambesi
RHODESIA
1965
ZIMBABWE
(Rep. 1980)
1980
MOÇAMBIQUE
(Rep.1974)
MADAGASCAR REP.
(1958)
RÉPUBLIQUE MALGACHE
1958
(Rep. 1960)
Atlantic Ocean
NAMIBIA
(UN Trust. SA admin.)
BOTSWANA
(Rep. 1966)
1966
BOPHUTHATSWANA
1977
SWAZILAND
(Rep. 1968)
UNION OF SOUTH AFRICA
(Fed. Rep. 1961)
1961
LESOTHO
(King. 1966)
1966
TRANSKEI
(Rep. 1976)
1976
VENDA
1979
CISKEI
1981
TRISTAN DA CUNHA
1918
1952
Indian Ocean

Modern Africa

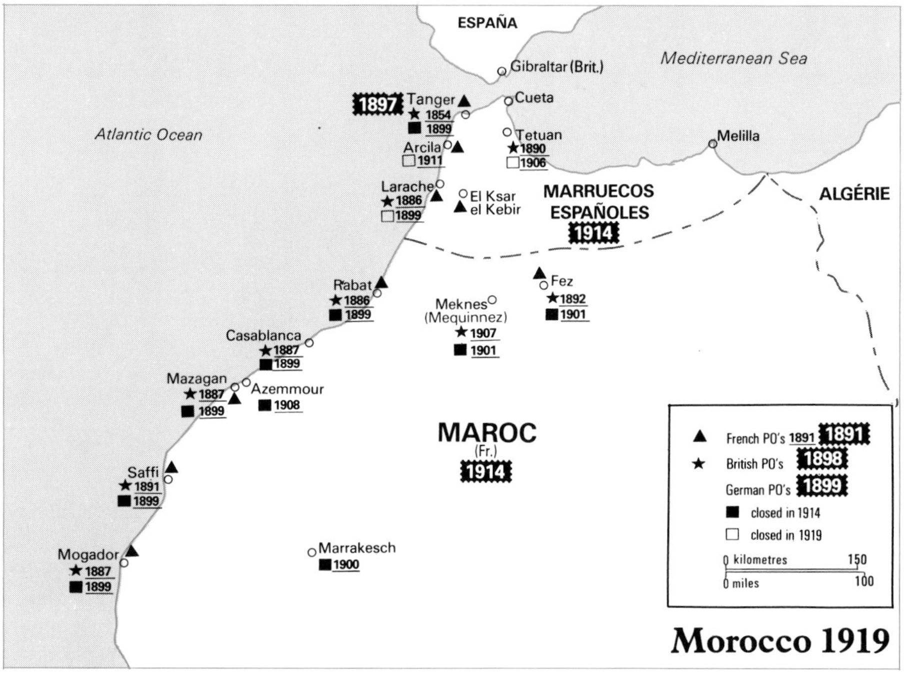
ESPAÑA
Gibraltar (Brit.)
Mediterranean Sea
Atlantic Ocean
1897 Tanger ★1854 ■1899
Cueta
Tetuan ★1890 □1906
Arcila □1911
Melilla
Larache ★1886 □1899
El Ksar el Kebir
MARRUECOS ESPAÑOLES 1914
ALGÉRIE
Rabat ★1886 ■1899
Fez ★1892 ■1901
Meknes (Mequinnez) ★1907 ■1901
Casablanca ★1887 ■1899
Mazagan ★1887 ■1899
Azemmour ■1908
MAROC (Fr.) 1914
Saffi ★1891 ■1899
Mogador ★1887 ■1899
Marrakesch ■1900
French PO's 1891
British PO's 1898
German PO's 1899
closed in 1914
closed in 1919
0 kilometres 150
0 miles 100
Morocco 1919

Morocco (Maroc)

The Barbary Coast, despite its organized piracy, attracted European consuls in the 16th century, but its decayed Muslim sultanate remained medieval into the 19th century. Various European aspirations were polarized by secret conventions in 1904 between Spain and France to partition Morocco. The French bought out German interests by concessions in the Congo. French and Spanish protectorates were established in 1912 and an International Zone in 1923. Opposition to French rule was suppressed by Lyautey in 1912-25 and Pétain in 1925-8. The protectorates were relinquished in 1956 and the international status of Tangier abolished later in the year. In 1957 the sultan assumed the title of king. Independent Morocco absorbed the northern part of Spanish Sahara in 1976 but this is still disputed by the Polisario.

In the 19th century posts were organized by European governments or private concerns.

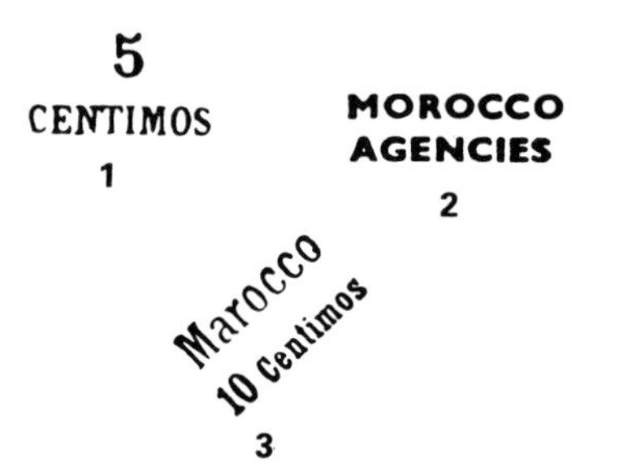
5
CENTIMOS
1
MOROCCO
AGENCIES
2
Marocco
10 Centimos
3

Overprints used in Morocco:
1 French Post Offices, 1891
2 British Post Offices, 1949
3 German Post Offices, 1899

• French POs in Morocco

FIRST STAMPS ISSUED 1 January 1891

CURRENCY

1891 100 centimos = 1 peseta

A French agency in Tangier passed mail via Oran, using a datestamp from c.1854. Used stamps of France from November 1862 (oblit. 5106 at Tangier).

Further offices opened in 1891 at Arzila, Casablanca, El Ksar el Kebir, Fez, Larache, Mazagan, Mogador, Rabat and Safi.

• Morocco Agencies (British POs in Morocco)

FIRST STAMPS Britain 1857-86
FIRST STAMPS ISSUED (stamps of Gibraltar overprinted) 1898

CURRENCY

1898 As Spain until 1956 or British currency
1917 As France until 1938

Used stamps of Britain 1857-86; stamps were cancelled at Gibraltar, and are only recognizably from Morocco if on cover.

POs were placed under control of Gibraltar 1886-1907; used stamps of Gibraltar 1886-98.

POs were under control of London 1907-56; used stamps of Britain overprinted, unsurcharged (whole period), or with currency surcharges in Spanish (entire period) or in French (1917-8 January 1938).

• German POs in Morocco

FIRST STAMPS ISSUED 20 December 1899

CURRENCY

1889 As Spain

Seven POs were opened in December 1899 and another eight subsequently. Those in the French zone were closed on 3 August 1914; the four on Spanish territory remained open until 16 June 1919.

• Spanish POs in Morocco

FIRST STAMPS Spain from 1860
FIRST STAMPS ISSUED 1903
Used only in Tangier (*see below*) after 1914

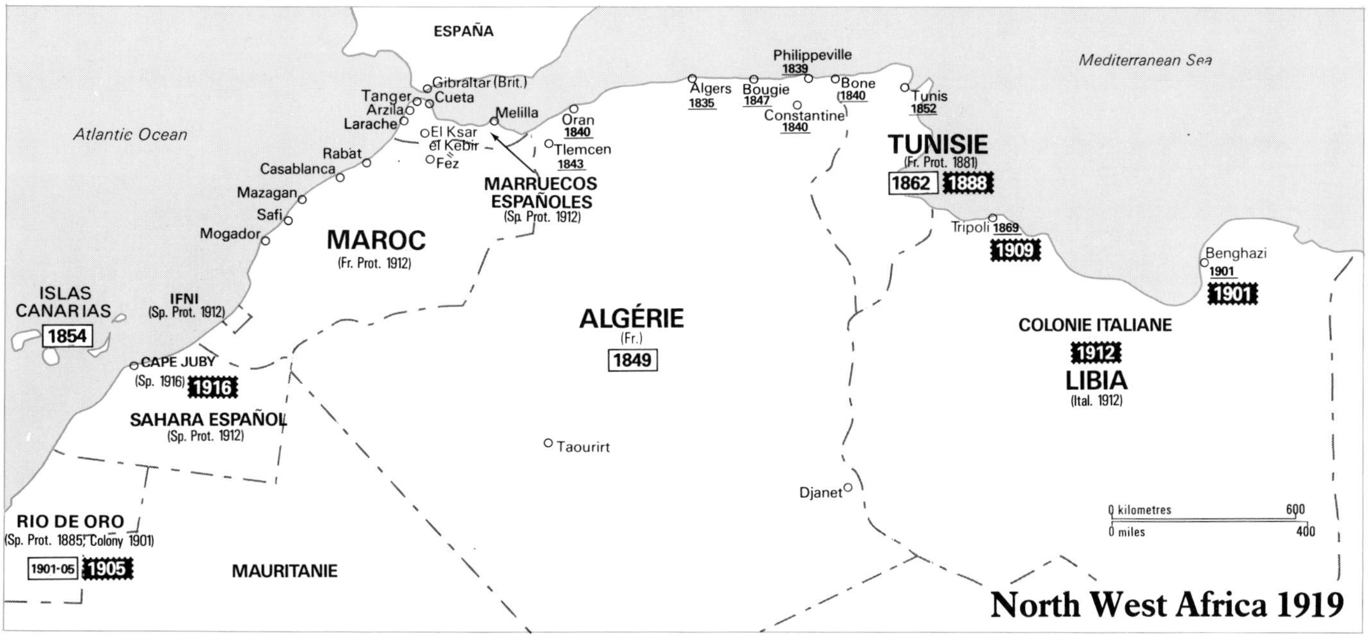
ESPAÑA
Mediterranean Sea
Atlantic Ocean
Gibraltar (Brit.)
Tanger
Cueta
Arzila
Larache
Melilla
Oran
1840
El Ksar
el Kebir
Fez
Tlemcen
1843
Rabat
Casablanca
Mazagan
Safi
Mogador
MARRUECOS
ESPAÑOLES
(Sp. Prot. 1912)
MAROC
(Fr. Prot. 1912)
Algers
1835
Bougie
1847
Philippeville
1839
Bone
1840
Constantine
1840
Tunis
1852
TUNISIE
(Fr. Prot. 1881)
1862
1888
Tripoli 1869
1909
Benghazi
1901
1901
ISLAS
CANARIAS
1854
IFNI
(Sp. Prot. 1912)
CAPE JUBY
(Sp. 1916)
1916
SAHARA ESPAÑOL
(Sp. Prot. 1912)
ALGÉRIE
(Fr.)
1849
COLONIE ITALIANE
1912
LIBIA
(Ital. 1912)
Taourirt
Djanet
kilometres
0
600
0 miles
400
RIO DE ORO
(Sp. Prot. 1885; Colony 1901)
1901-05
1905
MAURITANIE
North West Africa 1919

CURRENCY	
1903	As Spain

• Spanish Morocco

FIRST STAMPS ISSUED 22 July 1914
Withdrawn 7 April 1956

• Sherifian Post

FIRST STAMPS ISSUED 1912

CURRENCY
400 moussonats = 1 rial

An official post started in 1892 using octagonal cachets (operative throughout Morocco to 1915; in Tangier to 1919).

• French Morocco

FIRST STAMPS ISSUED 1 August 1914
Withdrawn 2 March 1956

CURRENCY	
1956	As France

The Sherifian post and former French offices were recognized as one system.

Morocco

Independent from France 2 March 1956; from Spain 7 April 1956; Tangier from international control 29 October 1956. For currency reasons the ex-Spanish and ex-French territories retained separate stamps to February 1958:

• Northern Zone

FIRST STAMPS 17 August 1956

• Southern Zone

FIRST STAMPS ISSUED 19 May 1956
FIRST STAMPS ISSUED for whole independent territory 20 April 1958

CURRENCY	
Until 1958 French	
After 1959	100 centimes = 1 dirham

TANGER
1

TANGIER
2

TANGIER
1857·1957
3

Overprints used in Tangier:
1 French Post Office, 1918
2 British Post Office, 1946
3 British Post Office, 1957

• Tangier (International Zone 1912- October 1956)

CURRENCY	
1918	As France

• French PO 1854-1918 *(see above)*

FIRST STAMPS ISSUED June 1897

Amalgamated with Spanish PO March 1942.

CORREOS
MARRUECOS
PROTECTORADO ESPAÑOL
75 ANIVERSARIO
U.P.U. 1874-1949
10
CTS
B
0^{15}
POSTES
+0^{25}
1970
ROYAUME DU MAROC
C
MAROC
50f
POSTES
S.M. MOHAMED V
D
25
25
A
20
Cs
CORREOS
E

A Post Sherifian 1912; **B** Spanish Morocco 1949; **C** Morocco:Kingdom 1970; **d** Morocco: Southern Zone 1956; **E** Spanish POs in Morocco 1909.

A
POSTES
15f
MAROC
MONUMENT DU SOUVENIR A CASABLANCA
40
40
MAROC
B
15
TANGER
MAROC
C

A French Morocco:Protectorate 1952; **B** French Morocco:Protectorate 1917; **C** French PO in Tangier 1918.

• **Spanish PO 1860-1914** (*see above*)

FIRST STAMPS ISSUED 1921

Continued to use stamps of ex-Spanish POs in Morocco 27 November 1914-1921.

Rival postal establishments of Nationalists and Republicans operated in 1936-40. Used stamps of Spanish Morocco 14 June 1940-11 October 1945.

• **British PO**
To 1927, *see* Morocco Agencies *above*)

FIRST STAMPS ISSUED 1927

Used also stamps of Britain without overprints (values of 2½*d* and above).

• **Ifni**

FIRST STAMPS ISSUED 1941

CURRENCY
Spanish

Spanish possession from 1860, stamps issued from 1941-69. From 1946, part of Spanish West Africa; in 1969 joined Morocco.

• **Rio de Oro**

FIRST STAMPS ISSUED 1905

CURRENCY
Spanish

Spanish protectorate 9 January 1885, administered from Canary Islands; colony, 1901; renamed Spanish Sahara (*see below*) in 1924. Used stamps of Spain 1901-5.

• **Spanish Sahara**

FIRST STAMPS ISSUED 1924

Later inscriptions as follows:
1924 POSESIONES ESPAÑOLAS DEL SAHARA OCCIDENTAL
1926 SAHARA ESPAÑOL
1943 (only), also in Arabic:
1960-75 ESPAÑA SAHARA

CURRENCY
Spanish

Known as Rio de Oro before 1924, the Spanish Sahara was a province of Spain until 31 December 1975.

When Spanish troops were withdrawn on 26 February 1976, the country was divided between Morocco and Mauritania; the border was agreed on 14 April 1976. Morocco had made her claim by the peaceful 'Green March' in November 1975. A so-called 'Saharan Arab People's Republic' was declared in opposition by Algerian-backed Rio de Oro guerrillas. Existing postal arrangements are not known.

• **Cape Juby**

FIRST STAMPS ISSUED 1916

CURRENCY
Spanish

Occupied by Spain, June 1916; incorporated in Spanish Sahara 1950.

Used stamps of Rio de Oro and Spanish Morocco in 1917-19.

• **La Agüera**

FIRST STAMPS ISSUED June 1920

CURRENCY

1920 As Spain

Occupied by Spain November 1920 as a military air base; incorporated in Spanish Sahara 1924.

• Spanish West Africa (Africa Occidental Española)

FIRST STAMPS ISSUED 9 October 1949-51

CURRENCY

1949 As Spain

Stamps inscribed AFRICA OCCIDENTAL ESPAÑOLA were used in both Spanish Sahara and Ifni.

COLONIA DE RIO DE ORO
CORREOS
PARA 1905
2 - PESETAS
A
1 PTA
CORREOS
CORREO ESPAÑOL TANGER
LA CRUZ ROJA ESPAÑOLA
MUESTRA
B
ALGERIE
1.00
C
25
CORREO AEREO
TERRITORIO DE IFNI (ESPAÑA)
D
25 CENTS
CORREOS
TERRITORIOS DEL AFRICA OCCIDENTAL ESPAÑOLA
E
REPUBLIQUE FRANCAISE
ALGÉRIE
1F50 POSTES 1F50
F
5 PTAS
ESPAÑA
SAHARA
CORREOS
PRO-INFANCIA 1971
G

A Rio de Oro 1905; B Spanish Tangier 1926; C Algeria: Independent; D Territory of Ifni 1943; F Spanish West Africa 1950; F Algeria: French Département 1924; G Spanish Sahara 1971.

Algeria

FIRST STAMPS France from 1849
FIRST STAMPS ISSUED 8 May 1924

CURRENCY

1924-64 French
After 1964 100 centimes = 1 dinar (parity with the franc)

French punitive expedition against Algiers pirates in 1830 led, after some indecision, to a war of conquest in 1840-8. A period of pacification followed until 1871 and then a period of peace in 1872-90 before the conquest of the Saharan oases. The early history and hence also postal history is military: civil administration did not begin until 1848, was not widespread until 1871, and only reached the desert provinces in 1902. Rivalry between military and civil authority extended to postal matters. The European population, c.600 in 1830, exceeded 10,000 in 1835 and 100,000 soon after 1845. Before 1881 there were more than 320,000 Europeans, and provision of state primary schools for the native

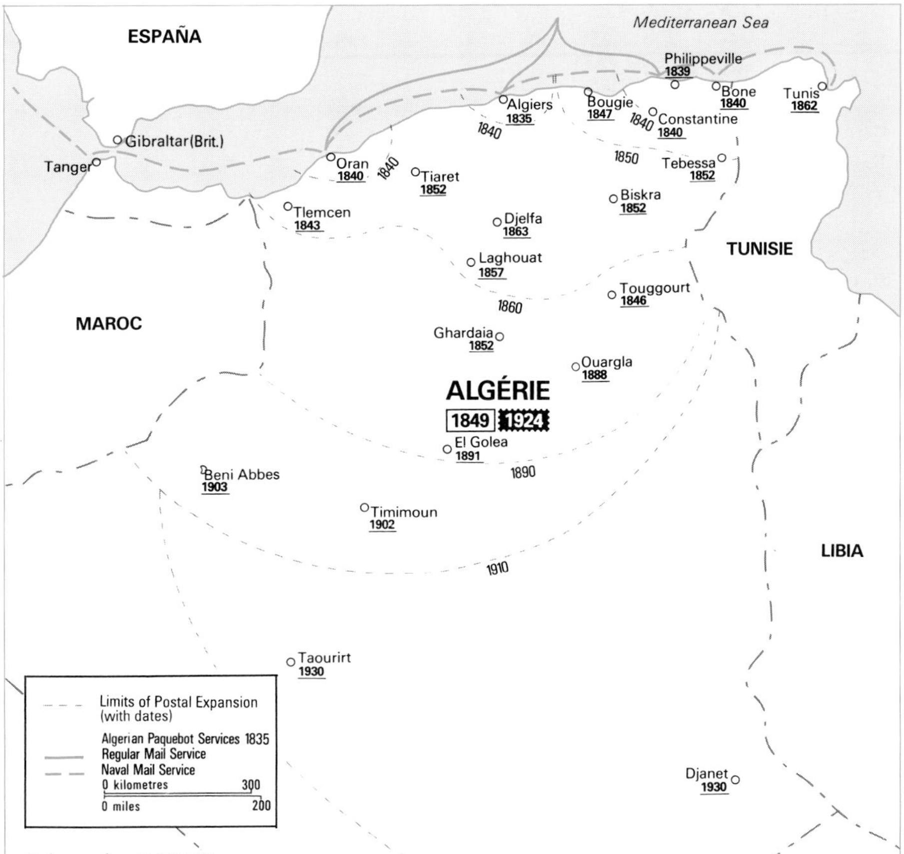
ESPAÑA
Mediterranean Sea
Philippeville 1839
Algiers 1835
Bougie 1847
Bone 1840
Tunis 1862
Constantine 1840
Gibraltar (Brit.)
Tanger
Oran 1840
Tiaret 1852
Tebessa 1852
Biskra 1852
Tlemcen 1843
Djelfa 1863
Laghouat 1857
TUNISIE
Touggourt 1846
MAROC
Ghardaia 1852
Ouargla 1888
ALGÉRIE
1849 1924
El Golea 1891
Beni Abbes 1903
Timimoun 1902
LIBIA
Taourirt 1930
Djanet 1930
Tamanrasset 1930
1840
1850
1860
1890
1910
1930
Limits of Postal Expansion (with dates)
Algerian Paquebot Services 1835
Regular Mail Service
Naval Mail Service
0 kilometres 300
0 miles 200

Algeria 1930

population had begun. A declaration that Algeria was to become an integral province of France led to open war on 1 November 1954 between Algerians and French troops backed by settlers, which lasted until a cease-fire on 18 March 1962. By referendum Algeria became independent on 3 July 1962.

Postal History

Letters from Europeans in Algiers are known at least from 1690, and a postal mark was used in Spanish-occupied Oran from 1749. But no regular service existed until 1830, when the military postal organization (*Trésor et Postes*) was introduced in Algiers. It was opened to civilians in 1835. Gradually the posts were separated from the paymaster branch and in 1860 they became autonomous. From 18 POs in 1845, the service grew to 97 offices in 1860 and 295 in 1880.

Postal services were initially by courier and by coastal steamboat service operated by the French navy. The coastal service passed to Messageries Maritimes in 1866, and from 1862 railways slowly pushed forward (Algiers-Oran opened 1871; Constantine-Philippeville 1870).

Military handstamps were used in 1830-9; datestamps bearing town names and dates were issued to POs after 1839.

Used stamps of France from 1 January 1849.

Oblit. 16 January 1849 – 31 December 1851 by dumb grille: stamps are identifiably from Algeria only on cover. After 1852 cancellation was by lozenge of dots with small figures (3710-4448) and after 1863 by similar lozenge with large figures (5000-5171). N.B. Most of these numbers, but not all, were issued to Algeria. Datestamps were used to cancel stamps from April 1876.

Used stamps of France 22 July 1958-27 June 1962.

Used locally overprinted stamps c. 4 July 1962-31 October 1962 until independence stamps were available.

There were 862 POs in 1969.

Tunisia

FIRST STAMPS France from 1862
FIRST STAMPS ISSUED 1 July 1888

CURRENCY

1888-October 1958 French
After 1 November 1958 1000 millièmes = 1 dinar

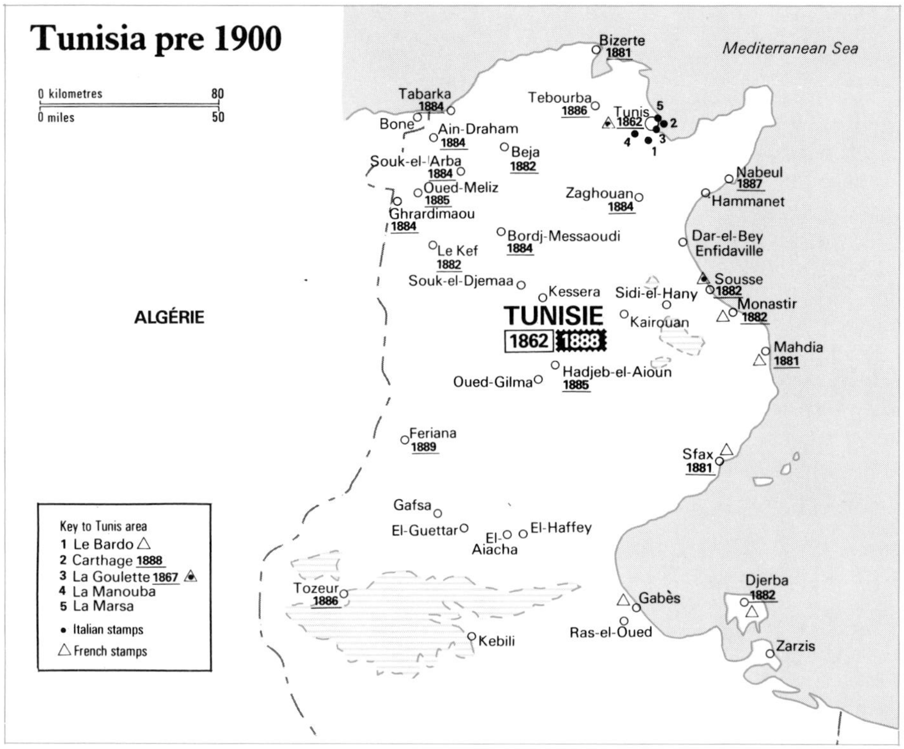
Tunisia pre 1900
0 kilometres 80
0 miles 50
Mediterranean Sea
Bizerte 1881
Tabarka 1884
Tebourba 1886
Tunis 1862
Bone
Ain-Draham 1884
Beja 1882
Souk-el-Arba 1884
Oued-Meliz 1885
Ghardimaou 1884
Zaghouan 1884
Nabeul 1887
Hammanet
Bordj-Messaoudi 1884
Le Kef 1882
Dar-el-Bey Enfidaville
Souk-el-Djemaa
Kessera
Sidi-el-Hany
Sousse 1882
Monastir 1882
ALGÉRIE
TUNISIE
1862 1888
Kairouan
Mahdia 1881
Hadjeb-el-Aioun 1885
Oued-Gilma
Feriana 1889
Sfax 1881
Gafsa
El-Guettar
El-Aiacha
El-Haffey
Tozeur 1886
Gabès
Djerba 1882
Ras-el-Oued
Kebili
Zarzis
Key to Tunis area
1 Le Bardo
2 Carthage 1888
3 La Goulette 1867
4 La Manouba
5 La Marsa
• Italian stamps
△ French stamps

Ruled by a hereditary dynasty of Turkish beys, the country was a centre of Mediterranean piracy. French interest was recognized by the Congress of Berlin (1878). After a short campaign a protectorate was established in May 1881. Tunisia was administered from Vichy from July 1940 to May 1943 when it was overrun by the Allies. After a period of self-government from 1 September 1955, Tunisia became an independent monarchy on 20 March 1956, and a republic on 25 July 1957.

Foreign POs were established in the 19th century.

A French agency in Tunis passed mail by sea via Bone from 1848 and had a datestamp from 1852.

Stamps of France used at Tunis from 1862 (oblit. 5107); at La Goulette from 1867 (oblit. 5121); also at Sousse (5259), Sfax (5262), Le Bardo (5308), Mahdia (5261), Gabès (5307), Djerba (5263) and Monastir (5260) from 1882. By 1888 there were c.42 POs.

Stamps of Italy (general issues for use abroad) are also known to have been used at Tunis (oblit. 235), La Goulette (3336) and Sousse (3364).

Inscription changed from TUNISIE to RÉPUBLIQUE TUNISIENNE from 8 August 1957.

In 1966 there were 381 POs.

Libya

FIRST STAMPS ISSUED 24 December 1951

CURRENCY

Until 1950 Italian
After 1950 1000 millièmes = 1 Libyan pound

A former *vilayet* of Turkey, captured by and ceded to Italy on 18 October 1912. Divided into two colonies from 26 June 1927 to 3 December 1934. Fought over in 1940-3, then under British military occupation until 1951. Independent 24 December 1951 (kingdom). Renamed Libyan Arab Republic in 1969 and Libyan Arab People's Republic in 1976.

• Italian POs

Tripoli opened January 1869.

FIRST STAMPS Italy from 1874
FIRST STAMPS ISSUED December 1909

Used general issues for Italian POs abroad from 1 January 1874.

Used stamps of Italian POs in the Turkish Empire from 1 June 1908.

Benghazi opened 15 March 1901.

FIRST STAMPS ISSUED July 1901

• Libya (Italian colony)

FIRST STAMPS ISSUED December 1912

Commemorative stamps for the two constituent parts (Tripolitania and Cyrenaica) were issued (concurrently with the general issues) before the official division and continued in use after the reamalgamation.

• Tripolitania

FIRST STAMPS 24 October 1923

CURRENCY	
1923	As Italy

• Cyrenaica

FIRST STAMPS 24 October 1923

CURRENCY	
1923	As Italy
1950	1000 mils = £1

Stamps also issued 16 January 1950-23 December 1951 during short period of autonomy.

Both parts used stamps of Britain overprinted M.E.F. in 1943-8.

Both parts used stamps of Britain overprinted B.M.A. TRIPOLITANIA from 1 July 1948 (B.A. TRIPOLITANIA for Tripolitania only 6 February 1950-December 1951).

• Fezzan

FIRST STAMPS ISSUED 16 May 1943

CURRENCY	
French	960 fr = 1 Libyan pound

Captured by Free French forces of Chad, 16 January 1943; under French military administration to 1951.

Used stamps of Algeria 1943-6.

• Ghadames

FIRST STAMPS ISSUED 12 April 1949

CURRENCY	
1949	As France

Both Fezzan and Ghadames became part of Libya on 24 December 1951.

BENGASI
1 PIASTRA 1
1
TRIPOLI
DI BARBERIA
2
TRIPOLITANIA
3

1 Overprint for use in the Italian PO at Benghazi, 1901
2 Overprint for use in the Italian PO at Tripoli, 1909
3 Overprint for use in the Italian Colony of Tripolitania, 1925

Libya (Independent)
Stamps inscribed in Arabic with or without the addition of L.A.R.

Egypt

FIRST STAMPS ISSUED 1 January 1866

CURRENCY	
1899	French
1921	Egyptian

A former province of the Ottoman Empire which became quasi-independent after the Napoleonic invasion (1798-1801) when Mehmet Ali of Kavalla established a dynasty of governors. His successors were granted the title of Khedive in 1867. From the Battle of the Nile (1798), British interest in guarding the route to India, improving imperial communications and suppressing the slave trade ensured continuing interference in Egyptian affairs. British troops occupied the country in 1882 to prevent the threat of the nationalist *Jehad* (holy war) spreading to the Suez Canal; a British resident and consul-general advised the Khedive. On 18 December 1914 (Turkey, to whom Egypt theoretically owed allegiance, being an enemy) Egypt was declared a British protectorate and the dynasty assumed the title of sultan. In 1922 Egypt became an independent kingdom, but a British presence was maintained until 1954. In 1952 a military *coup d'état* forced first the abdication of King Farouk and then of his infant son. A republic was proclaimed on 18 June 1953. The seizure (nationalization) of the Suez Canal in 1956 occasioned a disastrous Anglo-French attempt at reoccupation by force. Egypt federated with Syria on 1 February 1958 as the United Arab Republic; Syria left the Union on 28 September 1961, though Egypt clung to the name for another ten years. A similar attempt at federation with

KINGDOM OF LIBYA
A
SOCIALIST PEOPLE'S LIBYAN ARAB JAMAHIRIYA
TRIPOLI
INTERNATIONAL FAIR 1982
10
B
REPUBLIQUE TUNISIENNE
1831-1981
HEINRICH VON STEPHAN
150
C
C. 40
Libia
D
POSTS
CYRENAICA
E
POSTES
REGENCE DE TUNIS
15
F

A Libya:Kingdom 1952; **B** Libya:Republic 1982; **C** Tunis:Republic 1981; **D** Libya:Italian Colony 1922; **E** Cyrenaica:British Occupation 1950; **F** Tunis:French Protectorate 1888.

Libya did not make progress. Recent history has been of intermittent war against Israel with consequent *de facto* changes of boundary between the two followed by reconciliation.

Postal History

Government postal carriers date back far into the Islamic middle ages, and regular pigeon posts are said to have been started by Sultan Nureddin in 1146. In the early 19th century the need for external posts was felt only by foreign residents such as Greek merchants. Private posts to Europe (*Posta Europea*) were maintained by an Italian company, first organized in 1821 (handstamps). In 1857 this received government sanction to operate inland posts (already begun by local enterprise in Lower Egypt in 1843) until the concession was bought by the government in 1865. This explains why the first government cancellers are inscribed in Italian (POSTE VICEREALIEGIZIANE).

In 1835 Alexandria became the HQ of the 'Overland Route', Lieut. Waghorn's pioneer enterprise to speed the mails between Britain and India. The significance of Egypt to the British Empire was thus extended from the strategy of defence to the day-to-day business of communication.

Egyptian stamps with values in *paras* were used:

(a) in Northern Sudan,
(b) in Eritrea (Massawa) in 1869-85,
(c) on the Somali coast (Berbera and Zaila) in 1881-4, and
(d) in Ethiopia (Harar) in 1881-4.

Stamps bear inscriptions with EGYPT/EGYPTE in English or French; or Arabic; or Italian, POSTE KHEDIVIE EGIZIANE. Stamps used 1 March 1958-1 September 1972 bear the inscription UAR (*see also* Syria).

• British POs

Opened at consulates in Egypt in 1839 (Alexandria), 1847 (Suez) and 1859 (Cairo) to deal with mail carried by British mailboats. In 1860-79 stamps of Britain were used at Alexandria (oblit. B 01) and Suez (oblit. B 02).

• French POs in Egypt

FIRST STAMPS French 1857–99
FIRST STAMPS ISSUED 1899

•Alexandria

PO Opened 1830; closed 31 March 1931. Used stamps of France 1857-76 (numberred oblit. 3704 or 5080).

•Port Said

PO opened June 1867; closed 31 March 1931. Used stamps of France 1867-99 (numbered oblit. 5129).

A joint issue of 'Postage Due' stamps was used at both offices in 1928-30.

• Italian PO at Alexandria

In 1863-84 used an oblit. numbered 234 in an oblong of dots.

There were also Austrian, Russian and Greek POs in Alexandria.

• Suez Canal Company

A concession was granted in 1854, work started in 1859, and the Canal opened on 17 November 1869. The company transported mail free between Port Said and Suez in 1859-67. Between 18 July and 16 August 1868, a charge was made and special stamps were used. The Egyptian government then took over the service, and the charge was incorporated by treaty into the overall postage.

• British forces in Egypt (1932-41)

Concessional rates applied to letters home from service British troops. First 'seals' issued 1 November 1932, were followed in 1936 by stamps inscribed ARMY POST until April 1943 (these were used also in 1940 by some personnel in the Sudan).

Sudan

FIRST STAMPS USED Egypt 1867
FIRST STAMPS ISSUED March 1897
As independent republic
15 September 1956

CURRENCY

1897	Egyptian
1956	1,000 millièmes = 100 piastres = £1 Sudanese

The dynasty in Egypt laid claim to territories to the south as far as they were explored, appointing governors-general in Khartoum and later also in Equatoria. Their Sudanese armies penetrated as far as Uganda and Harar, and in 1875 even landed an expedition near Kismayu on the east coast of Africa until warned off by strong British opposition. The rise of Sudanese resistance under the Mahdi put an end to Egyptian dreams in the south. After the reoccupation in 1898, the Sudan became an Anglo-Egyptian condominium. After an interim period of self-government from 1954, on 1 January 1956 the country became the independent republic of Sudan.

POSTES EGYPTIENNES
SOUDAN
DEUX PIASTRES
MILLIÈMES
SUDAN POSTAGE
SUDAN
CATTLE
55 MMS
EGYPT POSTAGE
THREE MILLIEMES
EGYPTE
POSTES
1 MILL
AR EGYPT
POSTAGE
5 M
A
B
C
D
E
F
G

A Sudan:Egypt overprinted 1895; **B** Sudan:Anglo-Egyptian 1927; **C** Sudan:Independent 1962; **D** Egypt:Turkish Control 1866; **E** Egypt:Kingdom 1922; **F** Egypt:Republic 1953; **G** Egypt:Arab Republic 1971.

Right
Arrival of the Indian and Australian mails at Alexandria, 1853

Below right
Post and Telecom office, Rabat, Morocco

Below
Post-boxes, Cairo

ORDINARY MAIL
EXPRESS
POSTE AERIENNE

Postal History
Egyptian POs were set up in Suakim and Kassala c.1867; in Wadi Halfa, Khartoum, Berber and Dongola by 1873, and probably elsewhere by 1877. The system made use of camel post and Nile steamer. General Gordon extended the postal runner system to the farthest points of his Equatorial province but kept his posts offical and free of payment, so that no stamps were needed south of Khartoum. Letters from Gordon and others from Equatoria are known franked at and forwarded from Khartoum. Services were curtailed between 1882 and 1884 by the Mahdist War until the reconquest (1897-8). The postal service was run by the military (but with civil cancellation) until 1903. The characteristic 'retta' oblit. was used on mail collected from rural agencies. TPOs (steamer and railway) have continued to be a feature of the service.

• Eritrea

FIRST STAMPS Egyptian used in Massawa 1869-85
Italian POs abroad before 1883
FIRST STAMPS ISSUED 1 January 1893

CURRENCY	
Pre-1952	Italian
Post-1952	Ethiopian

Territorial acquisitions by the Italians from 1869 around Assab and Massawa were consolidated by Ethiopian recognition in 1889 and the colony of Eritrea was proclaimed on 1 January 1890. It became part of Italian East Africa in 1936-41. Eritrea was occupied by British forces in 1941 and administered by the British until it was federated with Ethiopia on 15 September 1952 (fully integrated ten years later). It still has a strong separatist movement.

Stamps in use in 1936 were equally valid throughout Italian East Africa and can be found used in Ethiopia and Italian Somaliland.

Used stamps of Italian East Africa in 1938-41.

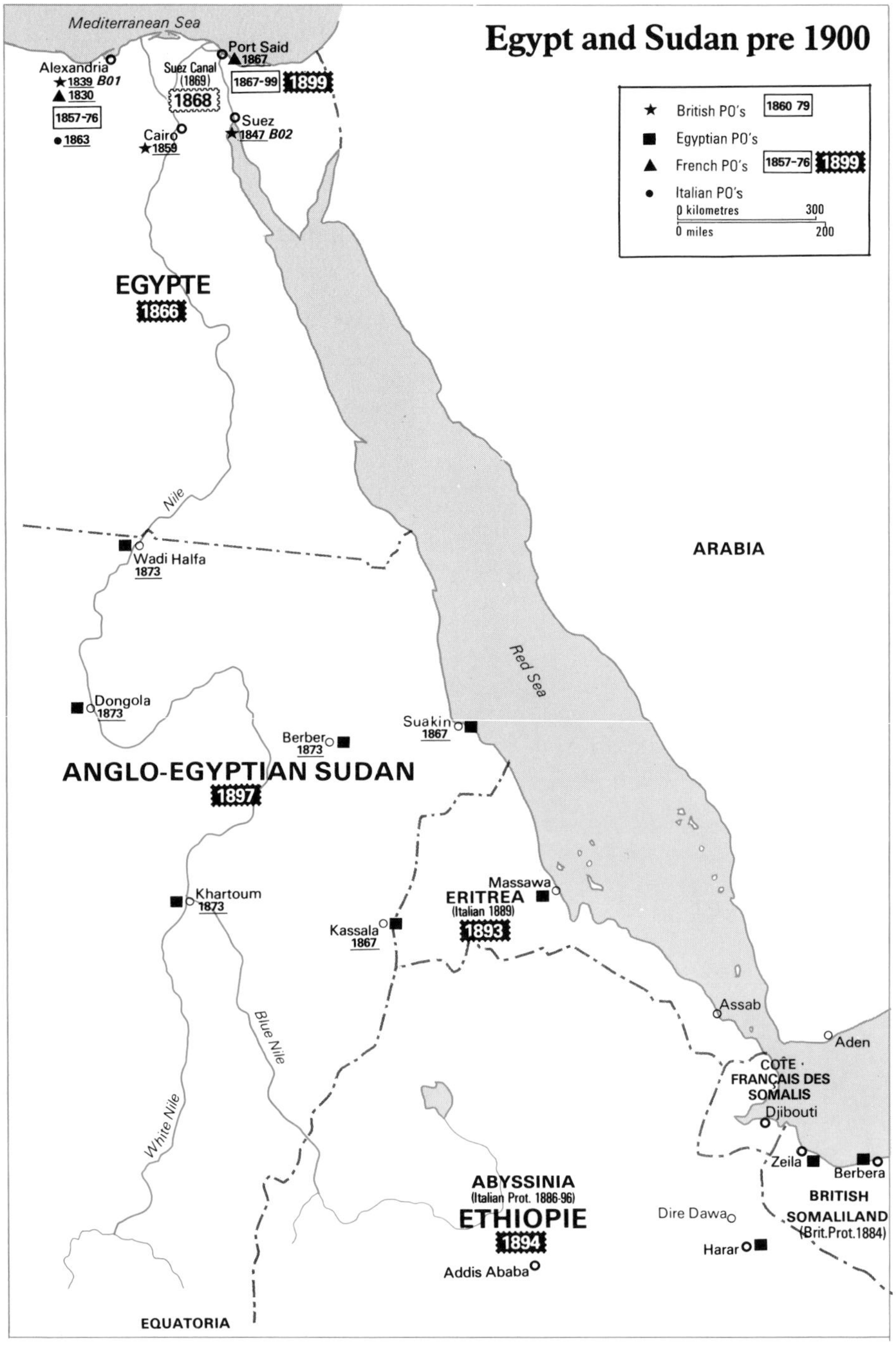
Egypt and Sudan pre 1900
British PO's
Egyptian PO's
French PO's
Italian PO's
1860 79
1857-76
1899
0 kilometres 300
0 miles 200
Mediterranean Sea
Alexandria
1839 B01
1830
1857-76
1863
Suez Canal (1869)
1868
Port Said
1867
1867-99
1899
Suez
1847 B02
Cairo
1859
EGYPTE
1866
Nile
Wadi Halfa
1873
Dongola
1873
Berber
1873
Suakin
1867
ANGLO-EGYPTIAN SUDAN
1897
Red Sea
ARABIA
Khartoum
1873
Kassala
1867
Massawa
ERITREA
(Italian 1889)
1893
Assab
Aden
Blue Nile
White Nile
CÔTE FRANÇAIS DES SOMALIS
Djibouti
Zeila
Berbera
BRITISH SOMALILAND
(Brit.Prot.1884)
ABYSSINIA
(Italian Prot. 1886-96)
ETHIOPIE
1894
Addis Ababa
Dire Dawa
Harar
EQUATORIA

British Occupation of Eritrea (1941-52)
Used stamps of Britain overprinted M.E.F. 2 March 1942.
Used stamps of Britain overprinted B.M.A. ERITREA in 1948-50.
Used stamps of Britain overprinted B.A. ERITREA 6 February 1950-14 September 1952.

Since federation in 1952 has used stamps of Ethiopia.

Stamps inscribed ERITREA purporting to come from 'areas liberated from Ethiopia' have been on the market in 1978 (mainly in Switzerland): it is not clear whether they are bogus, propagandist, or were prepared in hope of use. Evidence suggests that any mail from areas of Eritrea not under Ethiopian postal control is sent unstamped by unofficial runner into Sudan and posted there.

• Obock

FIRST STAMPS French Colonial General Issues from 1883
FIRST STAMPS ISSUED French Colonies overprinted 1 February 1892

CURRENCY	
1892	As France

A Somali coast town purchased in 1857 by the French Consul in Aden. Arrangement ratified by local chiefs in 1862 and area occupied by French from 1883. It lost all importance to Djibouti (q.v.) and the administration was moved there in 1894, when the Obock PO was closed.

Obock issues were used in Djibouti until supplies were exhausted.

• Djibouti

FIRST STAMPS Obock, and Obock overprinted, from 1893
FIRST STAMPS ISSUED 1894

CURRENCY	
1894	As France

Founded in 1888, the year in which the Côte Française des Somalis (French Somali Coast protectorate) was established. Became the capital in 1894. The boundaries of Côte Francaise were established between 1888 and 1901.

In 1902, stamps of Djibouti were replaced by issues bearing the title of the protectorate.

• French Somali Coast (Côte Française des Somalis)

FIRST STAMPS as Obock and Djibouti
FIRST STAMPS ISSUED August 1902

CURRENCY	
1902	As France

Established in 1888 and replaced the former areas of Obock and Djibouti. Developed slowly and in 1915 still had only one PO. Adhered strongly to Vichy France in World War II and was blockaded by British imperial forces until it surrendered in December 1942.

Stamps continued to be issued until 1967 but sometimes contained the title 'Djibouti' as well as the protectorate's full name — notably in the case of the Free French issue of 1943.

The French maintained a link through their territory to Ethiopia by rail, thus giving Ethiopia its only direct link to the coast. The Free French kept alive their civil air rights by running an airmail service between Djibouti and Madagascar in 1943-4.

• French Territory of Afars and Issas

FIRST STAMPS Obock, Djibouti and Côte Française des Somalis
FIRST STAMPS ISSUED 21 August 1967

CURRENCY	
1967	As France

A referendum was held in the Côte Française des Somalis in March 1967 and 60 per cent of the population

'The Post of the Desert', engraving by Horace Vernet, 1876

TERRITOIRE FRANÇAIS
POIGNARD AFAR
RF
30F
DES AFARS ET DES ISSAS
PROTECTORAT
CÔTE des SOMALIS
DJIBOUTI
POSTE ITALIANE
COLONIA ERITREA
CENT 20 VENTI
REPVBLIQVE FRANÇAISE
COLONIES POSTES
1F
OBOCK
POSTA AEREA
CENT. 50
ERITREA
B. A.
ERITREA
POSTAGE
REVENUE
10 CENTS
REPUBLIQUE DE DJIBOUTI
MER ROUGE
YEMEN DU NORD
YEMEN DU SUD
ETHIOPIE
DJIBOUTI
65F POSTES
REPUBLIQUE DE SOMALIE

A B C D E F G

A Afars & Issas:French Colony 1974; **B** Somali Coast:French Colony 1894; **C** Eritrea:Italian Colony 1893; **D** Obock:French Colony 1892; **E** Eritrea:Italian Colony 1936; **F** Eritrea:British Administration 1950; **G** Djibouti:Republic 1977.

POSTES ETHIOPIENNES
2 GUERCHES
ETIOPIA
9 MAGGIO 1936
CENT 50
POSTE COLONIALI ITALIANE

A B

ETHIOPIA 90c

C

A Ethiopia 1909
B Ethiopia 1936
C Ethiopia 1977

voted to continue association with France rather than for independence. The name was changed by decree on 5 July 1967. The territory attained independence as the Republic of Djibouti on 27 June 1977.

Republic of Djibouti

FIRST STAMPS ISSUED 27 June 1977

CURRENCY

1977	francs (Djibouti)

An independent state created on 27 June 1977 from the former French territory of Afars and Issas.

Ethiopia

FIRST STAMPS ISSUED 24 November 1894

CURRENCY

1894	16 guerche = 1 Maria Theresa thaler or talari
1905	100 centimes = 1 franc
1908	16 piastres = 1 thaler
1936	100 centimes = 1 thaler
1936	100 centesimis = 1 lira
1946	100 cents = 1 Ethiopian dollar

An independent sovereign state. Foreign embassies made sporadic contact with emperors and lesser warring chiefs in the 19th century. The imprisonment at Magdala of a British representative to King Theodore led to a celebrated rescue expedition in 1867-8. Various designs on Ethiopia by the Egyptians, French and Italians were resisted by diplomacy or force. It was attacked by Italy on 3 October 1935, invested and annexed on 9 May 1936. Transfers of territory from Ethiopia to Eritrea were made around Adowa, but all became part of Italian East Africa until liberated by Allied forces in 1941. The emperor was restored in January 1942. Further transfers of territory were made in 1948 near Gabredarre, but the Ogaden is still a point of conflict with Somalia. Eritrea was incorporated in 1952. A *coup d'état* on 12 September 1974 deposed the emperor, and a military régime is in power.

Postal History

Italian annexation issue (inscribed ETHIOPIA) 22 May 1936.

In 1936-41 part of Italian East Africa (q.v.) when stamps of Eritrea and Italian Somaliland were also indiscriminately valid and on sale. First stamps on restoration of independence were issued on 23 March 1942.

• French POs in Ethiopia

FIRST STAMPS ISSUED 1906-8 inscribed LEVANT but with values in French instead of Turkish currency

These operated at Harar and Dire Dawas (reached by railway from Djibouti c.1906) and at Addis Ababa, using stamps of Obock or French Somali Coast to frank mails going overseas. Registered mail is found with a triple combination including stamps of India applied at Aden. The French offices were closed in 1908 when Ethiopia joined the UPU.

Somalia:Independent 1981; Somalia: British Occupation 1948; Somalia: Italian Colony 1932; Somalia: Benadir 1903.

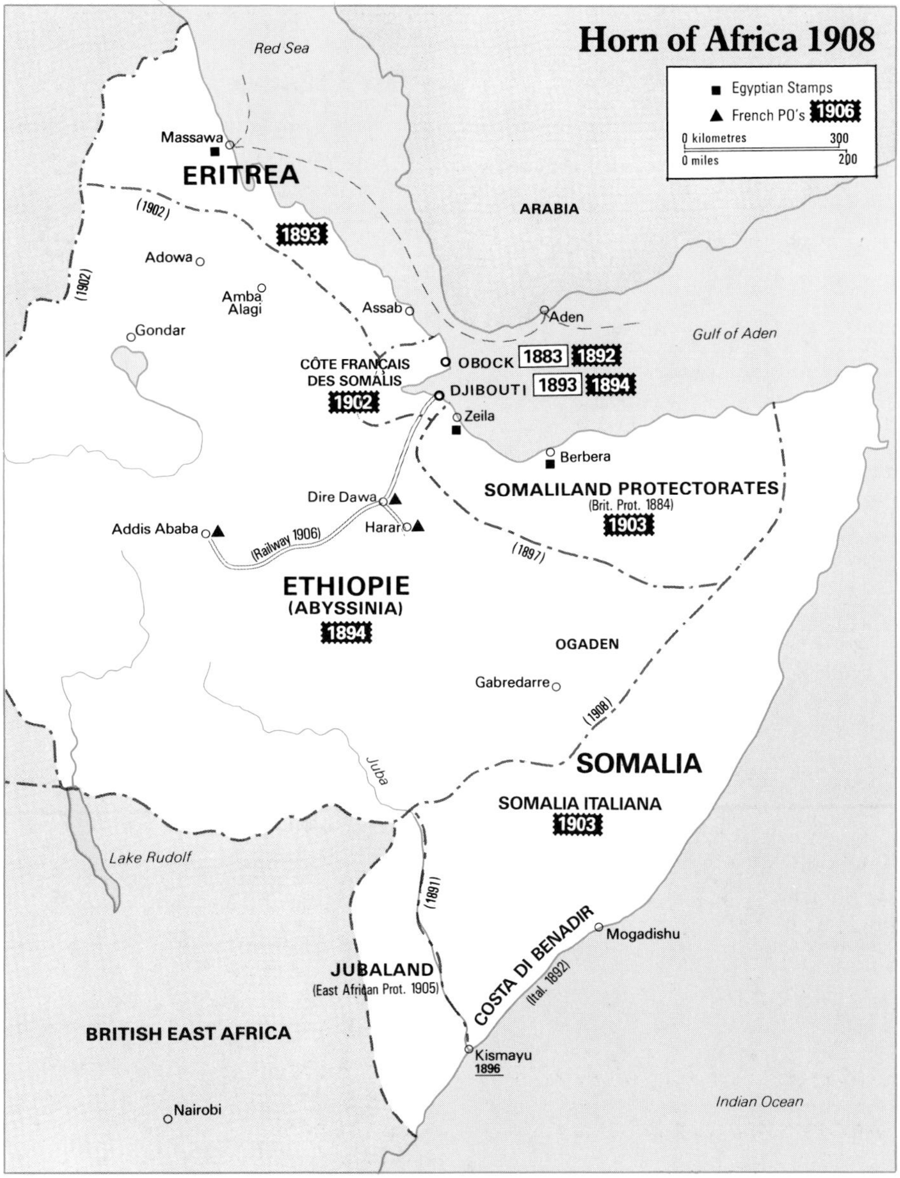
Horn of Africa 1908
Egyptian Stamps
French PO's 1906
0 kilometres 300
0 miles 200
Red Sea
Massawa
ERITREA
(1902)
1893
ARABIA
Adowa
(1902)
Amba Alagi
Assab
Aden
Gulf of Aden
Gondar
CÔTE FRANÇAIS DES SOMALIS
1902
OBOCK 1883 1892
DJIBOUTI 1893 1894
Zeila
Berbera
SOMALILAND PROTECTORATES
(Brit. Prot. 1884)
1903
Dire Dawa
Addis Ababa
(Railway 1906)
Harar
(1897)
ETHIOPIE
(ABYSSINIA)
1894
OGADEN
Gabredarre
(1908)
SOMALIA
Juba
SOMALIA ITALIANA
1903
Lake Rudolf
(1891)
Mogadishu
COSTA DI BENADIR
(Ital. 1892)
JUBALAND
(East African Prot. 1905)
BRITISH EAST AFRICA
Kismayu
1896
Indian Ocean
Nairobi

External mail pre-1908 is also known via British Somaliland, bearing triple frankings Ethiopia/British Somaliland/Aden.

Somalia (Somali Democratic Republic)

FIRST STAMPS ISSUED inscribed BENADIR 12 October 1903

Local chiefs had already placed themselves under Italian protection when in 1892 the Benadir coast was leased by the Italians from the sultan of Zanzibar. Sovereign rights were bought from the sultan and direct rule assumed 19 March 1905 under the name Italian Somaliland. Further territory was purchased from Ethiopia in 1908. Jubaland (*see below*) was added in 1925 as part of Italy's reward for joining the Allies in 1915.

Italian Somaliland, together with Eritrea and Ethiopia, became Italian East Africa (*see below*) 1 June 1936 to 1941. Occupied by British imperial forces in 1941, the territory was separately administered by the British until it was placed under United Nations trusteeship on 21 November 1949 with Italy as trustee nation for ten years. It became an independent republic in 1960, joining with ex-British Somaliland (*see* Somaliland Protectorate). After an army coup in 1969, it adopted a communist régime and the title Somali Democratic Republic.

Postal History

Unstamped Italian mail from the southern ports was handled in 1885-97 by an Italian consulate in Zanzibar, and in 1897-1903 by the PO at Kismayu where British East African stamps were applied.

Later stamps are overprinted or inscribed SOMALIA ITALIANA.

Stamps in use in 1936 were valid throughout Italian East Africa and can be found used in both Ethiopia and Eritrea. Also used stamps of Italian East Africa in 1938-41.

• Italian East Africa (Africa Orientale Italiana)

FIRST STAMPS for combined territories 7 February 1938

Subsequent issues were valid in parts of Italian East Africa remaining in Italian hands until the surrenders of 20 May 1941 (Amba Alagi) and 27 November 1941 (Gondar).

• Jubaland (Oltre Giuba)

FIRST STAMPS USED 1896
FIRST STAMPS ISSUED 29 June 1925

A province of Kenya ceded to Italy with effect from 29 June 1925 and incorporated into Italian Somaliland on 30 June 1926. Used stamps of British East Africa from opening of Kismayu PO c.1896.

From 1 July 1926 used stamps of Italian Somaliland.

British Occupation of Italian Somaliland

Civilian mail was handled at Mogadishu by a military office (EA APO 74), using stamps of Kenya, Uganda and Tanganyika, until Occupied Enemy Territory Administration (OETA) was operative.

Under OETA used stamps of Britain overprinted M.E.F. from 13 April 1942.

Used stamps of Britain overprinted E.A.F. from 15 January 1943.

Used stamps of Britain overprinted B.M.A. Somalia from 27 May 1848.

Used stamps of Britain overprinted B.A. SOMALIA from 2 January 1950. (Owing to lateness of availability, each of these issued overlapped into the following period of administration.)

• Somalia (Italian Trust Territory)

FIRST STAMPS 1 April 1950

• Somalia (Republic including ex-British Somaliland)

FIRST STAMPS 1 April 1960
later inscribed:
1973-JUM. DIM. SOMALIYA
from 1974pJAM. DIM. SOOMAALIYA

• Somaliland Protectorate (British Somaliland)

FIRST STAMPS ISSUED 1903

CURRENCY	
1903	16 annas = 1 rupee
1951	100 cents = 1 shilling

In Arab hands for centuries, the region came under Egyptian influence after 1870. When the Egyptian garrisons were withdrawn in 1884, the British government established a protectorate, garrisoned from Aden and administered by India until 1898. Control passed from the Foreign Office to the Colonial Office in 1905. Occupied by Italian forces in August 1940, it was liberated 16-24 March 1941 by a small force from Aden. Civil posts were restarted on 27 April 1942. By referendum the population opted for unification with newly independent Somalia on 1 July 1960.

Egyptian stamps used at Berbera and Zaila in 1881-4 (*see* Egypt).

Stamps withdrawn from sale 25 June 1960.

Used stamps of Somalia Trust Territory 25-30 June 1960, and thereafter stamps of Somalia.

• Wituland

A sultanate inland of Lamu under German protection 27 May 1885-30 June 1890. The local stamps 'issued' here with inscriptions in Swahili or Arabic have never had universal official recognition.

EAST AFRICA

The British East African group is complicated in that the postal history does not march in step with the politics, nor the stamps exactly with either. Though East Africa and Uganda combined their postal administrations in 1901, a planned political fusion never happened. A further union (involving other communications also) brought Kenya, Uganda, and Tanganyika together postally in 1933, but the three countries have always remained separate as protectorates, colonies, and independent states. Since 1976 their separateness has tended to extend to postal affairs as well. Until recently Zanzibar remained separate politically and postally.

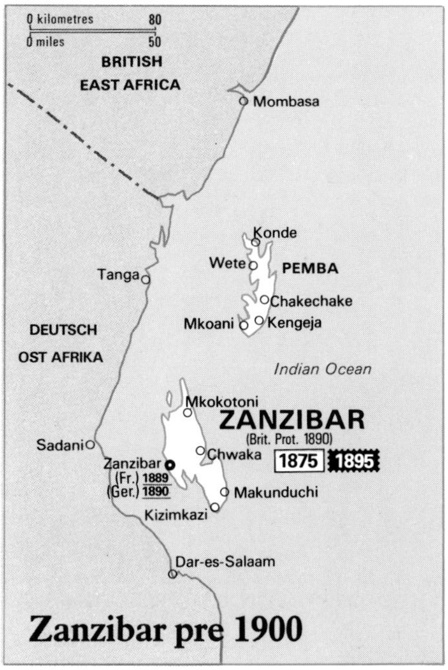
0 kilometres 80
0 miles 50
BRITISH
EAST AFRICA
Mombasa
Konde
Wete
PEMBA
Tanga
Chakechake
Mkoani
Kengeja
DEUTSCH
OST AFRIKA
Indian Ocean
Mkokotoni
ZANZIBAR
(Brit. Prot. 1890)
Sadani
Zanzibar
Chwaka
1875
1895
(Fr.) 1889
(Ger.) 1890
Makunduchi
Kizimkazi
Dar-es-Salaam

Zanzibar pre 1900

• Zanzibar

FIRST STAMPS India from (?) 1875
FIRST STAMPS ISSUED 10 November 1895 (Protectorate)
FIRST STAMPS inscribed ZANZIBAR TANZANIA 17 OCTOBER 1965

CURRENCY	
1895	As India
1908	100 cents = 1 rupee
1936	100 cents = 1 shilling

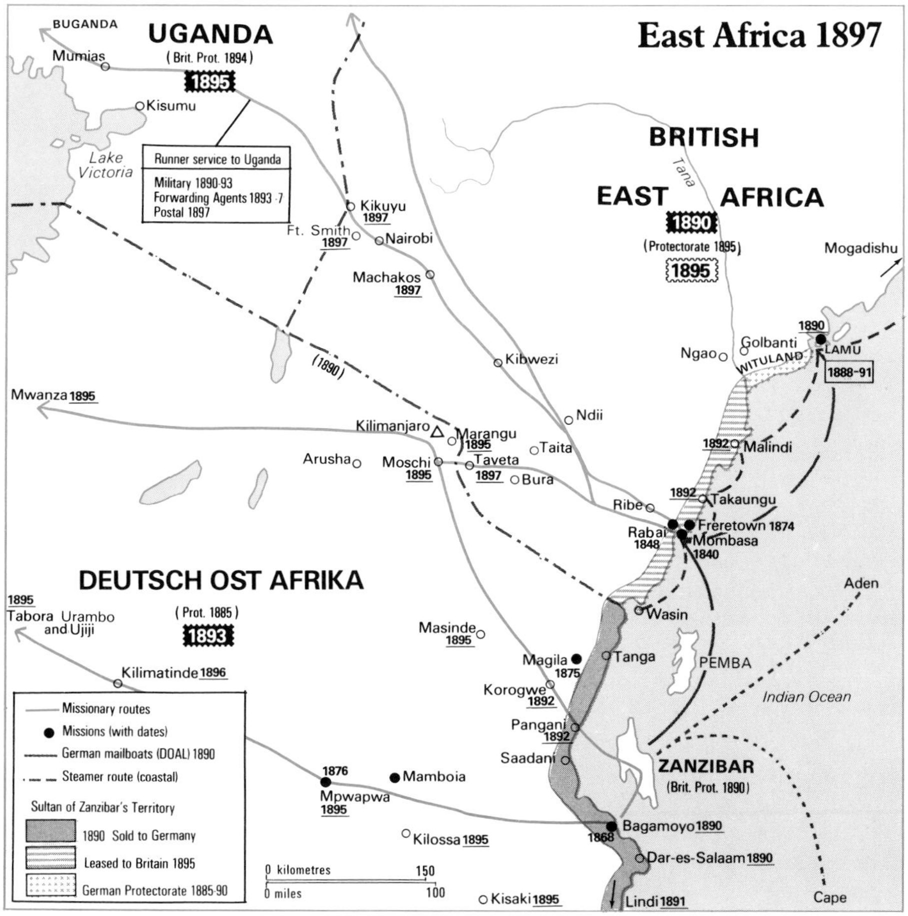
East Africa 1897
BUGANDA
UGANDA
(Brit. Prot. 1894)
1895
Mumias
Kisumu
Lake Victoria
Runner service to Uganda
Military 1890-93
Forwarding Agents 1893-7
Postal 1897
Kikuyu 1897
Ft. Smith 1897
Nairobi
Machakos 1897
BRITISH EAST AFRICA
Tana
1890
(Protectorate 1895)
1895
Mogadishu
1890
LAMU
Golbanti
WITULAND
1888-91
Ngao
Kibwezi
(1890)
Mwanza 1895
Ndii
Kilimanjaro
Marangu 1895
Taita
Arusha
Moschi 1895
Taveta 1897
Bura
1892 Malindi
1892 Takaungu
Ribe
Rabai 1848
Freretown 1874
Mombasa 1840
Aden
DEUTSCH OST AFRIKA
(Prot. 1885)
1893
1895 Tabora Urambo and Ujiji
Masinde 1895
Wasin
Magila 1875
Tanga
PEMBA
Indian Ocean
Korogwe 1892
Kilimatinde 1896
Pangani 1892
Saadani
ZANZIBAR
(Brit. Prot. 1890)
Missionary routes
Missions (with dates)
German mailboats (DOAL) 1890
Steamer route (coastal)
Sultan of Zanzibar's Territory
1890 Sold to Germany
Leased to Britain 1895
German Protectorate 1885-90
1876
Mpwapwa 1895
Mamboia
Kilossa 1895
1868
Bagamoyo 1890
Dar-es-Salaam 1890
0 kilometres 150
0 miles 100
Kisaki 1895
Lindi 1891
Cape

Sultans from Muscat colonized Zanzibar c. 1730 and transferred their capital there in 1832. They introduced the clove and controlled the slave markets. Foreign consulates followed in the wake of traders from the USA and Germany and missionaries from Britain. In 1856 the dynasty became independent of Muscat. Pressure was brought to bear by a British naval presence from the East Indies station that resulted in the Sultan closing the slave markets in 1873. British interests grew and in 1890 a protectorate was proclaimed. More direct rule was assumed in 1906 and on 1 July 1913 control passed from the Foreign to the Colonial Office. Political offices in the early days were closely linked (sometimes shared) with those of British East Africa.

On 10 December 1963 Zanzibar became an independent sultanate and a month later a republic. It federated with Tanganyika as a United Republic in April 1964, known as Tanzania after 17 November 1964.

Postal History

Though the island has no formal postal facilities, consular mails to Europe, carried to and from the Seychelles for onward transmission, either via Aden or Bombay, are known from 1829 (including letters from the explorers Burton, Speke, and Livingstone). In 1872 a regular packet service with Aden was started by the British India Steam Navigation Co. and from 1875 there was a regular PO (sub-office of Aden until 1878; under Bombay until 1895; independent from 10 November 1895 when Zanzibar entered the UPU in its own right). Was the most important East African port-of-call for all foreign mailboats until 1914; after airmails were established in 1931, it became a postal backwater. Internal services in the island started in 1897.

Zanzibar, not having been a member of the East African Postal Union, kept a separate postal administration after federation with Tanganyika until the end of 1967; stamps of the East African Postal Union 1964-67, inscribed KENYA UGANDA TANZANIA, were not valid in Zanzibar.

All Zanzibar stamps were withdrawn 1 January 1968 (but remained valid for a limited period). Thereafter Zanzibar used stamps of Tanzania.

• French PO in Zanzibar

FIRST STAMPS France January 1889-December 1893
FIRST STAMPS ISSUED 1894

CURRENCY

1894 As India

Opened January 1889. Despite repeated demands from 1895 by the British protecting power for closure, remained open (doing mainly 'philatelic' business) until 31 July 1904.

• German PA in Zanzibar

Opened on the arrival of Postsekretär Steinhagen in the *Reichstag*, which began the German mailboat service (D.O.A.L.) to East Africa, 27 August 1890. Closed by request of the British protecting power 31 July 1891.

Used stamps of Germany 27 August 1890-31 July 1891. Distinguishable by cancellation.

• Lamu

The principal mainland Arab settlement between Mombasa and Mogadishu attracted German traders from c. 1880. It was a British India Steamship Co. port-of-call. British influence in the area was recognized in 1890 whereafter it followed the fortunes of British East Africa.

BRITISH SOMALILAND
A
SOMALILAND PROTECTORATE
TWO ANNAS
B
SOMALILAND PROTECTORATE
OPENING OF THE LEGISLATIVE COUNCIL 1957
ONE SHILLING
BLACKHEAD SHEEP
C
ZANZIBAR
D
SOMALILAND PROTECTORATE
FOUR ANNAS
E
Sh 2/50
ASP
TENTH ANNIVERSARY OF THE AFRO-SHIRAZI PARTY
ZANZIBAR·TANZANIA
F
INDIA POSTAGE
Zanzibar
TWO ANNAS
G

A British Somaliland 1903; **B** British Somaliland 1938; **C** British Somaliland 1957; **D** Zanzibar 1952; **E** British Somaliland 1942; **F** Zanzibar 1967; **G** Zanzibar 1895.

Postal History
Correspondence to Germany is known (franked with Indian stamps via Aden or Zanzibar) from 1881. A German PA was set up on 22 November 1888. After a PO of the IBEA Co. was opened in May 1890, the Germans were requested to close theirs, but did not until 31 March 1891.

Used stamps of Germany 22 November 1888-31 March 1891. Distinguishable by cancellation.

• British East Africa

FIRST STAMPS ISSUED Imperial British East Africa Co. 23 May 1890
Protectorates 1 July 1895

CURRENCY

16 annas = 1 rupee (parity with India)

The coastal strip from Mogadishu to Lindi was under the protection of the Zanzibar sultans. The earliest European settlement (from 1844) was confined to a handful of missionaries in an area extending from Mombasa towards Mt. Kilimanjaro. The reputation of the Masai protected the interior from visitors until Thomson's journey of 1883. The Imperial British East Africa Company started operations under concession of the sultan in 1888. Territory administered by the company from 1888 to 30 June 1895 theoretically included Uganda from 1890 to 1893. With the company facing bankruptcy, the British government proclaimed a protectorate on 1 July 1895. The former eastern province of Uganda was transferred to British East Africa in 1902. Control passed from the Foreign to the Colonial Office in 1905 when the capital was moved from Mombasa to Nairobi, but the protectorate was not made a colony until 23 July 1920 when its name was also changed to Kenya.

Postal History
Early letters ('forerunners') are known (mostly in archives) from early missions (Rabai from 1848, Freretown from 1874); these were handled by forwarding agents at Zanzibar. POs were opened at Mombasa (HQ) and Lamu in May 1890; also agencies c.1892 at Malindi, Takaungu and Wasin. The protectorate joined the UPU in November 1895. The inland runner service of the transport department became a full postal responsibility when PAs were provided at Machakos and Kikuyu on 1 January 1897. Expansion followed the building of the Uganda Railway to Kisumu (1896-1902). Postal union was affected with Uganda in 1901, after which stamnps of British East Africa can be found used in Uganda.

During an acute shortage in August-September 1890, stamps of India were used.

On issue of protectorate overprints, the company stamps were demonetized (and stocks held in London remaindered in mint condition to the philatelic trade).

Protectorate stamps were overprinted locally overnight.

Used stamps inscribed EAST AFRICA AND UGANDA PROTECTORATES (*see below*) from 1903 (the King Edward VII registered envelope appeared before the stamps).

• Uganda (Before 1903)

FIRST STAMPS ISSUED March 1895
valid within borders only

CURRENCY

1895	Cowrie shells (c.200 = 1 rupee)
1896	16 annas = 1 rupee

The rival native kingdoms west of Lake Victoria were reached by Arab caravans in 1844 and by Europeans seeking the source of the Nile in 1862 (Speke and Grant). Following the almost simultaneous arrival in 1875 of Stanley from the south-east and Gordon's lieutenants (in Egyptian service) from the north, King Mtesa asked for missionaries from England. The first came in June 1877. Catholic White Fathers arrived in 1879. From the moment Bishop Hannington, arriving from the north-east, was murdered by order of Chief Luba in 1885, British intervention became inevitable. After trouble between warring factions, King Mwanga accepted the protection of an Imperial British East Africa

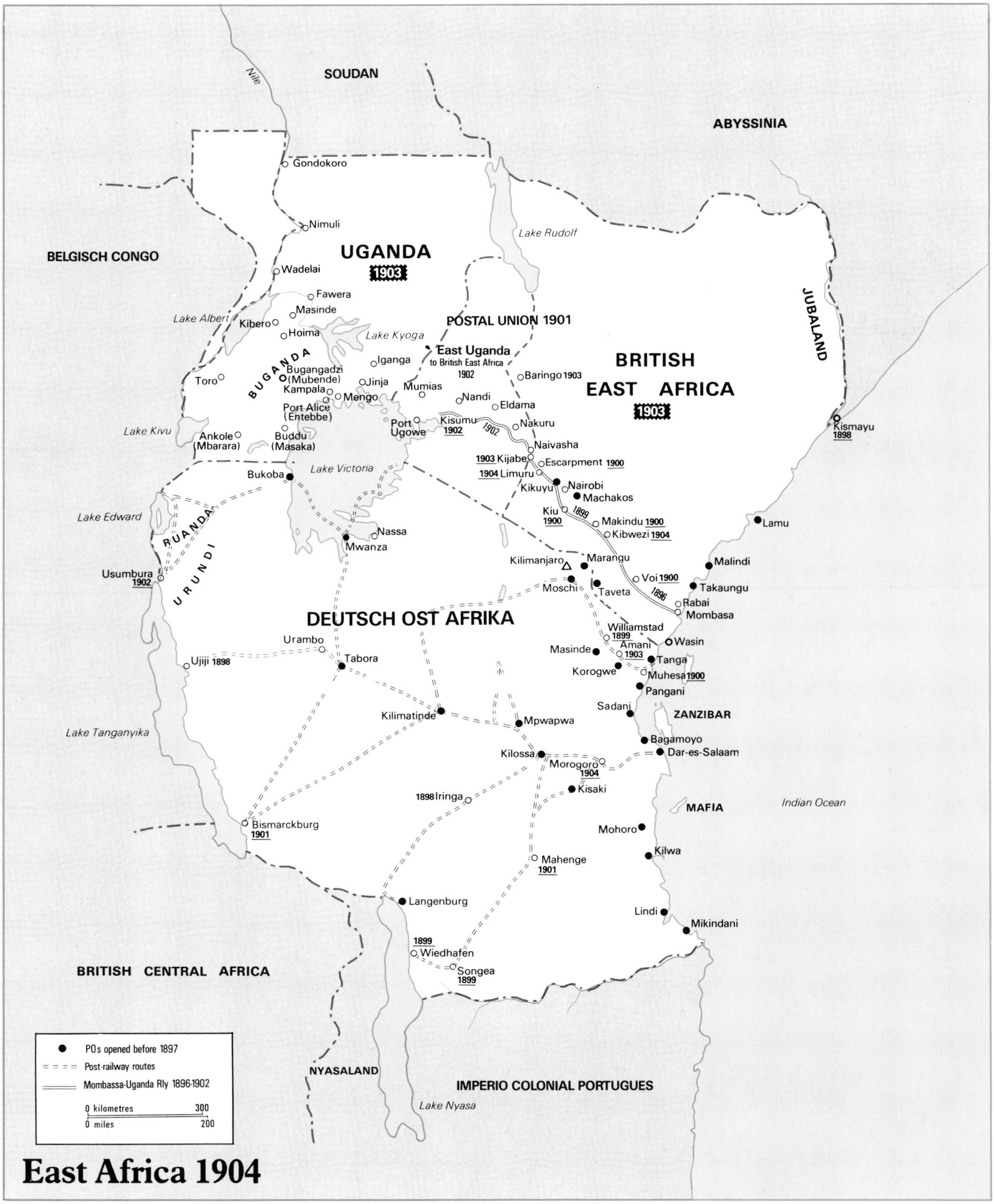
SOUDAN
Nile
ABYSSINIA
Gondokoro
Nimuli
BELGISCH CONGO
UGANDA
1903
Lake Rudolf
Wadelai
Fawera
Masinde
Lake Albert
Kibero
Hoima
Lake Kyoga
POSTAL UNION 1901
East Uganda
to British East Africa
1902
BUGANDA
Iganga
Bugangadzi
(Mubende)
Toro
Kampala
Jinja
Mengo
Mumias
Baringo 1903
BRITISH
EAST AFRICA
1903
JUBALAND
Nandi
Eldama
Port Alice
(Entebbe)
Lake Kivu
Ankole
(Mbarara)
Buddu
(Masaka)
Port
Ugowe
Kisumu
1902
1902
Nakuru
Naivasha
Kismayu
1898
Lake Victoria
1903 Kijabe
Escarpment 1900
1904 Limuru
Bukoba
Kikuyu
Nairobi
Machakos
Lake Edward
RUANDA
Kiu
1900
1899
Makindu 1900
Kibwezi 1904
Lamu
Nassa
Mwanza
URUNDI
Usumbura
1902
Kilimanjaro
Marangu
Malindi
Moschi
Taveta
Voi 1900
1896
Takaungu
Rabai
Mombasa
DEUTSCH OST AFRIKA
Williamstad
1899
Urambo
Amani
1903
Wasin
Masinde
Tanga
Tabora
Ujiji 1898
Korogwe
Muhesa 1900
Pangani
Sadani
ZANZIBAR
Kilimatinde
Mpwapwa
Lake Tanganyika
Bagamoyo
Dar-es-Salaam
Kilossa
Morogoro
1904
Kisaki
1898 Iringa
MAFIA
Indian Ocean
Bismarckburg
1901
Mohoro
Kilwa
Mahenge
1901
Langenburg
Lindi
Mikindani
1899
Wiedhafen
Songea
1899
BRITISH CENTRAL AFRICA
POs opened before 1897
Post-railway routes
Mombassa-Uganda Rly 1896-1902
0 kilometres 300
0 miles 200
NYASALAND
IMPERIO COLONIAL PORTUGUES
Lake Nyasa

East Africa 1904

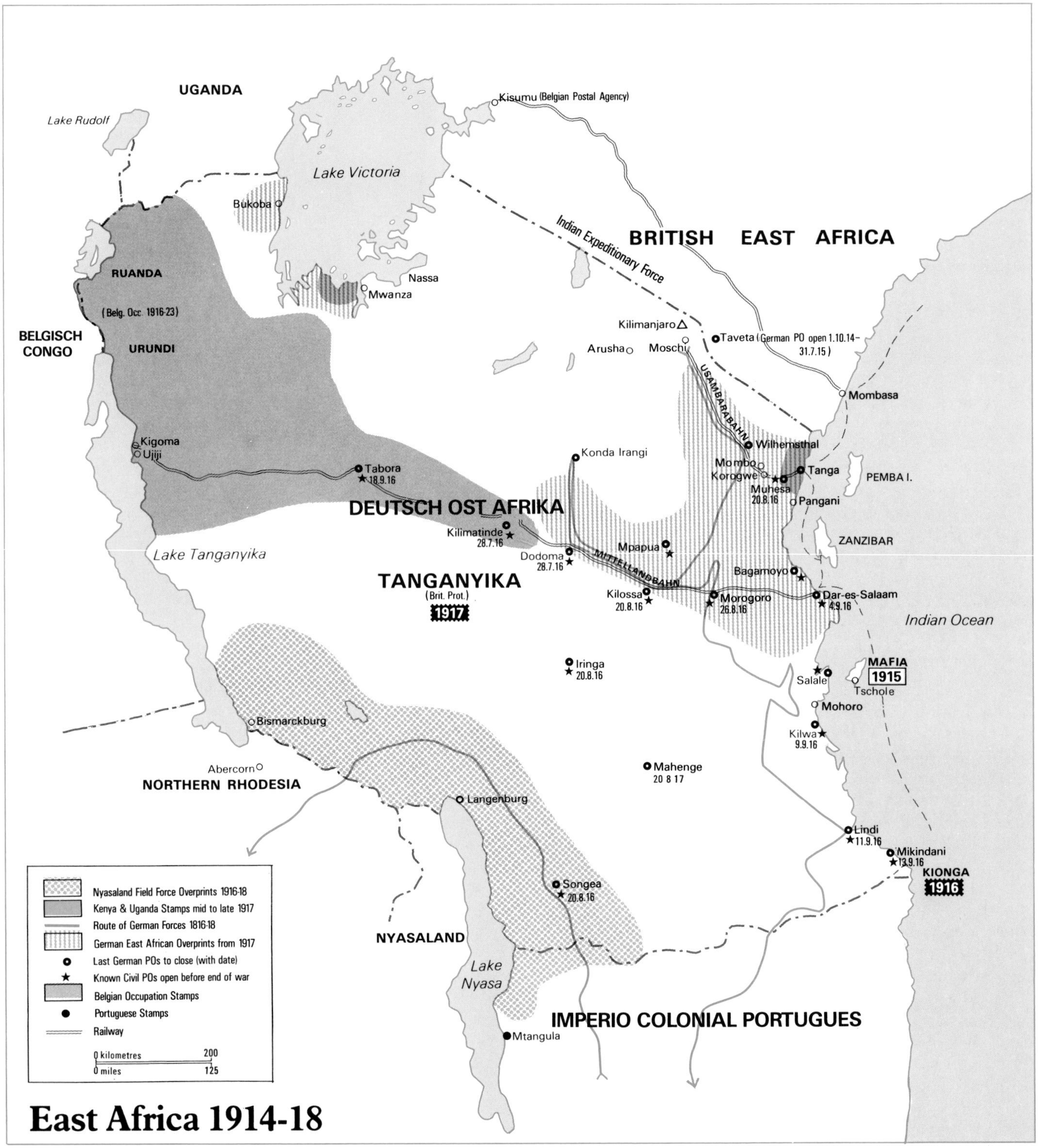
UGANDA
Lake Rudolf
Kisumu (Belgian Postal Agency)
Lake Victoria
Bukoba
Indian Expeditionary Force
BRITISH EAST AFRICA
RUANDA
(Belg. Occ. 1916-23)
Nassa
Mwanza
BELGISCH CONGO
URUNDI
Kilimanjaro
Taveta (German PO open 1.10.14–31.7.15)
Arusha
Moschi
USAMBARABAHN
Mombasa
Kigoma
Ujiji
Tabora
18.9.16
Konda Irangi
Wilhemsthal
Mombo
Korogwe
Tanga
PEMBA I.
Muhesa
20.8.16
Pangani
DEUTSCH OST AFRIKA
Kilimatinde
28.7.16
ZANZIBAR
Lake Tanganyika
Dodoma
28.7.16
Mpapua
MITTELLANDBAHN
Bagamoyo
TANGANYIKA
(Brit. Prot.)
1917
Kilossa
20.8.16
Morogoro
26.8.16
Dar-es-Salaam
4.9.16
Indian Ocean
Iringa
20.8.16
MAFIA
1915
Salale
Tschole
Mohoro
Bismarckburg
Kilwa
9.9.16
Abercorn
Mahenge
20 8 17
NORTHERN RHODESIA
Langenburg
Lindi
11.9.16
Mikindani
13.9.16
KIONGA
1916
Nyasaland Field Force Overprints 1916-18
Kenya & Uganda Stamps mid to late 1917
Route of German Forces 1816-18
German East African Overprints from 1917
Last German POs to close (with date)
Known Civil POs open before end of war
Belgian Occupation Stamps
Portuguese Stamps
Railway
0 kilometres 200
0 miles 125
Songea
20.8.16
NYASALAND
Lake Nyasa
IMPERIO COLONIAL PORTUGUES
Mtangula

East Africa 1914-18

Company flag in 1890. Lugard led an expedition in 1891-2 to sort out further religious-colonial strife. The British flag replaced that of the company in 1893. A formal British protectorate was proclaimed in 1894 and extended in 1896. A mutiny of Sudanese troops in 1897-8 caused disruption. In 1902 the eastern province was transferred to British East Africa. Control of Uganda passed from the Foreign to the Colonial Office in 1905. The border with Sudan was adjusted in 1914.

Postal History
Explorers' and missionary letters, carried by slavers' caravans, are known from 1862. In 1874-80 Gordon's Sudanese posts provided an outlet via the Nile, and after 1878 regular runner services via Bagamoyo or Saadani and Tabora were set up by Zanzibar forwarding agents for missionaries. This lasted till 1892 when Bishop Tucker transferred the Church Missionary Society service to the British East Africa route. Mail can sometimes be identified by initialled envelopes given stamps in Zanzibar or Mombasa. In March 1895 an internal service was started, but external mail still went unfranked by runner or caravan to Mombasa until 1896. In September 1896 prepayment to the frontier (Kikuyu) was made compulsory. The building of the Uganda Railway in 1896-1902 and the placing of steamers on Lake Victoria from Kisumu to Entebbe reduced the journey to the coast from eight weeks to eight days. The postal system was amalgamated with that of British East Africa from 1901 and run from Mombasa. This brought Uganda fully into the UPU.

Stamps of 1896 (valid internally and to the coast) were used on overseas mail in combination with stamps of British East Africa from 1896 to March 1899.

Specimen stamps of the November 1898 issue were supplied to Berne and correspondence franked with this issue was accepted almost everywhere though Uganda was not a member of the UPU until April 1901. For accountancy reasons separate stamps continued until 1903 and differential rates were charged for parcels.

• East Africa and Uganda Protectorates

FIRST STAMPS Common to both protectorates August-September 1903

CURRENCY	
1907	100 cents = 1 rupee
1922	100 cents = 1 shilling

Stamps in British East Africa were issued slightly earlier than in Uganda

The intention to adopt a currency based on florins rather than shillings in 1920-1 confused the postal rates; the change of name to Kenya about the same time led to many abandoned essays and proofs for new stamps and reprints of the old.

• German East Africa (Deutsch Ost Afrika)

FIRST STAMPS USED German 1890
FIRST STAMPS ISSUED 1 July 1893

German influence suddenly appeared with Carl Peters in 1884 and in a few months a virtual protectorate had been imposed on the south half of the Zanzibar mainland dominions. In 1890 a boundary was confirmed between British- and German-held territory (which remains today the border between Kenya and Tanzania).

The Arabs caravan route from the coast to Ujiji via Tabora was used by early explorers to return mail to Zanzibar (*see* Uganda) from at least 1858 (Burton), Livingstone's last letters to Stanley from Ujiji came by this route. By 1876 the Church and London Missionary Societies had regular runners serving Mambola, Mpwapwa and Urambo, making postal connection at Zanzibar. The earliest German expeditions (Wissman, etc.) used similar means.

PAs at Bagamoyo and Dar-es-Salaam (opened 4 October 1890) used stamps of Germany.

Last German PO (Mahenge) closed by *force majeure* 20 October 1917.

World War I: German occupation of Taveta (British East Africa).
Stamps of German East Africa used 1 October 1914-31 July 1915. This was strictly an FPO use, but (exceptionally) was given a named canceller for propaganda purposes.

Stamps of Germany salvaged from the crippled cruiser *Königsberg* (*see* Mafia Island *below*) were used in 1916 (when normal supplies were interrupted by British blockade) at Bagamoyo, Bukoba, Dodoma, Kilwa, Korogwe, Mohoro, Mombo, Pangani and possibly elsewhere.

Special Stamps during Allied Occupation
Stamps of India overprinted I.E.F. were used at FPOs from 1914 throughout the command (1914-16, mainly at bases along the Uganda Railway) 1916-18, at bases and on lines of communication in occupied territory); these can be identified (but not always located) by the numbers of the cancellers.

• Mafia Island

FIRST STAMPS ISSUED January 1915

An island off the coast of German East Africa taken by British forces in December 1914 as a base for attacks on the *Königsberg*.

Stamp stocks captured from Tschole PO were overprinted. Most of these (and many later imitations) fell into collectors' hands, but commercial mail is known franked with the later I.E.F. stamps further overprinted GR/POST/MAFIA.

Use ceased when the G.E.A. overprints became available for general use in the conquered territory.

Stamps of Nyasaland overprinted N.F. were used (also a few without overprint) by the Nyasa-Rhodesian Field Force operating in the southwest from 1916. A small remnant was used up after the war at civil offices. Stamps of Portuguese Nyassa cancelled by Nyasaland F.F. obliterator were used by that force at Mtangula.

0.50 F
ROYAUME DU BURUNDI
DEUTSCH-OSTAFRIKA
10 PESA 10
3.50f POSTES
R
1962
INDEPENDANCE
REPUBLIQUE RWANDAISE
A
B
C

A Burundi: Kingdom 1964; **B** German East Africa 1901; **C** Rwanda: Republic, Independent 1962.

• Kionga

FIRST STAMPS USED German East Africa
FIRST STAMPS ISSUED 1916

A province of German East Africa which was occupied by Portugal during World War I. It was incorporated into Mozambique.

• Tanganyika (1917-35)

CURRENCY	
1893	64 pesa = 100 heller = 1 rupee
1905	100 heller = 1 rupee
1915/16	16 annas = 1 rupee
1917	100 cents = 1 rupee
1922	100 cents = 1 shilling

FIRST STAMPS ISSUED October 1917

By 1917 a large enough part of German East Africa was securely in British hands for the application of civil administration. Control was exercised from Wilhelmstal until the capital was returned to Dar-es-Salaam in 1920. Shorn of Ruanda-Urundi and Kionga, the territory, mandated to Britain was renamed Tanganyika in 1920.

A few reopened POs (Tanga, Mwanza are known) used stamps of East Africa and Uganda protectorates in 1917.

Used postage-due stamps of Kenya and Uganda from 1 July 1933.

• Kenya and Uganda

FIRST STAMPS inscribed KENYA AND UGANDA 1 November 1922

Right
Post-box, Uganda

Below
Post office, Lamu, Kenya

LETTERS

On becoming a colony on 23 July 1920 the East Africa Protectorate was renamed Kenya.

After an experimental service in 1927 between Sudan and Lake Victoria had failed, the first regular airmail service (weekly) to East Africa was opened in February/March 1931, branching at Alexandria from the Imperial Airways route to India. This terminated at Mwanza (Tanganyika) until a Christmas proving flight of 1931 was followed in 1932 by a regular service through to South Africa.

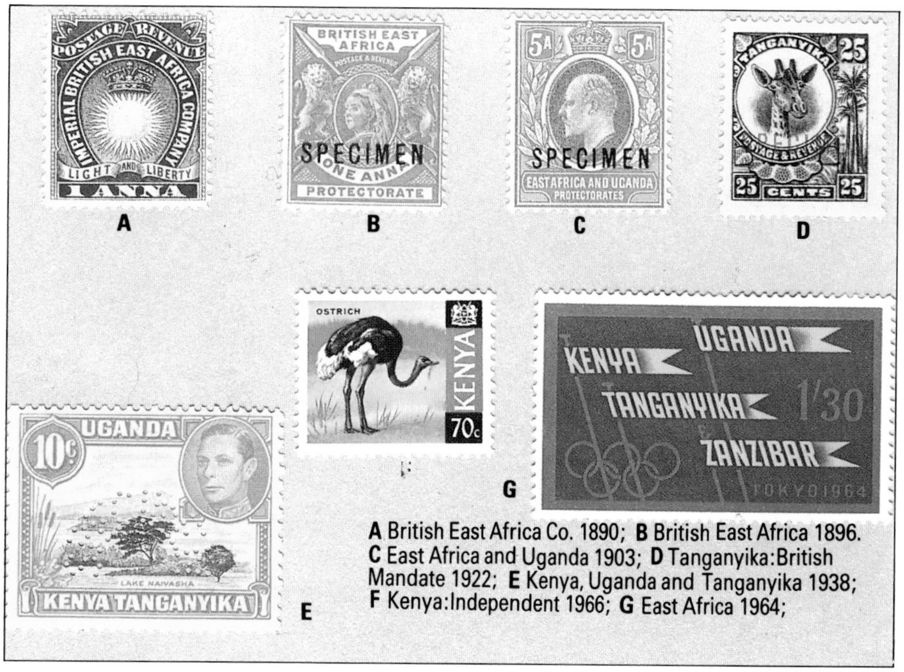
A
B
C
D
E
G
SPECIMEN
SPECIMEN
UGANDA
KENYA TANGANYIKA
KENYA
70c
UGANDA
KENYA
TANGANYIKA
ZANZIBAR
1'30

A British East Africa Co. 1890; **B** British East Africa 1896. **C** East Africa and Uganda 1903; **D** Tanganyika: British Mandate 1922; **E** Kenya, Uganda and Tanganyika 1938; **F** Kenya: Independent 1966; **G** East Africa 1964;

• Kenya, Uganda and Tanganyika

> **FIRST STAMPS** with joint inscription 1 May 1935

CURRENCY

1935 100 cents = 1 shilling

The East African Posts and Telecommunications Union formed on 1 July 1933 was confirmed as a commitment of the East African High Commission (1948). Postal HQ was placed at Nairobi. Joint operation did not necessarily imply adoption of rigid policy for all three countries. Whereas in Tanganyika German precedent was followed by the operation of TPOs on both main railways until 1959 as well as on Lake Tanganyika, in Kenya TPOs on the Uganda Railway which had ceased in 1924 were never resumed. Uganda had TPOs only on a few lake and river steamers. Runners have never been entirely superseded by motorized posts, as witness Kenyan successes in the Olympic Games.

The order of the inscription varies from design to design in order to give the three countries equal prominence.

Stamps overprinted OFFICIAL in 1959 were issued initially (July-October) in only nine main offices of Tanganyika (although later under pressure validated for general use).

• East Africa

After the successive independence of Tanganyika, Uganda and Kenya, the East Africa Common Service Organization (later Community) continued policy of the High Commission, issuing commemorative stamps for use in the three territories until it became a dead letter in 1976.

Stamps were inscribed KENYA UGANDA TANGANYIKA ZANZIBAR (issue of 21 October 1964 only) or KENYA UGANDA TANZANIA. (Despite the federation of Tanganyika and Zanzibar under one flag, these stamps were not valid in Zanzibar until 1 January 1968.)

N.B. Until 1976 the independent issues of each of the three constituent republics (*see below*) were valid in the other two, although placed on sale there only for the first two weeks to show validity.

• Tanganyika (1961-5)

> **FIRST STAMPS** independent Tanganyika 9 December 1961

CURRENCY

1961 100 cents = 1 shilling

Independent within Commonwealth 9 December 1961.

Tanzania

> **FIRST STAMPS ISSUED** inscribed TANZANIA 9 December 1965 (not valid in Zanzibar until 1968)

CURRENCY

1965 100 cents = 1 shilling

Tanganyika federated with Zanzibar in April 1964. It was known as Tanzania after 17 November 1964.

Uganda (After 1962)

> **FIRST STAMPS ISSUED** 9 October 1962

CURRENCY

1895	1000 couries = 2 rupees
1896	16 annas = 1 rupee
1962	100 cents = 1 shilling

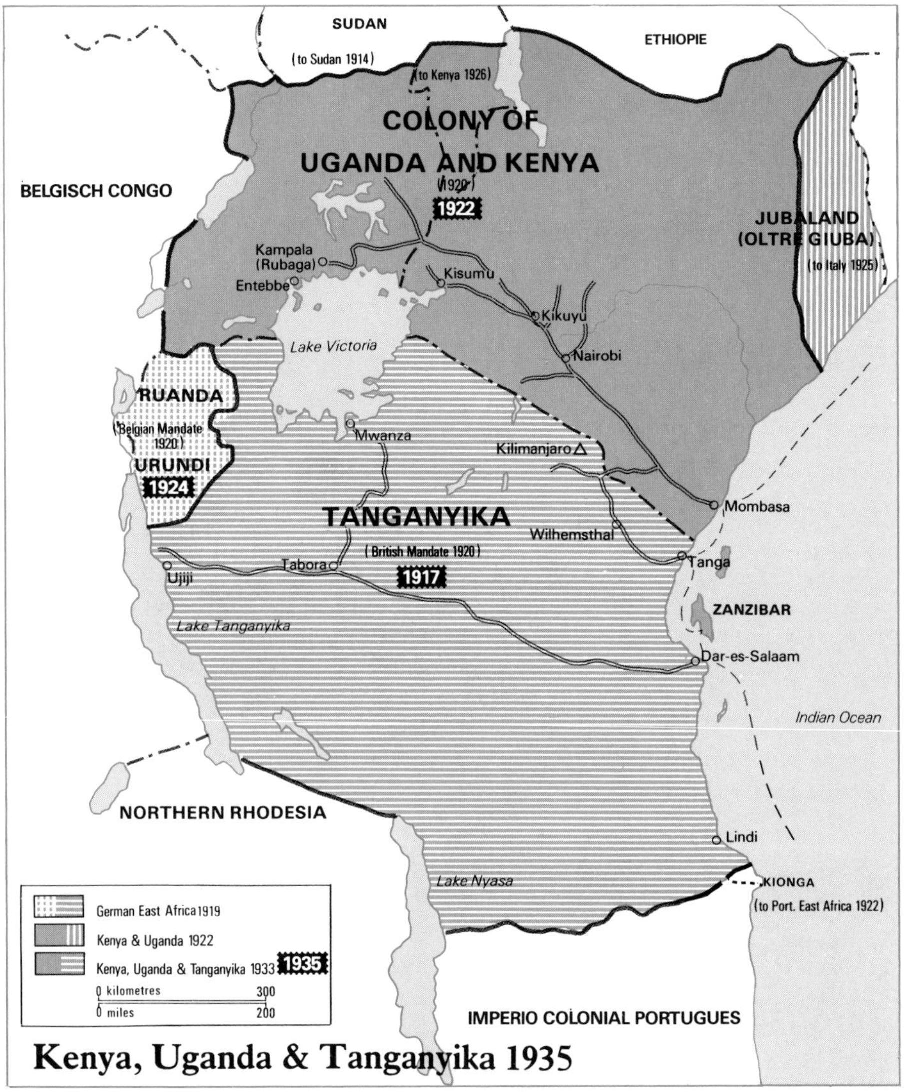
SUDAN
(to Sudan 1914)
(to Kenya 1926)
ETHIOPIE
COLONY OF
UGANDA AND KENYA
(1920)
1922
BELGISCH CONGO
JUBALAND
(OLTRE GIUBA)
(to Italy 1925)
Kampala
(Rubaga)
Entebbe
Kisumu
Kikuyu
Nairobi
Lake Victoria
RUANDA
(Belgian Mandate 1920)
URUNDI
1924
Mwanza
Kilimanjaro
Mombasa
TANGANYIKA
(British Mandate 1920)
1917
Wilhemsthal
Tabora
Ujiji
Tanga
ZANZIBAR
Lake Tanganyika
Dar-es-Salaam
Indian Ocean
NORTHERN RHODESIA
Lindi
Lake Nyasa
KIONGA
(to Port. East Africa 1922)
German East Africa 1919
Kenya & Uganda 1922
Kenya, Uganda & Tanganyika 1933
1935
0 kilometres 300
0 miles 200
IMPERIO COLONIAL PORTUGUES

Kenya, Uganda & Tanganyika 1935

Independent within the Commonwealth 9 October 1962.

Kenya

FIRST STAMPS ISSUED 12 December 1963

CURRENCY

1963 100 cents = 1 shilling

Independent within the Commonwealth 12 December 1963.

• Ruanda-Urundi

FIRST STAMPS under mandate 1 December 1924

Two African kingdoms ruled by German East Africa until World War I. Captured by Belgian troops in 1916. Stamps of Belgian Congo with dual overprints in French and Flemish were used at Belgian Field POs in the west sector, and as far east as Tabora from July 1916. It was mandated at the peace settlement to Belgium, and confirmed as a trust territory under the United Nations on 13 December 1946. On 1 July 1962 they became separately independent as Rwanda and Burundi (*see below*).

Rwanda

FIRST STAMPS 1 July 1962

Had become a republic while still under trusteeship, and stayed thus on independence.

Burundi

FIRST STAMPS 1 July 1962

Independent kingdom 1 July 1962; declared a republic 28 November 1966.

Mozambique

FIRST STAMPS ISSUED July 1876

CURRENCY

Portuguese

The Portuguese established trading posts in the 15th century, a long and varied history became a colony. Independence was agreed between Portugal and FRELIMO (Frente de Libertacap de Moçambique) on 7 September 1974 and a People's Republic was proclaimed on 25 June 1975.

Mozambique stamps were in use throughout Portuguese East Africa, except later in areas which had their own issues.

• Lourenço Marques

FIRST STAMPS ISSUED 28 July 1893

CURRENCY	
1895	As Portugal

• Zambezia

FIRST STAMPS ISSUED 28 July 1893

• Quelimane and Tete

Two provinces of Zambezia which had their own separate issues in 1913-20.

• Inhambane

FIRST STAMPS ISSUED 1 July 1895

From 1920 all the above territories reverted to the use of stamps of Mozambique.

• Nyassa Company

FIRST STAMPS ISSUED 1898

CURRENCY	
1898	As Portugal

Chartered to develop an area north of the River Lurio.

Stamps withdrawn 1929. Reverted to stamps of Mozambique.

• Mozambique Company

FIRST STAMPS ISSUED 1892

CURRENCY	
1892	As Portugal

Chartered to administer Manica and Sofala.

Stamps withdrawn 1942. Reverted to stamps of Mozambique.

Portuguese Colonies General Issues
General issues for use in Portuguese African colonies (after 1951 called overseas provinces) were made at intervals between 1 April 1898 and 1945. Their use (in Angola, Cabo Verde, Mozambique, Porguese Guinea, and São Tomé e Príncipe) ceased on 31 August 1958.

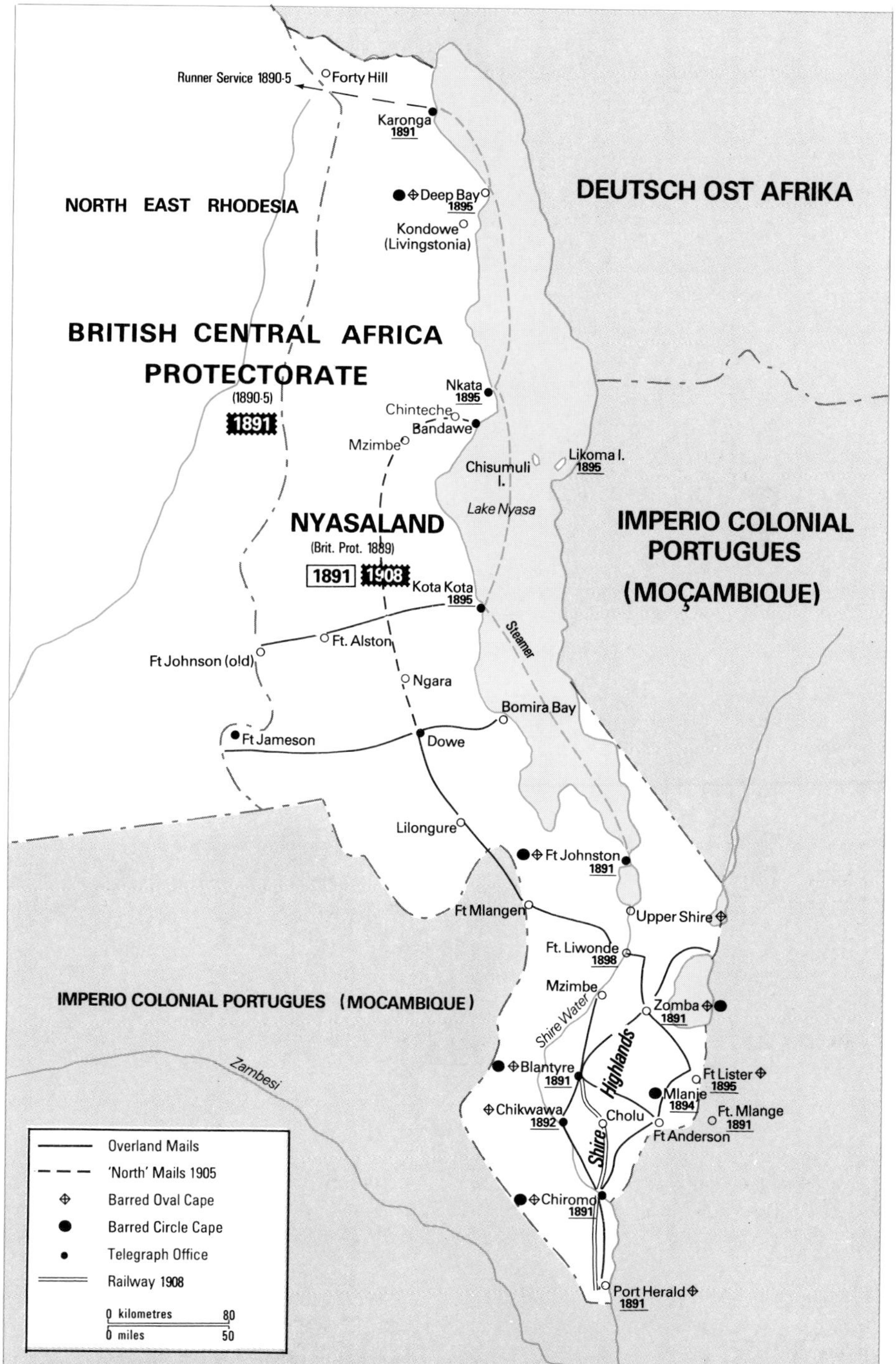
Runner Service 1890-5
Forty Hill
Karonga 1891
NORTH EAST RHODESIA
Deep Bay 1895
Kondowe (Livingstonia)
DEUTSCH OST AFRIKA
BRITISH CENTRAL AFRICA PROTECTORATE
(1890-5)
1891
Nkata 1895
Chinteche
Bandawe
Mzimbe
Chisumuli I.
Likoma I. 1895
Lake Nyasa
NYASALAND
(Brit. Prot. 1889)
1891 1908
IMPERIO COLONIAL PORTUGUES (MOÇAMBIQUE)
Kota Kota 1895
Steamer
Ft. Alston
Ft Johnson (old)
Ngara
Bomira Bay
Ft Jameson
Dowe
Lilongure
Ft Johnston 1891
Ft Mlangen
Upper Shire
Ft. Liwonde 1898
Mzimbe
IMPERIO COLONIAL PORTUGUES (MOCAMBIQUE)
Shire Water
Zomba 1891
Zambesi
Blantyre 1891
Highlands
Ft Lister 1895
Mlanje 1894
Chikwawa 1892
Cholu
Ft. Mlange 1891
Ft Anderson
Shire
Overland Mails
'North' Mails 1905
Barred Oval Cape
Barred Circle Cape
Telegraph Office
Railway 1908
0 kilometres 80
0 miles 50
Chiromo 1891
Port Herald 1891
Chinde

British Central Africa & Nyasaland 1908

• Nyasaland (British Central Africa Protectorate)

CURRENCY	
1891	British

FIRST STAMPS British South Africa Company (overprinted B.C.A.) 1891 (These were also used in North East Rhodesia, *see* Northern Rhodesia.)
FIRST STAMPS inscribed NYASALAND 22 July 1908

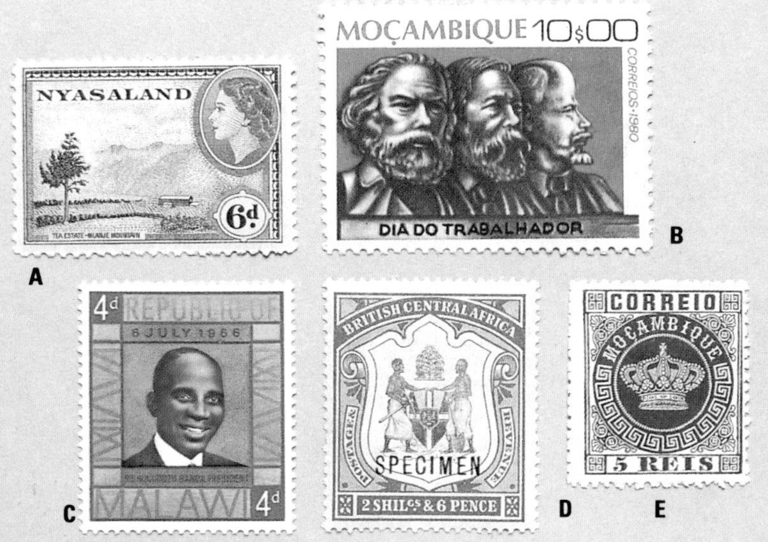
NYASALAND
6d
MOÇAMBIQUE 10$00
CORREIOS-1980
DIA DO TRABALHADOR
4d
6 JULY 1966
MALAWI
4d
BRITISH CENTRAL AFRICA
SPECIMEN
2 SHILGS & 6 PENCE
CORREIO
MOÇAMBIQUE
5 REIS
A
B
C
D
E

A Nyasaland:Protectorate 1953; **B** Mozambique:Independent 1980; **C** Malawi:Republic 1966; **D** British Central Africa 1895; **E** Mozambique:Portuguese Colony 1876.

The Shire River and Lake Nyasa were explored with the Zambezi by Livingston and Kirk in 1858-63. The Livingstonia mission was founded in 1874. Farther north the African Lakes Company operated between Lakes Nyasa and Tanganyika in 1880-5. A British Protectorate over Nyasaland was proclaimed in December 1889 to forestall the Portuguese in the Shire Highlands. In 1890-5, as British Central Africa Protectorate, it included North West and North East Rhodesia. Again in 1900-10 it administered North East Rhodesia. Name was changed back to Nyasaland on 6 July 1907. Became part of the Federation of Rhodesia and Nyasaland in 1954-63. A separate colony again in 1963, became independent within the Commonwealth on 6 July 1964 under name of Malawi (*see below*).

Postal History

Letters are known from Livingstone and others from the Shire Highlands and from officials of the African Lakes Company. The mail went by runner to Lake Nyasa, across it by steam launch, by runner again to the Shire River, then by boat to Quelimane or Chinde on the Indian Ocean. The first POs were opened at Chiromo and Port Herald in 1891. A British clearing office was opened in 1891 at Chinde (in Portuguese territory) which passed mail in sealed bags between Nyasaland and British or German mail steamers. Used stamps of Federation (*see* Rhodesia and Nyasaland) in 1954-63.

Separate issues (Nyasaland) resumed 1 November 1963 (withdrawn 5 July 1964).

Malawi

FIRST STAMPS ISSUED 6 July 1964

CURRENCY

Until 1971 British
From 1 January 1971 100 tambala = 1 kwacha

Name assumed by Nyasaland on independence 6 July 1964. Became republic (within the Commonwealth) 6 July 1966.

• British Bechuanaland

FIRST STAMPS ISSUED December 1885

CURRENCY

British

Became a British colony on 30 September 1885 until it was annexed to Cape Colony on 16 November 1895.

In 1885-6 mail was carried by runner or border police. PAs were opened at Banks Drift, Kuruman, Poedomoe, Setlagloi (1886), Palachwe (1888), Macloustie (1890), Vryburg Station and Keimoes (1891).

Used stamps of Cape of Good Hope from 16 November 1895 (while British Bechuanaland stamps continued in use in Bechuanaland Protectorate).

• Bechuanaland Protectorate

FIRST STAMPS ISSUED 7 August 1888

CURRENCY

Until 1961 British
From 14 February 1961 South African

From June 1890 to 1897 used stamps of British Bechuanaland (with which its postal administration was amalgamated in 1890-5). Further separate issues from 1897. All stamps withdrawn 29 September 1966.

Botswana

FIRST STAMPS ISSUED 30 September 1966

CURRENCY

1966 South African
1976 100 thebe = 1 pula

Formerly Bechuanaland Protectorate, achieved independence on 30 September 1966 as a republic.

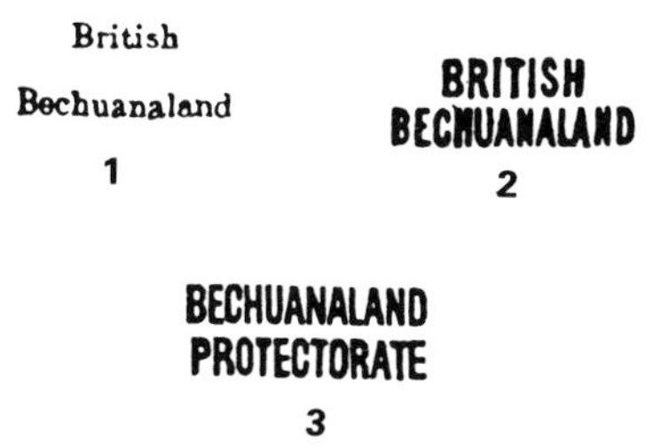
British
Bechuanaland
1
BRITISH
BECHUANALAND
2
BECHUANALAND
PROTECTORATE
3

1 Overprint of British Bechuanaland, 1885
2 Overprint of British Bechuanaland, 1891
3 Overprint of Bechuanaland Protectorate, 1897

2 cents
REPUBLIC OF BOTSWANA
BECHUANALAND PROTECTORATE
A
NORTHERN RHODESIA
1/-
B
C
1d 1d
NORTHERN RHODESIA
E
BECHUANALAND
PROTECTORATE
TWO PENCE
D
9n ZAMBIA
F
RHODESIA & NYASALAND
6d
POSTAGE
G

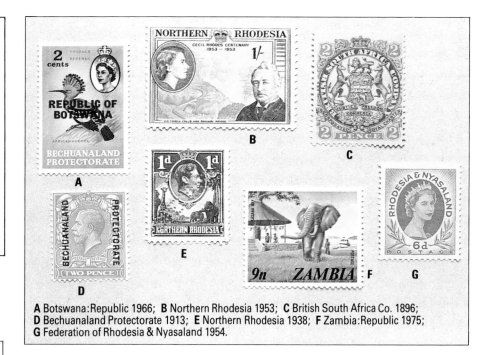

A Botswana:Republic 1966; **B** Northern Rhodesia 1953; **C** British South Africa Co. 1896; **D** Bechuanaland Protectorate 1913; **E** Northern Rhodesia 1938; **F** Zambia:Republic 1975; **G** Federation of Rhodesia & Nyasaland 1954.

• British South Africa Company (Rhodesia)

FIRST STAMPS (inscribed BRITISH SOUTH AFRICA COMPANY only) 2 January 1892. Issues valid throughout territory administered by the Company.
FIRST STAMPS (bearing also the word RHODESIA) 15 April 1909

A line of communication to Mashonaland (Salisbury) was established from Bechuanaland in the 1880s and fortified in 1890. Raids by the Matabele led to punitive measures in Matabeleland, Bulawayo being occupied on 4 November 1893. Matabeleland and Mashonaland became Rhodesia in 1898 (and later Southern Rhodesia). Railway links from Vryburg to Bulawayo, Beira-Umtali-Salisbury and Salisbury-Gwelo-Bulawayo were all established in 1897-1902. Rhodes' expansion northward met Johnston's westward from Nyasaland with some rivalry, and the resultant administrative complications confuse the postal history also (*see* Northern Rhodesia).

Postal History
Livingstone reached Matabeleland via Bechuanaland on his travels northward in 1841-53, during which he exchanged mails with Britain by runner or casual caravan via Colesberg and the Admiral in charge at Simonstown. Later missionary runner mails (1875-6) from Matabeleland reached the regular post at Linokana or Zeersut in Transvaal; but by 1880 a missionary postmaster at Gubulawayo was operating a service via Shoshong, which in August 1888 was made official under Rev. J.S. Moffat via Tati (Bechuanaland Protectorate) to Mafeking (British Bechuanaland). A horse post was set up in 1890 to Mashonaland, branching at Palachwe via Tuli to Salisbury. The occupation of Bulawayo brought a direct link to Salisbury. The route via Beira to the outside world began on 2 January 1892 and was shortened in 1898 by the arrival at Umtali of the railway from Beira.

Stamps of British Bechuanaland were used from British South Africa Company territory in 1888-92 (cancellations include GUBULAWAYO BECHUANALAND).

'Double Heads' portraying King George V and Queen Mary, which were current in 1910-13, were printed by Waterlows in colours which have rarely been equalled for choice. They were followed by the 'Admirals' in similarly well-contrasted shades. Earlier and some later issues were made by Bradbury, Wilkinson and Perkins, Bacon; but Rhodesia is unusual among British colonies in that — with a single exception (the Coronation 2*s* 6*d* of 1953) — it never had a stamp printed by De La Rue.

In 1924 remainders of issues 1892-1910 (2.7 million in all) were cancelled with back-dated genuine postmarks and sold to the stamp trade. The places and dates used are known and recorded.

• Northern Rhodesia

FIRST STAMPS ISSUED 1 April 1925

CURRENCY	
1925	sterling

Livingstone crossed the region from west to east on his trans-Africa journey of 1853-6. In 1890-5 the whole area was, in theory, administered by British Central Africa, but in 1895-1900 North East Rhodesia was separately administered. In 1895 North West Rhodesia (Barotseland) was placed under the control of the British South

Rhodesias 1909
(incl. Bechuanalands & Mozambique)

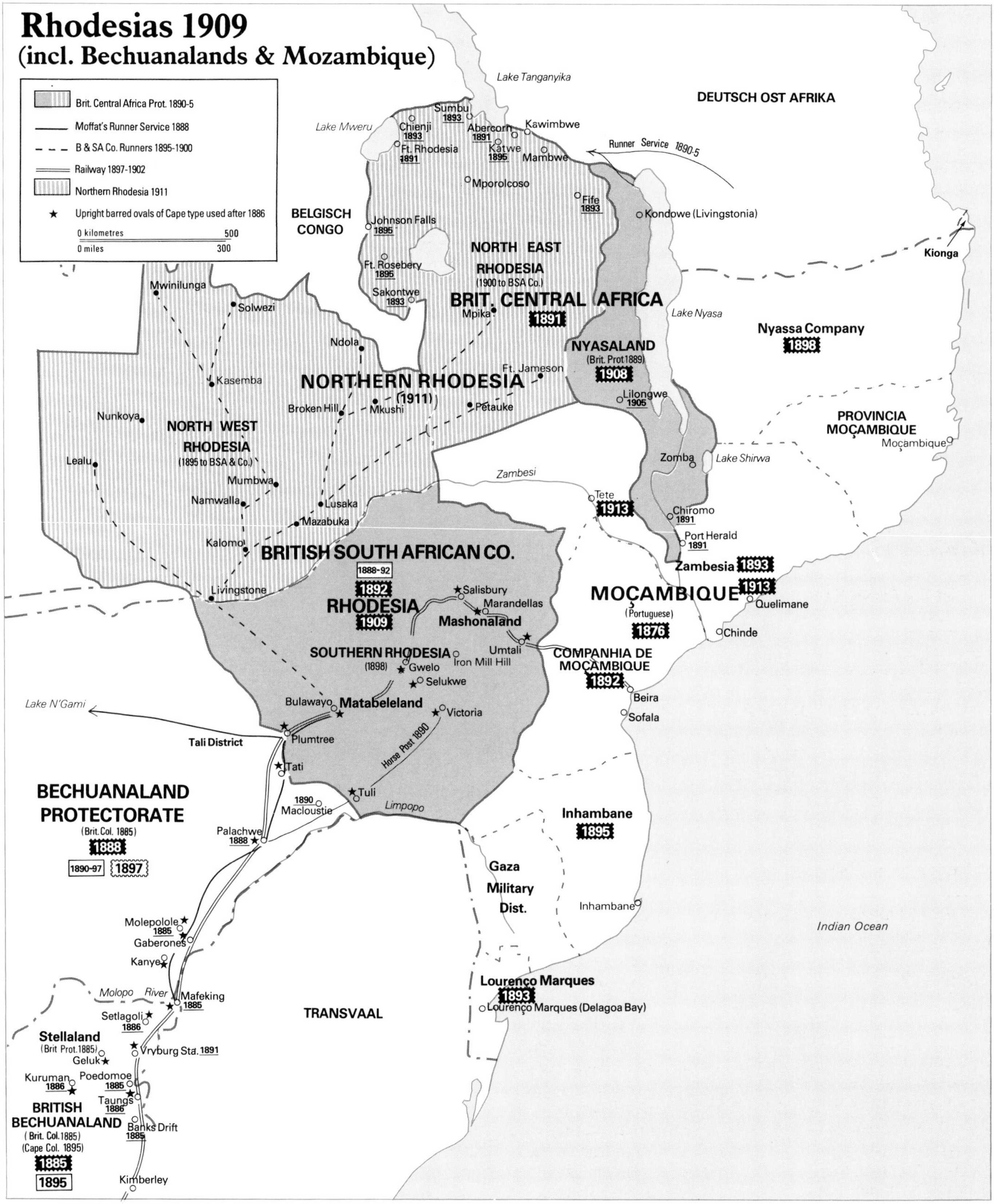
Brit. Central Africa Prot. 1890-5
Moffat's Runner Service 1888
B & SA Co. Runners 1895-1900
Railway 1897-1902
Northern Rhodesia 1911
Upright barred ovals of Cape type used after 1886
0 kilometres 500
0 miles 300
Lake Tanganyika
DEUTSCH OST AFRIKA
Lake Mweru
Sumbu 1893
Chienji 1893
Abercorn 1891
Kawimbwe
Ft. Rhodesia 1891
Katwe 1895
Mambwe
Runner Service 1890-5
Mporolcoso
Fife 1893
Kondowe (Livingstonia)
BELGISCH CONGO
Johnson Falls 1895
NORTH EAST RHODESIA (1900 to BSA Co.)
Kionga
Ft. Rosebery 1895
Sakontwe 1893
BRIT. CENTRAL AFRICA 1891
Mpika
Lake Nyasa
Nyassa Company 1898
Mwinilunga
Solwezi
Ndola
NYASALAND (Brit. Prot 1889) 1908
Ft. Jameson
Kasemba
NORTHERN RHODESIA (1911)
Lilongwe 1906
Broken Hill
Mkushi
Petauke
Nunkoya
NORTH WEST RHODESIA (1895 to BSA & Co.)
PROVINCIA MOÇAMBIQUE
Moçambique
Lealu
Zomba
Lake Shirwa
Zambesi
Mumbwa
Namwalla
Lusaka
Tete 1913
Chiromo 1891
Mazabuka
Port Herald 1891
Kalomo
BRITISH SOUTH AFRICAN CO. 1888-92 1892
Zambesia 1893 1913
Livingstone
Salisbury
RHODESIA 1909
Marandellas
MOÇAMBIQUE (Portuguese) 1876
Quelimane
Mashonaland
Chinde
Umtali
SOUTHERN RHODESIA (1898)
Iron Mill Hill
COMPANHIA DE MOÇAMBIQUE 1892
Gwelo
Selukwe
Beira
Lake N'Gami
Bulawayo
Matabeleland
Victoria
Sofala
Plumtree
Tali District
Horse Post 1890
Tati
BECHUANALAND PROTECTORATE (Brit. Col. 1885) 1888
Tuli
1890 Maclouste
Limpopo
Inhambane 1895
Palachwe 1888
1890-97 1897
Gaza Military Dist.
Inhambane
Indian Ocean
Molepolole 1885
Gaberones
Kanye
Molopo River
Mafeking 1885
Lourenço Marques 1893
Lourenço Marques (Delagoa Bay)
Setlagoli 1886
TRANSVAAL
Stellaland (Brit Prot. 1885)
Vryburg Sta. 1891
Geluk
Kuruman 1886
Poedomoe 1885
Taungs 1886
BRITISH BECHUANALAND (Brit. Col. 1885) (Cape Col. 1895) 1885 1895
Banks Drift 1885
Kimberley

Africa Company; North East Rhodesia followed suit in 1900. Combined as Northern Rhodesia in 1911, they passed to the British Crown in 1923. Northern Rhodesia achieved independence within the Commonwealth as Zambia (*see below*) on 24 October 1964.

The very little mail from North West Rhodesia in the 1890s came down by runner to Bulawayo. Mail from North East Rhodesia was routed via British Central Africa until 1895, and stamps overprinted B.C.A. were use at North East Rhodesian POs.

Used stamps of the Federation (*see* Rhodesia and Nyasaland) in 1954-63. Separate issues resumed 10 December 1963. Withdrawn 23 October 1964.

Zambia

FIRST STAMPS ISSUED 24 October 1964

CURRENCY

Until 1968 British

From 16 January 1968 100 ngwee = 1 kwathia

Name assumed by Northern Rhodesia on independence 24 October 1964.

• Rhodesia and Nyasaland

FIRST STAMPS valid throughout the Federation 1 July 1954

CURRENCY

British

Federation of Northern and Southern Rhodesia and the Nyasaland Protectorate was formed 1 August 1953 and dissolved 31 December 1963.

Stamps withdrawn 19 February 1964, after the three territories had resumed separate issues.

• Southern Rhodesia

FIRST STAMPS ISSUED 1 April 1924

CURRENCY

1924 sterling

Constituted a British Crown Colony with limited self-government on 1 October 1923. Became part of the Federation of Rhodesia and Nyasaland in 1954-63. On separation changed name to Rhodesia (*see below*).

Used stamps of Federation (*see* Rhodesia and Nyasaland) in 1954-65.

• Rhodesia (Zimbabwe-Rhodesia)

FIRST INDEPENDENT ISSUE 8 December 1965

Separate issues resumed 17 May 1965

CURRENCY

Until 1970 British

From 17 February 1970 100 cents = 1 dollar

After the break-up of the Federation, the former colony of Southern Rhodesia adopted the name Rhodesia in October 1964. On 11 November 1965 it unilaterally declared its independence (UDI) which was not recognized by Britain, the UN or other major powers.

While these applied economic sanctions 'Patriotic Front' guerrillas waged war on the régime from Mozambique and Zambia. The ruling white minority allowed limited black suffrage; elections brought to power a multiracial conservative government (which adopted the name Zimbabwe-Rhodesia) but increased opposition from radical and Communist rebels.

Stamps of Rhodesia were not recognized as valid by Britain and some other countries in 1965-71 and mail thus franked was treated on arrival as unpaid (the stamps were frequently gratuitously spoilt into the bargain).

Zimbabwe

FIRST STAMPS Rhodesia overprinted

FIRST STAMPS ISSUED 18 April 1980

CURRENCY

1980 100 cents = 1 dollar (Zimbabwe)

Following several atempts to achieve a compromise with the illegal government in Rhodesia, a meeting of Commonwealth Prime Ministers at Lusaka and a conference in London during 1979, agreed the basic principles. As a result, new elections were held after the guerrilla armies had been disarmed. The British Army with a Field PO in attendance supervised the transfer of power. Became independent on 18 April 1980.

Stamps inscribed 'Rhodesia' continued to be used until the new adhesives were released on Independence Day.

SOUTHERN AFRICA

• Cape of Good Hope (Cape Colony)

FIRST STAMPS ISSUED 1 September 1853

CURRENCY

British

To travellers in the 16th century the Cape was a landmark on the way to the Indies. Table Bay, a good watering place, was settled by a Dutch expedition under Jan van Riebeeck in 1652. Boer farmer commandos steadily subdued or pushed back the Bantu and Hottentot natives. When the French Revolutionary armies occupied the Netherlands in 1795, Britain took the Dutch colony under protection. It was returned to the Batavian Republic in

10D 10D
POSTAGE & REVENUE
SOUTHERN RHODESIA
A
SOUTHERN RHODESIA
2/6 2/6
CORONATION 1953
B
ZIMBABWE
3c
POSTAGE
AMETHYST
C
CAPE OF GOOD HOPE
2½d
POSTAGE 2 ½ PENCE
D
POSTAGE ONE SHILLING
CAPE OF GOOD HOPE
E
ZIMBABWE
40c
POSTAGE
BUNDI FALLS
F

A Southern Rhodesia: Self-Government 1924; **B** Southern Rhodesia 1953; **C** Zimbabwe: Independent 1980; **D** Cape of Good Hope 1892; **E** Cape of Good Hope 1855; **F** Zimbabwe: Independent 1983.

1803, but re-occupied in 1806 without disturbing the already traditional ways of the Boer farmlands. The Cape was given to Britain under the Treaty of Paris (1814). An influx of British settlers in 1820 and subsequently the adoption of English as the official language, the abolition of slavery in 1834 and the fixing of the territorial frontier drove the Boers into making the Great Trek northward. Cape Colony rapidly developed British institutions with responsible government by 1872. In 1910 it became part of the Union of South Africa.

Postal History
The first message recorded as having been passed from one vessel to another by leaving it under Post Office Tree (Mossel Bay) was in 1601. Letters are known from c.1619, but the earliest government postal system was set up by the Dutch in Cape Town on 28 September 1791. Prepayment was an early feature of the British system. Country POs linked by horse riders spread from 1816; by 1855 there were more than 100. Named 'Paid' handstamps were introduced in 1817, 'Ship Letter' and 'Packet Letter' handstamps a little earlier. Monthly steam packets to England were introduced in 1850, railway TPOs in 1883. Early triangular stamps were obliterated with a triangle of bars incorporating the initials CGH. Circular town date stamps, introduced in the 1850s, were placed alongside. The number of POs had risen to 500 by 1864 when the Cape numeral series of 'killers' was introduced to cancel the 'rectangulars'. Cape Colony joined the UPU in 1895 and adopted Imperial Penny Postage on 1 September 1899.

• Griqualand West

FIRST STAMPS Cape of Good Hope from 1871
FIRST STAMPS ISSUED March 1877

CURRENCY
British

Much disputed territory with a long history of strife between Griquas, Boers, the London Missionary Society and diamond prospectors, Griqualand West was annexed in October 1871 and administered as a British Crown Colony until incorporated into Cape Colony in October 1880.

Used stamps of Cape from October 1871 to 1877 including a MS overprint of September 1874 peculiar to Griqualand West. Oval date stamps are known of Diamond Fields, Du Toits Pan, De Beer's N R, and Kimberley. Stamps of Cape overprinted 'G' were issued in March 1877.

In October 1880 the remaining stamps overprinted 'G' were withdrawn from Kimberley and reissued to POs in Cape Colony for use.

• New Republic

FIRST STAMPS ISSUED January 1886

CURRENCY
British

Part of Zululand set up in 1884 as an independent state by secessionist Boers. A reduced area was demarcated and recognized by Britain in 1886. Annexed to South African Republic in 1888, transferred to Natal in January 1903.

Stamps had local validity only; letters leaving the Republic needed, in addition, stamps of Transvaal or Natal.

• Basutoland

FIRST STAMPS Cape of Good Hope from c.1880
FIRST STAMPS ISSUED 1 December 1933

CURRENCY
Until 1961 British
From 14 February 1961 South African

Lying between Cape Province and Natal, Basutoland became a British protectorate in 1843. Annexed by Britain in 1868 because of its constant strife with the Orange Free State, and joined to Cape Colony 1871-84. After a

G. W.
ZULULAND
1
2
GGGGGG
3

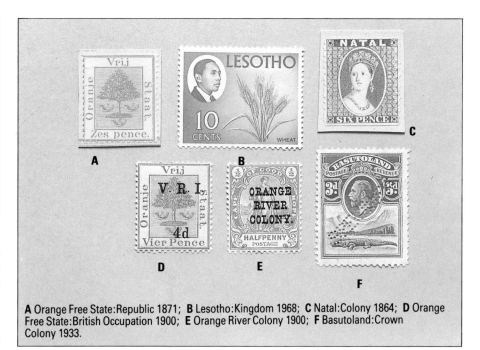

1 Overprint of Griqualand West, 1877;
2 Overprint of Zululand, 1888
3 Variety of overprints of Griqualand, 1877

general revolt in 1879-81, the Cape returned it to British imperial rule. It was not actively involved in the Second Boer War. Not incorporated in the Union in 1910 (though administered by the High Commissioner), it was granted self-government on 10 May 1965 and independence on 4 October 1966 as the kingdom of Lesotho *(see below)*.

Used stamps of Cape of Good Hope from c.1880. These can be recognized in the period before 1900 by date stamps or Cape numeral obliterators from nine offices: Thlotse Heights (317), later Leribe; Mafeteng (156); Maseru (281); Morija (277); Quthing (407); Mohaleschoek (210) Teyateyaneng (688); and Qachasnek; later offices can be identified by date stamps.

Used stamps of Union of South Africa from 1910 to 1933. All stamps inscribed BASUTOLAND were withdrawn on 31 October 1966.

Lesotho

Formerly Basutoland *(see above)*.

FIRST STAMPS ISSUED 4 October 1966

CURRENCY
South African

Vrij
Oranje
Staat.
Zes pence.
A
LESOTHO
10
CENTS
WHEAT
B
NATAL
SIX PENCE
C
Vrij
V. R. I.
Oranje
Staat.
4d
Vier Pence
D
ORANGE
RIVER
COLONY.
HALFPENNY
POSTAGE
E
BASUTOLAND
POSTAGE
REVENUE
3d
F

A Orange Free State:Republic 1871; **B** Lesotho:Kingdom 1968; **C** Natal:Colony 1864; **D** Orange Free State:British Occupation 1900; **E** Orange River Colony 1900; **F** Basutoland:Crown Colony 1933.

Left
South African post-runner with cleft stick, c.1900

Below
Post office, Mbabame, Swaziland

POST OFFICE
MBABANE

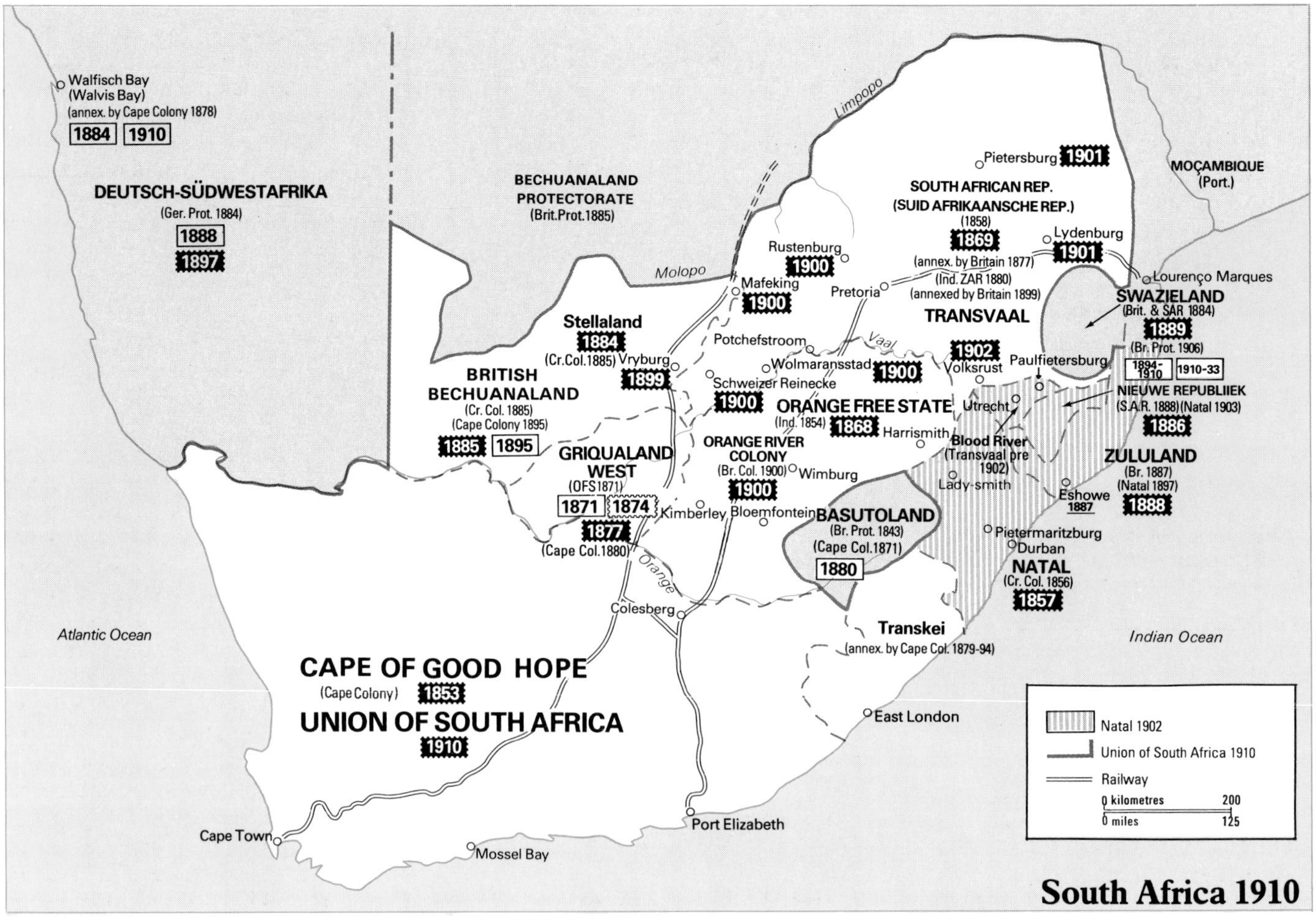
Walfisch Bay
(Walvis Bay)
(annex. by Cape Colony 1878)
1884 1910
DEUTSCH-SÜDWESTAFRIKA
(Ger. Prot. 1884)
1888
1897
BECHUANALAND
PROTECTORATE
(Brit.Prot.1885)
Limpopo
Molopo
Pietersburg 1901
MOÇAMBIQUE
(Port.)
SOUTH AFRICAN REP.
(SUID AFRIKAANSCHE REP.)
(1858)
1869
(annex. by Britain 1877)
(Ind. ZAR 1880)
(annexed by Britain 1899)
TRANSVAAL
Lydenburg
1901
Lourenço Marques
Rustenburg
1900
Mafeking
1900
Pretoria
SWAZIELAND
(Brit. & SAR 1884)
1889
(Br. Prot. 1906)
1894-1910
1910-33
Stellaland
1884
(Cr.Col.1885)
Vryburg
1899
Potchefstroom
Vaal
Wolmaransstad
1900
1902
Volksrust
Paulfietersburg
BRITISH
BECHUANALAND
(Cr. Col. 1885)
(Cape Colony 1895)
1885 1895
Schweizer Reinecke
1900
ORANGE FREE STATE
(Ind. 1854)
1868
Utrecht
NIEUWE REPUBLIIEK
(S.A.R. 1888)(Natal 1903)
1886
Harrismith
Blood River
(Transvaal pre
1902)
GRIQUALAND
WEST
(OFS 1871)
1871 1874
ORANGE RIVER
COLONY
(Br. Col. 1900)
Wimburg
1900
Lady-smith
ZULULAND
(Br. 1887)
(Natal 1897)
Eshowe
1887
1888
Kimberley
Bloemfontein
BASUTOLAND
(Br. Prot. 1843)
(Cape Col.1871)
1880
1877
(Cape Col.1880)
Orange
Pietermaritzburg
Durban
NATAL
(Cr. Col. 1856)
1857
Colesberg
Transkei
(annex. by Cape Col. 1879-94)
Atlantic Ocean
Indian Ocean
CAPE OF GOOD HOPE
(Cape Colony)
1853
UNION OF SOUTH AFRICA
1910
East London
Natal 1902
Union of South Africa 1910
Railway
0 kilometres 200
0 miles 125
Cape Town
Mossel Bay
Port Elizabeth

South Africa 1910

• Natal

FIRST STAMPS ISSUED 26 May 1857

CURRENCY

British

A British settlement was founded in 1824 and by 1835 its small town had been named D'Urban (later Durban) after the governor of the Cape. Piet Retief's breakaway from the Great Trek brought the Boers to Natal in 1837. After their massacre by Dingaan's Zulus and the reprisal at Blood River, the settlement was contested by British, Boer and Zulu in a three-cornered struggle that ended in annexation to Cape Colony in 1844. The Boer population trekked out to Transvaal in 1848. Natal became a separate colony in 1856. Zululand was incorporated in 1897, New Republic and Blood River Territories after 1902. Natal has been a state of South Africa since the Union of 1910.

Postal History

Private posts were run between stations of the American Missionary Service, while an external service to Cape Town by casual ship was started in 1846 by the *Natal Witness* with receiving offices at Pietermaritzburg and Durban. From 1849 an overland post route was operated every two weeks via Harrismith and Wynberg to Colesburg and the Cape. The first official inland horse-post began on 1 February 1850, but inland communications remained uncertain and slow until the coming of the railways in 1880. Regular monthly sailings to the Cape and England began in the 1860s. From 1872 both regular Cape packet services continued to Durban. A route via Mauritius existed in 1864-8, and in the 1870s there was a short-lived link via Zanzibar and Aden. From 1890 both western and eastern routes were continous.

Three local handstruck marks (for Pietermaritzburg, Durban and Ladysmith) are known from 1852. Date stamps incorporating the town name were used on covers from 1860, though stamps were obliterated with numeral cancellers. Combined numbered and dated marks followed, using the same numbers: the locations of 1-73 in these series are recorded.

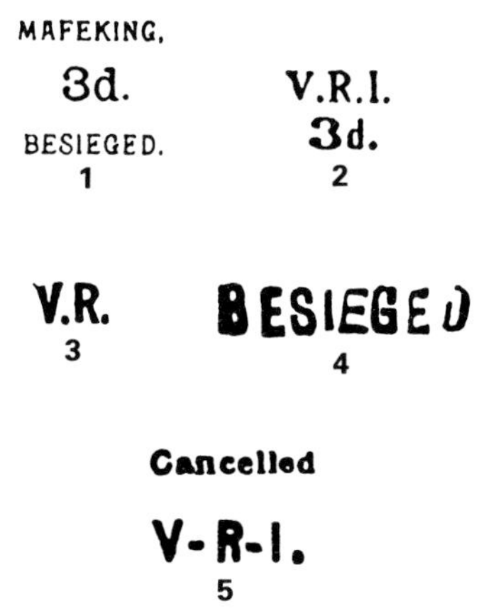
MAFEKING.
3d.
BESIEGED.
1
V.R.I.
3d.
2
V.R.
3
BESIEGED
4
Cancelled
V-R-I.
5

1 Siege of Mafeking, 1900
2 Occupation of Lydenburg, 1900
3 Occupation of Rustenburg, 1900
4 Siege of Schweizer Reinecke, 1900;
5 Occupation of Wolmaranssstad, 1900

• Zululand

FIRST STAMPS ISSUED 1 May 1888

CURRENCY

British

The Zulus exterminated their native rivals c.1820. After early clashes with British and Boers there continued an uneasy peace punctuated by border cattle raids from c.1840, until missionary interference and diplomatic incompetence provoked the Zulu War. In 1879 a British resident was appointed. On 9 May 1887 Zululand was declared British and on 31 December 1897 it was annexed to Natal.

Postal History
A postal service was started on 1 May 1888, Zululand being included with Natal in the UPU from that date. A PO had already been established at Eshowe in 1887. There were 21 POs open during the period of separate stamp issues. Use ceased on 30 June 1898, after which stamps of Natal were used.

• Orange Free State

FIRST STAMPS ISSUED January 1868

CURRENCY

British

The Boer settlements north of the Orange River, founded c.1828 and which grew as a result of the Great Trek, were recognized as an independent country in 1854. Despite previously friendly relationships with Cape Colony, it sided with Transvaal in the Second Boer War. Annexed to the British Empire on 24 May 1900 after Lord Roberts had occupied Bloemfontein, its name was changed temporarily to Orange River Colony. It has been a state of the Union since 1910.

In the 19th century most obliteration was by barred numeral or barred alphabetical cancellers, nearly all of which have been located and listed. In 1868-74 mail between Orange Free State and Cape Colony (and mail via Cape Colony going overseas) needed stamps of both countries in combination of rates.

The Free State became a British colony as Orange River Colony in 1900.

• Orange River Colony

FIRST STAMPS see Orange Free State
FIRST STAMPS ISSUED August 1900 (overprinted on Cape of Good Hope)

CURRENCY

1868 sterling

Formerly Orange Free State, this colony combined with other territories to form the Union of South Africa in 1910. Subsequently, the stamps of the territories were freely used throughout the Union; these were replaced by stamps of the Union in 1913.

• Transvaal (Zuid Afrikaansche Republiek)

FIRST STAMPS ISSUED August 1869 (Their delivery appears to have been delayed, and they were sold direct to collectors for cash to pay the printer, a very early example of the practice)

CURRENCY

British

Four Boer republics were founded by Voortrekkers who crossed the Vaal in 1836.

The Boers defeated the Zulus at Blood River in 1838, thereby avenging the treacherous slaughter of Retief and his followers in 1837. The Boers and the Zulus drove the Matabele beyond the Limpopo. The independence of the republics was recognized in 1852 and they united as the Zuid Afrikaansche Republiek (South African Republic) in 1858. Bankrupt and faced with imminent Zulu attack in 1877, this was annexed to Britain as Transvaal. Misrule led to revolt in December 1880 (First Boer War); Britain was defeated in battle and forced to restore independence to the ZAR ('Second Republic'). The country became divided between the ruling Calvinist Boers and the rich unrepresented taxpaying 'Uitlanders' of the newly discovered Gold District (Rand). The Second Boer War broke out on 12 October 1899, and Transvaal was again annexed on 31 May 1902. It became a state of the Union in 1910.

Postal History
Mail is known from 1859; handstruck town marks from 1864; and by 1866 there were 12 POs dependent on Potchefstroom. A full government service was started on 31 August 1869. Control was moved to Pretoria in 1870 and a mail-cart service instituted to Orange Free State and Natal. About 30 POs were given numeral obliterations in 1874. Until Transvaal joined the UPU in 1893, stamps of the transit country were needed in addition on mail destined for overseas.

£1
SPECIMEN
TRANSVAAL
A
DEUTSCH-SÜDWESTAFRIKA
B
10 SHILLING
C
RSA 4c
D
3d
E
F
SUIDWES-AFRIKA
4d SOUTH WEST AFRICA

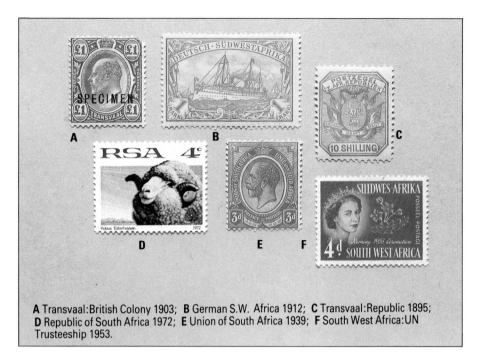

A Transvaal:British Colony 1903; **B** German S.W. Africa 1912; **C** Transvaal:Republic 1895; **D** Republic of South Africa 1972; **E** Union of South Africa 1939; **F** South West Africa:UN Trusteeship 1953.

Second Boer War (1899-1902)
Brought about by the intransigence of both Briton and Boer, this conflict was notable for its fluid guerrilla tactics and the bitterness with which it was fought. Boer prisoners were confined in Ceylon, Bermuda and St Helena. Censorship of mail was widespread for the first time. Much mail was captured, detained, or damaged in transit, and covers of the period are widely collected and studied by postal historians. Several places changed hands more than once, occasioning overprints (V.R.I., signifying Victoria Regina Imperatrix, was often used to show British occupation). During the numerous sieges stamps were produced locally in emergency.

• Mafeking
Town in Bechuanaland besieged 12 November 1899 by the Boers, relieved 17 May 1900.

> **STAMPS ISSUED** 24 March-17 May 1900

• Vryburg
Town in British Bechuanaland which changed hands twice.

> **STAMPS ISSUED** during brief Boer occupation November 1899, and during British occupation May 1900

• Pietersburg
Town in northern Transvaal to which Kruger's government withdrew from Pretoria.

> Authorized Boer provisionals, printed at the local newspaper office, were issued 20 March–9 April 1901

• Lydenburg
Town in eastern Transvaal occupied by British forces 6 September 1900.

> Stamps of Transvaal surcharged issued September 1900

• Rustenburg
Small town west of Pretoria invested by the Boers in June 1900 but relieved 22 June.

> Stamps of Transvaal overprinted V.R. issued 23 June 1900

• Schweizer Reinecke
Town southwest of Pretoria besieged 1 August 1900–9 January 1901.

> Stamps of Transvaal or Cape overprinted BESIEGED in rough uneven type were issued in August 1900

• Volksrust
Town in southern Transvaal near the Natal border.

> Revenue stamps of Transvaal overprinted V.R.I. were issued in March 1902

• Wolmaransstad
Town in western Transvaal, occupied by British troops, from which the Boers had removed all stocks of stamps.

> Stamps of Transvaal requisitioned from a local firm and overprinted were issued in June–July 1900

South Africa (Republic of South Africa)

> **FIRST STAMPS ISSUED** Union of South Africa 4 November 1910 (2½*d* value only; full definitives, 1913) Republic of South Africa 31 May 1961

CURRENCY
Until 1961 British
From 14 February 1961 100 cents = 1 rand

The Cape of Good Hope, Natal, the Orange Free State and Transvaal came together to form the Union of South Africa, with Dominion status, on 31 May 1910. The Union left the Commonwealth 31 May 1961 and became a republic (RSA).

Interprovincials
Stamps of the pre-Union colonies were

in use irrespective of origin throughout the Union from 18 August 1910 to 1 September 1913 (and were not demonetized until 31 December 1937).

Walfisch Bay (Walvis Bay)

FIRST STAMPS Cape of Good Hope from 1884

CURRENCY

1884 As Cape Colony
1910 As South Africa
1923 As South West Africa
1977 As South Africa

Claimed by the Dutch in 1796, this British settlement of 1800 was annexed to Cape Colony on 12 March 1878 and was incorporated into the Union of South Africa in 1910. Stamps used here can be recognized by cancellation.

Used stamps of Cape from 1884 (original oblit. barred oval 300).

Used stamps of South Africa from 1910 to 1922 (invalid after 31 January 1923).

Used stamps of South West Africa 1 January 1923-31 August 1977.

Since 1 September 1977 has used stamps of South Africa.

• German South-West Africa (Deutsch-Südwestafrika)

FIRST STAMPS 1888
FIRST STAMPS ISSUED March 1897

CURRENCY

German

Proclaimed a German protectorate on 24 April and flag raised 7 August 1884. Overrun by South African troops 1914-15.

Mail is known carried by casual ship between 7 August 1884 and 6 July 1888, when the first POs opened. Joined UPU in 1886. Used stamps of Germany from July 7 1888.

POs closed by captures August 1914-20 July 1915; PO at Olukonda was the last to fall.

EUROPEAN SWALLOW
45c CISKEI
Bophuthatswana 30c
VENDA
30c MIGRATORY BIRDS
E2
GIRAFFE
SWAZILAND
TRANSKEI 30c
SWAZI LAND
PROTECTORATE
POSTAGE
REVENUE

Bophuthatswana: 1984; Ciskei:Tribal Land 1984; Venda:Tribal Land 1984; Swaziland:Independent 1975; Transkei:Tribal Land 1984; Swaziland: Protectorate 1938.

South West Africa

FIRST STAMPS ISSUED 1 January 1923 Issues were bilingual in English and Afrikaans, but since 1970 have borne the abbreviations SWA instead.

CURRENCY

Until 1961 British
From 14 February 1961 South African

Ex-German colony mandated by the League of Nations to South Africa after World War I. Nazi activities by German settlers in 1934-5 led South Africa to administer it as a province. Despite United Nations' decisions to the contrary, this situation still obtains. Movements towards indepedence under the name Namibia have been blocked. The name Namibia has so far appeared only on stamps of sympathetic countries and on an issue of the United Nations publicly announcing by its inscription 'direct responsibility' for Namibia as a UN trust territory.

Used stamps of South Africa from c.19 September 1914 (at Lüderitzbucht) to 1922 (invalid after 31 January 1923).

Transkei

FIRST STAMPS ISSUED 26 October 1976

CURRENCY

South African

Territories under the protection of Cape Colony in 1858-65, then abandoned. Annexed to the Colony in 1879-94, but reserved to its black population from 1913. Transkei received internal self-government from South Africa in 1963 and was made an independent republic on 26 October 1976. It is not yet recognized by the UN or the UPU, but its stamps are accepted as valid.

Bophuthatswana

FIRST STAMPS ISSUED 6 December 1977

CURRENCY

South African

Tribal homeland territories of South Africa, lying west of Pretoria in the Rustenburg - Mafeking - Vryburg-Kuruman area, given autonomy in 1977.

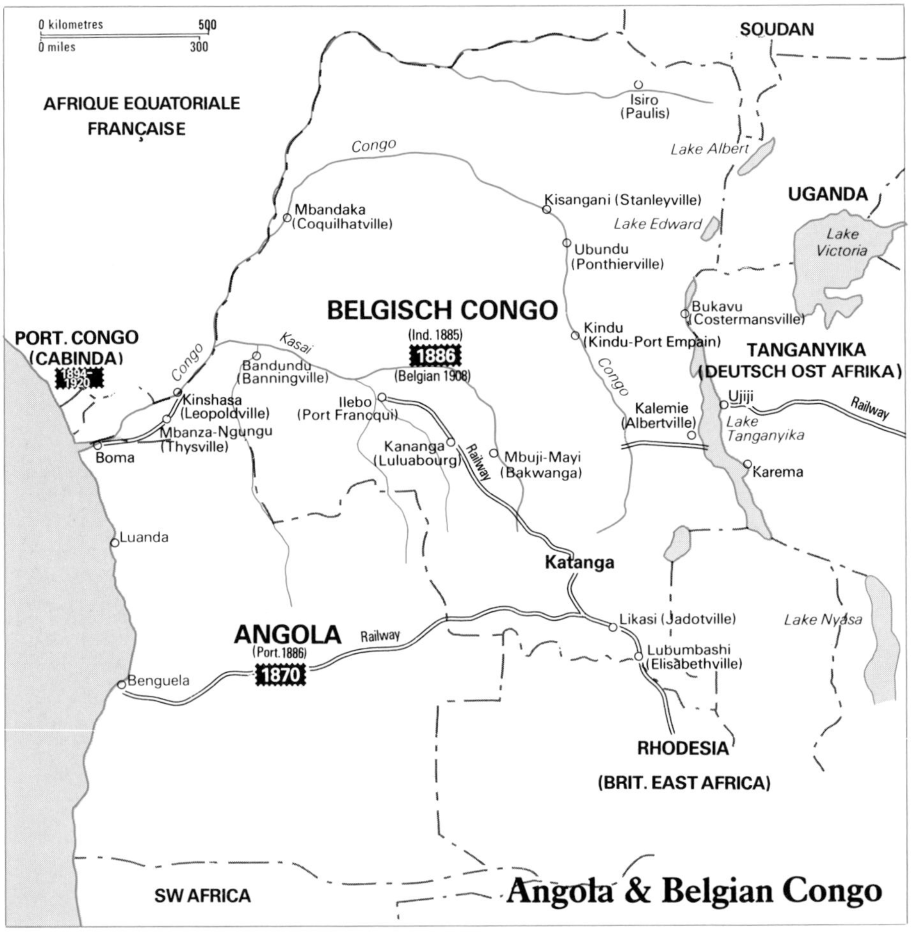
0 kilometres 500
0 miles 300
SOUDAN
AFRIQUE EQUATORIALE FRANÇAISE
Isiro (Paulis)
Congo
Lake Albert
UGANDA
Kisangani (Stanleyville)
Lake Edward
Lake Victoria
Mbandaka (Coquilhatville)
Ubundu (Ponthierville)
BELGISCH CONGO
(Ind. 1885)
1886
(Belgian 1908)
Bukavu (Costermansville)
Kindu (Kindu-Port Empain)
TANGANYIKA (DEUTSCH OST AFRIKA)
PORT. CONGO (CABINDA)
Kasai
Bandundu (Banningville)
Congo
Ujiji
Railway
Kinshasa (Leopoldville)
Ilebo (Port Francqui)
Kalemie (Albertville)
Lake Tanganyika
Mbanza-Ngungu (Thysville)
Kananga (Luluabourg)
Mbuji-Mayi (Bakwanga)
Boma
Karema
Railway
Luanda
Katanga
ANGOLA
(Port. 1886)
1870
Railway
Likasi (Jadotville)
Lake Nyasa
Lubumbashi (Elisabethville)
Benguela
RHODESIA
(BRIT. EAST AFRICA)
SW AFRICA
Angola & Belgian Congo

Venda

FIRST STAMPS ISSUED 13 September 1979

CURRENCY

1979 As South Africa

The Venda Territory Authority was established in 1969 and was granted internal self-government on 1 February 1973. Venda became fully independent on 13 September 1979.

Ciskei

FIRST STAMPS ISSUED 2 December 1981

CURRENCY

1981 As South Africa

Territorial authority within South Africa was established in 1961 and autonomous government was granted in 1972. Ciskei became fully independent on 4 December 1981. As in the case of Venda, this independence has not been accepted internationally, but stamps have been accepted for carriage of mail outside South Africa.

Swaziland

FIRST STAMPS ISSUED 18 October 1889
Withdrawn 7 November 1894
Separate stamps revived 2 January 1933

CURRENCY

Until 1961 British
From 14 February 1961 South African

Came under the joint protection of Britain and the South African Republic after 1884, then from 1902 solely under Transvaal (though not incorporated). On 1 December 1906 became a British protectorate, again administered from Cape Province. It was made a 'protected state' on 25 April 1967 and became an independent kingdom within the Commonwealth on 6 September 1968.

Used stamps of Transvaal 1894-1910.

Used stamps of South Africa after 1910.

• Stellaland

FIRST STAMPS ISSUED February 1884

CURRENCY

British

Free-booter Boer republic round the settlement of Vryburg set up on 10 January 1883. Annexed for Britain by Warren's Force, which reached Vryburg on 7 February 1885. Proclaimed part of British Bechuanaland as Crown Colony 30 September 1885.

Cancellation was by pen and ink. Stamps are known used by Warren's Force and cancelled at Kimberley in transit. Stocks withdrawn on 2 December 1885 were sold to Whitfield, King & Company of Ipswich.

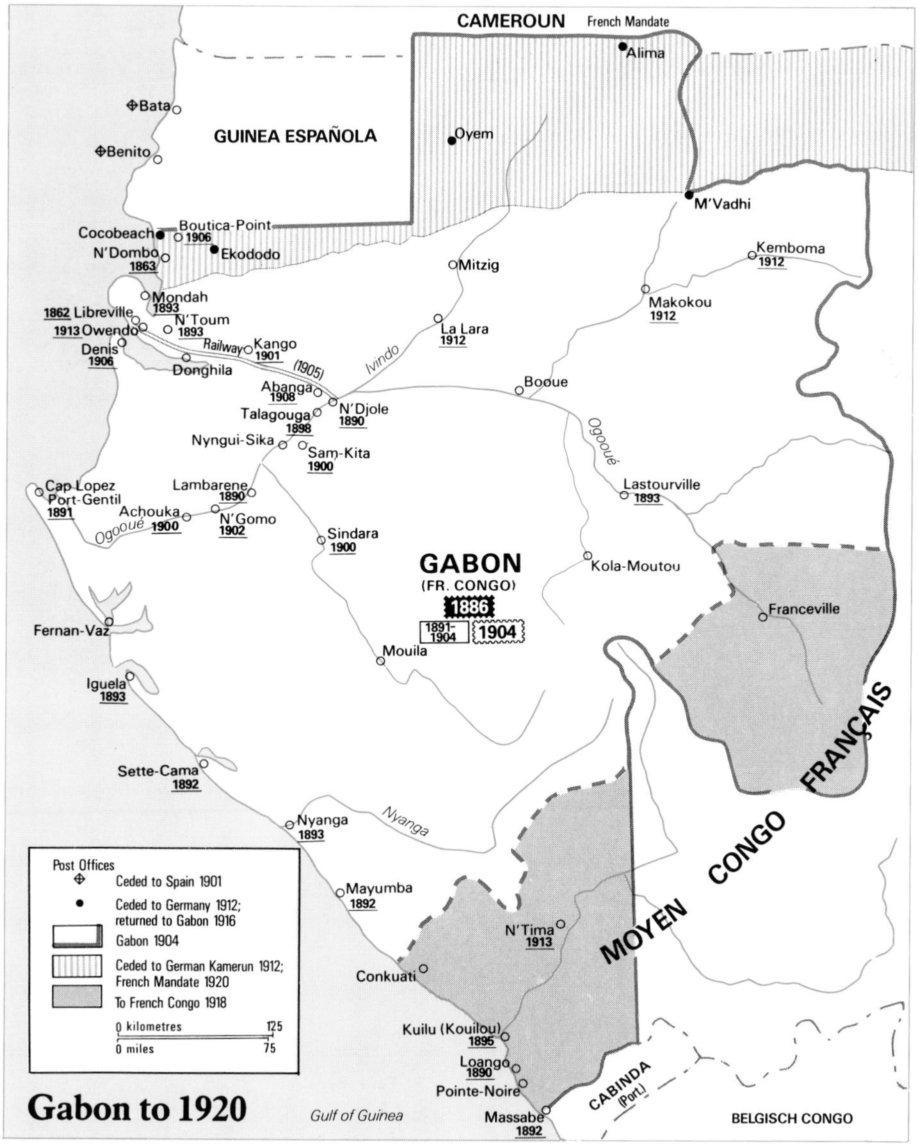

CAMEROUN French Mandate
Alima
Bata
Benito
GUINEA ESPAÑOLA
Oyem
M'Vadhi
Cocobeach
Boutica-Point 1906
N'Dombo 1863
Ekododo
Mitzig
Kemboma 1912
Mondah 1893
1862 Libreville
1913 Owendo
N'Toum 1893
Denis 1906
Railway
Kango 1901
(1905)
Donghila
Ivindo
La Lara 1912
Makokou 1912
Abanga 1908
Booue
N'Djole 1890
Talagouga 1898
Nyngui-Sika
Sam-Kita 1900
Ogooué
Cap Lopez
Port-Gentil 1891
Lambarene 1890
Achouka 1900
N'Gomo 1902
Ogooué
Lastourville 1893
Sindara 1900
GABON
(FR. CONGO)
1886
1891-1904
1904
Kola-Moutou
Franceville
Fernan-Vaz
Mouila
Iguela 1893
FRANÇAIS
Sette-Cama 1892
Nyanga 1893
Nyanga
CONGO
Post Offices
Ceded to Spain 1901
Ceded to Germany 1912; returned to Gabon 1916
Gabon 1904
Ceded to German Kamerun 1912; French Mandate 1920
To French Congo 1918
0 kilometres 125
0 miles 75
Mayumba 1892
N'Tima 1913
MOYEN
Conkuati
Kuilu (Kouilou) 1895
Loango 1890
Pointe-Noire
CABINDA (Port.)
Gulf of Guinea
Massabe 1892
BELGISCH CONGO

Gabon to 1920

Angola

FIRST STAMPS ISSUED 1 July 1870

CURRENCY

Until 1932 Portuguese
From 1932-54 100 centavos = 1 angolar
From 1954 Portuguese

Principal Portuguese possession in Africa was founded in 1576, but its boundaries were only gradually fixed after 1886. In 1935 was declared an integral part of Portugal, and after 11 June 1951 was treated as an overseas province. Proclaimed independent on 11 November 1975 and has been racked by civil war ever since. Neither the state of civil mails nor what arrangements exist for Cuban and Eastern European bloc forces involved is clear.

• Portuguese Congo

FIRST STAMPS ISSUED 5 August 1894

CURRENCY

Portuguese

The area now called Cabinda, north of the River Congo, was a separate administrative territory and had separate stamps from 1894 to 1920, when it was incorporated into Angola.

Zaire (Belgian Congo)

FIRST STAMPS inscribed ETAT DU CONGO 1 January 1886
FIRST STAMPS ISSUED inscribed ZAIRE 18 December 1971

CURRENCY

Until 1967 Belgian
From 1967 100 sengi = 1 likuta
100 makuta = 1 Zaïre

Although the mouth of the Congo was explored by British Admiralty expeditions from 1816 and became a steamer port-of-call on the Atlantic route to South Africa, all the knowledge and colonization came from the east side. A Belgian trading post was established at Karema on Lake Tanganyika in 1879 and similar posts along the Congo basin by H.M. Stanley. The independent state of the Congo was proclaimed at Boma on 1 July 1885 under the personal rule of Leopold II. Country annexed to Belgium on 15 November 1908. Independence as a republic on 30 June 1960 heralded chaos, the intervention of the UN and, after 1965, military dictatorship. Country changed its name to Zaïre on 27 October 1971.

• Katanga

FIRST STAMPS ISSUED 12 September 1960

Breakaway province 11 July 1960-15 January 1963, re-absorbed in Congo by 30 August 1964.

REPUBLIQUE GABONAISE
10F
2K
REPUBLIQUE DU ZAIRE
3k
REPUBLIQUE DEMOCRATIQUE DU CONGO
PROVINCIA DE ANGOLA
50 REIS 50
CERATOTHERIUM SIMUM
20c
CONGO
BELGISCH CONGO BELGE
2$50
REPUBLICA POPULAR
CORREIO AÉREO
ANGOLA
A
B
C
D
E
F

A Gabon:Republic 1969; **B** Zaire:Republic 1975; **C** Congo:Republic 1969; **D** Angola:Portuguese Colony 1886; **E** Belgian Congo:overprinted 1960; **F** Angola:Republic 1980.

REPUBLIQUE FRANÇAISE
2
POSTES
CONGO FRANÇAIS
A
DU CONGO
REPUBLIQUE POPULAIRE
100F
B

A French Congo 1900; **B** Congo:Popular Republic 1983.

Katangan town of Albertville was abandoned on 16 November 1961. In December 1961-March 1962 used stamps of Katanga locally overprinted CONGO until supplies arrived from Leopoldville.

• South Kasai

FIRST STAMPS ISSUED 20 June 1961

Another breakaway province that maintained autonomy 8 August 1960-2 October 1962.

Stamps exhausted or withdrawn by October 1961.

(Various other stamps of Congo overprinted SUD KASAI were sold in Brussels but never issued in Africa.)

Indian UN Force in Congo

United Nations force operated in Congo in 1964. Troops of many nations were involved, using their own military postal facilities and generally their national stamps. The Indian contingent in 1962-3 had (but doubtfully used) specially overprinted stamps.

EQUATORIAL AFRICA

Gabon

FIRST PROVISIONAL STAMPS 31 July 1886
FIRST STAMPS after new division 15 October 1904

CURRENCY

French

As part of anti-slavery activities, French established posts on the Gabon estuary and founded Libreville as a settlement for freed slaves. The explorations of Brazza extended the territory. A governor was appointed in 1886. Gabon was absorbed into French Congo between 11 December 1888 and 1 July 1904 and became part of French Equatorial Africa (*see below*) after 1910. Gabon became autonomous in 1958 and independent within the French Community in 1960.

Earliest office set up at Libreville in 1862 routed mail via the British PO at Fernando Po.

Used French Colonies General Issues from c.1862 (oblit. GAB in lozenge of dots applied at Libreville). Used stamps of French Congo (*see below*) from 1891-1904.

Used stamps of French Equatorial Africa (*see below*) 1936-59.

• French Congo

FIRST PROVISIONAL STAMPS ISSUED 24 March 1891
FIRST STAMPS inscribed MOYEN CONGO 1907

CURRENCY

1891 As France

Came under French control in 1880, when the capital Brazzaville was founded. Pointe Noire and Loango occupied in 1882 and the region was opened up towards Lake Chad in 1888. On 11 December 1888 was made a colony (incorporating Gabon,

REPUBLIQUE DU TCHAD
300F
POSTE AERIENNE 1983
CHARLES GREEN
Londres 1837
A
REPUBLIQUE FRANÇAISE
10 c
OUBANGUI-CHARI-TCHAD
MOYEN CONGO
B

A Chad:Republic 1983; **B** Ubangi-Shari-Chad: French Colony 1915.

Ubangi-Shari and Chad) called Gabon-Congo until 20 April 1891, Congo Français thereafter. Colony was redivided on 1 July 1904, and the central portion was renamed Moyen Congo. Territories were again combined on 15 January 1910 into French Equatorial Africa (this is not reflected in stamp issues until 1936, *see* French Equatorial Africa). Area became the Congo Republic (*see below*) on 28 November 1958.

Used French Colonies General Issues c.1881 (but there was very little postal activity before the absorption of Gabon). Used stamps of French Equatorial Africa 1937-59.

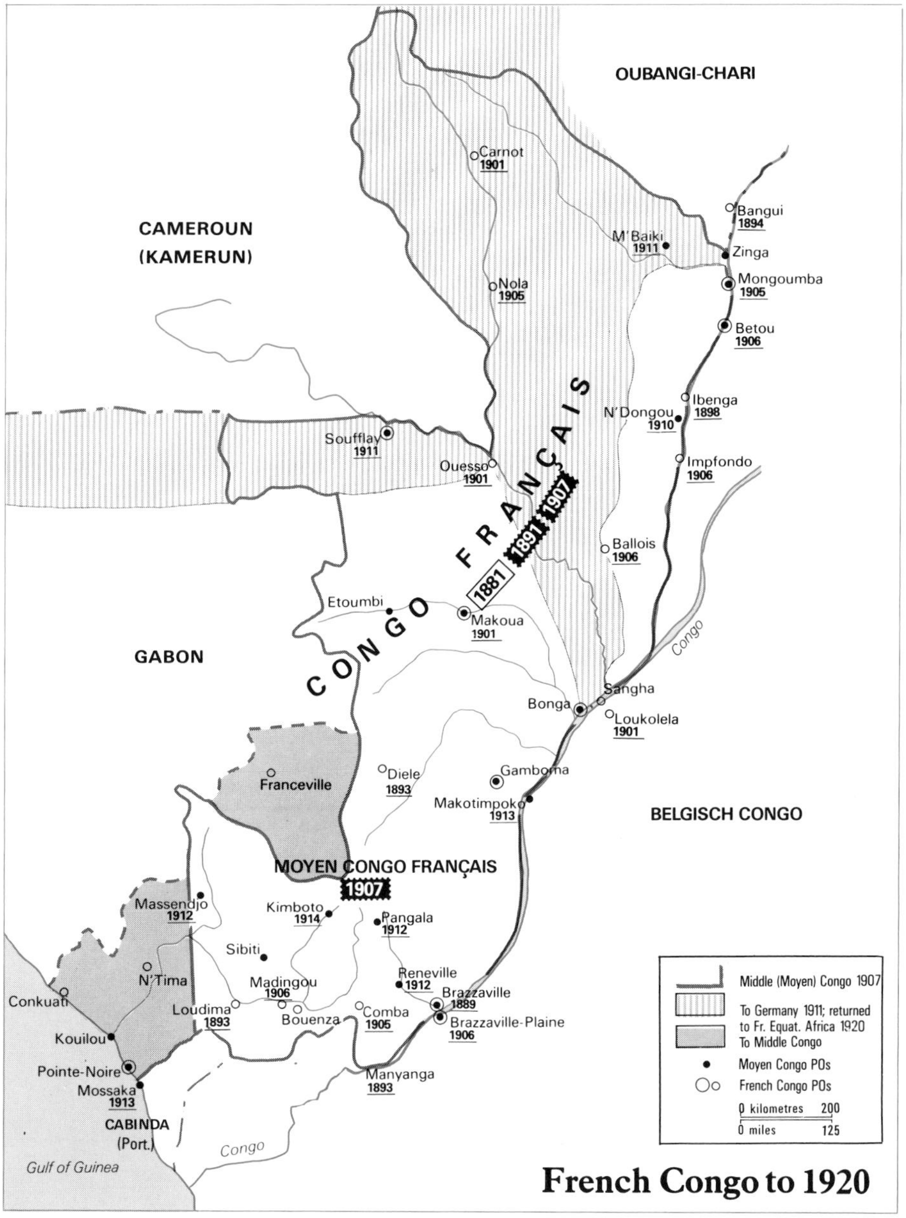
OUBANGI-CHARI
CAMEROUN
(KAMERUN)
GABON
BELGISCH CONGO
CONGO FRANÇAIS
1881
1891
1907
MOYEN CONGO FRANÇAIS
1907
Carnot 1901
Bangui 1894
M'Baiki 1911
Zinga
Nola 1905
Mongoumba 1905
Betou 1906
Ibenga 1898
N'Dongou 1910
Souffiay 1911
Ouesso 1901
Impfondo 1906
Ballois 1906
Etoumbi
Makoua 1901
Sangha
Bonga
Loukolela 1901
Franceville
Diele 1893
Gamboma
Makotimpoko 1913
Massendjo 1912
Kimboto 1914
Pangala 1912
Sibiti
N'Tima
Madingou 1906
Reneville 1912
Brazzaville 1889
Brazzaville-Plaine 1906
Conkuati
Loudima 1893
Bouenza
Comba 1905
Kouilou
Pointe-Noire
Mossaka 1913
Manyanga 1893
CABINDA
(Port.)
Congo
Gulf of Guinea
Middle (Moyen) Congo 1907
To Germany 1911; returned to Fr. Equat. Africa 1920
To Middle Congo
Moyen Congo POs
French Congo POs
0 kilometres 200
0 miles 125

French Congo to 1920

Congo Republic

FIRST STAMPS ISSUED 28 November 1970

CURRENCY

French

Autonomous 28 November 1958, with full independence within the French Community 15 August 1960. Became 'People's Republic of the Congo' on 3 January 1970.

• Ubangi-Shari-Chad (Oubangui-Chari-Tchad)

FIRST STAMPS French Colonies General Issues 1897
French Congo to 1915
FIRST STAMPS ISSUED 1915

CURRENCY

French

French influence was extended north of the Ubangi River by Brazza, and the territory of Upper Ubangui was formed in 1894, centred on the recently founded town of Bangui. The Shari area was occupied in 1898. Ubangi-Shari was part of French Congo until it was made a colony on 1 July 1904, but it was postally administered from

Chad & Ubangi-Shari to 1922

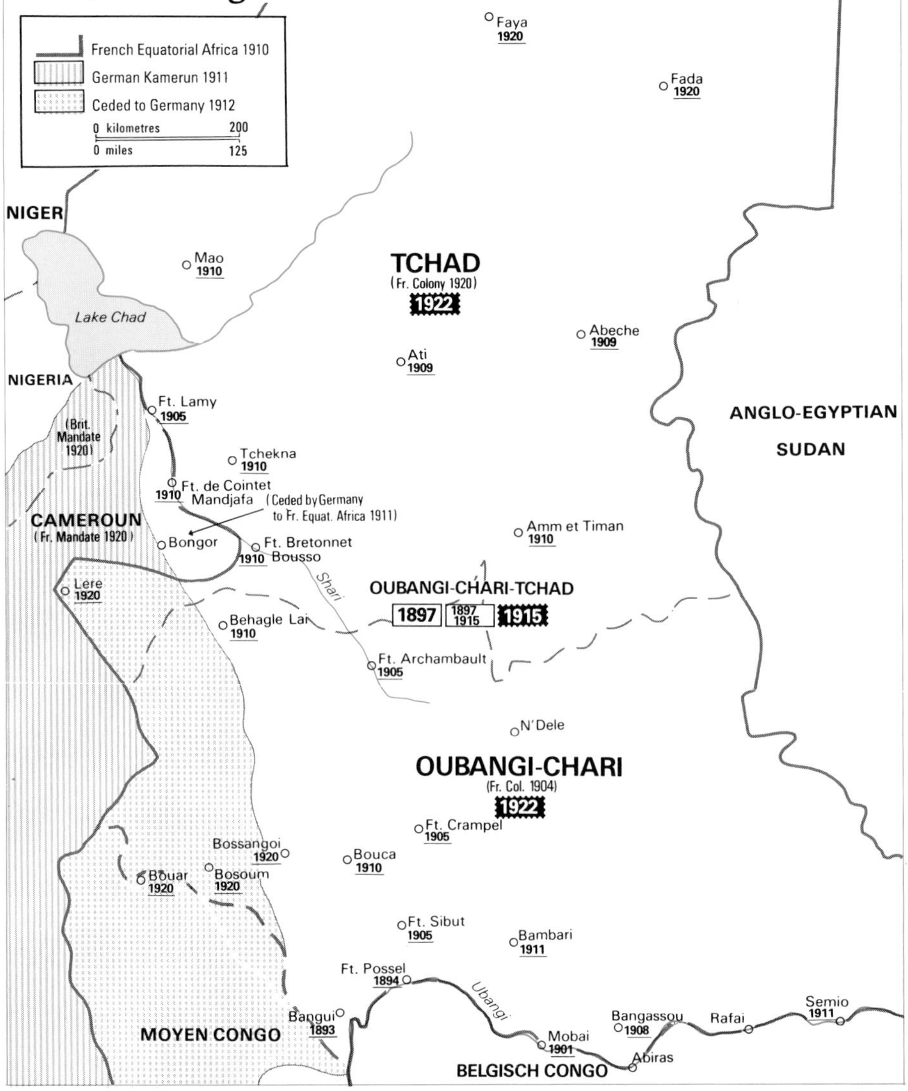
French Equatorial Africa 1910
German Kamerun 1911
Ceded to Germany 1912
0 kilometres 200
0 miles 125
NIGER
Lake Chad
NIGERIA
(Brit. Mandate 1920)
CAMEROUN
(Fr. Mandate 1920)
Faya 1920
Fada 1920
Mao 1910
TCHAD
(Fr. Colony 1920)
1922
Abeche 1909
Ati 1909
Ft. Lamy 1905
Tchekna 1910
Ft. de Cointet 1910
Mandjafa (Ceded by Germany to Fr. Equat. Africa 1911)
ANGLO-EGYPTIAN
SUDAN
Amm et Timan 1910
Bongor
Ft. Bretonnet 1910
Bousso
Shari
Lere 1920
OUBANGI-CHARI-TCHAD
1897
1897 1915
1915
Behagle Lai 1910
Ft. Archambault 1905
N'Dele
OUBANGI-CHARI
(Fr. Col. 1904)
1922
Ft. Crampel 1905
Bossangoi 1920
Bouar 1920
Bosoum 1920
Bouca 1910
Ft. Sibut 1905
Bambari 1911
Ft. Possel 1894
Ubangi
Bangui 1893
MOYEN CONGO
Bangassou 1908
Rafai
Semio 1911
Mobai 1901
Abiras
BELGISCH CONGO

French Congo until 1915. Both territories were incorporated into French Equatorial Africa in 1910. Chad became a separate colony on 17 March 1920.

• Ubangi-Shari (Oubangui-Chari)

FIRST STAMPS As Ubangi-Shari-Chad until 1922
FIRST STAMPS ISSUED November 1922

Although Chad became postally separate in 1920, the new stamps were not issued until 1922. The colony used the stamps of French Equatorial Africa in 1936-60.

Central African Republic (République Centrafricaine)

FIRST STAMPS ISSUED 1 December 1959

CURRENCY
French

Independent successor of Ubangi-Shari. Became a republic on 1 December 1958. Its ruler President Bokassa proclaimed himself emperor in 1976 and the country's name was changed to Central African Empire. Emperor overthrown in 1979 and title of republic reintroduced.

• Chad (Tchad)

FIRST STAMPS ISSUED November 1922

CURRENCY
French

A French military territory by 1900, Chad became dependent upon Ubangi-Shari until made a separate colony on 17 March 1920. Acquired independence in two stages in 1958 and 1960.

Used stamps of French Equatorial Africa in 1936-59.

Chad Republic (République du Tchad)

FIRST STAMPS ISSUED 28 November 1959

• French Equatorial Africa (Afrique Equatorial Française)

FIRST STAMPS ISSUED 16 March 1936

CURRENCY
French

Territories of Ubangi-Shari, Chad, French Congo and Gabon were federated in 1910 but retained certain separate services (including postal) until 1936. The region adhered to the Free French in 1940. In 1958 the federation broke up again into independent republics (*see above*).

Stamps ceased 1960, last used in Ubangi-Shari.

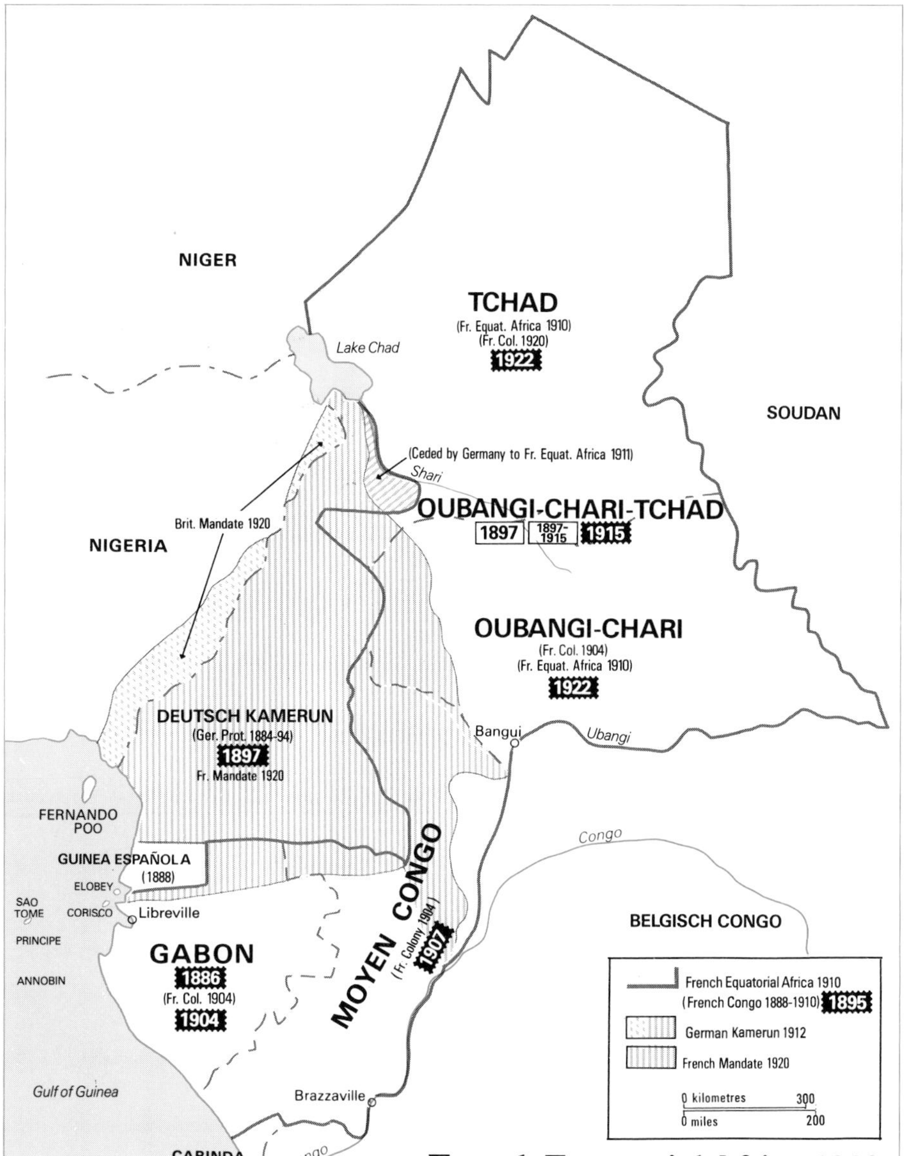
NIGER
TCHAD
(Fr. Equat. Africa 1910)
(Fr. Col. 1920)
1922
Lake Chad
SOUDAN
(Ceded by Germany to Fr. Equat. Africa 1911)
Shari
Brit. Mandate 1920
NIGERIA
OUBANGI-CHARI-TCHAD
1897
1897-1915
1915
OUBANGI-CHARI
(Fr. Col. 1904)
(Fr. Equat. Africa 1910)
1922
DEUTSCH KAMERUN
(Ger. Prot. 1884-94)
1897
Fr. Mandate 1920
Bangui
Ubangi
FERNANDO POO
GUINEA ESPAÑOLA
(1888)
ELOBEY
SAO TOME
CORISCO
Libreville
PRINCIPE
ANNOBIN
GABON
1886
(Fr. Col. 1904)
1904
MOYEN CONGO
(Fr. Colony 1904)
1907
Congo
BELGISCH CONGO
French Equatorial Africa 1910
(French Congo 1888-1910)
1895
German Kamerun 1912
French Mandate 1920
0 kilometres 300
0 miles 200
Gulf of Guinea
Brazzaville
CABINDA
(Port.)
Congo
French Equatorial Africa 1922

St Thomas and Prince Islands (São Tomé e Príncipe)

FIRST STAMPS ISSUED 1870

CURRENCY

1870 Portuguese

Two islands in the Gulf of Guinea discovered by the Portuguese in 1471 and populated by their exiled criminals and sugar planters. Portuguese colony until 11 June 1951 when the islands became an overseas province of Portugal. Independent republic from 12 July 1975.

• Fernando Po

FIRST STAMPS Britain from 1874
FIRST STAMPS ISSUED (as Spanish colony) 1 July 1868

CURRENCY

1874 Portuguese

Island in the Gulf of Guinea discovered by the Portuguese (1472), acquired by Spain in 1778, and in 1827-34 leased to Britain as an antislavery naval base. Became a separate Spanish colony until it merged in 1909 with Elobey, Annobon, Corisco and Rio Muni into Spanish Guinea (*see below*). On 30 July 1959 the island and Annobon were made a province of Spain, but on 12 October 1968 Fernando Po combined with Rio Muni to form Equatorial Guinea (*see below*).

Postal History
When British base was closed in 1834, the island, having a better climate than the coast, became a centre of British activity and a consul was appointed c.1850. The consul was made British packet agent in March 1859, when a 'Paid' handstamp was supplied. The agency was closed in 1877. The island was authorized to use stamps of Britain in April 1858-77, though none may have been supplied before 1874 (in 1874-7, oblit. 247).

Except for a special issue of 1929, used stamps of Spanish Guinea during 1909-60. Used separate stamps again 25 February 1960–11 October 1968.

• Elobey, Annóbon and Corisco

FIRST STAMPS ISSUED June 1903

CURRENCY

1903 As Spain

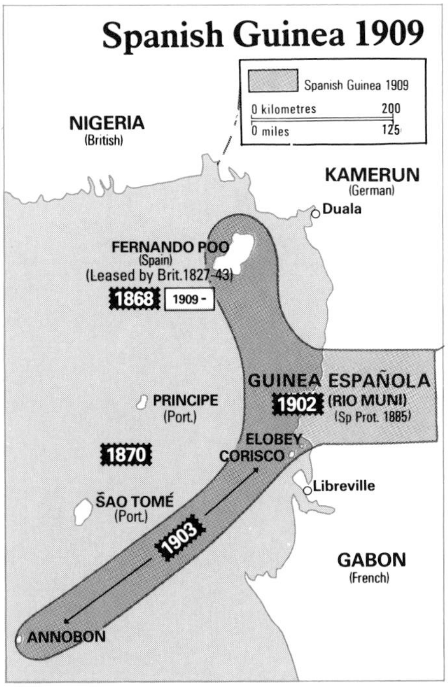
Spanish Guinea 1909
Spanish Guinea 1909
0 kilometres 200
0 miles 125
NIGERIA
(British)
KAMERUN
(German)
Duala
FERNANDO POO
(Spain)
(Leased by Brit.1827-43)
1868
1909 -
GUINEA ESPAÑOLA
1902
(RIO MUNI)
(Sp Prot. 1885)
PRINCIPE
(Port.)
1870
ELOBEY
CORISCO
Libreville
ŜAO TOMÉ
(Port.)
1903
GABON
(French)
ANNOBON

A
B
C
D
E
F
G

A Spanish Guinea 1917; B Sierra Leone:Independent 1963; D Liberia 1860; D Fernando Po:Spanish Colony 1907; E French Equatorial Africa 1937; F Sierra Leone:Crown Colony 1872; G Liberia 1974.

Three islands in Gulf of Guinea acquired from Portugal in 1778 and forming a Spanish colony. From 1909 to 1959 they were part of Spanish Guinea. In 1959 the islands were split, Annobón to Fernando Po and Elobey and Corisco to Rio Muni. Stamp issue ceased 1909.

• Spanish Guinea (Guinea Española)

FIRST STAMPS ISSUED 1902

CURRENCY

1902 Spanish

Spanish mainland territory (also known as Rio Muni) made a protectorate on 9 January 1885. During 1909-59 included Elobey, Annobón, Corisco and Fernando Po. On 30 July 1959 Annobón and Fernando Po were detached again. The mainland area, together with Elobey and Corisco, became an overseas province of Spain known as Rio Muni (*see below*).

Issues during 1909-49 bear the inscription TERRITORIOS ESPAÑOLES DEL GOLFO DE GUINEA.

The last issue inscribed GUINEA ESPAÑOLA appeared on 23 November 1959 (i.e., after the changes of 30 July).

• Rio Muni

FIRST STAMPS ISSUED 27 April 1960

CURRENCY

1962 Spanish

Overseas province of Spain from 30 July 1959, formerly part of Spanish Guinea (*see above*). On 12 October 1968 it recombined with Fernando Po to become Equatorial Guinea (*see below*).

Equatorial Guinea

FIRST STAMPS ISSUED 12 October 1968

CURRENCY

1902 Spanish

Former Spanish Guinea territories became an independent republic on 12 October 1968. Its despotism has been condemned by a UN Commission for crimes against human rights.

All issues since 1972 have been condemned by official philatelic bodies as undesirable.

WEST AFRICA

In common with the rest of Africa, settlements (and so posts) in West Africa started on the coast and were extended inland by exploratory penetration or conquest. Most inland boundaries were fixed by international commissions of European powers in the 1890s as settlement made it necessary.

Modern African states, here as elsewhere, have in consequence boundaries and land communications dependent upon colonial convenience rather than ethnic grouping. For example the modern state of Nigeria owes its multiracial composition to the British amalgamations of various territories based on the Niger.

Until 1879 each British colony had control of its own postal arrangements; the colonies all adhered together to the UPU in 1879 and adjusted uniform postal rates thereafter, but they continued to have individual stamps. French colonies were closer to the mother system using a general issue of stamps until local fluctuations in currency values forced its abandonment in 1892. German and Spanish colonies conformed more closely to regulations (including stamp designs) laid down by the mother country.

Liberia

FIRST STAMPS ISSUED 1860

CURRENCY

100 cents = 1 dollar

Originally a settlement formed in 1822 by American philanthropic societies for freed American slaves. Became an independent republic on 26 July 1847. Its boundaries were established by agreement with Britain in 1885 and later with France.

Sierra Leone

FIRST STAMPS ISSUED 21 September 1859
(oblit. B31 used at Freetown)

CURRENCY

Until 1964 British
From 1964 100 cents = 1 leone

British trading station was established here in 1672. The first settlement was at Freetown in 1787, for Africans rescued from slave ships. Colonized by the Sierra Leone Company in 1791, became a colony in 1808 and was extended inland by protectorate from 1892 to 1896. After becoming independent within the British Commonwealth on 27 April 1961, it underwent a series of military coups in 1967-8, and in 1971 was declared a republic.

Postal History
Casual letters are known from 1794. A regular packet operated from Falmouth from 1852. A PO agent was appointed to handle mail by British packets in July 1853. From 1854 mail from Freetown going to destinations abroad could be (and after 1860 had to be) prepaid; mail to UK was sent unpaid ('Bearing'). Datestamps and 'Paid' stamps were despatched to Freetown 21 March 1854 (no example of use is known before June 1855). The packet port moved to Liverpool in October 1858. An inland service was started in 1872. There were c. 137 POs in 1976.

The Gambia

FIRST STAMPS ISSUED March 1869

CURRENCY

Until 1971 British
From 1971 100 bututs = 1 dalasy

This early English settlement had a chequered existence and after the dissolution of the Africa Company was placed under Sierra Leone in 1821. In 1843 became a separate colony (though with a period of administration from Freetown, Sierra Leone, in 1866-88). British Crown Colony from 1888, it became self-governing in 1963 and independent within the Commonwealth on 18 February 1965. By referendum it became a republic within the Commonwealth on 24 April 1970. In 1981 there was a rising against the Government which was suppressed with the help of Senegalese troops. A federation of the two governments as Senegambia was proposed in 1982 but this has not been implemented and both countries continue to issue their own stamps.

A
GAMBIA
TWO PENCE
B
POSTAGE
GOLD
COAST
ONE PENNY
C
GOLD COAST
POSITION OF GOLD COAST
D
THE GAMBIA D1.25

A Gambia:Crown Colony 1880; **B** Gold Coast 1875; **C** Gold Coast 1948; **D** The Gambia:Republic 1979.

Postal History
'Ship letters' are known from 1836. Mail was sent via Sierra Leone in 1853. 'Paid' handstamps exist from 1861. There have been TPOs on government river steamers since 1922.

• Gold Coast

FIRST STAMPS 1 July 1875
Last issue overprinted GHANA on independence.

CURRENCY

British

Settled by various European powers after its discovery in 1471 by the Portuguese, by 1821 the area had gradually become predominantly British, the last European settlements being bought in 1850 and 1871. Gold Coast came under Sierra Leone until it was made a British Crown Colony in 1874, and itself controlled Lagos from 1874-

86. Ashanti, subdued in 1874, was annexed in 1901 after further revolts; territories farther north (already protected in 1896 to frustrate French ambitions) were also administered. On becoming a Dominion on 6 March 1957, it changed its name to Ghana (*see below*).

Postal History
Letters are known from the 18th century. Postal arrangements were administered by Sierra Leone (and incoming letters routed via Freetown); handstruck markings are known from 1855. Joined UPU January 1879.

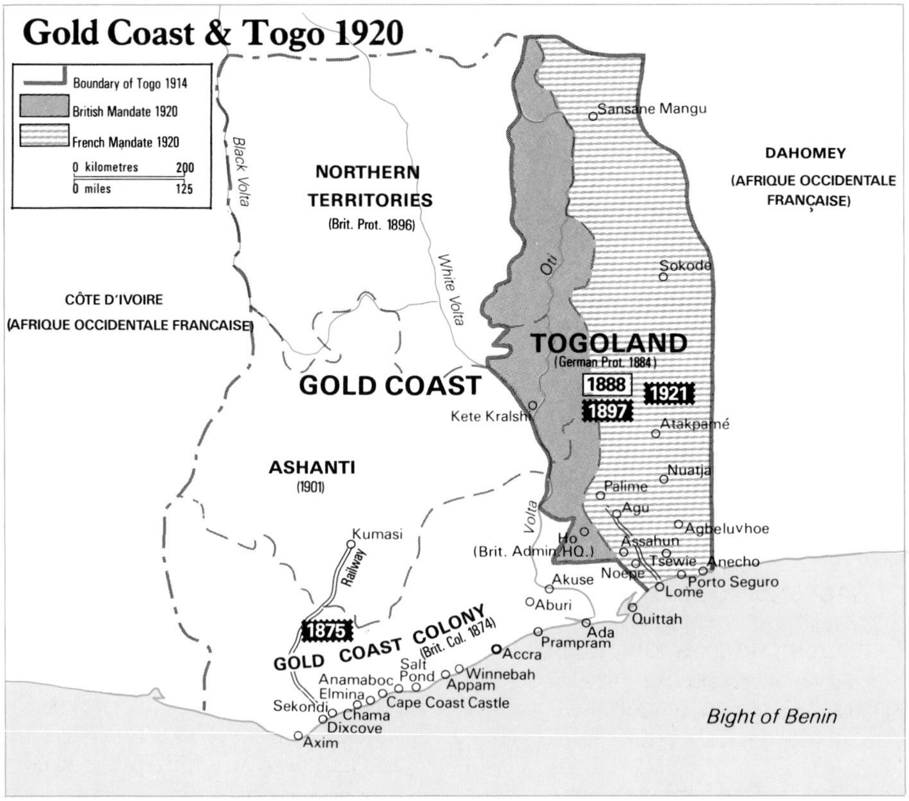
Gold Coast & Togo 1920
Boundary of Togo 1914
British Mandate 1920
French Mandate 1920
0 kilometres 200
0 miles 125
NORTHERN TERRITORIES
(Brit. Prot. 1896)
Black Volta
White Volta
Oti
Sansane Mangu
DAHOMEY
(AFRIQUE OCCIDENTALE FRANÇAISE)
Sokode
CÔTE D'IVOIRE
(AFRIQUE OCCIDENTALE FRANCAISE)
TOGOLAND
(German Prot. 1884)
1888
1921
1897
GOLD COAST
Kete Kralshi
Atakpamé
ASHANTI
(1901)
Nuatja
Palime
Agu
Agbeluvhoe
Kumasi
Railway
Volta
Ho
(Brit. Admin. HQ.)
Assahun
Tsewie
Anecho
Noepe
Porto Seguro
Lome
Akuse
Aburi
Quittah
1875
GOLD COAST COLONY
(Brit. Col. 1874)
Ada
Prampram
Accra
Salt Pond
Winnebah
Appam
Anamaboc
Elmina
Cape Coast Castle
Sekondi
Chama
Dixcove
Axim
Bight of Benin

Ghana

FIRST STAMPS ISSUED March 1957

CURRENCY

Until 1957 British

From 19 July 1965 100 pesewas = 1 cedi

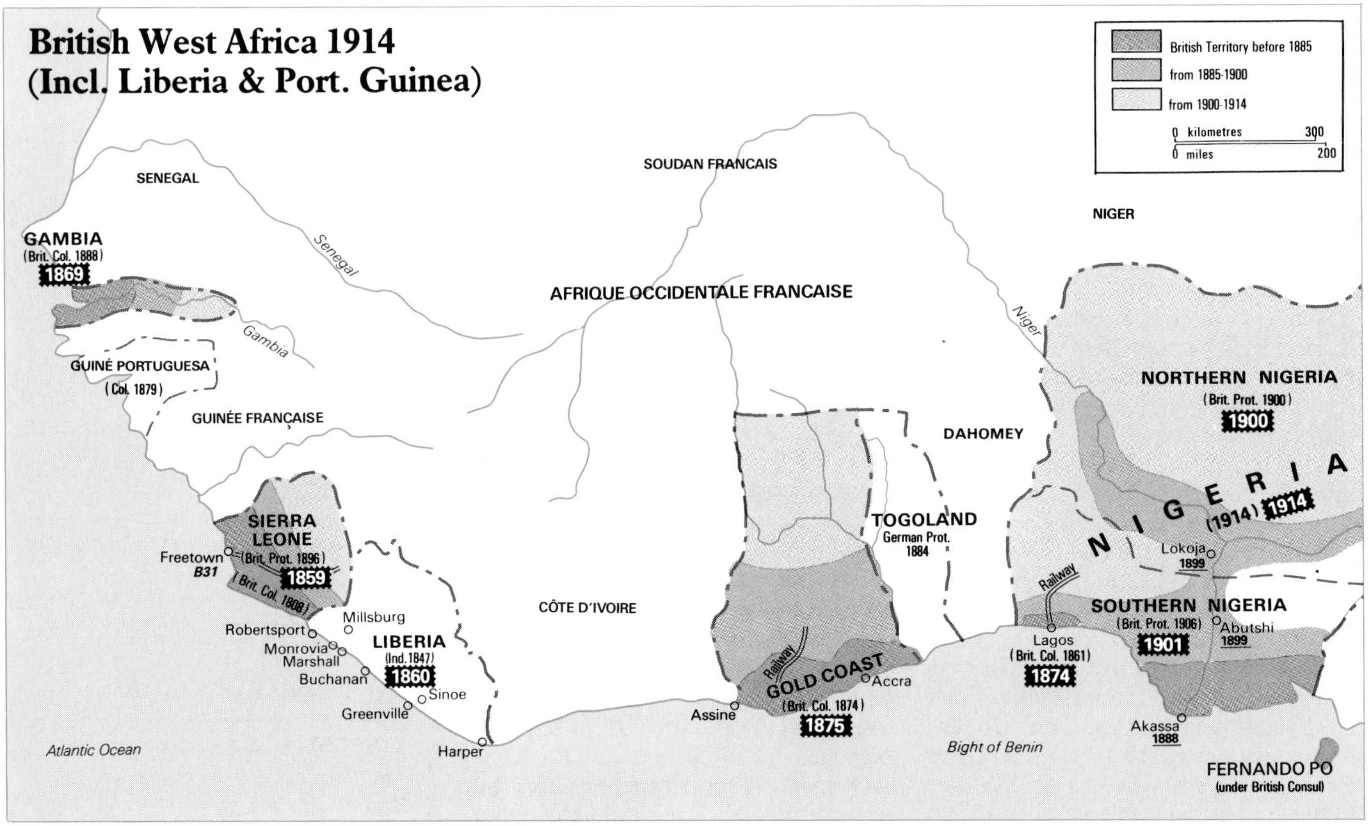
British West Africa 1914
(Incl. Liberia & Port. Guinea)
British Territory before 1885
from 1885-1900
from 1900-1914
0 kilometres 300
0 miles 200
SENEGAL
SOUDAN FRANCAIS
NIGER
GAMBIA
(Brit. Col. 1888)
1869
Senegal
AFRIQUE OCCIDENTALE FRANCAISE
Niger
Gambia
GUINÉ PORTUGUESA
(Col. 1879)
GUINÉE FRANÇAISE
NORTHERN NIGERIA
(Brit. Prot. 1900)
1900
DAHOMEY
NIGERIA
(1914) 1914
SIERRA LEONE
(Brit. Prot. 1896)
Freetown
B31
1859
(Brit. Col. 1808)
TOGOLAND
German Prot.
1884
Lokoja
1899
Railway
SOUTHERN NIGERIA
(Brit. Prot. 1906)
Abutshi
1899
1901
CÔTE D'IVOIRE
Millsburg
Robertsport
Monrovia
Marshall
LIBERIA
(Ind. 1847)
Buchanan
1860
Sinoe
Greenville
Lagos
(Brit. Col. 1861)
1874
GOLD COAST
Accra
(Brit. Col. 1874)
1875
Assine
Akassa
1888
Atlantic Ocean
Harper
Bight of Benin
FERNANDO PO
(under British Consul)

Dominion of the British Commonwealth from 6 March 1957, became a republic on 1 July 1960. Since 1975, apart from a period of civilian rule in 1979-81 it has been ruled by an army council chaired by Flt-Lieut. Rawlings.

In 1974 there were 237 POs and 710 PAs.

The distribution of cancelled remainders to the stamp trade in 1961 has killed interest for serious collectors.

Togo

FIRST STAMPS Germany 1 March 1888 (Klein-Popo. 1888: Lome 1890)
FIRST STAMPS ISSUED June 1897
15 July 1921 Under French Mandate
6 October 1947 As a Trust Territory
2 May 1955 As an Autonomous Republic

CURRENCY

1897	German currency
1914	As France ?
1915	sterling (British zone)

German merchants set up trading posts in 1878 at Anecho (Klein-Popo). By 1884 a protectorate was declared as a base for the German West African mailboats.

Traders' mail is known from 1885 carried by steamers of the Woermann Line (*see also* German Cameroons) and put into the German system at Hamburg.

Togo joined the UPU in 1886 with other German colonies. During German rule there were 17 POs and the last of these, Atakpamé, was overrun by the Allies on 26 August 1914.

Allied Occupation of Togo
Colony was seized by the Allies in August 1914 and administered jointly by Britain and France until divided between them on 10 July 1919. Lome was transferred from the British area to the French on 20 September 1920.

Stamps of German Togo overprinted in English issued: 1 October 1914.
Stamps of German Togo overprinted in French issued: 8 October 1914.

Later, British overprints were made on stamps of the Gold Coast (1915), and French overprints on stamps of Dahomey (1916). Some unoverprinted stamps of the Gold Coast were used during shortages in 1914-15.

After the territorial division, the British mandate used stamps of the Gold Coast (territory was absorbed into that colony and is now part of Ghana).

Mandates were confirmed by the League of Nations on 20 July 1922. The United Nations awarded the British zone to the Gold Coast on ethnic grounds.

French-mandated Togo declared for the Vichy Government in 1940. It was made a trust territory in 1946, became an autonomous republic within the French Community on 16 April 1955 and on 27 April 1960 an independent republic. There have since been palace revolutions.

Since independence there have been many issues from the country and, politically, it has been unstable.

In 1972 there were 39 POs and 16 PAs.

The Nigerias

• Lagos

FIRST STAMPS ISSUED 10 June 1874

CURRENCY

1874	sterling

Island centre of the slave trade occupied by treaty in 1851 and taken over by the British in 1861 as a Crown Colony. Amalgamated on 16 February 1906 with the Protectorate of Southern Nigeria.

A mail packet ran from 1852, but datestamp and 'Paid at Lagos' handstamp did not reach the Postal Agent until March 1859.

After 16 February 1906 used stamps of Southern Nigeria (*see below*); Lagos stocks on hand were also used up concurrently.

• Niger Territories

FIRST STAMPS Britain 1890-1900

CURRENCY

1892	sterling

Territories between the Forcados and Brass Rivers administered by the Royal Niger Company. On 1 January 1900 they were transferred to the British government.

In 1888 a special arrangement was made with the British GPO whereby mail franked with the company's handstamps would be delivered at single rates (instead of double charge). This did not always work.

Used stamps of Britain in 1890-1900; cancellation was by company handstamps at Akassa (1888); Burutu (opened 1896); Lokoja (June 1899); and Abutshi (October 1899).

• Oil Rivers Protectorate

FIRST STAMPS (overprinted GB) July 1892

CURRENCY

British

Protectorate assumed July 1884, confirmed 1885. Name changed on 12 May 1893 to Niger Coast Protectorate (*see below*).

PO was established at Old Calabar in November 1891 with sub-offices at Brass, Bonny, Opobo, Benin and Warri.

Used stamps of Britain November 1891-July 1892.

• Niger Coast Protectorate

FIRST STAMPS inscribed (by overprint) NIGER COAST PROTECTORATE November 1893

½ NIGER COAST PROTECTORATE ½
ONE HALF PENNY
THIRD ANNIVERSARY OF THE REVOLUTION 1966-1969
FREEDOM AND JUSTICE
12½np GHANA
BRITISH PROTECTORATE
OIL RIVERS
POSTAGE & REVENUE
HALF PENNY
REICHSPOST
Togo
PF. 25 PF.
REPUBLIQUE TOGOLAISE
30F
POSTES
A
B
C
D
E
F

A Niger Coast 1894; **B** Ghana:Independent 1969; **C** Oil River Protectorate 1892; **D** Lagos 1893; **E** Togo:German Colony 1897; **F** Togo:Independent 1974.

NORTHERN NIGERIA
POSTAGE & REVENUE
SPECIMEN
2½d
SOUTHERN NIGERIA
£1
SPECIMEN
ONE POUND
A
B

A Northern Nigeria 1900; **B** Southern Nigeria 1909.

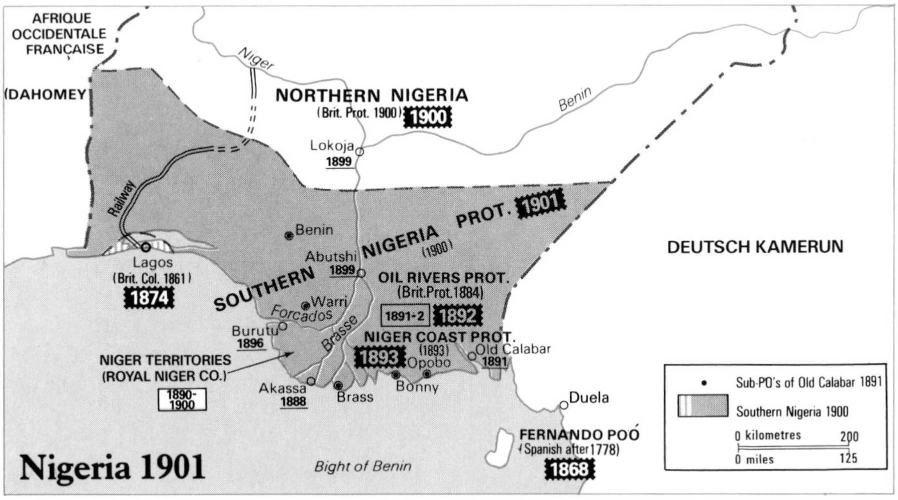

AFRIQUE OCCIDENTALE FRANÇAISE
(DAHOMEY
Niger
NORTHERN NIGERIA
(Brit. Prot. 1900) 1900
Benin
Lokoja 1899
Railway
SOUTHERN NIGERIA PROT. 1901
(1900)
Benin
Abutshi 1899
Lagos
(Brit. Col. 1861)
1874
Warri
Forcados
OIL RIVERS PROT.
(Brit.Prot.1884)
1891-2 1892
Burutu 1896
Brasse
NIGER COAST PROT.
(1893)
1893
Opobo
Old Calabar 1891
NIGER TERRITORIES
(ROYAL NIGER CO.)
1890-1900
Akassa 1888
Brass
Bonny
Duela
DEUTSCH KAMERUN
FERNANDO POÓ
(Spanish after 1778)
1868
Bight of Benin
Sub-PO's of Old Calabar 1891
Southern Nigeria 1900
0 kilometres 200
0 miles 125

Nigeria 1901

In 1906, when Lagos was amalgamated, stamps of Lagos were valid throughout Southern Nigeria.

Since 1914 has used stamps of Nigeria (*see below*).

• Northern Nigeria

FIRST STAMPS ISSUED March 1900

CURRENCY

British

Territories into which the Royal Niger Company had expanded were proclaimed a protectorate in 1900.

Since 1914 has used stamps of Nigeria (*see below*).

CURRENCY

British

Formerly Oil Rivers Protectorate. United with the chartered territories in 1900 to form the protectorate of Southern Nigeria (*see below*).

Stamps continued in use after the formation of Southern Nigeria until new stamps were ready.

• Southern Nigeria

FIRST STAMPS ISSUED March 1901

CURRENCY

British

During temporary shortages in 1902 used remainders of last Niger Coast Protectorate issue.

Nigeria

CURRENCY

Until 1971 British

Until 1973 (British, continuing nondecimal)

From 1973 100 kobo = 1 naira

Cameroons 1920
German Kamerun 1910
Ceded to French 1911
Gains from French 1912
British Mandate 1920
German PO's
by 1897
by 1911
Nigerian Stamps
French Cancels in 1916
0 kilometres 300
0 miles 200
Lake Chad
TCHAD
Ceded by Germany to Fr. Equat. Africa 1911
Mora
Maroua
NIGERIA
CAMEROON
Garoua
Ngaundere
Nsan
Kumba
Bafia
Bakebu
Ossindinge
Tinto
Bare
Rio del Rey
KAMERUN
(German Protectorate 1884)
1887
1897
Yoko
Br. 1915 Fr. 1915
CAMEROUN
(Fr. Mandate 1920)
N'Gila
Yabassi
Bonaberi
Duala
(Kamerun)
Buea
Bibundi
Viktoria
Tiko
Edea
Eseka
Jaundé
Akonolinga
Dume
Njassi
Abong-M'bang
FERNANDO POO
Lolodorf
Lomié
Jukadama
Kribi
Gross-Batanga
Makure
Ebolona
Sangmelina
Akoafin
Ambam
Souffley
GUINEA ESPAÑOLA
Ceded to Germany 1912
Ukoko
Ekododo
OUBANGI-CHARI
Buar
Ceded to German Kamerun 1912
Nola
Ikelemba
CONGO FRANÇAIS
AFRIQUE
EQUATORIALE
FRANÇAISE
Banga
GABON

FIRST ANNIVERSARY OF INDEPENDENCE 1st OCTOBER 1961
3d
NIGERIA
NIGERIA
POSTAGE & REVENUE
1s
REICHSPOST
Kamerun
25 PF.
A
B
C

A Nigeria:Crown Colony 1914; **B** Nigeria: Independent 1960; **C** German Cameroons 1897.

FIRST STAMPS ISSUED 1 June 1914

On 1 January 1914 all the Nigerian territories came under one administration (British Crown Colony and protectorate). The federation became independent within the Commonwealth 1 October 1960. Northern Cameroons were joined to it in 1961 and a republic was declared on 1 October 1963. After two military coups in 1966, the eastern states seceded as the Republic of Biafra (*see below*). The rebellion collapsed in 1970, but further military coups took place in 1975.

• Biafra

The eastern region of Nigeria waged a fruitless civil war against the Federal Republic from 1967 to 15 January 1970.

FIRST STAMPS 5 February 1968

CURRENCY

British

Biafran stamps were used mainly on internal mail, but latterly on external mail sent by air via Libreville.

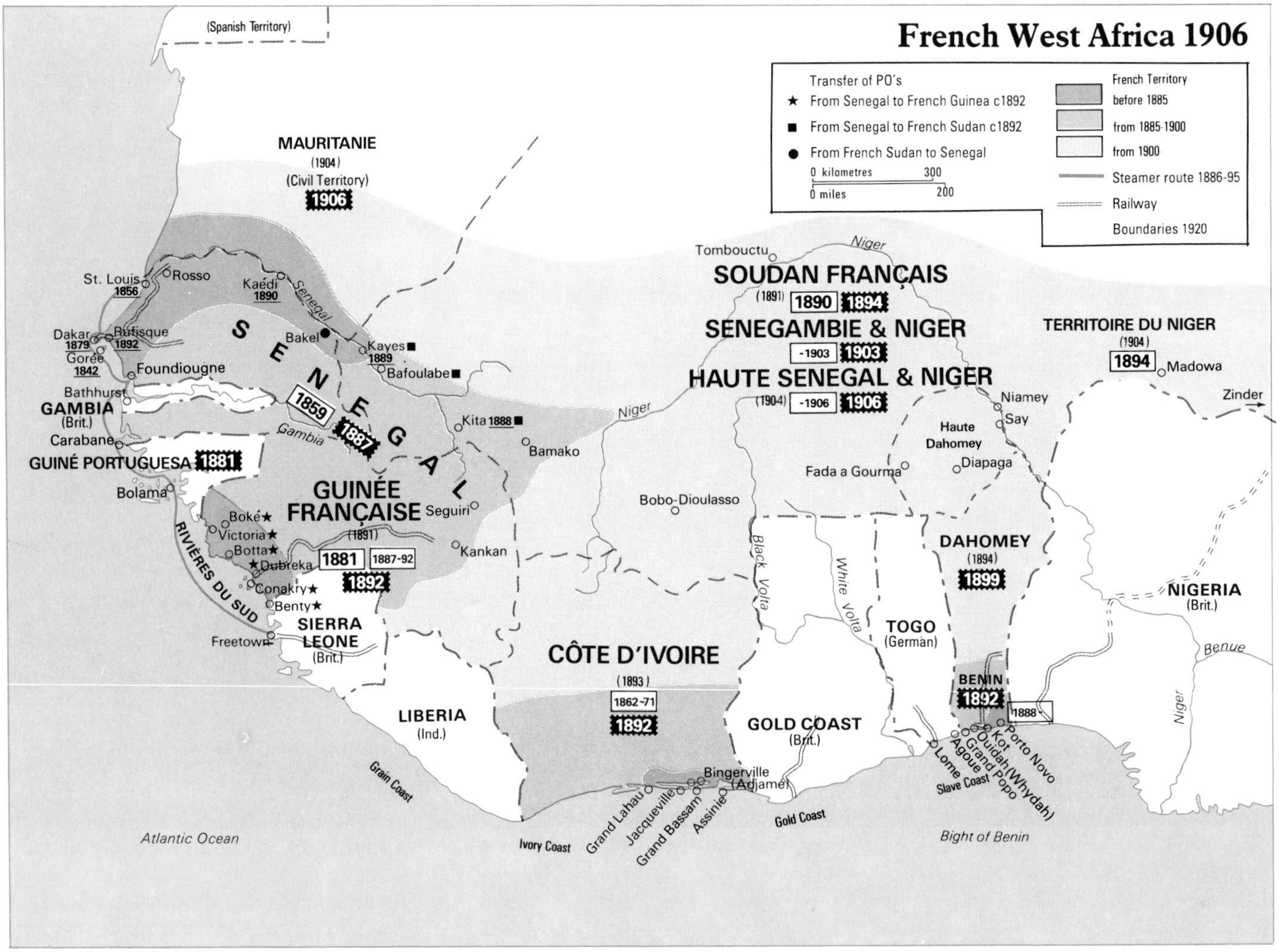
French West Africa 1906
Transfer of PO's
★ From Senegal to French Guinea c1892
■ From Senegal to French Sudan c1892
● From French Sudan to Senegal
0 kilometres 300
0 miles 200
French Territory before 1885
from 1885-1900
from 1900
Steamer route 1886-95
Railway
Boundaries 1920
(Spanish Territory)
MAURITANIE
(1904)
(Civil Territory)
1906
St. Louis
1856
Rosso
Kaédi
1890
Senegal
Dakar
1879
Rufisque
1892
Gorée
1842
Foundiougne
Bakel
Kayes
1889
Bafoulabe
SENEGAL
1859
1887
Bathhurst
GAMBIA
(Brit.)
Gambia
Carabane
GUINÉ PORTUGUESA 1881
Bolama
Kita 1888
Bamako
Niger
GUINÉE FRANÇAISE
(1891)
Seguiri
Boké
Victoria
Botta
Dubreka
1881
1887-92
1892
Kankan
Conakry
Benty
RIVIÈRES DU SUD
SIERRA LEONE
(Brit.)
Freetown
LIBERIA
(Ind.)
Grain Coast
Atlantic Ocean
Tombouctu
Niger
SOUDAN FRANÇAIS
(1891) 1890 1894
SENEGAMBIE & NIGER
-1903 1903
HAUTE SENEGAL & NIGER
(1904) -1906 1906
Bobo-Dioulasso
Fada a Gourma
Diapaga
Haute Dahomey
Niamey
Say
TERRITOIRE DU NIGER
(1904)
1894
Madowa
Zinder
Black Volta
White Volta
CÔTE D'IVOIRE
(1893)
1862-71
1892
GOLD COAST
(Brit.)
TOGO
(German)
DAHOMEY
(1894)
1899
BENIN
1892
1888
NIGERIA
(Brit.)
Benue
Niger
Bingerville
(Adjamé)
Grand Lahau
Jacqueville
Grand Bassam
Assinie
Ivory Coast
Gold Coast
Lome
Agoue
Grand Popo
Ouidah (Whydah)
Kot
Porto Novo
Slave Coast
Bight of Benin

• German Cameroons (Kamerun)

FIRST STAMPS Germany 1887
FIRST STAMPS ISSUED April 1897

CURRENCY
German

The Woermann shipping line set up an African base on the Kamerun River and by 1882 was running a mailboat service (Hamburg-Westafrika). A German protectorate of the coastal area round Duala (1884) was extended to Lake Chad in 1894. Further territory was acquired from France in 1911-12.

Mail from Kamerun before 1887 can be identified by shipping marks, sometimes on stamps of Germany supplied on board or on arrival in Hamburg.

Used stamps of Germany from 1 February 1887.

Six POs were opened before 1897: Kamerun (Duala), Victoria (1888), Bibundi (1891), Gross-Batanga (1893), Kribi (1894) and Rio del Rey (1897).

Allied Occupation
Duala was captured by Allied forces on 27 September 1914, but the campaign did not end until February 1916. (The last German PO to be overrun was at Mora on 18 February 1916). On 4 March 1916 the German colony was divided between Britain and France, an arrangement modified in 1919 when France reclaimed to Gabon and Moyen Congo the areas ceded in 1911-12. Two mandates were granted by the League of Nations based on the *de facto* partition line (*see below under* British Cameroons, Cameroun).

First British Occupation stamps July 1915.

First French Occupation stamps 10 November 1915.

• (British) Cameroons

FIRST STAMPS British Occupation 1915
Nigeria from c.1920

CURRENCY
British

From c.1920 used stamps of Nigeria.

This use can be recognized by cancellations of the following offices (of which those marked* were still open in 1960-1 *see* Southern Cameroons): *Victoria, Bakeba, Bamenda, *Buea, *Kumba, Malla, Maduri, Mnyuka, Ndjan, *Nsau, Nyasoso, Ossindinge, Rio del Rey, *Tiko and Tinto.

After World War II, divided into Northern and Southern Cameroons.

• Southern Cameroons

FIRST STAMPS ISSUED 1 October 1960

CURRENCY
British

These stamps continued until 30 September 1961 when Southern Cameroons joined Cameroun (*see below*) by plebiscite. (They were also valid in Northern Cameroons, which opted to rejoin Nigeria). Their inscription U.K.T.T. stands for United Kingdom Trust Territory.

Cameroun

FIRST STAMPS French Occupation 1915

CURRENCY
1897 As Germany
1915 As France also British Occupation CFA

French mandate and after 1946 trust territory. Became independent republic 1 January 1960. By the plebiscite of 30 September 1961 incorporated Southern Cameroons and took the name of Federal Republic, altered in June 1972 to United Republic.

Stamp issues were continous from 1915 (*see above* German Cameroons: Allied Occupation).

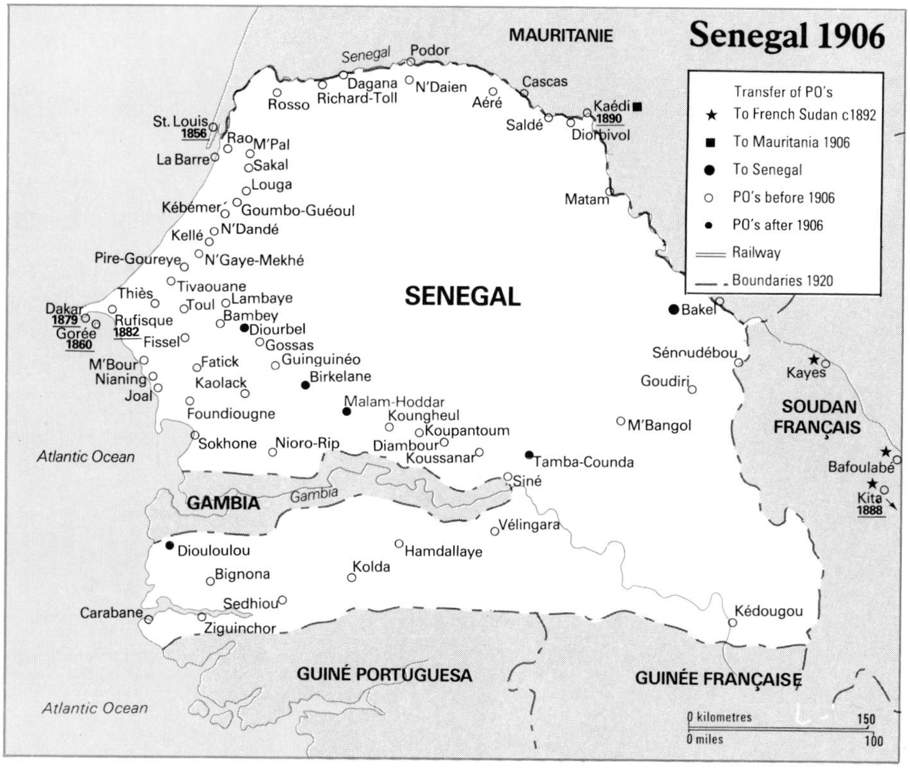

Senegal 1906
MAURITANIE
SENEGAL
GAMBIA
SOUDAN FRANÇAIS
GUINÉ PORTUGUESA
GUINÉE FRANÇAISE
Atlantic Ocean
Atlantic Ocean
Senegal
Gambia
Transfer of PO's
To French Sudan c1892
To Mauritania 1906
To Senegal
PO's before 1906
PO's after 1906
Railway
Boundaries 1920
Podor
Dagana
N'Daien
Rosso
Richard-Toll
Aéré
Cascas
Kaédi
1890
Saldé
Diorbivol
Matam
St. Louis
1856
Rao
M'Pal
La Barre
Sakal
Louga
Kébémer
Goumbo-Guéoul
Kellé
N'Dandé
Pire-Goureye
N'Gaye-Mekhé
Tivaouane
Thiès
Toul
Lambaye
Bambey
Dakar
1879
Gorée
1860
Rufisque
1882
Diourbel
Fissel
Gossas
M'Bour
Fatick
Guinguinéo
Nianing
Kaolack
Birkelane
Joal
Foundiougne
Malam-Hoddar
Koungheul
Koupantoum
Sokhone
Nioro-Rip
Diambour
Koussanar
Tamba-Counda
Siné
Vélingara
Bakel
Sénoudébou
Kayes
Goudiri
M'Bangol
Bafoulabé
Kita
1888
Diouloulou
Hamdallaye
Bignona
Kolda
Sedhiou
Carabane
Ziguinchor
Kédougou
0 kilometres 150
0 miles 100

• French West Africa

FIRST STAMPS ISSUED December 1944

CURRENCY
1944 CFA's

The French West African colonies were grouped together by decree in 1895 and, again, in 1904, under a governor-general at Dakar, but continued to have administrative autonomy, including separate stamps until 1944. These were valid for use in all French West African colonies: Dahomey, French Guinea, French Sudan, Ivory Coast, Mauritania, Niger, Senegal and Upper Volta from December 1944 until 1959-60. The stamps were used until each colony was independent or had issued its own stamps. The last issue (21 March 1959) was inscribed DAKAR-ABIDJAN and was used in Ivory Coast and Senegal only.

Senegal

FIRST STAMPS French Colonies General Issues from 1859 distinguished by a lozenge of dots with GOR or SEN
FIRST STAMPS ISSUED 1887

CURRENCY
1887 As France CFA

Traders from Dieppe had trading posts from 1826, but the earliest

French settlement, at St Louis, dated from 1659. In the 18th century the Senegal settlements were disputed between France and Britain, but were restored to France in 1817; Gorée Island had remained French throughout. In 1854 penetration inland began and by 1891 Senegal was exercising control over a large area of West Africa from St Louis or Dakar.

The Vichy régime survived an abortive Allied attempt to take Dakar (23-25 September 1940) until November 1942 when it became Free French. On 25 November 1958 Senegal accepted independence within the French Community, but joined with French Sudan on 4 April 1959 to form the Mali Federation. Senegal withdrew from this federation on 22 August 1960 and on 5 September became a republic within the French Community.

In 1842 Gorée was given the first postal service in French West Africa; it was not an integral part of Senegal until 1859. The first mainland PO was at St Louis (c.1856). By 1915, there were 55 POs in operation.

Senegal issues were also used in the region known as Rivières du Sud (after 1892, part of French Guinea) where known POs include Conakry, Benty, Boffa, Boké, Dubreka and Victoria; also at Kaédi and Rosso (after 1906 part of Mauritania), and at Kita and Kayes (later in French Sudan). Used stamps of French West Africa from 1944-59.

Mauritania

CURRENCY	
1906	As France
1973	100 cents = 1 ouguiya (um)

FIRST STAMPS Stamps of Senegal at Kaédi and Rosso only
FIRST STAMPS ISSUED 1906
FIRST STAMPS after Independence 20 January 1960

French influence spread north from Senegal and on 18 October 1904 Mauritania became a 'civil territory' dependency of French West Africa. Borders were pushed north in 1908-9, and colonial status was given on 1 January 1921. Administratively, Mauritania shared the same capital, St Louis, with Senegal. After two years of autonomy within the French Community, Mauritania became an independent Islamic republic on 28 November 1960. In 1976 it annexed the southern part of the former Spanish Sahara.

Before 1906 the only POs were at Kaédi and Rosso (closed before 1915),

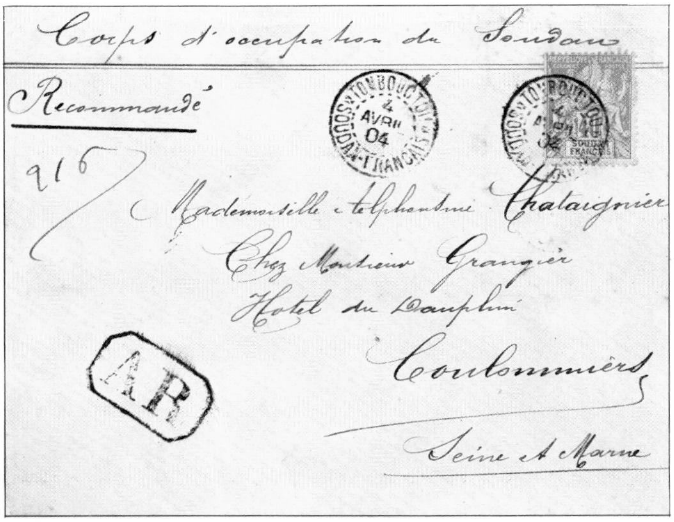
Corps d'occupation du Soudan
Recommandé
TOMBOUCTOU
SOUDAN FRANCAIS
4 AVRIL 04
AR
Coulommiers
Seine et Marne

Letter with stamp and postmark from Tombouctou, French Sudan, 1904

38. - Section de Mitrailleuses du 4e Sénégalais
Collection Barthès et Lesleur

French colonial troops in French Sudan c. 1904

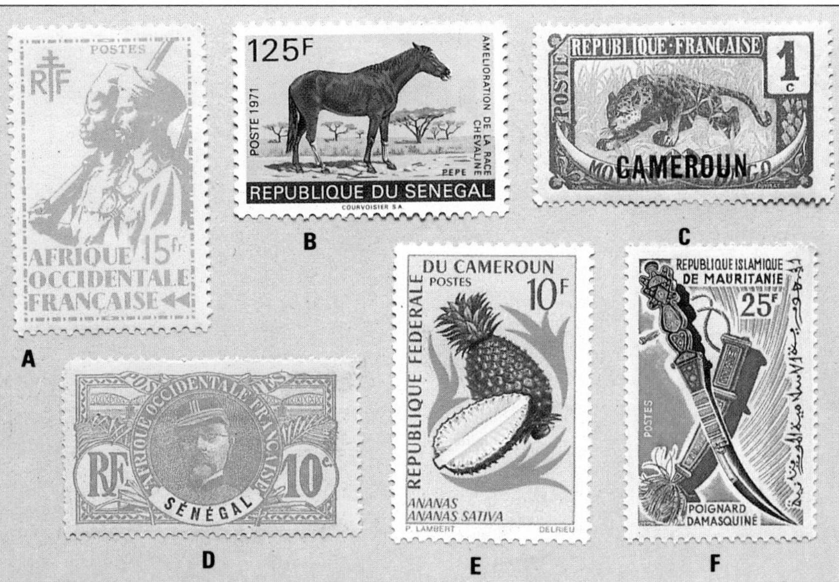
POSTES
RF
AFRIQUE OCCIDENTALE FRANÇAISE
15fr.
125F
POSTE 1971
AMELIORATION DE LA RACE CHEVALINE
PEPE
REPUBLIQUE DU SENEGAL
REPUBLIQUE FRANÇAISE
POSTE
1 c
CAMEROUN
RF
AFRIQUE OCCIDENTALE FRANÇAISE
SÉNÉGAL
10c
DU CAMEROUN
POSTES
10F
REPUBLIQUE FEDERALE
ANANAS
ANANAS SATIVA
REPUBLIQUE ISLAMIQUE DE MAURITANIE
25F
POSTES
POIGNARD DAMASQUINÉ

A French West Africa 1945; B Senegal:Independent 1971; C Cameroons:French Occupation 1921; D Senegal:French Colony 1906; E Cameroons:Federal Republic 1967; F Mauritania:Islamic Republic 1965.

4c
HAUT-SENEGAL NIGER
AFRIQUE OCCIDENTALE FRANÇAISE
FEDERATION DU MALI
POSTES
25F
COMMISSION DE COOPERATION TECHNIQUE EN AFRIQUE AU SUD DU SAHARA
Xme ANNIVERSAIRE

REPUBLIQUE DU MALI
POSTES
85F
CENTENAIRE DE LA CROIX ROUGE

A Upper Senegal and Niger 1914; B Federation of Mali 1960; C Republic of Mali 1963.

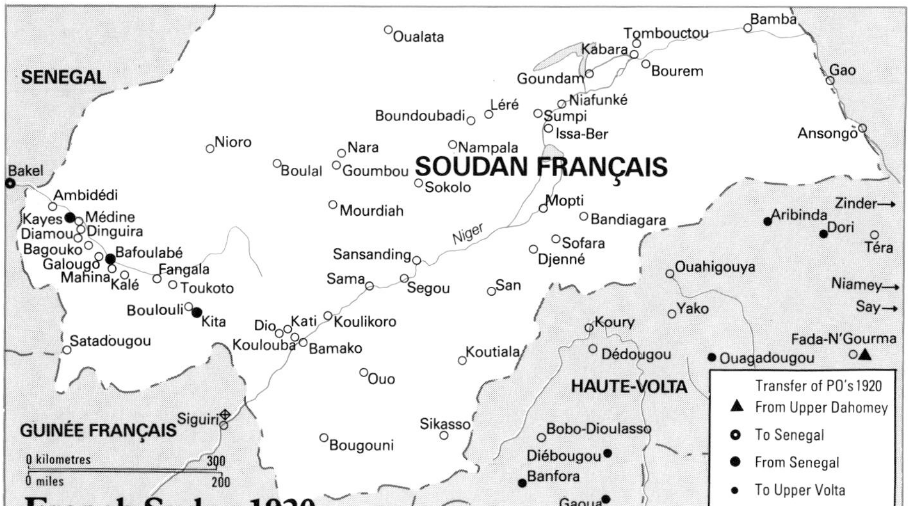
SENEGAL
SOUDAN FRANÇAIS
HAUTE-VOLTA
GUINÉE FRANÇAIS
CÔTE D'IVOIRE
Oualata
Tombouctou
Bamba
Kabara
Bourem
Gao
Goundam
Léré
Niafunké
Sumpi
Issa-Ber
Boundoubadi
Ansongo
Nioro
Nara
Nampala
Bakel
Boulal
Goumbou
Sokolo
Ambidédi
Kayes
Médine
Diamou
Dinguira
Mourdiah
Mopti
Bandiagara
Aribinda
Zinder
Dori
Téra
Bagouko
Bafoulabé
Galougo
Mahina
Kalé
Fangala
Toukoto
Sansanding
Niger
Sofara
Djenné
Ouahigouya
Sama
Segou
San
Niamey
Say
Boulouli
Kita
Dio
Kati
Koulikoro
Yako
Koury
Satadougou
Kouloubá
Bamako
Koutiala
Dédougou
Ouagadougou
Fada-N'Gourma
Ouo
Siguiri
Sikasso
Bobo-Dioulasso
Bougouni
Diébougou
Banfora
Gaoua
Boundaries 1920
0 kilometres 300
0 miles 200
Transfer of PO's 1920
From Upper Dahomey
To Senegal
From Senegal
To Upper Volta
To French Guinea

French Sudan 1920

administered from Senegal, whose stamps were used. In 1915 there were 10 POs in the colony.

Vichy stamps of Mauritania have been seen used in Senegal in 1944. Used stamps of French West Africa 1945-59.

• French Sudan (Soudan Français)

CURRENCY	
1894	As France

FIRST STAMPS French Colonies General Issues at Kayes 1890
FIRST STAMPS ISSUED 12 April 1894

French influence brought by explorer Faidherbe from the River Senegal to the Upper Niger was extended by conquest to the area of Tombouctou (1883) and stretched (without boundaries) as far as that influence could be maintained. The region was given the name Soudan Français in 1891 with its capital at Kayes.

It was shrunk in 1899 by transferring 11 of the southern provinces to French Guinea, Ivory Coast and Dahomey (though two provinces were returned in 1900). The remainder was broken up into three military districts based on Tombouctou, Bobo Dioulasso and Zinder (Niger). The other territories became Upper Senegal and Middle Niger.

In 1902 the non-military zone became Senegambia and Niger and in 1904 Upper Senegal and Niger. The capital was moved to Bamako.

In 1911 Niger became the only military district and began to separate from the main colony. It became an independent colony in 1922.

Prior to that, in 1919, the colony of Upper Volta had been created by detaching six of the southern provinces from Upper Senegal and Niger and, in 1920, the remainder returned to the original name of French Sudan. When Upper Volta was abolished in 1933, parts of the original provinces reverted to French Sudan. On 4 April 1954, French Sudan joined Senegal to make the Mali Federation.

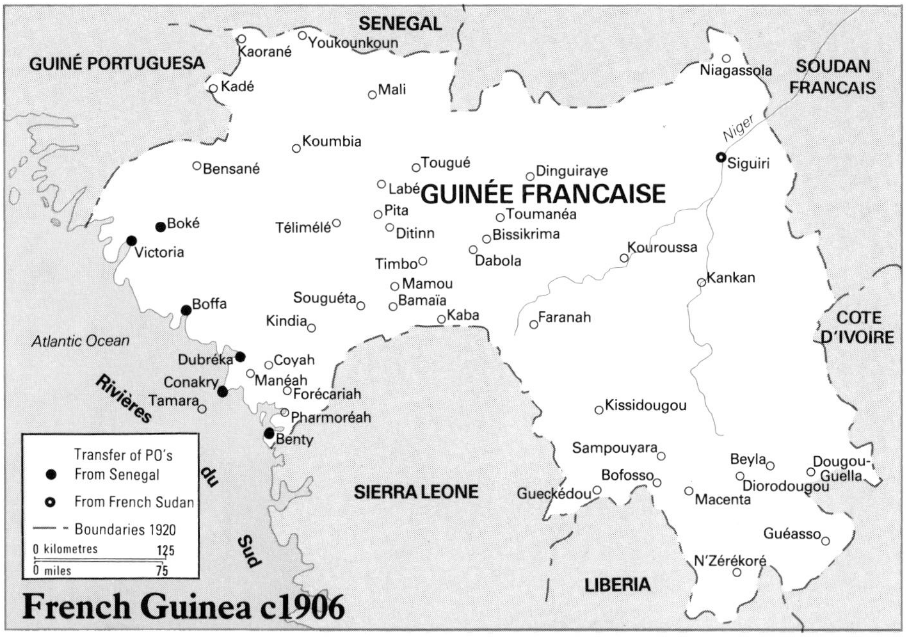
SENEGAL
GUINÉ PORTUGUESA
Kaorané
Youkounkoun
Kadé
Mali
Niagassola
SOUDAN FRANCAIS
Niger
Koumbia
Bensané
Tougué
Dinguiraye
Siguiri
Labé
GUINÉE FRANCAISE
Pita
Toumanéa
Boké
Télimélé
Ditinn
Bissikrima
Victoria
Timbo
Dabola
Kouroussa
Mamou
Kankan
Souguéta
Bamaïa
Boffa
Kindia
Kaba
Faranah
COTE D'IVOIRE
Atlantic Ocean
Dubréka
Coyah
Conakry
Manéah
Forécariah
Tamara
Pharmoréah
Rivières du Sud
Benty
Kissidougou
Transfer of PO's
From Senegal
From French Sudan
Boundaries 1920
0 kilometres 125
0 miles 75
Sampouyara
Beyla
Dougou-Guella
Bofosso
Diorodougou
SIERRA LEONE
Gueckédou
Macenta
Guéasso
N'Zérékoré
LIBERIA
French Guinea c1906

SOUDAN FRANCAIS
Deibougou
Banfora
HAUTE-VOLTA (1919)
Diefoula
Batie
Odienné
Tombougou 1905
Koroko 1905
Black Volta
Boundiali
Bouna
GUINEE FRANCAISE
Kong
Niangbo
Touba
Dabakala
Mankono
Katiola
Groumania
Séguéla
Bondoukou 1900
Man
Bouaké 1904
CÔTE D'IVOIRE
Logoualé
Kodiokofi 1904
Daloa
Assikasso 1900
Bouaflé
GOLD COAST
Dimbokro
Abehgourou
Sinfra
Toumodi 1904
Bongouanou
Issia
Ouessou 1904
Zaranou 1900
Adzope
Singorobo 1904
Bettié 1899
Agboville
Soubré
Tiassalé 1903
Ery-Makouguié 1905
LIBERIA
Divo
Azaguié
Alépé 1894
Aboisso 1904
Dabou 1903
Abidjan 1904
Bingerville 1901
Toupa
1890
Grand-Bassam 1890
Fresco
Jacqueville
Drewin 1906
1895 Grand Lahou
Assinie 1890
Sassandra 1901
Bérébi 1896
San Pedro 1847
PO's after 1906
Boundaries 1920
0 kilometres 80
0 miles 50
Cap Palmas
Tabou
Bliéron
Gulf of Guinea
Ivory Coast c1906

Upper Senegal and Middle Niger did not issue stamps. Stamps of French Sudan were used until 1903 when they were replaced by the stamps of Senegambia and Niger (q.v.).

In 1920 stamps of Upper Senegal and Niger (q.v.) were overprinted for use in French Sudan when it was reconstituted.

Used stamps of French West Africa 1944-59. Then became part of the Mali Federation.

• Senegambia and Niger

FIRST STAMPS French Sudan to 1903
FIRST STAMPS ISSUED July 1903
(inscribed SENEGAMBIE ET NIGER)

Postmarks of the colony were also altered in 1903 to read 'Senegambie et Niger'.

CURRENCY

1903 As France

• Upper Senegal and Niger

FIRST STAMPS French Sudan to 1903
FIRST STAMPS ISSUED 1906 (inscribed HAUT SENEGAL ET NIGER)

CURRENCY

1906 As France

Colony of French West Africa established in 1904 to replace Senegambia and Niger (q.v.). It absorbed the military districts except Niger, which became a separate military district in 1911 and independent in 1922.

Postmarks of the colony were worded 'Ht Senegal et Niger'; in Niger itself they were amended to read 'Territoire Militaire du Niger'. In 1915 there were 72 POs in the colony and 11 in the military territory of Niger. Stamps were overprinted for French Sudan when the name was changed again in 1920.

• Mali Federation (Fédération du Mali)

FIRST STAMPS ISSUED 7 November 1959

CURRENCY	
1959	CFA

Short-lived federation of French Sudan and Senegal from 4 April 1959, independent within the French Community from 20 June 1960 until 20 August 1960 when Senegal seceded.

Mali Republic (République du Mali)

FIRST STAMPS ISSUED September 1960

CURRENCY	
1959	CFA
later francs Maliennes	

After Senegal seceded from the Mali Federation (q.v.), the former French Sudan declared complete independence as the Mali Republic, September 1960.

• French Guinea

FIRST STAMPS French Colonies General Issues from 1881
FIRST STAMPS ISSUED November 1892

CURRENCY	
1892	As France

Local protectorates established between 1848 and 1865; extended in 1889 as Établissements des Rivières du Sud. Administered from Senegal but, after the fixing of boundaries, French Guinea became a separate colony on 17 December 1891. In 1899 it was extended inland by the transfer of a number of provinces from French Sudan. It was under Vichy until November 1942, then Free French.

By referendum, it was declared a republic under the name Republic of Guinea outside the French Community on 2 October 1958.

Initially used the French Colonies General Issues, which can be recognized by postmarks. Stamps of Senegal were used 1887-92 before the colonial standard issue in November 1892.

In 1915 there were 35 POs in the colony. Used stamps of French West Africa 1944-59.

Republic of Guinea

FIRST STAMPS ISSUED 5 January 1959

CURRENCY	
1959	As France
1973	100 cawry = 1 syli

Independent republic based on the colony of French Guinea. By referendum, elected to leave the French Community in October 1958.

Ivory Coast (Côte d'Ivoire)

FIRST STAMPS French Colonies General Issues at Assinie in 1862-71 (distinguishable by ASI in a lozenge of dots)
FIRST STAMPS ISSUED November 1892
As an autonomous republic 1 October 1959

CURRENCY	
1892	As France
	CFA

French trading posts were established briefly in 1700-7 and again from 1842. They were abandoned from 1871 to 1878 but reclaimed as Établissements de la Côte d'Or. After expeditions into the interior, a French colony was declared on 10 March 1893. About 1900 the capital was moved from Grand-Bassam to Bingerville (formerly Adjamé) after a severe outbreak of yellow fever. In 1934 the capital was again transferred, this time to Abidjan, the terminus of the railway.

On 1 January 1933 Upper Volta ceased to exist and six provinces were added to Ivory Coast. They remained part of the colony until Upper Volta was re-created in 1947. Ivory Coast became an autonomous republic within the French Community on 4 December 1958. Became independent on 7 August 1960.

Initially used the French Colonies General Issues at Assinie in 1862-71, and after the return special datestamps were used at Jacqueville, Grand-Bassam, and Assinie from 1889 inscribed 'Cote d'Or d'Afrique' (also, after 1892, at Grand Lahou).

By 1915 there were 38 POs in the colony and this number was increased in 1933 when certain provinces of Upper Volta were added to the colony. Used stamps of French West Africa from 1944-59.

• Benin

FIRST STAMPS French Colonies General Issues at Porto Novo from 1888
FIRST STAMPS ISSUED September 1892

CURRENCY
As France to 1894

Treaty of 1851 gave France possession of Whydah (Ouidah); control was extended to Grand-Popo in 1857, Porto Novo by 1863 and Cotonou by 1883.

Placed first under Gabon, then transferred to Senegal in 1886 under the name of Établissements Français du Golfe de Benin. They were in-

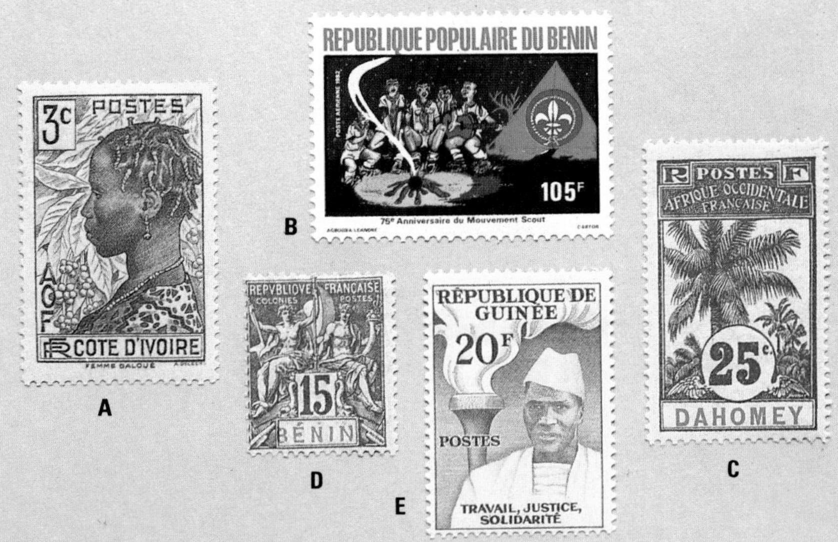
3c POSTES
A O F
COTE D'IVOIRE
REPUBLIQUE POPULAIRE DU BENIN
105F
75e Anniversaire du Mouvement Scout
POSTES
AFRIQUE OCCIDENTALE FRANÇAISE
25c
DAHOMEY
REPUBLIQUE FRANÇAISE
COLONIES POSTES
15
BENIN
RÉPUBLIQUE DE GUINÉE
20F
POSTES
TRAVAIL, JUSTICE, SOLIDARITÉ

A Ivory Coast:French Colony 1940; **B** People's Republic of Benin 1982; **C** Dahomey:French Colony 1906; **D** Benin:French Colony 1894; **E** Republic of Guinea 1959.

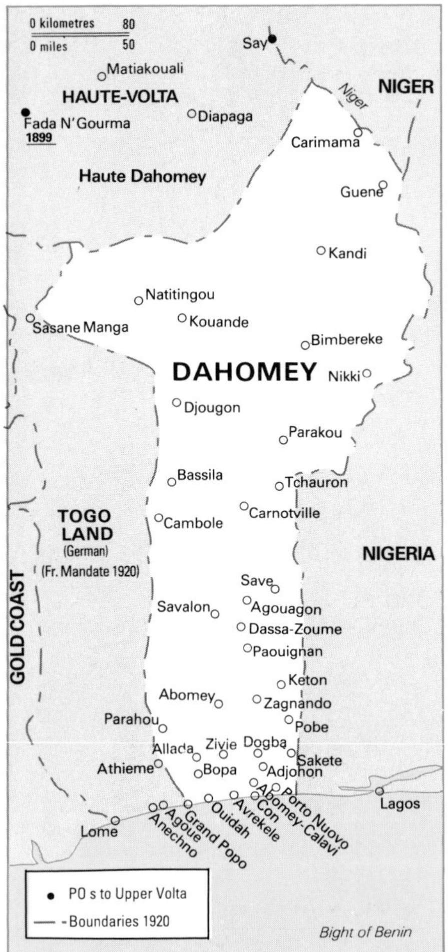
0 kilometres 80
0 miles 50
Say
Matiakouali
HAUTE-VOLTA
Fada N'Gourma
1899
Diapaga
NIGER
Niger
Carimama
Haute Dahomey
Guene
Kandi
Natitingou
Sasane Manga
Kouande
Bimbereke
DAHOMEY
Nikki
Djougon
Parakou
Bassila
Tchauron
TOGO LAND
(German)
(Fr. Mandate 1920)
Cambole
Carnotville
NIGERIA
GOLD COAST
Save
Savalon
Agouagon
Dassa-Zoume
Paouignan
Keton
Abomey
Zagnando
Parahou
Pobe
Allada
Zivie
Dogba
Sakete
Athieme
Bopa
Adjohon
Lagos
Lome
Agoue
Anechno
Grand Popo
Ouidah
Con
Avrekele
Abomey-Calavi
Porto Nuovo
POs to Upper Volta
Boundaries 1920
Bight of Benin

Dahomey pre 1920

corporated into Dahomey (*see below*) in 1899.

Cancellations inscribed BENIN are known from Aquoua, Kotonou (later Cotonou), Grand-Popo, Porto Novo and Whydah.

• Dahomey

FIRST STAMPS ISSUED 1899

CURRENCY

1899 As France CFA

Originally an independent African kingdom inland of the Benin settlements, subdued by the French in 1892-4. Ouidah was formally annexed 3 December 1892 and the rest of Dahomey was made a colony in 1894. In 1899 it absorbed the Établissements Français du Golfe de Benin and two provinces from French Sudan. These last were returned to the new colony of Upper Senegal and Middle Niger in 1900.

Dahomey remained within the French Community after autonomy was granted 4 December 1958, but left it at independence on 1 August 1960. Changed name to the People's Republic of Benin (*see below*) on 30 November 1975.

It is probable that only military offices existed up-country before 1899, but the provinces of French Sudan were issued with postmarks in 1899-1900 worded 'Haut Dahomey', which continued to be used after the provinces were detached. By 1915 there were 30 POs in the colony.

The stamps of French West Africa were used 1944-60. The first stamps issued as an independent republic were in 1960.

People's Republic of Benin

FIRST STAMPS ISSUED 3 April 1976

CURRENCY

1976 As France CFA

Independent republic based on the colony of Dahomey, which changed its name in 1975.

Upper Volta (Haute Volte)

FIRST STAMPS French Sudan from 1894
FIRST STAMPS ISSUED December 1920 (withdrawn 31 December 1932)

CURRENCY

1920 As France CFA

Separate French colony created from the south-eastern part of Upper Senegal and Niger on 1 March 1919. Ceased to exist on 1 January 1933, when its provinces were divided between French Sudan, Ivory Coast and Niger.

Revived in 1947, and on 10 December 1958 became an autonomous republic within the French Community. This it left on 5 August 1960 when it became independent. The name was changed to Burkina Faso in 1984.

Originally used the stamps of French Sudan (1894-1902), Senegambia and Niger (1902-4), Upper Senegal and Niger (1904-20). Postmarks changed on each occasion. When Upper Volta was broken up in 1933, the postmarks for each town were again changed to that of the colony to which they were transferred.

When Upper Volta was revived in 1947, the stamps of French West Africa were used until 1960. The first issue as an autonomous republic was on 11 August 1960. Upper Volta stamps continued to be used after the change of name in 1984 until new stamps were issued.

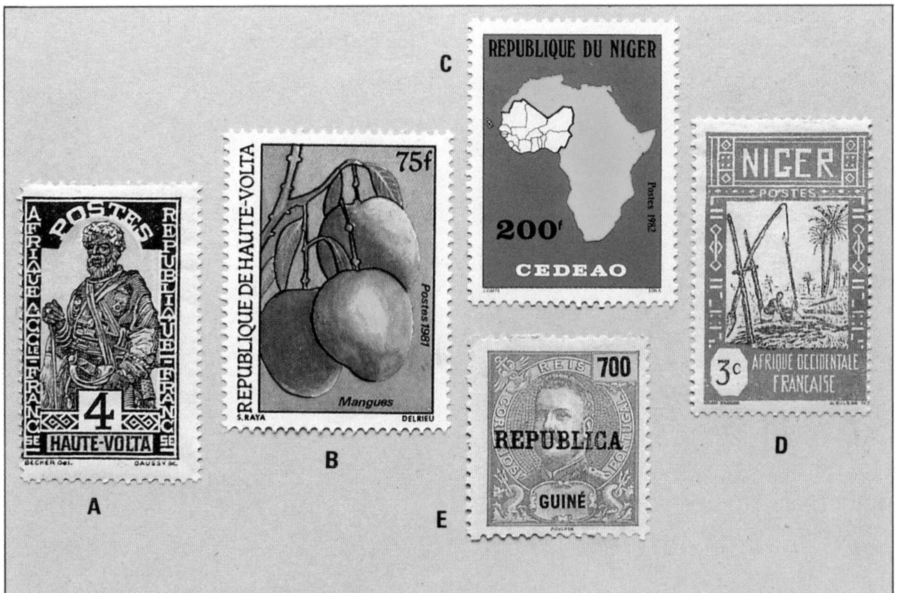
A
POSTES
4
HAUTE-VOLTA
B
REPUBLIQUE DE HAUTE-VOLTA
75f
Postes 1981
Mangues
C
REPUBLIQUE DU NIGER
200f
CEDEAO
Postes 1982
D
NIGER
POSTES
3c
AFRIQUE OCCIDENTALE FRANÇAISE
E
REIS
700
REPUBLICA
GUINÉ

A Upper Volta:French Colony 1928; **B** Upper Volta:Independent 1981; **C** Niger:Independent 1982; **D** Niger:French Colony 1926; **E** Portuguese Guinea:Republic 1911.

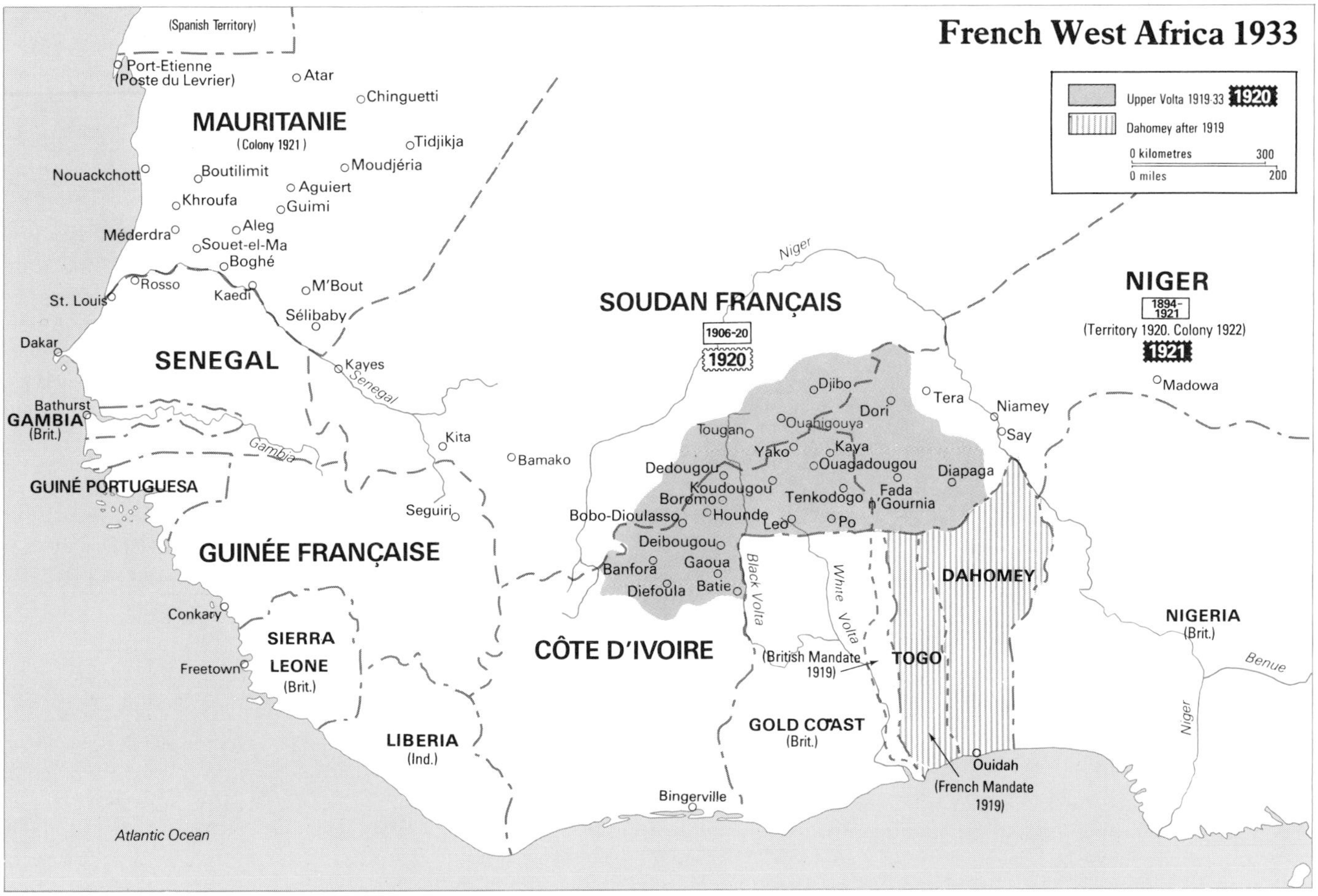
French West Africa 1933
Upper Volta 1919-33 1920
Dahomey after 1919
0 kilometres 300
0 miles 200
(Spanish Territory)
Port-Etienne
(Poste du Levrier)
Atar
Chinguetti
MAURITANIE
(Colony 1921)
Tidjikja
Nouackchott
Boutilimit
Moudjéria
Aguiert
Khroufa
Guimi
Méderdra
Aleg
Souet-el-Ma
Boghé
Rosso
M'Bout
St. Louis
Kaedi
Sélibaby
Dakar
SENEGAL
Kayes
Senegal
Bathurst
GAMBIA
(Brit.)
Gambia
Kita
Bamako
GUINÉ PORTUGUESA
Seguiri
GUINÉE FRANÇAISE
Conkary
SIERRA
LEONE
(Brit.)
Freetown
LIBERIA
(Ind.)
Atlantic Ocean
SOUDAN FRANÇAIS
1906-20
1920
Niger
Djibo
Dori
Tera
Ouahigouya
Tougan
Yako
Kaya
Ouagadougou
Dedougou
Koudougou
Boromo
Bobo-Dioulasso
Hounde
Tenkodogo
Fada N'Gournia
Diapaga
Leo
Po
Deibougou
Banfora
Gaoua
Diefoula
Batie
Black Volta
White Volta
CÔTE D'IVOIRE
(British Mandate 1919)
TOGO
DAHOMEY
GOLD COAST
(Brit.)
Bingerville
Ouidah
(French Mandate 1919)
NIGER
1894-1921
(Territory 1920. Colony 1922)
1921
Madowa
Niamey
Say
NIGERIA
(Brit.)
Benue
Niger

Burkina Faso

FIRST STAMPS see Upper Volta
FIRST STAMPS ISSUED October 1984

CURRENCY

1948 As Upper Volta

Formerly Upper Volta, the name was changed in July 1984. Continued to use the stamps of Upper Volta until new stamps were released in October.

Niger

FIRST STAMPS French Sudan on 3 August 1894
FIRST STAMPS ISSUED December 1921

CURRENCY

1921 As France

A French zone of influence and area of exploration extending east from the River Niger. It became a 'military territory' in 1900, based on Zinder, and part of French West Africa in 1904. It was administered as part of French Sudan and its successors until 1911 when it became the military territory of Niger. On 4 December 1920 became a separate territory, and a colony on 13 October 1922. In 1924 the capital was moved from Zinder to Niamey. Niger became an autonomous republic within the French Community on 18 December 1958 and an independent republic on 3 August 1960. In 1974 following a *coup d'état* a supreme military council was set up under President Kountché.

Used the stamps of French Sudan, Senegambia and Niger and Upper Senegal and Niger from 1894 to 1921. In 1915 there were 11 POs in the military territory.

Used the stamps of French West Africa 1944-59. The first stamps as an autonomous republic were issued in 1959.

• Portuguese Guinea

FIRST STAMPS ISSUED 1881

CURRENCY

1881 As Portugal

Previously a Portuguese dependency of the Cape Verde Islands, it became a separate colony in 1879 and had fixed its boundaries by 1886.

Guinea-Bissau

A revolutionary republic was in being in Portuguese Guinea before independence was recognized on 10 September 1974. The postal situation is now difficult to ascertain.

FIRST STAMPS ISSUED 1974

CURRENCY

1976 100 cents = 1 peso

Cape Verde Islands (Cabo Verde)

FIRST STAMPS ISSUED 1 January 1877

CURRENCY

Portuguese

Ten islands, lying off the western coast of Africa, annexed by Portugal in 1495. A Portuguese overseas province from 11 June 1951, whose inhabitants had Portuguese citizenship from 6 September 1961. Became independent on 5 July 1975.

THE SOUTH ATLANTIC

Ascension Island

FIRST STAMPS ISSUED 2 November 1922

CURRENCY

1922 sterling
1971 decimal currency

Previously administered by the British Admiralty as a naval base, the island became a dependency of St Helena in November 1922. At present it is on lease to the USA as a naval base and tracking station.

Postal History
A datestamp was supplied February 1858. Before 1887 the datestamp was usually applied to the cover rather than to the stamp. Regular surface mails were carried by the Union Steamship Co. and its successors from 1863 until 1977. Airmail services since 1972 have been routed to London in sealed bags by US military aircraft to Miami and thence by British Airways (earlier services were flown via Trinidad in 1958-60 or via Antigua in 1967-72).

Used stamps of Britain from 3 March 1867 to 1922.

The Island was an important staging point for the British Task Force in 1982.

St Helena

FIRST STAMPS ISSUED January 1856

CURRENCY

British

British Crown Colony with a population of c.5000. Revictualling station of the East India Company from 1673, the island was administered militarily during the exile of Napoleon (1815-21). Surrendered to the British Crown in 1834. Its importance declined with the opening of the Suez Canal. It housed Boer prisoners-of-war from 1900-2.

Postal History
Letters exchanged by ships before 1815 are known but rare. Early connections were generally via Cape Town; in late-Victorian days the mail to England by Union or Castle packet averaged 18-20 days. A 'Packet Letter' handstamp is known from 1816. The first datestamp was supplied in 1858. There was only one PO and no inland service before 1880.

Stamps used before 1912 are often found with fancy cancellations made locally from corks, and are seldom struck by datestamp before the 1880s.

Tristan da Cunha

FIRST STAMPS Britain from c.1918
FIRST STAMPS ISSUED 1 January 1952

CURRENCY
British
(Except for issue of 15 April 1961 in South African cents and rand; demonetized on evacuation)

Volcanic island group named after the Portuguese discoverer Tristão D'Acunha, colonized c.1817 from St Helena of which it is a dependency. Known as HMS *Atlantic Isle* in 1942-5. Evacuated from 10 October 1961 until April 1963 following a violent eruption.

Early mail (known from 1881) was sent unstamped by casual ship through a variety of ports of call (after 1935 mostly via South Africa) and charged on arrival.

Used stamps of Britain (when available) from c.1918. Cachet of origin (occasionally used to cancel stamps) from c.1918.

THE INDIAN OCEAN

The Indian Ocean has borne mail services since the earliest European settlements were made in India, so that here — as in the Atlantic — packet services were well established long before stamps were issued. British sailing packets served India, Ceylon and Australia; French packets Mauritius; Dutch sailing ships served the Indies. After the change to steam, mails were generally routed via Suez, though even after the opening of the Suez Canal (1869) important mail routes via the Cape served Durban, Mozambique

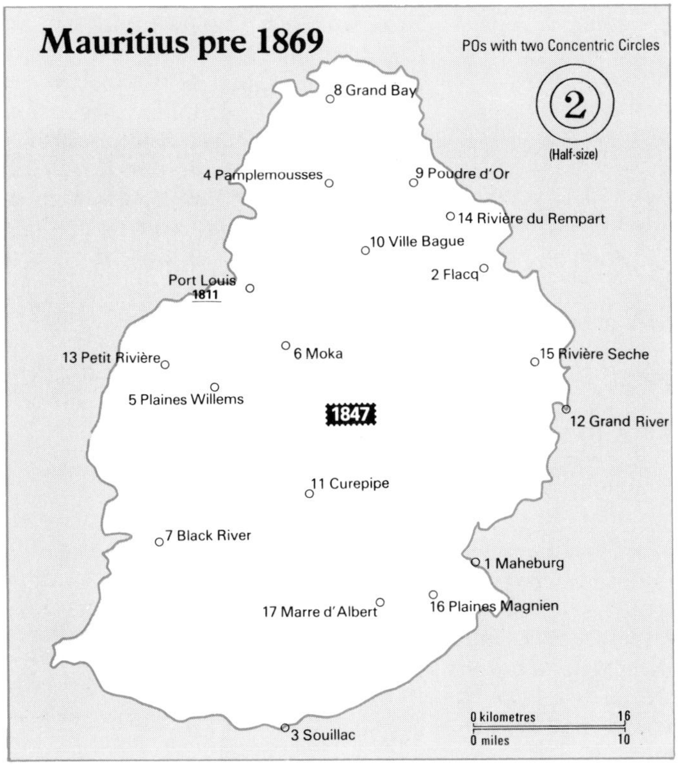
Mauritius pre 1869
POs with two Concentric Circles
2
(Half-size)
8 Grand Bay
4 Pamplemousses
9 Poudre d'Or
14 Rivière du Rempart
10 Ville Bague
2 Flacq
Port Louis
1811
13 Petit Rivière
6 Moka
15 Rivière Seche
5 Plaines Willems
1847
12 Grand River
11 Curepipe
7 Black River
1 Maheburg
17 Marre d'Albert
16 Plaines Magnien
3 Souillac
0 kilometres 16
0 miles 10

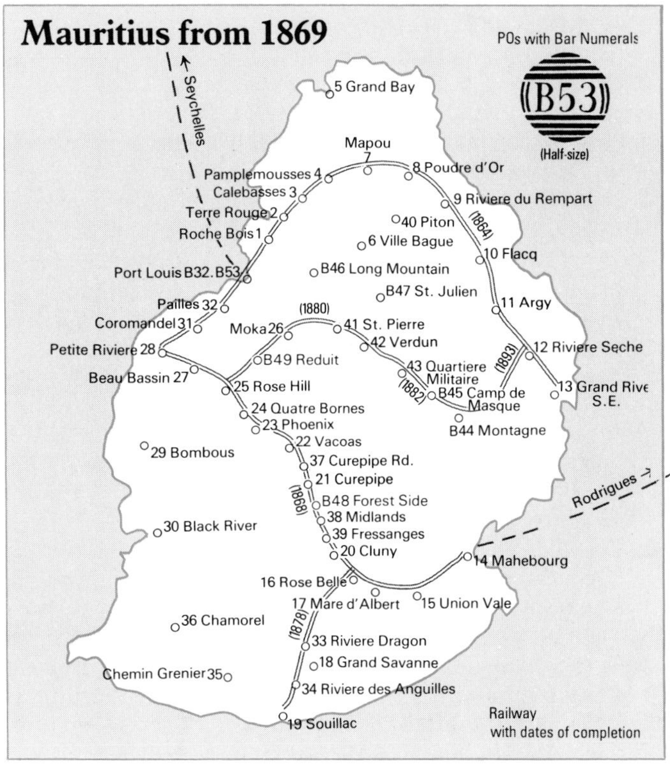
Mauritius from 1869
POs with Bar Numerals
B53
(Half-size)
Seychelles
5 Grand Bay
Mapou
7
Pamplemousses 4
8 Poudre d'Or
Calebasses 3
9 Riviere du Rempart
Terre Rouge 2
40 Piton
(1864)
Roche Bois 1
6 Ville Bague
10 Flacq
Port Louis B32. B53
B46 Long Mountain
B47 St. Julien
Pailles 32
(1880)
11 Argy
Coromandel 31
Moka 26
41 St. Pierre
42 Verdun
12 Riviere Seche
Petite Riviere 28
B49 Reduit
(1893)
43 Quartiere Militaire
13 Grand River S.E.
Beau Bassin 27
25 Rose Hill
(1882)
B45 Camp de Masque
24 Quatre Bornes
23 Phoenix
B44 Montagne
22 Vacoas
29 Bombous
37 Curepipe Rd.
21 Curepipe
(1868)
B48 Forest Side
Rodrigues
38 Midlands
30 Black River
39 Fressanges
20 Cluny
14 Mahebourg
16 Rose Belle
17 Mare d'Albert
15 Union Vale
36 Chamorel
(1878)
33 Riviere Dragon
18 Grand Savanne
Chemin Grenier 35
34 Riviere des Anguilles
19 Souillac
Railway
with dates of completion

A
B
C
D
E
F
G
ASCENSION
POSTAGE & REVENUE
CABO VERDE
VILA DA RIBEIRA GRANDE
$10
CORREIO
SIX PENCE
Bicentenary of the Death of Philibert Commerson 1973
Mauritius Rs2^50
TRISTAN DA CUNHA RESETTLEMENT 1963
6d
ST HELENA
ST HELENA
POSTAGE
SIX PENCE
ST HELENA
TRISTAN DA CUNHA
3d
THE COLONY'S BADGE

A Ascension Island 1934; **B** Cape Verde:Portuguese Colony 1948; **C** Mauritius:Crown Colony 1852; **D** Mauritius:Self-Government 1973; **E** St Helena 1963; **F** St Helena 1856; **G** Tristan da Cunha 1952.

and Zanzibar. The Germans operated a round-Africa service. The French routes via Suez served Madagascar and Réunion, Indo-China and New Caledonia; the British, India, Malaya and Hong Kong; the Germans, their Far Eastern and Oceanic possessions; Austrian-Lloyd ships carried mails to East Africa for a time. The most important exchange points were Aden, Zanzibar, Durban, Bombay, Calcutta and Singapore.

Mauritius

FIRST STAMPS ISSUED 21 September 1847

CURRENCY

1847 sterling
1878 100 cents = 1 shilling

Visited in turn by Arabs, Malays, and in the 16th century Portuguese, Mauritius was settled in the 17th century by the Dutch, who gave it its name. The French (1721) changed the name to Isle de France. The island fell to British arms in 1810 and was ceded to Britain in 1814, becoming Mauritius again. It was a Crown Colony until 1967, when it was given self-government, and on 12 March 1968 became independent within the Commonwealth.

Postal History
Letters are recorded from 1609; the contents of one are known, but the earliest surviving letters to and from Mauritius are dated 1638. After 1721 mails were carried by vessels of the French East India Company. In 1772 a government PO was placed at Port Louis. The government printer instituted an inland post linked to transmission by private ships. In 1783-8 a quarterly royal packet operated between Mauritius and (alternately) Bordeaux or Le Havre: from this period dates the first handstruck postal marking.

The first English PO was established at Port Louis in 1811, also with handstruck markings, but a stagecoach mail for internal distribution began only in 1834. In July 1847 PAs were opened in eleven districts. In June 1848 fast schooners were operated from Mauritius to take the mails via Ceylon. During the next decade mail was carried on various short-lived P&O Steamship Co. schedules via the Cape, Ceylon, or Aden, but only the arrival in 1864 of the packet-boats of Messageries Impériales brought a regular service to Europe via Aden. The same year saw the start of the railway network which served the island until World War II. POs were then relocated at or near railway stations and the 1869 series of numeral cancellations in oval of bars follows an order based on the railways (*see* right-hand map *p.323*). The previous series of numerals in two concentric circles (incorrectly recorded in the Robson Lowe *Encyclopaedia*) are located on left-hand map *p.323*. Mauritius joined the UPU in 1877.

Mauritius worked a sea-link to connect with the African airmail (via Mombasa-Nairobi) from 1933; the first (military) air service by landplane from Plaisance airfield was inaugurated in December 1943; and the first direct civil airmail (Air France) started between Mauritius and Nairobi in 1946.

First stamps were the famous 1*d* and 2*d* inscribed POST OFFICE, the design based on the 'penny black' of Britain, engraved by J. O. Barnard locally. The stamps remained undiscovered for years and the only specimens known on cover were found in 1897 in an Indian bazaar. The romance that surrounded them has perpetuated collectors' interest in the early and middle issues.

The island dependency of Rodriguez has had a branch PO since 1861, using stamps of Mauritius: these can be identified by cancellation B65 or, later, named datestamp.

Seychelles

FIRST STAMPS Mauritius 1861
FIRST STAMPS ISSUED 5 April 1890

CURRENCY

1890 100 cents = 1 rupee

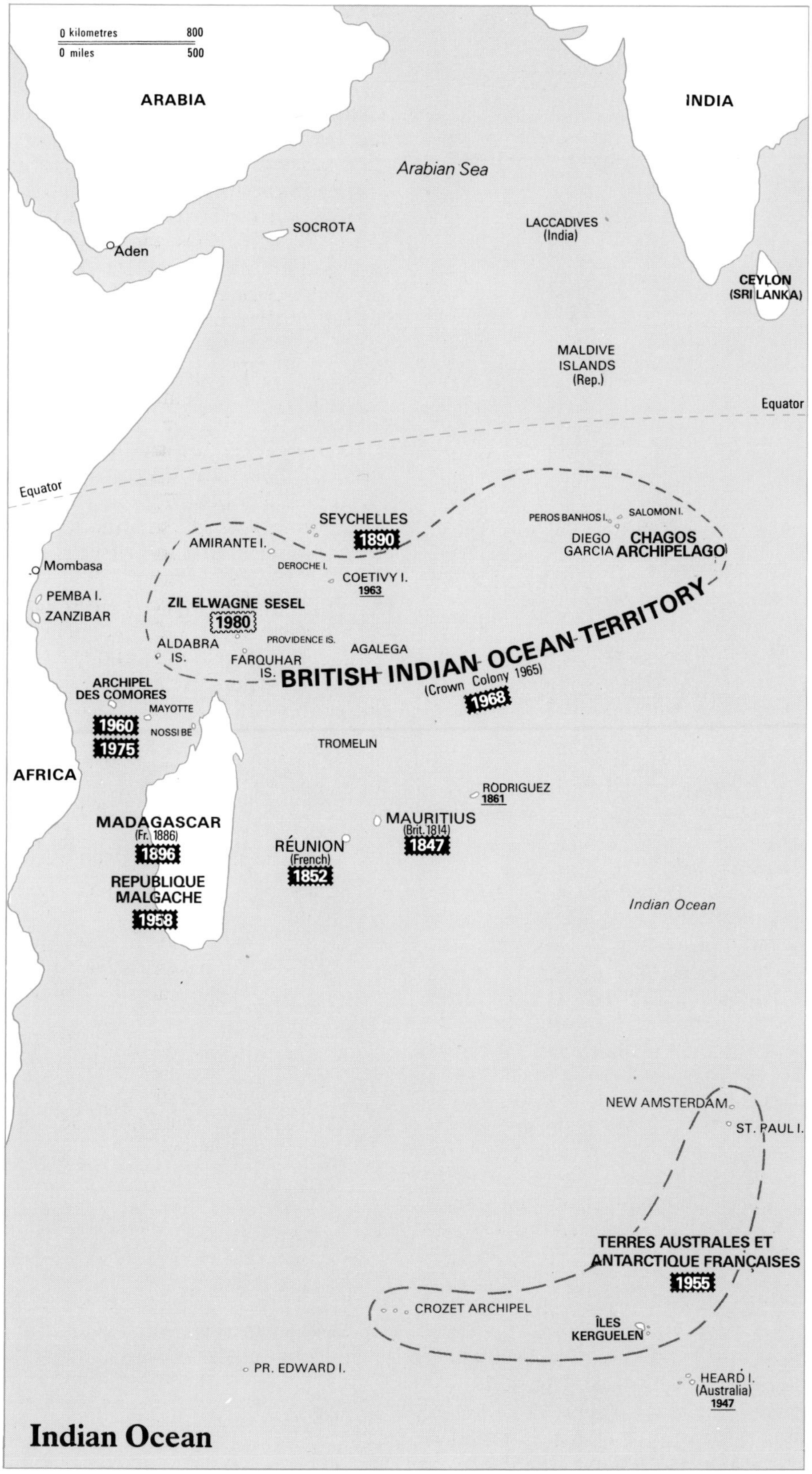
Indian Ocean
0 kilometres 800
0 miles 500
ARABIA
INDIA
Arabian Sea
Aden
SOCROTA
LACCADIVES
(India)
CEYLON
(SRI LANKA)
MALDIVE
ISLANDS
(Rep.)
Equator
SEYCHELLES
1890
AMIRANTE I.
DEROCHE I.
COETIVY I.
1963
PEROS BANHOS I.
SALOMON I.
DIEGO
GARCIA
CHAGOS
ARCHIPELAGO
Mombasa
PEMBA I.
ZANZIBAR
ZIL ELWAGNE SESEL
1980
ALDABRA
IS.
PROVIDENCE IS.
AGALEGA
FARQUHAR
IS.
BRITISH INDIAN OCEAN TERRITORY
(Crown Colony 1965)
1968
ARCHIPEL
DES COMORES
MAYOTTE
1960
1975
NOSSI BE
TROMELIN
AFRICA
RODRIGUEZ
1861
MAURITIUS
(Brit. 1814)
1847
MADAGASCAR
(Fr. 1886)
1896
RÉUNION
(French)
1852
REPUBLIQUE
MALGACHE
1958
Indian Ocean
NEW AMSTERDAM
ST. PAUL I.
TERRES AUSTRALES ET
ANTARCTIQUE FRANÇAISES
1955
CROZET ARCHIPEL
ÎLES
KERGUELEN
PR. EDWARD I.
HEARD I.
(Australia)
1947

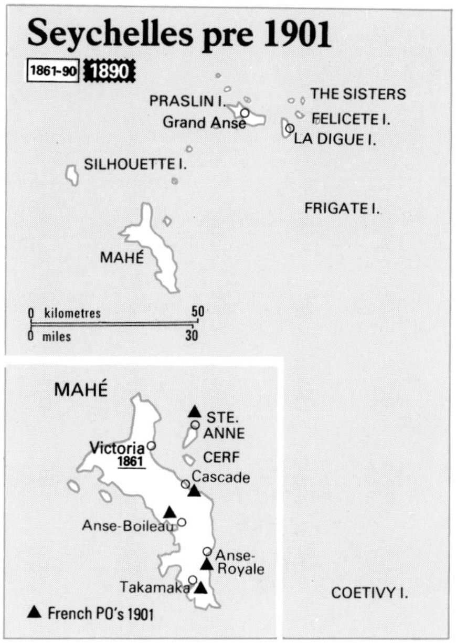
Seychelles pre 1901
1861-90
1890
PRASLIN I.
Grand Anse
THE SISTERS
FELICETE I.
LA DIGUE I.
SILHOUETTE I.
FRIGATE I.
MAHÉ
0 kilometres 50
0 miles 30
MAHÉ
STE.
ANNE
Victoria
1861
CERF
Cascade
Anse-Boileau
Anse-
Royale
Takamaka
French PO's 1901
COETIVY I.

Group of islands known to the Portuguese, explored by the French 1742-4, annexed by them in 1756, and settled (after an abortive attempt in 1768) in 1770. After changing hands in the Napoleonic Wars, they were administered from 1811 by Britain as a dependency of Mauritius. The islands, after intermediate stages, became a Crown Colony on 31 August 1903. Seychelles became independent on 29 June 1976.

Before 1861, mail was forwarded by a mail agent and bore no postal markings. The first PO opened at Victoria in 1861.

Seychelles was served by Ligne T packet-boats of Messageries Maritimes in 1864-95. Eight sub-POs were opened in 1901: on Mahé, Anse-Royale, Cascade (closed after 1916), Takamaka (closed c. 1907), Anse-Boileau (closed c. 1907), and Bel-Ombre (canceller supplied; not known in use); also Praslin Bay St Anne, Praslin Grand Anse, and La Digue. Later offices include La Misère (1968); Silhouette I. (1902-04; 1961); and Coetivy I. (1963).

Used stamps of Mauritius 1861-90. These can be recognized by oblit. B64 or Seychelles datestamp.

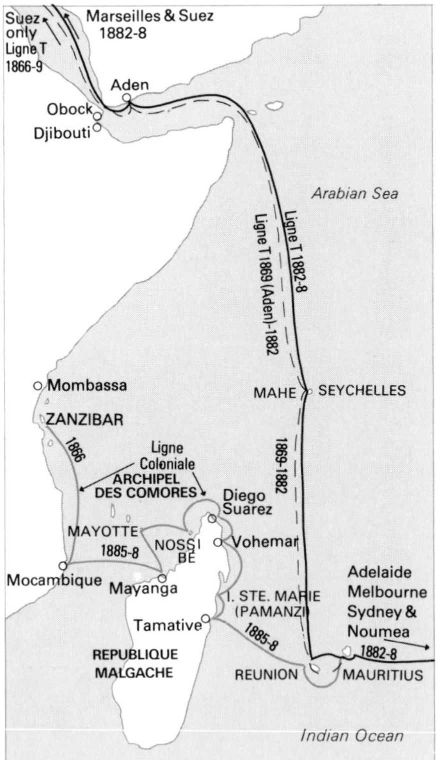
Suez only Ligne T 1866-9
Marseilles & Suez 1882-8
Aden
Obock
Djibouti
Arabian Sea
Ligne T 1882-8
Ligne T 1869 (Aden)-1882
Mombassa
ZANZIBAR
MAHE
SEYCHELLES
1866
Ligne Coloniale
ARCHIPEL DES COMORES
1869-1882
Diego Suarez
MAYOTTE
1885-8
NOSSI BE
Vohemar
Mocambique
Mayanga
I. STE. MARIE (PAMANZI)
Adelaide
Melbourne
Sydney &
Noumea
Tamative
1885-8
1882-8
REPUBLIQUE MALGACHE
REUNION
MAURITIUS
Indian Ocean

French Steamers to 1888

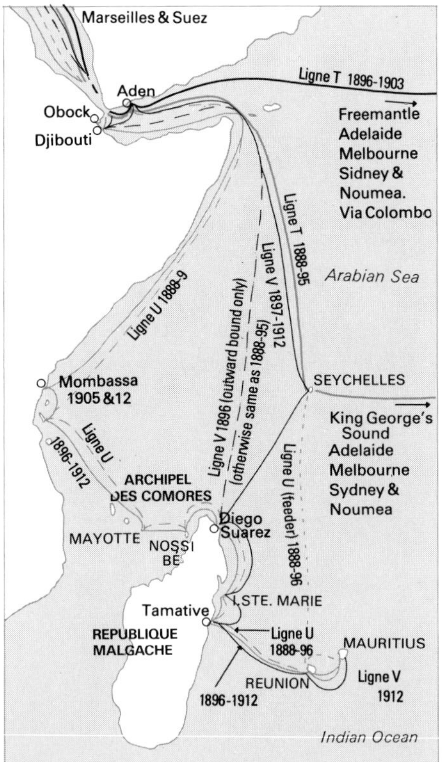
Marseilles & Suez
Ligne T 1896-1903
Aden
Obock
Djibouti
Freemantle
Adelaide
Melbourne
Sidney &
Noumea.
Via Colombo
Ligne T 1888-95
Arabian Sea
Ligne V 1897-1912
Ligne U 1888-9
Ligne V 1896 (outward bound only)
(otherwise same as 1888-95)
Mombassa 1905 & 12
SEYCHELLES
King George's Sound
Adelaide
Melbourne
Sydney &
Noumea
Ligne U
1896-1912
ARCHIPEL DES COMORES
Ligne U (feeder) 1888-96
Diego Suarez
MAYOTTE
NOSSI BE
I. STE. MARIE
Tamative
REPUBLIQUE MALGACHE
Ligne U 1888-96
MAURITIUS
REUNION
Ligne V 1912
1896-1912
Indian Ocean

French Steamers from 1888

British Indian Ocean Territory

For Zil Elwagne Sesel *see* after British Indian Ocean Territory.

> **FIRST STAMPS ISSUED** (locally) 17 January 1968 (released in London 15 January)

CURRENCY

100 cents = 1 rupee

A Crown Colony created on 8 November 1965 from territory previously administered by Mauritius (Chagos Archipelago; principally Diego Garcia) or Seychelles (Aldabra, Farquhar, and Desroches). The Chagos Islands came into prominence in 1942 when they were occupied to forestall the Japanese. Sparsely inhabited and visited from the parent island only two or three times a year, the islands again had strategic value when Aden became independent. In 1973 the civilian population of Diego Garcia was evacuated and the island leased to the USA as a naval air base. The other three groups were returned to Seychelles at its independence in June 1976.

Stamps of Mauritius or Seychelles were in theory valid before 1968 (though no postal facilities seem to have existed). POs opened at Aldabra, Farquhar, Desroches, Diego Garcia, Peros Banhos, and Salomon I.

Since 1969 mails have been carried by m.v. *Nordvaer,* with a TPO.

British Royal Navy personnel at the US base on Diego Garcia had no free privilege; their mail before June 1976 was franked with stamps of BIOT cancelled with the Diego Garcia handstamp. It was initially routed by USAF to Bangkok and thence by air to London; after the closure of US bases in Thailand, mail was routed to Clark AFB, Philippines, thence by air to San Francisco for London. Since 1976 all mail has been wholly military.

Since 1976 stamps of Seychelles have been used in Aldabra, Farquhar, and Desroches.

Zil Elwagne Sesel (Seychelles outer islands)

After 1976, the islands of British Indian Ocean Territory which were transferred to Seychelles used the stamps of that country. On 20 June 1980, stamps were issued inscribed ZIL ELOIGNE SESEL. These were sold from the m.v. *Cinque Juin* which operated as a TPO. From 22 July 1982 stamps were inscribed ZIL ELWAGNE SESEL.

Réunion

> **FIRST STAMPS ISSUED** 1 January 1852; also used French Colonies General Issues (mainly differenced by surcharges 1885-92)

CURRENCY

1852 As France

Claimed (while still uninhabited) by the French in 1638, named Ile de Bourbon in 1649 and settled in 1650 as a station for French ships en route for India. Renamed Réunion in 1793 (but reverted to Bourbon 1810-48). On 19 March 1946 it ceased to be a colony and became an overseas *département* of France; but since it had a local currency not at par with the French *franc*, it needed overprinted or differentiated stamps until the French metropolitan *franc* was adopted on 1 January 1975.

Bourbon shared a Royal French postal service with Isle de France in 1773 and had a separate postal administration from 1787. Handstamps were used from 1830. Before 1864 mail is known routed via Mauritius (q.v.), but from 1864 to 1940 Réunion was served by packet-boats direct from Marseille or Aden, via Seychelles or Zanzibar.

• Comoro Islands

> **FIRST STAMPS** 1864 (French Colonies General Issues)
> **FIRST STAMPS ISSUED** November 1892

CURRENCY

1950 100 centimes = 1 franc (Malagasy)

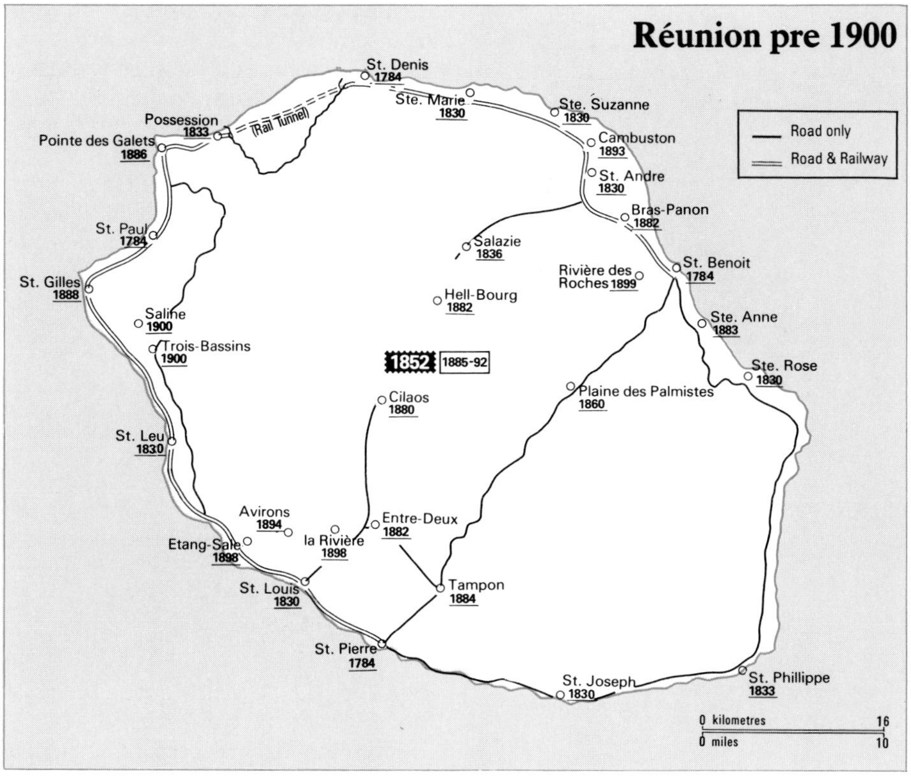
Réunion pre 1900
Road only
Road & Railway
St. Denis 1784
Ste. Marie 1830
Ste. Suzanne 1830
Cambuston 1893
St. Andre 1830
Bras-Panon 1882
St. Benoit 1784
Ste. Anne 1883
Ste. Rose 1830
Possession 1833
(Rail Tunnel)
Pointe des Galets 1886
St. Paul 1784
St. Gilles 1888
Saline 1900
Trois-Bassins 1900
Salazie 1836
Hell-Bourg 1882
Rivière des Roches 1899
1852 1885-92
Cilaos 1880
Plaine des Palmistes 1860
St. Leu 1830
Avirons 1894
Etang-Salé 1898
la Rivière 1898
Entre-Deux 1882
Tampon 1884
St. Louis 1830
St. Pierre 1784
St. Joseph 1830
St. Phillippe 1833
0 kilometres 16
0 miles 10

Mayotte, Anjouan, Grande Comore, and Mohéli came under French protection at various dates from 1841. They were separate colonies 1891-8, dependencies 1898-1912, colonies again from 25 July 1912 to 23 February 1914, when they became dependencies of Madagascar. They were captured from their Vichy sympathizers by British forces in 1942. On 9 May 1946 the islands became an autonomous overseas *département* of France. Mayotte is predominantly Catholic, the other islands Muslim Arab.

A separatist movement fostered in Tanzania was active in the 1960s and on 6 July 1975 the local chamber of deputies declared unilaterally for independence; all the Mayotte deputies abstained. Troops were flown in from Réunion pending a referendum, which on 22 December 1975 produced a similar result. The self-styled Etat Comorien celebrated with a couple of *coups d'état*. A second referendum in Mayotte showed an 80 per cent demand to become an integral part of France forthwith.

From c.1872 the Comoros and Nossi-Bé sent mail by a British India S. N. Co. steamer to Zanzibar. From 1880 a French sea link existed from Mayotte via Nossi Bé to Réunion. In 1885-8 Messageries Maritimes ran a 'Ligne Coloniale' between Mauritius and Mozambique via Madagascar and Comoro ports.

• Mayotte

FIRST STAMPS ISSUED November 1892

CURRENCY	
1892	As France

Ceased issuing stamps in 1914 when it became a dependency of Madagascar. Following a referendum in December 1974, and a *coup d'état* in 1975, Mayotte finally voted for the status of an overseas *département* of France. However, before the stamps of France became available in August 1976, the stamps of Comoro Archipelago (q.v.) were issued in Dzaoudzi in February 1976 before stamps were obtained from Réunion.

• Anjouan

FIRST STAMPS ISSUED November 1892

CURRENCY	
1892	As France

Came under French influence in 1843 and protection in 1866.

• Great Comoro (Grande Comore)

FIRST STAMPS ISSUED November 1897

CURRENCY	
1897	As France

• Mohéli

FIRST STAMPS ISSUED 1896

CURRENCY	
1906	As France

Initially a dependency of Anjouan, it received a PO c. 1902.

After 1914, stamps of the four islands were validated throughout Madagascar and dependencies and use up, after which stamps of Madagascar dependencies were used.

Comoro Archipelago (Archipel des Comores)

FIRST STAMPS ISSUED 1960 (inscribed ARCHIPEL DES COMORES)
FIRST STAMPS inscribed ETAT COMORIEN issued 1975 (in Anjouan, Grande Comore, and Mohéli), some of which have been declared 'undesirable'.

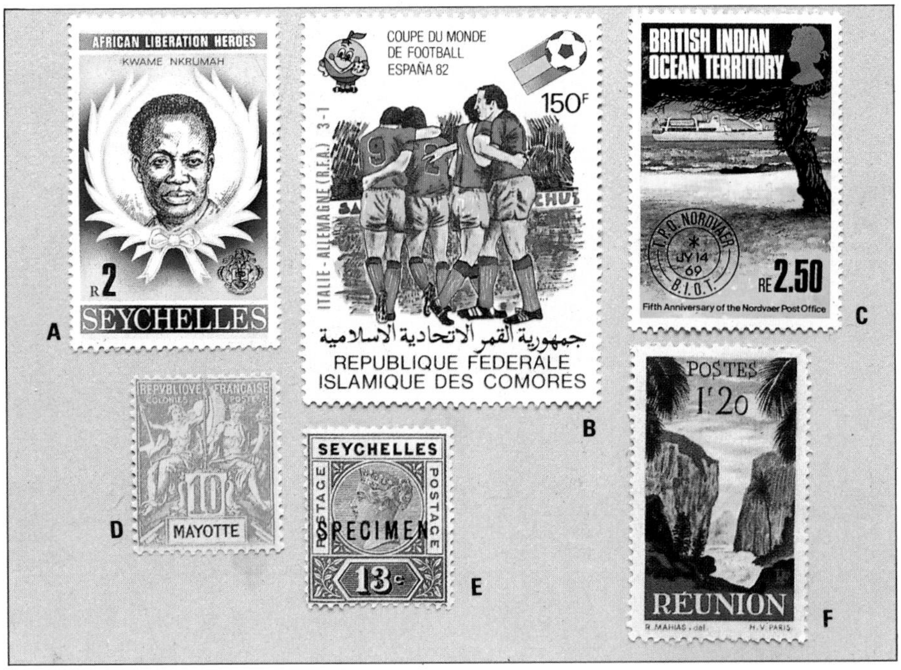
AFRICAN LIBERATION HEROES
KWAME NKRUMAH
R2
SEYCHELLES
A
COUPE DU MONDE
DE FOOTBALL
ESPAÑA 82
150F
ITALIE - ALLEMAGNE (R.F.A.) 3-1
جمهورية القمر الاتحادية الاسلامية
REPUBLIQUE FEDERALE
ISLAMIQUE DES COMORES
B
BRITISH INDIAN
OCEAN TERRITORY
RE2.50
Fifth Anniversary of the Nordvaer Post Office
C
MAYOTTE
D
SEYCHELLES
POSTAGE
SPECIMEN
13c
E
POSTES
1f20
RÉUNION
F

A Seychelles:Independent 1979; **B** Comoro Islands:Islamic Republic 1981; **C** BIOT 1974; **D** Mayotte:French Colony 1892; **E** Seychelles:Dependency 1892; **F** Reunion:French Overseas Département 1949.

• Madagascar

FIRST STAMPS French Colonies General Issues 1885
FIRST STAMPS ISSUED 1894

CURRENCY

French (but since 1966 the franc designated Fmg, reflected on stamps only since 1974)

Discovered by the Portuguese in 1500. The native population, settled perhaps 500 years earlier from South-East Asia, resisted the peripheral colonization of the French. In the 1880s other European nations also had aspirations. After a war in 1882-5 Diego Suarez (*see above*) was ceded to France and protected status without occupation extended to the whole island. This was recognized by Britain and Germany in 1890. In 1894 the French claimed the island. After the suppression of popular resistance, Tananarive was taken in September 1895 and a colony proclaimed on 30 May 1896. The Queen was deposed in 1897.

After the fall of France in 1940, Madagascar adhered strongly to Vichy. In 1942, fearing collaboration with the Japanese, the British seized the island by force and handed it to a Free French administration. The island became autonomous as République Malgache (q.v) on 14 October 1958 and an independent state as Malagasy Republic (q.v.) within the French Community on 26 June 1960. A series of *coups d'état* in 1975 led via military dictatorship to a left-wing régime, and the addition of 'Demokratika' to the country's official name.

Postal History
Up to 1881 the peripheral colonies shared the route to Zanzibar with the Comoro Islands. From 1881 they were served by a monthly steamer from La Réunion to Tamatave. Stamps (French Colonies General Issues, supplied from Réunion) were cancelled on board ship. French POs opened in 1885 at Tamatave, Tananarive, Fianarantsoa, Mahanoro, Majunga, Vatomandry, and Vohémar, which (with Ste Marie, Nossi Bé, and Diego Suarez) were served by the Ligne Coloniale de Mozambique.

Used French Colonies General Issues from 1885, including locally overprinted provisionals, some on stamps of France, March 1889-96.

A runner service (parcels from 1875; letters from 1888) was organized by the Norwegian Missionary Society which operated until 1899. A runner service from Tananarive to the French PO in Tamatave was organized by British residents before 1884 and made official by the vice-consul in 1884.

Used locally printed stamps March 1884-7, after which the service continued with handstruck markings to indicate payment.

In January-September 1895, during the French war of occupation, the British ran an inland mail service using special stamps.

Malagasy Republic (République Malgache)

FIRST STAMPS ISSUED December 1958

CURRENCY

1958	francs CFM
1976	5 francs = 1 ariary

• Madagascar and Dependencies

FIRST STAMPS ISSUED 1896

CURRENCY

1889 As France

• Nossi Bé

FIRST STAMPS ISSUED June 1889 (locally overprinted)

CURRENCY

1889 As France

A
£1
BRITISH ANTARCTIC TERRITORY
B
FALKLAND ISLANDS DEPENDENCIES
9D
ENDURANCE 1914-16
FALKLAND ISLANDS DEPENDENCIES
2½D
POSTAGE & REVENUE
C
BICENTENAIRE DE LA DECOUVERTE DES ILES CROZET
LE MARQUIS DE CASTRIES
24 JANVIER 1772
LE MASCARIN
RF
POSTE AERIENNE
100F
TERRES AUSTRALES ET ANTARCTIQUES FRANCAISES
South Georgia
2½d
CHINSTRAP & KING PENGUIN
D
E

A British Antarctic Territory 1963; **B** Falkland Island Dependencies 1954; **C** Falkland Island Dependencies 1949; **D** French Antarctic Territory 1972; **E** South Georgia 1963.

SUMMER SUPPORT
ROSS DEPENDENCY
8c
A
B
AUSTRALIAN
5D
1908-9
FIRST ATTAINMENT OF MAGNETIC POLE
ANTARCTIC TERRITORY

A Ross Dependency 1972; **B** Australian Antarctic Territory 1961.

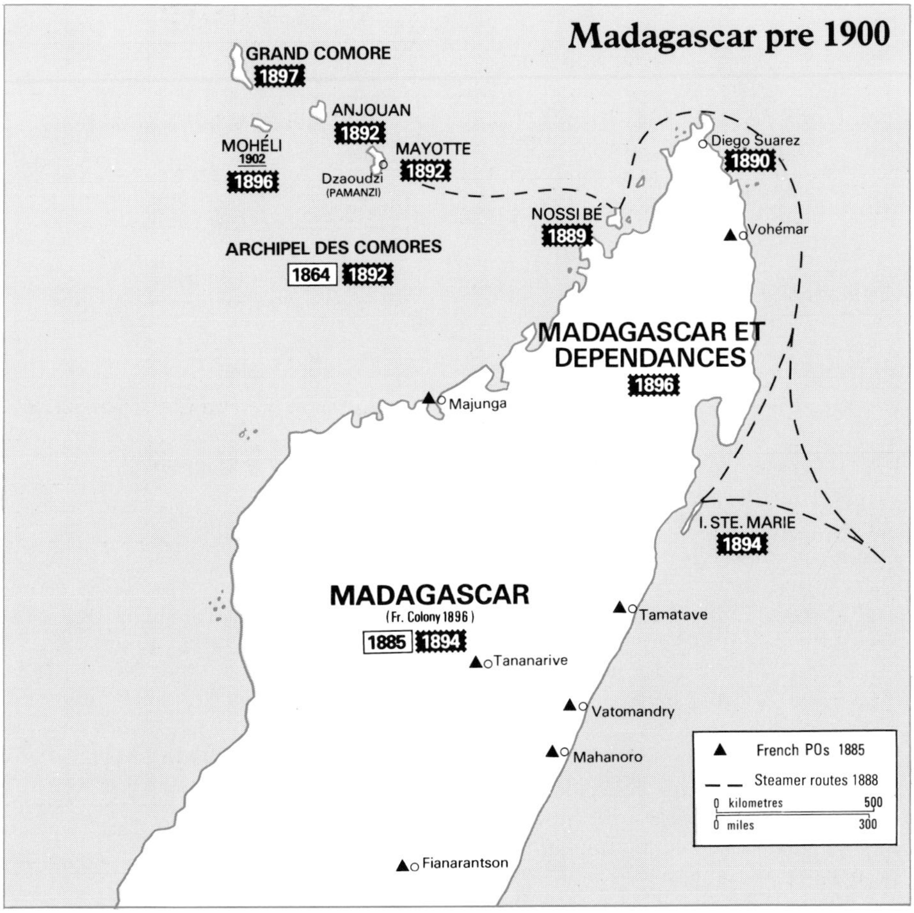
Madagascar pre 1900
GRAND COMORE
1897
ANJOUAN
1892
MOHÉLI
1902
1896
MAYOTTE
1892
Dzaoudzi
(PAMANZI)
Diego Suarez
1890
NOSSI BÉ
1889
Vohémar
ARCHIPEL DES COMORES
1864
1892
MADAGASCAR ET DEPENDANCES
1896
Majunga
I. STE. MARIE
1894
MADAGASCAR
(Fr. Colony 1896)
1885
1894
Tamatave
Tananarive
Vatomandry
Mahanoro
Fianarantson
French POs 1885
Steamer routes 1888
kilometres
0
500
miles
0
300

Island off north-west coast of Madagascar, French since 1841. A dependency of Mayotte until 1881, then of Diego Suarez, and, from 1901 an administrative part of Madagascar.

Used French Colonies General Issues from c. 1864 (oblit. NSB in lozenge of dots).

• Diego Suarez

FIRST STAMPS ISSUED 25 January 1890

CURRENCY

1890 As France

The fine harbour at the northern end of Madagascar became a French protectorate in 1840, was ceded in 1885, and incorporated in Madagascar in 1898.

Used French Colonies General Issues from c. 1885. Stamps validated after 30 May 1896 throughout Madagascar and dependencies.

• Sainte-Marie de Madagascar

FIRST STAMPS ISSUED April 1894 (withdrawn 18 January 1898)

CURRENCY

1894 As France

Port-of-call on the French route to India from 30 July 1750, treated as a dependency of Réunion, then from 1881 of Mayotte. Administered from Diego Suarez from 1888.

Used stamps of Diego Suarez from 1890.

ANTARCTICA

Falkland Islands Dependencies

- **Graham Land**

FIRST STAMPS ISSUED 12 February 1944

- **South Georgia**

FIRST STAMPS ISSUED 3 April 1944

- **South Orkneys**

FIRST STAMPS ISSUED 21 February 1944

- **South Shetlands**

FIRST STAMPS ISSUED 1944
FIRST GENERAL STAMPS for above four territories 1 February 1946
All stamps withdrawn 16 July 1963

CURRENCY

As Falklands

The most interesting period of their postal history was during the use of Falkland Island stamps (*see page* 174).

South Georgia
A British Antarctic Survey base (including the uninhabited South Sandwich Islands) which had a resident population of 22 in 1974.

Separate stamps resumed 17 July 1963.

The island was seized by the Argentinians during the occupation of Falkland Islands in 1982. It was the site of the first action between British and Argentinian forces in May of that year and was reoccupied.

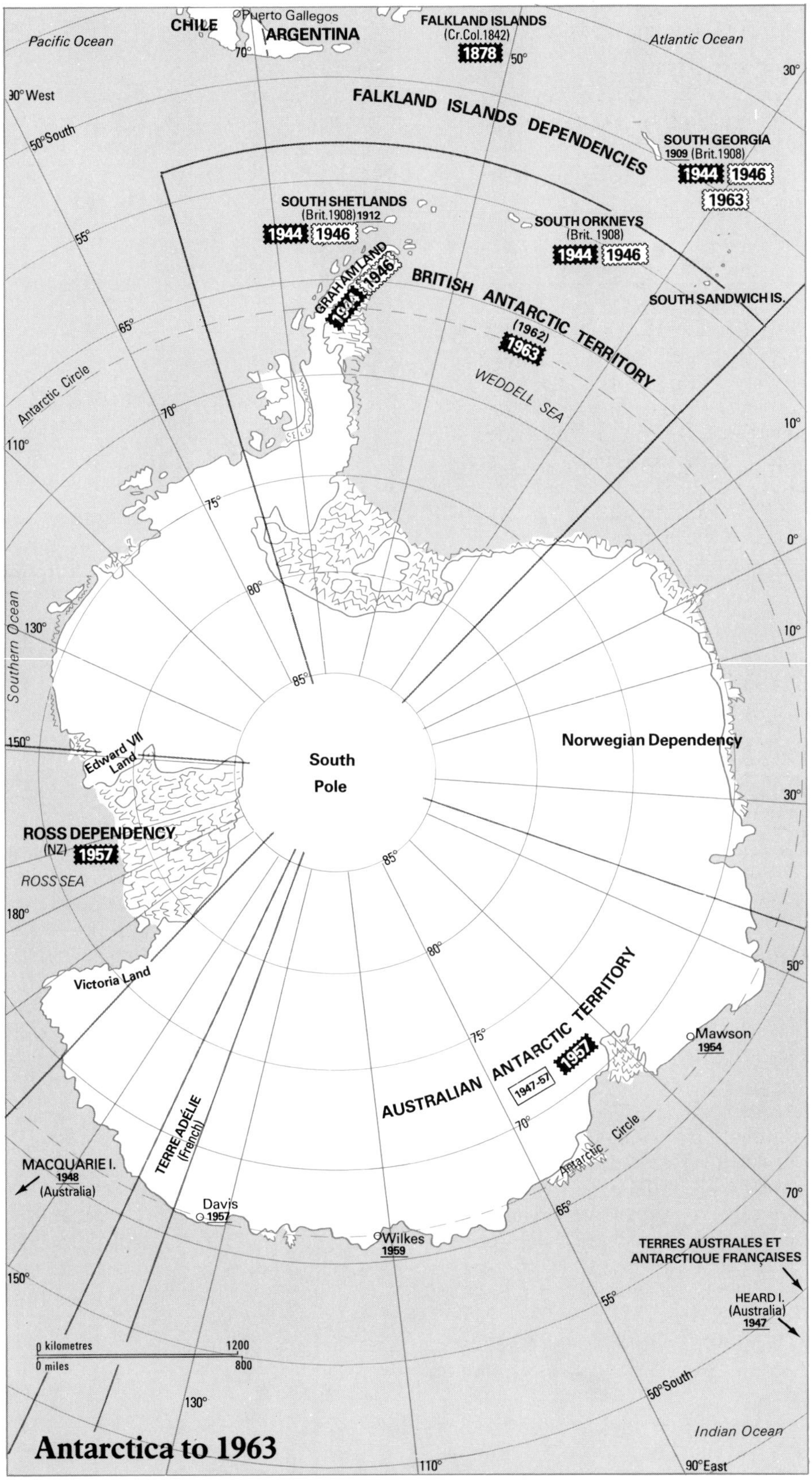

Puerto Gallegos
CHILE
ARGENTINA
FALKLAND ISLANDS
(Cr.Col.1842)
1878
Pacific Ocean
Atlantic Ocean
FALKLAND ISLANDS DEPENDENCIES
SOUTH GEORGIA
1909 (Brit.1908)
1944 1946
1963
SOUTH SHETLANDS
(Brit.1908) 1912
1944 1946
SOUTH ORKNEYS
(Brit. 1908)
1944 1946
GRAHAM LAND
1944 1946
BRITISH ANTARCTIC TERRITORY
(1962)
1963
SOUTH SANDWICH IS.
WEDDELL SEA
Antarctic Circle
Southern Ocean
Edward VII Land
South Pole
Norwegian Dependency
ROSS DEPENDENCY
(NZ) 1957
ROSS SEA
Victoria Land
AUSTRALIAN ANTARCTIC TERRITORY
1947-57
1957
Mawson
1954
TERRE ADÉLIE
(French)
MACQUARIE I.
1948
(Australia)
Davis
1957
Wilkes
1959
TERRES AUSTRALES ET ANTARCTIQUE FRANÇAISES
HEARD I.
(Australia)
1947
0 kilometres 1200
0 miles 800
Indian Ocean
90°East

Antarctica to 1963

British Antarctic Territory

FIRST GENERAL ISSUE 1 February 1963

CURRENCY

1963 sterling
1971 decimal currency

Designated 3 March 1962, comprising former Dependencies of Falkland Islands (except South Georgia) and Antarctica. Has a population of 81 scientists serviced by two Royal Research ships and two light aircraft. Deception Island was abandoned in 1969 after eruptions had partially wrecked the station.

French Southern and Antarctic Territories

(Terres Australes et Antarctiques Françaises)

FIRST STAMPS ISSUED 2 November 1955

CURRENCY

1955 100 centimes = 1 franc

French overseas territory consisting of the Crozet Archipelago (1772), the islands of St Paul, New Amsterdam (claimed by France 21 November 1924) and Kerguelen (reoccupied in 1949), and Adélie Land. This was created on 6 August 1955 owing to the imminent independence of Madagascar of which they had been dependencies. The territory is now administered from Réunion (q.v.).

Kerguelen used stamps of France in 1906-26 cancelled by the cachet of the Resident. Letters are known routed via Cape Town, Durban, Bumbury (Australia), or Madagascar.

Used stamps of Madagascar from c.1948 (A stamp of Madagascar was overprinted TERRE ADÉLIE on 26 October 1948 to honour its discovery in 1840).

Australian Antarctic Territory

FIRST STAMPS Australia 1947-57
FIRST STAMPS ISSUED 27 March 1957 (Australian release date; first day of issue in Antarctica 11 December 1957)
All stamps are valid for use in Australia

CURRENCY

1956 As Australia

Comprises all the islands and territory other than Adelie Land situated south of lat. 60°S. and between long. 160° and 45°E. Macquarie Island was claimed by New South Wales in 1810 and controlled from Tasmania by 1891. Visited since 1831, the mainland territory was claimed on 24 August 1936, though a base was not established until 11 February 1954. Heard Island had been visited at intervals by explorers and sealers from 1833, but effective control with a permanent base was not exercised until 26 December 1947 when the Australian flag was raised.

Mail is known from numerous Antarctic expeditions: Mawson in 1911 (used stamps of Tasmania), Shackleton in 1921-2 (used stamps of Britain), Mawson again in 1929-31 (used stamps of Australia), and the Australian National Antarctic Research Expeditions (ANARE) of 1947-65. The five permanent bases with POs are Heard Island (opened 25 December 1947); Macquarie Island (7 March 1948); Mawson (15 February 1954); Davis (14 January 1957); Wilkes (1 February 1959).

Used stamps of Australia 1947-57.

Ross Dependency

FIRST STAMPS ISSUED 11 January 1957

CURRENCY

1957 sterling
1968 100 cents = 1 New Zealand dollar

A sector of Antarctica and various islands between long. 160°E. and 150°W. and south of lat. 60°S. It includes the Ross Sea whose shores provided bases for Shackleton and Scott. Named after J. Clark Ross, who was knighted in 1831 for his discovery of the North Magnetic Pole. The region was formally claimed by Britain on 30 July 1923 on behalf of New Zealand, and was shortly afterwards made a dependency of New Zealand. A base was established from New Zealand by Sir Edmund Hillary.

Stamps of New Zealand overprinted KING EDWARD VII LAND were used by the Shackleton Expedition of 1908. Prior to leaving New Zealand the explorer had been appointed postmaster of King Edward VII Land by the postal department and had been issued with stamps and a cancellation.

Stamps of New Zealand overprinted VICTORIA LAND were used by the Scott Expedition of 1910-12. The party left London on 1 June 1910 and New Zealand on 29 November. Special stamps and a cancellation were provided. PO was opened at Cape Evans on 3 January 1911. Scott and his party died during their return from the South Pole early in 1912.

Index of Maps

General Index

Note

The following categories of information are listed in this index:

1. Names of stamp-issuing territories, usually used as section headings in the text or shown on the maps with dates of stamps issue.
2. Illustrations of stamps or overprints, listed under the names of the stamp-issuing territories.
3. Inscriptions or overprints cited in text or illustrations.
4. Indigenous names of the territories, cross-referred to the English form used in the text.

No illustrations other than of stamps or overprints are listed in the index.

Typographical distinction of entries:

1. Text and major references are listed and referred to in the index in roman type.
2. Page references for illustrations of stamps or overprints, listed under the name of the territories, are cited in (brackets).
3. Map titles, and page references for the maps, including for places shown with dates on the maps, are in *italics*.
4. Indigenous place-names giving only cross-references are in *italics*.
5. Inscriptions, postmarks and overprints cited only thus are in SMALL CAPITALS.
6. Continental divisions are in FULL CAPITALS.